JAMES BRADL

A

PRELIMINARY TREATISE

ON

EVIDENCE AT THE COMMON LAW

Elibron Classics series.

© 2005 Adamant Media Corporation.

ISBN 1-4021-9924-4 (paperback)
ISBN 1-4212-9965-8 (hardcover)

This Elibron Classics book contains the complete text of the
edition published in 1898 by Little Brown, and Company,
Boston.

CONTENTS

PREFATORY NOTE

The title-page and Introduction indicate the general character of this volume. It seeks, by means of some preliminary investigations, to help students of the law of evidence, whether young or old, towards a clear understanding of that subject.

By tracing the development of trial by jury, the author has endeavored to throw light on the beginnings and true character of our rules of evidence; by a more accurate analysis and a fuller illustration than is common, of the distinction between law and fact, to make plainer the respective functions of the jury and the court; and by an investigation of certain important topics, ordinarily, but, as it is believed, improperly treated as belonging to the law of evidence, to discriminate them from that part of the law, and set them in their proper place.

In dealing with these matters the author has not spared time or labor; and he trusts that his work may help to make clear the most difficult parts of what is ordinarily discussed in books on evidence. He has not sought to treat them with fullness, for they are here regarded as incidental to the main subject in hand; but to place them in the right focus, and to furnish such comment and illustration as may help to make their general scope and character intelligible.

A short summary of the existing law of evidence, and some suggestions as to the development of it, are given in the last chapter.

My indebtedness, in the earlier part of the chapters relating to the jury, to Brunner's admirable work, and to the learned collections of my friend Dr. Melville M. Bigelow, are duly acknowledged. I am under great obligations, also, to Francis Vaughan Hawkins, Esq., of Lincoln's Inn, the author of the well-known treatise on the Construction of Wills, for leave to reprint, in an appendix, his excellent paper on "The Principles of Legal Interpretation, with Reference especially to the Interpretation of Wills." I know of nothing on that subject so well worth reading.

J. B. T.
Law School of Harvard University,
September 15, 1898.

INTRODUCTION

I have long intended to write a treatise on the law of evidence, for practical use. But in setting out to do this, many years ago, I found at once the need of going much deeper into the history of the subject, and into an exact analysis of many familiar terms, than I had supposed would be necessary. It soon became apparent that it was impossible to write anything which would satisfy my own conceptions of what was needed, without a careful examination of the older law of trials, and without adding to this a critical study of a considerable number of related topics, crudely developed and half understood, as it appeared and still appears to me, which overlie and perplex the main subject in hand. It was necessary that these collateral matters should be detached from the law of evidence, carefully scrutinized and discriminated, and set in their true places. The chapters which follow are the partial outcome of some of these preliminary investigations. They are to be regarded, therefore, as incidental and auxiliary studies in the course of an examination of the law of evidence in English-speaking countries.

At once, when a man raises his eyes from the common-law system of evidence, and looks at foreign methods, he is struck with the fact that our system is radically peculiar. Here, a great mass of evidential matter, logically important and probative, is shut out from the view of the judicial tribunals by an imperative rule, while the same matter is not thus excluded anywhere else.[1] English-speaking countries have what we call a "Law of Evidence;" but no other country has it; we alone have generated and evolved this large, elaborate, and difficult doctrine. We have done it, not by direct legislation, but, almost wholly, by the slowly accumulated rulings of judges, made in the trying of causes, during the last two or three centuries, — rulings which at first were not preserved in print, but in the practice and tradition of the trial courts; and only during the last half or two-thirds of this period

---

[1] It is not forgotten that an exclusion of *witnesses* is ancient and universal. In this respect the peculiarity of the English common law lay in shutting out fewer classes of persons than other systems. Bat this peculiarity, as we shall see, has its explanation in the same cause which produced the other.

have they been revised, reasoned upon, and generalized by the courts *in banc*[2].

When one has come to perceive these striking facts, he is not long in finding the reason for them. Indeed the very structure of the system thus produced points to the reason, when we observe its constant, anxious, and overanxious endeavor to prevent the tribunal to which the evidence is principally addressed from being confused and misled, and from dealing with questions which it has no right to deal with. It might seem strange and not worth while to keep alive so long a tribunal which has needed so much watching and so many safeguards, if one did not recall the immense persistence of legal institutions and usages, as well as the deep political significance of the jury and its relation to what is most valued in the national history and traditions of the English race. It is this institution of the jury which accounts for the common-law system of evidence, — an institution which. English-speaking people have had and used, in one or another department of their public affairs, ever since the Conquest. Other peoples have had it only in quite recent times, unless, indeed, they may belong to those who began with it centuries ago, and then allowed it to become obsolete and forgotten. England alone kept it, and, in a strange fashion, has developed it.

This institution, the jury, which is thus the occasion of our law of evidence, and which is also at the bottom of our *system* of pleading and procedure, and of very much in all brunches of, the substantive common law, has a peculiar interest for us, in the United States, in being lodged beyond the reach of ordinary legislation, in our national and state constitutions. I have endeavored in the following pages, for the first time, as I believe, however briefly, to trace the history of the English jury through the earlier judicial records and the Year Books, so far as these are yet in print; and thus to connect what is well known in our modern English law with the admirable researches of Dr. Brunner into the early continental history of the jury.[3] In order to set a historical background for this ancient tribunal, and to bring clearly into view the conceptions which

---

[2] The text-writers have, no doubt, contributed to shape the law. Bat these are modem. Gilbert, whose book was published in the middle of the last century, was our first important writer on Evidence ; and there was little else before the present century.

[3] *Die Entstehung der Schwurgerichte,* von Dr. Heinrich Brunner, Berlin. Weidmannsche Buchhandlnng, 1872.

were originally involved in the notion of trial by jury, or rather, as it was then thought of, proof by jury, — I have given some, account of the older modes of trial, and of their survival and ultimate dying out in England. I hope that those who attentively consider the long and strange story, of the development of the English jury and the immense influence it has had in shaping our law, will find here a basis for conclusions as to the scope and direction of certain much-needed reforms in the whole law of evidence and procedure.

A system of evidence, like ours, thus worked out at the forge of daily experience in the trial of causes, not created, or greatly changed, until lately, by legislation, not the fruit of any man's systematic reflection or forecast, is sure to exhibit at every step the marks of its origin. It is not concerned with nice definitions, or the exacter academic operations of the logical faculty. It is attending to practical ends. Its rules originate in the instinctive suggestions of good sense, legal experience, and a sound practical understanding; and they are seeking to determine, not what is or is not, in its nature, probative, but rather, passing by that inquiry, what, among really probative matters, shall, nevertheless, for this or that practical reason, be excluded, and not even heard by the jury. From the diversity and multitude of the casual rulings by the judges, — rulings often hastily made, ill-considered, and wrong, — from the endeavor to follow these as precedents and to generalize and theorize upon them, from the forgetting by some courts, in making this attempt, of the accidental and empirical nature of much in these determinations, and the remembering of this fact by ethers, there has resulted plenty of confusion. The pressure under which a ruling most be made is often unfavorable to clear thinking, and the law of evidence, largely shaped at *nisi prius,* took on a general aspect which was vague, confused, and unintelligible. One thing in particular added greatly to the confusion, namely, the habit of assuming, whenever evidential matter was rejected or received, that the result was attributable to some principle of the law of evidence; while, very often indeed, the reason lay wholly in the rules of pleading, procedure, or substantive law which happened to control the case. In this way the law of evidence came to be monstrously overloaded, and was made to swallow up into itself much which belonged to other branches of law, or to the wide regions of logic and legal reasoning. Thus, not only were many of these other subjects clouded and thrown out of focus, but the law of evidence itself was intolerably perplexed.

In the following papers, after the account of the older modes of proof and of the development of the English jury, to which I have already referred, there will be found an attempt to discriminate several of the topics, thus improperly absorbed into the law of evidence, and to state their true nature, and their relation to other parts of the law. In trying to do this, it was necessary to endeavor to define the law of evidence itself, as well as other fundamental conceptions, such as those of "fact" and "law," with which it is bound up. Some of these inquiries, *e. g.,* those into the nature of presumptions, judicial notice, the burden of proof, and what is called "the parol evidence rule," involve matters of a very wide scope, reaching, in some cases, into every part of the law.

At first it was my intention to connect and combine these papers, most of which were originally prepared for publication as separate articles,[4] into a systematic whole. But, upon reflection, it has seemed wiser to let them stand in the general shape in which they were first written, — restoring some parts which were then omitted for lack of room, carefully revising the whole, adding much, and especially adding, for completeness, one or two chapters constructed upon a plan similar to that of the other papers. What may thus be found wanting in orderly treatment will be made up, it is hoped, in freshness of interest.

I have a good hope, when the present volume is completed, of supplementing it, before long, by another, in similar form but of a more immediately practical character, giving a concise statement of the existing law of evidence.

---

[4] See volumes three to seven, inclusive, of the Harvard Law Review (1889-1893).

PART I

CHAPTER I
THE OLDER MODES OF TRIAL

When the Normans came into England they brought with them, not only a far more vigorous and searching kingly power than had been known there, but also a certain product of the exercise of this power by the Prankish kings and the Norman dukes; namely, the use of the inquisition in public administration, *i. e.,* the practice of ascertaining facts by summoning together by public authority a number of people most likely and most competent, as being neighbors, to know and tell the truth, and calling for their answer under oath. This was the parent of the modern jury. In so far as the business of judicature was then carried on under royal authority, it was simply so much public administration; and the use of the inquisition came to England as an established, although undeveloped, part of the machinery for doing all sorts of public business. With the Normans came also another novelty, the judicial duel, — one of the chief methods for determining controversies in the royal courts; and it was largely the cost, danger, and unpopularity of the last of these institutions which fed the wonderful growth of the other.

The Normans brought to England much else, and found that much of what they brought was there already; for the Anglo-Saxons were their cousins of the Germanic race, and had, in a great degree, the same legal conceptions and methods, only less worked out. Looking now at these and at the Norman additions, what were the English modes of trying questions of fact when the jury came in, and how did they develop and die out? Some account of these things will serve as a background in trying to make out the Jury.

I. The great fundamental thing, to be noticed first of all, out of which all else grew, was the conception of popular courts and popular justice. We must read this into all the accounts of our earliest law. In these courts it was not the presiding officers, one or more, who were the judges; it was the whole company: as if in a New England town-meeting, the lineal descendant of these old Germanic moots, the people conducted the judicature, as well as the finance and politics, of the town. These old courts were a sort of town-meeting of judges. Among the Germanic races this had always been so; nothing among them was more ancient than the idea and practice of popular justice.[5] This notion among a rude people carried with it all else that we find, — the preservation of very old traditional methods, as if sacred; a rigid adherence to forms; the absence of a development of the rational modes of proof. Of the popular courts Maine says, in the admirable sixth chapter of his "Early Law and Custom," while speaking of the Hundred Court and the Salic Law: "I will say no more of its general characteristics than that it is intensely technical, and that it supplies in itself sufficient proof that legal technicality is a disease, not of the old age, but of the infancy of societies." The body of the judicial business of the popular courts, seven and eight centuries ago, lay in administering rules that a party should follow this established formula or that, and according as he bore the test should be punished or go quit. The conception of the trial was that of a proceeding between the parties, carried on publicly, under forms which the community oversaw. They listened to complaints which often must follow with the minutest detail certain forms *"de verbo in verbum,"*[6] which must be made probable by a "fore-oath," complaint-witnesses, the exhibition of the wound, or other visible confirmation. There were many modes of trial and some range of choice for the parties; but the proof was largely "one-sided," so that the main question was who had the right or, rather, the privilege of going to the proof. For determining this question there were traditional usages and rules,

---

[5] Maine, Early Law and Custom, c. 6; Pop. GOV., pp. 89-92; Essays in Anglo-Saxon Law, 2-3.

[6] So often in our older records. This rigor survives now chiefly in the fading rules of criminal pleading. It is interesting in the great Statute of Wales, 12 Edw. I. (1284), to see the contact of our old law with the customs of a region still less advanced. In certain pleas (s. 8), the demand is to be set forth in words stating the fact, without any exception for mistake in words, *non observata ilia dura consuetudine, Qui c dit a syllaba, cadit a tata causa.*

Of course it is to be remembered that in this husk of formalism lay, often, the safeguard of men's rights. "We may say with the great Romanist of our own day, that formalism is the twin-born sister of liberty." 2 P. & M., Hist. Eng. Law, 56).

and the decision of it was that famous *Beweisurtheil*,[7] which disposed of cases before they were tried. Since the trial was a matter of form, and the judgment was a determination what form it should take, the judgment naturally came before the trial. It determined, not only what the trial should be, but how it should be conducted and when, and what the consequence should be of this or that result.

In these trials there are various conceptions: the notion of a magical test, like the effect of the angel's spear upon Milton's toad —

> "Him thus intent, Ithuriel with his spear
> Touched lightly;... up he starts,
> Discovered and surprised;"

that of a call for the direct intervention of the divine justice *(judicium Dei, Gottesurtheil); that* of a convenient form or formula, sometimes having a real and close relation to the probable truth of fact, and sometimes little or no relation to it, like a child's rigmarole in a game — good, at all events, for reaching a practical result; that of regulating the natural resort of mankind to a fight; that of simply abiding the appeal to chance. There was also, conspicuously and necessarily, the appeal to human testimony, given under an oath, and, perhaps, under the responsibility of fighting in support of it. But what we do not yet find, or find only in its faint germs, is anything such as we know by the name of a trial, any determination by a court which weighs this testimony or other evidence in the scale of reason, and decides a litigated question as it is decided now. That thing, so obvious and so necessary, as we are apt to think it, was only worked out after centuries.[8]

II. Something must be said of a preliminary matter, of that institution of the complaint-witness, — called also, as some other things were called, the *Secta*,[9] — which has been the source of much confusion. This had a function which was a natural and almost

---

[7] Brnnuer, *Die Entstehung der Schwurgerichte,* 174; Von Bar, *Beweisurtheil, passim.* As regards the German books I am greatly indebted to my friend and cousin, Gamaliel Bradford, of Boston. With lavish generosity he read to me the whole of the two books just cited and several others.

[8] The reasons which still make it go difficult to refer international controversies to the rational mode of trial may help us to understand our older law.

[9] See Brunner, Schw. 428 *et seq.; P. & M.,* Hiat. Eng. Law, ii. 603 *et seq.*

necessary feature of the formal system of proof.[10] When the proof
was "one-sided," and allotted to this man or that as having merely
the duty of going through a prescribed form to gain his case, it was a
very vital matter to determine which party was to have it. If there
was to be a trial, it might, indeed, be a privilege to go to the proof;
and yet, as the form was often clogged with technical detail and had
little or no rational relation to the actual truth of what was involved
in the charge, it might be very dangerous and burdensome to be put
to the necessity of going through with it. The forms of trial might
also involve bodily danger or death. Not every complaint or
affirmative defence, therefore, was allowed to put an antagonist to
his proof: there must be something to support it. This notion is fixed
in the text of John's Magna Carta (art. 38), in 1215: *Nullus ballivus
ponat de cetero aliquem ad legem*[11] *simplici loquela sua, sine
testibus fidelibus ad hoc inductis.*[12]

---

[10] Brunner, Schw. 170 *et seq;* 175. Lea, Sup. and Force, 4th ed. 95-6.

[11] *As to* this term *lex,* see *infra,* 199-201.

[12] Brunner's explanation of this passage is found in Schwurg., 199-200.
"If a lord appears with a complaint-witness against his vassal, in his own court,
the vassal must answer, although no witnesses are brought. . . . Sometimes this
privilege was limited so that the lord had it but once a year. The privilege of the
fisc [or, as we should say, the crown] in this respect was unlimited. If a royal
officer appears as plaintiff in a complaint belonging to his chief, he need not
produce any witness. . . . Even if Much a complaint only called for the oath of
purgation from the defendant, yet for this there was need, not merely of a clear
conscience, but compurgators, and the painful formalism of the oath might only
too easily bring the swearer to grief. Article 38 in Magna Carta may have owed it
origin to such considerations when it provided, 'Nullus ballivus,' " etc. See also
Brunner in Zeitschrift der Savigny-Stiftung (Germ. Abt.), ii. 214. Compare
Glanv. ix., 1, and *ib.* Beames's trans. 222 n. 1. Compare also Bracton, 410 (say
A.D. 1258). *Ad simplicem vocem querentis non habent judices necesse, nec pars
de qua queritur, defendere se per legem.* And Bract. N. B. ii. case 260 (1227): *Et
quia . . . predictus Rogerus nichil ostendit . . . nec sectam producit, nec cartam
profert, nec aliquid aliud nisi simplicem vocem suam,* &c. See also *ib.* case 425,
and *ib.* iii. case 1565.

The meaning of this article of Magna Carta seems to have been the
subject of dispute very early. In *Y. B.* 32 & 33 Edw. I. 516 (1304), after quoting
the principal words and setting forth two interpretations, it is added: *Alius
intellectus et melior, quod defendens in brevi de debito et in aliis brevibus
consimilibus non ad legem ponatur nisi querens arramaverit sectam versus eum.*
The handwriting of the MSS. of this passage is said to be of the time of Edw. II.
(1307-1327). Compare Coke (2 Inst. 44), citing the "Mirror."

Holt, C. J., in City of London *v.* Wood, 12 Mod. 669, 678, 679 (1700-
1), ventured upon some dubious explanations of this article, in the course of

This sort of "witness," it must be noticed, might have nothing to do with the trial; he belonged to that stage of the preliminary allegations, the pleading, where belonged also profert of the deed upon which an action or a plea was grounded. But just as rules belonging to the doctrine of profert crept over in modern times, unobserved, into the region of proof, under the head of rules about the "best evidence"[13] and "parol evidence," so the complaint-witnesses were, early and often, confused with proof-witnesses — a process made easy by the ambiguity of the words *"testis," "secta,"* and "witness." The complaint-proof was thus confused with the old "one-sided" witness-proof, with the rational use of witnesses by the ecclesiastical courts, and with the proof by oath and oath-helper.

One complaint-witness seems originally to have been enough, and in the procedure leading to the duel or the grand assize one was always enough; but generally two or more were required; and as in the duel the witness might be challenged, so in other trials the defendant could stake his case on an examination of the complaint-witnesses, and if they disagreed among themselves he won. Apart from this, the complaint-witnesses need not be sworn; they might be relatives or dependents of the party for whom they appeared. As they were not necessarily examined at all, so in later times they were not even produced, and only the formula in the pleadings was kept up. In this form, as a mere expression in pleading, *et inde producit sectam,* the *secta* continued to live a very long life; so that within our own time we read as the third among Stephen's "principal rules of pleading," that "the declaration should, in conclusion, lay damages and allege production of suit.... This applies to actions of all classes.... Though the actual production — has for many centuries fallen into disuse, the formula still remains,... 'and therefore he brings his suit,' " etc.[14] It even survived the Hilary rules of 1834.

---

which he truly said: "The witnesses mentioned by the statute are not to be produced after issue joined, or to be cross-examined, but only to give proof of a probable cause of action, that is, such proof as we now require of a *modus decimandi,* when we grant a prohibition to stay a suit for tithes *in specie."* Compare Webb *v.* Petts, Noy, 44, where in a question on a modus, " it was agreed that a proof (by hearsay) was good enough to maintain the surmise within the statute 2 Edw. 6." [c. 13, s. 14.]

[13] See Thayer's Cas. Evid. 726.

[14] Pleading (Tyler's ed., from the 2d Lond. ed. of 1827), 370-2.

It was the office of the *secta* to support the plaintiff's case, in advance of any answer from the defendant. This support might be such as to preclude any denial, as where one was taken "with the mainour" and the mainour produced in court,[15] or where the defendant's own tally or document was produced, or, as we have noticed, where a defendant chose to stake his case on the answers of the *secta*. Documents, tallies, the production of the mainour, the showing of the wound in mayhem, all belong under this general conception. The history of our law from the beginning, of it is strewn with cases of the profert of documents. This last relic of the principle of the Saxon fore-oath and the Norman complaint-witness was not abolished in England until 1852.[16]

A few cases will illustrate what has been said about these things. In 1202[17] in the King's Court, an appeal was brought for assaulting the plaintiff and wounding him with a knife in the jaw and arm, "and these wounds he showed,[18] and this he offers to prove... by his body." In 1226[19] William seeks to recover of Warren twelve marks on account of a debt due from his father for cloth, *et inde producit sectam que hoc testatur.* Warren comes and defends, and asks that William's *secta* be examined. This is done, and the *secta*

---

[15] Palgrave hag a lively thirteenth century illustration of this in his fiction founded on fact, "The Merchant and the Friar," 173; see also Palg. Eng. Com., ii. p. clxxxvii, pl. 21 (1221); s. c. Maitland, Pl. Crown 'for Gloucester, 92, pi. 394 ; ib. 45, pi. 174, and notes pp. 145, 150; Pike's Hist. Crime, i. 52. It is an entire misapprehension to suppose, as Stephen does. Hist. Cr, Law, i. 259, that this is a trial. The very point of the matter is that trial is refused. Compare Ass. Clarend., s. 12 (1166), Ass. North., s. 3 (1176), 3 Br. N. B., case 1474 (1221), Stat. Wall. s. 14 (1284). This principle also covered cases that were not so plain; as in 1222 (Br. N. B. ii., case 194), in an action for detaining the plaintiff's horse which he had sent by his man to Stamford market for sale, it is charged that the defendant had thrown the man from the horse in the market, imprisoned him five days, kept the horse so that afterwards he was seen in the Earl of Warenne's harrow at Stamford, etc., *et inde producit sectam* (giving ten or eleven names). The defendant defends the taking and imprisonment and all, word for word, etc. "But because all the aforesaid witnesses testify that they saw the horse in the seisin of Richard and in the harrow of the Earl, and this was done at Stamford market," the defendant had his day for judgment. The author of the note-book hag a memorandum on the margin at this cage: *Nota quod ea que manifesta sunt non indigent probacione.*

[16] St. 15 & 16 Vic., c. 76, s. 55.

[17] Maitland, PL Cr. i., case 87.

[18] This was good old Germanic usage. Brunner, Schw. 201. Compare LL. H. I., xciv, 5 (Thorpe, i. 608).

[19] Bracton's Note Book, iii., case 1693.

confess that they know nothing of it, and moreover they do not agree *(diversi sunt in omnibus rebus);* and William has no tally or charter and exhibits nothing, and it is adjudged therefore that the defendant go quit. In 1229[20] Ada demands of Otho eleven pounds, which her father had lent him, and makes profert of a tally, and produces a *secta* which testifies that he owes the money. Otho denies it, and is adjudged to make his proof with compurgators — *defendat se duodecimo manu*[21] ease in 1323 draw attention to the exact effect of the complaint-proof.[22] A woman claimed dower, alleging that her husband had endowed her *assensu patris,* and put forward a deed which showed the assent. The defendant traversed; some discussion followed as to how the issue was to be tried, and as to the effect of the deed. Counsel for the defendant said, "The deed which you show effects nothing beyond entitling you to an answer"... Counsel for the plaintiff: "True, but... he can only have such issue as the deed requires."

With the gradual discrediting of party proof and the formal procedure, the *secta* steadily faded out. The "Mirror," which appears to have been written not long before 1290,[23] says: "It is an abuse that a plaint should be received and heard where there are no suitors presented to testify that the plaint is true."[24] As early as 1314[25] we find counsel saying that the Court of Common Bench will not allow the *secta* to be examined. Yet ten years later,[26] a demand for examining the *secta* reveals the fact that the plaintiff has cone; and this defeats his claim, as it had defeated a plaintiff's claim in 1199.[27] Finally, in 1343,[28] in an action of debt for money due, partly under a bond and partly by "contract," the court refused an examination of

---

[20] Bracton's Note Book, ii., case 325.

[21] As to the meaning of this phrase, see P. & M. Hist. Eng. Law, ii., 598, n. 4. *De* Gruchy, Anc. Coau. de Norm., 192, n. 6. The common meaning in England appears to have been that of the Statute of Wales (in 1284), *cum undecim secum jurantibus,* — in Coke's phrase "an eleven and himself," 2 Inst. 45. And in 1454-5 Needham, Serjeant, says (Y. B. 33 H. VI. 8): "The tenant shall bring his law *de duodecimo, manu,* that is to say, eleven and himself." Compare King *v.* Williams, 2 B. & C. 538 (1824); s. c. 4 D. & R. 3, *infra,* p. 33; also Laws of Canute, c. 66, Lea, Sop. & Force (4th ed.), 48.

[22] Y. B. Ed. II 507.

[23] Maitland, "Mirror," p. xxiv.

[24] *Ib.* 162, 71. Compare P. & M. Hist. Eng, Law, ii., 213.

[25] Y. B. Ed. II. 242.

[26] Ib. 582.

[27] 2 Rot. Cur. Reg. 102.

[28] Y. B. 17 Ed. III. 48, 14.

the *secta.* We read: *"Rich:* As to the obligation, we cannot deny it; as to the rest, what have you to show for the debt? *Moubray:* Good suit *(secta). Rich: Let* the suit be examined at our peril. *Moubray:* Is that your answer? *Rich:* Yes, for you furnish suit in this case of contract in lieu of proof of the action. *Moubray:* Suit is only tendered as matter of form in the count; wherefore we demand judgment. Sh. (J.):[29] It has been heard of that suit was examined in such cases, and this opinion was afterwards disapproved *(reprove).* SH. (J.): Yes, the same Justice who examined the suit on the issue *[pur issue]* saw that he erred and condemned his own opinion. *Gayneford:* In a plea of land the tendering of suit is only for form, but in a plea which is founded on contract that requires testimony, the suit is so examinable *[tesmoinable]* that, without suit, if the matter be challenged, the [other] party is not required to answer. SH. (J.): Certainly it is not so; and therefore deliver yourselves. *Rich:* No money due him," etc. The thing is evidently antiquated by this time. And yet, as we saw, it continued as a form in pleading for nearly five centuries longer.

III. The old forms of trial (omitting documents) were chiefly these: Witnesses; The party's oath, with or without fellow-swearers; The ordeal; Battle. Of these I will speak in turn. They were companions of trial by jury when that mighty plant first struck its root into English soil, and some of them lived long beside it. But, as we shall see, while that grew and spread, all of these dwindled and died out.[30]

---

[29] Whether Shardelowe or Shareshull, both judges of the Common Bench at this time, I do not know. Selden seems to have misconceived this matter when he said (Note 8, Fortescue de Laud., c. xxi), after citing a case of trial by witnesses, in 1234 *(infra,* p. 21), printed for the first time in Maitland's invaluable "Bracton's Note Book" : "The proofs of both aides are called *secta.* It was either this or some like case that Shard [elowe] entended in 17 Ed. III., fol. 48 b, in John Warrein's case — speaking of a justice that examined the snit. And it appears [he adds truly] there, that under Ed. III., the tendering of suit or proofs was become only formal as at this day, like the *plegii de prosequendo."*

[30] For certain other model of "trial" we Stephen, Pl. (Tyler's ed.), 114, 129, and 3 Blackstone, Com. 329.

I use the word *"trial,"* because it is the word in common *use* daring recent centuries. But as applied to the old law this word is an anachronism. The old phrases were *probatio, purgatio, defensio;* seldom, if ever, in the earlier period, *triatio.* In those days people "tried" their own issues; and even after the jury came in, *e.g.* in the early part of the thirteenth century, one is sometimes said to clear himself *(purgare se)* by a jury; just as a man used to be said in our colonies to "clear himself" and "acquit himself" by his own oath, as against some accusations and testimony of an Indian. Plym. Col. Rec. xi. 234, 235 (1673); 1

(1) *Trial by Witnesses.* — This appears to have been One of the oldest kinds of "one-sided" proof. There was no testing by cross-examination; the operative thing was the oath itself, and not the probative quality of what was said, or its persuasion on a judge's mind.[31] Certain transactions, like sales, had to take place before previously-appointed witnesses. Those who were present at the church door when a woman was endowed, or at the execution of a charter, were produced as witnesses. In case of controversy it was their statement, sworn with all due form before the body of freemen who constituted the popular court, that ended the question.[32] In order to show the purely formal character of this sort of proof in the period of the Frankish kings, even where counter-witnesses were allowed, Brunner refers to a capitulary of Louis le Débonnaire, of the year 819, quoted below in a note. It will be observed that while he who suspects that witnesses produced against him are false may bring forward counter-witnesses, yet if the two gets differ hopelessly, the only solution of the difficulty that offers is to have witnesses from each side fight it out together.[33]

Prov. Laws Mass. 151 (1693-4). *Triare,* from the French *trier,* is, indeed, seen, although very seldom, in our early books, *e.g.* in Bracton, f. 105 (say 1259); Fleta, iv., c. 11, ss. 4 and 5 (say 1290); Britton, f. 12, and the "Mirror," iii., c. 34 (Troth near the same date as Fleta); but Pollock and Maitland (Hist. Eng. Law, ii., 596, n, 2) point out a more probable MSS. reading in Bracton, of *terminandae,* instead of *triandae,* and suspect the text of Fleta. In Y. B. 30 & 31 Ed. I., 528 (1302), it is said of challenges to several jurymen *triebantur per residues de duodecim.* In that century the word grew common. In 1353 (Rot. Parl., 1., 248, 12) it is said that if there be a plea before the Mayor of the Staple *et sur ceo pur trier ent la verite enqueste ou proeve soil a prendre,* if both are foreigners, *soit trie per estranges; if* both are denizens, soit *trie per denzeins,* etc. In 1382 the St. R. II. st. 1, c. 6, provides that *rei veritas . . . per inquisitionem trietur.* Everybody knows how familiar the word has become in the last three centuries.

[31] Brunner, Schw. 54-59, 84 *et seq.,* 195 *et seq..* Big. Pl. A. N. xx., Stat. Wall. § 14, Lyon, Hist. Dover, ii., 292, 294.

[32] As to dower, see Brunner, Schw. 342-344, 432-434; Pl. Ab. 21, col. 2 (1198).

[33] Si quis cum altero de qualibet causa contentionem habyuerit, et tegtes contra eum per judicium product! fuerint, si ille falsos eos esse suspicatur, liceat ei alios testes, quos meliores potuerit, contra eos opponere, ut veracium testimonio falsorum testium perversitas superetur. Quod si ambæ partes testium ita inter se dissenserint, ut nulla tenus una pars alteri cedere velit, eligantur duo ex ipsis, id est, ex utraque parte unus, qui cum scutis et fustibus in campo decertent utra pars falsitatem, utra veritatem suo testimonio sequatur. Et campioni qui victus fuerit, propter perjurium quod ante pugnam commisit, dextera manus amputetur. Cæteri vero ejusdem partis testes, quia falsi apparuerint, manus suas

An English illustration of the old trial by witnesses, of the date of 1220 — 1, and bearing marks of antiquity then, is found in the Liber Albus,[34] where, before Hubert de Burgh and his associate justices, the citizens of London answer as to the way in which certain rents may be recovered in London, viz., by writ of "Gavelet," in which, if the tenants deny the *servitium,* the claimant shall name *sectam suam, scilicet duos testes,* who are to be enrolled, and produced at the next hustings. "And if on this day he produce the witnesses and it is shown by them *ut de visu suo et auditu,...* the complainant shall recover his land in demesne." This is also incorporated in the "Statute of 'Gavelet' " usually referred to as 10 Edward II. (1316).[35]

But even earlier than this, here, as also in Normandy,[36] the old mere party proof by witnesses had, in the main, gone by. Things indicate the breaking up and confusing of older forms; anomalies and mixed methods present themselves. The separate notions of the complaint *secta,* the fellow-swearers, the business witnesses, the community witnesses, and the jurors of the inquisition and the assize run together. It is very interesting to find that, as the Norman law contemporaneous with our earliest judicial records shows the same breaking up and confusion as regards this sort of trial which we remark in England, so it is the same classes of cases in both countries that preserve the plainest traces of it. "In my opinion," says Brunner,[37] "undoubtedly we are to include under the head of the formal witness-proof these: (1) The proof of age; (2) The proof of death; ... (3) The proof of property in a movable chattel."

(a.) Age. — In a case of 1219, in the Common Bench,[38] where the defendant alleged the minority of the plaintiff, the plaintiff replied that he was of full age, and thereof he put himself on the inspection of the judges, and if they should doubt about it he would

---

redimant; cujus compositionis duæ partes ei contra quem testati sunt dentur, tertia pro fredo solvatur. — (Capitulare Primum Ludovici Pii, A.D. 819, *Baluze,* Capitularia Regum Francorum, I. 601.) Compare Henry II. of England in 1186, when charters were produced on both sides: *"Iste carte ejusdem antiquitatis sunt et ab eodem rege Aedwardo emanant. Nescio quid dicam: nisi ut carte ad invicem pugnent!"* Big. Pl. A. N. 239, citing Chron. Joc. de Brakel. 37 (Camden Soc.).

[34] Mun. Gild. Lond. i. 62.

[35] But in 1 St. Realm, 222, it is put as *"temp. incert."*

[36] Brunner, Schw. 189.

[37] Schw. 205.

[38] Bracton'a Note Book, ii., case 46; cited in Bracton, f. 424 b.

prove it either by his Bother and his relatives, or otherwise, as the court should adjudge. The judges were in doubt, and ordered that he wove his age by twelve legal men, and that he come with his proof "on the morrow of souls."[39] Now these twelve are not at all a "jury," for the party selects them himself. At the page of Bracton's treatise where he cites this case, he tells us that in these cases the proof "is by twelve legal men, or more if there be need, some of whom are of the family... and some of whom are not;" and he gives the form of oath, which is a very different one from that of the jury. First, one of them swears that the party is or is not twenty-one if a man, or fourteen or fifteen if a woman — *sic me Deus adjuvet et sancta, Dei evangelia;* and then in turn each of the others swears that the oath thus taken is rue.

In a peculiarly interesting part of his great work on the jury, Brunner points out that the old witness-proof was in some cases transformed at the hands of the royal power into an inquisition, so that the witnesses were selected by the public authority, as they were in the ordinary jury.[40] We seem to see this way of blending things in the English process *de aetate probanda.* In 1397[41] we read, after the statement that the king's tenants, on coming of age, in Order to recover their lands must sue out a writ *de aetate probanda,* that those who serve on the inquest must be at least forty-two years old, "and shall tell signs to prove the time of the birth, as that the same year there was a great thunder, tempest, or pestilence, and the like; and all these signs shall be returned by the sheriff." And the reporter puts it as a query whether, since this is proof by witnesses *(per proves),* there may be less than twelve. The requiring of the age of forty-two points to the idea that they must have been of an age to be a witness when the child was born. By 1515 [42] this doubt seems to have been settled: "It was agreed that the trial of his age shall be by twelve jurors; but in giving their verdict every juror should show the reason inducing his knowledge of the age, such as being *son gossipe,* or that he had a son or daughter of the same age, or by reason of an earthquake or a battle near the time of

---

[39] See also *ib.* iii., case 1131 (A. D. 1234), and case 1362 (in 1220).
[40] See *infra,* 102, 103.
[41] Bellewe, 237.
[42] Keilwey, 176-7.

the birth, and the like." Quaint illustrations of these examinations, of the year 1409, are found in the *Liber de Antiquis Legibus*.[43] In one of these cases, relating to a woman's age, each of the twelve makes his statement separately, and each is asked how he knows it. One, sixty years old, says that he fixes the age by the fact that he saw the child baptized; they had a new font, and she was the first person baptized from it. Another, a tailor of the same age, says that he held a candle in the church on the day of baptism, and also made the clothes which the mother wore at her purification. Two others, over fifty, fix the day by a great rain and flood which made the river overflow, and filled the hay with sand. Two others recollect that their hay from six acres of meadow was carried away by the flood. Two others remember it by a fire that burned a neighbor's house. Another by the fact that he was the steward of the child's grandfather, and was ordered by him to give the nurse who told him the news twenty shillings; and so on. Similar details may be found in a record of 1297[44] and in manorial documents of 1348.[45] It is easy, then, to see how in this sort of case the old proof by witnesses should gradually fade out into trial by jury; for the old jury was nothing but a set of triers made up of community witnesses selected by the king's authority. The old mode of trying age by the inspection of the judges, which we saw in 1219, was practised long; but the general rule became established in all such cases that the judges, if in doubt, might refer the matter to a jury.[46]

(b.) Ownership of Chattels. — There were other sorts of transformation. We have seen[47] how the old law could admit counter-witnesses without destroying the formal nature of the proof. With the refinement of procedure, affirmative defences came to be more distinctly recognized; each party had to produce a complaint *secta.* There grew up the practice (whether by

---

[43] pp. cxlix-cliii. Camden Soc. (1846).

[44] Pl. Ab. 293, col. 1.

[45] Baigent, Crondal Records, 431-436.

[46] Y. B. 21 H. VII. 40, 58. Brooke's Ab. Trial, 60. In 1375-6 (Y. B. 50 Edw. III. 6, 12), cavendish, Chief Justice of the King's Bench, being asked to view a woman, and determine her age or nonage, declined, with the prompt remark: "There is not a man in England who can rightly adjudge her of age or under age. Some women who are thirty years old will seem eighteen."

[47] *Ante,* p. 17.

consent of parties or otherwise) of disposing of the case by examining these, and deciding it according as one *secta* was larger than the other, or composed of more worthy persons; and, if it was impossible to settle it on such grounds, of going to the jury. The *secta* in such cases turned into proof-witnesses. It was chiefly such a class of cases, presently to be mentioned, that brought down into our own century the *name* of "trial by witnesses," and the fact of a common-law mode of trial which had not sunk into the general gulf of trial by jury.

In 1234 — 5[48] there came up to the king's court a record of proceedings in the hundred court of a manor of the Bishop of Salisbury. A mare had been picked up in the manor, and one William claimed her in the hundred court and took her, on producing a sufficient *secta* and giving pledges to produce the mare and abide the court's order for a year and, a day, according to the custom of the manor. One Wakelin de Stoke then appeared as claimant, and the steward required each to come on a day with his *secta.* They came, *et Wakelinus producit sectam quod sua est, et similiter Wilhelmus venit cum secta sua, dicens quod sua fuit et ei pullanata (i. e;* foaled). The hundred court, finding itself puzzled and not knowing *cui incumbebat probacio,* postponed judgment *pro afforciamento habendo (i. e; semble,* in order that the parties might increase their sectas). Then Wakelin appeared with a writ removing the case to the king's court at Westminster. At Westminster William produced his *secta,* and they differed *in multis, et in tempore et in aliis circumstanciis,* some of them saying that William bought the mother of the mare four years ago, and she was then pregnant with her and had a small white star on her forehead; and some that it was six years ago and she had no star; and some agreeing in the time but differing about the mark, — some of them saying she had no star, but only some white hairs on her forehead, and some that she bad no star at all. Wakelin produced a *secta* that wholly agreed, all saying that on such a day, four years tack, Wakelin came and bought a sorrel *(soram)* mare with a sucking colt, and gave the colt to one John to keep. They were questioned about marks, and entirely agreed in saying that the colt had the left ear slit and part of the tail cut off, and that she was black. A view was taken of the colt, and she was not more than four years old at most, or three years and a half at least.

---

[48] Bracton's Note Book, iii., case 1115.

Then an official of the manor, Thomas de Perham, said that Wakelin, before he saw the mare in question, told her color and all the marks by which she could be identified, and that William, when he was questioned, did not know her age, and said nothing distinct, except that she was foaled to him. The case, however, went down again for judgment, because the Bishop of Salisbury claimed his jurisdiction; *et quia secta quam Wilhelmus producit non est sufficiens nec aliquid probat et quia loquela incepta fuit infra libertatem episcopi... concessa est ei et teneat unicuique justiciam.*[49]

(c.) *Death.* — But the typical sort of case, and the longest-lived, is what Selden instances[50] when he says: "But some trials by our law have also witnesses without a jury; as of the life and death of the husband in dower and in *cui in vita.*" This continued in England until the end of the year 1834. A case or two will illustrate this proceeding.

In 1308 [51] Alice brought a *cui in vita,* and Thibaud, the tenant, answered that the husband was living. The woman offered proof that he was dead, hanged at Stamford; the tenant the same, that he was alive, *issint que celui que mend provereit mend avereit.* "Alice came and proved her husband's death by four *juretz,* who agreed in everything; and because Thibaud's proof was *mellour et greyneure* than the woman's proof, it was adjudged that she take nothing by her writ." In Fitzherbert,[52] what seems to be the same case is briefly referred to, and there we read that they were at issue, *issint cesti yue mieulx prove mieulx av.;* and the tenant proves by sixteen men, etc., and the demandant by twelve; and because the tenant's proof *"fuit greindr* than the demandant's, it was awarded," etc. If we take Fitzherbert's account to be accurate, it might appear that the twelve men oil each side cancelled each other, and left a total of four to the credit of the tenant, a result which made his proof the better.[53] This old catch of *qui mieulx prove mieulx av.,* a pretty certain badge of antiquity, appears again sixty years later. A woman,

---

[49] For the theory of such cases see Brunner, Schw. 431. See also, *supra, p. 15, n. 7.*

[50] Selden, Fortescue de Land., c. 21, n. 8. For early cases, see Wm. Salt Soc. Coll. (Staffordshire), iii. 120-121 (1203),and Br. N. B. ii. case 356 (1229).

[51] Y. B. Edw. II. 24.

[52] Trial, 46.

[53] Dyer, 185 a, pi. 65, quotes this case as showing four witnesses for the woman and twelve for the tenant.

brought an appeal for her husband's death. The defendant said he was alive. The parties were directed to bring their witnesses, *et celui qui meuch prova meuch av.*[54] In 1560, in the interesting case of Thorne *v.* Rolff,[55] we have an instance where, in. dower, issue was taken on the death or life, and the parties were called on to inform the court "*per proves, [i. e;* witnesses] *ut oportet.*" The demandant brought two, "who were sworn and examined by Leonardo, second prothonotary." These statements are entered in full on the record, which is all given in Benloe's report. The two statements occupy about a page of the folio. Then it is recorded that the tenant produced no witnesses, and the court admits what is offered, as *bonam, probabilem et veram probationem,* and gives judgment for the demandant. Dyer connects this with the old law by citing Bracton, 302, where he speaks of deciding in such cases according to the *probatio magis valida.* The number, rank, and position of the witnesses are what Bracton alludes to.[56] But it is probable that by the time of Thorne *v.* Rolff the rational method of conducting the "trial by witnesses" had taken place; for Coke, half a century later,[57] in enumerating "divers manners of trials," designates this as "trial *by the justices* upon proofs made before them;" and so Comyns, a hundred years afterwards.[58] Blackstone, however, later in the last century,[59] and Stephen,[60] pour back again this new wine into the old bottles and call this wholly modern thing by the old name of "trial by witnesses." Blackstone's explanation of it shows little knowledge of its history. At last this venerable and transformed relic of the Middle Ages was abolished in England, when real actions came to an end by the statute of 1833.

(2.) *Trial by Oath.* — As the Anglo-Saxons required from a plaintiff the taking of a fore-oath, so the defendant was allowed sometimes to clear himself merely by his own oath; the case was "tried" by that alone. But the great mediæval form of trial by oath

---

[54] Lib. Ass. 273, 26; Brooke, Ab., Trial, 90, makes the phrase read *cesty qui nient provera nient avera.*

[55] Dyer, 185 a, (ed. 1601); s. c. Old Benloe, 86. Compare Bastall'a Entries (ed. 1579), Dower, Barre, 1, for another case in 1559.

[56] Compare Pl. Ab. 287. col. 1-2 (1292, 20 Edw. I.).

[57] Case of the Abbot of Strata Mercella, 9 Co. 30 b.

[58] Digest, Trial, (B). For a specimen of what might be called trial by witnesses, see St. 5 & 6 Edw. VI. c. 4, s. 3 (1552).

[59] Com. iii., c. 22.

[60] Pleading, Tyler's ed. (from the 2d Eng. ed., 1827), 114, 131.

was where the party swore with oath helpers — compurgation. In the Salic Law, that "manual of law and legal procedure for the use of the free judges in the oldest and most nearly universal of the organized Teutonic courts, the court of the hundred,"[61] in the fifth century, we find it.[62] It continued among the Germanic people in full force. These fellow-swearers were not witnesses; they swore merely to the truthfulness of another person's oath, or, as it was refined afterwards, to their belief of its truth. It was not requisite that they should have their own knowledge of the facts. Although constantly called by the ambiguous name *testis,* they were not witnesses. They might be, and perhaps originally should be, the kinsmen of the party.[63]

In our own early books this was a great and famous "trial," and its long survival has made it much more familiar to the modern English student than some of its mediaeval companions. It was the chief trial in the popular courts, and as regards personal actions, in the king's courts, where, in real actions also, it was resorted to in incidental questions.[64] In the towns it was a great favorite. An early and quaint illustration of it is found in the Custumal of Ipswich, drawn up about the year 1201 by way of preserving the old usages of the town, and again compiled a hundred years later because of the loss of the older copy.[65] In debt between citizens of the town, the party who had to prove his case was to bring in ten men; five were set on one side and five on the other, and a knife was tossed up in the space between them. The

---

[61] Maine, Early Law and Custom, 144.

[62] Hessels & Kern col. 208, xxxvii; and see ib. Extravagantia, B, p. 421; Lea, Sup. and Force, 4th ed. 34,42.

[63] Lea, Sup. and Force, 4th ed. Mr. Lea's excellent book is full of instruction. Lewis, Anc. Laws of Wales, 30, 112.

[64] Palgrave, Eng. Com. i. 262-3. Glanv. viii, 9, Bigelow, Pl. A. N. xviii. For its extensive use in the manor courts, see Selden Soc. Publications, vols. ii. and iv. The highly formal character which it sometimes took on, and the perils which attended it, are illustrated in a passage from an unpublished treatise of the fourteenth century, preserved by Professor Maitland in *ib.* vol. iv. p. 17. All comes to naught if the principal withdraws his hand from the book while swearing, "or does not say the words in full as they are charged against him. ... If a defendant fails to make his law he has to pay whatever the plaintiff has thought fit to demand." We are told (Lea, Sup. and Force, 4th ed. 78) that in the city of Lille, down to the year 1351, the position of every finger was determined by law, and the slightest error lost the suit irrevocably.

[65] Black Book of the Admiralty, ii. 170-173.

five towards whom the handle lay were then set aside; from the other five one was removed, and the remaining four took the oath as compurgators.

In criminal cases in the king's courts, of the graver sort at any rate, compurgation is thought to have disappeared in consequence of what has been called "the implied prohibition" of the Assize of Clarendon, in 1166.[66] But it remained long in the local and in the ecclesiastical courts.[67] Palgrave[68] preserves as the latest instances of compurgation in criminal cases that can be traced, some cases of 1440 — 1, in the Hundred Court of Winchelsea in Sussex. They are cases of felony, and the compurgation is with thirty-six neighbors. They show a mingling of the old and the new procedure. On April 4,1435, Agnes Archer was indicted by twelve men, sworn before the mayor and coroner to inquire as to the death of Alice Colynbourgh. Agnes *adducta fuit in pleno hundredo... modo felonico, nuda capite et pedibus, dis-cincta, et manibus deligatis; tendens manum suam dexteram altam, per communen clericum arrelnata fuit in his verbis* (and then follows in English a colloquy): "Agnes Archer, is that thy name? which answered, yes.... Thou art endyted that thou... felonly morderiste her with a knyff fyve tymes in the throte stekyng, throwe the wheche stekyng the saide Alys is deed.... I am not guilty of thoo dedys, ne noon of hem, God help me so.... How wylte thou acquite the?... By God and by my neighbours of this town." And she was to acquit herself by thirty-six compurgators to come from the vill of Winchelsea, chosen by herself.[69]

---

[66] Pike, Hist. Crime, i. 130: "The mode of trial was to be what it had been before the Conquest, with the difference that compurgation was no longer permitted in those cases which were of sufficient importance to be brought before the justices in eyre." See Stubbs, Select Charters (6th ed.) 142, Palg. Com. i. 259, Pike, Hist. Crime, i. 122, 123.

[67] Compare Palgrave, Merchant and Friar, 182-3. As to this "trial" in the ecclesiastical courts, see Pollock and Maitland, Hist. Eng. Law, i. 426, Compare Dr. Hooke's case, Gardiner, Star Chamber and High Commission Cases (Camd. Soc.), 276.

[68] Com. ii., p. cxvi, note; compare *ib.* i. 217.

[69] Sometimes it was the rule that twelve of the thirty-six produced by the accused were set aside on the king's behalf, and twelve by the town, and that only the remaining twelve swore with the accused. See the custumals of Winchelsea, Dover, Romney, Bye, and Sandwich in John Lyon's History of Dover, ii. 265. I am indebted to my colleague Dr. Charles Gross for this reference.

The privilege of defending one's self in this way in pleas of the crown was jealously valued by the towns; it was easier and safer than the jury. London had it in its charters. In the few Anglo-Saxon words of the first short charter granted by the Conqueror and still "preserved with great care in an oaken box amongst the archives of the city,"[70] there is nothing specific upon this. But in the charter of Henry I., s. 6, the right of a citizen is secured in pleas of the crown, to purge himself by the usual oath; and this is repeated over and over again in charters of succeeding kings.[71] Henry III., in his ninth charter, cut down the right, by disallowing a former privilege of the accused to supply the place of a deceased compurgator by swearing upon his grave.[72] There was the "Great Law," in which the accused swore with thirty-six freemen (six times, each time with six), chosen, half from the freemen of the east side of the rivulet of Walbrook, and half from the west; they were not to be chosen by the accused himself, nor to be his kinsmen or bound to him by the tie of marriage or any other. The accused might object to them for reasonable cause; they were chosen and *struck,* much after the way of a modern special jury. The "Middle Law" and "Third Law" were like this, but had eighteen and six compurgators respectively.[73] In civil cases of debt and trespass, compurgation with six others was the rule in London; or, if the defendant was not a resident, with only two others. If he had not two, then the foreigner was to be taken by a sergeant of the court to the six churches nearest, and to swear in each.[74]

In the king's courts the earliest judicial records have many cases of this mode of trial; *e.g.* in 1202, in the Bedfordshire eyre, where, in an action for selling beer in the borough of Bedford by a false measure, the defendant was ordered to defend herself "twelve-handed;" and she gave pledges to make her "law" *(vadiavit*

---

[70] Norton's London, 324, note. Palgrave, Merchant and Friar, 180.

[71] Of Henry II., Richard, John, Henry III., the three Edwards, and Richard II. For the charters, see Liber Albus, Mun. Gild. Lond. i. 128 *et seq.*

[72] Lib. Alb., Mun. Gild. Lond. i. 137-8; *ib.* Riley'a ed.. 123, note.

[73] Lliber Albus, Mun. Gild. Lond. i., 57-59, 92, 104, 203; *infra,* 199.

[74] A good Anglo-Saxon method. Fleta, Lib. 2, c. 63, s. 12, gives the merchants' way of proving a tally by his own oath in nine churches. He was to swear to the same thing in each, and then return to Guildhall for judgment. As to the tally, see Y. B. 20 & 21 Edw. I. 68, 304, 330, Y. *B.* Edw. II. 278, Black Bk. Adm. ii. 126.

legem).[75] In 1382,[76] among the measures of relief from litigation following acts done in the recent insurrections, people charged with trespasses are allowed *purgare se* by three or four fellow-swearers. In Wales the *assache* was in existence in 1413, requiring the oath of three hundred persons, and it was found necessary in St. 1 Henry V. c. 6, to relieve those who had been loyal in a late rebellion from the hardships of so formidable a "trial."

From being a favored mode of trial, this "law," or, as it is commonly called, "wager of law," from its preliminary stage of giving pledges to perform it, steadily tended to become a thing exceptional; not going beyond the line of the precedents,[77] and within that line being a mere privilege, an optional trial alongside of the growing and now usual trial by jury. In the newer forms of action it was not allowed, and finally it survived mainly in detinue and debt.[78] Yet within a narrow range it held a firm place.[79] In 1440,[80] in debt for board, Yelverton, for plaintiff, tried to maintain that the defendant could not have his law of a thing "which lies in the conusance of the pais." But the court held otherwise and the defendant had his law. In 1454 — 5,[81] there was a great debate among the judges over a demurrer to a plea of non-summons in a real action, with "ready to aver *per pais.*" It was insisted by Prisot (C. J.) that this lay in the knowledge of the pais, and that all such things should in reason be triable by the jury. He admitted, however, that the practice had been otherwise. His associates, Danvers and Danby, agreed with him; while Moile and Ayshton pressed strongly the more conservative doctrine. "This will be a strong thing," said Moile; "it has not been done before." "Since waging law," said

---

[75] Maitl. Pl. Cr. i., case 61; s. c. Palg. Com. ii., p. cxix, note. And so elsewhere abundantly in the earliest records; *e. g.* in 1198-9, Rot. Car Beg. i. 200. And see Glanvill, Bk. 1, cc. 9 and 16 (1187), Bracton, 410.

[76] St. 6 Rich. II. c. 5.

[77] See Pl. Ab. 291, col. 1 (1293-4).

[78] Steph. Pl. (Tyler's ed) 131-2.

[79] It was allowed sometimes where it seemed desirable to relieve a party against a burdensome or unfair claim; *e g.* in 1363, against the claim of Londoners that another was indebted to them, when they had taken no tally or deed, and offered to prove it merely *par lour papirs. So* in 1403 (St. 5 H. IV. c. 8) it is protected against contrivances for depriving one's adversary of it, and driving him to an inquest of unfriendly neighbors. Jenkins, Rep. ix, among "Abases of the Law," numbers "the taking away wager of law upon contracts."

[80] Y. B. 19 H. VI. 10, 25.

[81] Y. B. 33 H. VI. 7, 23.

Ayshton, "has always been practised, and no other way, this proves, in a way, that it is *un positive ley.* All our law is directed *(guide)* by usage or statute; it has been used that no one wages his law in trespass, and the contrary in debt; so that we should adjudge according to the use," etc. No decision in the case is reported. But Brooke, in his Abridgment, in the next century, gives the latter view as *optima opinio.*[82]

In 1492,[83] Sebastian Giglis, "merchaunt of Venyce," complains to the Chancellor against Robert Welby, as having exposed him to the repayment of money advanced to Robert by a third party at the plaintiff's request, by waging his law "as an untrue Cristenman," when sued for it by this third party, who has now come upon the plaintiff and demands it of him. Robert had signed a "bill" for it, but nothing under seal. Robert's answer admitted receiving the money, but set forth that he was acting as an agent of King Richard III. and "wrote a bill of receipt... to the intent that the said bill... might have been a remembrance to the said late King for repayment of the said sum." After a hearing the Chancellor decreed that inasmuch as the defendant admitted receiving the money and showed no payment or exoneration, or any reasonable ground for being exonerated, he should pay the money to *the plaintiff.* The effect of this case seems to be overstated by Spence,[84] in saying that the merchant was relieved "from the consequences of the defendant having waged his law.... This interference of the Court of Chancery no doubt had its effect in causing this ancient mode of proof... to go into disuse." The case is, indeed, very significant, but it will be remarked that the court by no means directly relieved the party himself, who had lost by a good and established form of trial. It relieved Sebastian, and not the plaintiff in the other litigation.

A century later, in 1587,[85] when compurgation had become less usual, and, in the eyes of the Chancellor, almost archaic, we read that the Star Chamber refused to deal with one who was alleged to have sworn falsely in making his law; "the reason was because it was as strong as a trial. And the Lord Chancellor demanded of the

---

[82] For the established rule in such cases see 2 Rot. Cur. Reg. 125 (1198), Bracton, 334 *b.,* 366, Y. ,B. 30 & 31 Edw. I. 189 (1302), Y. B. 15 Edw. III. 299 (1341).

[83] Cal. Proc. in Chanc. i. ccxx-cxxii; cited in Spence Eq. Jnr. i. 696.

[84] *Ubi supra.*

[85] Goldsborough, 51, pi. 13; Doctor and Student, ii. c. 24, end.

Judges if he were discharged of the debt by waging of his law; and they answered 'yea.' But Manwood (C. B.) said that it was the folly of the plaintiff, because that he may change his action into an action of the case upon an assumpsit, wherein the defendant cannot wage his law." In his report of Slade's Case (1602) Coke remarks[86] that courts will not admit a man to wage his law without good admonition and due examination.

After another century this procedure still keeps its place, but it is strange, and the profession has lost the clue. In 1699, in the Company of Glaziers Case,[87] in debt on a bylaw, the defendant had his law. When he came with his compurgators, the plaintiff's counsel urged that the court need not receive him to his oath if he were swearing falsely or rashly; *"sed, per* Holt, C. J., 'We can admonish him, but if he will stand by his law, we cannot hinder it, seeing it is a method the law allows.' " The reporter takes the pains to describe the details of the proceedings, as if they were unfamiliar;[88] and at the end of it all he adds: *"Per* Northey (plaintiff's counsel), this will be a reason for extending indebitatus assumpsits further than before. Holt, C. J. We will carry them no further." In the next case,[89] where, in a similar matter, two or three years later, the court refused wager of law in debt on a by-law, Holt, C. J., said that the plaintiff's counsel yielded too much in the Glaziers Case: "It was a gudgeon swallowed, and so it passed without observation." In 1701 — 2 came a great case,[90] where, in debt on a city by-law, for a penalty for refusing to serve as sheriff, the defendant offered to make his law

---

[86] 4 Rep., p. 95.

[87] Anon., 2 Salk. 682.

[88] The defendant was set at the right corner of the bar, without the bar, and the secondary asked him if he was ready to wage his law. He answered yes; then he laid his hand upon the book, and then the plaintiff was called; and a question thereupon arose whether the plaintiff was demandable? And a diversity taken where he perfects his law instanter, and where a day is given in the same term, and when in another term. As to the last, they held he was demandable, whether the day given was in the same term or another. Then the court admonished him, and also his compurgators, which they regarded not so much as to desist from it; accordingly, the defendant was sworn, that he owed not the money *modo et forma, as* the plaintiff had declared, nor any penny thereof. Then his compurgators standing behind him, were called over, and each held up his right hand, and then laid their hands upon the book and swore, that they believed what the defendant swore was true.

[89] London v. Wood, 12 Mod. 669, 684.

[90] London *v.* Wood, 12 Mod. 669.

with six freemen of the city, according to the custom of London. The plaintiff demurred. Much that was futile was said of wager of law. We are told by Baron Hatsell[91] that it lies only "in respect of the weakness and inconsiderableness of the plaintiff's... cause of demand... in five cases: first, in debt on simple contract, which is the common case; secondly, in debt upon an award upon a parol submission; thirdly, in ah account against a receiver;... fourthly, in detinue;... fifthly, in an amerciament in a court baron or other inferior courts not of record." Holt rationalized the matter in a different way:[92] "This is the right difference, and not that which is made in the actions, viz., that it lies in one sort of action and not in another; but the true difference is when it is grounded on the defendant's wrong;... for if debt be brought and... the foundation of the action is the wrong of the defendant, wager of law will not lie." And again,[93] "The secrecy of the contract which raises the debt is the reason of the wager of law; but if the debt arise from a contract that is notorious, there shall be no wager of law."

In the latter half of the eighteenth century it was nearly gone. Blackstone tells us: "One shall hardly hear at present of an action of debt brought upon a simple contract," but of assumpsit for damages, where there could be no wager of law; and so of trover instead of detinue. "In the room of actions of account a bill in equity is usually filed.... So that wager of law is quite out of use;... but still it is not out of force. And therefore when a new statute inflicts a penalty and gives... debt for recovering it, it is usual to add 'in which no wager of law shall be allowed;' otherwise an hardy delinquent might escape any penalty of the law by swearing that he had never incurred or else had discharged it." [94]

---

[91] *Ib.* p. 669-70.

[92] Ib. p. 677.

[93] *Ib.* p. 679. Perhaps this came from Coke, who shows little knowledge of the history of the matter. In Inst. ii. 45 (printed about 1642, several years after Coke's death), he says: — "The reason wherefore in an action of debt upon a simple contract, the defendant may wage his law is for that the defendant may satisfy the party in secret, or before witness, and all *the* witnesses may die; ... and this for aught I could ever read is peculiar to the law of England."

[94] Com. iii. 347-8. This clause had already been found in English statutes for three centuries and more; it appeared also on this side of the water, in our colonial acts, even in regions like Massachusetts, where it is said that wager of law was not practised. Dane's Ab. i., c. 29, art. 8. In Childress *v.* Emory, 8 Wheat. 642, 675 (1823), Story, J., is of opinion that "the wager of law, if it ever

The validity of this ancient trial was, indeed, recognized by the Court of Common Pleas in 1805,[95] but in 1824, when for the last time it makes its appearance in our reports,[96] it is a discredited stranger, ill understood: "Debt on simple contract. Defendant pleaded *nil debet per legem*.... Langslow applied to the court to assign the number of compurgators.... The books [he says] leave it doubtful.... This species of defence is not often heard of now.... Abbott, C. J. The court will not give the defendant any assistance in this matter. He must bring such number of compurgators as he shall be advised are sufficient.... Rule refused. The defendant [say the reporters] prepared to bring eleven compurgators, but the plaintiff abandoned the action." It had turned out, then, to be not yet quite a ghost; and so in 1833[97] it was at last enacted by Parliament "that no wager of law shall be hereafter allowed." Palgrave[98] had lately pointed out with accuracy the old and the later legal situation: "An inquest or jury, in civil causes, was never adopted according to the usual course of the popular courts of Anglo-Saxon origin, unless by virtue of the king's special precept." In an action begun there by the writ which empowered the sheriff to act as the king's justiciar, an inquest might be summoned, "but if the suit was grounded upon a plaint the opinion of the suitors or the compurgatory oath constituted the common-law trial.... The same rule was observed in the manorial courts, in which by common, right all pleas were determined by wager of law.... Even in the king's court the incidental traverses in a

---

had a legal existence in the United States, is now completely abolished." "Trial by oath," however, was not unknown here. See *supra,* 16, n. 1. See also the effect of the defendant's oath as neutralizing the plaintiff's shop-books in Plym. Col. Laws, 196 (1682). By a statute of Massachusetts (St. 1783, c. 55) on a charge of usury a like purgation was given, at a time when a party to the suit could not be a witness. When, later, he was admitted, in such cases, to testify, we find Shaw, C. J., in Little v. Rogers, 1 Met. 108, 110 (1840), describing the situation *as* one where "the trial by jury has been substituted for the old trial by oath." Compare Fry *v.* Barker, 2 Pick. 65. Lea, Sup. and Force, 4th ed. 87-88, quotes cases from the English colony of Bermuda in 1638 and 1639, where, at the assizes, persons "presented upon suspicion of incontinency," are sentenced to punishment unless they purge themselves by oath.

[95] Barry *v.* Robinson, 1 B. & P. (N. B.), p. 297: "If a man," argued counsel, "were now to tender his wager of law, the court would refuse to allow it." ... "This was denied by the court," adds the reporter.

[96] King *v.* Williams, 2 B. & C. 538 ; s. c. 4 D. & B. 3. 3

[97] St. 3 & 4 Wm. IV. c. 42, s. 13.

[98] Com. i. 262-3.

real action, such as the denial of the summons by the tenant, were always determined by compurgators; and in all personal actions wager of law was the regular mode of trial, until new proceedings were instituted which enabled the judges to introduce the jury trial in its stead. But this silent legislation, has not destroyed the Anglo-Saxon trial [his preface is dated Feb. 1,1832]; it is out of use, but not out of force; and it may, perhaps, continue as a part of the theory of the law until some adventurous individual shall again astonish the court by obtaining his privilege, and by thus informing the legislature of its existence, insure its abolition."

(3) *The Ordeal.* — Of trial by the ordeal (other than the duel) not much need be said. Nothing is older; and to this day it flourishes in various parts of the world. The investigations of scholars discover it everywhere among barbarous people, and the conclusion seems just that it is indigenous with the human creature in the earliest stages of his development.[99] Like the rest, our

---

[99] Patetta, *Ordalie,c.* 1. See Inst. of Narada, Jolly's Trans. 44-54. This book is attributed to some period between the second and ninth centuries before Christ; "but the materials of our work," says the translator (p. xx), "are of coarse much older, and many of the laws it contains belong to the remotest antiquity." Beginning at Part I. c. 5, s. 102, and ending at Part II. (pp. 44-54), we have the doctrine of ordeals. After speaking of the situation where there are neither writings nor witnesses, and of the examination of the defendant, it is said that "If reasonable inference also leads to no result," the defendant is to be put to the ordeal. "He whom the blazing fire burns not, whom the water soon forces not up, or who meets with no speedy misfortune must be held veracious in his testimony on oath. Let ordeals be administered if an offence has been committed in a solitary forest, at night, in the interior of a house, and in cases or violence and of denial of a deposit. . . . The balance, fire, water, poison, and sacred libation are said to be the five divine tests for the purgation of suspected persons." Then follows an account of each of these ordeals. 1. After describing the scales and the first weighing of the accused, it is said: "And having adjured the balance by imprecations, the judge should cause the person accused to be placed in the balance again. 'O balance, thou only knowest what mortals do not comprehend. This man being arraigned in a cause is weighed upon thee. Therefore mayest thou deliver him lawfully from his perplexity.' . . . Should the individual increase in weight, he is not innocent; if he be equal in weight or lighter, his innocence is established." 2. In the ordeal of fire seven circles with a diameter equal to the length of the man's foot, and thirty-two inches distant from each other, are marked on the ground. The circles are smeared with cows' dung, and the man, having fasted and made himself clean, has seven *açvattha* leaves laid on his hands and fastened there, and takes in his hands a smooth ball of red-hot iron, weighing fifty *palas,* and walks slowly through the seven circles. He then puts the ball on the ground. " If he is burnt, his guilt is proved; but if he remain wholly unburnt,

ancestors had it. Glanvill,[100] for instance (about 1187), lays it down that an accused person who is disabled by mayhem *tenetur se purgare... per Dei judicium... scilicet per callidum ferrum si fuerit homo liber, per aquam si fuerit rusticus.*[101] This was found to be a convenient last resort, not only when the accused was old or disabled from fighting in the duel, but when compurgators or witnesses could not be found or were contradictory, or where for any reason no decision could otherwise be reached.

In our earliest judicial records the ordeal is found often. The earliest of these cases which is assignable to any precise year is one of 10 Rich. I. (1198 — 9),[102] where, on an appeal of death, by a maimed person, two of the defendants are adjudged to purge themselves by the hot iron. But within twenty years or so this mode of trial came to a sudden end in England, through the powerful agency of the Church, — an event which was the more remarkable

---

he is undoubtedly innocent. . . . 'Thou, o fire, dwellest in the interior of all creatures, like a witness. Thou only knowest what mortals do not comprehend. This man is arraigned in a cause and desires acquittal. Therefore mayest thou deliver him lawfully from his perplexity.' " 3. In the ordeal of water, the man wades out into the water up to his navel, and another shoots an arrow. The man dives or ducks into the water, and if he remains wholly under while a swift runner gets and fetches back the arrow he is innocent. The adjuration to the water is similar to the above, in the case of fire and the balance. 4. In the ordeal by poison elaborate directions are given about the choice of the poison and the time of year for administering it. The invocation runs; "Thou, O poison, art the son of Brahma, thou art persistent in truth and justice; relieve this man from sin, and by thy virtue become as ambrosia to him. On account of thy venomous and dangerous nature thou art the destruction of all living creatures; thou art destined to show the difference between right and wrong like a witness," etc., etc., much as in the other cases above. "If the 'poison is digested easily, without violent symptoms, the king shall recognize him as innocent, and dismiss him, after having honored him with presents." S. In the ordeal by sacred libation, "the judge should give the accused water in which an image of that deity to whom he is devoted has been bathed, thrice calling out the charge with composure. One to whom any calamity or misfortune happens within a week or a fortnight is proved to be guilty." Sir Henry Maine, writing in 1880 (Life and Speeches, 426), 'after saying that "perjury and corruption are still deplorably common in India," adds: "Ordeals are perpetually resorted to in private life."

[100] Book xiv., c. i. See also cases from Domesday Book and other eleventh century sources in Bigelow, Pl. A. N. *passim.*

[101] And so the *Dialogus de Scaccario,* ii. 7, written ten rears earlier; Pollock and Maitland, Hist. Eng. Law, i. 154, n. 7.

[102] Rot. Cur. Reg. i. 204. See several cases of uncertain date in the reign of Rich. I. in Pl. Ab. 13-17.

because Henry II., in the Assize of Clarendon (1166) and again in that of Northampton (1176), providing a public mode of accusation in the case of the larger crimes, had fixed the ordeal as the mode of trial. The old form of trial by oath was no longer recognized in such cases in the king's courts. It was the stranger, therefore, that such quick operation should have been allowed in England to the decree, in November, 1215, of the Fourth Lateran Council at Rome. That this was recognized and accepted in about three years (1218 — 19) by the English crown is shown by the well-known writs of Henry III. to the judges, dealing with the puzzling question of what to do for a mode of trial, *cum prohibitum sit per Ecclesiam Romanam judicium ignis et aquae,*[103] I find no case of trial by ordeal in our printed

---

[103] *Sacros. Conc.* xiii. ch. 18, pp. 954-5. Rymer'a *Foedera* (old ed.), 228, it. (Rec. Com. ed.) 154, has one of these writs. Maitland quotes it in his Gloucester Pleas, p. xxxviii. How promptly it was obeyed by the ecclesiastics in the local courts is seen in a case of 1231 (2 Br. N. B. case 592), where on a writ of false judgment to the court of the Abbot of St. Edmunds in an appeal of felony for wounds it appeared that the' case had been tried by jury, without the king's warrant. The Abbot's steward being asked *quo warranto faciunt talem inquisitionem de vita et membris,* said that since the war [1215-1217],this had been usual in the Abbot's court. Before the war, it is added, they had the ordeal of fire and water.

Patetta, *Ordalie, 312,* doubts the accepted opinion that the disappearance of the ordeal in England was thus due to the Lateran Council decree. He remarks, truly, that the action of the Council merely forbade ecclesiastics to take part in the ordeal, and adds that there is mention of the ordeal in Henry the Third's Magna Carta of 1224-5. Compare also Bigelow, Hist. Proc. 323-4. But one is inclined to doubt whether Dr. Patetta had in mind the king's writs above referred to; those and the sudden cessation of the cases seem conclusive. As regards the mention of *legem manifestam* as late as the Magna Carta of 1224-5, it may, probably, be explained by the circumstance that this was a reissue of an earlier document; the mere *legem ot* the former documents had already become *legem manifestam nec adjuramentum,* in the second reissue of 1217. This was not in the reissue of 1216. Its appearance in 1217 is not an unnatural or untimely expansion of the term *legem.* The new phrase was also used for the battle as well as the ordeal in its narrower sense — the sense now under consideration. See Brunner's interesting comment on this passage of Magna Carta in Zeits. der Sav.-Stift. (Germ. Abt.) ii. 213. In 1291 *legem manifestam* is used in the sense of the duel. In an appeal of mayhem, the appellor made default. The appellee being then put on his defence to the king's prosecution, set up the point that the only way of proving a mayhem was by having the party maimed inspected, and in the absence of this denied that any one *poni debet ad legem manifestam.* Pl. Ab. 285, col. 1. There occurs a reference to the ordeal in a record of 1221, but on examination it proves to be a statement that one Robert underwent the ordeal at a previous trial, which may well have been some years

records later than Trinity Term of the 15 John (1214). We read then of several cases.[104] One Ralph, accused of larceny, is adjudged to purge himself by water; he did clear himself, and abjured the realm. And so in another exactly like case of murder. It was the hard order of the Assize of Clarendon that he who bad come safely through the ordeal might thus be required to abjure the realm, a circumstance which recalls the shrewd scepticism of William Rufus when he remarked of the *judicium Dei* that God should no longer decide in these matters, — he would do it himself.[105] In a third case a person was charged with supplying the knife with which, a homicide was committed, and was adjudged to purge himself by water of consenting to the act. He failed, and was banged.

In England, then, this mode of trial lived about a century and a half after the Conquest, going out after Glanvill wrote, and before Bracton. The latter is silent about it. The "Mirror," written, as Maitland conjectures, between 1285 and 1290, regrets that it has gone by. "It is an abuse," says the writer, "that proofs and purgations are not made by the miracle of God where no other proof can be had." [106] In 1679 a defendant astonished the court by asking to be tried by the ordeal.[107]

The conception which, was at the bottom of the ordeal and compurgation is often misunderstood. Thus Palgrave [108] says that under the arrangements of the Assize of Clarendon "the ordeal was, in fact, only a mode of giving to the culprit a last chance of escaping the punishment of the law." And so Stubbs:[109] "The ordeal, in these circumstances being a resource following the verdict of a jury acquainted with the fact, could only be applied to those who were to all intents and purposes proved to be guilty." No, the ordeal was

---

earlier. Maitland's Gloucester Pleas, cage 383, and p. xxii; and notes on this case at p. 150, and on case 434, at p. 151.

[104] Plac. Ab. 90, col. 2. One of these cases and another separate one are found in Maitland, Sel. Pl. Cr. i., case 116. In this volume there follow three others, 119, 122, and 125, "of uncertain date."

[105] Eadmer, Hist. Nov. (Rolls Series), 102, Pollock and Maitland, Hist. Eng. Law. ii. 597, Brunner, Schw. 182. Compare the cool sense of Frederic II. in 1231, Lea, Sup. and Force, 4th ed. 422.

[106] Maitland, "Mirror," 173 (Book 5, c. i. s. 127).

[107] Whitebread's case, 7 How. St. Tr. 383; cited by Stephen, 1 Hist. C. Law, 253 n.

[108] Com. ii. 177.

[109] Sel. Charters, 6th ed. 142.

simply a mode of trial; or, as they phrased it in those days, of clearing one's self of a charge. And so, while it gave way, after the Lateran Council decree, to trial by jury, the old accusing jury persisted and still persists.

Modern civilization occasionally feels nowadays the want of some substitute for these old tests, in cases where there is very strong ground of suspicion, but full legal proof is wanting. Compare the convenient ecclesiastical compurgation, *e.g.* in the sentence of the Archbishop of Canterbury, in 1631, in Hooke's case.[110] After deciding against Hooke on some points he adds: "For his simony I vehemently suspect him, and therefore [he is] to purge himself *manu.*"

(4) *Trial by Battle.* — This is often classified as an ordeal, "a God's judgment," but in dealing with our law it is convenient to discriminate it from the ordeals, for the battle has other aspects than that of an appeal to Heaven. Moreover, it survived for centuries the ordeal proper. It had, also, no such universal vogue. Although it existed among almost all the Germanic people, the Anglo-Saxons seem not to have had it;[111] but with the Normans it came into England in full strength. In Glanvill, a century after the Conquest, we see it as one of the chief modes of trial in the king's courts: "A debt... is proved by the court's general mode of proof, viz., by writing or by duel."[112] "They may come to the duel or other such usual proof as is ordinarily received in the courts," etc.[113] Of the inferior courts, also, we are told that in a lord's court a duel may be reached between lord and man, if any of the man's peers makes himself a witness and so champion.[114] He, also, who gave the judgment of an inferior court might, on a charge of false judgment, have to defend the award in the king's court by the duel, either in person or by a champion.[115] And so elsewhere.

There is sufficient evidence that it was, at first, a novel and hated thing in England. In the so-called "Laws of William the Conqueror," it figures as being the Frenchman's mode of trial, and

---

[110] Gardiner's Star Ch. and High Com. Cases, 259.
[111] Pollock and Maitland, Hist. Eng, Law, i. 16.
[112] Lib. 10,c. 17.
[113] Lib. 13, c.11.
[114] Lib. 9, c. 1.
[115] Lib. 8, c. 9. See generally *St. de Magn. Ass. et Duel!is, St.* Realm, i.

not the Englishman's. In a generation after the Conquest, the charter of Henry I. to the city of London grants exemption from it; and the same exemption was widely sought and given, *e.g.*, in Winchester and Lincoln.[116] The earliest reference to the battle, I believe, in any account of a trial in England, is at the end of the case of Bishop Wulfstan *v.* Abbot Walter, in 1077.[117] The controversy was settled, and we read: "Thereof there are lawful witnesses... who saw and heard this, ready to prove it by oath and battle." This is an allusion to a common practice in the Middle Ages, that of challenging another's witness;[118] or perhaps to one method of disposing of cases where adversary witnesses were allowed, and these contradicted each other. Brunner [119] refers to this, with Norman instances of the dates 1035, 1053, and 1080, as illustrating a procedure which dated back to the capitulary of 819, quoted above.[120] Thus, as among nations still, so then in the popular courts and between contending private parties, the battle was often the *ultima ratio,* in cases where their rude and unrational methods of trial yielded no results.

In a great degree it was for the purpose of displacing this dangerous, costly, and discredited mode of proof that the recognitions — that is to say, juries in their first organized form — were introduced. These were regarded as a special boon to the poor man, who was oppressed in many ways by the duel.[121] It was by enactment of Henry II. that this reform was brought about, first in his Norman dominions (in 1150 — 52), before reaching the English throne, and afterwards in England, sometime after he became king, in 1154. Brunner (to whom we are indebted for the clear proof of this) remarks upon a certain peculiar facility with which the jury

---

[116] Mun. Gild. Lond. i. 128, s. 5, and Thorpe, i. 502 — quod *nullus eorum faciat bellum.* Pl. Ab. 26, col. 2, Lincoln; Pike, Hist. Crim. Law, i. 448; Patetta, *Ordalie,* 307, 308.

[117] Essays in Anglo-Saxon Law, 379; s. c. Bigelow, Pl. A. N. 19; Brunner, Schw. 197, 400-1.

[118] Lea, Sup. and Force, 4th ed. 120.

[119] Schw. 197-8; Ib. 68, 401. citing Glanvill, lib. 10, c. 12; lib. 2,c. 21.

[120] *Supra,* p. 17 n.

[121] See *e.g.* the recitals in the St. of Vouchers (20 Edw. I. gt. I) of 1292. So also we are told that "Saint Louis abolished battle in his country because it happened often that when there was a contention between a poor man and a rich man, in which trial by battle was necessary, the rich man paid so much that all the champions were on his side, and the poor man could find none to help him." *Grandes Chroniques de France, vol.* 4, p. 427, 430, al. 3, cited in Brunner, Schw. 295, note.

made head in England, owing, among other reasons, to the facts (1) that the duel was a hated and burdensome Norman importation, and (2) that among the Anglo-Saxons, owing to the absence of the duel, the ordeal had an uncommonly wide extension, so that when, a generation later than the date of Glanvill's treatise, the ordeal was abolished, there was left an unusually wide gap to be filled by this new, welcome, and swiftly developing mode of trial.[122] The manner in which Glanvill speaks of the great assize is very remarkable. In the midst of the dry details of his treatise we come suddenly upon a passage full of sentiment, which testifies to the powerful contemporaneous impression made by the first introduction of the organized jury into England.[123]

Selden has remarked upon the small number of battles recorded as actually fought.[124] The society which bears his honored name is now bringing to light cases of which he probably never heard.[125] Such traces of the duel and the ordeal in England as are found before Glanvill's time are collected in Bigelow's valuable *Placita Anglo Normannica.* Very early cases from Domesday Book, compiled by William within twenty years of the

---

[122] Schw. 300-304. Compare Bigelow, Pl. A. N. xxvii n.

[123] Glanvill, lib. 2, c. 7. This well-known passage runs in substance thus: The Grand Assize is a royal favor, granted to the people by the goodness of the king, with the advice of the nobles. It so well cares for the life and condition of men that every one may keep his rightful freehold and yet avoid the doubtful chance of the duel, and escape that last penalty, an unexpected and untimely death, or, at least, the shame of enduring infamy in uttering the hateful and shameful word ["Craven"] which comes from the mouth of the conquered party with so much disgrace, as the consequence of his defeat. This institution springs from the greatest equity. Justice, which, after delays many and long, is scarcely ever found in the duel, is more easily and quickly reached by this proceeding. The assize does not allow so many essoins as the duel; thus labor is saved and the expenses of the poor reduced. Moreover, by as much as the testimony of several credible witnesses outweighs in courts that of a single one, by so much is this process more equitable than the duel. For while the duel goes upon the testimony of one sworn person, this institution requires the oaths of at least twelve lawful men.

[124] *Duello,* cc. 8 and 13.

[125] If the lawyers knew how much they could promote the cause of legal learning, and thereby improve our law, by becoming members of this excellent society (it costs a guinea a year), they would not neglect the opportunity. The American Secretary and Treasurer is Mr. Richard W. Hale, of No. 10, Tremont St., Boston.

Conquest, are found here.[126] Selden refers to a civil case in Mich. 6 Rich. I. (1194), as "the oldest case I have read of." [127] This may be the case in Vol. I. of the *Rotuli Curiae Regis,* 23 — 24, 26, which appears to be the earliest one reported in the judicial records. Although the demandant here *hoc offert probare versus eum per Radulphum filium Stephani, qui hoc offert probare ut de visu patris sui per corpus suum sicut curia consideraverit,* and the defendant came and defended the right and inheriting of (the plaintiff), *et visum patris Radulphi filii Stephani, per Johannem... qui hoc offert defendere per corpus suum consideracione curiae,* — yet the case appears to have gone off without the battle, on another point. But this record shows the theory of the thing. The plaintiff offers battle and puts forward a champion who is a complaint-witness, and who speaks as of his personal knowledge or, as in this case, on that of his father,[128] and stands ready to fight for his testimony. Before the battle the two champions swear to the truth of what they say.

In the mother-country, Normandy, one might hire his champion; but in England, theoretically, it was not allowed. In 1220 one Elias Piggun was convicted of being a hired champion, and lost his foot — *consideratum est quod amittat pedem.*[129] What was thus forbidden seems, however, to have been much practised, and finally, in 1275, the struggle to prevent it came to an end by abandoning any requirement that the champion be a witness. The St. West. I., c. 41, reads: "Since it seldom happens that the demandant's champion, is not forsworn in making oath that he or his father saw the seisin of his lord or ancestor and his father commanded him to *deraign,* it is provided that the demandant's champion be not bound to swear this; but be the oath kept in all other points."

---

[126] pp. 41, 42, 43, 61, 305.

[127] *Duello,* C. 13.

[128] Glanvill, lib. 2, c. 3, sets forth that in this class of cases the plaintiff cannot be his own champion, for he mast have a good witness, who shall speak of his own knowledge or that of his father. So in the recognition, substituted for the battle, the jurymen — the twelve witnesses of Glanvill's eulogy, so much better than the one battle-witness — are to speak of their own personal knowledge, or by the report of their fathers, *et per talia quibus fidem teneantur habere ut propriis. Ib.* lib. 2, c, 17. Compare Brunner, Schw. 180.

[129] Maitland, Sel. Pl. Cr. i. 192; s. c. Bracton, 151 b.

The Year Books indicate small use of the trial by battle in later days. One sign is the particularity with which the ceremonial is described, as if it were a curiosity. Thus in 1342 — 3, and again in 1407,[130] in criminal appeals, the formalities of the battle oath and subsequent matters are fully given. And in 1422[131] the ceremony in a battle between champions is described with carious details, down to the defaulting of the tenant on the appointed day. In 1565 Sir Thomas Smith[132] tells us, of this mode of trial, that it was not much used, but "I could not learn that it was ever abrogated." This was only six years before the famous writ of right, in Lowe *v.* Paramour,[133] which furbished up this faded learning. Dyer has a pretty full and good account of that case; but Spelman's Latin[134] is fuller and very quaint. The trial in a writ of right, he tells us, repeating with precision the doctrine of four centuries and a half before, is by duel or the assize; *utrunque genus hodie insuetum est sed duelli magis.*[135] Yet, he goes on, it chanced that this last was revived in 1571, and battle was ordered, *non sine magna jurisconsultorum perturbatione.* Then comes a curious detailed account, setting forth, among other things, how Nailer, the demandant's champion, in his battle array, to the sound of fifes and trumpets, on the morning of the day fixed for the battle, *Londinum, minaciter spatiatur.* It has been said that Spelman was present at Tothill Fields on that day with the thousands of spectators that assembled; he does not say so, I believe, but he writes with all the vivacity of an eye-witness. The demandant made default. Another like case occurred as late as 1638, but again there was no fight.[136] Efforts to abolish the

---

[130] Y. B. 17 Edw. III. 2, 6; 8. c. Lib. Ass. 48, 1; Y. B. 9 H. IV. 3, 16.

[131] Y. B. 1 H. VI. 6, 29.

[132] Com. England, bk. ii. c. 8.

[133] Dyer, 301.

[134] Glossary, *sub vac. Camus* (A. D. 1625).

[135] How rusty the lawyers were in 1554, as regards the Grand Assize, is shown in Lord Windsor *v. St.* John, Dyer, 98 and 103 b.

[136] Cro. Car. 522; Rushworth's Coil. ii. 788. Milton, a contemporary of this case, has gravely entered in his Common Place Book, the following, having reference to a case of the last preceding century: *"De Duellis :* Not certain in deciding the truth, as appears by the combat fought between 2 Scots before the L. Grey of Wilton in the market place of Haddington, wherein Hamilton, that was almost if not cleerly known to be innocent, was vanquish't and slain, and Newton the offender remained victor and was rewarded by the Ld. Grey. Holinsh. p. 993."

judicial battle were made through that century and the next, but without result. At last came the famous appeal of murder in 1819,[137] in which the learning of the subject was fully discussed by the King's Bench, and battle was adjudged to be still "the constitutional mode of trial" in this sort of case. As in an Irish case in 1815,[138] so here, to the amazement of mankind, the defendant escaped by means of this rusty weapon. And now, at last, in June, 1819, came the abolition of a long-lived relic of barbarism, which had survived in England when all the rest of Christendom had abandoned it.[139]

As to the grand assize, also, — that venerable early form of the jury which Henry II. established, with its cumbrous pomp of choosing for jurymen knights "girt with swords,"[140] — it is

---

[137] Ashford v. Thornton, 1 B. & Ald. 405.

[138] Neilson, Trial by Combat, 330.

[139] Stat. 59 Geo. III. c. 46, — reciting that "appeals of murder, treason, felony, and other offences, and the manner of proceeding therein, have been found to be oppressive; and the trial by battle in any suit is a mode of trial unfit to be used; and it is expedient that the same should be wholly abolished." The statute went on to enact that all such appeals "shall cease, determine, and become void and . . . utterly abolished, [and that] in any writ of right now depending or hereafter to be brought, the tenant shall not be received to wage battle, nor shall issue be joined or trial he had by battle in any writ of right."

[140] "The writs of parliament are," said Coke, nearly three centuries ago (2 Inst. 597), "to return two knights for every county *gladiis cinctos,* not that they should come to the parliament girt with swords, but that they should be able to do knight's service." But the courts always kept up the real thing. The ceremony of choosing the knights is described in 1406 (Y. B. 7 H. IV. 20, 28) thus: "The four knights were called, who came to the bar girt with swords ["girt with swords above their garments," says Dyer in Lord Windsor *v. St.* John, Dyer, 103 b. A. D. 1554] and were charged ... to choose twelve knights girt with swords from themselves and others, ... and the justices ordered the parties to go with the knights into a chamber to choose and to declare their challenges of the others chosen by the four, for after the return of the panel so made by the four knights the parties shall have no challenge to panel or polls before the justices."

In Y. B. 30 & 31 Ed. I. 117 (1302), the oath of the four electing knights is.: "I will lawfully choose sixteen knights girt with swords, from among myself and the others," etc. This appears to have been the rule, to choose twelve and to add the four, — so that the whole assize was sixteen. (Brunner, Schw. p 365). The old cases show the full number, but sometimes only a part of the four electors are included, and sometimes none of them, perhaps owing to challenges. See cases of 1198-9 in 1 Rot. Cur. Reg. 197, 198, 200, and 201, a case of 1199 in 2 *ib.* 27, and one of 1269 in North. Ass. Rolls (Surtees Soc.) 137. Stephen (Pleading, 129, Tyler's ed.) says: "These knights [the four] and twelve of the recognitors elected, together making a jury of sixteen, constitute what is called the grand assize."

convenient to notice, at this point, that it went out at the end of 1834, with the abolition of real actions.[141]

We have now traced the decay of these great mediaeval modes of trial in England. What, meantime, had been happening to the jury?

---

[141] Except as a belated case or two of a writ of right may have remained over for trial at a later date. The latest case appears to have been that of Davies *v.* Lowndes, reported as of April, 1835, in 1 Bing. N. C. 597, and, at a second trial, as of November and December, 1838, in 5 *ib.* 161 (Forayth, Tr. by Jury, 139).

CHAPTER II
TRIAL BY JURY AND ITS
DEVELOPMENT

Some account has now been given of early Germanic conceptions of proof and modes of trial, and of their place, development, and disappearance in English judicature. Something also has been very briefly said as to the emergence, in the midst of all these things, of the trial by jury, and of its pedigree, as growing out of certain practices in public administration inherited by the Normans from the Frankish, kings, and brought into England at the Conquest.

We are now to trace this earlier history, transmigration, and development of the jury in England, and to follow its strange and wholly peculiar course for some six or eight centuries, to our own time. This will be done in a summary manner, for the main purpose now in hand is not that of writing a history of the jury, but of elucidating the English law of evidence, which, is the child of the jury.

I. 1. "The capitularies and documents of the Carlovingian period," says Brunner,[142] "have a procedure unknown to the old Germanic law, which has the technical name of *inquisitio.* The characteristic of it is that the judge summons a number of the members of the community, selected by him as having presumably a knowledge of the facts in question, and takes of them a promise to declare the truth on the questions to be put by him.... This inquisition... was applied both in legal controversy and in administration, and we must observe that the departments of administration and justice were then considerably united." After the conquest of Neustria by Rollo the Norman, in 912, that province, although acquiring new rulers, retained its old institutions. Where the laws of the conquerors, the Normans, were fundamentally so nearly related to those of the people whom they had conquered, the two "could not long exist by the side of each other. The less cultivated must be absorbed by the other, and the narrower the fundamental difference the quicker the process of absorption."[143] Thus the

---

[142] Schw. 84.
[143] Brunner, Schw. 159-130.

Norman law was mainly Frankish law; and with the rest we find there the inquisition.

Where royal power was vigorous, as among the Franks, it required safer and director ways of settling those matters of fact on which its revenues depended than the rude, superstitious, one-sided methods which were followed in the popular courts. In a capitulary of Louis I. *(le débonnaire)* in 829,[144] it is ordered that every inquiry relating to the royal fisc shall be made, not by witnesses brought forward [by the party], but *per illos qui in eo comitatu meliores et veraciores esse cognoscuntur, — per illorum testimonium inquisitio fiat, et juxta quod illi inde testificati fuerint, vel contineantur vel reddantur.* This, it will be noticed, is not merely ascertaining facts, it is determining controversy by a mode of "trial;" taxes are laid, services exacted, personal status fixed, on the sworn answer of selected persons of a certain neighborhood. Such persons were likely to know who was in possession of neighboring land and by what title; they knew the *consuetudines* of the region, the free or servile status of the neighbors, their birth, death, or marriage. An enlightened principle had come in as regards revenue which was likely to extend and did extend to judicature, for that was only another part of royal administration.[145]

Only the crown, the royal or ducal power, could have accomplished so great an innovation as this.[146] The popular courts were hopelessly caught in the web of custom; within narrow limits they moved forever round and round in the ancient track. The crown alone could compel parties who wished to abide by the old formal procedure to give it up, or enforce the attendance of the community witnesses who made up the inquest and compel them to take an oath.[147] The popular law had left it to the parties to

---

[144] Baluze, i. 673, vi.; Anc. Lois Franc, i. 69; Brunner, Schw. 88, note.

[145] "So intimate is the connection of judicature with finance under the Norman kings that we scarcely need the comments of the historians to guide us to the conclusion that it was mainly for the sake of the profits that justice was administered at all." Stubbs, Const. Hist. Eng. i. 385-6. See the partial separation of judicature from the other business of government at Plymouth in 1646. Plym. Col. Bee. xi. 54.

[146] Brunner, Schw. 255-62.

[147] See St. 52 H. III. c. 22 (1267): *Nullus de cetera possit . . . nec jurare libere tenentes suos contra voluntatem suam, desicut hoc nullus facere potest sine precepto domini regis.* Compare Customs of Kent, 1 St. Realm 225, and the

produce their witnesses. The maxim that only royal authority
could put a man to an oath made and kept trial by jury the special
possession of the royal courts. Only such as received the power
by delegation from the crown, as the Church, great men, or royal
officials presiding over popular courts, could try in this way.

All this is but an illustration of what Maine has said,[148]
that in early times the king was the great law-reformer. Beginning
as an auxiliar of the popular courts, enforcing their decisions and
exercising an "ultimate residuary authority" in correcting their
errors, the king administered "that royal justice which had never
been dissociated from him... [and] was ever waxing while the
popular justice was waning.... In those days whatever answered to
what we now call the spirit of reform was confined to the king
and his advisers; he alone introduced comparative gentleness into
the law and simplified its procedure.... [This] was once the most
valuable and indeed the most indispensable of all reforming
agencies; but at length its course was run, and in nearly all
civilized societies its inheritance has devolved upon elective
legislatures."

2. In the latter half of the eleventh century the Normans
brought over to England a strong type of this royal power. They
brought also the inquisition. Through the whole of the next
century and more, the growth and use of it in the Norman
dominions on both sides of the channel were much the same. But
from the beginning of the thirteenth century, when John lost his
southern territory to the French, the inquisition, mainly dying
slowly out in France, began its peculiar, astonishing development
in England. In trying to follow its English history we remark at
once that for more than a century there is little clear, authoritative
information. We get our knowledge mainly from the scattered
accounts of cases in Domesday Book, and in chronicles and
histories. These have been collected by a competent and careful
hand in the *Placita Anglo-Normannica* of Dr. Bigelow.[149] The
noble series of extant English judicial records does not begin until

---

proceedings against the Abbot of St. Edmunds for trying a criminal case by jury
without royal authority, in Br. N. B. ii. case 592.

[148] Early Law and Custom, c. vi.

[149] Boston: Little, Brown, & Co. 1879. "This volume [Preface, p. iii] is
not a selection of cases, but contains all, of a temporal nature, that are of any
value in the known legal monuments of the period."

1194 (Trin. 5 Rich. I.)[150] Our first law treatise, Glanvill, was written not before 1187.[151] Our existing law reports begin not earlier than two centuries and a quarter after the Conquest, in 1292.[152]

(a) During this earliest period there are many illustrations of the use of the inquisition in ordinary administration. The conspicuous case is that of the compilation of Domesday Book in 1085 — 6. This was accomplished by a commission, making inquiry throughout England, by sworn men of each neighborhood, responsible and acquainted with the facts. Domesday is a record of all sorts of details relating to local customs, and the possession, tenure, and taxable capacity of the land owners. "Questions of title to land and services, and disputes over the status of persons were of constant occurrence before the commissioners, and the results are briefly stated."[153] Incidentally much else came in, as where an inquest[154] relates in its answers the proceedings of a litigation in the popular court, and how, upon Ralph's failure to appear on a day fixed by the sheriff, the men of the hundred had adjudged *(dijudicaverant)* the land to his adversary. The disputes and offers of proof before the Commissioners themselves are sometimes reported.[155]

Of the use of the inquisition in judicature there is an instance, in 1080, or soon after,[156] when, in order to settle a litigation as to certain lands held of the Church of Ely, turning on the question

---

[150] J. H. Round, *Earliest English Plea Rolls,* Eng. Hist. Rev. xi. 102,103.

[151] *Glanvilla, Tractatus de Legibus et Consuetudinibus Regni Angliue,* Lib. viii. c. iii. A fine is cited here as enrolled on the Monday next after the feast of Simon and Jude, in 33 H. II.; this feast was Oct. 28, 1187. I do not take account of the rather special treatise known as *Dialogus de Scaccario,* written not before 1176-7. For something newly discovered, — "what we may believe to be our oldest legal text-book" (Maitland, in Law Quart. Rev. viii. 75), see the "*Quadripartitus,* an English law book of 1114," edited by Dr. Liebermann (Halle, 1892). Other later discoveries and contributions of the same learned writer are mentioned in Pollock and Maitland, Hist. Ting. Law, i. xxi. and 75 *et seq.*

[152] Y. B. 20 & 21 Edw. L

[153] Bigelow, Pl. A. N. xlix; Palg. Com. i. 271-3. "Not even an ox nor a cow, nor a swine was there left which was not set down in his records," says a Saxon chronicler quoted by Palgrave.

[154] Ranulf *v.* Ralph, Bigelow, Pl. A. N. 307, citing Domesday, i. 424.

[155] Illustrations of this sort of thing, taken from Domesday, may be seen in Bigelow, Pl. A. N. pp. 37-61, and *ib.* 293-307.

[156] Bigelow, Pl. A. N. 24, citing Lib. Eliensis, 256.

of who held when Edward the Confessor died, the king directs the
summoning of three shires and various nobles, and orders that out of
these, several (*plures)* English be chosen to tell, under oath, the facts;
and it is directed (with certain qualifications), that matters shall be
adjusted according to the answers. Of uncertain date in the reign of
the Conqueror, who died in September, 1087, is the case of Gundulf,
Bishop of Rochester, *v.* Pichot, Sheriff of Cambridge,[157] in which on
a great controversy as to whether certain lands belonged to the king
or "St. Andrew," the king ordered that it be referred to the judgment
of all the men of the county, — in other words, to the county court.
The county awarded it to the king. The presiding officer, Odo,
Bishop of Bayeux, doubted this award, and directed that the county
should. choose twelve of their number to confirm it by oath.[158] These
retired, and then returned and swore to what had been said by the
county court. A year afterwards a monk who had once been steward
of the region in question, and knew this to be false, raised some
question about it; this resulted in confessions of perjury from the one
who led in the oath, and from another; and in the condemnation and
punishment of all who swore.[159] This case shows the Anglo-Saxon
procedure, which was that of the Germanic popular courts, viz.,
judgment by the whole assembly. Bat it also shows the interference
of the king's representative, and a resort to an inquest of twelve,
chosen under his orders by the county from its own members, and
speaking under oath. In the reign of "William Rufus, in 1099,[160] we
have what Bigelow has called "the earliest record of anything like a
modern judicial iter by the royal justiciars."[161] It does not appear by
what methods the judges proceeded. In another case a writ of

---

[157] Bigelow, PI. A. N. 34, citing *Anglia Sacra,* 338, Hickes, Dis. Ep.
33; s. c. Essays in Anglo-Saxon Law, 374 (with the date 1072-1082). Reeves
(Hist. Eng. Law, Finl. ed. i. 137) refers to this as being "the earliest mention of
anything like a jury."

[158] *So* in the reign of Henry I. (1100-1135) the king in his writ gives
express authority to require the oath, if dissatisfied with the unsworn answer, *"Its
et videte divisas . . et facite recognoscere per probos homines de comitatu et
dividere. . . . Et si bene eis* non *credideritis, sacramento confirment quod
dixerint."* Palg. Eng. Com. ii. 184, note; s. c. Bigelow, PI. A. N. 139.

[159] Those who had not confessed were adjudged perjured,
guandoquidem ille, post quem alii juraverant se perjurum esse fatebatur.

[160] The King v. The Abbot of Tavistock, Bigelow, PI. A. N. 69, citing 2
Monasticon, 497 (ed. 1846).

[161] Hist. Proc. 93.

William Rufus, of uncertain date, directs the sheriff to assemble the shire and take its judgment on a dispute as to lands, and to adjust the matter accordingly. A writ of execution in the same case indicates that it was decided by a jury, — *sicut testimoniata et jurata fuit.*

In the reign of Henry I., in 1122, the king directs that a controversy as to land be referred to the declaration of men of a certain neighborhood. Seven, hundred were assembled, and the Sheriff of Dorset and Somerset presided. Sixteen men swore *se veram affirmationem facturos de inquisitions terrae illius... quorum assertioni cuncti adquiescentes... sua jura conquerentibus adjudicabant,* &c. The names of those who swore are added. We see here again the hundred court giving the judgment upon the statement of those members who were chosen to swear.[162]

(b) With the reign of Henry II. (1154 — 1189) we reach the period when all this irregular, unorganized use of the inquisition begins to take permanent shape at the hands of a great and sagacious king. Through the text of certain of his ordinances (assizes), and through the treatise ascribed to Glanvill, the last of his chief justices, we shall soon get more definite instruction. A chronicler describes an early controversy in this reign, of the year 1158,[163] between the men of Wallingford and Oxford, and the Abbot of Abingdon, as to the right to a market. The king, being in Normandy, had been persuaded to forbid the defendant to sell any but small articles until his return. The defendant asserted full rights of market. The king, on further complaint made to him in Normandy, directed the Earl of Leicester (Chief Justiciar from 1154 to 1162) to assemble the county of Berkshire and cause twenty-four of the older men to be chosen to answer on oath; if they should swear that the defendant had full market in the time of Henry I. he should have it: otherwise not. This resulted in favor of the defendant. The plaintiffs then went to the king, who had returned, and complained that this oath was false, and that among those who swore had been some of the defendant's men. The king thereupon ordered an assembly of the Wallingford men and of the whole county of Berkshire at Oxford, before the justices, and that oath should be made to the truth by the older men. chosen by both sides *(ex utraque parte),* excepting that none should belong to

---

[162] Pal. Com. ii. 183; Bigelow, Pl. A. N. 119.
[163] Bigelow. Pl. A. N. 198, citing 2 Hist. Mon. Abingd. (Rec. Com.)

the Abbey. At this assembly the jury were separated *(congregati... universi, et segregate qui jurarent),* and they differed — the Wallingford men swearing that there was only a market for bread and ale, the Oxford men for more things, but not a full market; and the men of the county, that it was a full market, with possibly one exception. The Earl of Leicester, who presided *(qui justitia et judex aderat),* was unwilling to give judgment on these differing statements, but reported matters to the king, adding the information that he himself had lived at Abingdon when he was a boy, and that he had seen a full market there in the time of King Henry I. This satisfied the king *(tanti viri testimonio delectatus),* and he decided in favor of the defendant.

(c) But we had better leave now these unauthoritative reports of the chroniclers[164] and wait, as regards cases, until solid ground is reached in the judicial records, half a century later. Meantime it will be profitable to consider two or three things.

(1.) It is interesting to remark how the English kings, in their capacity as Dukes of Normandy, were using there this same machinery. While they had brought it to England, they had also left it at home.[165] Dr. Brunner speaks of having carefully examined many Norman documents of the twelfth century, little studied before and never printed, and remarks[166] that they enable one to contradict the view that Anglo-Norman law had taken the lead and Norman law followed. Up to Glanvill the English law was constantly fructified from the Norman. Henry was Duke of Normandy before he was Justiciary and then King of England. It was not, Brunner adds, until near the end of the union between the two countries (in 1206), that England took the lead. It is not surprising, then, to find that Henry II. began the work of developing and organizing the inquisition as Duke of Normandy before he came to the English throne, and as early as the year

---

[164] The chroniclers preserve many valuable documents. As regards their narratives we have to remember their bias and their ignorance of technical law, recalling Coke's warning at the beginning of the third volume of his reports: "And for that it is hard for a man to report any part or branch of any art or science justly and truly which he professeth not, and impossible to make a just and true relation of any thing that he understands not, I pray thee beware of chronicle law," etc.

[165] Brunner, Schw. 148, 207-8.

[166] Brunner, Schw. 135.

1152.[167] This work lay in. establishing it as a right to have this method of proof in certain classes of cases, and in making it obligatory. Before this, it had been granted merely as matter of royal favor in particular instances; it now became, in some cases, matter of right to have the king's writ ordering it.[168] The phrase now became "recognition" rather than "inquisition," — the two terms ill reality importing two aspects of the same thing, one, the inquiry, the other, the answer.

These "recognitions" were so many new modes of trial on particular questions, established by a dead lift of royal power. In the case of the "great assize" this trial was optional with the tenant, but not with the demandant. As regards the other recognitions they were required, in specified sorts of cases, and were equally obligatory upon both parties. In theory, such recognitions might have been established in other cases, *e.g.*, in criminal matters, by the same authority. If anybody should be inclined to wonder why this was not done, he should bethink him of the extraordinary nature of the actual achievement. The real wonder is that so much was done; for the introduction of a compulsory procedure of this sort was very foreign to the conceptions of the older law. By that, men had "tried" their own cases. To put upon a man who had the right to go to the proof, — instead of the *probatio, defensio, purgatio,* of the older law, where he produced the persons or the things that cleared him, — the necessity of submitting himself to the test of what a set of strangers might say, witnesses selected by a public officer, — this was a wonderful thing.[169]

A portentous thing was it that any ruler should set himself above the old *lex et consuetude.* More than a century later, when we find the king claiming this power, we see also how firmly he is

---

[167] Brunner, Schw. 300-304; hut compare Bigelow, Pl. A. N. xxvii n. Brunner here makes the interesting remark that "the need of innovation must have already made itself felt, for the reason that a dangerous rival to the rude and inelastic procedure of the temporal courts was growing up, in the canon law. ... It may therefore be regarded as no mere coincidence that Henry II., the reformer of procedure, was the man who first succeeded in forcing the ecclesiastical jurisdiction into narrower limits." See the remark of Bereford, J., in 1303 (Y. B. 30 & 31 Edw. I., 492).

[168] Brunner, Schw. 394-5.

[169] A friend reminds me of the many signs,such as outlawry and distress, that survived even to recent times, of the inability of the old law to compel a man directly to submit to judicial authority.

resisted. In 1291 — 2 it was sought, in ascertaining certain facts, to put some great men to their oath. They all answered that it was unheard of that they or their ancestors should be compelled to take an oath. It was set forth to them that in many cases, for the common welfare, the king is above the *leges et consuetudines in regno suo usitatas;* and thereupon many times was the book held out to them, but they refused.[170] In old times this denial of the *king's* power of compulsion was a denial of such power anywhere. And it is in this sense probably that we are to understand the "Mirror," at about the date last named, in enumerating abuses: *"La primier et la soveraigne abusion est que le Roy est oustre la ley."*[171] The writer of this book though it an abuse that one should not be allowed to try his case by battle or the ordeal.[172] And again, as to a class of criminal cases: "It is an abuse that the justices drive a lawful man to put himself on the country when he offers to defend himself against the approver by his body."[173]

(2.) Of the phrases that we meet so often, *recognitio* and *assisa,* some illustration may be convenient. The solemn declaration, in certain, matters affecting the clergy, made in 1164 and ordinarily called the Constitutions of Clarendon, is styled, in the document itself, *ista recordatio vel recognitio;* while in chapter ix. provision is made for settling certain cases *recognitione duodecim legalium hominum.* In the Assize of Northampton (1176) at § 4, relating to the writ of mort d'ancestor, it is directed that the justices cause a *percognitionem* to be taken by twelve lawful men, *et sicut recognltum fuerit ita,* etc.

The word *recognitio,* meaning thus a solemn acknowledgment, declaration, or answer, came to be mainly limited to "the inquisitions which under the ducal ordinance *(secundum assisam)* were started by a ducal writ."[174] Of the term "assize," Brunner says, "In England the technical expression '*assisa*' got established for recognition in the narrower sense. *Assisa* means, in the first place, the *thing,* the assembly, as well judicial as legislative. In its extended sense, it means what belongs to or comes from such

---

[170] Pl. Ab. 227, col. 2.

[171] Book 5, c. 5, a. 1.

[172] Book 5, c. 5, ss. 126, 127.

[173] *Ib. s.* 19.

[174] Brunner, Schw. 293-4. And see a French document of 1267, specifically giving this meaning to the word, *ib.* 294-5.

an assembly, the judgment or the ordinance. As to these specific assizes which introduced the recognitions, the term 'assize' has passed over to them." [175] Of the use of the word "*assisa*" as meaning the ordinance itself, we see illustrations both in the title and the text of the assizes of Clarendon and Northampton,[176] of the Assize of Arms (1181), and the Assize of the Forest (1184). *Item justitiae... faciant fieri recognitionem de dissaisinis factis super assisam, etc. Haec est assisa... de foresta, etc.*[177] On the other hand, the use of it in the sense of a particular remedy, or form of action, or mode of proceeding, and also in the sense of the tribunal, the recognitors, is sufficiently illustrated if we recall the *Magna Assisa,* the several assizes of Novel Disseisin, Mort d'ancestor, and the rest, and the common expressions, *cadit assisa in juratam.*

(3.) These ordinances of Henry II. (or, perhaps, as it has been conjectured, only a single ordinance applicable to a variety of cases,) are not preserved; but the character of them as acts of royal legislation sufficiently appears in the ordinances already named,[178] as well as in Glanvill[179] and elsewhere. In speaking of proceedings under them to recover possession, called assizes, and also recognitions, Reeves[180] following Glanvill, or rather paraphrasing him with comment, mentions eight; and he remarks[181] that, "Of all the assizes in use in Glanvill's time it was only that *de morte antecessoris* and that *de nova disseisina* that were original writs." All the others are here supposed to be auxiliary to a proceeding already pending. But the more accurate statement, doubtless, is that of Pollock and Maitland.[182] After speaking of the proprietary action and the grand assize, they add: "In four other cases a plaintiff may begin proceedings by obtaining a royal writ which will direct that an

---

[175] *Ib.* 299. Littleton, s. 234, says: "This name assize is women *equivocum,* for sometimes it is taken for a jury [quoting the beginning of the record of an assize of novel disseisin, *assisa venit recognitura,* etc.]. . . . And sometimes it is taken for the whole writ of assize. . . . And sometimes assize is taken for an ordinance." Compare Mirror (Whittaker's, Selden Soc. ed.) 65 (c. 25).

[176] Ass. North, a. 5.

[177] Ass. North, a. 5.

[178] Stubbs, Charters (6th ed.), 135, 140, 150, 156.

[179] ii. c. 7, and c. 19, and xiii. c. 1.

[180] Hist. Eng. Law (Finl. ed.), 223-232. Glanv. xiii, c. 1 and 2.

[181] P. 230.

[182] Hist. Eng. Law, i. 128.

inquest shall be sworn to answer a particular question formulated in the writ. These four cases are the subject-matter of the four petty assizes, (1) the assize *utrum, (2)* the novel disseisin, (3) the mort d'ancestor, (4) the darrein presentment. It is probable that for a short while a few other cases were met in a similar fashion; but in a little while we have these four and only these four petty assizes. Only in these four instances does the writ which is the first step in the procedure, 'the original writ,' direct the empanelling of an inquest."[183]

That these proceedings originated with Henry II. Is neatly indicated by a charter of King John, granted in 1202, to the church of Beverly, and recited in a later *Inspeximus,* confirming the rights of that church as against any *assisas vel recognitiones vel constitutiones postea factas;* so far as recognitions or assizes are necessary as touching what belongs to the reeve of Beverly, they are to be held in his court, where such matters were pleaded *tempore regis Henrici patris nostri, vel tempore Henrici Regis avi patris nostri, antequam recognitiones vel assisae in regno nostro essent constitutae.*[184] The assizes or recognitions, *i. e.,* the inquisitions provided for by royal ordinance, compulsory and obtainable as of right, existed, as was said before, only in a limited number of cases. But the old method of obtaining this mode of relief by special permission in other cases, still held; and it was had by consent. Having regard to the powerful favor of the crown, and to the experience of the advantages of this rational mode of determining questions of fact, as compared with the duel and the old, one-sided, formal proof, one might easily guess at the great and rapid extension of it that followed. Questions raised by the *exceptio,* and other incidental matters, were largely disposed of in this way, either by consent of parties or order of court; but to some extent the body of men thus procured was in early times distinguished by a different name from that which assembled under the king's ordinance; it appears as the *jurata.*[185] Where the ordinance did not extend, and where a party would not consent to a *jurata,* the old formal methods of proof prevailed; and some of them continued for centuries.[186] But this again, among other causes, led to a resort to

---

[183] See Mirror, c. xxv. (Whittaker's, Selden Soc. ed.), p. 65.

[184] Houard. Anc. Loix, ii. 287-8; cited by Brunner, Schw. 301.

[185] See Pollock and Maitland, Hist. Eng. Law, 128. Compare Pike, in Y. B. 12 & 13 Edw. III. pp. xxxix-lxx.

[186] *Supra, c.* ii.

new forms of action, and in these the only mode of trial was the jury. By its intrinsic fairness as contrasted with older modes, and by the favor of the crown and the judges, it grew fast to be regarded as the one regular common-law mode of trial, always to be had when no other was fixed.[187]

(4.) Some further mention should be made of the fragmentary legislation of this reign.[188] In the Constitutions of Clarendon, in 1164, — *ista recordatio vel recognitio cujusdam partis consuetudinum et libertatum et dignitatum antecessorum suorum,* — matters between the king and the church, were regulated. In c. i. controversies about presentation and advowson *(de advocatione et presentatione ecclesiarum)* are placed under the jurisdiction of the king's court, — "for the decision of which the assize of darrein presentment was issued, the only vestiges of which *[i. e.,* of the assize or ordinance itself] are preserved in Glanvill."[189] In c. vi. a jury of accusation is provided for, — *faciet jurare duodecim legates homines de vicineto... quod inde veritatem secundum conscientiam suam manifestabunt.* In c. ix. the assize *Utrum* appears, — *recognitione duodecim legalium hominum.*[190] In the Assize of Clarendon, in 1166, provision is made for taking inquests throughout England by local juries of accusation, and for the trial of the chief cases by the ordeal. Such juries are also required in the Inquest of Sheriffs (1170), and the Assize of Arms (1181). In the Assize of Northampton (1176), "a reissue and expansion of the Assize of Clarendon... drawn up in. the form of instructions to the six committees of judges who were to visit the circuits now marked out," the fourth article provides for continuing in the heir of a freeholder the seisin that his father had, and, if the lord refuse it, for what appears to be the assize of mort d'ancestor, — *Justitiae... faciant inde fieri percognitionem per duodecim legales homines qualem seisinam defunctus inde habuit die quo fuit vivus et mortuus: et sicut recognitum fuerit, ita haeredibus ejus restituant.* Article five requires the taking of assizes of novel disseisin; or, to give it just as it is expressed, the taking of a recognition on the Assize *super*

---

[187] In 1275 (St. West. I. c. 12), one accused of felony, and refusing to pat himself on a jury, is dealt with as refusing "the common law of the land."

[188] For this see Stubbs, Charters.

[189] Stubbs, Charters (6th ed.), 136.

[190] See Pollock and Maitland, Hist. Eng. Law, i. 123; also *ib.* 218, in treating of Frankalmoin.

(Assisam),[191] of disseisins made since the king came to England after the peace between him and his son. This important assize is now traced to the year 1166.[192]

(5.) To the end of the period now under consideration belongs Glanvill. In this book we find frequent mention of the *assisa, recognitio, jurata, patria, visinetum,* as a mode of proof, — in other words, of trial by jury. Glanvill takes up first the writ of right,[193] and after dealing with a variety of preliminary matters, such as the essoins, getting the parties into court and the plaintiff through his declaration, he tells us[194] that the tenant now has his election to defend himself *per duellum, vel ponere se inde In magnam assisam domini Regis et petere recognitionem quis eorum majus jus habet in terra illa.* If the tenant puts himself on the great assize, and the plaintiff assents in court, he cannot withdraw. If he does not assent, he must show a good reason, as that the parties are both descended from the same line as the inheritance;[195] and if this be disputed he must establish it (c. 6). Glanvill here pauses (c. 7) to praise the assize in the well-known, passage in which this *"constitutio"* is attributed to the royal goodness, and is contrasted with the duel as regards its justice, reasonableness, speed, and economy.[196] He goes on to explain that the tenant, appealing from the local court to the king's court, so as to have the benefit of this assize, may have a writ of prohibition to the lower tribunal.

It was when the proceedings under the original writ had taken this turn that the plaintiff might have his auxiliary writ (cc. 10

---

[191] In view of the use of this phrase here and in Glanvill, as referring to legislative ordinances no longer extant, it is interesting to notice it in a record of 1201 as meaning the Assize of Clarendon: *Nicholaus purget se per aquam, per assisam,* — "Let Nicholas purge himself by [the ordeal of] water according to the Assize." Maitland, Pl. Cr. 1. This Assize ("The most important document, of the nature, of law or edict, that has appeared since the Conquest," Stubbs, Const. Hist. i. 469) was discovered by Palgrave sixty years ago in a MSS. copy of Glanvill in the British Museum. Pal. Com. ii. 166.

[192] Pollock and Maitland, i. 124, 125.

[193] Lib. i. c. 5.

[194] Lib. ii. c. 3.

[195] See Stat. *de magnis assists et diiellis (inc. temp.)* St. Realm, i. 218.

[196] *Supra,* p. 42; Reeves, Hist. Com. Law (Finl. ed.), 187-8. An interesting question exists as to whether the word *magna* belongs in this passage. Reeves, i. 187, note; Beames's Glanv. 54, note. Whether it belongs here or not, it is found elsewhere in Glanvill and in our other early books, as designating this particular recognition.

and 11) for summoning four knights of the county and neighborhood to choose twelve others of the same neighborhood *qui melius veritatem sciant, ad recognoscendum super sacramentum suum utrum M. an R. majus jus habeat.* The details of this election and of the summoning of the twelve knights are then given (cc. 12, 14,15).

It is remarkable how free from technicality and how liberal in tone are the provisions of this ordinance of the king and the practice under it, as explained by Glanvill (c. 12). When once the twelve knights have assembled (cc. 17, 18), it is first ascertained by their oath whether any of them are ignorant of the fact *(rei veritatem).* If there be any such, they are rejected and others chosen. If the twelve differ in their verdict, others are added until there are twelve who agree, on one side or the other.[197] The knowledge required of them is their own perception, or what their fathers have told them, or what they may trust as fully as their own perceptions *(per proprium visum et auditum... vel per verba patrum suorum, et per talia quibus fidem teneantur habere ut propriis).* The knights may either say, directly and shortly, that one party or the other has the greater right, or merely set forth the facts, and thus enable the justices to say it, — what we call a Special verdict. The interesting fact is stated (c. 19) that the king's ordinance provides a punishment for the false swearing of these persons; viz., the loss of all chattels and movable goods, but not the freehold. They are also to be imprisoned, for at least a year, and to lose their *legem terrae,* being no longer the *legalis homo,* and becoming forever infamous.[198]

It will be observed that the writ of right had no necessary relation to the new modes of trial; the regular trial was the old one, the duel. It was only when the tenant claimed the benefit of the statute that the case was tried by the inquisition, or, as it is more usually called in this relation, the recognition. The writ which secured this was merely an auxiliary writ of summons obtained by the plaintiff to meet the emergency in his case which had thus developed. But Glanvill, later on,[199] speaks in detail of a different

---

[197] As to the rule of adding the four electors to the twelve, making the triers a jury of sixteen, see *supra,* p. 46, n.

[198] Legalis, *in jure nostro de eo dicitur qui stat rectus in curia, non exlex seu utlagatus, non excommunicatus, vel infamis &c., sed qui et in lege postulet et postuletur. Hoc sensu vulgare illud in formulis juridicis, probi et legales homines.* Spelman, Gloss.

[199] Lib. xiii. c. I.

thing when he comes to possessory writs: "Now we are to speak of the usual proceedings where seisin only is in question. And since these usually go forward by a recognition, by favor of that ordinance of the kingdom which is called the assize (*ex beneficio constitutionis regni que assisa nominatur*), it remains to speak of the various recognitions." Eight recognitions are then named (c. 2), viz.: *de morte antecessoris, de ultima presentatione, utrum tenementum sit feudum ecclesiasticum vel laicum, utrum seisitus de feodo vel de vadio, utrum sit infra etatem*[200] (c. 16), *utrum seisitus de feodo vel de warda* (c. 14), *utrum presentaverit occasione feodi vel warde, de nova disseisina;* and the writs for these are given in succession. Glanvill also plainly says that in other ways the recognition is reached; as regards incidental points they are ordered, sometimes by assent of the parties and sometimes by the order of the court (*et si que sunt similia quo in curia frequenter emergunt presentibus partibus, tunc ex consensu ipsarum partium, tunc etiam, de consilio curie consideratur ad aliquam controversiam terminandam).* In dealing with the first of these writs, Glanvill explains, once for all, the procedure. The writ directs the sheriff to summon twelve *liberos et legales homines de visineto de illa villa* to appear, ready on their oath *recognoscere si... et interim terram illam videat...* (c. 3). The sheriff is to select these men, in the presence of the parties, if they choose to attend (c. 5). Only two essoins (excuses for delay) are allowed in any possessory recognition, and none at all in the writ of novel disseisin. In considering various dilatory pleas to which the tenant may resort, it is said that the question of fact thus raised may be disposed of by a resort *ad duellum, vel ad aliam usitatam probationem. As* regards the mode in which the twelve are to arrive at their verdict Glanvill simply says (c. 11) it is *sub forma prescripts in hoc libro,* — meaning, perhaps, the explanations about the writ of right in the second book; it is only there that he gives any such explanations.

Glanvill's last book (xiv.) deals with criminal cases, — *de criminalibus restat tractandum.* Here, as yet, the jury has penetrated little; but here also it has come. In such cases the ordinary common-law *(per legem terrae)* mode of accusation is the private one, by appeal and the ordinary mode of trial is battle or the ordeal; for, in criminal cases, compurgation in the king's courts seems to

---

[200] In this case the recognition is by eight.

have disappeared by the Assize of Clarendon. But sometimes one is accused by "public fame," *i.e.,* the accusing jury. In this case the judge must inquire carefully into the basis of this accusation *per multas et varias inquisitiones et interrogationes coram justic faciendas inquiretur rel veritas, et id ex verisimilibus rerum indiciis et conjecturis, mine pro eo nunc contra eum qui accusatur facientibus.*[201] Sometimes the accused has an election whether to submit to the ordeal; and sometimes he is forced to it, as in homicide, where lie has been taken in flight by a pursuing crowd, if this be attested in court by a jury, — *si... hoc per jura-tam patrie fuerit in curia legitime testatum* (c. 3). One may decline battle for the reason of being sixty years old or over, or being maimed. But then he is driven to the ordeal (c. 1).

Glanvill often, throughout his work, speaks of referring incidental questions *ad visinetum,* of determining them *per juratam patriae vel visineti.* What has already been said may serve to show that this was sometimes under the king's ordinance *(juxta assisam)* by a recognition, and sometimes that it came about, as a consequence of the judge's control over the procedure, by the outright award of the court, by agreement of parties, or by the mere order of the crown. In 1200 [202] an entry on the judicial rolls begins abruptly, *Jurata venit recognitura,* &c. The jury finds that the sons of S. are the inheritors of a certain estate, *ut eis videtur;* and it is added, *et notandum quod haec inqiiisicio facta fult per preceptum domini Regis, non per consideracionem curiae vel secundum consuetudinem regni."*

II. We now come to the time when there are printed records, and cases can be cited. Henceforward we are on more solid ground, and may hope to trace more clearly the development of things. A student is struck at once with the rapid growth of the new mode of trial during the next century. The evil practice of exacting a large and uncertain fee for granting a recognition, even when it was matter of right,[203] which continued

---

[201] Compare the office, in civil cases, of the *secta* — to make a charge probable. *Supra,* p. 10. These preliminary inquiries must not be confounded with the trial; Stephen appears to fall into this error. Higt Crim. Law, i. 259-60.

[202] Rot. Cur. Reg. ii. 189.

[203] Bigelow, Hist. Proc. 187-90. In 1199 (1 Rot. Cur. Reg. 354) the Abbot of Colchester, defendant in an assize of mort d'ancestor, offers the king

throughout the twelfth century, was forbidden by John's Magna
Carta, in 1215. The Barons had demanded in their "Articles,"[204] *Ne
jus vendatur, vel differatur vel vetitum sit;* and in art. 40 of the
Charter the king had promised *"Nulli vendemus, nulli negabimus aut
differemus rectum aut justiciam."* Then the multiplication, in civil
cases, of new writs and forms of action, available as of right and all
of them calling for a trial by jury, gave it a great increase. As to the
king's right to issue new writs, the abridgment of the right in 1258,
and the enactment in 1285 of that fruitful provision,[205] whereby the
clerks in chancery were empowered to issue new writs *in consimili
casu,* — authorizing actions on the case and providing the channels
through which a vast proportion of the flood of subsequent litigation
has flowed, — I can merely allude to these things.[206] Even without
all this and before it, there had been an extraordinary growth; for
instance, trespass, occasionally resorted to in John's reign or
earlier,[207] became apparently a writ of course after the middle of the
thirteenth century.[208] In this, as well as in all cases which were not
covered by established rules, the jury was the mode of trial. "And
since in a plea of trespass the defendant can hardly escape making
his defence by the country, the justice, by consent of parties, shall
make inquiry of the truth by lawful inquest," says the Statute of
Wales hi 1284 (c. xi.).[209] "To avoid the perilous risk of battle it is
better to proceed by our writs of trespass than by appeals, says
Britton (A. D. 1291 — 2).[210] In 1304[211] battle was offered and

---

one silver mark to have the assize made up *de senioribus et legation bus
hominibus de ipso visineto.* And in the same year *(ib.* 375) the men of "Docking"
offer the king ten marks *pro habenda jurata de consuetudinibus quas antiquiter
consueverunt,* &c.

[204] No. 30; Stubbs, Charters (6th ed.), 293.

[205] St. Westm. 11. c. 24.

[206] See Bigelow, Pl. A. N. Introd. xxviii-xxx.

[207] Bigelow, Hist. Proc. 160.

[208] Professor Ames in Harv. Law Rev. iii. 29, note; confirmed by
Professor Maitland in his valuable article on the "Register of Original Writs," 26.
177-9, 217: "At the end of the Barons' war ... we suddenly come upon a large
crop of such actions." In Pollock and Maitland, Hist. Eng. Law, ii. 524 n. it is
said: "After looking through some unprinted rolls we feel entitled to say that this
action was still uncommon in 1250, but was quite common in 1272."

[209] 1 St. Realm, p. 66. See Heselrigg's case in 1291 (Pl. Ab. 285, col. 1).

[210] f. 49 ; Nichola, i. 123. A learned friend suggests that by the middle
of the thirteenth century there were no cases where a defendant on his trial might

accepted in trespass, but the court refused to allow it. In 1308, a bull of Pope Clement V. against the trying of ecclesiastics in English secular courts shows the jury in use in criminal cases and gives us a glimpse of it as seen through Continental eyes: *Contra dictos clericos duodecim laid admittuntur in testes, qui si,dicunt se credere illos super quo accusantur commississe delictum, testibus creditur indubitanter eisdem; et ex hoc ad mortem ut praemittitur condemnantur.*[212] By the year 1436, in a statute[213] for relieving against certain crying abuses of trial by jury, we find a recital that it has now spread over the whole field. "Our said Lord the King, considering that the trial of the life and death, lands and tenements, goods and chattels of every one of his subjects in this kingdom, touching matters of fact, remains and stands, and from day to day probably is to be had and made by the oaths of inquests of twelve men duly summoned in his courts," &C., &c.

But the inquisition had its most interesting extension, and the one which it will be most profitable to trace, in criminal cases. Of one aspect of this a very interesting account is given by Brunner.[214] Here, as in civil cases, the incidental questions raised by an *exceptio* were often referred, by consent of the parties, or by the king's grace obtained by the offer of money, to an inquisition. Many instances of such offers for a jury to try the question, upon a special plea in criminal cases, are found in the reign of John. The commonest case of this sort, so far as our printed records show, was the plea, on an appeal, that it "was brought maliciously, to disinherit or otherwise injure the appellee, whose innocence is also alleged, — the *exceptio de otio et atia.*[215] These pleas often involved practicailly a decision

---

not regularly have a jury if he applied for it, and no case where a plaintiff might not have it except debt, detinue, and the writ of right, — allowing, of course, for situations where documents were the proper mode of trial. There were other situations, or rather perhaps, certain specific inquiries, to which the jury was thought inapplicable, as in a case in 1295 (Pl. Ab. 289, col. 1), where we read that, *Dominus Rex in hoc casu non vult super intellectum sive conscienciam ipsorum Johannis et Rogeri aliquam patriam admittere.* Compare Hengham, C. J., in Alein *v* Simon, Y. B. 32 & 33 Edw. I. 60 (1304).

   [211] Y. B. 32 & 33 Edw. I. 318-320.

   [212] Wilkins, *Concilia,* ii. 322; cited in Palgrave, Com. i. 246.

   [213] Stat. 15 H. VI. c. 5.

   [214] Schw. 469-474.

   [215] Instances of this, in 1200, may be seen in Rot. Cur. Reg. ii. 30, 97, 230, and 265; the last-named case reappears, in 1207, in Pl. Cr. (Maitland) i., case 54. In this last volume interesting instances, of the years 1202-5, are found, at

of the main question of guilt or innocence. By the Magna Carta of
King John (art. 36) such writs "were no longer to be sold and bought,
but given as of right.[216] In this way, then, it seems to have been
possible, even before the decree of the Fourth Lateran Council, in
this same year of 1215, to apply the jury to criminal cases whenever
the accused asked for it. But how if he did not ask for it? The Assize
of Clarendon, in 1166, with its apparatus of an accusing jury and a
trial by ordeal is thought to have mainly done away in the king's
courts with compurgation as a mode of trial for crime;[217] and now
the Lateran Council, in forbidding ecclesiastics to take part in trial by
ordeal, was deemed to have forbidden that mode of trial, as well in.
England as in all other countries where the authority of the Council
was recognized.[218] The king's judges would naturally turn to the
inquest, as was done irregularly m some of the nobles' courts.[219] But
this had not been used heretofore in criminal cases without the
consent of the accused; and the action of the judges took the course
of gaining his consent and stimulating it. Somehow or other it
eventually became the received opinion that one accused of crime
could not be tried by the country unless he should plead, and put
himself on that mode of trial. It was so in Normandy;[220] and this may
well suggest that the fundamental reason of it was one common to
both countries; viz., a struggle of the old formalism in adjusting itself
to the new procedure. But there was an unsettled time at first, and

---

cases 81, 87, 91, 92. See also case 161, in 1221. In case 79 (1203), on a plea to an
appeal, of a previous concord and settlement, the appellee offers two marks to the
king for an inquest, and has it.

[216] *Nichil detur vel capiatur de cetero pro brevi inquisitionis de vita vel
viembris sed gratis concedatur et non negetur.*

[217] See supra, p. 26.

[218] "The next eyre . . . took place in the winter of 1218-19. The judges
had already started on their journeys when an order of the king in council was
sent round to them . . . . : 'When yon started on your eyre it was as yet
undetermined what should be done with persons accused of crime, the Church
having forbidden the ordeal. For the present we must rely very much on your
discretion to act wisely according to the special circumstances of each case.' "The
judges were then given certain general instructions: Persons charged with the
graver crimes, who might do harm if allowed to abjure the realm, are to be
imprisoned, without endangering life or limb. Those charged with less crimes,
who would have been tried by the ordeal, may abjure the realm. In the case of
small crimes there must be pledges to keep the peace. Maitland, Glouc. Pleas,
xxxviii.

[219] See Br. N. B. ii., case 592; s. c. *supra,* p. 26.

[220] Brunner, Schw. 474.

some persons were tried by jury and hanged who never had consented to the jury.[221] There was ground for this course in the usages of the king's court in both civil and criminal cases. If the tenant in a writ of right put himself on the grand assize, the question as regards the demandant was not whether he consented, but whether he had a good reason for refusing to consent.[222] So in the petty assizes, there was no choice. As regards exceptions Britton tells us (218 b), *en tels cas soit la assise tourné en juree, et en plusours autre cas, si les parties se assentent, et si noun, soit jugé contre cely qe assenter ne se vodera.* As we saw in Glanvill, one might be compelled to the ordeal against his will. In the nature of things it could not really be left to the option of an accused person whether he would be tried or not. It is not strange then to find that the judges, using the large discretion confided to them by the crown after the Lateran Council, sometimes forced a jury upon an unwilling prisoner.[223] The two cases cited by Emlyn in his note to Hale's Pleas of the Crown, which are above referred to, are clear instances of it. Seven cases in Gloucester, however, during the same iter in which these occurred, preserved by Maitland, are, as he says, "provokingly inconclusive."

Maitland's researches among the rolls in preparing the "Select Pleas of the Crown" (A. D. 1200 — 1225), which make the first volume of the publications of the Selden Society, lead him to make[224] the important remark regarding Emlyn's two cases, that "no other cases to the same effect have as yet been found." Yet Bracton's opinion seems to have been in accord with them. In very interesting passages, quoted by Maitland, Bracton [225] argues for this doctrine on the analogy of what happens (citing two cases of 1226), in an appeal where the appellant is a woman, an old person, or one maimed. In such cases there can be no battle, and, since the Lateran Council, no ordeal; the process is the jury, — *cogendus est igitur appellatus quod se, defendat per patriam.* On an indictment, also, after describing the proceedings (143 b), in saying that these

---

[221] Cases of this sort, of the period 1220-1222, may be found in Hale, PL Cr. ii. 322, note; s. c. Maitland, Pl. Cr. i., cases 153,) 57; Maitland, Glouc. Pleas, xxix. Compare St. Wall. c. xi. (1284) as to personal trespasses. *Infra,* p. 78.

[222] Glanv. ii. 6.

[223] Glouc. Pl. xxxix. See Pollock and Maitland ii., 648.

[224] P. 99, note.

[225] Lib. iii., cc. 21, 22.

forms are to be followed in all cases of homicide where one has put himself on an inquisition, his expressions are, *sive sponte, sive per cautelam inductus, sive per necessitatem.* None of Bracton's citations in this part of the work, viz. in the treatise *De Corona,* are later than 1231 — 2, except one of 1262, which appears to be an interpolation; and this is esteemed the oldest part of the book.[226] "The main part of it seems to have been written between 1250 and 1258."[227] Down, then, to the middle of the thirteenth century, or later, it seems to have been thought possible by high authority, as well in criminal cases as in civil, to try a man by jury, or, at any rate, to convict him, whether he consented or not. But the doctrine was contrary to settled ideas, it was not an established one, the precedents were few, and it was supported rather on analogy than any body of direct authority. An obvious course, in case of refusal, was that of treating the party as confessing. There had, indeed, always been cases where one was hanged without any trial at all, as where a man was taken in the fact. In 1222,[228] one of two alleged robbers puts himself on a jury and is substantially acquitted. The other refuses; but it appears that he was found in possession of part of a tunic lately stolen, and *omnes de comitatu et de visneto* say that he is a thief, and has been in complicity with thieves, that he is not in frank-pledge, and has no lord to vouch for him, and that there is no good thing in his favor; accordingly it is adjudged, "*convictus est, ideo,* etc.," *i.e.,* he is to be hanged. In 1226,[229] Henry le Dreys is appealed by an approver in whose company he had been taken. He is not in frank-pledge, and has no lord to vouch for him, and does not offer in any way to purge himself, *et ideo suspendatur,* etc.

There was irregularity and looseness. In 1219,[230] the itinerant justices are punished for hanging men without trial, who were not taken with the mainour, had not confessed, and apparently had not put themselves on a jury: they had carried the current practices too far, and applied them to persons who had, indeed, befriended a near relative who appeared to be a thief, and who, while not confessing, had not satisfactorily denied receiving

---

[226] Twiss, Bracton, i. xiv, xv; *ib.* xlviii, citing Güterbock.
[227] 1 Pollock and Maitland, Hist. Eng. Law, 185.
[228] Br. N. B. ii. case 136.
[229] Br. N. B. iii. case 1724.
[230] *Ib.* ii. 67.

the stolen goods. The twelve jurors of the hundred had been referred to, and had given them a bad name, had "heard say" that the stolen goods were divided on their land, etc. Whether by reason of this sort of loose practice, or the prevalence of old ideas, or for whatever reason, it seems to have become the rule that standing mute was not confession, and that the accused could not be put on his trial by a jury without his consent.[231] Of course the matter might have been covered by an "assize." But it was not; on the contrary, towards the end of the century we find a remarkable

---

[231] Maitland's Court Baron (4 Seld. Soc. Pub.) preserves certain forms and of a date not later than 1268, for helping stewards and others to hold their local courts, and illustrates the current methods and opinions of that period on the subject in hand. At p. 62 we have proceedings against one William for the larceny of a mare. He has offered battle; then the steward addresses the accused: —

"William, now answer me by what device thou earnest by this mare; for at least thou canst not deny that she was found with thee, and that thou didst avow her for thine own."

"Sir, I disavow this mare, and never saw I her until now."

"Then, William, thou canst right boldly put thyself upon the good folk of this vill that never thou didst steal her."

"Nay, sir, for these men have their hearts big against me and hate me much because of this ill report which is surmised against me."

"Thinkest thou, William, that there be any who would commend his body and soul to the devils for thee or for love or for hatred of thee? Nay, verily, they are good folk and lawful, and thou canst oust from among them all those whom thou suspectest of desiring thy condemnation. But do thou what is right and have God before thine eyes, and confess the truth of this thing and the other things that thou hast done, and give not thyself wholly to the enticement of the devil, but confess the truth and thou shalt find us the more merciful."

At p. 64, W. of M. is arrested for receiving and concealing stolen oxen. He says they are his own, bought at a fair; and he offers battle. The steward then addresses him: "And if thou didst buy them with thy money in the fair of C., whither come merchants with divers merchandises to buy and sell, as thou hast said, why didst thou hide them so secretly for so long a time? It seemeth to me that thou didst come by them in some evil manner. It is seemly, therefore, that thou shouldst acquit thyself in other wise, for that there is an evil presumption against thee; and of this and of all other matters thou shonldst put thyself upon the good folk of this vill."

"Nay, sir, I am not put to that as it seemeth to me, for that I am ready to defend by my body the aforesaid beasts as my own proper chattel."

The steward insists that even if no one will prove the thing against the accused, "we have good hope and hold it for truth (nos *avumus bone esperaunce e pur voirs le sentums)* that thou didst come by these beasts wrongfully. Therefore answer in some other wise if thou thinkest well so to do." The accused holds out, but renews his offer of battle, and is ordered back to prison.

statute which seems to recognize the doctrine that consent was necessary, and provides a punishment *(peine)* for refusal, of a nature to induce consent. The Statute of Westminster the First (3 Edw. I. c. 12) enacts, in 1275, that "Notorious felons, openly of ill fame, who will not put themselves on inquests for felonies with which they are charged before the justices at the king's suit, shall be put in strong and hard imprisonment *(en le prison forte et dure)* as refusing the common law of the land. But this is not to be understood of persons who are taken on light suspicion." This appears to be the first mention of what came to be known as the *peine forte et dure.*

Of the long continuance of this practice until its abolition in 1772,[232] and the tardy adoption then, and in 1827,[233] of Bracton's opinion and the method of the cases in 1221; and of the strange and barbarous variations upon this penalty brought about by judges' or jailers' authority, I need not say much. But a few words may be interesting. I have given all the language of the statute. In Britton (about 1291 — 2), we find details which are not in the statute: "That they be barefooted, ungirt and bareheaded, in the worst place in the prison, upon the bare ground continually night and day, that they eat only bread made of barley or bran, and that they drink not, the day they eat, nor eat, the day they drink, nor drink anything but water, and *(il soint enfyrges)* that they be put in irons."[234] Fleta,[235] a book which the writer of Britton is supposed to have had in his hands, says nothing of putting in irons. In the middle of the next century it was found possible by a woman to live forty days under the penance;[236] so that although a miracle is intimated, in saying of this woman that she lived "without food or drink," it has been supposed that they did not yet *press* the prisoners. But this is probably a mistake; the penance may have been varied in the case just referred to. Pressing appears to be mentioned in the "Mirror;" and in the Cornish iter of 1302 we find what appear to be two cases of this sort, and one or two other cases of the *graunt penance,* in which

---

[232] St. 12 Geo. III. e. 20, s. 1.

[233] St. 7 & 8 Geo. IV. c. 28.

[234] Nichols, i. 26, 27.

[235] See lib. i. c. 34, s. 33.

[236] Pike, Hist. Crime, i. 211, Bl. Com. iv. 328. Barrington, Obs. Stat. 62, gives the date as 31 Edw. I., and founds an inference on the mistaken time.

the full details are not given.[237] The penance is described in the case of John de Dorley and Sir Ralph Bloyho[238] thus: "that he should be put in a house on the ground in his shirt, laden with as much iron as he could bear *(charge de tant de fer cum il poit porter),* and that he should have nothing to drink on the day when he had anything to eat, and that he should drink water which came neither from fountain nor river." In 1406,[239] we find Gascoigne, by advice of all the justices, awarding the penalty with further details. Two appealed of robbery and "mute of malice, to delay their death," are to lie on the ground naked, save trowsers, to have put upon them as great a weight of iron as they can bear and more *(tant de ferr et pois come ils puissent porter et pluis),* and to have for food only the poorest bread that can be found, and standing water from the place nearest to the jail, and these only on. alternate days, bread only on one day, and only water on the next, — and so to lie till death. In 1464,[240] at the Nottingham assizes, the judges had a long struggle with one Robert Eypton, appealed of larceny, who, when asked how he would acquit himself, persisted in the strange answer, "By God and our lady St. Mary and holy church." After repeated importunities from the judges, extending over several hours, he finally yielded, and was found guilty. Danby, C. J., in setting forth the consequences of holding out said: "You will be sent to the prison from which You came to us, and will have on your body a weight of stones and iron as great as you can bear and greater; and one day bread, namely brown bread *(pain, s. browne bred)* and another day water, until you be dead; and besides the water will be from the water running next the prison." In 1474,[241] on an appeal, the terms of the judgment are given: "Needham went to Newgate and asked judgment *in forma quae sequitur.*

---

[237] Y. B. 30 & 31 Edw. I. 510. See also *ib.* pp. 498, 502, 531.

[238] *Ib.* 510.

[239] Y. B. 8 H. IV. 1, 2.

[240] In 1505 (Keilwey, 70, pi. 4), at the jail delivery at Southwark the judgment was that two persons accused should lie prostrate and have as much weight put on them, &c., &c., and that their heads should not touch the earth, and they would only have *Rye bread, et le prochein ewe standing at dit prison;* "it shall not be running water, and they shall stay so until they are dead." See Coke, C. J.'s, long wrangle with the prisoner in Weston'a case, a How. St. Tr. 911 (1615).

[241] Y-B.4 Edw. IV. n, l8.

That the appellee be remanded to his prison... and be put in a cell, and be naked on the bare ground without litter or rushes, or cloth or anything, and shall lie there naked on his back,... his head and feet covered, and that one arm be drawn with a cord to one quarter of the cell, and the other to the other quarter, and that one foot be drawn to one quarter of the cell and the other to the other, and that on his body be put a piece of iron as much as he can bear, and more *(un péece de ferre tant come il poit suffre et port sur luy, et pluis),* and the first day after, he shall have three morsels of barley bread without any drink, and the second day he shall thrice drink, without bread, as much as he can of water standing near the prison, and this shall be his diet until he be dead."[242] At Newgate two centuries later, in 1662,[243] they had made other changes. Kelyng, C. J., tells us that "George Harley, being indicted for robbery, refused to plead, and his two thumbs were tied together with whipcord that the pain of that might compel him to plead, and he was sent away so tied, and a minister persuaded to go to him to persuade him; and an hour after he was brought again and pleaded. And this was said to be the constant practice at Newgate." This method was sometimes accompanied by the press; at this period also a sharp stone or stake was placed under the prisoner's back. The tying with whipcord was kept up at Newgate at least as late as 1734.[244]

So long, and longer, did this stupid, needless barbarity last. Indeed, in 1708, in a statute assimilating some parts of the

---

[242] Y. B. 14 Edw. IV. 8, 17.

[243] Kelyng (old ed.), 27.

[244] Pal. Com. ii. 189-191, Barrington, Obs. on Stat. (2d ed.) 61-66. As is well known, there was a reason for enduring this horrid torture, in the doctrine that one who was not formally adjudged guilty did not forfeit his lands. In 1565, Sir Thomas Smith (Com. Eng. book 2, c. 26) writes: "His condemnation [for standing mute] is to be pressed to death, which it one of the cruelest deaths that may be. He is laid upon a table, and another upon him, and so much weight of stones or lead laid upon that table, while as his body be crushed and his life by that violence taken from him. This death some strong and stout-hearted man doth chose; for, not being condemned of felony, his blood is not corrupted, his lands nor goods confiscate to the Prince," &c. Mr. Pike's account (Hist. Crime, ii. 194-5; t'6. 283-5) of Strangeways' sufferings in 1658, of Burnworth's, in 1726, under nearly four hundredweight, and of John Durant's case, in 1734, are horrible, but interesting.

For what is known of the case of Giles Corey, pressed to death at Salem in Massachusetts, in 1692, see Upham, Salem Witchcraft, ii. 334.

criminal law in England and Scotland, while it is provided that after July 1, 1709, no person accused of crime in Scotland shall suffer torture, it is with the express proviso, that the law "shall not extend to take away that judgment which is given in England against persons indicted of felony who shall refuse to plead or decline trial."[245] But at last came the abolition of it all in 1772, and the adoption then and in 1827 of the rules that had been advocated and a little followed five centuries before.[246] It is impossible to review these facts and not agree with Palgrave when he says: "It is a singular proof of the want of attention to any general principles of legislation that a custom equally foolish and barbarous should have continued so long unaltered. And the subject is one, among others, which shows that the English law must forfeit many of the encomiums... which have so long passed current amongst us."[247] It is melsucholy to think what might have been done some centuries earlier, when we compare the enlightened provisions, in 1284, of the Statute of Wales, c. xi. as to smaller matters of personal trespass, where the damages exceeded forty shillings: "And since in a plea of trespass the defendant can hardly escape defending himself by the country, the judge is to inquire, by consent of parties, into the truth of the matter by a good inquest.... Mention is made above of the consent of parties, but it may happen that the defendant will refuse an inquest of the country. In that case, if the plaintiff offer to prove by the country the trespass done him, and the defendant reject it, let him be held as convicted, and punished as if he had been convicted by the country." As

---

[245] St. 7 Ann. c. 21, s. 5.

[246] "For the more effectual proceeding against persons standing mute on their arraignment for felony or piracy . . . s. 1. If [he] shall stand mute or will not answer directly to the felony or piracy . . . [he] shall be convicted, etc. . . . The court shall thereupon award judgement and execution ... as if ... convicted by verdict or confession. . . ." (Stat. 12 Geo III. c. 20). "S.1. If any person, not having the privilege of peerage, being arraigned upon any indictment for treason, felony, or piracy, shall plead thereto a plea of not guilty, he shall by such plea, without any further form be deemed to put himself upon the country for trial. . . . s. 2. If any person, being arraigned for treason, felony, piracy, or misdemeanor, shall stand mute of malice, or will not answer directly ... it shall be lawful for the court ... to order the proper officer to enter a plea of not guilty. . . ." (Stat. 7 & 8 Geo. IV. c. 28). In 1700 (St. 11 & 12 Wm. III. e. 7, s. 6) the same thing was provided in an act for the suppression of piracy.

[247] See also Sir J. F. Stephen's observations, in Hist. Cr. Law, i. 300.

regards the origin of these singular practices, it may be conjectured that the *prison forte et dure* of the St. West. I. c. 12, in 1275, is to be understood by reference to what Palgrave calls the "temporary ordinance" of the King's Council,[248] in 1219, after the Lateran Council. The judges, as we have seen, were then ordered, as regards the worst cases, to imprison, — but not in such a way as to imperil life or limb, — *teneantur in prisona nostra et salvo custodiantur; ita quod non incurrant periculum vitas et membrorum occasions prisonae nostrae.*[249] The later statute seems to refer to this caution, and to remove it. It is 'the bad cases also that this statute purports to deal with, "notorious felons and such as be openly of evil name," and the order is, that if these persons will not put themselves on the inquest, *soient mises en la prison forte et dure.* Apart from the order of 1219, it was matter of course that those who, according to the ideas of the period, could not be tried without their own consent, should still be kept in prison; and it is highly probable that, without any statute for it, some persuasions would be adopted to induce consent. It was so in Normandy, where the prisoner was put on short diet, and where the judges even authorized torture.[250] But if the order of 1219 operated as a restraint upon. these endeavors, the later statute would seem to have changed this; something might now be added to the old imprisonment, and the description of it is found only in these words, *forte, et dure.*[251] It is certain that not until after this statute do we hear of the "penance," and then we find it very soon.[252] As might be expected, it varies from time to time. We hear nothing of pressing at first; but seem to find it as early as 1302.[253] This,

---

[248] Com. i. 266.

[249] Rymer, Foed. (old ed.) 228. As regards this word *prison,* compare a note of the reporter in Y. B. 20 & 21 Edw. I. (1292): *Nec debet duci ad barram in ferris, quia dam est inferris est in prisona.*

[250] Brunner, Schw. 474; Pal. Com. ii. 190; *ib.* i. 268.

[251] For certain *unlawful,* practices of sheriffs and jailers, in putting appellees of good fame en *vile et dure prisone,* see Stat. 5 Edw. II. c. 34 (1311).

[252] *Supra,* p. 74.

[253] In 1291-2, of accused, parties who refused to put themselves on the country, the record says, *habeant penam statuti.* Staffordshire Coll. (Wm. Salt Soc.) vi. 279. Palgrave (Com. ii. 189) cites a statement of 1293, in the "Chronicle" of the Priory of Dunstable (ii. 609): *Eodem anno justiciarii itinerantes apud Eboracum valde rigide se gerebant; et quendam nobilem . . . de*

with the whole matter of the "penance," is the subject of bitter complaint in the "Mirror," a book written, as is now supposed, about 1289. It is declared[254] an abuse to load *(charge)* a man with iron and put him in penance before he is attainted of felony. Again,[255] the Statute "West. I. is said to be abused in that the penance is pushed so far as to kill people without regard to their condition, when perhaps a man might acquit himself (se *purra per* cas *aider et acquiter)* otherwise than by the country; and he ought not to be punished till he has been attainted. This book declares chargeable with homicide those who kill a man adjudged to penance, by excess of *"peyne."*[256]

But other matters remain to be mentioned touching the trial of criminal cases, except those minor offences which in early times were very summarily disposed of.[257] In most cases, the difficulty about a want of consent, by one accused of the graver crimes, to that new mode of trial which the abolition of

---

multis feloniis arrestatum ad poenitentiam statuti posuerunt, quia vere dictum patriae recusavit; et mortuus est in prisona. Immediately after this a great robbery is mentioned, for which some knights and gentlemen were hanged; *quidam autem eligentes poenitentiam secundum statutum miserabiliter defecerunt.* It will be noticed that the Chronicler refers the penance to the statute. And so the Mirror. Palgrave (Com. ii. 189) says that at about the period of the Mirror the chroniclers "record the fate of many criminals who perished under the infliction." It should be mentioned that Palgrave, in saying that *Bracton* describes the penance, doubtless suffers from a misprint; it should read Britton. Bracton does not mention it. In 1323 the records show half a dozen deaths of prisoners at the prison of the castle of Northampton resulting from hunger, cold, or privation. One case was that of a prisoner undergoing penance for refusing to put himself on the country. Gross, Coroners' Rolls (Selden Soc.), 79-81.

    I ought at least to refer to the fact that Coke (2d Inst. 179) and Hale (Pl. Cr. ii. 321-2) mention weighty considerations in support of their opinion that the *peine forte et dure* existed before the statute. What I have said would indicate that in a sense this may he so, but not in their sense; in other words, that imprisonment existed before the statute, hut not any lawful *prison forte et dure.* On the whole subject, see Pollock and Maitland, Hist. Eng. Law, ii. 647.

    [254] Mirror, lib. 5, c. 1. s. 54.

    [255] *Ib.* lib. 5, c. 4, g. 12.

    [256] Mirror, lib. i. c. 9 (p. 24).

    [257] "So far as we can see, if the justices in eyre receive a presentment of any of the minor offences [lower than felony] they give the incriminated person no chance of denying his guilt, but at once declare him to be 'in mercy.' . . . We believe that in Henry III.'s day anything that we could call the trial of a man upon an indictment for misdemeanor was exceedingly rare." Pollock and Maitland, Hist. Eng. Law, ii. 649. Compare ib. 510, 520.

the ordeal had brought forward, did not arise; he did consent to be tried by the country. But there were marked peculiarities about "the country" that tried a criminal case. "The reader will note the contrast," says the editor of certain selections from criminal pleas of 1292 — 3,[258] "between these juries and a petty jury of the present day. The jurors at these assizes, with one or two exceptions, were knights, or heads of knightly families." The explanation lies in the fact that the trial jury in criminal cases was generally made up of those who made the presentments, and these, under the Assize of Clarendon, were required to be made *per xii legaliores homines de hundredo, et per iv legaliores homines de qualibet villata.* "As we read the rolls and Bracton's text," says a high authority upon this difficult subject,[259] "what normally happens is this: the hundred jury, without being again sworn, — it has already taken a general oath to answer questions truly, — is asked to say in so many words whether this man is guilty or no. If it finds him guilty, then 'the four townships' are sworn and answer the same question. If they agree with the hundredors, sentence is passed. This we believe to have been the normal trial. But there were many juries about, for every hundred had sent one, and upon occasion the justices would turn from one to another and take its opinion about the guilt of the accused. By the end of Henry III.'s reign [1272] it is common that the question of guilt or innocence should be submitted to the presenting jury, to the jury of another hundred, and to the four vills. They are put before us as forming a single body, which delivers an unanimous verdict." The accusing jury, it has been said,[260] is not strictly an accusing body, and perhaps not even a suspecting one; it is, perhaps, reporting the mere fact that the party is suspected; "when asked, therefore, to say directly *(praecise dicere)* whether he is guilty or no, they may acquit him." In 1279[261] we see a trial jury made up by a combination of accusing juries and a specially elected

---

[258] Staffordshire Collections (Wm. Salt Soc.), vi. part 1, 280, n.

[259] Pollock and Maitland, Hist. Eng. Law, ii. 644. The learned authors speak after an examination of many unpublished records. See also Dr. Charles Gross's excellent remarks in his recently published Select Coroners' Rolls (Seld. Soc. Pub. vol. 9), pp. xxvii-xliii.

[260] Pollock and Maitland, Hist. Eng. Law, ii. 645.

[261] North. Ass. Rolls (Surtees Soc.), 374.

one: *Et juratores... tam de illis qui fuerunt juratores coram praefatis* [the judges] *quam de illis qui modo electi fuerunt ad coronam dicunt,* &c.

It came, indeed, to be allowed to the accused to challenge those who had served on the presenting jury.[262] And so, about 1302,[263] the accused, a knight, says, *in pares meos consentiam sed non in duodecim per quos sum accusatus;* and he is allowed the challenge. It seems, nevertheless, long to have been the approved practice to try an accused person by some, at least, of those who had indicted him. In 1340,[264] in an irregular proceeding against Willoughby, a deposed justice, he is charged, "by the commonalty of the county of Lancaster," with certain corrupt practices about indictments. Parning, J., says: "In such cases the inquest should be taken by the indictors and others.... Certainly if indictors be not there it is not well for the king." But, at last, in 1351 — 2,[265] it was formally enacted "that no indictor be put on an inquest upon the deliverance of one indicted for trespass or felony, if he be challenged for this cause by the party indicted."

The form of statement in the early records as to the composition, of the criminal jury varies. In 1221,[266] sometimes the record reads simply that the accused put himself on a jury. "The jurors [or the xii jurors] say," etc. At others it runs: "the jurors, and the vill of S., and the coroner, and all the other of the county, say precisely," etc.; or "the jurors say [etc.], and so say the vills of C., L., and H.;" or perhaps four or five vills are named; or we read that the accused "put themselves on the verdict of the twelve jurymen and the vills;" or that "all the jurors both of the vill and of the hundred say," etc. In 1220,[267] a party begins

---

[262] "When the defendants have put themselves upon the country, and the jurors are come into court, they may be challenged in the following form: 'Sir, this man ought not to be upon the jury, because he indicted me, and I presume of him and all those who indicted me, that they still bear the same ill-will against me as when they indicted me.' And we will," adds the supposed royal author, "that where a man's life is at stake. this exception shall be allowed." Britton, 12; *ib.* Nichols ed. 29-30 (A. D. 1291).

[263] Y. B. 30 & 31 Edw. L 531. See *infra,* p. 113.

[264] Y. B. 14 & 15 Edw. III. 261.

[265] St. 25 Edw. III. 5, c. 3.

[266] Maitland, Gl. Pl. cases 100, 101, 213, 228, 229, 326, 330. See also Maitland, Sel. Pl. Cr. i. *passim.*

[267] Maitland, Sel. Pl. Cr. i. case 193.

by putting himself "on the county of Essex or of Norfolk or Southampton or all of them," and afterwards "puts himself on the county of Surrey or on all men in England who know him." At Easter came twenty-four knights from Surrey, at the king's summons, who declared him to be a robber. "And since he put himself upon these, let him be hanged." [268]

---

[268] See also many cases in the valuable selections from the Plea Rolls, in the Staffordshire Collections, published by the Wm. Salt Archaeological Society. (London: Harrison & Sons.) In Vol. VI., Pt. I. 269 (1292-3), we read: "The jury of this hundred and the neighboring villa say he is guilty" i6 278: "The jury of this hundred, together with the jury of Newcastle said," &c.; *ib.* 279: "The jury of the hundred of Offelowe, together with the nearest villa, say," &c.; *ib.* 280,-twelve jurors are named *ib* 281 fourteen jurors are named, "elected *ad hoc;"* *ib.* 284, it is "the jurors of the two hundreds" of P. & C. In 1356 *(ib.* vol. xii. 146), we find something that sounds more like conforming to the usage in civil cases "a jury of the vicinage being tried and sworn (trati *el jurati)* stated" &c. This, it will be noticed, was four or five years after the Statute of 25 Edw. III. Again, in 1372, when parties charged with felony had put themselves on a jury, we read that *juratores ad hoc electi, triati et jurati dicunt,* &c. Gross, Coroners' Rolls, 121.

CHAPTER III
TRIAL BY JURY AND ITS
DEVELOPMENT (*CONTINUED*)

Now, having seen this new and reformed method of proof, what we call trial by jury, fairly afoot in England and started on its great and strange career, it will be profitable to run over certain leading facts in its history during several centuries. These arrange themselves, conveniently enough, under two heads, I. The methods of informing the jury, and of securing and improving that quality in them which made them a fit body to "try" the facts in issue, *i. e.,* to decide them by their answers; and II. The methods of controlling the jury, of preventing the access of improper influence, of punishing them, and of reviewing their action.

But before beginning on these things one or two other matters should be briefly mentioned.

(a). As to the number of the jury. In early times the inquisition had no fixed number. In the Prankish empire we are told of a great variety of numbers.[269] Among the Normans, also, it varied much, and "twelve has not even the place of the prevailing *grundzahl.*"[270] It may have been the recognitions under Henry II. that established twelve as the usual number;[271] and even there the number was not uniform. In the technical "inquest of office," it always continued to be uncertain: "This is done," says Blackstone, [272] "by a jury of no determinate number; being either twelve, or less or more." In 1199 [273] there is a jury of nine. In Bracton's Note Book, at dates between 1217 and 1219, we see juries of 9, 36, and 40, — partly owing, indeed, to the consent of litigants. We have already noticed that the grand assize was sixteen, made by adding the four electors to the

---

[269] We read of 66, 41, 20, 17, 13, II, 8, 7, 53, 15, &c. Brunner, Schw. 111, 112.

[270] There, also, the documents show all sorts of numbers, — 4,5, 6,12,18, 21, 27, 30, and so on. *Ib.* 273, 274.

[271] *Ib.* 363.

[272] Com. iii. 258, cited by Brunner.

[273] Rot. Cur. Reg. ii. 114.

elected twelve,[274] and that recognitions as to whether one be of age were by eight.[275] The attaint jury was usually twenty-four; but in the reign of Henry VI. a judge remarked that the number was discretionary with the court.[276]

(b). The rule of unanimity in giving a verdict was by no means universal at first. A doctrine had a considerable application in Normandy and survived in England, that it was enough if eleven agreed; the ground of this being the old rule that a single witness is nothing — *testis unus testis nullus.*[277] Then in certain cases a majority of the twelve was enough; as in the assize of novel disseisin, in which only seven were necessarily present, these seven being then required to be unanimous. Brunner's remark is very likely true, that "Only in the second half of the fourteenth century did the principle get established that in all inquests the twelve must agree in order to a good verdict."[278] The Mirror appears to assert an opinion which I have not observed elsewhere, that "since two witnesses are enough, according to the Word of God" *(solonque le dit de Dieu),* a verdict should be held good if two only are found to agree.[279] But we are perhaps to understand this courageous, or, it may be, fantastic writer as asserting his opinion of what ought to be law. Thus regarded, his statement seems to overlook the fact that the jury were more than witnesses; they were triers as well; and the explanation of their number being usually greater than the scriptural "two or three" lies probably in those historical considerations to which Brunner[280] refers, such as the desire to make up not merely by quality but by

---

[274] *Supra,* p.46 n.

[275] *Supra,* p. 64 n.

[276] For other variations in England and Normandy, see Brunner, Schw. 364, and Hargrave's note, Co. Lit. 155. "The grand jury," says Bacon's Abridgment, in 1740, "may consist of thirteen or any greater number." 3 Bac. Abr., "Jnries," A.

[277] As to this rule, see Best, Evid. ss. 597-600.

[278] For Brunner's very interesting account of all this, see Schw. 364-371; he cites Bracton, 184 b, 255 b, and 179 b. The last citation relates to the mort d'ancestor, and runs thus: "The assize is to proceed by twelve jurors . . . and not fewer, as it may in the assize of novel disseisin, by seven at least. . . . And so here let the assize proceed by twelve at least." In the French rise of the inquest, the principle of a majority decision prevailed.

[279] Whittaker, Mirror (Selden Soc.), lib.3, c. 34, lib. 5, c. 1, s. 136. But see the editor's note at p. 116. As to this remarkable book, and Andrew Horn's relation to it, see Maitland's introduction to Whittaker's edition.

[280] Schw. 112.

quantity for the lack, in the case of the jury, of that amenability to counter proof and the battle which sometimes existed in the case of the older witnesses.[281]

In 1286 the jurors in an assize of novel disseisin were unevenly divided,[282] but the judgment is given in these words: *et quia dicto majoris partis jur, standum est, consideratum est,* etc. This doctrine of giving judgment with the majority is laid down generally, in the trial of felony, by Britton (12 b): "If they cannot agree let them be separated and examined why. If the greater part know the truth and a part not, let judgment be given with the majority." The case given in Emlyn'a note [283] and those cited below give much reason to believe that this was at first the general rule, in civil cases also. In 1318 — 19, Bereford, C. J., when the twelfth juryman on an inquest had not appeared, asked the parties whether they would agree to going on with eleven. The reporter notes it as a question, whether this can be done by assent in "pleas of assize and attaints."[284] In 1291, in trespass for assault, the parties, by consent, had a jury of ten.[285] In 1367, on the taking of an assize, one juryman would not agree with the other eleven, and the justices took a verdict from these and imprisoned the twelfth. On moving for judgment,

---

[281] Supra, p. 17.

[282] "*X jur. dicunt unum, et* xi. *dicunt alium contrarium,*" says the account in Pl. Ab. 279, col. 1, Kanc. We must surmise that xi. is a misprint for ii. Since the foregoing was written, I find this case given more fully in one of Emlyn's valuable notes, in Hale's Pl. Cr. ii. 297. It is there said that the whole jury consisted of eleven, that it stood ten to one, and that "both verdicts are recorded: *Decem jurati dicunt quod,* &c. & *undecimus juratorum scilicet Johannes Kineth dicit, &'c.*"

Emlyn in this note supports by several cases the opinion that it was anciently the general rule in civil cases, when the jury was divided in opinion, to examine each side, to cause both verdicts to be recorded, and then to give judgment *ex dicto majoris partis juratorum.* He gives from the rolls a case of 1271 or 1272, where in a writ of right the jury stood eleven to one, and this course was followed; and also the above-named case of 1286. Another case, of 1292, where a verdict of eleven had been taken in 1288, the twelfth disagreeing, is given in full by Emlyn, and seems to support his view. This case is briefly given also in Pl. Ab. 286, col. 2, Norf. To these may be added an imperfect case of 1199 (Rot. Cur. Reg. ii. 105; s. c. shortly given in Pl. Ab. 23 col. 2, Suff.), which seems to be explained by what is said in Emlyn's note. Compare also a case of 1202, in Maitland, Sel. Pl. Cr. i. case 241.

[283] *Supra,* p. 87, note 4.

[284] Y. B. 12 Edw. II. 373.

[285] Pl. Ab. 285, col. 1, Ebor.

when counsel urged that it had formerly been adjudged in trespass
that a verdict of eleven might be good, "and this we will show you
by record," — Thorpe, C. J., said: "It is fundamental *(let ley fuit
fondue)* that every inquest shall be by twelve... and no fewer....
Though you bring us a dozen records, it shall not help you at all;
those who gave judgment on such a verdict were greatly blamed."
Moubrey, J.: "As the verdict was by eleven and judgment cannot be
rendered, sue out a new inquest and let the man imprisoned be
discharged."[286]

---

[286] Y. B. 41 Edw. III. 31, 36; s. c. 41 Ass. 11, Hale, PL Cr. ii. 297. It
will be useful to follow up the cases given by Emlyn with a few which will
connect them with the case of 1367, last above-mentioned. In 1334 (8 Ass. 35),
where a verdict had been reached, but it is not stated by how many, it is added
that "because one juryman had delayed his companions a day and a night, without
agreeing with them, and this without reason, it was awarded that he stay in the
Fleet. Afterwards he was bailed until the court should be advised what it would
do with him." In 1355 (29 Ass. 4), on a challenge to the array in an assize, three
triers were sworn who could not agree during a whole night. Whereupon the court
said that if they would not agree, it would take the verdict of the two, and would
order the third to prison, as in case of an inquest. The Reporter adds, *quaere si sit
lex.* Compare another case of disagreement among the triers of a challenge, where
one was challenged and the eleven already sworn were the triers. They stood ten
to one. Counsel urged that the eleventh might be disregarded, and added that if
they were trying the principal case, and the twelfth would not agree with his
associates, "yon would take the verdict of the eleven." The court in effect
followed this course. In 1367 (41 Ass. 11), in what appears to be another report of
the case last quoted in the text, we read as follows: "In another assize before the
game justices [Ingelby and Cavendish] at Northampton, the assize was sworn.
They were all agreed, except one, who would not agree with the eleven. They
were remanded and stayed there all that day and the next, without drink or food.
Then the judges asked him [the one who stood out] if he would agree with his
associates, and he said never, — he would die in prison first. Whereupon they
took the verdict of the eleven, and ordered him to prison, and thereupon a day was
given upon this verdict in the Common Bench. *Kirketon* [Serjeant] prayed
judgment on the verdict. Thorpe [Robert, C. J. C. B.] said, they were all agreed
that this verdict, taken from eleven, was no verdict, and that a verdict could not be
taken from eleven. But *Kirketon* told how Wilughby [a judge from 1328 to about
1357] in trespass took the verdict of eleven and sent the twelfth to prison; and the
attaint was sued against the eleven. And also W. Thorpe [a judge and Chief
Justice from 1328 to 1350] in an assize in the twentieth year of the present king
[1345 — 6] took the verdict of eleven. Thorpe. That is no example for us; he was
heavily reproached for that. . . . And afterwards by assent of all the justices it was
declared that this was no verdict. It was therefore awarded that this panel be
quashed and annulled, and that he who was in prison be enlarged, and that the
plaintiff sue a new *venire facias. . . Note,* that the justices said they ought to have
taken the assize with them in a wagon until they were agreed."

The requirement of twelve in the petit jury, unless by consent, and the need of unanimity, seemed now to have become the settled rule.[287] And, by-and-by, we shall read in Duncomb's Trials *per Pals* (1665),[288] this account of the sanctity and foreordained character of the number twelve:

"And first as to their [the jury's] number twelve: and this number is no less esteemed by our law than by Holy Writ. If the twelve apostles on their twelve thrones must try us in our eternal state, good reason hath the law to appoint the number of twelve to try our temporal. The tribes of Israel were twelve, the patriarchs were twelve, and Solomon's officers were twelve. 1 Kings iv. 7.... Therefore not only matters of fact were tried by twelve, but of ancient times twelve judges were to try matters in law, in the Exchequer Chamber, and there were twelve counsellors of state for matters of state; and he that wageth his law must have eleven others with him who believe he says true. And the law is so precise in this number of twelve, that if the trial be by more or less, it is a mistrial."

Let us come now to the two great heads under which we are to consider what remains to be said of the jury.

I. As to informing the jurors, *(a)* In the first place, they were men chosen as being likely to be already informed; in this respect, as well as others, they were a purged and selected body.[289] This selection came about in some degree by way of a statutory correction of abuses, as in the St. of 13 Edw. I. (West. 2) c. 38, in 1285, reciting a practice of putting on diseased, decrepit men, and poor men, and sparing the rich; and in a statute of 21 Edw. I. in 1293,[290] reciting like troubles, and "the sparing of such as are richer and more likely to know the fact." I pass by the matter of property qualification, and the precautions, by way of challenge, to keep off persons unsuitable by reason of favor to a party, or of want of property or social standing. Always they were from the neighborhood — *de visineto*.

The edition of the Book of Assizes of 1679, the one now most commonly used, and also an, earlier one of 1606, make *Kirketon* say that W. Thorpe "took the verdict of xii." But in the edition of 1561 it reads, "the verdict of xi;" and this is necessary to make sense.

[287] See Pollock and Maitland, ii. 623 — 625.

[288] Eighth ed. (London, 1766) p. 92.

[289] See Maitland, Sel. Civil Pleas, i. case 221, where an official is in mercy for putting a villein on an assize of novel disseisin.

[290] See Maitland, Sel. Civil Pleas, i. case 221, where an official is in mercy for putting a villein on an assize of novel disseisin.

This expression was not precisely defined, beyond its meaning from the same county; but in practice it went much further. It became the rule to require that a certain number of the jury should come from the particular hundred in question; and these men were expected to inform the others. In an important case of 1374, Belknap, C. J., says: "In an assize in a county, if the court does not see six, or at least five, men of the hundred where the tenements are, to inform the others who are further away, I say that the assize will not be taken. *A multo fortiori,* those of one county cannot try a thing which is in another county."[291] A statute of 1543 required six hundredors.[292] In 1585 this was reduced, in personal actions, to two.[293] "The most general rule," said Coke, early in the seventeenth century, "is that every trial shall be out of that town, parish, or hamlet... within which the matter of fact assignable is alleged, which is most certain and nearest thereunto." [294] Much trouble was caused by going into this detail, and at last in 1705 it was enacted that in civil cases it should be enough to summon the jury from "the body of the county."[295] In criminal cases the same result appears to have been worked out in practice.[296] Of the conceptions of the earlier period, as to this matter, we may see a lively illustration in a passage from Sir Francis Palgrave's "The Merchant and the Friar" (1837), in which, under the guise of a pleasant fiction, he presents curious details of English life in the thirteenth century.[297] Long afterwards it was regarded as the

---

[291] Y. B. 48 Edw. III. 30, 17; s. c. Lib. Ass. 48, 5.

[292] St. 35 H. VIII. c. 6, s. 3.

[293] St. 27 Eliz. c. 6, s. 5.

[294] Co. Lit. 125.

[295] St. 4 Ann, c. 16, s. 6.

[296] For details as to this, see Note 191, Co. Lit. 125.

[297] These are being explained, so he fables, by an English friar, Roger Bacon, to an Italian merchant, Marco Polo, while showing the stranger over London. They are at Guildhall, and the trial of one of the alleged robbers of the king's treasury, in 1303, is beginning. "Sheriff, is your inquest in court ?" said the mayor. "Yes, my Lord," replied the sheriff; "and I am happy to say it will be an excellent jury for the crown. I myself have picked and chosen every man on the panel. . . . There is not a man whom I have not examined carefully. . . . All the jurors are acquainted with [the prisoner], ... I should ill have discharged my duty if I had allowed my bailiff to summon the jury at haphazard. . . . The least informed of them have taken great pains to go up and down in every hole and corner of Westminster, — they and their wives, — and to learn all they could hear concerning his past and present life and conversation. Never had any culprit a better chance of having a fair trial," etc.

right of the parties to "inform" the jury, after they were empanelled and before the trial. In 1427, we read in the St. 6 H. VI. c. 2, that in certain cases the sheriffs must furnish the parties with the jury's names six days before the session, if they ask for it, since (it is recited as a grievance) defendants heretofore could not know who the jury were, "so as to inform them of their right and title before the day of the session," *(pur eux enformer de lour droit et titles devaunt, etc.)*. This statute supplements an earlier general statute of 42 Edw. III. c. 11 (1368), mentioned in 3 Bl. Com. 353, which deals with the mischief that parties cannot be ready with their challenges. Probably Coke's remark about the St. H. VI., in 3 Inst. 175, that both parties must have been meant to be present when this information was given, was a misapprehension; but, of course, a party had to keep outside the line of embracery.

It was a little later than the time of Palgrave's story when Thomas Makerill and his brother, in 1317, were arrested for assaulting an officer of the court in "Fletestrete," and twelve men of the court, in whose presence this took place, and also twelve men of the *visne* of "Fletestrete" were summoned for a jury.[298] So in 1347 — 8, where the defendant pleaded a release, and the plaintiff replied infancy, and that he was born in Fleet Street and prayed for a jury thence; the defendant rejoined that the release was made when the plaintiff was of full age and in "Tamestreet," and prayed for a jury thence. The court awarded a jury from both places.[299] About 1356, when a judge of the Common Bench complained in the Exchequer against a woman for calling him "traitor, felon, and robber," the case went to an inquest of "attorneys of the Common Bench and the Exchequer." [300]

(b). These cases may illustrate a common method of securing for the jury a better knowledge of matters in issue, viz., that of combining men of different *visnes,* who might inform each other. This existed in Normandy. We notice it in our own earliest records, as in 1199.[301] A remarkable instance of the use of separate juries for

---

[298] Pl. Ab. 331. col. I.

[299] Y. B. 22 Edw. III. 1, 2.

[300] 30 Ass. 19. And so when an appellor disavowed his appeal, and alleged duress, Scrope, C. J., in 1338, inquired by those "nearest to the jail." Fitz. Corone, 118.

[301] Rot. Cur. Reg. ii. 10. Compare the practice of bringing viewers before a jury, 29 Ass. 70; 40 *ib.* 4.

amassing their several contributions of knowledge by separate verdicts is found in the proceedings on occasion of the great robbery of the royal treasury at Westminster Abbey in 1303. Mr. Pike, to whom we owe this information, cites the case as illustrating the progress made in separating the accusing and the trial jury.[302] The king appointed a commission of inquiry. "A jury was empanelled for every ward of the city of London, and for every hundred of Middlesex and Surrey — and in addition to these there was a jury of goldsmiths and aldermen." They charged certain persons. Five justices were then directed to try the accused. "Juries were summoned from the same hundred and wards as before, but in obedience to a different commission." It is not clear, in this case, just how the separate juries were used at the trial. In general, separate panels in such cases were combined in one. In 1230,[303] seven from Surrey and seven from London were united into one jury by consent. It was the practice, later on, at any rate,[304] where two panels were summoned from different counties, to choose one juror alternately from each.

   (c). Moreover, as among eligible persons, there seems always to have existed the power of selecting those especially qualified for a given service. Jurors are summoned not merely from closer or less close neighborhoods, but *de senioribus et legalioribus,* as asked in 1198;[305] from Florentine merchants living in London, where there was an issue, in 1280, as to an act done in Florence;[306] and from experts and men of particular trades, like the London juries of cooks and fishmongers, where one was accused of selling bad food.[307] What we call the "special jury" seems always to have been

---

[302] Hist. Crime, i. 198 — 200, 207, 208, 466.

[303] Br. N. B. ii. case 375.

[304] *As* in 1402, Y. B. 4 H. IV. 1, pl. 2; and in 1619, Hob. 330.

[305] Rot. Cur. Reg. i. 354.

[306] Pl. Ab. 201, col. 2., and s.c. MSS. copy from the Record Office.

[307] Ryley, Mem. London, 266 (1351); *ib.* 536 (1394); Palgrave, Merch. and Friar, 190 — 194. The jury of the "half tongue," *de medietate linguae, was* founded on considerations of policy and fair dealing, rather than a wish to provide a well-informed jury. See "Ordinance of the Staples," 27 Edw. III. St. 2, c. 8 (1353); and St. 28 Edw. III. c. 13 (1354). In 1348, in debt on a contract, the defendants, German merchants, had put forward a charter from the king, allowing them in such cases to have half the jury made up of German merchants, and it was allowed. This benefit, it is said, before the statutes, "was wont to be obtained by grant of the king made to any company of strangers." Molloy, De Jur. Mar. Bk. iii. c. 4 ; Staunf. Pl. Cr. lib. iii. c. 7. We read of it in 1280-81. "9 Edw. 1. A

used. It was a natural result of the principle that those were to be summoned who could best tell the fact, the *veritatem rei.* And so we read that in 1645 — 6, in the King's Bench, "The court was moved that a jury of merchants might be retained to try an issue between two merchants, touching merchants' affairs, and it was granted, because it was conceived they might have better knowledge of the matters in difference which were to be tried than others could who were not of that profession." [308] Nearly three centuries earlier, in 1363, the St. 37 Edw. III. c. 16, in providing for proof of certain facts in Gascony by a certificate of magistrates there, added that if the certificate be contradicted, it shall be tried by merchants frequenting those parts and others who best know about it *(la certification soit trie par marchantz usantz celles parties et autres gentz qe meuth ont de ceo conisance).*

In the grand assize, as we have seen, knights were regularly the jurors. So in the jury of attaint, the writ read, *sumoneas,... xxiv legales milites de visneto.[309]* In 1323, [310] when it was objected that there were no knights on the jury, Herle, J., said, "You never saw such a jury taken without a knight," and ordered a *venire facias* of knights and others. In Coke's time, we read that "in au attaint there ought to be a knight returned of the jury."[311]

Trials at bar often required special juries. Indeed, Blackstone [312] is willing to say that "special juries were originally introduced in trials at bar, when the causes were of too great nicety for the discussion of ordinary freeholders; or where the sheriff was suspected of partiality, though not upon such apparent causes as to warrant an exception to him." The itinerant method of administering justice, as it developed into the *nisi prius* system, resulted in sending

---

Jew had his trial *per medietatem linguae, scilicet* of Jews; and they were sworn upon the five books of Moses, holden in their arms, and by the name of the God of Israel, who is merciful." Dyer, 144 b. editor's note in margin.

[308] Lilly ' Pract. Reg. ii. 154.

[309] Bract. 291.

[310] Fitz. Ab. Attaint, 69.

[311] Inst. 156. The challenge for this defect is supposed to have been abolished in 1751 by St. 24 Geo. II. c. 18, s. 4, although the recital in this section deals with another sort of case, that of a peer of the realm being a party. In such cases at least one knight was required. (Fitz. Ab. Chall. 115, in 1339, affirmed in Plowd. 117, in 1554.) In Blackstone's time (Com. iii. 351), the rule in attaint was "twenty-four of the beat men in the country."

[312] Com. iii. 357.

down most actions to be tried in the counties rather than at Westminster;[313] but in 1285, in regulating this system, the St. West. II. c. 30, expressly provided: *Sed inquisitiones de grossis et pluribus articulis, qui magna indigeant examinatione, capiantur coram justiciariis de bancis, nisi ambae partes,* etc.[314] For the handling of these greater and more complicated causes, there was picked out a better class of jurymen; and there was allowed to the parties themselves a considerable hand in the selection.[315]

As regards special juries in general, we seem to observe the transition from the older, unregulated system to the modern one soon after a case in 1724,[316] where, on a motion for a special jury in the King's Bench, and a question whether this could be had without consent of the parties, "the master of the office was ordered to search for precedents, and he reported that about thirty years ago there were several precedents for special juries upon trials for nice points, without the consent of the parties, but that in the last thirty years there were several motions made for that purpose, but always denied.... Three of the judges (out of four) were of opinion that a special jury might be granted 'to try a cause at bar without the consent of the parties, but never at the *nisi prius* unless very good cause was shewed (and not shewed here); therefore, since the high sheriff is the proper officer to return juries, and there is no imputation against him... the court would not vary from him without the consent

---

[313] *Ib.* 352 — 4.

[314] And so in 1699 (Lord Sandwich's case, 2 Salk. 648), per Holt, C. J., "Where there is value or difficulty, we are bound of common right to grant trials at the bar," citing this passage from St. West. II. In 1453 (Y. B. 32 H. VI. 9, 14), *"Laicon* came to the bar and prayed a *nisi prius* in a writ of trespass between the Bake of Exeter and the Lord of Cromwell." *Billing* objected: "You well know that here in the Hall when the writ was returned there was a great *rout,* and it seemed that great mischief would follow; and greater would ensue if the nisi *prius* should be there [in the country], for my Lord of Exeter is a great and *prepotent* prince in that country. *Laicon.* It wonid be a great relief for the jurors to have the *nisi prius* there. But Prisot said that it should not be, and they were ousted of the *nisi prius."*

[315] In 1661 (Wheeler *v.* Honour, 1 Keble, 166) we read: "which Windham, *J.,* agreed: and trials at bar are to the end to have the most discreet persons, and therefore to clap on ordinary person upon a tales in such cases was not fitting." In 1738 (Smith d. Dormer *v.* Parkhurst, Andrews, 315), on a question of granting a new trial, after a trial at bar, counsel argue: "The evidence of one or two witnesses ought not to overturn the finding of twelve gentlemen of figure and fortune, who might, too, be governed by their own knowledge."

[316] The King *v.* Burridge, 8 Mod. 245.

of the parties." Thereupon, by a declaratory statute in 1730,[317] it was enacted that either party in any case, as well criminal as civil, may have a special jury, oil motion, at his own expense. And the matter was further regulated by later acts.

(d). From the beginning of our records, we find cases, in a dispute over the genuineness of a deed, where the jury are combined with the witnesses to the deed. This goes back to the Franks; and their custom of requiring the witness to a document to defend it by battle also crossed the channel, and is found in Glanvill.[318] As regards these earlier details, and the significance and relation to the old law of this fact of allowing one's self to be thus preappointed as a witness, I must merely refer to very interesting passages of Brunner.[319] In these cases the jury and the witnesses named in the deed were summoned together, and all went out and conferred privately as if composing one body; the witnesses did not regularly testify in open court. Cases of this kind are found very early, *e. g.* in 1208 — 9.[320] In 1208,[321] there is an offer of the defendant to put himself on *legalem juratam patrie,* and on the witnesses to a deed, eleven of whom are named, and it is added, *et alii multi.* Some light is thrown on the conception at the bottom of this introduction of so many names as witnesses, when we observe that people wrote down the names of absent friends and got their consent afterwards. It was only a few years after these cases when one of John's barons, being in prison and desirous of raising money, wrote to three distinguished friends asking, as they could not be present at the execution of his deeds, and as their names had been written in as witnesses, that they would consent to this.[322] A witness to a deed, according to the popular conception, was not necessarily one who had seen it executed, but one who was willing to give it credit by his name.. This may account for its turning out so often, when witnesses were questioned, that they knew nothing about the matter.

---

[317] St. 3 Geo. II. c.25, s. 15.

[318] Lib. x. c. 12.

[319] Schw. 197-8; ib. 434-6. Brunner cites the case of Bishop Wulfstan *v.* Abbot Walter, which is in Bigelow, Pl. A. N. 16, 287; a. c. Essays in Angl. Sax. Law, 377.

[320] Pl. Ab. 63, col. 1, Berk.

[321] *Ib.* 56, col. 2, Suff.

[322] *Quia ad cartas faciendas . . . presentiam vestram habere non potuimus, precamur . . . ut de cartis nostris in quibus ob securitatem obtinendam testes estis ascripti, testes esse velitis.* Ellis's Letters, 3d Series, i. 25.

In 1219, certain parties put themselves on the witnesses and a jury. The order is *"fiat inde jurata per...* (seven witnesses) *et per...* (nine others) *et veniat... ad recognoscendum,"* etc.[323] The jury, it will be noticed, is said to be composed of the two; and as the jury proper are often questioned by the court in giving their verdict, so the witnesses are sometimes thus questioned separately. A very interesting instance of this occurs in 1236,[324] where the whole combination answers that they never heard of the deed till it was brought and read publicly to the county court and the persons named in it were asked to give testimony. Then the witnesses are questioned separately, and all but three say this again, and add that they never knew that they were named till in the county court. Three, differing somewhat from the others in their account, say that they had seen the deed several years ago, and had been asked by the maker to be witnesses and furnish testimony. As to seisin, the three say that they know nothing more than what they have answered *cum aliis juratoribus in communi.* Then all, *tam juratores yuam testes,* are questioned as to something else, and say they do not know, but rather think, *(melius credunt)* etc. Asked how they know that the said Abbot was not seised,... they say that they know this well and it is very clear because the same G. enfeoffed a certain R. of the site of a horse-mill at Michaelmas, etc. And more of the same sort.[325] In 1318,[326] on a question arising incidentally in an action of trespass as to an alleged release of the plaintiff, the parties put themselves on a jury and on the four witnesses named in the deed. The jury answer, that they have examined the witnesses, that these differ, and they cannot make out from this examination what the fact is. But they give reasons for suspecting the credibility of the witnesses, and therefore make their definite answer *(dicunt precisè)* that the release is not the plantiff's deed. The justices then, *ut rei veritas... apercius et evidencius sciretur,* immediately question the four witnesses

---

[323] Br. N. B. ii. case 51. The case illustrates the old proof of document! by comparison of seals, — *Prior ponit se super testes et super alia sigilla ipsius Nicholai, &c.*

[324] Bracton, N. B. iii. case 1189.

[325] See also a good case in 1227 (Br. N. B. ii. case 249), where four witnesses and nine jurymen are summoned. Separate answers are recorded. Compare Bracton, 366, as to the examination of summoners, *qui more testium diligenter et separatim examinati,* &c.

[326] Pl. Ab. 331, col. i. London; s. c. MS. copy from the Record Office.

separately, in curious detail; they find them discordant, and give judgment on the verdict.[327]

In the earlier cases these witnesses sometimes appear to have been conceived of as a constituent part of the jury; it was a combination of business-witnesses and community-witnesses who tried the case, — the former supplying to the others their more exact information, just as the hundredors, or those from another county, did in the cases before noticed. But in time the jury and the witnesses came to be sharply discriminated. Two or three cases in the reign of Edward III. show this. In 1337, 1338, and 1349 [328] we are told that a person under age may be a witness; that witnesses cannot be challenged; that the two classes are charged differently; the charge to the jury is to tell the truth to the best of their knowledge *(a lour ascient),* while that to the witnesses is to tell the truth and loyally inform the inquest, without saying anything about their knowledge *(sans lour scient);*[329] "for the witnesses," says Thorpe, C. J., in 1349,

---

[327] "The justices immediately called the four witnesses before them and examined each of them separately as to the making, sealing, and place and time how and when, and other necessary circumstances touching the deed." They were discordant and untrustworthy, "for [continues the record] three of the said witnesses . . . said before the justices that they were not present at the making, or sealing, nor ever saw the deed or knew of it until on a certain Thursday they came all together to the manor . . . and found there this said Richard, who showed them the said writing and said it was his deed. Each of them was asked, separately and by himself, at what hour they came there, and in what building in the manor Richard showed them the writing, and how he was dressed. One of them said that they came there in the morning before sunrise, and that the writing was shown to the four witnesses in the queen's chamber of the manor; and Richard was dressed in a German tunic *de Medleto,* and was shod in white shoes. The second said that they came at six o'clock *(hora diei prima)* and the writing was shown to the four witnesses at this hour, in the hall of the manor. The third said that they came, all at the same time, at nine o'clock *(hora diei quasi alta tertia),* and Richard showed them the writing in the stable of the manor, and he had on a black cloak. The fourth witness, William de Codinton, said that he never came to the manor with the said three witnesses, and never knew or heard of the making of the writing, or whether it was or was not Richard's deed, except from the report of the three witnesses, who gave him to understand, and swore to it, that the writing was Richard's deed." The judgment was against the deed, reciting the jury's verdict and the worthlessness of the witnesses' testimony.

[328] Y. B. 11 & 12 Edw. III. 338; Y. B. 12 & 13 Edw. III. 4; 12 Ass. 34, 12; s.c. Fitz. Ab. Challenge, 9; 23 Ass. 11.

[329] "It is an abuse," says the Mirror, a little earlier than this, "to use the term 'a *lour escient'* in the oath, and make jurors decide upon thoughts *(quiders),* since the principal word in their oath is that they will say the truth." c. 5, s. 1, 135.

"should say nothing but what they know as certain, *i. e;* what they see and hear. If a witness is returned on the jury, he shall be ousted. A challenge good as against a juryman is not good against a witness. If the witnesses and the jury cannot agree upon one verdict, that of the jury shall be taken, and the defeated party may have the attaint against the jury; had they followed the information of the witnesses the attaint would not lie, unless they found against the deed." In that case it might, for it was conceived that a negative could not be certainly known to the witnesses.[330] This method proved inconvenient. Among other reasons, the number of the witnesses was often large. So long as the trial could not proceed without them, there was great inconvenience endlessly; and the twelve jurymen made quite enough of that. Accordingly by the statute of York, in 1318, it was provided that while process should still issue to the witnesses as before, yet the taking of the inquest should not be delayed by their absence.[331] In this shape the matter ran on for a century or two. By 1472,[332] we find a change. It is said, with the assent of all the judges, that process for the witnesses will not issue unless asked for.

As late, certainly, as 1489, we find witnesses to deeds still summoned with the jury.[333] I know of no later case. In 1649 — 50 Brooke, afterwards Chief Justice of the Common Bench, argues as if this practice was still known:[334] "When the witnesses... are joined to

---

Professor Maitland, to whose labors legal scholars are so greatly indebted, in giving some account of the earliest (manuscript) Register of Writs which he has seen, one of 1227 (3 Harv. Law Rev. 97, 110 *et seq.),* prints from it an interesting note relating to the grand assize. *In hac assisa non ponuntur nisi milites et debent jurare precise quod veritatem dicent, non audito illo verbo quod in aliis recognitionibus dicitur, scilicet a se nescienter."* Doubtless, as Maitland suggests, this last is a misreading of the barbarous law French a son *ascient.* Almost the same words are found in Maitland's "Glanvill Revised," ii. 11 and 17 (Harv. Law Rev. vi. 9); but the old law French in both places is now corrupted into *amuncient (i. e. a mun scient).* These passages show exactly what Shareshulle, J., meant in the next century, when he said (Y.B. 11 & 12 Edw. III. 341), of the witnesses, *lour serement est a dire veritt tut atrenche, auxi com ils sunt jures en un graunt assise, et nemye a lour ascient.* Of the queer phrase, *tut atrenche,* Selden surmises that it is a corruption from *tout oultrance.* Note 43, Hengham, Magna, c. xii.

[330] See Thorpe, C. J., in 23 Ass. 11. Compare Ingleby, J., and Fitzjohn in 40 Ass. 23 (1366).

[331] St. 12 Edw. II. c. 2.

[332] Y. B. 12 Edw. IV. 4, 9.

[333] Y. B. 5 H. VII. 8.

[334] Reniger v. Fogossa, Plow. 1, 12.

the inquest," etc.; and I do not observe anything in his Abridgment, published in 1568, ten years after his death, to indicate that it was not a recognized part of the law during all his time. It may, however, well have been long obsolescent. Coke says of it, early in the seventeenth century, "and such process against witnesses is vanished;"[335] but when or bow he does not say. We may reasonably surmise, if it did not become infrequent as the practice grew, in the fifteenth century, of calling witnesses to testify to the jury in open court, that, at any rate, it must have soon disappeared when that practice came to be attended with the right, recognized, and, as it seems, first granted, in the statute of 1562 — 3,[336] to have legal process against all sorts of witnesses.

(e). But in the earlier-times there were other combinations of the community-witnesses who ordinarily composed the jury, with business-witnesses and the like. In 1225,[337] on a question of villeinage, six are summoned from the neighborhood *ad recognoscendum cum parentibus... quas consuetudines,* etc. In 1226,[338] on a question relating to a partition, the sheriff is ordered to find out who were present at the partition *et ex illis et aliis venire facial xii., etc., ad recognoscendum,* etc. In 1227,[339] in a case of dower, the sheriff is directed to find out who were present at the endowing and from these and others to summon twelve. In an interesting case of 1323,[340] in a case of dower *assensu patris,* counsel for plaintiff says: "We put forward a deed which testifies the assent; but that naturally lies *en proeve (i. e.,* in proof by witnesses) and not *en averrement (i. e.,* proof by jury), for it is not in the conusance of the country but of those who were present, and we are ready to aver the consent by them and others *(i.e.,* by a jury with them).... bereford, C. J. We have nothing to do here with the witnesses named in the deed, for it is not denied; but we will cause those to come whom you will name as present when you were endowed, together with a jury *(ovesque bon pays). Aldeburgh* (for

---

[335] Inst. 6 b.

[336] St. 5 Eliz. c. 9, g. 6. See *infra,* p. 129.

[337] Br. N. B. iii. case 1041.

[338] *Ib.* case 1707.

[339] *Ib. case* 1919. For the form of the writ, see Bracton, 304 b. Other cases are Br. N. B. ii. cases 91,154. See also *ib.* case 456; S. C. ib. case 595 (1230); ib. case 631 (1231); Bracton, 380.

[340] Y. B. Edw. II. 507. See also a case of 1315, Y. B. Edw. II. 278.

defendant). That will be hard, for he may name *ses cosyns et ses auns,* who by his procurement will decide against us." But it was allowed. This sort of thing seems to have been a mingling of the old procedure and the new. The proving by witnesses present at the endowing was the old *lex recordamenti.* An account of it in Normandy is found in Brunner.[341] A case of 1236 — 7 probably belongs to this class, where on a question relating to an alleged gift and seisin of a manor by the father of a tenant *in capite* now claiming it, the sheriff is to summon twelve from the *visne* of the manor *ad recognoscendum utrum... dedit... et... fuit in seisina... et quod venire faceret coram predictis liberos homines... ad recognoscendum utrum, etc.* It seems probable that this passage is corrupt and should read *cum predictis.*[342]

In 1326 — 7, by St. 1 Edw. III. c. 4, it was provided that when a record comes up to the king's court on a writ of false judgment, and it is denied, an averment shall be received by a jury and those who were present in court when the record was made. It was added, after the method of the statute of York, nine years before, in dealing with witnesses to deeds, that if the others do not come, the jury shall proceed without them.[343]

With this sort of case may be compared that of the proof of age. The two appear to represent different results in a combination of the old and new modes of proof.[344]

---

[341] Schw. 342, 343.

[342] Br. N. B. iii. case 1187. The original roll is not extant (Br. N. B. i. 161). But Professor Maitland, the editor of the Note Book, who did me the great kindness of examining again the original of that, at the British Museum, declares that there can be no doubt that the copyist has made it *coram.*

[343] The old mode of trial in such cases is shown in Br. N. B. ii. cases 40 (1219) and 243 (1227), where battle is offered. Compare Rot. Cur. Keg. i. 356.

[344] *Supra,* pp. 19, 20; and compare a case of 1375-6, in Staffordshire Coll (Salt. Soc.), xiv. 739. And see Brunner, Schw. 343, 433.

Before leaving this class of cases, it is interesting to notice that two centuries ago and over, the people of New England used now and then, out of policy, when they were trying a case relating to an Indian, to add Indiana to the jury; *e.g.* in a criminal case in 1682. Plym. Col. Records, vi. 98. So in 1675 (*ib.* vol. v. 167 — 8), six Indians were added to the jury of twelve, on the trial of three Indians for the murder of another one. "It was judged very expedient by the Court that . . . some of the most indifferentest, gravest, and sage Indians should be admitted to be with the said jury, and to help to consult and advise with, of and concerning the premises." The verdict ran thus: "We of the jury, one and all, both English and Indians do jointly," etc. See Harv. Law Rev. *is..* 7, 8,105 (*f*). Our earliest records show the practice of exhibiting charters and other writings to the jury. These things, *par excellence,* used to be known as "evidence" and "evidences." In a great degree, they belonged to the stage of pleading, — in so far as they were wholly or in part the ground of action or defence, or a negation or qualification of it. A record, and so a fine or recognizance, or a charter under seal, bound one who was a party to it and sometimes one who was not. Should such a thing he produced in pleading, the execution of it must be admitted or denied. If admitted, that was the end of the matter. If denied and put in issue, then the question was on the genuineness of it, not on its truth or operative quality; and it was detained in court and delivered to the jury to examine.[345] Such documents, if admitted, must be met by others of equal force. When the pleadings were over, it might well be that they should be delivered to the jury or shown to them in illustration of the exposition made by counsel; in fact, this was often done, "to inform the jury." Other documents also were shown to the jury, — any which might illustrate or support the statements of counsel. And these statements themselves were "evidence." It must be held in mind that all through the period when the jury went on their own knowledge, they listened to perfectly unsupported narratives of fact from counsel, not under oath.

How if one who should have pleaded a charter or record did not plead it, relying, perhaps, on the jury, who might know of it? Could they find a matter of record or a deed without having it shown them? If they knew of it, must they find it, — being sworn to tell the truth? And how if they knew the fact to be otherwise than as this deed or record represented it? How if they knew the fact to be otherwise than as the pleadings represented it? Were they not perjured if they did not tell the truth? These were serious questions, and some of them troubled the lawyers for centuries.

Let us look at some of the cases: In a case of about the year 1200, the jury, if we may trust a lively and intelligent chronicler, made short work of a charter. The plaintiff claimed seisin of certain lands in right of a ward, as her inheritance; the defendant relied on a deed of the father of the ward. The deed was read to the assize in open court. Their verdict, as it is reported, was "that they knew nothing of our chartularies or private agreements *(juramento facto,*

---

[345] Y.B. 38 H. YI. 13,27.

dixerunt milites se nescire de cartis nostris, nec de privatis conventionibus), but that they believed that Adam and his father and grandfather, for a hundred years back, had held the manors in fee one after the other. And so we were disseised by the judgment of the court."[346]

In our earliest reports we find the use of documents merely as evidence to the jury. In 1294,[347] there is a case in which a doctrine was applied which had led to a struggle a little earlier, viz., that although one had lost in a possessory assize, this was no bar to his recovering, in a writ of right.[348] In an assize of mort d'ancestor, where the tenant's defence was that plantiff's ancestor had enfeoffed him by a charter and did not die seised, the assize found this true, and gave their verdict for the tenant. The demandant, nevertheless, brought a writ of right and was upheld in it, and it was said that the defence must be by battle or the great assize and not by the charter: "Yet the charter may be put forward as evidence *(en evidence)* to the grand assize."[349]

Where a charter gave a ground of action or defence, it must regularly, as we said, be pleaded; if admitted, it might save going to the assize. If it were not pleaded, one could not regularly use it in evidence to the jury. But the jury could have it if they wished. In 1292 we find this stated in a note by the reporter.[350] Of course this in principle is just as much helping the jury by evidence as if a witness came before them to testify. The fact that they might be ignorant of such things was noticed in the St. West. II. c. 25, in providing against certain dangers from the *festinum remedium* of the novel disseisin: If the defendant against whom the assize may have passed in his absence afterwards show the justices charters or releases "in which the jury were not examined, nor could be, because not mentioned in

---

[346] Forsyth, Tr. by Jury, 129 — 130, citing Jocelyn de Brakelonde. The perplexities that were caused sometimes by conflicting charters (forgery even by holy men was very common) are illustrated by the humorous exclamation of Henry II. when charters were produced before him by both sides. *Supra,* p. 18, n.

[347] Y. B. 21 & 22 Edw. 1.450.

[348] *Ib.* 428.

[349] See Lowe *v.* Paramour, Dyer, 301 (1571).

[350] Note. — If a charter be put forward to inform the assize after they are sworn and charged, the charter will not be received unless the assize ask for it. To have the charter inform the assize, one should plead on the charter and say this: 'He did not die seised, etc., for he enfeoffed us by this charter, and then put forward the charter to inform,' " etc. Y. B. 20 & 21 Edw. I. 20.

pleading, and probably they might be ignorant of such writings," —
the jury and the parties were to be resummoned.

In 1339[351] Scharshulle, J., is reported as saying that since a
warranty requires a specialty, if it be not pleaded or put in evidence,
a finding of it by the assize shall not hold. It was the rule in attaint, as
well before as after witnesses were allowed to testify to jurors, that
the plaintiff should give nothing in evidence to the "grand jury," as
they called it, additional to what the first jury had had; for the
question was whether, upon what these knew and ought to know,
their verdict was false. In 1351 — 2,[352] counsel complains of his
adversary in attaint, that he is putting forward in his pleading a
release not pleaded in the first case, of which, therefore, the first jury
could not have had cognizance. But he is answered that there was no
opportunity to plead it, and that it *was* given in evidence to the
former jury.

A distinction was made between matters of record or sealed
writings and others. The former were authenticated by the record and
the seal; the others were not "authentic." Yet, just as counsel might
freely make statements of fact to the jury, unsupported otherwise, so
they might exhibit to them unsealed writings. The jury could carry
out with them only writings under seal. The presence of the writing
at the private consultation of the jury seems to have been conceived
of as if it were a witness to a deed, or one of those who testified to a
view, or those present at the giving of dower; it must be an
"authentic" paper that could testify there. A specialty was different in
kind from a writing unsealed. Often it was an operative, *constituting*
instrument; and it was conceived of generally as authentically
establishing what it purported. Other documents were "testimonial"
only.[353] And so, in 1352,[354] we find that on a question as to the
prescriptive title to tithes of the Master of St. Cross at Winchester, an
ancient register of tithes, of a hundred years back, was put forward
in. evidence, and because it was not sealed, the jury only inspected it
and gave it back before they went out.[355]

---

[351] Y. B. 13 & 14 Edw. III 80. Compare 11 & 12 Edw. III 620 — 622;
12 Ass. 16.

[352] 26 Ass. 12.

[353] *Infra,* 393.

[354] 26 Ass. 4. Compare 21 Edw. IV. 37 — 38 (1481).

[355] Gawdy, J., in Vicary *v.* Farthing, Cro. El. 411 (1595), said, "It is
also clear that writings or books which are not under seal cannot be delivered to

One or two more cases may be cited in order to bring down the showing of documents to the jury to the modern form. As the practice of submitting writings to them was far older than that of admitting ordinary witnesses, so the conditions and qualifications of it were earlier fixed. In 1340,[356] the assize, in novel disseisin, had found in a special verdict that the tenant had previously brought an action for the same land and had recovered; the tenant had pleaded this, but had not produced the record. The judges asked the jury how they knew this, "since" (to quote the record) "pleas and judgments of the king's court are of record and outside the notice and cognizance of a jury of the country. They said that they had not any certain knowledge (of it)... and would not positively say that there was such a plea,... but by reason, of the summons and resummons... and the view... and its being commonly said in the country that there was such a plea and such a judgment rendered in the said form, and because the sheriff had a writ... to put the said John... in seisin, as he said, and did put him in seisin, they understood that there was such a plea and such a judgment rendered between the said parties." The report adds: "Scharshulle, J. The assize has expressly said (&c.)... and what they say about a recovery does not lie within their cognizance" etc. It turned out that the jury were substantially right; there was such a record, but owing to a slight variance between the form of it and the pleading, judgment was finally given for the plaintiffs.

It was, then, as it would seem, improper for a jury to find, specifically, matter of record without evidence.[357] And in 1419 —

---

the jurors without the assent of both parties." So Olive v. Guin, 2 Sid. 145 (1658). Collier's Case, 7 How. St. Tr. col. 1207 (1680), Style Pract. Reg 177 (1655). This was law in New Jersey down to 1797. State *v.* Raymond, 53 N. J. (Law) 260 (1891). We find it laid down still in Lofft's Gilbert (ed. 1795), i. 21, accompanied by that sort of baffling and inadequate reasoning which Gilbert often sets forth regarding matters not understood. For the way of talking about these matters in the sixteenth and seventeenth centuries, see Newis v. Lark (Scolastica's case), Plowd. 403, 410, 411 (1571); Finch, Com. Law, 61 b. (1613); Olive *v.* Guin, ubi *supra.*

[356] Y. B. u Edw. III 25 — 34. See Mr. Pike's careful statement of the case (Introd. Xxxvii — xl).

[357] Br. Ab. Assize, 258. But it was competent for a jury, at the peril of the attaint, to find a general verdict which might coyer such a matter, and might rest merely upon their general knowledge of it. In this last case, if they had chosen, they could have answered definitely (precise), no disseisin. See Vin. Ab. Trial, Q. f. Newis *v.* Lark, ubi *supra.* Compare 28 Ass. 3. As to a question relating

20,[358] in a case much debated, it was held, with some difference of opinion among the judges, that a jury cannot in a special verdict find a deed which has not been pleaded or given in evidence: "Hull [J.]. This deed is only the private intent of a man, which can be known only by writing; and if the writing be shown, it may lawfully be avoided in several ways, as for *non sane* memory, being within age, imprisonment, or because it was made before the ancestor's death, and the like — things which the party cannot plead unless he have *over* of the deed, and it be shown."

An important step in the use of writings to the jury is recorded in other cases of this period. In earlier times, it seems to have been legitimate for the parties to talk with the jury after they had retired to consult.[359] But in 1361,[360] in a real action, after the jury had gone out, and been put in charge of an officer, the defendant gave the officer a box, containing a deed, and asked him to give it to the jury; this was done. The plaintiff made complaint, and an examination was made by the court. The officer admitted receiving and delivering the box, but knew not what was in it. The jury admitted finding the deed in the box, and examining it, but said they had already found their verdict, and did not change it, but were more confirmed in it. The court imprisoned the officer and the jury, and fined both them and the defendant. The editor of the record does not tell us about the further disposition of the case.

In 1389,[361] in two actions of trespass, "the panel was cancelled" for similar misconduct. "The jury being asked if the said William Broun had spoken to them or shown them any evidence, stated that he had done so, and had shown them a deed under the seal of William Stanleye.... It was therefore considered that the panel should be cancelled," etc. In 1409,[362] "The plaintiff in an assize gave a writing *(escrowment)* to a juror who had been empanelled, as evidence of his matter. After the juror with the others was sworn and put in a house to agree on the verdict, he showed the writing to his companions; and the officer in charge of the inquest stated the matter

---

to a difference between the general issue and other issues, see Dowman's case, 9 Co. 7 b., 11 b. — 14 (1586).

[358] Y. B. 7 H. V. 5, pl. 3.
[359] See a case of 1221 in Br. N. B. iii. case 1963.
[360] Staffordshire Coll. (Salt Soc.), xiii. 6 — 7
[361] *Ib.* xv. 23.
[362] Y. B. II H. IV. 17, 41. See *supra,* p. 92.

to the court. Whereupon the justices took the writing from the jurors, took their verdict, questioned the jurors as to the time of giving the writing, and found as stated above. The plaintiff had a verdict and now prayed his judgment. Gascoigne, C. J; and Huls, J., said that the jury, after they were sworn, ought not to see or take with them any other evidence than that delivered to them by the court and put forward by the party in court on the showing of his evidence. And since he did the contrary... he should not have judgment. The plaintiff said that the writing proved merely what he had given in evidence to the jury at the bar; and it was not so bad as if he had not spoken to them *en evidence. Et non allocatur.*" In 1481[363] we read that, "Then Brian [C. J.] delivered [to the jury] all the evidences of both parties which could influence the jury as to the truth of the issue; and all the evidences which were not material he would not allow to be delivered."

It has been justly remarked by Starkie that "the exercise of this kind of control was in truth the foundation of that system of rules concerning evidence before juries which has since constituted so large and important a brunch of the law of England."[364] But long after this, if there were no misconduct of the parties in furnishing the evidence, it was clearly held that juries might act on their private knowledge, and even on documents not known to the court or the parties, *e. g.* in a case of 1598,[365] cited with approval in Bushel's case, in 1670.[366] In the last case, after saying that it is absurd to fine a jury, since the judge does not know the evidence it goes upon, Vaughan, C. J., added, "For the better and greater part of the evidence may be wholly unknown to him; and this may happen in most cases, and often doth, as in Graves and Short's case. Error of a judgment in the Common Bench. The error assigned was, — the issue being whether a feoffment were made and the jurors being gone together to confer of their verdict, one of them showed to the rest an escrow *pro petentibus,* not given in evidence by the parties; *per quod* they found for the demandment. Upon demurrer, adjudged no error; for it appears not to be given to him by any of the parties, or

---

[363] Y. B. 21 Edw. IV. 38, I.

[364] "Trial by Jury," Little & Brown's ed. 39; reprinted from (English) Law Review, ii. 370. For a good illustration of this sort of control, see Y. B. 21 Edw. IV. 37 — 38, 1 (1481).

[365] Graves v. Short, Cro. El. 616.

[366] Vaughan, 135, 149. See Woodward *v.* Leavitt, 107 Mass. 453, 466.

any for them; it must be intended he bad it as a piece of evidence about him before, and showed it to inform himself and his fellows, and as he might declare it as a witness that he knew it to be true. They resolved, if that might have avoided the verdict, which they agree it could not, yet it ought to have been done by examination, and not by error."

(g). There were other ways of informing the jury. Of guiding and restraining them I shall say more hereafter. The judge gave them their "charge," and each party or his counsel explained to them his contention. In our early reports a charge from the judge precedes the statements of counsel. In the first case in our extant Year Books,[367] there is a charge to the jury, but no report of any address on either side. In the same volume and year, in an assize of mort d'ancestor, the defendant is told by the judge to omit something from his oral pleading and plead only to the points of the assize: "What you say about your pledges, say it in evidence to the assize *(dites ceo en evidence de lasise)*."[368] In 1302,[369] after the "great assize" was sworn, Berewyk, J., said to them: "John de Kilcayt heretofore brought a writ of right against William de Bodom and demanded eighteen perches, &c., whereupon W. came and put himself on God and the great assize. We have [370] the record, how they pleaded. You have nothing to say except only what you are charged with — as to the right." Then Mutford (counsel) speaks for John, setting forth that J.'s grandfather was seised of the land "as of fee and right," that it descended to his son John and from him "to this John who demands it as his son. And such is his right." Hunt then speaks for William: "This same John enfeoffed G. of the advowson of the church of C. with its appurtenances; and this land is appurtenant to the church of C. And this is William's right and the right of his church." The great assize then went out.[371] Of the same

---

[367] Y. B. 20 & 21 Edw. I. 3 (1292).

[368] *Ib.* 242. Compare Shardelowe, counsel, in 1324, Y. B. Edw. II. 614.

[369] Y. B. 30 & 31 Edw. I. 116 — 118.

[370] One of three manuscripts used in preparing this volume, as we are told (p. 119, note; compare *ib.* xlix.), says, "we have;" the others, "we have not." The former reading seems the more probable.

[371] The report closes thus: "The great assize went out. Then came back two knights and wished another knight. Berewyk [J.] to the marshall, — 'Don't allow any of them to come in unless all come together.' The great assize: 'Sir, we say that W. has better right to hold as he holds, than his adversary as he demands.' Brumpton [J.]. 'Therefore the court awards that W. retain the same

period[372] is a charge in a criminal case. One W., the stabler of J.'s horse, had been kicked while trying to mount, so that he died. J. was charged by the jury of accusation with retaining the horse, although he had thus become a *deodand,* and with having buried W. without calling in the coroner. He denied both charges and put himself on the country. The judge, turning, probably, to the same jury that had accused the defendant, replied: *"Ecce hic bona patria de duodecim.* Bead the names and save him every sufficient challenge." Some challenges were made, *que triebantur per residues de duodecim.* The judge proceeded to charge the jury thus: "If W. died from the kick of the horse, the horse would be *deodand.* If not it would be John's. If the king should lose through you what rightly belongs to him, you would be perjured. If you should take away from John what is his, you would commit a mortal sin. Therefore, by the oath you have made, disclose and tell us the truth, whether the said W. died of the horse's kick or not. If you find that he did, tell us in whose hands is the *deodand* horse and what he is worth; and whether the said W. was buried without a view of the coroner."

It will be noticed that the charge had the effect not merely to bring clearly to the jury's mind what they were to pass upon, but also to prevent their wandering away into irrelevant matters — matters which were admitted, or were outside the issue. Exactly what was admitted by the pleadings, or what was the scope of the issue, it was not always easy to say. It was for the judges to keep the jury within proper limits. "Good people," said Bereford, J., in 1306, "you have only to inquire whether any of the predecessors of the aforesaid Prior presented the last person," etc.[373]

(A). And now a very interesting matter, — the beginnings of special pleading. We are apt, nowadays, to miss some of the chief and controlling conceptions of the time when the rules of pleading were taking shape. We still know, indeed, the fear that a jury may go off on some misapprehension of law or fact; that has always been a familiar difficulty. But in the days when a chief reliance of juries, as

---

land as his right and the right of his church of C. to the end of the world *(a remenaunt de monde)* quit of J. and his heirs forever; and that J. be in mercy.' "

[372] Y. B. 30 & 31 Edw. I. 528.

[373] Y. B. 33 — 35 Edw. I. 166. In Y. B. 30 & 31 Edw. I. 132 (1302), Brumpton, J., after reciting the process: "Good people the points of the assize are agreed on. You have only to say," etc. Compare Hankford, J., in Y. B. 7 H. IV. 11, 3, cited in Dowman's case, 9 Co. pp 12 and 14.

regards matters of fact, was their own knowledge, when witnesses to
the jury were in general not received at all, or, if received, were little
regarded, and when it was recognized that everything might lawfully
be settled upon the jury's private knowledge, — the matter of getting
exact facts and shadings of fact, in a case which was at all delicate,
clearly and permanently set down on the record, and in a shape to fix
them in the jury's mind, had a very great and conspicuous
importance. Otherwise, even if stated to the jury by counsel, and in
the judge's charge, they might easily be forgotten or slighted. We
find early in the Year Books the beginning of a discussion which is
forever going on in the fifteenth century, as to how far one can go in
his pleading; what should be pleaded, and what is merely "evidence"
of the facts to be pleaded; what shall be entered on the record, and
what shall be left to be "said in evidence to the jury." We say
nowadays that "facts" are to be pleaded, and not the evidence of
facts.[374] That was early said, but it was very far indeed from being
rigidly enforced. Often we find the courts allowing one to set forth
his case fully, "for fear of the laymen," *i. e.,* in order that the jury
might not pass upon questions of law, and might not go wrong
through any misapprehension of the facts. Much "evidence" was
thus entered on the records; once there, it got recited to the jury when
they were sent out, and was clearly brought to the notice of all who
had occasion to address the jury, as well the counsel as the court.[375]
Sometimes, also, this served the purpose of preserving a memorial,
in case of further litigation, of exactly what was involved in any
given case. Of the last we see an instance in 1306,[376] where a
defendant found put forward against him a deed of release by his
father of certain rent now claimed. He met this by a long statement,
setting forth that his grandfather had a rent of double this amount;
that it descended in halves to two sons; that his father, one of these,
had released his rent, but subsequently his uncle's share had
descended to him. He went on to admit the release, but prayed that

---

[374] See the often quoted language of "the serjeants at the bar," in
Dowman's case, 9 Co. 7 b., 9 b. (1586); also Steph. Pl. 310, 360 (Tyier's ed.) as
to pleading evidence, and the general issue.

[375] Thus, in 1481 (Y. B. 21 Edw. IV. 37 b. I): "Then the jury appeared
and the parties, and the jurors were tried and sworn, the record was read to them,
and the point of the issue recited, viz. [&c.]. And now *Touwsend* shows in
evidence to them," &c.

[376] Y. B. 33 — 35 Edw. I. 118 — 120.

this statement "might be entered, on the roll so that we be not foreclosed on another occasion from demanding the same services. And it was granted by the court. "

In 1305,[377] the plantiff demands tenements of the defendant, tracing title by descent from his great-grandfather. The defendant answers that the land is part of a manor of which plaintiff's grandmother was seised, and that she gave this land in tail to the defendant's father, from whom the defendant takes his inheritance. The plaintiff replied that his great-grandfather had separated from the manor the land now demanded, and given it in frank marriage to R. M., who was seised of this land until after the deed of the grandmother was given, and so she was not seised when she gave her deed. The defendant insisted that his assertion of the grandmother's seisin should be traversed as simply as he had alleged it, without limiting) it to time. And Bereford, J., said to the plaintiff, "It is fit that you traverse him; and what you give in answer shall be in evidence that she was not seised because *U.* M. was seised; and it shall be entered and the inquest shall be charged thereon." In 1302,[378] in a similar dispute, Brumpton, J.) said to the defendants, charged as owners in common with others, and setting up that the others, a husband and wife, held as the wife's dower: "Nothing shall be entered on the roll but this, viz.; that you do not hold in common. But state this by way of information and evidence to the inquest."

The Year Books of the next century, and especially those of Henry VI., are full of discussions over this matter. The judges used a large discretion as to entering on the record evidence, *i. e.,* explanatory, discriminative, and probative allegations, and they gave as a reason for entering it, the danger that the jury would go wrong, from not apprehending the facts and from not separating fact from law. Once entered on the record, there could be no doubt of its being brought to the jury's knowledge; and in case of an attaint, it fixed them with notice of it. Observe how this is spoken of. In 1409 — 10,[379] Hankford, J., said that formerly in actions of debt on account, the defendant usually pleaded simply the general issue, and by reason of the too great generality of the issue, the jurors would sometimes give their verdict against the defendant, if he were

---

[377] *Ib.* 100, 107.
[378] Y. B. 30 & 31 Edw. I. 228.
[379] Y.B. 11 H. IV. 50, 27.

indebted to the plaintiff on arrears of account, or on some other contract. Afterwards the practice was to traverse the account specially and to take issue on this. In 1430,[380] where, in an action of trespass, the defendant sought to plead specially, it was refused. "We pray," says counsel, "that all may be entered for evidence. Martin [J.], You have alleged only what you can give in evidence. Paston [J.], If this matter be not entered, the party is in danger of great mischief, for where one pleads merely not guilty, the jury has no regard to the place where the trespass is done; that is the common way of jurors. Martin [J.], We cannot adjudge the law according to the understanding of jurors. If they find him guilty of trespass in another county, clearly the attaint lies for the defendant." Only a little later,[381] in an action of waste, the defendant objected to the particularity of the declaration: "It has not until lately been the practice to count so, but generally.... Martin [J.], It is a good practice, for if he counts generally and the other pleads, *nul wast fait,* the laymen perhaps will find no waste." In 1436,[382] in trespass, the defendant urged these same reasons for entering his special plea: Juyn (J.), "I will not say that we cannot enter all this matter, but if we should it would bring great *comberance to* the court. If.we do it in this case we must in all others; and if we should enter such things we shall not have clerks enough in this place."[383] Only the general issue was entered. In 1482,[384] in trespass for taking and carrying away goods at Dale in Middlesex, *Lodworth* (apprentice), for defendant, said that long before the fact in question the owner of the goods in possession of them bailed them to the plaintiff to keep safely at Sale in Durham; afterwards the owner directed the defendant to take them from the plaintiff's possession at Sale for safe keeping; and in virtue of that, he went to the said Sale and there took the goods and delivered them to the owner, without this, that he took them at Dale in Middlesex. *Vavasour,* for the plaintiff, said that this was merely not guilty at Dale in Middlesex. A Middlesex jury cannot have notice of this taking in another county. "Fairfax [J.], When the defendant has a matter to help him of which he can only have advantage by evidence given at the day [of trial], if it is part of his

---

[380] Y. B. 9 H. VI. 63,16.

[381] Y.B. 11 H. VI. 1,2.

[382] Y. B. 14 H. VI. 23, 67.

[383] For the court's discretion as to this, see Brooke, Ab., Gen. Issue, 16

[384] Y. B. 22 Edw. IV. 39, 24.

plea and entered on the roll, the jurors will give more attention to it.
And so there is much reason for his having this as part of his plea....
Hussey [C. J.],... As to his having this special matter by plea, he shall
have it; for where it is useful to him and not hurtful to the plaintiff,
there is the greater reason for his having it by plea. And so he did
have it *quod nota bene, &c.*"[385]

In the Year Book 19 H. VI. 21, 42 (1440), a valuable little
note, or small treatise, on "Color" is preserved, in which the need of
entering special matter is pointed out in order to prevent the laymen
from passing on questions of law. This great, specific reason, that of
separating law from fact, and helping one to refer questions of law to
the court, was mingled with the more general one, of preventing the
jury from going wrong on impulse or misapprehension; and finally,
to the obscuring of the subject, it came to supersede and displace it,
in the discussions of our books. In 1504,[386] in an action of
conspiracy, the defendant pleaded that he had given his testimony at
the assize in answer to the proclamation calling on all who knew,
etc., to come forward and inform the justices; and that this was the
conspiracy charged upon him. The plaintiff denied the right to plead
this in justification of conspiracy. Fairfax, counsel for the defendant,
argued that this was a good answer, just as when two juries are
charged to inquire together for the king [juries of accusation], each
may inform the other, and this may be pleaded. And, he added, "by
reason of distrust of the laymen *(per le doubt de les Iais)* one shall
have special matter in many cases.... Rede, J., There is reason for
pleading the special matters. For doubt of the laymen *(per les
ambiguites de les lais gens)* who do not know the law, and to put
these things in the judgment of the justices.... Fineux, O. J.,... He
shall not be driven to the general issue, for it is special matter and
triable by the justices. To put this, which is matter of law, into the
mouth of laymen will be perilous. He shall have the plea." In 1529 in
an action under a statute for driving animals in parks,[387] the
defendant answered that the plaintiff had no park in the place
supposed. One justice denied that this was a good plea, but Richard
Brooke, J., said: "To plead not guilty will be a dangerous issue to put
in the mouth of lay people; for if the truth be that the plaintiff had

---

[385] See also Y. B. 10 H. VII. 29, 27 (1494).
[386] Y. B. 20 H. VII. 11, 21; s. c. Keilwey, 81 h. 3, 83 b. 6.
[387] Keilwey, 202 b. 1.

no park there, but a close with wild beasts, and the defendant did chase them in fact," and this appear in evidence, the lay people will consider little or nothing whether he had a park there or not; but they will regard the chasing. And they do not know the law, whether the plaintiff, since he has no park, has misconceived his action or not; and so, inasmuch as he [defendant] did chase them in fact, it will be a great color for them to find him guilty."[388]

We are not, then, to suppose, when witnesses were not in general called to testify to a jury, that therefore the jury did not receive any evidence. The original simple conception of them as a body of witnesses, who "tried" the case by their answer, was, as we see, always qualified and always undergoing more qualification. Great pains, to be sure, was taken in early times to require publicity as regards matters which might be the basis of legal right, and to fix rights by connecting them with easily known facts; the endowing at the church door, the requirement, in case of curtesy, of hearing the child cry within the four walls, the sale before witnesses, and the law of hue and cry, are instances. See what was expected of a defendant in 1306,[389] who turned up at court a day late, and offered the excuse that he was hindered by a flood. He was first questioned as to where and when it happened. He couldn't have got here any way, says the demandant's attorney. The tenant: "I travelled night and day. Mallore, J.: What did you do when you came to the water and could not pass? Did you raise the hue and cry and *menée?*[390] For otherwise the country would have no knowledge of your hindrance. The tenant: No, sir, for I did not know so much law; but I shouted and yelled." *(Sire, nay, qe jeo ne savoye mie tant de ley, mes jeo criay e brayay).*[391] It will be remembered, then, in addition to what has now been said, that a jury from any neighborhood was a body of persona far more likely to be already informed than such a body would be to-day.[392]

---

[388] See also Y. B. 10 H. VI 20, 67 ; 11 *ib.* 2, 4 ; *ib.* 35, 27 ; 14 *ib.* 21, 63 (end); 19 *ib.* 31, 59; 22 *ib.* 35, 54; 39 *ib.* 9, 14; 9 Edw. IV. 49, 7 ; 10 H. VII. 15, 13 ; *ib.* 29, 27.

[389] Y. B. 33 — 35 Edw. I. 122.

[390] And so Britton, f. 20, in speaking of the hue-and-cry: *oveke la menée des corns et de bouches.* Nichols translates: "with the company of horns and voices."

[391] See Prisot, C. J., in Y. B. 39 H. VI. 16, 20 (1460).

[392] Palg. Com. i. 247 — 8

(i). The arrangements of the courts allowed of giving information in another way. As already said, the explanatory oral statements of the party or his counsel always contained the element of adding to what the jury knew. As time went on this increased. We are to remember that the jury, in a general way, knew the facts already, and that they were able to judge of the truth of these conflicting statements. In 1302,[393] when the jury gave their verdict, Brumpton, J., said: "Tell us the damages. The assize: Ten shillings Poleyn [counsel, breaking in]: There was a chest worth two marks, and other goods," etc. The judge warns the jury to be careful, for an attaint lies (since 1275) for damages, as well as the matter in chief. But the jury repeat their finding. We see this process well in a full and a valuable case of 1465, a trial at bar,[394] in an assize of novel disseisin. This case shows us witnesses testifying openly to the jury; that practice had come in now. And it also shows us the counsel putting in evidence freely by mere allegations to the jury. Littleton, Fairfax, and others, serjeants, make long narratives for the plaintiff. Yong does the same for the defendant. Sometimes a witness is called, and examined by the court. Sometimes he is only referred to as being present and ready to testify. Sometimes a document is put in. But mainly the statements of counsel are put forward as being in themselves evidence. We notice that the judges suggest to the defendant's counsel discharging the inquest and demurring upon the evidence, — then, probably, a pretty new thing in pleading; the plaintiff's counsel were ready for this, but the others declined; and the verdict went against the defendants. If they had demurred to the evidence they would have demurred to the allegations of counsel. A century later, in 1571,[395] in a famous demurrer upon evidence in an assize of novel disseisin, there is a long set of recitals of what William Bendloe, the plaintiff's serjeant, "said in evidence," and "gave in evidence," and "showed in evidence; " and then the defendants say that "the evidence and allegations aforesaid are insufficient in law," etc. And so, two centuries later than that, in Cocksedge *v.* Fanshaw.[396] In the great case of Gibson

---

[393] 1 Y. B. 30 & 31 Edw. I. 122 — 4.

[394] Babington *v.* Venor, Long Qnint (5 Edw. IV.) 58.

[395] Newis v. Lark, Plow. 403, 407. This form, with others, is given in Rastell's Entries, 318 — 319 a.

[396] Doug. 119 (1779).

v. Hunter, in 1793,[397] in which the demurrer upon evidence, as a workable part of legal machinery in England, after its life of about three centuries and a half, came to an end, we find a note by the reporter seeking to reconcile this case with Cocksedge *v.* Panshaw; the record in that case, it is said, "is agreeable to the ancient mode adopted in. demurrers to evidence, in which it was usual to enter both the allegations of counsel in favor of the party offering the evidence and the evidence itself on the record, and to demur as well to the allegations as the evidence." This note is only wrong in its intimation that the allegations in former times were in any way a thing different from the "evidence." On the contrary, in early times they appear to have been a leading and well-recognized kind of evidence. But in 1645 it had been laid down that such allegations are "no evidence to the jury."[398]

(j). But not yet have I spoken of the method of informing the jury by witnesses testifying publicly in court, our chief way in modern times, — without which, indeed, it is difficult for us even to conceive of trial by jury. Always, as we see, there had been, in some cases, a mingling of the jury with witnesses in their private deliberations. Why did they not have more help of this sort? It is evident that any general practice of sending out witnesses with the jury to testify privately to them, witnesses such as either party might choose to call, could readily be abused; it would lend itself easily to irregular and corrupting influences. If such witnesses were to be used at all, one would guess that their communications would come in like those made by the respective parties, or by counsel in their addresses to the jury; they would have the character of statements confirmatory of these and supplementary, and like them would be publicly made in court. And that seems to have been the course of the development. I know of no reason to suppose that a party's casual witnesses[399] were originally sent out with the jury. There was legal process for the document-witness and others of the preconstituted class, but none for the other. How and when did this great change of introducing witnesses to testify publicly to the jury come about? No one as yet can tell with exactness. Let me mention a few things that may help in tracing the matter.

---

[397] 2 H.Bl. 187, 209 — 11.
[398] Style, Pract. Reg. 171.
[399] Bentham's convenient phrase for the ordinary witness, as distinguished from the "preappointed" one.

There was certainly one sort of trial in which witnesses were publicly examined before the jurors at an early period; and this may well have been. a provocation to the same thing in the regular jury trial. I mean the case of challenges to the jurors. These "triers," generally two of the unchallenged jurors, might question the challenged men. on oath, and might be sworn and charged to say whether these were telling the truth. We see this in the hard-fought case of Wike v. Gernon, reported as of 1371 — 1375.[400] There had been a struggle over empanelling the jurors, involving questions about taking an unequal number from two counties, and about challenges to jurors as being in the service of a party and as having given their verdict beforehand[401] by telling their opinion, and for other reasons. The reporter adds: "And yet the persons who were challenged were sworn to give evidence to the jurors [i.e., those jurors who were trying the challenges]; and so it may be where the challenge sounds not in their reproach or dishonor. But where the challenge was for taking money of the party, it was determined by the triers, without having evidence, by their oath. In 1401,[402] a juror was challenged as not having enough freehold, and at the request of the triers he was sworn to tell the value of his freehold, and he said five shillings; "and then the triers were charged on the question whether he told the truth, and they said that he was sufficient."

We find among the Parliament Rolls, in 1354, a remarkable petition, of which an explanation may perhaps be found in a case of the year 1353.[403] Several persons, including one of the justices, had been accused of conspiracy in indicting J. as a felon, who was acquitted. H. answered that he was a justice at the sessions, and

---

[400] Lib. Ass. 301, 12 ; S. C. *ib.* 304, 5, and also in 315, 1, 315, 5, and Y. B. 48 Edw. III. 30, 17. An assize of novel disseisin. The parties were at issue as to whose son the defendant was, Alice G.'s or Alice *W.'s;* and there was a great debate over the question of what jury should try the question, a jury from Essex, where the defendant said he was born, or from Lincoln, where the land was. It was finally determined to take it from both counties. The jury were out three days before agreeing, and when they came to give their verdict all went for nothing by the plaintiff's becoming nonsuit. In 1382 Belknap, C. J., who had been of counsel with the plaintiffs here, asserted emphatically this power of becoming nonsuit a *chesc. temps avant plein verdict dit.* Bellewe, 251, 2.

[401] *Adevant main!* and so elsewhere often. Had the statute of 1362 (13 Edw. III. c. 15), requiring the pleading to be in English, hurt, just a little, the parity of the reporter's French?

[402] Y. B. 3 H. IV. 4, 18.

[403] 27 Ass. 12.

bound to inform the jury for the king to the best of his ability.[404] Four others said that they were indictors. Another one said that when the indicting jurors made their oath *(quand les jurors sur l'enditement fir. serment)* he was sworn to inform them. This one was driven to plead not guilty; and all the others did the same. The king's counsel only wished a verdict as to two, and these (both of the last class) were found guilty. The justice seems to have pleaded *nolo contendere,* and the indictors were held excused. It may well have been this and like cases that led to a petition[405] to the king and council, in 1354, reciting the false and malicious charging of people with conspiracy and maintenance, and irregular practices in procuring juries, both of accusation and trial, and praying, for the correction of these evils, "that hereafter when any people are at issue and the inquest is charged and sworn, all evidence which is to be said *(totes evidences que sont a dire)* be openly said at the bar, so that after the inquest departs with its charge, no justice or other person have conference *(parlance)* with them to move or procure the said inquest, but that they say the fact upon. their own peril and oath." This petition was granted. It seems to promise a public offering at the bar of whatever evidence was to be given. But, observe, it does not inform us that, in fact, any other evidence was given, as yet, than such as we have heretofore considered.[406]

A case like that of 1353 is seen again in 1406, an action of conspiracy, against the bailiff of the Savoy and an accusing jury; it is stated in the margin.[407] Such cases draw attention to a remarkable

---

[404] "It is the custom for the justice to go to the in dieters to encourage and inform them" *(de les conforter et enformer).* Willoughby, in Y. B. 14 & 15 Edw. HI. 261 (1340). See *supra,* p. 83.

[405] Part. Rolls, ii. 259, col. 2.

[406] See Y. B. 11 H. IV. 17, 41, quoted *supra,* p. 110.

[407] Y. B. 9 H. IV. Mich. pl. 24; s. c. 8 *ib.* 6, 8. The bailiff said that by the order of the Sheriff of Middlesex he had caused twelve men to come to inquire of divers articles for the King. They were sworn, and he was in attendance on the court, as in duty bound, and was ordered by the court to attend the jurora and tell them what he knew of the matter for which the plaintiff was indicted. "He was compelled by the court," says his plea, "to swear and inform them on this side, and so it was done by reason of his oath and the compulsion of the law. . . . The others said that they were sworn in the said inquest to inquire for the King and [so] indicted the plaintiff for the matter comprised in his bill; and so they did this by reason of their oath and the compulsion of the law." The plaintiff replied that the bailiff had done more than his duty required, and that the jurors procured themselves to be empanelled. In another part of the reports [Y. B. 8 H. IV. 6, 8] it

fact, which I have not seen alluded to, namely, the part played by proceedings for maintenance and conspiracy in checking the development of trial by jury. In 1433[408] we find something still more distinct and instructive, something which indicates that it was by this time a well-known thing to testify publicly to the jury, and which shows, also, the grave perils that attended this act, and signally helps us to understand the slow emergence of the practice and the slight indications of it that we find thus far. A writ of maintenance was brought in the King's Bench against one B, charging that in an assize of rent between the plaintiff and C, the defendant had "maintained" C. B answered that long before C had anything in the said rent he himself owned it; and he bad granted it to C. When the said assize was brought against C, the latter came to B, the present defendant, and. asked him to come to the assizes with him and bring his evidences relating to the rent; and accordingly B came with these and delivered to C certain ancient evidences to plead in bar against the plaintiff in discharge of his warranty of the rent; this was all the maintenance. In discussing whether this really constituted maintenance, and if so whether it was justifiable, it was insisted that the defendant should not have come voluntarily, but only by way of voucher to warranty. There was some difference of opinion among the judges, and the case was adjourned without a decision.[409] But the judges said interesting things. Hals, J., said, "In a tort of maintenance it is a good plea to say that he who is charged came and prayed us, since we were an old man of the region and had knowledge of the title of the land of which he was impleaded, that we would be with him to inform the jury about the title; and so we did, etc. So here it is good. Cheyne [C. J.], It will be adjudged a maintenance in your cases, because he has no cause or privity for maintaining the controversy more than the merest stranger in the world unless the other had cause of warranty against him. And as to what you say of

---

appears that one of the jury who simply pleaded not guilty was acquitted. The plaintiff's counsel asked judgment against the bailiff and the others on the pleadings; but Gascoigne, C. J., held, as to the jurymen, that they were unquestionably excused of conspiracy by their oath; and, as to the bailiff, that if it were admitted that his plea did not excuse him, yet, being the only one left, he could not be convicted, for *un sole ne poit conspirer.* See Y. B. 20 H. VII. 11, 21 (1504), 27 H. VIII 2, 6 (1536).

[408] Y.B. 11 H. VI. 43, 36.

[409] Brooke, Ab. Maintenance, 51, says, "*et fuit in manor agree que il est bon barre.*"

its being a good plea in maintenance that he is an old man of the region, and having better knowledge of the right and title of this rent, and his coming with the defendant to declare his right in the said rent, etc., I say that this is a real maintenance; for on such a ground everybody could justify a maintenance, and that would be against reason. But if he had shown a ground of the maintenance on which the law presumes him bound to be with the party, then. this would not be adjudged a maintenance, — as if he were with his relation *(cosin),* or came with one because he was his servant or his tenant. He is bound to be with his servant or tenant; but it is not so in other cases."[410] And so in the course of many other discussions as to whether a given thing were maintenance, and, if it were, whether it were justifiable. In 1442 — 3, in. the case of Pomeray *v.* the Abbot

---

[410] In the same year (Y. B. 11 H. VI. 42, 37) came an interesting case illustrating the giving of evidence to the jury and also their power to disregard it. Parties were at issue on the life or death of a woman. She and her husband had formerly recovered judgment against the plaintiff in a writ of maintenance, but the plaintiff now alleges that she was dead before the judgment. "And the inquest was taken at the bar, and the parties appeared and the woman whose death was alleged was brought to the bar and shown to the jury in evidence that this was the woman whose life or death they were to try; and the woman herself said that she was the same person; and several others who were there well knew that this was the same woman whose death was alleged, and they showed it to the jury. And then the jury was charged; and when they were agreed they came to give their verdict, and found that the woman died on the day the plaintiff said in his assignment of error. And all the court and all the bystanders marvelled much at this false verdict, that they should find the woman dead who was ready here at the bar in full life. And then the writ of maintenance was inspected, and in the writ it was proved that on the day of the nisi *prius* the woman appeared in her own person and the record made mention of it. Cheyne, C. J. . . . It is proved by matter of record that she was alive four days after the day when the verdict finds her to be dead, and so it seems to me that this verdict is null (*riens a purpose)* and a mere *jeofail,* in trying a thing contrary to the record; and so that the defendant is not to suffer by this verdict. And afterwards Cheyne assembled on this matter all the judges of both benches [and they agreed with him that] a matter of record . . . shall be tried by the record itself; . . . the verdict cannot defeat the record; . . . and if the court had been As to a jury contradicting the record, compare Goddard's case, 2 Co. 4 6 (1583 — 4), where it is said by the court that while parties may be estopped to say the troth, "yet the jurors, who are sworn to say the truth, shall not be estopped. . . . But if the estoppel or admittance be within the same record in which the issue is joined upon which the Jurors shall give their verdict, then they cannot find anything against that which the parties have affirmed and admitted of record, although the truth be contrary; for the court may give judgment upon a thing confessed by the parties, and jurors are not to be charged with any such thing, but only with things in which the parties differ."

of Bukfast,[411] where the Abbot was charged with maintenance of his servant in a suit against the plaintiff, Pole, Serjeant, argued: "If the Abbot had told the jury the truth of the matter and had openly shown them evidence for his servant, it would not be adjudged maintenance, any more than it would be if another person should tell the jury the truth of the matter at his request. "Paston, J." It is well to avoid maintenance as thoroughly as possible.... As to what is said that there is no maintenance in showing the jury the truth of the matter, in some cases there is and in some there is not. If one who has no reason to meddle in the matter and who is not learned in the law shows the jury, or the party himself, or his counsel, the truth of the matter and opens evidence of it as well and as fully as one who was learned in the law could, yet this is a maintenance in his person." The perils of an ordinary witness are still further illustrated in a case of 1450,[412] in which it was sought to hold certain persons sworn on an inquest, for maintenance. Littleton (counsel) said: "What a man does by compulsion of law cannot be called maintenance; as where a juror passes for me and against you, etc." Fortescue, C. J., agrees to this, and adds, "If a man be at the bar [*i. e.* in court] and say to the court that he is for the defendant or plaintiff, that he knows the truth of the issue and prays that he may be examined by the court to tell the truth to the jury, and the court asks him to tell it, and at the request of the court he says what he can in the matter, it is justifiable maintenance. But if he had come to the bar out of his own head *(de son teste demesne)* and spoken for one or the other, it is maintenance and he will be punished for it. And if the jurors come to a man where he lives, in the country, to have knowledge of the truth of the matter, and he informs them, it is justifiable; but if he comes to the jurors or labors to inform them of the truth, it is maintenance, and he will be punished for it; so Fortescue said, and it was admitted by the court."[413]

The doctrine of maintenance seems to have scared, witnesses in Chancery. It is to the period of 1450 — 60 that a

---

[411] Y. B. 21 H. VI. 15, 30 ; 8. c. 22 *ib.* 5,7.

[412] Y. B. 28 H. VI. 6,1.

[413] And so in 1504, Y. B. 20 H. VII. 11, 21, *per* Rede, J. The reasoning in this case illustrates the way in which the law on these subjects found a chance to grow.

petition belongs [414] in which a plaintiff asks the Chancellor to issue a subpoena to a certain witness to appear and declare the truth, setting forth that the "same Davyd will gladly knawelygge the treweth of the same matiers, bot he wald have a maundement fro yowe for the cause that he shuld noght be haldyn parciall in the same matter."

One may observe, then, in the unsettled state of the law of maintenance a reason, likely to have been very influential, for the slow development of the practice of testifying to the jury. No process seems then to have been. issued for such witnesses. The rule applicable to compurgators as stated by Needham, Serjeant, in 1454 — 5, probably applied here: "No process shall issue against them, nor can [the party] compel any man to swear with him." [415]

It is, of course, abundantly plain that by this time witnesses, if they pleased, could testify in open court to the jury; and it seems also plain that this was by no means freely done. Furthermore, it is pretty certain that this feature of a jury trial, in our day so conspicuous and indispensable, was then but little considered and of small importance. "We see this in Fortescue's famous and interesting book, *"De Laudibus Legum Angliae,"* written in Latin, not long, probably, before 1470. Fortescue had been Chief Justice of the King's Bench from 1442 — 1460; after being in exile with the queen and son of Henry VI., he returned to England, and was alive as late as 1476, — dying, it is said, at the age of ninety. In this book, written in the form of a dialogue between the Prince of Wales in exile and "a certain grave old knight, his father's Chancellor, at that time in banishment with him," the excellence of English laws is set forth, as compared with the "civil law," *i. e.,* the law of other European countries, founded on the Roman system. The first point in this comparison is the method of determining controversies of fact; more than a quarter of the book is taken up with showing how much better, in this respect, the English system is than that of the continent, where two witnesses are enough: "Slender, indeed, in resource must he be

---

[414] Calendars of the Proceedings in Chancery, i. p. xix.

[415] Y. B. 33 H. VI. 8,23. In 1481 (Y. B. 21 Edw. IV. 28,1) "a man offered himself to be sworn that he was present at the execution of one of the releases. Brian [C. J.], I will not compel him to this, but if he will of his own accord he shall be received. And so he was sworn and questioned and testified as above."

thought, and of less industry, who out of all the men he knows cannot find two so void of conscience and truth as to be willing for fear, favor or advantage to go counter to the truth in anything.... Who then can live secure in property or person under law like this, giving such aid to any one who would harm him." (c. 21.) Under that system (c. 23), justice constantly fails from the death or failure of witnesses. In England, on the other hand (cc. 25, 28), the witnesses must be twelve; they are chosen by a public official of high standing acting under oath, from among persons of the neighborhood where the matter in question is supposed to exist or take place, men of property, indifferent between the parties, subject to challenge by both, acting under oath. They are informed of the controversy by the court, and the parties or their counsel, and their witnesses, and confer together afterwards privately and with deliberation, and return and give their answer publicly in court.[416] After this verdict, an aggrieved party, by the writ of attaint, through the oath of twenty-four men of much better estate than the twelve, may convict the latter of a false oath, and subject them to the severest punishment. And then (c. 26), Fortescue sums up: "Here no one's cause or right fails by the death or failure of witnesses. No unknown witnesses are produced here, no paid persons, paupers, strangers, untrustworthy, or those whose condition or hostility is unknown. These witnesses *(jisti testes)* are neighbors, able to live out of their own property, of good name and unsullied reputation, not brought into court by a party, but chosen by an official who is a gentleman and indifferent, and required *(compulsi)* to come

---

[416] Fortescue's statement of the mode of proceeding at the trial is too interesting to be omitted: "The whole record and process will be read to them [the twelve] by the Court, and the issue upon which they are to certify the Court will be clearly explained to them. Then each party personally or by his counsel, in the presence of the Court, will state and show to the jurors all the matters and evidences which he thinks can instruct them *as to* the truth of the issue thus pleaded. And then each may introduce before the justices and jurors all the witnesses that he wishes to produce on his side, who, being charged by the justices on the holy evangelists of God, shall testify all that they know bearing upon the matter of fact *(probantia veritatem facti)* which is in controversy. If need be, witnesses of this sort *(testes hujusmodi)* may be separated until they shall have deposed what they will, so that the saying of one shall not inform another, or stir him to the giving of like testimony." Thereupon the jurors go out and deliberate.

before the judge. These men know everything which witnesses can tell them; these are aware of the trustworthiness or untrusworthiness, and the reputation of the witnesses who are produced."

In this account it is obvious how great a figure that old quality of the jury still plays, which made them witnesses; it is the chief thing; the point of all this elaborate contrast is the greater number and better quality of the English witnesses, and the greater security there is in the impartial methods of procuring them. They may, indeed, be informed by other witnesses, produced by either party, yet they themselves also are witnesses; and one remarks the small place that these informing witnesses have in the picture. The point of view here referred to clearly appears in what follows. By and by the prince is wholly satisfied of the excellence of the English law, — one scruple only remaining. The Scriptures say that "the testimony of two men is true;" and "bring with you one or two, so that in the mouth of two or three every word be established." If the Lord says two or three, why require more? No one can get any better or other foundation than the Lord has set. This is what troubles me a little, — *hec sunt,' Cancellarie, que aliquantulum me conturbant.* The Chancellor is ready with his answer; If the testimony of two is true, *a fortiori* that of twelve should be thought true; according to the rule, *Plus semper in se continet quod est minus.* All that the Scriptures mean, he goes on, is that not less than two shall serve. "In no case can this mode of proceeding fail for lack of witnesses; nor can the testimony of witnesses, if there be any, fail of its due effect, etc."

The slight importance of witnesses and their testimony is also indicated in what one of the judges says in a case of 1499:[417] While the parties were putting in their evidence, there came up a storm *(tempest de thunder et de pluye)* and the jury separated without leave of the justices; and one of them talked with a friend of one of the parties. They returned, and the case went on, and they gave a verdict. Then these facts came out, and there was a doubt as to the validity of the verdict. Ultimately [418] this was held good, but now, in expressing his opinion against it, Vavasour, J.,

---

[417] Y. B. 14 H. VII. 29, 4.
[418] Y. B. 20 H. VII. 3, 8.

said that it was not material that the evidence was not given before the jury separated: "Evidence is only given to inform their consciences as to the right. Suppose no evidence given on either side, and the parties do not wish to give any, yet the jury shall give their verdict for one side or the other. And so the evidence is nut material to help or harm the matter."

Almost contemporaneous with Fortescue's book is the case of Babington v. Venor, in 1465,[419] in which, for the first time in the Year Books, we have something like a full report of the arguments, and the putting in of the case before the jury. It was an assize of novel disseisin. Littleton for the plaintiff "shows in evidence" for the plaintiff a long story. Towards the end of it he says as to one point, "a man is here at the bar, an esquire, who spoke with her, etc.... and he will declare it. And also here is the general attorney of the Lord [Bishop] of W., who says in his Lord's name that, etc." There is nothing to show that either of these witnesses was actually put on. "Then Yong, for the defendant, shows evidence to the assize," — going on with another long story; and then he says, "The defendant's farmer is here at the bar ready to show to the Court *(al Court)* how, etc.,... and this will the farmer declare to you, and also the rent-collector." Then he shows certain documents, nothing being said of any examination of witnesses as yet. Then Catesby, for the plaintiff, makes counter statements, *e. g;* how the plaintiff entered, in the presence of several men here at the bar, etc., etc.; and he concludes by praying that the farmer may be examined. "The farmer came into Court and was sworn on a book to tell the truth to the Court as to that on which he should be examined; and he was examined by the Court.... and he shows, etc.... And. the rent-collector was also examined on a book as to this," etc. Then Guy Fairfax, counsel for the plaintiff, tells another story as to what took place at the view. Then came some discussion on points of law. Then the judges suggested to the defendant's counsel that if they wished to rest upon the plaintiff's evidence as not denied by them, they might discharge the inquest and demur upon the evidence; or if they were willing to run the risk of what the jury would say, the

---

[419] Long Quint (Edw. IV.), 58; S. C. Y. B. 5 Edw. IV. 5, 24. *Supra,* p.121

evidence might stand just as it was. The defendants preferred to go to the jury. Then came a discussion over a point of law, and then. the charge: "Sirs, you have had much evidence from both parties. Do in this matter as God will give you grace and according to the evidence and your conscience. You will not be compelled to say, precisely, disseisin, or the contrary, but you may find the fact, *i. e.,* the special matter, so as to give a special verdict on that and pray the judgment of the Court. And so go together, etc." The jury found for the plaintiff. One observes that only the defendant's farmer and rent-collector seem to have testified; these owed him a duty and might safely speak; all others are merely ready at the bar, prepared to affirm what the counsel says, if any one wishes to question them. The statements of counsel as to what his witness had to say, accompanied by the production of these, served as a method of putting in evidence.

In passing from this matter of the ways of informing the jury, it must be remembered, that although we have now reached modern methods, we are very far indeed from having reached the modern conception of trial by jury. Look, for instance, at Coke's ideas, a century and a half later, when he is explaining certain statutes as to treason and perjury.[420] The statutes of 1 Edw. VI. c. 12 and 5 & 6 *ib. c.* 11, had required two accusers (t. *e;* witnesses), in order to a conviction of treason. And then a statute of 1 & 2 Ph. & M. c. 10, had enacted that all trials for treason should thereafter be "had and tried only according to the due course and order of the common law." Coke says that this last statute does not repeal the others, for it "extends only to trials by the verdict of twelve men *de vicineto* of the place where the offence is alleged; and the indictment is no part of the trial, but an information or declaration for the king; and the evidence of witnesses to the jury is no part of the trial, for by law the trial in that case is not by witnesses but by the the verdict of twelve men; and so a manifest diversity between the evidence to a jury and a trial by jury." "Albeit by the common-law trials of matters of fact are by the verdict of twelve men, etc., and deposition of witnesses is but evidence to them, yet, for that most commonly juries are

---

[420] *3* Inst. 26, 27; ib. 163.

led by deposition of witnesses,"etc. For an instance of a trial by witnesses, expressly contrasted with trial by twelve men, see the St. 5 & 6 Edw. VI. c. 4, s. 3, where, *inter alia,* one who should strike another with a weapon in a church or churchyard should lose an ear, or, upon the grim supposition of the statute, if he "have none eares," be branded, — if convicted by the verdict of twelve men, or by his own confession, or by two lawful witnesses.[421]

---

[421] Compare many passages in the statutes of the sixteenth century, *e. g.,* St. 27 H. VIII. c. 4 (1535) for changing the mode of trial for piracy. It is recited here that "pirates, thieves, robbers and murderers upon the sea often escape unpunished because they are tried before the Admiral after the course of the civil laws, the nature whereof is that before any judgment of death can be given . . . either they must confess, . . . which they will never do without torture or pains, or else their offences be so plainly and directly proved by witnesses indifferent, such as saw their offences committed, which cannot be gotten but by chance at few times," and it is then enacted that hereafter such offences shall be inquired into and tried under the King's commission to the Admiral and others, in such shires as the King shall name, "after the common course of the law of the land," — after indictment "by the oaths of twelve good and lawful men, . . . that the trial of such offence . . . shall be had by twelve men inhabited in the shire limited within such commission . . . and no challenge to be had for the hundred."

In farther illustration of the conceptions of Coke's time, see the remarkable provisions of the St. 4 Jac. I. c. 1, s. 16 (1606). In composing the relations between England and Scotland, it was provided in s. 6 that certain offences committed in Scotland by Englishmen should be tried in the northern counties of England, and that the accused might have witnesses in his behalf under oath. This was a great step *(infra,* p. 159). In s. 16, after reciting the unusual dangers of perjury on the border, and the fact that the jurymen in these cases were to have special property qualifications and so to be specially well fitted for their office, these juries are authorized "to receive and admit only such sufficient good and lawful witnesses upon their oaths, either for or against the party arraigned, as shall not appear to them or the greater part of them to be unfit and unworthy to be witnesses in that case, either m regard of their hatred and malice, or their favor and affection, either to the party prosecuting or to the party arraigned, or of their former evil life and conversation."

This, it will be observed, is not merely allowing the jury to refuse credence to the witnesses, a thing always allowed; it is permitting them to refuse to hear the witnesses.

CHAPTER IV
TRIAL BY JURY, AND ITS
DEVELOPMENT *(CONTINUED)*

II. We come now to consider the mode of controlling the jury and correcting their errors. We have seen how the ways of adding to their knowledge were gradually increased, until at last witnesses called in by the parties were regularly admitted to testify publicly to these other witnesses, summoned by the sheriff, whom we call the jury. This mounting witnesses upon witnesses was a remarkable result and teemed with great consequences. The contrast between the functions of these two classes became always greater and more marked. The peculiar function of the jury — as being triers — grew to be their chief, and finally, as centuries passed, their only one; while that of the other witnesses was more and more defined, refined upon, and hedged about with rules. It is surprising to see how slowly these results came about. The attaint, which long held its place as the only way of remedying a false verdict, proceeded on the theory that the first jury had willfully falsified, and so was punishable. An independent, original knowledge of the facts was attributed to the jury, and not a merely inferential and reasoned knowledge. So long as this theory was true and was really a controlling feature of trial by jury, witnesses must needs play a very subordinate part. They were not necessary in any case. When they appeared, the jury could disregard all they said, and should, if it were not accordant with what they knew. Gradually it was recognized that while the jury might not be bound by the testimony, yet they had a right to believe it, and that they were the only ones to judge of its credibility. It became, then, the chief question whether they had such evidence before them as justified their verdict. If they had, they were not punishable; if they had not, why punish them for what, perhaps, they did not know? And so the attaint jury was not allowed to have more or other evidence making against the first jury's verdict than what that jury had had before them. But so much evidence they could have; and this points to the fact that evidence and witnesses produced to a jury, operated as fixing the jury with knowledge which otherwise might not so certainly be

imputed to them.[422] Still if they might believe what was thus testified
to them, it was equally true that they might disbelieve it, or any part
of it; and an attaint jury must often find it hard to say that it was a
wilful falsehood, to go against a mass of evidence which *admitted* of
being thought only partly true, or of being wholly disbelieved. The
attaint grew unworkable. For one reason or another people were
unwilling to resort to it, and jurors of attaint were unwilling to find
the former jury guilty, In 1451 the inhabitants of Swaffham asked
Parliament to annul a verdict and judgment in novel disseisin,
alleging perjury in the jurors by reason of "menaces," and setting
forth that the said inhabitants, for pity and remorse of their
consciences, were loth to use a writ of attaint, since "the said assize
durst not, for dread of the horrible menaces of the said Sir Thomas,
otherwise do but be foresworn in giving their verdict in the same
assize."[423] In 1565 Sir Thomas Smith[424] tells us: "Attaints be very
seldom put in use, partly because the gentlemen will not meet to
slander and deface the honest yeomen, their neighbors; so that of a
long time they had rather pay a mean fine than to appear and make
enquest.... And if the gentlemen do appear, gladlier they will confirm
the first sentence, for the cause which I have said, than go against it.
"The Star Chamber was resorted to for the purpose of supplying the
defects of the attaint and securing punishment for jurors who gave
false or corrupt verdicts. The judges of the common-law courts went
a certain way in the same direction of fining and imprisoning jurors
who went against the evidence. Of this I shall speak later. It is
enough here to quote what Hudson in his Treatise on the Star
Chamber, written in the early part of the seventeenth century, says of
that court.[425] He is claiming for it a very ancient jurisdiction; and

---

[422] Y. B. 7 Edw. IV. 29, 14 (1467 — 8); s. c. Brooke, Abr. Attaint, 87:
"Littleton, J. A man recovers against S. in an assize, and he brings attaint and
shows in evidence to the grand jury a record which was not shown to the petty
jury. There the petty jury may say that this was not given to them in evidence; for
if it was not given them in evidence they are not bound to find it."

In 1662 (Frankland *v.* Saville, 1 Keble, 249), *"per curiam,* though one
consent to have a letter read, yet the jury in pain of attaint are not hound to find
it." See *supra,* pp. 107,108.

[423] Draft of a petition from the town of Swaffham. "Paston Letters"
(Gairdner's ed.), No. 151.

[424] Com. of Engl., Bk. 3, c. 2.

[425] Part i. s. 4; p. 11, as printed in Collectanea Juridica. Hudson was
called to the bar in 1605, and died not later than 1635.

after speaking of certain acts of Henry IV. he adds: "When a corrupt jury had given an injurious verdict, if there had been. no remedy but to attaint them by another jury, the wronged party would have had small remedy, as it is manifested by common experience, no jury having for many years attainted a former."

In time courts adopted the method of granting new trials when the verdict was unreasonable, without punishing the jurors. A step had then been taken which made it important that the court should know, so far as possible, all that the jury knew; and accordingly the old doctrine of their going on private knowledge began more and more to give way. The jury were told that if any of them knew anything relating to the case, they ought to state it publicly in court. This lay long in the shape of a moral duty of the jurors, not enforceable; but after a time it was enforced, and the court assumed that, in general, nothing was known to the jury except what was publicly stated in court, — adding to this, under the notion of judicial notice, what they were legally supposed to know and what was known to everybody. This brought matters down to the state of things in which we are now living. The jury became merely judges upon evidence.

(a) Let us turn back, and trace the working out of these results. For centuries the great check upon the jury was the attaint, *i. e;* a proceeding in which the original parties and also the first jury were parties, and where a, larger jury, made up of knights or other more considerable persons than the first, passed again on the same issue. If they found contrary to the first finding, then the first jury was convicted of perjury and heavily punished; and the first judgment was reversed. We see in one of our earliest cases[426] the punishment of a jury who, by confession of their leader and others, were adjudged to have perjured themselves, and also a reversal of the first judgment. It is probable that punishment generally attended the proof of "perjury" in the use of the inquisition. But it is not likely that in the older law a reversal of the judgment would always follow. In Glanvill there is no mention of the attaint, even as regards the possessory assizes,[427] yet he says conspicuously that in the ordinance establishing the great assize provision is made *(eleganter inserta)* for

---

[426] Gundulf *s.* Pichot (1072 — 1082), Big. Pl. A. N. 34; 8. c. *supra,* pp. 51 — 52.

[427] Brunner (Schw. 422, note) remarks this.

the punishment of those who swear falsely.[428] But there seems always to have been the same finality in the procedure by the grand assize as in the duel: *Ea enim que in curia... per duellum semel fuerint terminata negotia perpetuam habent firmitatem.*[429] And so in the earliest extant Year Book, in 1292,[430] the reporter has a memorandum, "Note: After the great assize an attaint never lies." The attaint *(convictio)* seems to have originated in England, but is not traceable to any extant legislation. Whether it may have been a part of the ordinances of Henry II. establishing the recognitions, or whether it developed from the *pena* mentioned by Glanvill in speaking of the great assize, or whether it was granted in the discretion of the king and his justices, seems not to be ascertained. This at least is true, that while it is not in Glanvill, and while the first express mention of it in legislation appears to have been in 1268,[431] we find it in the judicial records as early as 1202,[432] and it is fully discussed in Bracton half a century later.

On the other side of the channel, they had punishment for jurors who swore falsely. Brunner[433] cites an undated capitulary of the eighth or ninth century which shows this. But the attaint went beyond this: it was a procedure which also secured the reversal of the previous verdict, as a proceeding for error in law might secure the reversal of a judge's decision. This, we are told, was a thing unknown in Normandy. As regards the *stabilia,* the petitory action corresponding to the writ of right, Brunner quotes a Norman case of 1248, in which the jury by mistake gave a verdict in favor of one William, and the court gave judgment accordingly; whereupon the jury came back with the information: *Quod non bene dixerunt, quia,*

---

[428] *Pena autem in hac assisa temere jurantium ordinaria est et ipsi regali institutioni eleganter inserta.* Glanv. ii. 19. He goes on to say that if the jurors are convicted of perjury *(perjurasse)* or confess, they lose all chattels and movables to the king, are imprisoned for at least a year, and that henceforth, losing their *legem,* they shall incur perpetual infamy. The point of the *eleganter inserta* seems to be intimated when it is added that this punishment is uniform with that of the champion; it is rightly imposed, in order that all who put forward a false oath in this sort of case — whether champion (Glanv. ii. 3) or juryman — may suffer a like punishment.

[429] Glanv. ii. 3.
[430] 20 Edw. I. 18.
[431] See *infra,* p. 146.
[432] *Infra,* p. 143.
[433] Schw. 89.

Robertus maius ius habebat in terra illa quam W. The court, however, would not change their judgment; William kept the land, and the jurymen had to pay Robert the value of it.[434] The same rule applied in other recognitions. Brunner cites a record of about the year 1200, in which a litigant in Normandy gives the king (John) twenty besants that a recognition upon a recognition be not made in a certain case, *injuste et contra consuetudinem Normanniae.'* In England the continental rule held as regards the writ of right; in this the great assize ended the controversy as absolutely as the duel which it displaced. Whatever is settled in the king's court by the duel, says Glanvill,[435] is settled forever. And again,[436] where a matter is settled by the great assize, *tam finaliter quam per duellum terminabltur negotium.* Yet, none the less, even here, as we have seen, was a punishment provided for perjury by the assize jury — that *pena eleganter inserta* already mentioned.

In 1227,[437] a certain prior had lost, in a writ of right of an advowson, — the great assize finding for the defendant, *quia non viderunt quod idem Prior* or any of his predecessors presented a clerk at the church in question. Thereupon the prior came, alleged that there was a false oath, and put forward half a dozen charters which seemed to prove it. The defendant, relying on the finality of the former trial, simply declined to answer and demanded judgment. Yet the case seems to have been thought doubtful, for it was postponed, to give time for a conference with the king and with other

---

[434] Schw. 371. It would have been strange if this rigor had not existed in early days, when form bound every man by the exact words he uttered in court. This subject is well illustrated in Brunner's essay on "Word and Form," in the old French procedure, published in the Proceedings of the Imperial Academy of Vienna, Vol. 77. A translation of this may be found in the *"Revue Critique de Legislation et de Jurisprudence,"* (New Series), Vol. I. Of the formalism of the old law many traces yet remain, such as the necessity for using specific words in criminal pleading. One sees an authentic bit of it in 1284 in the Statute of Wales, c. VIII. (St. Realm, i. 64), where it is said of certain real actions, that the demandant shall count in words that express the truth, without being subject to any challenge for words, — *non observata ilia dura consuetudine, qui cadit a sillaba cadii a tota causa. See* also the rigor which was customary before the statutes of jeofail, as indicated by St. 14 Edw. III. c. 6. The curious discussions over this statute, in Y. B. 40 Edw. III. 34, 18, and 11 H. IV. 70, 4, are worth remarking.

[435] Lib. ii. c. 3.

[436] *Ib. c.* 6.

[437] Br. N. B. ii. case 262.

justices. The prior did not appear at the day given, and the defendant had judgment. This seems to have been an irregular attempt at attainting the jurors of the great assize; for these jurors appear to have been summoned, and at the postponement the order was *et juratores sine die donec aliud audiverint.* The annotator also remarks upon the margin: "Note, that not easily may the jurors in the great assize be attainted:" *Nota, quod juratores in magna assisa non poterunt convinci de facili.* In his treatise Bracton[438] says that in all assizes, except the grand assize, the *convictio* (attaint) lies; and for this exception he gives the reason that the tenant has consented to the grand assize and can. not go back upon his own proof.[439] Perhaps the true reason was that in this case the old rule of finality had not been changed.[440]

The origin of the attaint in the possessory recognitions, is attributed by Brunner, reasonably enough, to the mere favor of the king, and he refers to a case of 1347 or 1348,[441] in which a disappointed suitor offers the king twenty shillings for an attaint jury. Other early cases point the same way. The earliest one, so far as I observe, was in 1202,[442] and there the defeated party offers the king forty shillings for a jury of twenty-four knights. In the same year a like offer of twenty shillings is made.

Not merely were jurors punished, in this way, for a false verdict, and this and any judgment upon it reversed: the judges also were sometimes punished for errors in law and their judgments reversed. The judges, according to the very old law, had to defend their judgment by the duel. The same ideas survive in our early records. In 1231,[443] certain special justices who had taken an assize of mort d'ancestor between Oliver as demandant and William, a prior, as tenant, were summoned at the complaint of the tenant to record the proceedings, and the jurors to certify their verdict. The justices say that the jury found that Roger, a brother of Oliver, died

---

[438] 290, 296 *b.*

[439] Such was, indeed, the rule, that where one had put himself on any mode of proof, lie must abide the result; and so, originally, the *jurata,* aa contrasted with the *assisa,* was not subject to the attaint. Pollock and Maitland, ii. 540, 621.

[440] *Supra,* p.141.

[441] Schw. 372; cited by him from Biener, Eng. Geschw. i. 72; 8. c. Pl Ab. 124, col. 2. Pollock and Maitland, Hist. Eng. Law, 662, n. 1.

[442] Maitland, Sel. Civ. Pl. i. case 216.

[443] Br. N. B. ii. 564.

seised of the land, and that Oliver was next heir, and so judgment was given for Oliver. The jurors were asked if this was the record. While admitting it in part, they said that Oliver had an older brother, Ralph, who was living, and therefore they had doubted whether Oliver was the nearest heir, and they set forth a former litigation as explaining their doubt. Oliver was then asked if this were so, and did not deny it. The justices, however, did deny it at first; but afterwards they admitted that the jurors said that Oliver had an older brother. Now, under these circumstances, according to a doctrine set forth by Glanvill,[444] while the younger brother has a superior claim in a writ of right, yet he cannot maintain a mort d'ancestor, for the older brother, and not he, is the nearest heir. It was, therefore, wrong in the justices to give judgment for the younger brother. Accordingly it was now adjudged as follows: "Because the justices acknowledge that the jurors said that the said Oliver had an older brother named. Ralph, and therein have absolved the jurors, and the justices adjudged that Oliver was the next heir on the ground that the said Ralph could not be *dominus et heres,* whereas this (namely, being *dominus et heres)* has regard to *jus* and not to *possessio* or to the assize of mort d'ancestor, it is adjudged that the said justices erred in making that judgment, and made a false judgment; and therefore the justices are amerced, and the jurors go without day, and Oliver is amerced, and the prior recovers his seisin."[445]

(V) It was sometimes found, in preparing to give judgment, that the verdict of the jury was obscure or incomplete; the judges below had not questioned them enough. In such cases they were resummoned to the court in banc *ad certificandum.* This was called the *certificatio.* One sees it in 1232,[446] and 1237.[447] In 1290 — 1,[448]

---

[444] Lib. vii. c. 1.

[445] In 1235 — 6 (Br. N. B. iii. case 1166), there is a complaint to the king of an error, committed by the justices at Westminster, in giving judgment too quickly against a defendant on default, "whereas many distraints should follow . . . before the said Thomas should have recovered on the default." The justices appeared and admitted the facts, but pleaded ignorance, *nesciverunt in dicto negocio melius procedere.* The judgment was reversed. There was no jury in this case, and nothing is said of any punishment of the judges; "but observe," says the editor in his note (vol. iii. p. 179), "that proceedings in error are a complaint against the judges who have erred."

[446] Br. N. B. ii. case 887.

[447] *Ib.* iii. case 1226.

[448] Pl. Ab. 284, col. 2, Suff.

one who had caused the jury to be resummoned for this purpose, being asked in what the jury had been insufficiently questioned or had spoken obscurely, answered by merely repeating their verdict, which he seems to say is wrong. His adversary replied that the the verdict is not obscure, and for a plain verdict *non potest esse certificatio set poems attincta;* and she asks judgment and has it. In 1556,[449] we read that "Because the [special] verdict was not full and perfect, the plaintiff sued a certificate of assize to make the jurors come again to be more fully examined; who came again and made their verdict more certain."

(c) The attaint at first was but a limited remedy, given only in assizes, but it grew by statute and by the discretion allowed to the judges. The first mention, of it in the statutes is a mere mention in 1268,[450] cutting down general exemptions from serving on "assizes, juries and inquests," in cases where necessity requires the service, — as it may, said the statute, in the great assize, or where the party is a witness to a deed, *aut in attinctis,* etc. In 1275,[451] it is recited that people lose their estates because some "doubt not to make a false oath; "and it is enacted. that, on inquests in pleas of land or freehold or what touches freehold, the king, *de son office,* when it shall seem needful shall hereafter give attaints.[452] This statute is supposed to have extended the remedy beyond the case where the assize jury answered merely on the point of the assize, to the case where it answered on incidental or newly developed questions, *in modum juratae,* and to all juries in real actions.[453] In 1302 Berewik, J., calls

---

[449] Panel *v.* Moor, Plowd. 91, 92.

[450] St. Marl. 52 H. III. c. 14.

[451] St. West. I. 3 Edw. I. c. 38.

[452] "Not that the king shall grant these writs whenever applied for, *ex merito justitiae* [Coke's view, 2 Inst, 237], (a sense which the words *ex officio* surely never bore in any writer of Latin, whether good or had), but that the king shall *ex officio,* without being sued and applied for, grant," etc. Reeves, Finl. ed. ii. 34. And so in 1292 (Y. B. 20 & 21 Edw. I. 110) Spigornel (counsel) says: "We understand, sir, that no attaint shall pass upon an inquest without the special order of the king." In 1294 (Y. B. 21 & 22 Edw. I, 330) the reporter has a note "that justices itinerant may grant attaints upon assizes which pass before them, but not on inquests." Coke (2 Inst. 130) thinks that the attaint lay, at common law, in pleas both real and personal, — a view which Reeves (ii. 33) justly discredits.

[453] In Pollock and Maitland, ii. 621, after quoting Bracton as saying that when a man has chosen his own proof "he cannot reprobate it," it is said in a note: "Therefore *a jurata* cannot be attainted. When this role was altered in 1275 (St.

on the assize in novel disseisin to tell him the damages, and warns them that there may be an attaint for damages as well as the principal matter, "and, nowadays, out of this Court, without the need of seeking it in the Chancery."[454] This seems to rest on the statute of 1275; at common law, the rule is given by Bracton,[455] *de damnis nulla erit convictio sed... locum habet certificatio.*

The Mirror, towards the end of the thirteenth century, wished attaints extended and made easier: "It is an abuse that attaints are not granted without difficulty in the Chancery to attaint all false jurors, as well in all other actions real, personal and mixed, as in the petty assizes."[456] Before Andrew Horn's death[457] there came an instalment of this desired reform. In 1326 — 7,[458] after a recital of "great mischiefs, damages and destructions of divers persons, as well as of the men of holy church, by the false oath of jurors in writs of trespass," the writ of attaint is allowed for the principal matter and also for damages in trespass, and the chancellor is to grant such writs *sanz parler au Roi.* In this fast-breeding action of trespass, the writ of attaint was further extended in 1331,[459] to cases where the proceeding was informal and without writ, if the damages pass forty shillings; and then in 1354, it was enacted that "the writ of attaint be granted without regard to the amount of damages, as well upon a bill of trespass as upon a writ of trespass." [460]

West. I. c. 38) it was already becoming evident that the consensual origin of the *jurata* was a fiction." *Supra,* p. 143.

[454] Y. B. 30&31 Edw. I. 124.

[455] 290 b.

[456] Lib. v. c. i. s. 77.

[457] Which was in 1328. Black Book of the Adm. i. Introd. lix. note. As to whether Horn really was the writer of the Mirror, see Maitland's excellent Introduction to that strange book.

[458] St. 1 Edw. III. c. 6.

[459] St. 5 Edw. III. c. 7.

[460] *St.* 28 Edw. III. c. 8. The word "bill" imported an informal document. In the "Paston Letters" the word is constantly used for a letter; *e. g., in No.* 813 (1478) Sir John Paston's mistress writes that she is in good health "at the making of this sympyll byll," and asks for an answer by "the brynger of my byll." So in 1440 — 1 (Y. B. 19 H. VI. 50, 7), Paston, J.: If a bill be good in substance it is enough; *car un bill n'ad aucun forme.* In 1315 (Y. B. Edw. II. 277) a party had averred by Domesday Book, and a mandate was issued by Bereford, C. J., to the treasurer and barons of the exchequer, to certify as to the contents of Domesday. They would not certify, because the mandate was only un *bille* sealed with the seal of William de Bereford; whereupon the latter sent a writ *[brief),* and this brought an answer. Beeves, Hist. C. L. Finl. ed. ii. 97, note; 16. 99, note.

Earlier than this, in 1347,[461] the commons had petitioned for the attaint in writs of debt and all other writs and bills where the demand or damage amounted to forty shillings, but the answer came, "Let the old law stand till the king be better advised." At last, in 1360, came full relief in a statute providing, "against the falsehood of jurors, that every man against whom they shall pass may have the attaint both in pleas real and personal."[462] Later in the fourteenth century the benefit of the attaint was extended in other ways, e. g; by giving it to a reversioner when the life tenant had lost.

(d) The attaint was now a general remedy, for litigants in the king's courts, but it was found to be a very inadequate one. The next century is full of complaints, loud, bitter, and constant, of the wretched working of the jury and the attaint; perjury, bribery, and ruinous delays are set forth as inducing the increase of the property qualifications of jurors, and imposing new penalties upon them. Two remarkable statutes, of 1433 and 1436 respectively,[463] must be noticed. The first recites mischief, damage, and disherison from "the usual perjury of jurors," increasing by reason of gifts made them by the parties to suits, so that the greater part of people who have to sue *(quont a suer)* let go *(lessent)* their suits by reason of the said mischief and especially on account of the delays in writs of attaint. When the grand jury[464] appears and is ready to pass, a tenant or defendant or one of the petit jury pleads false pleas not triable by the grand jury, and so delays proceedings until this be tried. When this is

---

[461] Parl. Rolls, ii. 167,23.

[462] St. 34 Edw. III. c. 7. The statute goes on: "And that the attaint be granted to the poor who shall swear that they have nothing wherefrom to pay therefor except their *countenance,* without payment *(fine);* and to all others by an easy payment." The true historical place and nature of the attaint, and indeed of this whole ancient business of trial by jury itself, are sometimes oddly misconceived. See, e. g., the remarks of Shaw, C. J., in Com. *v.* Anthes, 5 Gray, 185,198 (1855): "This, like many anomalies of the like kind, . . . shows how little the true nature and principle of jury trial in its perfection were understood. . . . But these abuses and anomalies have long since passed away, and both in Great Britain and in this country the principle of jury trial is well understood." It would have sounded strangely to the lawyers of the fourteenth and fifteenth centuries to hear the attaint called an anomaly. *Their* jury trial was different in kind from ours.

[463] St. 11 H. VI. c. 4, and St. 15 *ib. c.* 5. For the corresponding petitions in Parliament and the answers, see Parl. Rolls, iv. 408; *ib.* 448 (47); and *ib.* 501 (26).

[464] Then the usual name of the attaint jury, as it is now of the larger criminal jury.

settled for the plaintiff, another pleads a like false plea since the last continuance; and so each of the defendants, tenants, or jurors, one after another, may plead and delay the grand jury; and, although all be false and feigned, the common law has no penalty. This has caused great vexation and travail to the grand juries, and plaintiffs have been so impoverished that they could not pursue their cases, and jurors are more emboldened to swear falsely. It is, therefore, ordained that plaintiffs may recover [against] all such tenants, jurors, and defendants the damages and costs thus suffered. The other statute, after reciting that by the law of the realm trials in matters of life and death and as to all sorts of questions, as regards matters of fact *(touchant mailers en fait),* are likely to be "by the oaths of inquests of twelve men;" that great, fearless, and shameless perjury horribly continues and increases daily among common jurors of the realm; that in proportion as men are more sufficient in land, the less likely they are to be corrupted; that in every attaint there must be thirteen defendants at least, unless some die, each of whom may have separate answer triable in any county, and the attaint may be delayed until all these are tried, and so delays to the plaintiffs in the said attaints for ten years *par commune estimation,* — goes on to provide for an increase of the property qualification of the attaint jurors, and that an adverse decision in any "foreign plea," *[i. e.,* one triable elsewhere than the issue in attaint] shall give the whole attaint against the one pleading it.

But not only was the size and the machinery of the attaint jury cumbrous and well adapted to delays and frauds, but the attaint jurors were unwilling to find the petit jurors guilty, the punishment was so harsh. Now that witnesses were produced before a jury and they were expected to judge of the truth or falsity of the witnesses, things had changed. The testimony of these witnesses to the jury, like writings not under seal which might be submitted to them, did, indeed, tend in one way to assist the application of the attaint, for it helped to fix upon the jury a knowledge of the facts which were thus publicly brought home to them.[465] Yet in another way it must have steadily operated to bring the attaint into discredit. The 'essential nature of the jury's function as being something different from that

---

[465] It was still true that they were not legally bound to believe what was thus brought home to them. "But, *per curiam,* though one consent to have a letter read, yet the jury in pain of attaint are not bound to find it." Frankland v. Savill, 1 Keble, 249 (1662). And so Olive *v.* Guin, 2 Sid. 145 (1658).

of these new witnesses, something more than being mere testifiers to what they had seen and heard, as being always in a degree judges, drawing conclusions from what their senses presented and what others testified to them, — all this must have rapidly grown plain; and so the extreme severity and unfitness of the punishment. The punishment mentioned by Glanvill,[466] three centuries before, continued to be applied in the attaint, and. was even increased; the convicted juryman, lost all his movable goods to the king; he was imprisoned for a year at least; he lost his *lex terrae* and became infamous. Bracton[467] repeats this in substance, making their lands and chattels seized by the king until redeemed, and adds, "Never thereafter may they be received to an oath for they shall not afterwards be *othesworth."* It came also to be expressed as a part of the judgment that their wives and children should be turned out of doors, and their lands laid waste.[468]

The wisdom of providing some milder punishment was seen, — something that would not seem excessively severe and grossly unjust. Accordingly in. 1495,[469] in providing the attaint for the first time, in the city courts of London, the punishment is limited to a fine of twenty pounds, "or more, by the discretion of the mayor or aldermen," imprisonment for six months or less, and "to be disabled forever to be sworn in any jury before any temporal judge. "In the same year,[470] there is a general statute which was afterwards

---

[466] Lib. ii. c. 19.

[467] 292 *b.*

[468] Fortescne, *De Laud, c.* 26. In 1496 (Y. B. 12 H. VII. 4, 2) Danvers and Wood, Justices, said that "the reason why a juryman is to have a freehold when he is sworn is that the law intends that he will more take care to speak the truth than one who has none; and if he do not say the truth he will be punished in attaint and his land wasted."

[469] St. 11 H. VII. c.21.

[470] Ib. c. 24. "Made in favor of the subjects, namely, for the qualification of the rigorous and terrible judgment of the common law in attaint," said the court in Austen *v.* Baker, Dyer, 201a (1561). "This parliament," says Lord Bacon, in his History of Henry VII., in speaking of the eleventh year of H. VII., "was made that good law which gave the attaint upon a false verdict between party and party, which before was a kind of evangile, irremediable." In what appears to be Lord Bacon's Latin: *His etiam comitiis lata est lex illa bona quae breve de attincta vocatum introduxit per guod judicia juratorum, quae veredicta vocantur, falsa rescindi possint; quae ante illud tempus, evangelii cujusdam instar erant, atque plane irrevocabilia.* Mr. Justice Gray, in citing this in Sparf v. U. S. 156 U. S. 51, 116, remarks upon the strange error of "assuming that the attaint was introduced by the St. 11 H. VII. c. 24." This is, indeed, a

continued several times, and then, having expired, was temporarily revived in 1531, by St. 23 H. VIII. c. 3, and finally made perpetual in 1571 by St. 13 Eliz. c. 25. It continued in substance to be the law governing this matter until the abolition of attaints in 1825. This statute, after the usual recital of continuing perjury [of jurors] and its mischiefs, provides that a party grieved by an untrue verdict, where the demand and verdict reach forty pounds shall have an attaint jury of the same number as heretofore. The petit jury shall (with certain exceptions) have no answer except that their verdict was true. If the issue be found against them they shall be fined twenty pounds, one-half for the king, the other for the party suing. They shall also "make fine and ransom by the discretion of the justices; "and they" shall never after be of any evidence, nor their oath accepted in any court." The party may plead any good bar to the attaint, but that is not to delay the trial of the petit jury's plea and issue. If the party's plea, whatever it be, is found against him, then the plaintiff in attaint is "to be restored to that he lost with his reasonable costs and damages." If the verdict be in a personal action and under forty pounds, the qualifications of the attaint jury are less, and the fine shall be only five pounds.

(e) The statutes of Henry VII. however, while providing something new, did not repeal the old common-law attaint; "so that," says Blackstone,[471] "a man may now bring an attaint either upon the statute or at common law, at his election, and in both of them reverse the former judgment." Either way the punishment was very severe; and it plainly appears that this, with other causes, was working fast to make the attaint wholly inoperative. I have referred to the "pyte and remorce of their concyencez" which kept the people of Swaffham, in 1451, from bringing a writ of attaint;[472] and to a part of what Sir Thomas Smith[473] said in 1565: "Attaints be very seldom put in use, partly because the gentlemen will not meet to slander and deface the honest yeomen, their neighbors, so that of a long time

---

remarkable error. It is hard to account for it. Possibly Lord Bacon, who specifies no chapter, had in mind the provisions of c. 21, as Spedding seems to conjecture by citing it in his edition of Bacon's works (Vol. 6, 160, ed. Spedding & Ellis). Chapter 21, in providing for the attaint in the London city courts, recites that "none atteint ne other sufficient punysshement is for such perjured persones before this tyme purveyed, and ordeyned within the same Citie."

[471] Com. iii. 404.
[472] *Supra,* p.138.
[473] Com. of England, book iii. c. 2.

they had rather pay a mean fine than to appear and make the inquest. And in the meantime they will in-treat, so much as in them lyeth, the parties to come to some composition and agreement among themselves; as lightly they do, except either the corruption of the inquest be too evident, or the one party is too obstinate and headstrong. And, if the gentlemen do appear, gladlier they will confirm the first sentence for the causes which I have said than go against it." A century later, in 1665,[474] Hyde, C. J., "seeing the attaint is now fruitless," declared with vehemence in a civil case that jurors ought to be fined. And after another century, Blackstone said,[475] "I have observed very few instances of an attaint in our books later than the sixteenth century." "The writ of attaint," said Lord Mansfield at about the same time, in 1757,[476] "is now a mere sound in every case." In 1825 it was at last enacted that in all cases attaints should "henceforth cease, become void and be utterly abolished."[477]

A case or two will illustrate the working of the attaint in its decrepitude. In 1542,[478] more evidence for the plaintiff in attaint had in fact been given to the attaint jury than was given below; but this was held to be wrong, and Shelley, J., "admonished the jury to look to the evidence which was given to the first jury upon which they passed; for if they had pregnant and manifest proof and evidence to confirm the matter, although that were in fact false and the truth of the matter was contrary, still they ought not to regard, that, but ought to weigh in their consciences what themselves would have done upon the same strong evidence as the first jury did; for *homines sunt mendaces et non angeli,"* etc.[479] In 1593,[480] the attaint jury gave a

---

[474] 1 Keble, 864, 6. In 1738, in Smith d. Dormer *v.* Parkhurst, Andrews, 315, Lee, C. J., in discussing the question of granting a new trial, after a trial at bar, said: "As the duty of courts, therefore, is to do justice, and as in actions that are final where there is a false verdict the only remedy was an attaint, which has been considered as no remedy ... by reason of the difficulty of the proceedings and the severity of the punishment, the courts have gone into the easier remedy of granting new trials." In 1740, it is said in 3 Bac. Abr. 278, "Since the attaint is only disused and not taken away, we shall here set down," etc.

[475] Com. iii. 404.

[476] Bright v. Eynon, 1 Burr. p. 393.

[477] St. 6 Geo. IV. c. 50, § 60.

[478] Rolfe *v.* Hampden, Dyer, 53 *b.*

[479] *Supra,* p. 138.

[480] Queen *v.* Ingersall, Cro. El. 309. A proceeding formerly said not to be good. In 1467 — 8 (7 Edw. IV. 29, 14). "In attaint the jurors asked if they

special verdict. The defendant in a *qui tam* action had been charged with buying cattle out of market, viz., of one Pearepoint. On a plea of not guilty the jury below had found for the defendant. On attaint, the twenty-four in their special verdict set forth that the petit jury had the evidence of one Whitworth that the defendant bought of him, out of market, the cattle of Pearepoint. The attaint jury finds that the cattle were really bought of Whitworth as Whitworth's cattle; but this was not given in evidence, and they ask the court's judgment as to the law. The court holds against the attaint; since the jury finds that the evidence below was false in part, the first jury might properly enough disbelieve it all.

(*f*) Of course it must be remembered that there were other grounds for punishing juries, and other grounds for giving new trials. The court always held towards the jury a relation of control, and the books are full of traces of ordinary discipline. In 1293, the jury appeared to be answering subtly, so as to conceal something. The judge calls for a better answer, or he will shut them up over night.[481] If the jurors took out food with them, or violated any of the ordinary rules, they were always subject to punishment; and in such cases new trials were granted.[482] Not a few statutes also were passed,

---

might give their verdict at large, as in an assize; and the justices said no." But it was sustained in 1561; Burham *v.* Heyman, Dyer, 173.

[481] Y. B. 21 & 22 Edw. I. 273. In an assize of mort d'ancestor, a tenant set up the existence of an older heir, William, and an alienation by him. The jury found that this William entered as oldest son and heir, and as next heir. "Roubury [J.]. How say you that he is next heir? The Assize. Because he was born and begotten of the same father and the *same* mother, and his father on his death-bed acknowledged that he was his son and his heir. Roubury [J.]. Yon shrill tell us in another fashion how he is next heir, or stay shut up, without food and drink, till to-morrow morning. And then they said that he was born before the ceremony [of marriage] and after the betrothal." This, at common law, made him a bastard.

[482] In 1577 — 8, in Welcden *v.* Elkington, Plowd. 516, 518, we read, "And for that a certain box of preserved barberries, and sugar, called sugar-candy, and sweet roots, called liquorish [sic], were found with the aforesaid John Mucklow, one of the jurors aforesaid, after he had departed from the bar here to advise together with the other jurors aforesaid . . therefore the same John Mucklow is committed to the prison ... of the Fleet, until he shall have made a fine with the lady the Qneen. &c." He was fined twenty shillings. "There are instances in the Year Books of the reigns of Edward III., Henry IV., and Henry VII. of judgments being stayed (even after a trial at bar), and new *venires* awarded, because the jury had eat and drank without consent of the Judge, and because the plaintiff had privately given a paper to a juryman before he was sworn." (Bl. Com. iii. 387 — 8).

especially in the fourteenth century, giving actions or criminal process against jurymen receiving bribes and taking part in embracery. Of other less obvious but extremely important modes of controlling the jury, and their consequences, something will be said later.[483]

(g) It will have been noticed, perhaps, that nothing has been said of the attaint for a false verdict in criminal cases. At the beginning we saw that there was no assize, *i. e.,* no statutory jury, in such cases, and it seems to have been only in assizes that the attaint was first allowed. The jury in criminal cases came in gradually, and by way of the consent of the accused, willing or forced.[484] The doctrine, in all cases where one had consented, was that such party could not have the attaint, for this would be *facere probationem suam nullam;* as we say now, one cannot blacken his own witness. The king, however, it was said, might have the attaint if the case went against him. Bracton[485] tells us this, and four hundred years later we read it in Sir M. Hale.[486] But the silence of the books as regards actual cases of the exercise of this power in criminal cases may lead us to some doubt about it. The words of Bracton are satisfied by such cases as those relating to the king's revenues, and such as the *qui tam* action of 1593.[487] As regards appeals, the common-law mode of trial was by battle. It is, perhaps, reason enough for denying the attaint to the plaintiff in an appeal, that historically the battle was a final thing, and here, as in the grand assize, whatever trial took the place of it shared this

---

[483] *Infra,* pp. 162, 169, 175.

[484] *Supra,* p. 68 *et seq.*

[485] Bracton, 290 *b; Supra,* p. 143. Pollock and Maitland, Hist. Eng. Law, ii. 621.

[486] P. C. ii. 310 (written 1660 — 1676) citing Fitz. Attaint, 60; s. c. 16. 64; But this is contemporaneously denied by Vaughan, C. J., in Bushel's case (Vaughan, 146), in 1670: "For there is no case in all the law of such an attaint, nor opinion, but that of Thirning's, 10 H. IV., ... for which there is no warrant in law, though there is other specious authority against it." What Thirning, C. J. (Vanghan's predecessor at the head of the Common Bench), is shortly reported to have said, in 1409, is this: "One indicted of trespass and found guilty by the other inquest shall not have attaint nor a petition in the nature of attaint, because in a way *(en maner)* twenty-four have given the verdict [i. e., two juries], and the two verdicts agree; but if he be acquitted the King shall have attaint by prerogative." Fitz. Attaint, 64. This reason, as to two verdicts, was probably invented (although one sees it in the Year Books), and not the true historical reason.

[487] Supra, p. 154.

character.[488] One other remark may be made as regards all criminal cases. Always scope was allowed to the sentiment that there should be mercy and caution in such cases. We read in a report of 1302, *Et hoc nota quod melius est nocentem relinquere impunitum quam innocentem punire;*[489] and so Fortescue,[490] in a chapter where he celebrates the felicity of the English in having so many safeguards against injustice in criminal trials: "Truly I would rather that twenty guilty men should escape through pity than that one just man should be unjustly condemned." But even in England the king, in criminal cases, was no mere ordinary party to an action; the procedure was heavily weighted in his favor. In treason and felony the accused could not have counsel; later, when witnesses could be had for the king, the accused could not have them; and still later, when he also could have them, his witnesses could not be sworn.[491] The king, therefore, had small

---

[488] And the attaint was not extended by statute to appeals. In 1347 — 8 (Lib. Ass. 102, 82), in an appeal of mayhem, "Thorpe [J.], said that the defendant should never have attaint in an appeal of mayhem, any more than in a felony; for the statute gives attaint only in a writ of trespass and a bill of trespass." Not only, then, was it true, as Britton said (f. 49), that, "for avoiding the perilous risk of battle, it is better to proceed by our writs of trespass, than by appeals," But one got the benefit of the attaint in that way.

[489] Y. B. 30 & 31 Edw. I. 538. From the Digest, 48, 19, 5: *Divus Traianus . . . rescripsit, satius enim esse impunitum relinqui,* etc.

[490] *De Laud.* c. 27.

[491] Sir Thomas Smith, writing in 1565, in his Commonwealth of England, Book II. c. 26, preserves a lively picture of the trial of a capital case in his time. After the inquest is full, "Then [the crier] saith aloud: 'If any can give evidence, or can say anything against the prisoner, let him come now, for he standeth upon his deliverance.' ... If they which be bound to give evidence come in, first is read the examination which the justice of the peace doth give in; then is heard, if he be there, the man robbed, what he can say, being first sworn to say the truth; and after, the constable and as many as were at the apprehension of the malefactor and so many as can say anything, being sworn. . . . The judge, after they be sworn, asketh first the party robbed if he know the prisoner, and biddeth him look upon him. He saith yea; the prisoner sometime saith nay. . . And so they stand awhile in altercation, then he telleth all that he can say; after him likewise all those who were at the apprehension of the prisoner, or who can give any indices or tokens, which we call, in our language, evidence, against the malefactor. When the judge hath heard them say enough, he asketh if they can say more. If they say no, then he turneth his speech to the inqnest, 'Good men,' saith he, . . . 'ye have heard'" [etc.] — giving the charge. Nothing, whatever, is said of any evidence *for* the accused. And so Staunford Pl Cr. lib. iii. c. 8 (1557): *A*

doner evidence, chescun seira admitte pur le Roy; saying nothing of any witnesses for the accused.

In Throckmorton's case, 1 How. St. Tr. 869, 884 (1554), the accused, on trial for treason, asked that one John Fitzwilliams should be "called to depose in this matter what he can." Then John Fitzwilliams drew to the bar and presented himself to depose his knowledge in the matter in open Court. *Attorney.* I pray you, my lords, suffer him not to be sworn, neither to speak.; we have nothing to do with him. *Throckmorton.* Why should he not be suffered to tell the truth? And why be ye not so well contented to hear truth for me as untruth against me? *Hare* [Master of the Rolls]. Who called you hither, Fitzwilliams, or commanded yon to speak? You are a very busy officer. *Throckmorton.* I called him, and do humbly desire that he may speak and be heard as well as Vaughan [a witness for the crown], or else I am not indifferently used; especially seeing Master Attorney doth so press this matter against me. *Southwell* [a Privy Councillor], Go your ways, Fitzwilliams, the Court hath nothing to do with you. Peradventure yon would not be so ready in a good cause. Then John Fitzwilliams departed the Court and was not suffered to speak." Thereupon Throckmorton sagaciously turned this rejection to account: "Since this gentleman's declarations may not be admitted, I trust you of the jury may perceive it was not for anything he had to say against me; but, contrariwise, that it was feared he would speak for me." Later on he appealed, unsuccessfully, to the judges again (887 — 888): "And notwithstanding the old error amongst yon which did not admit any witness to speak, or any other matter to be heard in the favor of the adversary, her Majesty being party, her Highness's pleasure was that whatsoever could be brought in the favor of the subject should be admitted to be heard. . . . *Bromley* [Chief-Justice]. Yon mistake the matter; the queen spake those words to Master Morgan, Chief-Justice of the Common Pleas; but you have no cause to complain, for you have been suffered to talk at your pleasure."

In Udall's case, in 1590 (1 How St. Tr. 1271,1281), in a trial for felony the defendant offered some witnesses, "'And further, if it please you, my lords, here are some witnesses that upon their oaths will testify how diversely he [Thompkins, a witness for the crown] hath reported of his confession to this thing, if it please your lordships to accept them.' And the witnesses offering themselves to be heard, were answered that because their witness was against the queen's majesty, they could not be heard." After conviction (1304), when brought up for sentence, being asked "Why did yon not plead these things to the jury?" he answered, "I did so; and offered to produce sufficient proof for it; but your lordships answered that no witnesses might be heard in my behalf, seeing it was against the queen; which seemeth strange to me, for methinks it should be for the queen to hear all things on both sides, especially when the life of any of her subjects is in question."

Coke, in his Third Institute, 79 (published in 1648; he died in 1633), recites and comments on the St. 31 Eliz. c. 4 (1589), making it felony for those in charge of the queen's armor, ordnance, etc., to "imbesile" it, but allowing the accused to make any lawful proofs that he can, by lawful witnesses or otherwise. He cites, also, and comments on the St. 4 James I. c. 1, s. 6 (1606), allowing to the accused in certain felonies, witnesses on oath "for the better information of the consciences of the jury and justices." And then Coke adds: "To say the truth, we never read in any act of Parliament, ancient author, book case, or record, that in criminal cases the party accused should not have witnesses sworn for him; and therefore there is not so much as *scintilla juris* against it." Of this statute of 1606, Blackstone says (Com. iv. 360): "The House of Commons were so sensible of this absurdity that in the bill for abolishing hostilities between England and Scotland when felonies committed by Englishmen in Scotland were ordered to be tried in one of the three northern counties, they insisted on a clause and carried it against the efforts of both the crown and the House of Lords, against the practice of the courts in England and the express law of Scotland, that in all such trials, for the better discovery of the truth, and the better information [as above], there shall be allowed unto the party so arraigned the benefit of such witnesses, only to be examined upon oath, that can be produced for his better clearing and justification as hereafter in this Act are permitted and allowed.'" I have changed Blackstone's quotation from the statute by making it exact.

The practice, however, in general, was the old one; and we may observe, in 1613 (The King v. Thomas, 2 Bulst. 147), that even Coke, as Chief-Justice, in reciting certain "slanders of the Jesuits against our common law," including the denial to the accused in capital cases of counsel, and witnesses upon oath, while counsel and witnesses upon oath were allowed for the king and against the accused, did not deny any of these things, but merely pat forward against them the duty of the judge, by the English practice, to take care of the prisoner's interests. This same defence he set up afterwards in his third Institute, in speaking of the matter of refusing the prisoner counsel in capital cases on a plea of not guilty: "The true reasons of the law in this case are, first, that the testimony and the proofs of the offence ought to be so clear and manifest, as there can be no defence to it; secondly, the court ought to be instead of counsel for the prisoner," etc. (p. 29). So again (p. 137), "the evidence to convince him should be so manifest, as it could not be contradicted." And on p. 210 he lays down "the rule of law. *Quod in criminalibus probationes debent essee luce clariores.*" These, words of Coke, as we shall see, were quoted by Scroggs, C. J., in 1679, as the reason for refusing to allow the defendant's witnesses to be sworn.

But for some reason the practice of the courts as regards witnesses softened; perhaps, owing to the public sentiment that had forced these provisions into the statute of 1606, and had driven the Chief-Justice, in 1613, to make apologies from the bench. At any rate, in 1632 — 3, before Coke's death (Tyndal's case, Cro. Car. 291), in a case of felony, "divers witnesses were produced by the defendant which were heard, without oath." And then follows this remark: "Bat some of them witnessing matter which the attorney-general [Noy] conceived would make for the king, were, upon the desire of the said attorney, sworn, and after ordered upon their said oaths to deliver their knowledge.

And so this became the practice, that in capital cases, witnesses might be heard for the accused, but not upon oath. We hear of witnesses for the accused, produced or proposed, in Strafford's impeachment for treason (3 How. St. Tr. 1428) in 1640; in Land's case, in 1643 (4 *ib.* 342); in Macguire's case, in 1645 (i'6. 667); in Love's case, in 1651 (5 *ib.* 136); in Vane's case, in 1662 (6 *ib.* 152); and in Turner's case, in 1664 *(ib.* 605, 613); but in none of these cases is there any discussion over their not being sworn. In 1679, however, (Whitebread's case,

need of the attaint in criminal cases; and the doctrine was ancient that one should not be twice put in jeopardy of life or limb for the same offence.

How then were juries kept in check in such cases? Probably the influence of the crown was sufficiently strong to prevent much injustice as against the prosecution. On the other side, the king could pardon,[492] and moreover the natural sympathy of the jury with accused persons, and the operation of humane maxims and sentiments, secured a tolerable fairness. And, no doubt, the judges disciplined the jury in one way or another. An early instance of this,

---

7 How. St. Tr. 311, 359), in a trial for high treason, one of the accused asked to have his witnesses sworn, it was refused by North, C. J., Com. Pl., and Scroggs, C. J., added: "In no capital case against the king can the witnesses for the prisoner be sworn; but I will say this to the jury, that [the reason] they are not sworn is because they cannot; but the jury is to take great heed of what they say, and to be governed by it according to the credibility of the person and the matter." Thereupon another of the accused cited the foregoing passage from 3 Coke's Inst. 79. *North, C. J.,* "We know that the constant usage and practice is so, and yon cannot produce any man, that in any capital case had his witnesses sworn against the king. *L. C. J. [Scroggs],* My Lord Coke says otherwise that the evidence should be BO plain that nothing could be answered to it; and therefore no evidence should be sworn against the king. *Gavan.* My lord, those are the words of my Lord Coke. *L. C. J. Scroggs.* Yon argue against the known practice of all ages. *L. C. J'. North.* There was never any man, in a capital case, sworn against the king." And so in Fitzharris's case, 8 How. St. Tr. 223, 373 (1681), for high treason'; and Oates's case, 10 it. 1280 (1685).

Sir Matthew Hale, who died on Christmas Day, 1676, had been Chief-Justice of England from 1671 to 1676. In his Pleas of the Crown, ii. 283, he says: "Regularly the evidence for the prisoner in cases capital is given without oath, though the reason thereof is not manifest; but [otherwise it is] in all cases not capital, though it be misprision of treason; neither is counsel allowed him to give evidence to the fact, nor in any case, unless matter of law doth arise."

But this whole matter was cured in 1695, as regards treason, by the St. 7 Win. III. c. 3, s. I. In 1701, by St. 1 Anne, c. 9,s. 3, in felony, also, witnesses for the accused were allowed to be sworn. But not until 1836 (St. 6 & 7 Win. IV. c. 114) was there statutory authority in England, for a full defence by counsel in cases of felony. "A long step in that direction was, however, made by the practice which grew up in the course of the eighteenth century to allow counsel to cross-examine witnesses in cases of felony — an indulgence which . . . was not allowed by the House of Lords to Lord Ferrers (in 1760), though his defence was insanity." Steph. Gen. View Cr. Law (2d ed.), 46. Stephen cites a case of rape in the reign of Edw. L (Y. B. 30 & 31 Edw. I. 529, 530; cf. p. xliv), where in refusing to allow counsel, to the prisoner, the general rule to that effect is announced. Rape was made a felony in 1285.

[492] Hale, Pl. Cr. ii. 309, 310.

in 1302, is found in Y. B. 30 & 31 Edw. I. 522. A man was indicted for homicide, and said that he had been previously acquitted of the same death; it was found by the rolls that it was as he said, and that he had the king's writ *de bono et malo.* It was adjudged that he should go quit, and that five of the [indicting] inquest should go to prison as "attainted," and that the sheriff should take their lands and chattels into the king's hands. Berewyk, J., goes on to make some remarks which appear to mean (the text seems corrupt) that while these men cannot be attainted (*i. e.,* convicted) by a jury of twenty-four, yet they are attainted out of their own mouths, for they were on the inquest which formerly acquitted this man of the death, and now on a jury which accuses him of it. It is added by the reporter that the justices were the harder on them because they could not suggest any one else as guilty. So, in 1329,[493] a jury was amerced for undervaluing the goods of a felon who fled.

When the criminal jury came to act on the evidence of witnesses, the punishing of them must often have seemed harsh and out of place. It could not last, but it was hard to give it up. In 1500, for refusing to convict on what was regarded by the court as sufficient evidence, the jury were imprisoned until they gave a bond to appear before the king and council, and were then fined eight pounds apiece. But Sir Richard Empson was afterwards punished for this.[494] The fining and imprisonment of jurors were authorized, in 1534, by the statute 26 H. VIII. c. 4, but only in a particular place, viz., in "Wales and the Marches thereof." Certain irregularities in those parts were recited, and these punishments were authorized in case of acquittal or giving "an untrue verdict against the king, contrary to good and pregnant evidence ministered to them by persons sworn before the justices," etc. Vaughan, in Bushel's case, draws the inference from this statute that this treatment would not be legal without it, or where it did not extend. But the Star Chamber accounted it legal enough for them. "In the reigns of H. VII., H. VIII., Queen Mary, and the beginning of Queen Elizabeth's reign," says Hudson in his Treatise on the Star Chamber (s. vii.), "there was scarce one term pretermitted but some grand inquest or jury was fined for

---

[493] Fitz. Cor. 287.
[494] Hardres, 98 — 9.

acquitting felons or murderers; in which case lay no attaint." In Throckmorton's case, in 1554,[495] when the jury acquitted the accused of treason, after his vigorous and shrewd defence of himself, "The Court, being dissatisfied with the verdict, committed the jury to prison. Four of them afterwards made their submission, and owned their offence... and were delivered;... but the other eight were detained... and on the 26th of October [the trial was on April 17] were brought before the Council in the Star Chamber. The Lords, extremely offended at their behavior," sentenced the foreman and another to pay £2,000 apiece within a fortnight, and the other six a thousand marks each, and all were sent back to prison. On December 12, five jurors were discharged on paying £220 apiece, and nine days later the rest, on paying £60 apiece.

We may see how the whole matter was regarded by a sagacious and well-informed statesman, only ten or eleven years after Throckmorton's case, in Smith's Commonwealth of England.[496] If, he says, a jury improperly find a man guilty, the judges moderate this by reprieving and recommending a pardon. "If, having pregnant evidence, nevertheless, the twelve do acquit the malefactor, which they will do sometime,... the prisoner escapeth, but the twelve not only rebuked by the judges, but also threatened of punishment.... But this threatening chanceth oftener than the execution thereof. Yet I have seen in my time, but not in the reign of the queen now,[497] that an inquest for pronouncing one not guilty of treason contrary to such evidence as was brought in, were not only imprisoned for a space, but an huge fine set upon their heads; ... another inquest for acquitting another, beside paying a fine of money, put to open ignomiy and shame. But these doings were even then by many accounted very violent, tyrannical, and contrary to the liberty and custom of the realm of England. Wherefore it cometh very seldom in use: yet so much at a time the inquest may be corrupted that the prince may have cause with justice to punish them, for they are men and subject to corruption and partiality as others be."

We are told of many precedents in the Court of Wards for punishing juries who refused to find as directed by the courts, and

---

[495] 1 How. St. Tr. 869; s. c. 1 Jardine's Crim. Trials, 62.

[496] Book iii. c. 1.

[497] He was writing in Elizabeth's seventh year. Throckmorton's trial was in Queen Mary's first year.

the reporter specifies five of them running from 1571 down to 1597, "this Easter term 39 Eliz."[498] In 1600,[499] in an appeal of death, the foreman and seven others of the jury were heavily fined; but there was here an element of real misconduct, besides going against the instructions of the court. In 1602,[500] for acquitting of murder, the jury were "committed and fined and bound to their good behavior," and the reporter does not omit to mention that Popham, Gawdy, and Fenner (the judges) *fuerunt valde irati.* In 1607[501] it is said, whether by the reporter or the Star Chamber is not quite clear, that, "when a jury hath acquitted a felon or traitor against manifest proof there they may be charged, in the Star Chamber, for their partiality in finding a manifest offender not guilty, *ne maleficia remanerent impunita."* In 1664,[502] six of a jury were fined for refusing "to find certain Quakers guilty according to their evidence." In 1665, in Wagstaffe's case, a famous one, in which the reporters differ about various details,[503] we learn from the judge himself [504] that the jury were fined for acquitting, against law and evidence, certain Quakers charged with being at an unlawful conventicle. Two were fined five marks apiece, and the other ten a hundred marks apiece. After failing to get relief at the hands of the Court of Exchequer and the King's Bench, the jurymen, says Sir Matthew Hale, "brought their *habeas corpus* in the court of Common Bench, and all the judges of England were assembled to consider of the legality of this fine and the imprisonment thereupon.... It was agreed by all the judges of England (one only dissenting) that this fine was not legally set upon the jury, for they are the judges of matters of fact, and although it was inserted in the fine that it was *contra directionem curiae in materia legis,* this mended not the matter, for it was impossible any matter of law could come in question till the matters of fact were settled, and stated, and agreed by the jury, and of such matters of fact they were the only competent judges."[505] The dissenting judge was

---

[498] Moore, 730, 731.

[499] Watts *v.* Braines. Cro. El. 778.

[500] Wharton's case, Yelverton, 243; s. c. Noy, 48.

[501] Floyd v. Barker, 12 Co. 23.

[502] Leach's case, T. Raymond, 98.

[503] Hardres, 409; s. c. 1 Sid. 272; 1 Keble, 938; T. Raym. 138; Hale P. C.il. 312, 313.

[504] J. Kelyng, Rep. 3d ed. 69.

[505] Hale, P. C. ii. 312. Hale's book is supposed to have been written in 1660 — 1676. It was not printed for sixty years after his death.

probably Kelyng. Had the judges met a little earlier there would have been another dissenter, *viz.,* Chief-Justice Hyde, who died on the the first of the same May wherein Wagstaffe was punished. What his views were may be seen in a civil case just before, on "Friday, April 14," [506] where in arranging for a new trial in a case where a verdict had been given contrary to evidence, he "ordered the sheriff should return a good jury in the new trial;" and the reporter adds, "Hyde, Chief-Justice, conceived jurors ought to be fined if they would go against the Hare [law?] and direction, take bit in mouth and go headstrong against the court; and said, that by the grace of God he would have it tried, seeing the attaint is now fruitless." The ardor of these expressions may be understood from what this same judge had done before, and the reception his action had met with. In a civil case he had fined the jurors five pounds apiece three years before, but the exchequer judges had refused to enforce the fine as being illegal, and "the greater part of the rest of the judges" had agreed with them.[507] The doctrine of a few years later, that wherever an attaint will lie upon a verdict it is illegal to fine or imprison, was referred to the case where Hyde had fined the jury: "All the judges have agreed upon a full conference at Serjeant's Inn in this case. And it was formerly so agreed by the then judges in a case where Justice Hyde, etc.,... that a jury is not finable for going against their evidence where an attaint lies... for it may be affirmed and found upon the attaint a true verdict."[508]

But in criminal cases, at any rate, fining was still kept up; although there was a difference in the power allowed to different courts.[509] In 1666[510] Kelyng, now Chief-Justice, fined a jury five pounds apiece for a verdict of manslaughter where he had directed them that it was murder; "but after, upon the petition of the jurors, I took down their fines to 40*s.* apiece, which they all paid." In 1667,[511] Kelyng fined eleven of the grand jury twenty pounds apiece for refusing to indict for murder, and the judges of the King's Bench held this good. The reporter makes the judges add, "And when the petty jury, contrary to directions of the court, will find a murder

---

[506] 1 Keble, 864.

[507] Hale, P. C. ii. 160, 311.

[508] Bushel's case, Vaughan, pp. 144 — 5.

[509] Hale, P. C. ii. 313.

[510] Kelyng, old ed. 50.

[511] King *v.* Windham, 2 Keble, 180.

manslaughter... yet the court will fine them. But, "adds the reporter," because they were gentlemen of repute in the country, the court spared the fine; yet in Parliament the Chief-Justice was fain to submit, being by Sir H. W[indham] accused."[512] Finally, at the Old Bailey, in 1670, the jurors who acquitted William Penn and William Mead on a charge of taking part in an unlawful assembly, etc., were fined and imprisoned. But on *habeas corpus* in the Common Pleas,[513] they were discharged, and Vaughan, C. J., pronounced that memorable opinion which soon ended, the fining of jurors for their verdicts, and vindicated their character as judges of fact. "A witness," he says, "swears to but what he hath heard or seen, generally or more largely to what hath fallen under his senses. But a juryman swears to what he can infer and conclude from the testimony of such witnesses by the act and force of his understanding to be the fact inquired after."[514] As regards the charge that the jury went against the instruction of the court in law, — a court, Vaughan says, does not charge a jury with matter of law in the abstract, but only upon the law as growing out of some supposition of fact. This matter of fact is for the jury; it is not for the judge, "having heard the evidence given in court (for he knows no other)," to order the jury to find the fact one way rather than the other; for if he could, "the jury is but a troublesome delay, great charge, and of no use." The judge cannot know all the evidence which the jury goes upon; they have much other than what is given in court. They are from the vicinage, because the law supposes them to be able to decide the case though no evidence at all were given in court on either side. They may, from their private knowledge, of which the judge knows nothing, have ground to discredit all that is given in evidence in court. They may

---

[512] For the proceedings in the House of Commons, see 6 How. St. Tr. 993. The House appears to have passed a resolution (after hearing the Chief-Justice in his own defence) condemning the fining or imprisoning of jurors *as* illegal. But a bill which was brought in, to the same effect, did not pass the House.

[513] Bushel's case, Vanghan, 135; 8. c. 6 How. St. Tr. 999; for Penn and Mead's case, see *ib.* 951. Vaughan's opinion, as it has come down to us, seems to be an unfinished draft. As to the jurisdiction of the Common Pleas in such cases, see Wood's case, 3 Wils. 172.

[514] "A verdict," says Lee, C. J., in 1738 (Smith d. Dormer v. Parkhurst, Andrews, 322), "is only a judgment given upon a comparison of proofs." That brings us into a modern atmosphere.

proceed upon a view.[515] "A man cannot see by another's eye, nor hear by another's ear; no more can a man conclude or infer the thing to be resolved by another's understanding or reasoning." It is absurd that a judge should fine a jury for going against their evidence, when he knows but part of it, "for the better and greater part of the evidence may be wholly unknown to him; and this may happen in most cases, and often doth, as in Granby and Short's case." [516]

(h) Two things stand out prominently in Vaughan's opinion in Bushel's case: 1. The jury are judges of evidence. 2. They act upon evidence of which the court knows nothing; and may rightfully decide a case without any evidence publicly given for or against either party. It was now two hundred years since Fortescue wrote his book and showed witnesses testifying in open court to the jury; and as we see, not yet has the jury lost its old character, as being in itself a body of witnesses; indeed, it is this character, and this fact that the judge cannot know the evidence upon which they go, that make one of the chief pillars upon which Vaughan's great judgment rests. This double character of the jury was no novelty. As we have seen, the jury had much evidence long before the parties could bring in their witnesses, and in so far as they acted on evidence they were always

---

[515] For the modern way of dealing with this matter of the view, see Tully *v.* Fitchburg R. R. Co., 134 Mass. 499, 503. As regards difficulties that some courts have felt in harmonizing the function of the court in setting aside verdicts, with that of the jury in acting upon a view and in dealing with the evidence of experts, see Topeka *v.* Martineau, 42 Kansas, 389 — 91; Hoffman *v.* R. R. Co., 143 Pa. 503; Parks *v.* Boston, 15 Pick. 209 — II, and. the excellent remarks of Shaw, C. J., in Davis *v.* Jenney, 1 Met. X22 — 3; Shoemaker *v.* V. S. 147 U. S. 282, 304, 305.

[516] Cro. El. 616 (1598). Bushel's case marks the end of the anachronism of punishing jurors for their verdicts *as* being against evidence. It should be said, however, that some reservations were made. Hale, P. C. ii. 310 — 314, St. Bar *v.* Williams, 3 Keble, 351 (1674). Although the attaint was not abolished until 1825, it was but a name. Yet Vaughan's successor. Sir Francis North, afterwards Lord Keeper, did not at all like this result. In that very interesting book, "The Life of the Lord Keeper Guilford," his brother, Roger North (i. p. 131), preserves a remark by the Lord Keeper that the doctrine "that juries cannot be fined for slighting evidence and directions [is] contrary to reason and the whole course of precedents." Roger North adds, "This was popular, and the law stands so settled. The matter is trust, whether the court or jury. The Court may abuse & trust in an undue punishment of jurymen, as in any other acts of justice; and on the other side, juries may abuse their trust. . . . The precedents run all for the trust on the side of the court; what reason to change it (which was changing the law) but popularity."

judges. This side of their function had been slowly growing, until now it was a great, conspicuous thing. But the old one had not gone; that also continued a leading part of their function. Yet it had begun to diminish, and by the end of another century it would be mainly gone.

(i) As things stood after Bushel's case, how should the jury be controlled? The attaint was obsolete, and fining and imprisonment were no longer possible. In no way could they be punished for giving verdicts against law or evidence. The courts found a remedy by a simple extension of their very ancient jurisdiction of granting new trials in case of misconduct. If a jury should accept food from one of the parties while they were out, or should take from him a paper not delivered to them in court, and should afterwards find for him, the court would refuse judgment, and grant a new *venire.* And so for other sorts of miscarriage.[517] Why not, then, if the jury should go plainly counter to law, or should give an irrational, absurd, or clearly false verdict, do the same thing? This was done. It was hazardous, for it was, in some cases, undertaking to revise the action of the jury in a region belonging peculiarly to them, and was going beyond anything that had formerly been done. Moreover, how should the court know that the jury's verdict was against evidence? And how should they know what the law was until they knew what the facts were, since the law, as applicable to the case, was inextricably bound up with some definite supposition of fact? Evidently the keen arguments of Vaughan's opinion were applicable also to the granting of new trials, for going against law and evidence. But, nevertheless, the step had been taken at least as early as the first half of the seventeenth century.

In order to make it effective it was necessary to accompany this practice by an endeavor to make the jury declare publicly their private knowledge about the cause. This effort prospered but slowly. The old function of the jury was too deeply ingrained to give way in any short time; the judges long contented themselves with advice, with laying it down as a moral duty that the jury should publicly declare what they knew. But while the

---

[517] In Lady Herbert *v.* Shaw, 11 Mod. 118, Holt, C. J., "cited a case in the time of Edward the Third, where a new trial was granted because a great lord concerned in the cause sat upon the bench at the trial"

jury's right to go upon their private knowledge was emphatically recognized in 1670, and continued to be allowed in the books well on into the next century, yet the enlarged practice of granting new trials, and the growth and development of it in the seventeenth and eighteenth centuries, was steadily transforming the old jury into the modern one; and at last it was possible for the judges to lay it down for law that a jury cannot give a verdict upon their private knowledge.[518]

(j) Let me now run over a few of the cases relating to the new way of controlling the jury, speaking first of civil cases, and then of criminal. The first reported case of the modern new trial is said (I suppose truly) to be that of Wood v. Gunston, in 1655, in the "Upper Bench."[519] The jury, in an action for calling a man a traitor, had given fifteen hundred pounds damages; a motion was made to set this aside *as* excessive, and give a trial. It was granted after full debate, — Glynne, C. J., saying, "If the court do believe that the jury gave a verdict against their direction they may grant a new trial." Although this is the first reported case of allowing a new trial for the modern reasons, perhaps it was not the first one decided. Holt, C. J., in 1699, in Argent v. Sir Marmaduke Darrell,[520] where a new trial was moved for in a trial at bar, on the ground that the verdict was against evidence, said: "The reason of granting new trials upon verdicts against evidence at the assizes is because they are subordinate trials appointed by the Statute West. II. c. 30.... And there have been new trials anciently, as appears from this, that it is a good challenge to the juror that he hath been a juror before in the same cause. But we must not make ourselves absolute judges of law and fact too; and there never was a new trial after a trial at bar, in

---

[518] "It remained," says Mr. Pike (Hist. Crime, ii. 368 — 9), "for Lord Ellenborough, in the year 1816, to lay clearly down the maxim, that a judge who should tell jurors to consider as evidence their own acquaintance with matters in dispute would misdirect them. The true qualification for a juror has thus become exactly the reverse of that which it was when juries were first instituted. In order to give an impartial verdict, he should enter the box altogether uninformed on the issue which he will have to decide." Perhaps the effect of this case, which I take to be R. v. Sutton, 4 M. & S. 532, *is* overstated here. But this, at least, is true, that the court here clearly assumes the truth of this doctrine. See 3 Harv. Law Rev. 300; McKinnon v. Bliss, 21 N. Y. 215; Chattanooga R. R. Co. v. Owen, 90 Ga. 265.

[519] Style, 466; s. c. 462.

[520] Salk. 648.

ejectment."[521] And Lord Mansfield, in the case of Bright *v.* Eynon,[522] in 1757, said: "It is not true 'that no new trials were granted before 1655;' as has been said from Style, 466. "He was referring, apparently, to the argument of Serjeant Maynard, in that case (Wood *v.* Gunston), who" said that after a verdict the partiality of the jury ought not to be questioned, nor is there any precedent for it in our books of the law." Lord Mansfield added: "The reason why this matter cannot be traced farther back is, 'that the old report books do not give any accounts of determinations made by the court upon motions.' "In support of what he says, Lord Mansfield relies on. the language of Glynne, C. J., in Wood *v.* Gunston: "It is frequent in our books for the court to take notice of miscarriages of juries and to grant new trials upon them." But we are dealing with an extension of this old practice. As regards the challenge of which Holt, C. J., speaks, it may indicate a new trial for ordinary' misconduct; or it may have been the challenge to jurors, in criminal cases, who had served on the grand jury.[523] We may assume, probably, that the new practice came about not long before Wood v. Gunston. In 1648, in Slade's case,[524] judgment had been stayed upon a verdict, on a certificate from the judge presiding at the trial, who certified that "the verdict passed against his opinion." A motion was now made for judgment; but "Hales, of counsel with the defendant, prayed that this judgment might be arrested, and that there might be a new trial, for that it hath been done heretofore in like cases."[525] Rolle, J., "It ought not to be stayed, though it have been done in the Common Pleas, for it was too arbitrary for them to do it, and you may have your attaint against the jury, and there is no other remedy in law for you, but it were good to advise the party to suffer a new trial for better satisfaction." We may take it, then, that in the early part of the seventeenth century the practice of revising and setting aside the verdicts of juries, as being contrary to the evidence, was first introduced, or, at any rate, clearly recognized and established.[526]

---

[521] But as to this also the law developed. R. *v.* Bewdley, 3 P. Williams, 207 (1712); Smith d. Dormer *v.* Parkhurst, Andrews, 315 (1738).

[522] 1 Burr. 390.

[523] *Supra,* p. 82.

[524] Style, 138.

[525] Hales is probably Sir M. Hale, who was occasionally so called, and was then a leading barrister.

[526]526 A very interesting fact should be noted here, that the common-law courts were probably stirred up to granting new trials not only by the

obsolescence of attaints and the need of controlling juries which resulted from that, but by the abolition of the Star Chamber, and the interference of Courts of Equity. The Star Chamber had long punished jurors for false verdicts. "Not so few as forty juries have been punished in this court for perjury in their verdicts within fifty years," says Hudson, speaking early in the seventeenth century (Treatise on the Star Chamber, Coil. Jurid. 115). Compare *supra*, p. 139. The Star Chamber was abolished in 1640 (St. 16 Car. 1, c. 10), about five years after Hudson's death. In Martyn v. Jackson (1674), on the motion to set aside a verdict on the parol affirmation of Hale, C. J., that it was against evidence, Twisden, J., and Wilde, J., refused a new trial Rainsford, C. J., was for it: "Juries are wilful enough, and denying a new trial here will but send parties into the Chancery." 3 Keble, 398. See 1 Spence, Eq. Jur. Ch. 700. A little later than this case of 1674, in a trial at Guildhall, the counsel agreed upon a special verdict, and drew up the notes for it. "Thereupon the Chief-Justice told the jury that, it being matter in law, it was by the counsel on both sides left to the determination of the court. The foreman of the jury . . . told the Chief-Justice that the court nor counsel should not make any verdict for them, — they, as an English jury, would make their own verdicts themselves; and, thereupon, gave a general verdict for the defendant. But there being a bill in Chancery depending about this matter, and an injunction moved for, after this verdict, the Lord Chancellor Finch declared that he had formerly so great an opinion of London juries that if his whole estate lay at stake, he would willingly try it by a London jury. But, says he, they have so misbehaved themselves in this cause that I had rather see my house on fire than hear of such another verdict. And therefore he granted a perpetual injunction." 2 Lilly's Abr. (ed. 1745) 798. Lord Nottingham had been "the Lord Chancellor Pinch" from 1675 to 1681. A new trial was granted in 1712, after like behavior of a jury in a trial at bar. R. v. Bewdley, 3 P. Williams, 207. Compare the strong language of Holt, C. J., in granting a new trial, in Ash v. Ash (Comb. 357).

For the older law of attaints, reviews, and new trials in our American colonies, especially in Massachusetts, see a learned note by Horace (Mr. Justice) Gray, Quincy's Rep. 558 — 560, 565, 567; 6 Dane's Ab. c. 189; Angier a. Jackson, Quincy, 84 (1763), 9 Pick. 569 — 571; Miller v. Baker, 20 Pick. 285, 288 — 290. In Massachusetts, in May, 1672, a law was passed in regard to the verdicts of juries in civil cases, providing that in general they should be accepted by the courts, "unless, upon apparent corruption or error in the jury giving in their verdict contrary to law or evidence, the party cast shall in open court attaint the jury," and give bond with surety to prosecute the jury in an action of attaint in the Court of Assistants. In that case, the action shall be tried by a jury of twenty-four, and if "manifest error and mistake" be found, the party complaining is to be repaid "his full damage from the other party to the original suit." If bribery, conspiracy, or other corruption be found in the jury attainted, they are to be punished by fine or imprisonment; but, if the former jury be "acquitted," they are to have double costs from the accusing party, and their verdict is to stand good. Rec. of Mass. iv. Part 2, 508. Twelve years later, on September 11, 1684, a stringent and effectual restraining statute was passed, which, after reciting that this provision for attaints is attended with various mischiefs, provides that the attainting party shall state in writing "for what cause, and show how the same doth appear so to be;" and if the former verdict be confirmed that he shall pay "to

Now, as I have said, in order to enforce effectually the granting of new trials on the new grounds, it was important that the jury should disclose publicly what they knew, so that the court could tell whether they really did go against evidence or not. The courts acted accordingly. In 1598,[527] we see it recognized that a juryman may communicate to his associates privately any oral or written, information that he has, if not induced thereto by either of the parties. But in 1650, in Bennett v. Hartford,[528] it was laid down that a juror ought to state publicly in court on oath any such information, and not to give it in private to his companions. In 1656,[529] a barrister, being returned of the jury, and "having been at a trial of the same cause about twenty years past, in the exchequer, and heard there great evidence," asked whether he ought to inform the rest of the jury privately of this, or conceal it, or declare it in open court. The court ordered him to make public declaration of it. He did so, and upon merely his juryman's oath. Half a century later, in 1702,[530] the same duty is reported to have been laid down in general terms for the whole jury: "If a jury give a verdict on their own knowledge, they ought to tell the court so, that they may be sworn as witnesses. And the fair way is to tell the court before they are sworn that they have evidence to give." And so our modern doctrine grew up.[531]

As regards criminal cases, the doctrine of new trials had to pay regard to the pleasure and interests of the crown, on the one side,

---

the country" a fine of ten pounds, and also pay forty shillings to each of the attainted jurymen. And, further, if corruption were charged against the first jury, they shall have an action for slander, jointly or severally, against the attainting party, and he shall be further fined, *as* the court thinks meet, and shall pay double costs to the other party and double interest on the former verdict. Rec. of Mass. v. 449. This statute suddenly checked attaints, and it may, perhaps, have put an end to them. Immediately before, the records show many cases. Afterwards three cases are recorded, in the following March, and, about a year later, one case. In examining the records of the Court of Assistants for several years after this. I saw no other case.

[527] Graves v. Short, Cro. El. 616. Compare Vanghan, 135, 149.

[528] Style, 233; s. c. *semble,* Style's Reg. (2d ed.), 176.

[529] Duke v. Ventris, a trial at bar, Trials per Pais. c. 12 (8th ed. p. 258).

[530] Powys v. Gould, 7 Mod. I; s. c. Anonymous, 1 Salk. 405; Holt, 404.

[531] *Supra,* p. 170, n. The giving of testimony by the jury, although not common, is now well recognized. I am tempted to mention a recent case in New York, reported to me by a friend. In the United States Circuit Court, in the City of New York, in 1892, in a criminal case, one of the jurymen who understood French, was sworn to act as interpreter, and served in the double capacity through the whole trial. *Ex relatione* Lloyd McKim Garrison, Esq., of the New York bar.

and, on the other, to considerations of mercy for the accused, and especially to the ancient maxim that saved a man from being put a second time in jeopardy of life or limb. And so that extension of the scope of new trials which went on during the seventeenth century had only a partial operation in criminal cases. As regards a new trial after acquittal, "It was never yet known," said Chief-Justice Pratt, in 1724,[532] "that a verdict was set aside by which the defendant was acquitted, in any case whatsoever, upon a criminal prosecution." And as to a new trial upon a conviction, it has been said that the case of "Simons, the Jew," in 1752, for perjury, was the first one in which a new trial had been allowed "to any person who had been convicted of a criminal offence."[533]

Both of these statements must be qualified. In 1660,[534] "two cases were cited, wherein new trials had been granted on the king's behalf." These cases, indeed, were disposed of by Twisden, J., as having been "in the late troublesome times, and by the party's assent;" and in the principal case, one of acquittal on an indictment for perjury, it was held, that no new trial could be had on the king's behalf. But Wyndham, J., a lawyer of great experience and a very able judge, "held it grantable, it not being touching life." The doctrine of the last case was held in later cases, in 1661 and 1663.[535] In one of these,[536] on an application for a new trial, after an acquittal of perjury, Wyndham, Justice, dissenting, said that a new trial might be granted in perjury; "the books are only to the point that a man's life shall not be twice in jeopardy for one fault; but in this case the punishment does not reach to life." But the view of the majority (Hyde, C. J., Kelyng, and Twisden, J.), as stated in a MSS. of Kelyng, was that "no [new] trial ought to be where the party was once acquitted for any crime that concerns life or member, or which would make the party infamous;" and the reasons are given that "on a new trial his adversary would see where he failed and might use ill means to prove what he failed in before; and that upon search no

---

[532] The King. *v.* Jones, 8 Mod. 201, 208. And so in 1691 in R. *v.* Paris, 1 Shower, 336, "a new trial was denied, for that the court said there could be no precedent shown for it in case of acquittal."

[533] 19 How. St. Tr. 692, n.

[534] The King *v.* Read, 1 Lev. 9.

[535] Ib. Also r. v. Bowden, 1 Keble, 124. The King *v.* Jackson, 1 Lev. 124.

[536] The King v. Fenwick and Holt, 1 Sid. 153 (1663); s. c. 21 Viner's Abr. 478.

precedent was found that ever any new trial was granted in such case," except the two above-mentioned.[537]

On the other hand, as to the case of one who had been convicted, — in 1663, in a case growing out of the same transaction as that in the King v. Fenwick,[538] viz.: in a criminal information against Sir John Jackson, for subornation of perjury,[539] a new trial was refused, for one who had been found guilty. This was followed in repeated cases, and it was declared that "there can be no trial *de novo* for or against the king." [540]

But this was not a permanent state of things. Cases of great hardship appeared, and in a few years the course changed. In 1671,[541] on an application for a new trial, after a conviction on an information for perjury, the court of King's Bench was evenly divided, Twisden and Rainsford still adhering to their former views, while Sir M. Hale, the new Chief-Justice, and Moreton, "conceived that after a conviction a new trial may he had on such circumstances," — viz., of surprise. In this case, however, it was found that the allegation of surprise was untrue. But two years later,[542] after a conviction on an indictment of perjury, a new trial was granted and precedents were found for it: "Though upon Sir John Jackson's case it were held that no new trial can be after acquittal, yet, *per curiam,* in cases of conviction a new trial may be; and so was Turner's case, who after conviction of barratry had a new trial and was acquitted, and so was Primate's case, Abbot's man. And *per curiam* a new trial was granted." [543] Hereafter this doctrine was followed; and so, in 1681,[544] on a like application, we read that, "On precedents cited by Dolben, Justice, that in the time of Lord Hale [Chief-Justice from 1671 to 1676] a verdict against one Jackson, of Worcestershire, for perjury in a case of simony,[545] but given against the evidence was set aside, and other precedents shown to the same purpose, — by the whole court this verdict against Smith

---

[537] 21 Viner's Abr. 478, 5, margin. Compare s. c. 1 Keble, 546.

[538] Supra, p. 175.

[539] Primate v. Jackson, 1 Keble, 538, 638, 639.

[540] The King v. Lewin, 2 Keble, 396; The King v. Marchant, *ib.* 403 (both in 1668). See *supra,* p. 163.

[541] The King v. Hannis, 2 Keble, 765.

[542] R. v. Latham, 3 Keble, 143.

[543] And so again in 1675, in R. v. Cornelius, 3 Keble, 525.

[544] R. v. Smith, T. Jones, 163; s. c. 2 Shower, 165.

[545] Probably the King v. Hannis, *supra.*

was set aside likewise, with consent of the Lord Pemberton. [lately become Chief-Justice] who at first doubted as a thing unusual. And a new trial was awarded."

It was only after these doubts and vicissitudes that the practice in criminal cases came to be settled in its existing shape. It became possible at length for Hawkins, in 1721,[546] to say: "It is settled that the court cannot set aside a verdict which acquits a defendant of a prosecution properly criminal, as it seems that they may a verdict that convicts him, for having been given contrary to evidence and the directions of the judge, or any verdict whatever for a mistrial." [547] "As to acquittals, the practice of the courts," said the court (Lord Coleridge, C. J.), in 1881, in Queen v. Duncan,[548] "has been settled for centuries, and is that in all cases of a criminal kind where a prisoner or defendant is in danger of imprisonment no new trial will be granted if the prisoner or defendant, having stood in that danger, has been acquitted."

Even after a conviction, the English practice allowed no new trial in capital cases. A single case to the contrary, Queen v. Scaife,[549] in 1851, was explained away in the Privy Council, in K. v. Bertrand,[550] and was never followed in England. In the last-named case, from New South Wales, Sir John T. Coleridge for the court said: "The course of the general argument for the respondent was of this sort: It seemed not to be very seriously denied that, except for the precedent of The Queen v. Scaife the court below, in making absolute the rule for a new trial, had introduced a new practice; but it was said that this was in analogy with the whole proceeding of our courts of justice in regard to new trials; that as to these, as in many other instances, a wholesome improvement in our law had been made and established; that this improvement had been made in the exercise of a wise discretion, and perhaps inherent powers, for the advancement of justice; that new trials had commenced in civil matters, and advanced in them gradually, and upon consideration,

---

[546] P. C. ii. c. 47, s. 11 (1st ed.).

[547] In a mistrial, the theory is that the accused has not been put in jeopardy; Arundel's case, 6 Coke 14 b, in 1596, where one was found guilty of murder, but judgment was arrested and a new *venire* awarded, on account of a mistrial, — the first jury being of a wrong venue.

[548] 7 Q. B. D. 198.

[549] 17 Q. B. D. 238.

[550] L. R. 1 P. C. 520 (1867).

from one class of cases to another; that thence they had passed to criminal proceedings, first where the substance was civil, though the form was criminal, and thence to misdemeanors, such as perjury, bribery, and the like, where both form and substance were criminal. Hitherto it was admitted that they had, except in the instance of The Queen *v.* Scaife, stopped short of felonies, but that the principle in all was the same; and that, where there was the same reason, the same course ought to be permitted. There may be much of truth in this historical account; and if their lordships were to pursue it into details, it might not be difficult to show how irregular the course has been, and what anomalies, and even imperfections perhaps, still remain. But they need not do this; it is enough to say they cannot accept the conclusion: what long usage has gradually established, however first introduced, becomes law; and no court, nor any more this committee, has jurisdiction to alter it."

In this country, after a conviction, new trials are generally allowed in all criminal cases. After an acquittal, they are not allowed; but even here there are exceptions, as in Connecticut.[551]

We have now traced the attaint to its end, and have brought out its modern substitute. During the last two or three centuries many interesting things have grown out of the changes in the jury.

The statutes of the sixteenth and seventeenth centuries, requiring two witnesses in certain cases, or sometimes one witness, were a limitation upon the power of the jury; before, they need have no witnesses at all.[552]

---

[551] State *v.* Lee, 65 Conn. 265, in 1894. For a carious provision in Iowa by which, in case of acquittal, questions of law may be carried up by the State, but without any power in the court to reverse the action of the lower court, see McClain's Annot. Code of Iowa, s. 5924, Wambaugh, Study of Cases, 2d ed. s. 63. The game thing was, in fact, done in Com. *v.* Steimling, 156 Pa. 400 (1893), a singular case, for which I am indebted to my colleague, Professor Beale. See Quincy's Rep. 558, 559, 565, for matter relating to our colonial period.

[552] For the statutes relating to treason, see Foster, Disc. of High Treason, c. iii. s. 8. In 1623, a statute was passed (St. 21 Jac. I. c. 27) punishing with death "as in case of murder," the mothers of bastard children concealing the (leath of the children, unless "by one witness at least," it were proved that the child were born dead. Hale (P. C. ii. 289) tells us that "I have always taken it to be a proof by one witness," if one who had seen the child testified to circumstances, such as having no hair or nails, which made it probable that the child was born dead, — a humane construction which regarded sufficiently the main purposes of the statute. It should be added that this statute was aimed at the same mischief as a similar French one of 1556, in the reign of Henry II., imposing death unless the

The process of laying down rules of presumption and fixing upon evidence a *prima facie* or conclusive quality, — always an incident of judicature, — was yet immensely stimulated by the jury. A legislative illustration of this is seen in the "Statute of Stabbing," [553] in 1603, fixing upon certain acts the quality of malice aforethought, "although it cannot be proved;" a law made, as the judges declared in 1666, in Lord Morley's case,[554] "to prevent the inconveniences of juries, who were apt to believe that to be a provocation to extenuate a murder which in law is not."

There is reason to surmise that a leading motive in the enactment of that comprehensive, but strange and very un-English piece of legislation, the Statute of Frauds, was found in the uncertainty that hung over everything at a period when the law of proof was so unsettled. It will be remembered that it was then a very critical time; that the attaint as an operative thing had vanished, while the law of new trials was in its infancy, and the rules of our present law of evidence bat little developed.[555]

But the greatest and most remarkable offshoot of the jury was that body of excluding rules which chiefly constitute the English "Law of Evidence." If we imagine what would have happened if the petit jury had kept up the older methods of procedure, as the grand jury in criminal cases did, and does at the present day,[556] — if, instead of hearing witnesses publicly, under the eye of the judge, it had heard them privately and without any judicial supervision, it is easy to see that our law of evidence never would have taken shape; we should still be summing it all up, as Henry Finch did at the beginning of the seventeenth century,[557]

---

woman should have declared her state and called in witnesses (*tesmoignage suffisant*) of the events in question. This requirement was the usual and familiar one of the early periods of our own law. See, for example, Bracton, 147, as to the required complaint in case of tape.

[553] *St.* 1 Jac. I.c. 8.

[554] Kelyng (old ed.) 55.

[555] See Harv. Law Rev. iv. 91. I am inclined to the conjecture that like reasons helped to the enacting of "An Act for Determining Differences by Arbitration," St. 9 Wm. III. c. 15 (1698).

[556] Two centuries ago the grand jury came near losing its ancient methods. In Shaftesbury's case, 8 How. St. Tr. 759 ('November, 1681), they were, in fact, compelled to receive their evidence publicly in court. But the vigorous protests of the jury and the fruitless outcome of the attempt led to an abandonment of it.

[557] *Nomotechnia,* 61 *b* (1613).

*L'evidence al jurie est quecunque chose que serve le partie a
prover l'issue pur luy.* This it is, — this judicial oversight and
control of the process of introducing evidence to the jury, that
gave our system birth; and he who would understand it must keep
this fact constantly in mind.

In closing this long story of the development of the jury,
one or two remarks present themselves. Perhaps the reader may
have found himself wondering that the enlightened ideas of proof
which prevailed in Rome should not have survived, in some
sufficient degree to have saved the men of the Middle Ages from
repeating all over again the ancient experience of Rome in its days
of barbarism, la such cases we have to remind ourselves not only
of the astonishing persistence of national habits, but also of the
fact that human experience is incommunicable when men. and
nations are not prepared to learn from it. Civilization is not a
matter of particular centuries, — the later ones; but of a particular
stage of human development. It is as Dr. Arnold said: "The largest
part of that history which we commonly call ancient is practically
modern, as it describes society in a stage analogous to that in
which it now is, while on the other hand most of what is called
modern history is practically ancient, as it relates to a state of
things which has passed away." [558]

And again, if the reader, in running over these chapters,
has wondered that the movement was so slow, that men should lie
enslaved to forms and habits so long after the meaning had left
them, that they should fail to make some obvious, slightly-new
application of principles already grasped, and should wait for
centuries before this is done, we may reflect that this same thing
appears all through human history. Perhaps it will be otherwise as
the superior and elect minds of our race come to find an audience
among the men of their own day — a thing more and more
happening as swift means of communication make all men.
neighbors. But, meantime, we are helped, to understand this
fumbling and wandering of the human mind, in the region which
we have been considering, and the strange lingering, just out of
reach, of conceptions and modes of proof which seem to us the
only possible ones, by noticing what has happened elsewhere. Of
the art of printing Palgrave has said: "The most remarkable point

---

[558] Thucydides, i. Appendix I.

in the history,of this art, which has been destined, to change the moral aspect of the globe, is not its so-called discovery by Gutenberg or Koster, but the great length of time which elapsed before it was put in use by the nations of western Christendom."[559] This bit of human history, then, which we have been studying, is simply of a piece with all the rest.

---

[559] Thucydides, i. Appendix I.

PART II

CHAPTER V
LAW AND FACT IN JURY TRIALS

In tracing the long history of the jury and the way in which it has come to be a body of judges, we have remarked the necessity of separating law from fact, and have seen how great a part this requirement has played in shaping our whole legal system.

Sometimes the discrimination between law and fact in its relation to jury trials is identified, in legal discussions, with the distinction between what matter is for the court and what for the jury. When that happens attention is drawn at once to an important hint, namely, that the inquiry relates only to the issue, — to the law and fact which are complicated in the ultimate proposition in dispute. It is only with the issue that juries have any necessary concern; as regards everything else, no question need arise as to what is for the jury and what for the court. But beyond this suggestion we have got no real help, in attempting to fix the meaning of law and fact, from this identification. To be told that law is for the court and fact for the jury, to hear again the familiar Latin that *ad guaestionem facti non respondent judices, ad quaestionem juris non respondent juratores,* enlightens us not at all as to the true discrimination between fact and law. How then shall we arrive at the right distinction?

I. In trying to answer that question let us ask what exigency it was that called for juries, inquests, and assizes. Why were they created? The answer to this question is intimated when we read their oath, and the old precept to the sheriff for summoning them. He was to summon those "who best can and will" *veritatem dicere.* The jurors in the assize of novel disseisin swore, one after another, as Bracton gives it in his Latin,[560] *"Hoc auditis, justitiarii, quod veritatem dicam... de tenemento de quo visum feci;"* and their verdict was this promised *veritatis dictum.* They were wanted, in a pending legal controversy, where the parties were at issue on some question of fact, to say what the fact was, and the phrase for this matter of fact

---

[560] Fol. 185.

was *"rei veritas."*[561] The truth of the thing about what? About all sorts of questions. Was a party in possession of something? Did he disseise somebody? Had he put his seal to a paper? Did he enfeoff another of land? and what land? What was the *consuetudo,* the custom, of such a place? Was a person legitimate, a *nativus,* an idiot, or insane? These are the same questions that juries pass on to-day, having in them the same elements of opinion and of law, compounded with those simpler features which catch the eye and ear; questions of "fact," as we say.[562]

Now although juries had only to do with an *issue* of fact, yet questions of fact, in any exact sense, were by no means limited to the issue. The courts settled a great many questions of fact for themselves; they could not take a step without passing upon such questions. Was the deed that was put forward in pleading "rased" or not? If a party claimed, the right to defend himself as a maimed person, was it really mayhem? Was a person who presented himself and claimed to be a minor, really under age? A stream of questions as to the reality, the *rei veritas,* the fact, of what was alleged before the justices was constantly pouring in. A prisoner, for example, had confessed; on being brought into court, he declared that it was by duress of his jailer. Was this so? To find this out the justice took the short cut of sending for several of the fellow-prisoners and the jailer, and questioning them all in the prisoner's presence; and he found that it was not true.[563] This, again, is just as it is to-day. Courts pass upon a vast number of questions of fact that do not get on the record, or form any part of the issue. Courts existed before juries; juries came in to perform only their own special office; and the courts have always continued. to retain a multitude of functions which they exercised before ever juries were heard of, in ascertaining whether disputed things be true. In other words, there is not, and never was, any such thing in jury trials as an allotting of all questions of fact to

---

[561] Very early instances of the use of the term *rei veritas,* for our word "fact," may be seen in Brunner, Schw. 88, 95, and 109, and Bigelow, PI. A.N. 114, 200,208, 211,258.

[562] Doubtless the old customary law knew little of our distinction of law and fact. Brunner, Schw. 47 — 48, 395. The finding of the old *consuetudines* may be likened to ascertaining the *factum* of a statute in modern times. See Brunner, Schw. 385, P. & M. Hist. Eng. Law, i. 81.

[563] Y. B. 30 & 31 Edw. I. 543 (circa A. D. 1300). *"Ecce,"* says the justice, *"socii vestri in prisona testificantur coram vobis. . . . Vis tu aliud aliquid dicere?"*

the jury. The jury simply decides some questions of fact. The maxim *ad quaestionem facti non respondent judices, ad quaestionem juris non respondent juratores,* was never true, if taken absolutely.[564] It was a favorite saying of Coke, in discussing special verdicts; and in Isaack *v.* Clark[565] he attributes it to Bracton; but that appears to be an error; a careful search for it in Bracton has failed to discover it. It seems likely that this formula took shape in England in the sixteenth century.[566] But the maxim was never meant to be taken absolutely.

---

[564] This *"decantatum,"* as Vaughan called it, in his famous opinion in Bushell's case (Vaughan, 135), appears in a variety of forma; a common one is that in the text. Bulstrode (ii. 204 and 305) makes Coke say *jurisperitus* (and so Rolle, i. 132), and *jurisprudentes,* instead of *judices.*

[565] Rolle, i. p. 132; s. C. 2 Bulst. p. 314 (1613 — 14).

[566] Biener, Eng. Geschw. i. ch. 2, s. 25; ch. 5, g. 40. Best, Ev. s. 82, note, seems to be in error when he understands Bonnier, *Preuves,* 5th ed., i. s. 119, to say that the maxim "has been long known on the Continent." Bonnier, in discussing the question whether the judge is bound by the answers of experts, does indeed refer to "le vieil adage mal à propos reproduit per certains auteurs modernes, *ad quaestionem facti respondent juratores, ad quaestionem juris respondent judices;"* but this writer spoke as one familiar with the phrases of English legal literature. The absence of any reference to the maxim in other continental authors to whom I have had any reference or access, leads me to think that Bonnier was merely quoting *le vieil adage* from our law. Coke seems to have spawned Latin maxims freely. Is this also his? and so his reference to Bracton merely to an authority for the doctrine, and not the phrase? In those days of polyglot law it was easy for a man to slip back and forth between his English, and his Latin and law French. *"Come Bracton est"* is the expression that Rolle puts into his month. Bulstrode merely has it, "As Bracton."

It has been suggested, inasmuch as Bulstrode makes Coke, after giving the Latin maxim, say: "as Bracton, commentaries in Amy Townsend'a case, fol. iii.," that Bracton may be a misprint for "Plowden," whose reports, after the usual fashion of that period, he cites as "commentaries." But this does not help matters. While it is true that in the case of Amy Townsend counsel deal with the subject, and point out the different duties of court and jury, yet neither in Plowden's original French nor in the English translation, is any maxim given, whether Latin or other. Bulstrode's punctuation is nothing; it is always meaningless. Moreover, if we could dispose of Bulstrode's report in the way suggested, it would still leave unexplained the come *Bracton est* of Rolle's report. Amy Townsend's case was argued in 1553, in the first year of Mary. Buller, J., in the Dean of St. Asaph's case, 21 How. St. Tr. 947 (1783), in charging the jury, after having cited a case at the end of the seventeenth century, says, "If one goes still farther back, we find it settled as a principle which admits of no dispute, and laid down so early as the reign of Queen Elizabeth as a maxim, that ad *quaestionem facti respondent juratores, ad quaestionem juris respondent judices.* And in ... Bushell's case the same maxim is recognized negatively, namely, *ad quaestionem facti non respondent judices,"* etc. Buller gives no more definite reference to his authority

As I said, it is limited to questions with which the jury has to do; it relates only to issues of fact, and not to the incidental questions that spring up before the parties are at issue, and before the trial; and so of many of those which present themselves during the trial. The maxim has nothing to do with matters of evidence, but only with a limited class of questions of fact; namely, questions raised by the pleadings, questions of ultimate fact.[567]

If, then, we limit the inquiry to the issue, in what sense and how far is the maxim true? It is true, *(a)* As stating the great, general rule that the regular common-law mode of trying questions of fact is by jury. For example, it is accurately said by Coke:[568] "The most usual trial of matters of fact is by twelve such men; for *ad quaestionem facti non respondent judices;* and matters in law the judges ought to decide and discuss; for *ad quaestionem juris non respondent juratores.*" *(b)* In a sense that is intended to emphasize the limitations of the jury, to say that it is *only* fact which they are to decide. *"Non est juratoribus judicare"* was the judgment of the court in 1554, when an inquest of office had found a conclusion of law;[569] or as the counsel expressed it in another report of the case:[570] "The office of twelve men is... not to adjudge what the law is; for that is the office of the court, and not of the jury." (c) In a sense which emphasizes the right of the jury in all cases to limit themselves to their own province, of fact, and to leave with the

---

in Elizabeth's time, so that this does not carry us back of Coke's reports, in which the maxim frequently occurs, *e. g.,* in Priddle and Napper's case, 11 Co. 8b, 10b (1612), in Edward Altham's case, 8 Co. 148,155 (1610), the Abbot of Strata Mercella's case, 9 Co. 24, 25 (1590 — 1), and Dowman's case, 16. 7 b, 13 (1586). It should, be remarked of Coke's reports that although the maxim is sometimes found, as in the last-named case, in the course of a statement of a judge's opinion, that is no clear indication that these are the judge's words. Coke's method of reporting thickly interlards the statement of both court and counsel with his own discursive talk. A comparison, for example, of his report of Dowman's case with what other reporters give, tends to confirm the opinion that it is Coke who is talking when he gives this maxim, and so that lie remains still our earliest authority for it.

[567] Bartlett *v.* Smith, 11 M. & W. 483; Bennison *v.* Jewison, 12 Jurist, 485; s. c. 1 Ames, Bills and Notes, 512.

[568] Co. Lit. 155 b.

[569] Dyer (ed. 1601), 106b; and see Hill *v.* Hanks, 2 Bulst. p. 204 (1614); Isaack v. Clark, ib. p. 314 (1614 — 15); King v. Poole, Cas. t. Hardwicke, p. 28 (1734).

[570] Plowden, p. 114.

judges the determination of the law applicable to the facts thus returned; their right to give a special verdict. And so, "It was resolved by Sir Ed. Andersen, chief justice, and all the justices of the bench, that the special verdict was well founded; they held that in all pleas... and upon all issues joined,... the jury may find the special matter... [and] pray the opinion of the court... by the common law, which has ordained that matters in fact shall be tried by jurors, and matters in law by the judges; and as *ad quaestionem,"* etc.[571]

It is true that Coke had a way of generalizing the matter and quoting the maxim as if it represented a limitation upon the judges as wide and full and exact as that upon the jury.[572] But although it

---

[571] Dowman's Case, 9 Co. pp. 12 — 13 (1586).

[572] And accordingly he sometimes gets quoted in this country for a doctrine that would have much amazed him or any other English judge, from the beginning down; namely, for the notion that the court, at common law, has no right to indicate to the jury its own views of the facts. See, for example, the dissenting opinion of Daniel, J., in Mitchell v. Harmony, 13 Howard, 115, 141 — 148. This doctrine has widely found expression in the statutes of our States. "In 1796 the North Carolina legislature amended the common-law rule by prohibiting judges from expressing an opinion on the facts." Walter Clark, in 4 Green Bag, 457, 472, who quotes the excellent adverse comments on this practice, by Ruffin, J., in State *v.* Moses, 2 Dev. 452. In Massachusetts this change was introduced in 1860 (Gen. St. c. 115, s. 5), in the form that "The courts shall not charge juries with respect to matters of fact, but may state the testimony and the law." It is not too much to gay of any period, in all English history, that it is impossible to conceive of trial by jury as existing there in a form which would withhold from the jury the assistance of the court in dealing with the facts. Trial by jury, in such a form as that, is not trial by jury in any historic sense of the words. It is not the venerated institution which attracted the praise of Blackstone and of our ancestors, but something novel, modern, and much less to be respected.

In the Federal courts the common-law doctrine on this subject has always held. "In the courts of the United States, as in those of England, from which our practice was derived, the judge, in submitting a case to the jury, may, at his discretion, whenever he thinks it necessary to assist them in arriving at a just conclusion, comment on the evidence, call their attention to parts of it which he thinks important, and express his opinion upon the facts. . . . The power of the courts of the United States in this respect is not controlled by the statutes of the State forbidding judges to express any opinion upon the facts." Gray, J., for the court, in Vicksburg, etc. R. R. Co. *v.* Putnam, 118 U. S. 545, 553 (1886). And so McLanahan *v.* Ins. Co., 1 Pet. 170, 182 (1828), and Simmons *v. V.* S., 142 U. S. 148, 155 (1891). In U. S. *v.* Phil. and Reading R.R.Co., 123 U. S. 113, 114 (1887), the court said: "Trial by jury in the courts of the United States is a trial presided over by a judge, with authority, not only to rule upon objections to evidence, and to instruct the jury upon the law, but also, when in his judgment the due administration of justice requires it, to aid the jury by explaining and

became thus a loose rhetorical flourish and ornament of his pedantic speech, we must not be misled by that. Its true significance may still be drawn out thus: In general, issues of fact, and only issues of fact, are to be tried by a jury. When they are so tried, the jury, and not the court, are to find the facts; and the court and not the jury is to give the rule of law. The jury are not to refer the evidence to the judge and ask his judgment upon that, but are to find the facts which the evidence tends to establish, and may only ask the court for its judgment upon these. That this determination by the jury involves a process of reasoning, of judgment and inference, makes no difference; for it is the office of jurors "to *adjudge upon their evidence* concerning matter of fact, and thereupon, to give their verdict; and not to leave matter of evidence to the court to adjudge, which does not belong to them."[573]

II. Having now a general conception of the scope and meaning of the old maxim, let us come closer to our questions, and try to find some definition of "fact," and to reach a clear legal discrimination between fact and law.

To define fact is, indeed, a *"perylous chose,"* as they say in the Year Books; and some persons think it unnecessary.[574] It is certainly true that the term is widely used in the courts, much as it is used in popular speech, — that is to say, in a tentative, literary, inexact way. But as our law develops it becomes more and more

---

commenting upon the testimony, and even giving them his opinion upon questions of fact, provided only he submits those questions to their determination."

[573] Littleton's Case (1612), cited in 10 Co., p. 56 b. "A verdict is only a judgment given upon a comparison of proofs," said Lee, C. J., in Smith d. Dormer v. Parkhurst, Andrews, 315, 332 (1738). And Lord Bacon, in his Life of Henry VII. *(supra,* 151, n. 6), characterized verdicts as *Judicia juratorum, quae veredicta vocantur.*

[574] For instance, as to definitions in general, a very able writer in the Solicitors' Journal (vol. 20, 869) says: "A definition is the most difficult of all things. There is far greater probability of a correct use of terms than of a correct definition of them. The best definition, therefore, is that by use. A correct use renders definition unnecessary, because the law will speak plainly without it. And where it is unnecessary to define, it is also dangerous, because an incorrect definition will confound the correct use," etc. That is a true utterance of the inherited instinct of English-speaking lawyers and judges. But it is quite certain that as our law grows it must be subjected more and more to the scrutiny of the legal scholar, and that it will profit by any serious and competent effort to clarify and restate it.

important to give definiteness to its phraseology; discriminations multiply, new situations and complications of fact arise, and the old outfit of ideas, discriminations, and phrases has to be carefully revised. Law is not so unlike all other subjects of human contemplation that clearness of thought will not help us powerfully in grasping it. If terms in common legal use are used exactly, it is well to know it; if they are used inexactly, it is well to know that, and to remark just how they are used.

1. "Fact" and its other forms, *factum, fait,* stand in our law books for various things, *e. g.,* (a) for *an act;* just as the word "fact" does in our older general literature. "Surely," says Sir Thomas Browne,[575] "that religion which excuseth the fact of Noah, in the aged surprisal of six hundred years," etc., and so Bracton:[576] "Since he is not the agent of the one who made him essoiner, it is not for him to prove another's status or another's act" *(factum). (b)* For that completed and operative transaction which is brought about by sealing and executing a certain sort of writing; and so for the instrument itself, the deed *(factum).* (c) As designating what exists, in contrast with what should, rightfully, exist, — *de facto as* contrasted with *de jure.* "The whole condition of things in the insurgent States was matter of fact, rather than matter of law," said the Chief Justice of the United States in 1868.[577] *(d)* And so, generally, as indicating things, events, actions, conditions, as happening, existing, really taking place. This last is the notion that concerns us now. It is what Locke expresses[578] when he speaks of "some particular existence, or, as it is usually termed, matter of fact." The fundamental conception is that of a thing as existing, or being true. It is not limited to what is tangible, or visible, or in any way the object of sense; things invisible, mere thoughts, intentions, fancies of the mind, when conceived of as existing or being true, are conceived of as facts. The question of whether a thing be a fact or not, is the question of whether it is, whether it exists, whether it be true. All

---

[575] *Pseudodoxia Epidemica,* Book v. ch. xxiii. s. 16; on the Vulgar Error that "It is good to be drunk once a month." So in St. 33 H. VIII. c. 21, s. l, — "Have detested her for this fact." And so Governor Bradford in his "History of Plymouth Colony," in speaking of the first execution in the colony, that of John Billington, for murder: "His fact was that he . . . shot him with a gun." Page 180; (ed. 1898) 330.

[576] Fol. 337.

[577] Thorington *v.* Smith, 8 Wall. 1, 13.

[578] Human Understanding, Bk. iv. c. 16, s. 5.

inquiries into the truth, the reality, the actuality of things, are inquiries into the fact about them. Nothing is a question of fact which is not a question of the existence, reality, truth of something; of the *rei veritas.*[579]

But this, it may be said, is a portentous sort of definition; it is turning every question into a question of fact. That is true, so far as any question asks about the existence, the reality, the truth of something. But, obviously, in actual legal use the term has other limitations. As regards the present discussion, we have noticed that "fact" is confined to that sort of fact, ultimate fact, which appears in the pleadings and is the subject of the issue. Moreover, even in the issue, that kind of fact which we call "law" is discriminated, and set apart under its own name.

---

[579] Bentham, who is not very instructive here, defines thus: "By a fact is meant the existence of a portion of matter, inanimate or animate, either in a state of motion or in a state of rest." But he divides facts into physical and psychological; events and states of things; positive and negative; adding that "the only really existing facts are positive facts. A negative fact is the non-existence of a positive one, and nothing more." (Works, vi. 217 — 218.) And so Best, Ev. ss. 12, 13. Holland (Jurisprudence, 8th ed. 92) simply says: "'Facts' (*Thatsachen, Faits*), which have been inadequately defined as 'transient causes of sensation,' are either 'Events' or 'Acts.'" Sir Wm. Markby (Law Mag. and Review, 4th Series, ii. at p. 312), in a neat and valuable discussion of "Law and Fact," after remarking that he would rather not pledge himself to any final definition of what a fact is, adopts for his immediate purpose Stephen's definition in the first two editions of his Digest of Evidence, art. 1 namely, "'Fact' means everything capable of being perceived by the senses, every mental condition of which any person is conscious." But Stephen afterwards withdrew this definition. He had been keenly criticised by a writer in the Solicitors' Journal (vol. xx. 869, 870; Sept. 9,1876), who said, "The proper subject of affirmation and negation is not 'facts,' but propositions;" and, among other valuable remarks, inquired how it was with such matters as negligence, custom, ownership, the defamatory quality of a writing, and the qualities of persons and things generally. "The phraseology," he added, "is really applicable only to the rudest form of jurisprudence." The writer himself thought that no definition is necessary. These criticisms took effect; in his third edition, and all later ones, Stephen dropped any attempt at definition, and substituted in art. 1, this: "'Fact' includes the fact that any mental condition of which any person is conscious exists;" and in his preface to the third edition, after saying that he "had been led to modify the definition of fact by an acute remark made on this subject in the Solicitors' Journal," he added that "The real object of the definition was to show that I used the word 'fact' so as to include states of mind." See the learned consideration whether a thing be *quid facti or quid juris,* in Menochins, *De Praesumptionibus,* Lib. 1, qu. 11. See definitions of fact as contrasted with opinion, in Sir George Cornewall Lewis's "Influence of Authority in Matters of Opinion."

2. What, then, do we mean by "law"? We mean, at all events, a rule or standard which it is the duty of a judicial tribunal to apply and enforce. It is not my present purpose to discuss the nature or origin of law.[580] How the rule or standard comes into existence, where it is found, just what the nature of it is, how far it is the command of a supreme political power, and how far the silently-followed habit of the community, — these and other like questions there is no occasion to consider now. It is enough, here, to say, that in the sense now under consideration, nothing is law that is not a rule or standard which it is the duty of judicial tribunals to apply and enforce. I do not need to consider whether all general standards that courts apply are to be called law; that matter I pass by;[581] it is enough for our present purpose to say, that unless there be a question as to a rule or standard which it is the duty of a judicial tribunal to apply, there is no question of law. The inquiry whether there be any such rule or standard, the determination of the exact meaning and scope of it, the definition of its terms, and the settlement of incidental questions, such as the conformity of it, in the mode of its enactment, with the requirements of a written constitution, are all naturally and justly classed together and allotted to the same tribunal; and these are called questions of law.[582]

III. We must discriminate further. Besides questions of fact and law, there are questions of which Austin has remarked[583] that they are questions neither of law nor of fact, — questions of reasoning, of the application of law to fact, questions of method, of procedure. "It is the office of jurors to adjudge upon their evidence;" so the court is reported to have said in Littleton's case.[584] That

---

[580] See James C. Carter's "The Ideal and the Actual in Law," Reports of the American Bat Association, vol. xiii 217; Holmes, Common Law, 35 — 38,150 — 1, and "The Path of the Law," 10 Harv. L. Rev. 457; Markby, Elements of Law, c. 1, ss. 1 — 31; Holland, Elements of Jurisprudence ec. ii. — vi. inclusive; Austin, Jurisp. (London, Murray, 1873) i. 103 — 106; Maine's Ancient Law, cc. 1 and 2; Christian's note to 1 Bl. Com. 74; Lord Esher, M. R., in Cochrane v. Moore, 25 Q. B. D. 57; E. R. Thayer, "Judicial Legislation," 5 Harv. L. Bev. 172.

[581] Markby, *ubi supra.* If a jury cannot, in point of reason, find a verdict, they cannot as a matter of law; and such questions go up on exceptions. Denny v. Williams, 5 Alien, 1; Lane v. Moore, 151 Mass. 87, 91.

[582] See *infra,* 257.

[583] Jurisp. i. 236 (ed. 1873); *infra,* 251.

[584] Supra, 189.

remark brings out a fundamental point, so obvious as hardly to need stating; namely, that it is no test of a question of fact that it should be ascertainable without reasoning and the use of the "adjudging" faculty; much must be conceived of as fact which is invisible to the senses, and ascertainable only in this way. Of course, by the judges this function of reasoning has constantly been exercised; the sentence just quoted makes it apparent that it must also be discharged by juries. We are not, then, to suppose that a jury has found all the facts merely because it has found all that is needed as a basis for the operation of the reasoning faculty; the right inference or conclusion, in point of fact, is itself matter of fact, and to be ascertained by the jury. As regards reasoning, the judges have no exclusive office; the jury also must perform it at every step.[585]

There comes up for consideration, then, this matter of reasoning: a thing which intervenes, *e. g.,* in questions of negligence and the like, between the primary facts, what may be called the raw material of the case, and the secondary or ultimate facts; just as it intervenes, in the court's questions of the interpretation of statutes and other writings, between the bare words of the document and the ascertainment of its legal meaning.[586] It would be straining our word "procedure" beyond due limits to say that reasoning is part of the procedure, for reasoning is essential everywhere in the law; yet one may get a useful hint by regarding it, for a moment, in that light. As the procedure, and method of trial, are to be discriminated from both law and fact, which make up the subject-matter that is to be dealt with in these ways and methods, — so we may separate from law and fact the process by which conclusions are reached; namely, the process of reasoning. As both court and jury must take notice

---

[585] "It is not because facts are admitted that it is therefore for the judge to say what the decision upon them should be. If the facts which are admitted are capable of two equally possible views, which reasonable people may take, and one of them is more consistent with the case for one party than for the other, it is the duty of the judge to let the jury decide between such conflicting views." Bowen, L. J., in Davey *v.* London & S. W. Ry. Co., 2 Q. B. D. 70, 76 (1883). In citing this passage with approval, Williams, J., in Pearce *v.* Lansdowne, 69 L. T. Rep. 316 (1893), said: "I do not believe that because the facts are admitted the functions of the jury as to drawing inferences from them are altered at all."

[586] *As* in determining what was covered by the word "place," in a statute forbidding betting in any "house, office, room, or other place;" a matter which was the subject of elaborate discussion by six judges, and of dissent, in Powell *v.* Kempton Park Co. [1897], 2 Q. B. 242.

without proof, of much that is assumed as known to all men, and especially to all who are concerned in judicial inquiries, so each must conduct the familiar, if unobserved, processes of reasoning in accomplishing the ends of its own department. It is true that the jury was not brought into existence because the court needed help in the mere business of reasoning, but simply to report upon the fact, the *rei veritas;* reasoning, however, founded upon general and particular experience, was unavoidable. Courts might always have done their own reasoning, after a fashion, if they had been in possession of a full supply of primary fact; but they were not; and when once juries were called in, at no period of their history could they discharge their special function of ascertaining and reporting facts, without going through a process of reasoning. "While the juror's oath," said Bracton,[587] "has in it three associated things *(comites),* truth, justice, and judgment, it is truth that is to be found in the juror, *justitia etjudicium* in the judge. But sometimes judgment seems to belong to jurors, since they are to say on their oath, yet according to their belief, whether so and so disseised so and so, or not." And again,[588] "If the jurors state the fact as it is *(factum narraverint sicut veritas se habuerit),* and afterwards judge the fact according to their statement of it, and err, they make a mistaken judgment rather than a false one, since they go upon a belief that such a judgment follows such a fact."

Bracton uses the expression "they judge the fact." We can observe the real nature of this operation by looking at the case of expert witnesses to fact. What is their function? It is just this, of judging facts and interpreting them. They are called in because, being men of skill, they can interpret phenomena which other men cannot, or cannot safely, interpret. They "judge" the phenomena, the appearances or facts which are presented to them, and testify to that which in truth these signify or really are; they estimate qualities and values. We say that they testify to opinion. In truth, they are "judging" something, and testifying to their conclusion upon a matter of fact. It is perfectly well settled, in our law, and, as it would seem, elsewhere,[589] that such opinions or judgments are merely those

---

[587] Fol. 186 b.

[588] Fol. 290 b.

[589] "It is not true, as is so generally claimed, . . . that on the Continent the opinion of the expert is binding on the court. ... I do not find it to be the case by law, anywhere, that the opinion of the expert may encroach on the functions of the court, whatever the result attained, due to placing the expert in a more

of a witness; they are simply to aid the final judges of fact, and not to bind them. The last judgment is still for the jury, or other judge of fact;[590] that judgment is not one of law. In Germany, this discrimination is clearly expressed: "Experts judge only of the relation of phenomena perceived by the senses to general rules of their art or science; but not at all of the relation of a fact to legal rules *(Rechtswahrheiten);* that is merely the judge's affair.... In contrast with his judgment, what the expert decides is simply a fact; it is no more nor less than a mere witness's declaration; and this fact, like every other, the judge has to refer to the appropriate rule of law. For this reason experts are called *judices facti, — judices* as opposed to ordinary witnesses, *judices facti,* because they do not judge as to the law, but their judgment or opinion only gives as its result a fact."[591]

We have thus noticed a *tertium quid,* the process of reasoning, which we have set aside as relating to processes and methods in arriving at law or fact. Another thing was brought to notice in the passage from Littleton's case and is constantly presenting itself, namely, "matter of evidence." The jury, it was there said, "are not [by a special verdict] to leave matter of evidence to the court to adjudge;" they are themselves "to adjudge upon that evidence concerning matter of fact."

Now, "matter of evidence" is here discriminated from "matter of fact." Of course it is not to be classed with "matter of law," and although properly designated, in ordinary cases, as "matter of fact," it is not matter of fact in the sense which is specially involved in the present discussion. What, then, is it? It is something incidental, subsidiary, belonging where the matter of reasoning belongs. Indeed, it is only the material and basis for reasoning. When

---

responsible and trustworthy position, may be. Ober-meyer's book teaches this doctrine throughout, and all the codes I have seen, or seen quoted, so provide. For instance, Art. 323 of the [Frencli] Code *de proc.: Les juyes ne saint astreints a suivre l'avis des experts, si leur conviction s'y oppose. . . .* See also Art. 377 of the Code of the German empire." — Clemens Herschel, *Experts in Judicial Inquiries.* Boston, Alfred Madge, Printer, 1886.

[590] Head v. Hargrave, 105 U. S. 45; Olsen v. Gjertsen, 42 Minn. 407 (1890); and so in France; Bonnier, *Preuves,* 5th ed. *s.* 119.

[591] Dr. W. H. Puchta in *Zeitschrift fur Civilrecht und Prozess,* iii. 57. Compare *Das Archiv. fur die Civilistische Praxis,* xxvi. 255 — 6. For these and some other German references I am indebted to my friend, Mr. Fletcher Ladd. See also Bonnier, *Preuves, ubi supra.* There was formerly a maxim *Periti potius judices sunt quam testes.* — Herschel, *ubi supra.*

it is said that fact is for the jury, the fact intended, as we have seen, is that which is in issue, the ultimate fact, that to which the law directly annexes consequences, that thing which, in a special verdict, the jury must plainly find, and not leave to the court to find. Issues are not taken upon evidential matter. Of evidence, the same thing is to be said which we have already said of the reasoning that is founded upon it; namely, that it is for both court and jury, according as either has occasion to resort to it.

I have spoken of evidence and reasoning as belonging to the region which dealt with the processes and methods of arriving at the law and fact that are involved in an issue. In expressing this, it has been said, with what may seem a certain violence of phrase, that they belong with procedure. It will be useful to indicate here, a little more plainly, just what is meant by this. Procedure deals with the machinery by which legal controversies are settled. Reasoning, as we have already seen,[592] the rational method of settling disputed questions is the modern substitute for certain formal and mechanical "trials," or tests, which flourished among our ancestors for centuries, and in the midst of which the trial by jury emerged. When two men to-day settle which is the "best man" by a prize-fight, we get an accurate notion of the old Germanic "trial." "Who is it that" tries "the question? The men themselves. There are referees and rules of the game, but no determination of the dispute on grounds of reason, — by the rational method. So it was with "trial by battle" in our old law; the issue of right, in a writ of right, including all elements of law and fact, was "tried" by this physical struggle; and the judges of the Common Pleas sat, like the referee at a prize-fight, simply to administer the procedure, the rules of the game. So of the King's Bench in criminal appeals; and so Richard II. at the "trial" of the appeal of treason between Bolingbroke and Norfolk, as Shakespeare represents it in the play. So of the various ordeals; the accused party "tried" his own case by undergoing the given requirement as to hot iron, or water, or the crumb. So of the oath; the question, as regards both law and fact, was "tried" merely by the oath, with or without fellow-swearers. The old "trial by witnesses" was a testing of the question, in like manner, by their mere oath. So a record was said to "try" itself. And so, when out of the midst of these methods first came the trial by jury, it was the jury's oath, or rather their verdict, that "tried" the case. But now, when we use the phrases "trial" and "trial by jury," we mean a rational ascertainment of facts, and a rational ascertaining and application of rules. What was formerly "tried" by the method of force or the mechanical following of form, is now "tried" by the method of reason.

At an earlier page[593] we have seen that in the older days the word "law," *lex,* sometimes indicated a form of procedure; not law, in our sense of substantive law, but a mode of trial. This comes out clearly in an exposition of the phrases *lex et consuetudo* in the old custumal of Normandy, where we read: *"Consuetudines* are customs, followed from ancient times, allowed by rulers and kept up by the people, determining whose anything is or where it belongs. But *Leges* are what is instituted by rulers and kept up by the people in the country, for settling particular controversies. *Leges* are a sort of legal instrument for declaring the truth of controversies. Usages *(Usus)* relate to the *leges;* for *usus* are the ways in which we use the *leges.* To illustrate: the *consuetudo* is, that a widow has the third part of the fief that her husband possessed at the time of the marriage. But if a controversy arises as to whether he did then possess the fief in which she claims dower, it is to be settled *per legem inquisitionis,* and the like. And the *usus* are the ways in which such a *lex* is to be performed, namely, by twelve persons, under oath, worthy of credit, who have inspected the fief."

Readers of Sir Henry Maine's books will recall the emphasis which he puts upon procedure in early systems of law. The Salic law, he tells us, "deals with thefts and assaults, with cattle, with swine, and with bees, and, above all, with the solemn and intricate procedure which every man must follow who would punish a wrong or enforce a right." And again: "So great is the ascendency of the Law of Actions in the infancy of courts of justice, that substantive law has at first the look of being gradually secreted in the interstices of procedure; and the early lawyer can only see the law through the envelope of its technical forms." [594] Our inherited system, as we have already seen,[595] kept in existence until a period within living memory a phrase which comes straight down from those early days. Until the year 1833[596] certain cases in England could be tried *per*

---

[593] *Supra,* 28.
[594] Early Law and Custom, 168, 389.
[595] *Supra, c.* i.
[596] Stat. 3 & 4 Wm. IV. c. 42, s. 13, *supra,* p. 34.

legem; a man waged his law *(vadiare legem),* i. e., gave pledges for performing it; and afterwards performed his law *(facere legem).* In the old Germanic law there were many of these *leges,* or modes of trial. Trial by battle was the *lex ultrata;* by the ordeal, the *lex apparens, manifesto,* or *paribilis;* by the single oath, the *lex simplex;* by the oath with compurgators, the *lex probabilis,* or the *lex disraisinae;* by record, the *lex recordationis;* by inquest, or the assize, *lex inquisitionis* and *recognitionis.*[597] Our phrase "law of the land" comes down out of the midst of all this. "A man," says Glanville, "may make his villein free, so far as his relations to himself or his own heirs are concerned. But if the villein should be brought into court against a stranger *ad diracionationem faciendam... vel ad aliquem legem terre faciendam,"* etc. "By *lex terrae* is meant," says Brunner,[598] "the procedure of the old popular law." This old use and conception of *lex* is to be explained by what Sir Henry Maine has said at the end of his "Early Law," from which I have already quoted. All the primitive codes "seem to begin with judicature, and to distribute substantive law into 'heads of dispute.' " "The authority of the Court of Justice overshadowed all other ideas and considerations in the minds of those early code-makers." "It must have been a man of legal genius who first discerned that law might be thought of and set forth, apart from the Courts of Justice which administered it, on the one hand, and apart from the classes of persons to whom they administered it, on the other."

Turning back, now, from these old conceptions to our own, we may observe again that while, of course, there are rules

---

[597] On this subject see Brunner, Schw. pp. 168 *et seq.;* Spelman, Gloss. *sub voc. Lex;* Ducange, *ib.*

[598] Schw. 254, 325, 180. Selden's notes to Fortescue, *De Laud.* c. 26. In the *Dialogus de Scaccario,* ii. 7 (1176 — 1177), the writer says that by *judicia,* he means *leges candentis ferri vel aquae.* Glanvill, xiv. c. 1, says the accused person is to clear himself *per del judicium, scilicet per callidum ferrum vel per aquam. Ib. c.* 2, as regards the hiding of treasure trove, *ob infamiam autem non solet, juxta legem terre, aliquis per legem apparentem se purgare,* etc. In 2 *Rot. Cur. Reg.* 173 (1199 — 1200) one defendant is adjudged to defend himself by the judgment of fire and another by the duel. Of the first it is said, *vadiavit legem.* Of the second, *vadiavit duellum.* And then both are called *leges,* — a day is given them for making *leges suas.* Bracton, 410, in speaking of compurgation, says, *Formantur autem verba legis secundum formam recordi, sicut in omnibus aliis legibus faciendis observat* etc.

and laws of procedure, and while, of course, these are to be ascertained by the judges, they are not what is meant (still less' is meant a mode of trial) when we contrast the law and fact that are blended in the issue. There the conception of law is purely that of the substantive law which is applicable to the "facts," namely, the ultimate facts that are in question, — of the legal consequences and implications that are bound up with these facts.

And we may also remark again that equally the topics of evidence and of reasoning, dealing, as they do, with the processes and methods of our modern "trials," and being, as they are, a part of the machinery and procedure by which these trials reach their ends, belong one side of our subject.

IV. We have now made our definitions and principal discriminations.[599] But, as I said at the outset, the allotment to the jury of matters of fact, even in the strict sense of fact which is in issue, is not exact. The judges have always answered a multitude of questions of ultimate fact, of fact which forms part of the issue. It is true that this is often disguised by calling them questions of law. In the elaborate and carefully prepared codification of the criminal law, which has long been pending in the British Parliament, we are told, of "attempts to commit offences," that "the question whether an act done or omitted with intent to commit an offence is or is not only preparation... and too remote to constitute an attempt... is a question of law."[600] In a valuable letter of Chief Justice Cockburn, addressed to the Attorney-General, and commenting on the Draft Code,[601] he justly criticised this passage: "To this I must strenuously object. The question is essentially one of fact, and ought not, because it may be one which it may be better to leave to the judge to decide than to submit it to a jury, to be, by a fiction, converted into a question of law.... The right mode of dealing with a question of fact which it is thought desirable to withdraw from the jury is to say that it shall, though a question

---

[599] As regards what are called mixed questions of law and fact, see *infra*, 225,251.

[600] Report of Criminal Code Bill Commission (1879), Draft Code, s. 74.

[601] Dated Jane 12, 1879, and printed by order of the House of Commons.

of fact, be determined by the judge." The same sort of thing which is thus objected to is extremely common in judicial language here.[602]

Among questions of fact which are commonly treated in this way a conspicuous illustration is found in the construction of writings. It is not uncommon to call the interpretation and construction of writings "a pure question of law." [603] That it is a question for the judge there is no doubt. But when we consider to what an extent the process of interpretation is that of ascertaining the intention of the writer, — his expressed intention, — irrespective *of* any rules of law whatever, and when we come to undertake the details of such an inquiry, it is obvious that most of this matter is not referable to law but to fact. The judge has to ascertain the usual meaning of words in the vernacular language, and what modifications of that meaning are allowable as a mere matter of the fair use of language; also, the fair meaning or the permissible meaning of the composition of these words, — how far one part relates to and modifies another, and how far the general sense of the whole controls, displaces, or supersedes the more common effect of any particular words and phrases. Such questions are addressed to the trained faculties of an educated man, acquainted with the use and the rules of language, and with the sort of business to which the writing relates, and may be settled merely by a critical reading of the paper. Moreover "the meaning of words varies according to the circumstances of and concerning which they are used."[604] When once these circumstances are known, *i. e.,* all the extrinsic facts which may legally affect the interpretation, then the courts exercise the right to determine the bearing of these facts on the words of the writing, and the combined effect of words and facts as touching the

---

[602] As when we are told: "I apprehend that whether an instrument of writing be under seal or not, is a question of law, to be solved by the court from the inspection of the instrument itself." — Kennedy, J., for the court, in Duncan *v.* Duncan, 1 Watts, 322, 325.

[603] Hamilton v. Ins. Co., 135 U. S. 242, 255. Just as it is sometimes said of another well-known question, "What facts and circumstances amount to probable cause is a pure question of law." Stone *v.* Crocker, 24 Pick. 84. In Lyle *v.* Richards, L. B. 1 H. L. 222, 241, Lord Westbury said: "It is no doubt true that the construction of written instruments is matter of law, and that when a written instrument is laid before jurymen they are bound to receive the interpretation of the effect of that instrument from the judge."

[604] Blackburn, J., in Allgood *v.* Blake, L. B. 8 Ex. 160.

expression of intention. This may not involve any question of law in the exact sense, for the answer may depend on no legal rule, but only on the rules, principles, or usages of language and grammar, as applied by sense and experience. So far, then, as the meaning of a document is to be determined merely by reading it in the light of ascertained facts, attending the making of it, we are presented with no question of law, in any strict sense of the word; it is a question for the court, but not a question of law.

But of course the construction of writings has always to take account of whatever rules of law may be applicable to the subject; and always there is a question to be determined by the courts, how far any such rules of law exist in the particular instance; such as the important rules which limit the process to the text alone, as illustrated by the circumstances to which, either in terms or tacitly, it refers; and which determine when and how far extrinsic matter may be used in aid of interpretation. There are also many specific legal rules, presumptive or absolute, for the interpretation of particular words or phrases. So that, of course, the mere grammatical process of interpretation has to be carried on, shaped, and restrained, in conformity with these rules of law, whatever they may be. And sometimes these legal rules, technical and strict, exclude all search after the actual intention of the writer; for although, in some instances where only the interests of the writers are concerned, this intention may well be a decisive consideration, in other writings, designed to affect the rights of third persons, and successive generations of them, it may not be permissible to allow the strict and technical meaning of the terms to be varied by any reference to what the writer really meant.

The subject, however, is too large and intricate for anything more than a passing reference at this point. [605] Any general statements about writings must be subject to deductions, for there is a great diversity of them. There are "records," judicial and legislative, such as statutes, judgments, pleadings, — the proving, use, and application of which were the subject of legal rules before juries were born. These rules largely hold their place to-day, for reasons of sense and convenience. There are written texts of law, questions about which (some of them at least, those of the domestic forum) belong to the judges. There are deeds, charters, and wills,

---

[605] See *infra,* c. x.

operative instruments, which are the subjects of specific legal rules as to their constitution, form, and phraseology. There is negotiable paper, of which the like is true. There are the ordinary contracts in writing, or written memoranda, required by law. There are writings not required by law, but made by choice of the parties to be a memorial of a transaction. And there are other writings of a merely casual nature, like ordinary correspondence. Many writings used to be regarded as in themselves constituting, or rather furnishing by the mere inspection of them, a mode of "trial" for what they reported; as records did. If such a writing were once authenticated, it closed inquiry. On the other hand such writings, even records and statutes, might be merely evidential; as when a deed, in a question of prescription, went to the jury as evidence of the fact of ancient possession, and not to show the date of its beginning.[606] But, whatever their character, and however used, the construction of writings, when once the facts necessary for fixing it have been ascertained, whether properly to be called a matter of fact or of law, was a matter for the courts and not for the jury.[607] This has always been so. Writings came into general use and got into the courts, mainly through the Roman ecclesiastics,[608] and it was natural that the Roman methods of dealing with them should be adopted; and, once

---

[606] Y. B. 34 H. VI. fol. 30, pl. 7 (1456); s. c. Thayer's Cas. Evid. 210.

[607] Parke, B., in Hutchinson v. Bowker, 5 M. & W. 535, 542, "The law I take to be this, — that it is the duty of the court to construe all written Instruments; if there are peculiar expressions used in it, which have in particular places or trades a known meaning attached to them, it is for the jury to say what the meaning of these expressions was, bat for the court to decide what the meaning of the contract was." And again the same accurate judge stated the matter in Neilson v. Harford, 8 M. & W. 806, 823, "The construction of all written instruments belongs to the court alone, whose duty it is to construe all such instruments, as soon as the true meaning of the words in which they are couched, and the surrounding circumstances, if any, have been ascertained as facts by the jury; and it is the duty of the jury to take the construction from the court, either absolutely, if there be no words to be construed as words of art, or phrases used in commerce, and no surrounding circumstances to be ascertained; or conditionally, when those words and circumstances are necessarily referred to them. Unless this were so, there would be no certainty in the law; for a misconstruction by the court is the proper subject by means of a bill of exceptions, of redress in a court of error; but a misconstruction by the jury cannot be set right at all effectually." And so see Key v. Cotesworth, 7 Ex. 595; Brown v. McGran, 14 Peters, 479,493; Smith v. Faulkner, 12 Gray, 251, 254; Graham v. Sadlier, 165 111. 95.

[608] Anglo-Saxon Law, 230.

adopted, that they should not be changed when new modes of trial, such as the trial by jury, came in. Often the jury could not read.[609] It may be added that an established judicial usage like this has always been powerfully supported by considerations of good sense and expediency. Of a great part of the writings brought under judicial consideration, it is true that they were made, as Bracton says, to eke out the shortness of human life, *"ad perpetuam memoriam, propter brevem hominum vitam."* Such things, so important to a short-lived race of creatures, so long enduring, should have a fixed meaning; should not be subject to varying interpretations; should be construed by whatever tribunal is most permanent, best instructed, most likely to adhere to precedents.

On this and similar grounds of policy, and especially, and more and more so as time went on, for fear the jury should decide some question of law that was complicated with the fact, many other questions of fact have been retained by the judges, either studiously and by design, or as a more or less accidental result of practice. Whether there is malice in cases of homicide, and what is sufficient "cooling-time" where there was provocation;[610] and, in actions for malicious prosecution, whether the cause for instituting the prosecution is "reasonable and probable,"[611] are well-known illustrations of this. From like motives courts refused to allow juries to find a general verdict in cases of criminal libel.[612]

V. If it be asked how the judges, sometimes with and sometimes without the cooperation of the parties, have been able to work all this out, it must be remembered that in England the judges have always, in theory, been great ministers of the Crown; and that even to this day much of the reality and many visible signs and symbols of this high place and power remain. Here, also, as well as there, the function of directing the administration of justice, of steadying and making it consistent

---

[609] See, *e. g., as* late as 1790 the reasoning of Lord Kenyon in Macferson *v.* Thoytes (Peake, 20), "Comparison of hands is no evidence. If it were so, the situation of a jury who could neither write nor read would be a strange one, for it is impossible for such a jury to compare the handwriting."

[610] R. v. Oneby, 2 Lord Raymond, p. 1494.

[611] Abrath *v.* N. E. Ry. Co., 11 App. Cas. 247.

[612] Com. *v.* Anthes, 5 Gray, 212 — 219.

by rules binding on juries no less than on judges and litigants, and of ascertaining and construing the substantive law, carries with it great power. Let us look at the operation of this in some of its particulars.

1. In the exercise of their never-questioned jurisdiction of declaring the common law, during all the long period of its secular growth in England and America, there has arisen constant occasion for specifying the reach of definite legal rules, and so of covering more and more the domain of hitherto unregulated fact. This has consisted, in a great degree, in declaring the scope and operation of sound reason, wherein the common law so largely consists.[613] With the growth of knowledge and human experience, and with the multiplied new application of maxims of reason and sense to combinations of fact, both new and old, the judges, in such a system as ours, are thus forever advancing, incidentally, but necessarily and as part of their duty, on the theoretical province of the legislator and the juryman.[614]

2. Especially has this function come into play in supervising and regulating the exercise of the jury's office. Herein lies one of the most searching and far-reaching occasions for judicial control — that of keeping the jury within the bounds of reason. This duty, as well as that of preserving discipline and order, belongs to the judge in his mere capacity of presiding officer in the exercise of judicature. Reason is not so much a part of the law, as it is the element wherein it lives and works; those who have to administer the law can neither see, nor move, nor breathe without it. Therefore, not merely must the jury's verdict be conformable to legal rules, but it must be defensible in point of sense; it must not be absurd or whimsical. This, of course, is a different thing from imposing upon the jury the judge's own private standard of what is reasonable. For example, when the original question for the jury is one of reasonable conduct, and a court is called on to revise the verdict, the judges do not undertake to set aside the verdict because their own opinion of the conduct in question differs from the jury's.[615] They are not an appellate jury.

---

[613] *Go.* Inst. 97 b.

[614] For illustrations of this, see E. R. Thayer, *Judicial Legislation, 5* Harv. Law Rev. 172.

[615] Stackus v. R. R. Co., 79 N. Y. 464; Stevenson *v. U. S.,* 162 U. S. 313. But the Courts in this class of cases are making new doctrines of law, e. g., in requiring people to stop, look, and listen before crossing a railway; as in Pa. R.

The question for the court is not whether the conduct ultimately in question, *e. g.,* that of a party injured in a railway accident, was reasonable, but whether the jury's conduct is reasonable in holding it to be so; and the test is whether a reasonable person could, upon the evidence, entertain the jury's opinion. Can the conduct which the jury are judging, reasonably be thought reasonable? Is that a permissible view? [616]

R.. *v.* Beale, 73 Pa. 504; and the "bicycler's stop" will not serve; he must dismount. Robertson *v.* Pa. R. R. Co., 180 Pa. 43. In Vermont a party need not stop. Manley *v.* Canal [R. R.] Co., 69 Vt 101.

[616] *Infra,* 223. This matter has been neatly and accurately handled by Lord Halsbury, in the House of Lords.

A few years before, in Solomon *v.* Bitton, 8 Q. B. D. 176 (1881), in an action of trover the substantial question for the jury was whether they believed the plaintiff's or the defendant's witnesses. On an application by the defendant fur a new trial on the ground that the verdict was against the weight of evidence, the trial judge. Sir N. Lindley, expressed himself as dissatisfied with the verdict, and a new trial was ordered. On appeal this order was reversed, the court (Jessel, M. B., and Brett and Cotton, L.JJ.) saying that the rule in such cases ought not to depend on whether the judge who tried the case was dissatisfied with the verdict or would have come to the same conclusion, "but whether the verdict was such as reasonable men ought to come to."

In 1886, in The Metropolitan Railway Company *v.* Wright, 11 App. Cas. 152 (1886), in a case involving the question of negligence, the Divisional Court (Lord Coleridge, C. J., and Stephen, J.), had ordered a new trial on the ground that the verdict was against the weight of evidence. The Court of Appeal (Selborne, L. C., Brett, M. R., and Lindley, L. J.) reversed this decision; and the House of Lords sustained the reversal. The Lord Chancellor Herschell laid down the principle that "the verdict ought not to be disturbed unless it was one which a jury, viewing the whole of the evidence reasonably, could not properly find." And then Lord Halsbury, in a short and excellent statement, put the matter with precision: "My Lords, the facts of this case may of course be differently viewed by different minds. I am content with the view of the facts as stated by the Lord Chancellor, and I am disposed to think that I should have found the same verdict. But what I take to be of supreme importance, as defining the functions of judges and juries, is the principle upon which a new trial can be granted, upon the ground that a verdict is against the weight of evidence. Now I think that the principle laid down in Solomon *v.* Bitton is erroneous, as reported, in the use of the word 'ought.' If a court — not a Court of Appeal in which the facts are open for original judgment, but a court which is not a court to review facts at all — can grant a new trial whenever it thinks that reasonable men ought to have found another verdict, it seems to me that they must form and act upon their own view of what the evidence in their judgment proves. This, I think, is not the law. If reasonable men *might* find (not 'ought to,' as was said in Solomon *v.* Bitton) the verdict which has been found, I think no court has jurisdiction to disturb a decision of fact which the law has confided to juries, not to judges. My noble and

We might anticipate that this clear but delicate line would often be overstepped. It often has been. It is the line which was under discussion in an important modern suit for libel,[617] when, in considering the power of the court, on a motion in arrest of judgment, Lord Penzance insisted that a court could not take the case from the jury, if the publication was reasonably capable of a libellous construction. On the other hand it was laid down by Lord Blackburn that the court, on this particular question, unaffected by Pox's Act, was to judge for itself; and he added, "It seems to me, that when the court come to decide whether a particular set of words, published under particular circumstances, are or are not libellous, they have to decide a very different question from that which they have to decide when determining whether another tribunal, whether a jury or another set of judges, might not unreasonably hold such words to be libellous." That this vital discrimination has been neglected, in a great many cases where the court has had to review the action of the jury, there is abundant reason to believe.[618]

The point may be further illustrated by cases on the subject of necessaries for an infant. Formerly, in such cases, the plaintiff, in reply to the plea of infancy, put upon record the facts which were thought to identify the articles as necessaries. Nowadays these facts are not pleaded. The former practice tended to give the parties the court's opinion; now they get the jury's, which may be a very different matter. The jury's verdict is, indeed, subject to the court's

---

learned friend on the woolsack has put the proposition in a form which is not open to objection, but which perhaps leaves open for definition in what sense the word 'properly' is to be used. I think the test of reasonableness, in considering the verdict of a jury, is right enough, in order to understand whether the jury have really done their duty. If their finding is absolutely unreasonable, a court may consider that that shows that they have not really performed the judicial duty cast upon them; but the principle must be that the judgment upon the facts is to be the judgment of the jury and not the judgment of any other tribunal. If the word 'might' were substituted for 'ought to' in *Solomon* v. *Bitton,* I think the principle would be accurately stated."

[617] Capital and Counties Bank *v.* Henty, 7 App. Cas. 741; a. c. 31 W. R. 157; Hazy *v.* Woitke, 23 Col. 556.

[618] This distinction is of fundamental importance in constitutional law, where courts are reviewing the action of legislatures and considering whether they have kept within the limits of legislative power. Compare Terry *v.* Anderson, 95 U. S. 628, 633, 634, *per* Waite, C. J. Thayer, Origin and Scope of the American Doctrine of Constitutional Law (Little, Brown, & Co), 17 — 22; 7 Harv. Law Rev. 129.

revision; but at that stage, as we see, the court asks merely that "very different question," which Lord Blackburn mentions, whether the jury could reasonably find the supplies to be necessaries. In Makarell v. Bachellor,[619] in 1597, the plaintiff sued in debt for supplying apparel, and, upon a plea of infancy, replied that the defendant "was one of the gentlemen of the chamber to the Earl of Essex, and so it was for his necessary apparel; and it was thereupon demurred. The court held that they were to adjudge what was necessary apparel; and such suits... cannot be necessary for an infant, although he be a gentleman." In Ryder v. Wombwell,[620] in 1868, where a like question went to the jury and was found for the plaintiff, the court, in granting a nonsuit on the ground that there was no evidence sufficient to warrant the verdict, laid down the general principle that the court may always say, whether, *prima facie,* having regard to "the usual and normal state of things," which is known to judges as well as to juries, certain things "may be" necessaries; and, that if evidence is offered of special circumstances, changing the usual state of things, the question for the court is whether, upon the evidence, the jury could reasonably find them necessaries. On both points, it will be observed, the court is simply holding the jury and the parties within the limits of reason.

       3. In exercising their presiding function, the judges have had to invoke presumptions and to lay down rules of presumption. They have thus, imperceptibly and inevitably, modified the jury's action in dealing with questions of fact, and have narrowed the number and range of questions coming under the jury's control. These presumptions are sometimes not so much rules of law, as formulated advice, indicating what judges recognize as permissible or desirable in the jury; but often they are strictly rules for the decision of questions of fact. A fuller statement on this subject will be found in a later chapter.[621] It is the characteristic of a presumption, in dealing with a disputed question of fact, to make a *prima facie* decision of the question. In the long history of trial by jury this process has forever gone on, sometimes as a mere natural, unobserved step in the work of a tribunal which regards precedent and seeks for consistency in administration, sometimes as a sharp and short way of bridling the

---

[619] Cro. El. 583.

[620] L. R. 4 Ex. 32.

[621] *Infra, c.* viii.

jury. Such things were done as being mere administration; as rightly belonging to officials who had, what the juries had not, the responsibility of supervising the conduct of judicature, and of securing the observance, not merely of the rule of law, but of the rule of right reason. None the less, however, are we to notice that the actual working of this process has transferred a great bulk of matter of fact from the jury to the court by the simple stroke of declaring that it shall no longer be dealt with merely as matter of fact, but shall be the subject of rules, — rules of practice, rules of good sense, *prima facie* rules of law, even conclusive rules of law, even so far do the courts go in this process. In cases of prescriptive rights, for instance, it was perceived how hard it often is to prove them, *propter brevem hominum vitam,* and the judges established the rule that when once you had given evidence running back through the term of living memory, the rest of the long period of legal memory might be spanned by a presumption. It was admitted to be. a question of fact and for the jury, whether the truth was so or not; but the judges were not content to leave it there; for a grave matter of policy was involved, and immense property interests; and they perceived the very slender proportions of the evidence. "No doubt," said Mr. Justice Blackburn,[622] "usage for the last fifty or sixty years would be some evidence of usage seven hundred years ago; but if the question is to be considered as an ordinary question of fact, I certainly, for one, would very seldom find a verdict in support of the right as in fact so ancient." And so, in such cases, the judges instructed the jury that they "ought" to find what was thus presumed; and, what was more, they enforced this duty on the triers of fact, whether *nisi prius* judges or juries, by granting new trials if it was disregarded.

4. Closely allied to the process just dealt with is that of the definition of language. This has a great reach. In fixing the meaning of legal terms, the judges have often assumed the determination of matters of fact. Such phrases as "malice," "false pretences," "fraud," "insanity," "reasonable notice," and the like, whether statutory expressions or other, have required a definition. The judges alone could give it; and they have sometimes given it, as in the case of

---

[622] Bryant *v.* Foot, L. R. 2 Q. B. p. 172; Jenkins *v.* Harvey, 1 Cr., M. & R. 877. "Presumptions do not always proceed on a belief that the thing presumed has actually taken place. Grants are frequently presumed . . . from a principle of quieting the possession." *Per* Sir Wm. Grant, M. R., in Hillary *v.* Waller, 12 Ves. 239, 252.

insanity, in a manner to close questions of fact which might well have been left open.[623]

From the earliest times until now much of the law is expressed in terms of what is reasonable. A widow shall have reasonable dower; she may have reasonable estovers; a party shall give reasonable notice; he shall act reasonably, etc., etc. The pages of Glanvill and Bracton are as full of this sort of thing as those of our latest volume of reports. It is the judges who have had to define what was reasonable, or else to determine how it should be defined; just as they had to say what "a long time" should mean in regard to adverse possession. *Quam longa esse debent,* says Bracton,[624] *non definitur a jure sed ex justitiariorum discretione.* "Reasonableness in these cases," says Coke,[625] "belongeth to the knowledge of the law, and therefore to be decided by the justices." But in exercising this function the judges gave definitions which called in the jury, by referring to non-legal standards, like that of the conduct of the prudent man. It is clear that, even in the old days, one may find reasonableness passed on by the *secta,* and the jury.[626]

Of these judicial definitions our books are full.[627] Sometimes they begin by fixing, in particular cases, an outside limit of what is rationally permissible, as in many of the cases about reasonable time and the like; and then grow more precise. In this

---

[623] See the observations of Mr. Justice Doe in dissenting opinions in State r. Pike, 49 N. H. 399, 430, 442, and Boardman *v.* Woodman, 47 N. H. 120, 146 — 150; and the opinion of the court (Ladd, J.) in State *v.* Jones, 50 N. H, 369.

[624] Fol. 51 b.

[625] Co. Lit. 56 b.

[626] Bracton, 315 — 316 b. As to what ought to be adjudged waste and what not, in point of quantity, says Bracton, *habet quaelibet patria* suum *modum, constitutionem et consuetudinem.* What conformed to this standard in such a case would be defined by the court as reasonable. Of course, in so far as questions of reasonableness relate to procedure, or other topics which belong peculiarly to the court, it is easy to see that they are for its own decision. *Infra,* 230, n. 4. But the general statement that, in our older law, questions of reasonableness were always for the judges has often been accepted with too little discrimination.

[627] See, e. g., Twyne's case (3 Co. 80 b), defining phrases in St. 13 Eliz. c. 5, s. 2, as to fraudulent conveyances; Calder *v.* Bull, 3 Dall. 386, and Hartung *v.* The People, 22 N. Y. 95, defining the term *ex post facto;* McCulloch *v,* Maryland, 4 Wheat. 316, defining the words "necessary and proper," in the Constitution of the United States; Russell *v.* Russell [1897], A. C. 395, defining the statutory word "cruelty;" State *v.* Stevens, 69 Vt. 411, defining the phrase "a set line," in a statute relating to fishing; and Taylor *v.* Horst, 52 Minn. 300, defining "book-account." There is no end to such cases, old and new, in every part of the law.

way the legal rule as to what is reasonable notice of the dishonor of a bill of exchange was established: juries were resisted by the court when they sought to require notice within an hour, and, on the other hand, when they tried to support it if given within fourteen days, or within three days, when "all the parties were within twenty minutes' walk of each other;"[628] and so the modern rule was fixed, that ordinarily notice is sufficient if given on the following day. In the case of uncertain fines in copyholds, the courts had previously gone through a like process of regulating excess, until at last, not without the aid of courts of equity, they had fixed a specific outside limit.[629] The process is now going on as regards the question of timely notice to the, indorser of a demand note.[630]

So far as the phrases to be defined occur in contracts or similar writings, they become subject to the rule already mentioned, that the construction of writings is matter for the court. So far as they are found in statutes or our American constitutions, the courts have control of the definition not merely on. this ground, but on another, namely, that it is one of those incidental questions, relating to a law, which, being attracted to the main one, are themselves regarded as questions of law.[631] Courts do, indeed, when engaged in this process of definition, sometimes take the opinion of the jury; and their acceptance of the verdict, which in reality may mean nothing more than an allowance of the jury's opinion as one that the court is willing to accept, is sometimes inaccurately thought to involve a ruling that the question itself belongs of right to the jury. And again, a decision of a court *in bane* that it is not error in law thus to take the opinion of the jury is supposed to mean that it is the duty of the judge to do it. But sometimes this matter is more accurately dealt with. In a criminal case in Massachusetts, involving the question whether a certain game was a lottery, within the meaning of a statute, this question was left to the jury.[632] Four years later, in a similar case, the same court said: "This having been determined to be a lottery in Commonwealth *v.* Wright, it is not necessary to go on forever taking

---

[628] Tindal *v.* Brown, 1 T. R. pp. 168 — 9.

[629] Per Lord Loughborough, Doug. 724, n.; Co. Lit. 59 b. Compare Maine, *Early Law and Custom,* 315.

[630] Ames, Cases on Bills and Notes, i. 783 n.; Paine *v.* B. R. Co., 118 U. S.152, 160.

[631] *Supra,* p. 193.

[632] Com. v. Wright, 137 Mass. 250.

the opinion of the jury in each new case that comes up. Whether or not a definitely described game falls within the prohibition of the statute is a question of law. The defendant was bound to know at his peril. Whatever practical uncertainty courts may have felt upon a subject with which they are less well acquainted than some others of the community, in theory of law there is no uncertainty, and the sooner the question is relieved from doubt the better."[633]

---

[633] *Per* Holmes, J., in Com. *v.* Sullivan, 146 Mass. 142,145. See Holmes, Common Law, 123 n. It has an odd effect to call this a question of law, and at the same time speak of the court feeling a practical uncertainty about it which leads them to consult the jury . What is meant is that it is a question for the court. Compare a recent less accurate English case, Pearce *v.* Lansdowne, 69 Law Times Rep. 316 (1893), where a potman at a public house had sued his employer under an Employers Liability Act, contending that he was a "workman" within the meaning of the Act; and not "a domestic or menial servant," who was a personage excluded from that category by the terms of the statute. In one of the county courts the jury found for the plaintiff, subject to the question, which the judge reserved for himself, whether the potman was "a domestic or menial servant." The judge heard evidence as to the nature and circumstances of the plaintiff's employment, and held that he was "a domestic or menial servant." The evidence was uncontradicted, and showed that the duties of the potman at the public house "were to sweep out the bar, to wash the bar and the pewter pots, to dust round, to clean the windows, to put fresh sawdust down, and to take beer out to customers. He did not sell anything. He slept at his own house, at some distance from the public house, and returned home three times a day for meals." The plaintiff appealed, and in the Queen's Bench Division the appeal was dismissed. But the court (Williams and Collins, JJ.) found much difficulty in dealing with the case. They declared that the judge below had usurped the place of the jury, and that the strictly proper course to be observed at the present stage would be that of sending the case back to be given to a jury; but that, as both sides wished the matter to be finally disposed of now, the court would, under an established but irregular rule of practice in dealing with motions for a new trial, take on itself the jury's function and declare that the judge below had reached a right result. Mr. Justice Williams, who gave the principal opinion in the case, said: "I do not quite know why the functions of the judge and those of the jury are not kept properly separate in dealing with these Acts of Parliament, but there seems to be a sort of notion that if the facts of the particular case are admitted, the result is that the functions of the judge and the jury are thereby altered, that the jury cease to be the tribunal which is to draw the necessary inferences of fact, and that it becomes the duty of the judge to draw them. ... I do not believe that because the facts are admitted, the functions of the jury as to drawing inferences from them are altered at all. . . . . There is no dispute here as to what were the duties performed by the plaintiff or as to the circumstances under which he performed them." Then the judge quotes as authority for what he is saying the language of Lord Justice Bowen in a case of negligence, not adverting, in doing so, to a real difference between such a case and one where the court is construing

5. The rules of practice and the forms of pleading and procedure were under the control of the judges.

(a) The judges often compelled special verdicts. It was the old law that a jury, if it chose to run the risk of a mistake, and so of the punishment by attaint, always might find a general verdict.[634] But the judges exerted pressure to secure special verdicts; sometimes they ordered them, and enforced the instruction by threats, by punishing the jury, and by giving a new trial.[635] As matter of history, we know that the jury, on the whole, successfully stood out against these attempts; and that in most cases their right was acknowledged.[636] But now it is remarkable bow judges and legislatures in this country are unconsciously travelling back towards the old result of controlling the jury, by requiring special verdicts and answers to specific questions.[637] Logic and neatness of legal theory have always called loud, at least in recent centuries, for special verdicts, so that the true significance of ascertained facts might be

---

a statute. In Davey *v.* Lond. & S. *W.* Ry. Co., 12 Q. B. D. 70, 76, the Lord Justice had said: "It is not because facts are admitted that it is therefore for the judge to say what the decision upon them should be. If the facts which are admitted are capable of two equally possible views which reasonable people may take, and one of them is more consistent with the case for one party than for the other, it is the duty of the judge to let the jury decide between such conflicting views. "After citing this, Williams, J., proceeds: "It is impossible to state the law with more accuracy and clearness; and, to apply it here, I say that no one can doubt that on the facts it is possible that reasonable persons may take different views as to whether the plaintiff was . . . 'a domestic or menial servant.' Under these circumstances I wish to say, as emphatically as I can, that it seems to me here that the county court judge took upon him self the functions of the jury without any occasion for so doing."

[634] Co. Lit. 228 a; 2d Inst. 425; Dowman's case, 9 Co. 7 b, 12 b.

[635] Chichester's case, Aleyn, 12 (1644); Gay *v.* Cross, 7 Mod. 37 (1702); R. *v.* Bewdley, 1 Peere Williams, 207 (1712). Compare Baker's case, 5 Co. 104 (1600).

[636] Mayor of Devizes *v.* Clarke, 3 A. & E. 506.

[637] See Mr. W. W. Thornton's article in 20 Am. Law Rev. 366, on "Special Interrogatories to Juries." At pp. 381 and 382 the writer says: "The practice of submitting a vast number of interrogatories to a jury is frequently criticised by the courts; nevertheless the practice continues, and in fact is growing worse. ... All the statutes provide that if [the answers to] the special interrogatories are inconsistent with the general verdict, they shall prevail over the latter." See Maceman *v.* Equitable Co., 72 N. W. Rep. Ill (Minn., July, 1897). In Atch. R. R. Co. v. Morgan, 22 Pac. Rep. 995 (Jan. 1890, Kansas), seventy-eight questions were put to the jury, filling nearly three octavo pages of fine print and double columns.

ascertained and declared by the one tribunal fitted to do this finally and with authority. But considerations of policy have called louder for leaving to the jury a freer hand. The working out of the jury system has never been shaped merely by legal or theoretical considerations. That body always represented the people, and came to stand as the guardian of their liberties; so that whether the court or the jury should decide a point could not be settled on merely legal grounds; it was a question deeply tinged with political considerations. While it would always have been desirable, from a legal point of view, to require from the jury special verdicts and answers to special questions, that course would have given more power to the king and less to the people. It is one of the eccentricities of legal history that we, in this country, while exalting in some ways the relative function of the jury far beyond all English precedent, are yet, in some parts of the country, greatly cutting down their powers in the particular here referred to.[638] Doubtless the judges at common law have always exercised a limited power of questioning the jury about their verdicts. But the general, common-law right of the jury to refuse to answer such questions and to give a short, general verdict has been acknowledged. It was conspicuously recognized in a recent English case, where, in a criminal trial of great importance, for a violation of the Foreign Enlistment Act, such questions were put to them and answered. I quote from the account of a competent observer who was present at the trial:[639] "Then... came the charge of the court by the Lord Chief Justice, at the conclusion of which he propounded to the jury seven questions.... Sir Edward Clarke [for the defence] endeavored to interpose an objection to the propounding of these questions, but he was silenced in the most peremptory manner by the Lord Chief Justice, who said that he would permit no interruption at that stage. The jury were then told that they were only requested by the court to answer the questions; they could not be compelled to answer them. They could, if they chose, bring in a general verdict of guilty or not guilty; but in refusing to answer the questions they would be assuming a grave responsibility, inasmuch as questions of law were involved."

---

[638] *Supra,* 188 n., 218 n.

[639] Reg. v. Jameson *et al.,* 6 Yale Law Journal, 32, 9S, an article by Professor Wurts, of Yale University.

(b) Again, under this general power of shaping the rules and forms of pleading and procedure, the courts, as we have noticed already,[640] used to enable a party to spread upon the record the particulars, and even the evidence, of his case, with a view to a better control of the jury. This gave much into the hands of the judges, on a demurrer, and on a motion in arrest of judgment; and sometimes it greatly enlarged their power at the trial. The operation of this may be illustrated by the former law of libel. Chief Justice Shaw, in explaining the old controversy on that subject, in an important case,[641] after stating the rules of pleading, says: "The theory of those judges who held that the jury were only to find the fact of publication and the truth of the averments, colloquia, and innuendoes, was this: that when the words of the alleged libel are exactly copied, and all the circumstances and incidents which can affect their meaning are stated on the record, inasmuch as the construction and interpretation of language, when thus explained, is for the court, the question of the legal character of such libel... would be placed on the record, and therefore, as a question of law, would be open, after verdict, on a motion in arrest of judgment." The fierce struggle that went on over this question and ended in the statute, recognizing the jury's right, as in other cases, so in cases of criminal libel, to give a general verdict,[642] illustrates the immense practical importance of the question who should have the opportunity to apply the law to the fact. The history of the jury is full of such illustrations. To leave to the jury, on the one hand, what is unhappily called a mixed question of law and fact, with the proper alternative instructions as to what the law is upon one or another supposition of fact; and, on the other hand, to have such a question remain with the court after the jury have reported upon the specific questions of fact, — are two exceedingly different things. Within permissible limits there is generally a good range of choice in matters of intendment and inference; it makes a great difference who is to make the choice, even when these just limits are observed; and since mistakes are possible, and even wilful error, the reasons for wishing for one of these tribunals rather than the other are greatly increased.

---

[640] *Supra,* 114 — 19.

[641] Com. *v.* Anthes, 5 Gray, 185, 214.

[642] St. 32 Geo. III. c. 60. Capital and Counties Bank *v.* Henty, 7 App Cas. 741; a. c. 31 W. R. 157.

(c) Resulting, also, from this general control of the courts over the procedure, is a peculiar doctrine in actions for malicious prosecution, and for false imprisonment. The former of these is the modern representative of the old action of conspiracy. At an earlier page we have seen an instance, in conspiracy, of the way in which the defendant was allowed to set forth his matter of defence on the record, out of regard to the uncertainties of the jury.[643] The same thing is seen about a century later,[644] where Gawdy, J., doubted whether this sort of thing were a plea, "because it amounts to a *non culpabilis....* But the other justices held that it was a good plea, *per doubt del lay gents.*" Besides the old "formed action" for conspiracy, there appeared early the action on the case in the nature of conspiracy; in which, however, a real conspiracy was not necessary to be proved even when alleged.[645] There was always great anxiety on the part of the court lest this action should be abused. It was said that while it was true that when two conspire maliciously to indict and there is an acquittal, the action lies; yet it ought not to be so where only one prosecutes, — "for then every felon that is acquitted will sue an action against the party;[646]" and at any rate, if the action does lie, it can only be where the defendant had no probable cause; and the defendant, on his side, should plead his reasons.[647]

Afterwards the scope of the action was enlarged so as to include a prosecution for a "trespass," *i.e.,* a misdemeanor, and also the bringing of a civil action; and the settled form of pleading became that of the plaintiff specifically alleging malice and want of reasonable and probable cause, and the defendant pleading the

---

[643] *Supra,* 118; a case of 1504.

[644] Pain *v.* Rochester, Cro. Eliz. 871 (1601 — 2). See also Chambers *v.* Taylor, *ib.* 900.

[645] Skinner *v.* Gunton, Saunders, 228, 230 a, and *per* Holt, C. J., in Roberts *v.* Savill, S Mod. 405, 407 (1698): "For really it is an action on the case, and no action of conspiracy."

[646] Shute and Gawdy, JJ., in Knight *v.* German, Cro. Eliz. 70 (1587).

[647] S. c. Cro. Eliz. 134 (1589). In this case, an action for maliciously causing the plaintiff to be indicted for felony, the defendant had pleaded the general issue. Error was brought on a judgment for the plaintiff. "Gawdy, Justice. If the defendant did it upon good presumptions, he ought to plead them; as that he found them in the house, etc., or the like cause of suspicion; but no such thing is pleaded. Otherwise every one shall be in danger of his life by such practices. Wray, Chief Justice, agreed."

general issue.[648] Ceasing to enter the facts on the record removed from the court the opportunity to determine, on demurrer or motion, in arrest of judgment, whether these facts, assuming them to be true, constituted reasonable and probable cause. But otherwise, it left the respective duties of court and jury as they were before; it did not, in theory, touch the question of who is to pass upon the effect of the facts when they are not assumed or admitted to be true. To say that such. and such a thing will not support a jury's verdict, and such and such another will, is only to speak of those bounds of reason within which the judge of fact must always keep; it sets up these limits on one side and the other, but so long as they are observed it says nothing as to who shall constitute this tribunal, whether jury or court. But it was easy to be inexact about this. To-day and always courts have tended to be thus inexact, and in speaking of they own function, namely, that of deciding whether a certain conclusion is permissible, whether it *can be* reached by a jury, — not merely to call it a question of law (which often it is not), but loosely to identify it with the jury's question. This subtle error has been and now is one of the commonest in our books.[649] Whether it came about by way of this

---

[648] Atwood *v.* Monger, Style, 378 (1655); Roberts *v.* Savill, 5 Mod. 394, 405, 410 (1698); s. c. 1 Salk. 13; Jones *v.* Gwynn, 10 Mod. 214 (1713); S.C. Gilbert, 18&; Johnstone *s.* Sutton, 1 T. K. 493, 495, 544 (1786); Cotton v. Browne, 3 A. & E. 312 (1835); Panton *v.* Williams, 2 Q. B. 169 (1841). It is to be remarked, however, that in the action of trespass for false imprisonment, the defendant still continued to plead in full the facts of his justification. Baynes *v.* Brewster, 2 Q. B. 375 (1841); Spencer *v.* Anness, 32 N. J. Law, 100 (1866); Burns *v.* Erben, 40 N. Y. 463 (1869). See the complaints of Lord Denman in Baynes *v.* Brewster, *ubi supra.*

[649] *Supra,* 209. To take an illustration from two cases in the same court. In Carroll *v.* The Interstate Rapid Transit Co., 107 Mo. 653, 660 (1891), the question arose on the defendant's demurrer upon the evidence. The opinion is expressed thus: "In the present action the question mast be determined whether plaintiff exercised ordinary care for his own safety; or to put the statement into a somewhat more practical form, whether his conduct, in the opinion of the court, was such as a person of ordinary prudence and caution, in the same circumstances, would have exhibited, according to the usual and general experience of men." It is obvious from what follows in the opinion that the court did not mean to take to itself the jury's question, but only to ask what conclusions were permissible, as a matter of sound reason. In a later case (Keown *v.* St. Louis R. Co., 41 S. W. Rep. 926, July, 1897), the same distinguished judge in a similar case says: "The next question is whether or not Willum was guilty of a breach of duty ... in starting the car. . . . Was he, then, bound to anticipate Keown's presence there, or to look towards the rear of the car for him before starting the

confusion of two different questions, or however it happened, it became one of the settled phrases of the courts to say, not merely that the fixing of these outside limits is a question of law for the court, but to say also, broadly, that determining reasonable and probable cause itself is a question of law for the court. In the case of 1504, above referred to, Fineux, O. J., says of the facts allowed to be pleaded there: "He shall not be driven to the general issue, for it is special matter, and triable by the justices.[650] In 1785, Buller, J., declared that what is reasonable or probable cause is matter of law."[651] And this was repeated and elaborately laid down in a leading English case in the Exchequer Chamber in 1841. And the same thing often, as in a Massachusetts case, in 1832: "What facts and circumstances amount to probable cause is a pure question of law. Whether they exist or not, in any particular case, is a question of fact. The former is exclusively for the court; the latter for the jury."[652] No one, indeed, ever treated it as a question for the court in the full sense in which a preliminary question as to the admissibility of evidence is for the court, namely, in the sense that all the facts necessary to determine it must be passed on by the court.[653] As in the case of the interpretation of writings, where the extrinsic facts are to be ascertained by the jury, so here, it is common to say that the facts are for the jury, and the conclusion upon those facts is for the court. Thus in a great case in 1786 the Chief Justices Lord Mansfield and Loughborough said: "The question of probable cause is a mixed proposition of law and fact. Whether the circumstances... are true

---

car? It must be confessed that this query has given us some trouble to answer, and we express our conclusion on it with some misgivings. . . . Conceding the full force of plaintiff's evidence it does not tend to prove the essential fact. . . . Whether submitted testimony tends to establish negligence is a question of law," etc. A motion for a rehearing was made, and counsel pressed a point as to the Court's, misgivings, and urged that these showed that the case was one about which fair-minded men might differ, and so was for the jury. But the court (*ib.* 929) adhered to its decision, saying that its " misgivings " related only to *its own* question and not to the jury's: " The question whether or not, in any case, given testimony tends to prove negligence, is a question for the courts. And though it may sometimes be difficult of solution, the court is bound to solve the difficulty as best it can," etc. I use these illustrations because the language, in both cases, is that of one of the soundest and most accurate of American judges.

[650] *Supra,* 119.

[651] Candell *v.* London, cited by counsel in 1 T. R. 520. *Infra,* 226.

[652] Stone *v.* Crocker, 24 Pick. 81, 83.

[653] Bartlett *v.* Smith, 11 M. & W. 483; Gorton *v.* Hadsell, 9 Cush. 511.

and existed, is a matter of fact; but whether, supposing them true, they amount to a probable cause, is a question of law."[654] Baptizing the question of reasonable and probable cause with this name, as a "mixed question of law and fact," common and almost universal as it is, has only added to the confusion. All questions of fact, for a jury or for a court, are mixed questions of law and fact; for they must be decided with reference to all relevant rules of law; and whether there be any such rule, and what it is, must be determined by the court. Now since this mixture of law and fact is thus common to a variety of different situations, it is an uninstructive circumstance to lean upon when one seeks for guidance in discriminating these situations.[655]

The place of this question of reasonable and probable cause might be truly intimated, by a turn of phrase borrowed from the familiar expression just commented upon, — if one should call it *a mixed question of fact;* "mixed" in the sense that the two tribunals are blended in deciding it, that the issue of fact is divided between them. We must observe that this is not what happens in ordinary questions of reasonable conduct and negligence; these now go to the jury as being mere questions of fact; to be determined, indeed, according to such rules and definitions of law as the judge lays down. But in such cases it is the jury that applies these rules of law to the facts, whenever the facts are disputed, or when, although "the facts are agreed," as we say, yet the inference from them, in any point of fact, is disputable. These questions of negligence, also, are continually styled mixed questions of law and fact. But in regard to the question of reasonable and probable cause as it arises in malicious prosecution and false imprisonment, as well as in regard to that of the true meaning of writings, it is the established doctrine that while the jury are to find the specific facts from which the

---

[654] Johnstone v. Sutton, 1 T. R. 493, 545. And so very commonly, as in Munns *v.* Dupont, 3 Wash. C. C. 31 (1811); Humphries v. Parker, 52 Me. 500 (1864); Ash v. Marlow, 20 Ohio 119 (1851).

[655] See the valuable remarks of Duer, J., in Bulkeley *v.* Smith, 2 Duer, 261. He truly says that this phrase is a deceptive one, either wholly unmeaning, or intelligible and true only in a sense equally applicable to every question of law that a judge in the prosecution of a trial can be required to determine. Misled by this expression, he says, judges often content themselves with defining reasonable and probable cause, and then leaving everything to the jury . This, of course, is dealing with the matter just as negligence is now ordinarily dealt with. See *infra,* 231 n., 250. 15

conclusion, is to be drawn, yet, these being ascertained, the conclusion of reasonable and probable cause or the absence of it is to be ascertained only by the judge.

Call it what you will, the question itself is exactly the same which arises in all cases of negligence, — has one conformed to the standard of the prudent and reasonable man?[656] Such questions, a hundred years ago, were often called questions of law, and the method then and now applied to reasonable and probable cause in malicious prosecution was also applied to other like questions, as ordinary questions of negligence. The case of Tindal *v.* Brown[657] was decided only six months before the decision of the Exchequer Chamber in Button *v.* Johnstone.[658] In the former case Lord Mansfield and. the other judges said that reasonableness of time when the general facts were ascertained was a question of law for the court. In the latter, they said the same of reasonable and probable cause. But in modern times this same *general* question, of what is reasonable notice, arising in Tindal *v.* Brown, — like questions of reasonable conduct in general, is clearly recognized as a question of fact for a jury. Doubtless the particular question there discussed has become the subject of a judicially legislated rule of law. But only ten years after the decision of the King's Bench in Tindal *v.* Brown, Lord Kenyon, in granting a new trial, said of the general question: "I cannot conceive how this can be a matter of law. I can understand that the law should require that due diligence shall be used, but that it should be laid down that the notice must be given that day or the next, or at any precise time, under whatever circumstances, is, I own, beyond my comprehension." [659] And four years later, in refusing a new trial, the same judge said, after objecting to the rule imputed to Tindal *v.* Brown, "Whether reasonable notice have or have not been given, must depend on the circumstances of the case, of which the jury will judge."[660] But now, whatever be the exact shape of any specific question of this sort, there is no doubt about the matter of

---

[656] See a definition which is very widely applied in this country in Munns *v.* Dupont, 3 Wash. C. C. 31 (1811); compare Humphries *v.* Parker, 52 Maine, 500.

[657] 1 T. R. 167 (May, 1786). *Supra,* 215.

[658] T. R. 493, 544 (Nov. 1786).

[659] Hilton v. Shepard, cited in note to 6 East, 3.

[660] Hopes *v.* Alder, cited in note to 6 East, 3. But compare Wyman *v.* Adams, 12 Cush. 210.

reasonableness in general. "The questions raised at the trial were questions of fact, and of fact only," said Lord O'Hagan in an important accident case, involving questions of negligence.[661] The characteristic of all such questions is the same. The only rule of law is one which appeals to an outside standard, that of general experience; and the application of it, by whatever tribunal made, calls for a preliminary determination of something for which there is no legal test, — a matter of fact, and not a matter of law, — namely, the behavior, in a supposed case, of the prudent man. If the settling of such a question be matter of fact in ordinary cases of negligence, it is equally so in cases of malicious prosecution and false imprisonment; for saying this, notwithstanding the careless phraseology of our books, there is abundant authority. See, for

---

[661] Dublin, etc. By. Co. *v.* Slattery, 3 App. Cas. 1155, 1181 (1878). In a similar case in the Supreme Court of the United States, Fuller, C. J., for the court, quoted with approval the language of an earlier case before the same tribunal: "The policy of the law has relegated the determination of such questions to the jury, under proper instructions from the court. . . . When a given state of facts is such that reasonable men may fairly differ upon the question whether there was negligence or not, the determination of the matter is for the jury." Bait. &0. R. R. Co. *v.* Griffiths, 159 U. S. 603 (1895). Compare Holmes, J., in Doyle *v.* B. & A. R. R. Co., 145 Mass. 386. In Phipps *v.* Lond. & N. W. Ry. Co. [1892], 2 Q. B. 229, on an appeal from the Railway Commissioners, under a statute forbidding a railway company to give "any undue or unreasonable preference or advantage to or in favor of any particular person or company," etc., etc., and limiting the right of appeal to questions of law, the court declined to consider the question of reasonableness, because it was merely a question of fact. "It cannot be doubted," said Lord Herschell, "that whether in particular instances there has been an undue or unreasonable prejudice is a question of fact. ... I should say that the decision must be arrived at broadly and fairly . . . looking at all the circumstances which are proper to be looked at; ... keeping in view all the circumstances which may legitimately be taken into consideration, then it becomes a mere question of fact." The only question of law in this case was whether, on a complaint of undue preference to a particular trader, the commissioners could rightly take into account the circumstance that this party had access to a competing route; and it was held that they could. Under the Interstate Commerce Act of the United States there is no such restriction on the right of appeal, and the Supreme Court of the United States, while entertaining jurisdiction on both the questions alluded to in the English decision above quoted, yet distinctly agrees with it, and relies upon its authority in adopting both of its conclusions above mentioned: "It cannot be doubted," says Shiras, J., for the court, "that whether in particular instances there has been an undue or unreasonable prejudice or preference ... are questions of fact depending on the matters proved in each case." Int. Com. Comm. *v.* Alabama Ry. Co., 168 *V. S.* 144, 170 (1897). Of this class of cases something more is said, *infra,* 249.

example, the weighty *seriatim* opinions of the law Lords in a case of false imprisonment, in 1870.[662] Lord Chelmsford said: "My Lords, there can be no doubt since the case of Panton *v.* Williams,[663] in which the question was solemnly decided in the Exchequer Chamber, that what is reasonable and probable cause in an action for malicious prosecution, or for false imprisonment, is to be determined by the judge. In what other' sense it is properly called a question of law I am at a loss to understand. No definite rule can be laid down for the exercise of the judge's judgment. Each case must depend upon its own circumstances, and the result is a conclusion drawn by each judge for himself, whether the facts found by the jury, in his opinion, constitute a defence to the action. The verdict in cases of this description, therefore, is only nominally the verdict of a jury." In the same case Lord Westbury added: "The existence of reasonable and probable cause is an inference of fact. It must be derived from all the circumstances of the case. I regret, therefore, to find the law to be, that it is an inference to be drawn, by the judge, and not by the jury. I think it ought to be the other way."[664]

---

[662] Lister v. Perryman, L. R. 4 H. L. 521.

[663] 2 Q. B. 169.

[664] In the same case, *per* Lord Colonsay, a Scotch Lord: "I have frequently had to deal with cases of this kind in the other end of the island; but there this question of want of reasonable and probable cause is treated as an inference in fact to be deduced by the jury from the whole circumstances of the case, in like manner as the question of malice is left to the jury. If I had tried the case there I should have left this matter to the jury; and if the jury had found a verdict for the defendant, I should have approved of that verdict for reasons I am about to explain. . . . But in England it is settled law that this is a matter for the court to deal with. The court deals with it as an inference to be drawn by the court from the facts, but whether an inference of law or an inference of fact does not, I think, appear from the reports. I do not see clearly whether it is called an inference of law merely because it is left to the court, or whether it is left to the court because it is really an inference of law. But, undoubtedly, it appears to be settled law in this country that want of reasonable and probable cause is matter for the court. . . . Probably it became so from anxiety to protect parties from being oppressed or harassed in consequence of having caused arrests or prosecutions in the fair pursuit of their legitimate interests, or as a matter of duty, in a country where parties injured have not the aid of a public prosecutor to do these things for them. Finding that I had to deal with this as a matter of inference in law, I was desirous to ascertain what were the rules or principles of law by which the court ought to be guided in drawing that inference. I did not find that there were any. Neither in the very able argument we heard from the bar, nor in the judgments set oat in these papers, nor in the cases that have been referred to, are any such rules or principles enunciated. . . . And upon a careful consideration of the decisions, it

The, reasons which have availed to keep this particular question, of fact, in actions for malicious prosecution and false imprisonment, in the hands of the court, are easily to be seen, and have already been suggested. It is the danger so often recognized by the courts, e. g., by Lord Colonsay,[665] lest those who would come forward in aid of public justice should be intimidated or discouraged. For this reason the judge used to refuse to give out copies of indictments for felony unless on a special order, "for the late frequency of actions against prosecutors (which cannot be without copies of the indictments) deterreth people from prosecuting for the King upon just occasions."[666] Such orders were refused where there appeared to the court to have been probable cause for the prosecution. In 1697, *per* Holt, Chief Justice, if A be indicted of felony and acquitted, and he has a mind. to bring an action, the judge will not permit him to have a copy of the record, if there was probable cause of the indictment, and he cannot have a copy without leave."[667] And, in the last half of the next century, Blackstone tells us that, "in prosecutions for felony it is usual to deny a copy of the indictment, where there is any, the least, probable cause to found such prosecution upon."[668]

---

seems to me impossible to deduce any fixed and definite principle to guide and assist the judge in any case that may come before him. Chief Justice Tindal's rule seems almost the only one that can be resorted to, namely, that there must have existed a state of circumstances upon which a reasonable and discreet person would have acted. Now, in the system to which I have already alluded it is thought that twelve reasonable and discreet men (as jurors are supposed to be) can judge of that matter fur themselves, and that lawyers are not the only class of persons competent to determine whether the information was such as a reasonable and discreet man would have acted upon. For what is it that a judge would have to determine lie would have to determine whether the circumstances warranted a reasonable and discreet man to deal with the matter, that is to say, not what impression the circumstances would have made upon his own mind, he being a lawyer, but what impression they ought to have made on the mind of another person, probably not a lawyer." To a similar effect was the opinion of the Lord Chancellor Hatherley. And so Barton v. By. Co., 33 Minn. 189. See also Newell, Malic. Pros. 277.

[665] *Supra,* 229.

[666] Orders of the Judges in 1664, Kelyng (old ed.), 3.

[667] Groenvelt r. Burrell, I Ld. Raym. 252; s. c. Carthew, 421, "for the court will never help any litigious suit."

[668] 3 Com. 126. Of course in such situations reasonable and probable cause is for the court. *Supra,* 214, n. 3.

The plain truth, then, about the matter now under consideration is, that for reasons of policy the courts still continue to retain the determination of a part of the total issue of fact. If this were confessed, instead of disguising a question of fact for the court under the name of a question of law, much. confusion would be avoided.[669] From the beginning there has been confusion. Throughout, the right to decide whether, on the pleadings or evidence, there was any case of reasonable and probable cause, has tended to be confounded with that of deciding whether in fact it is proved to have existed. There is much reason for believing that the leading modern case of Panton *v.*

---

[669] See, for instance, such cases as Bulkeley *v.* Smith, 2 Duer, 261; Ball v. Rawles, 93 Cal. 222; and Hess *v.* Oregon German Bank, 49 Pac. Rep. 803 (Oregon, Aug. 1897): and compare Rowlands *v.* Samuel, 11 Q. B. 38, 41 n.; Douglass *v.* Corbett, 6 El. & Bl. 511, *per* Coleridge, J.; and Stephen, Malic. Pros., *passim.* What is regarded as the true method of handling this question is set forth in a very recent case, correcting a common method which some courts have followed, — that of leaving a definition to the jury, with instructions to say whether, on that definition, there was reasonable and probable cause. Herbert Stephen, in his little book on Malicious Prosecution (pp. 70 — 83), citing Abrath *v.* N. E. Ry. Co., 11 App. Cas. 247, conceives that this is the true modern practice, and that therefore the old anomaly is now in effect done away with. But, in a case just referred to, Hess *v.* Oregon German Bank (*ubi supra),* p. 805, the court, with accurate discrimination, remarks: ' "Probable cause is in the nature of a judgment to be rendered by the court upon a special verdict of the jury,' says Judge Harrison in Ball *v.* Rawles, 93 Cal. 227, 'and is not to be rendered until after the jury has given its verdict upon the facts by which it is to be determined.' It is not, however, necessary that the facts be found by the jury in the form of a special verdict. The court may instruct them to render their verdict for or against the defendant, according as they shall find the facts designated to it, which the court may deem sufficient to constitute probable cause. But it is necessary for the court, in each instance, to determine whether the facts that they may find from the evidence will or will not establish that issue. Neither is it competent for the court to give to the jury a definition of probable cause, and instruct them to find for or against the defendant, according as they may determine that the facts are within or without that definition. Such an instruction is only to leave to them in another form the function of determining whether there was probable cause. The court cannot divest itself of its duty to determine this question, however complicated or numerous may be the facts. It must instruct the jury upon this subject in the concrete, and not in the abstract, and must not leave to that body the office of determining the question, but must itself determine it, and direct the jury to find its verdict in accordance with such determination. The court should group in its instructions the facts which the evidence tends to prove, and then instruct the jury that, it they find such facts to be established, there was or was not probable cause, as the case may be, and that their verdict must be accordingly."

Williams[670] should have been decided the other way, and that the weight of authority at that time supposed to exist in its favor would have been found, on a more critical examination, to shrink to slender proportions.[671]

(d) A singular product of the old ways of withdrawing questions from the jury was developed in the subtle doctrine of "color" in pleading.

The word "color" seems formerly to have designated the sort of reason which, would justify one in pleading specially, where his duty was, *prima facie,* to plead the general issue; he could do this if he could show some ground, in point of law or fact, on which the jury would naturally be misled, if he were to follow the general rule, not setting out the special matter in his pleadings. This might be a purely fictitious ground. Illustrations of this are found in a note on color in the Year Books of the year 1440, before referred to.[672] In this we are told that "this color is always matter in law, or some other difficulty for the lay people;... as in case I bring assize against you, and you say that you yourself leased the same land to one for the term of his life, and then granted the reversion to me, and then the tenant for life died, and I am claiming the reversion by force of this grant, — but the tenant never attorned; this special matter is allowable because it is dangerous to plead *nul tort,* since the laymen will try the matter on the theory that the reversion passes by force of the grant, without attornment.... But where the special matter is not a matter of law or of difficulty, the tenant, as defendant, must take the general issue; as, if the tenant says that he was seised until he was disseised, whereupon he re-entered, this plea is not allowable, because all men know well that the tenant in that case is no disseisor; or if he says that the plaintiff claims as a younger son, for everybody understands that the younger son cannot inherit before the older," etc., etc. If not originally, at any rate later, "color," sometimes called

---

[670] 2Q. B. 169 (1841).

[671] How easy it has been to slip, while not meaning to depart from the usual doctrine, may be seen in the case of Wass *v.* Stephens, 128 N. Y. 123, 127 (1891): "The question of probable cause may be a question of law for the court, or of fact for the jury, depending upon the circumstances. If the facts are undisputed and admit of but one inference, the question is one of law; if disputed, or if capable of opposing inferences, the question is for the jury." Andrews, J., citing James *v.* Phelps, 11 A. & E. 483. And so Burns *v.* Erben, 40 N. Y. 463; Ash *v.* Marlow, 20 Ohio, 119.

[672] Y. B. 19 H. VI. 21, 42. *Supra,* 118.

"express color," came to designate a purely fictitious ground of right on the other side, put forward by one who was constructing a plea of confession and avoidance. "Color," said Fulthorpe, J., "is nothing but giving a party *un couleur de droit* and also an entry, but the color need not be rightful in fact, for such color would be bad for the defendant."[673]

In St. Germain's quaint dialogue of the "Doctor and Student," there is an amusing, grave discussion as to the morality of the fiction of color, and incidentally an explanation of it by the Student.[674] The discussion ends by the suggestion of the Student that it is a man's duty, out of love to his neighbor, to save the jury from the peril of a wrong finding, by avoiding the general issue wherever he can, — an argument which the Doctor agrees to ponder. In setting forth this matter, the Student states the rule that one must not plead detail which amounts only to the general issue; and yet in some cases if he do plead the general issue, he will have to leave a point of law "to the mouths of twelve laymen, which be not learned in the law; and, therefore, better it is that the law be so ordered that it be put in the determination of the judges than of laymen." Accordingly, the party was permitted to turn his traverse into a confession and avoidance, by alleging and admitting some fictitious ground of right on the other side, not quite defensible in point of law, and then avoiding it by detailed matter which really was only an argumentative general issue. This got his facts on the record, and at the same time the rule that one must either traverse or confess and avoid, moulted no feather. Form was preserved, for the party had confessed and avoided; to be sure he had set up a mere fiction; hut the other party was not allowed to deny it, and he had kept to the rules.[675]

(e) Under this same head, I may mention the demurrer upon evidence. Very soon, as it seems, after the general practice began of allowing witnesses to testify to the jury, this interesting contrivance

---

[673] Y. B. 19 H. VI. 19, 41; cf. Y. B. 21 & 22 Edw. I. 616, 618 (1294).

[674] II. c. 53. This book was published in 1518. As to the morality of color, it is said of Robert Hale, the father of Sir M. Hale, that "he gave over the practice of the law because he could not understand the reason of giving color in pleadings which, as he thought, was to tell a lie; and that with some other things," etc. Burnet's Life of Sir Matthew Bale, 2.

[675] Stephen, Pleading, Tyier's ed. 206-215. Compare 2 Reeves, Hist. Eng. Law (Finl. ed.), 349, 629; Warner *v.* Waiasford, Hob. 127.

for eliminating the jury came into existence. Such demurrers, like others, raised only an issue in law. They had the effect to withdraw from the jury all consideration of the facts, and, in their pure form, to submit to the court two questions, of which only the second was, in strictness, a question of law; namely, whether a verdict for the party who gave the evidence could be given, as a matter of legitimate inference from the evidence; as a matter of law. Of this expedient I do not observe any mention earlier than the year 1456.[676] Near the end of the last century demurrers upon evidence got their death blow in England, by the decision in the case of Gibson v. Hunter, carrying down with it also the great case of Lickbarrow v. Mason, which, like the former, had come up to the Lords upon such a demurrer.[677] It was there held that in cases of complication or uncertainty in the evidence, the party demurring must specify upon the record the facts which he admits.

This decision got rid of the first question, at least of its chief difficulties, and left only the second. It compelled the demurring

---

[676] Y. B. 34 H. VI. 36, 7. It is interesting, less than a century and a half later, to observe Bacon's conceptions about evidence and demurrers upon evidence. In his Maxims of the Law, Reg. III., in discussing the rule that words are taken strictly, against the party who uses them, after putting a case of a demurrer, and remarking the liberal construction of the recorded evidence, as compared with the construction of pleadings, he goes on thus: "And the reason thereof cannot be, because a jury may take knowledge of matters not within the evidence, and the court, contrariwise, cannot take knowledge of any matter not within the pleas: for it is clear that if the evidence had been altogether remote and not proving the issue, there, although the jury might find it, yet a demurrer might well be taken upon the evidence. But I take the reason of difference to be, between pleadings, which are but openings of the case, and evidences, which are the proofs of an issue : for pleadings, being but to open the verity of the matter in fact indifferently on both parts, have no scope and conclusion to direct the construction and intendment of them, and therefore must be certain; but in evidence and proofs, the issue, which is the state of the question and conclusion, shall incline and apply all the proofs as tending to that conclusion. Another reason is, that pleadings must be certain, because the adverse party may know whereto to answer, or else he were at a mischief; which mischief is remedied by demurrer : but in evidence, if it be short, impertinent, or uncertain, the adverse party is at no mischief, because it is to be thought the jury will pass against him: yet, nevertheless, because the jury is not compellable to supply the defect of evidence out of their own knowledge, though it be in their liberty so to do, therefore the law alloweth a demurrer upon evidence also."

[677] Gibson v. Hunter, 2 H. Bl. 187; Lickbarrow v. Mason, ib. 211. See Lord Blackburn's comments on these cases in Sewell v. Burdick, 10 App Cas. 74, 99 (1884).

party to abandon wholly a notion, which seems to have existed in the profession, that by this proceeding he was shifting to the court the duty of "judging the facts," and was thus avoiding the uncertainties of the jury. Always it had been the theory of this sort of demurrer that the demurring party admitted all the evidence of the other side, and all the conclusions therefrom which a jury might lawfully and rightly reach. As regards conclusions of fact, the whole field of rational inference was open to a jury, and a demurrer admitted all that could rationally be found against the party demurring. The decision in Gibson *v.* Hunter, so far as the advisory opinion of the judges may be thought to give the true reasons for it (for this is all we have to go by), had this effect: namely, it compelled the parties to reach an agreement and specification as to what was thus admitted by the demurrer, before the case came to the court *in banc.* The rule now laid down had the effect to adjust below, before the single judge, all debate over this question; the demurring party was required to say, at that stage, exactly what he was admitting; the single judge might compel a joinder in demurrer, when proper admissions were made, and might compel the making of proper admissions by allowing a refusal to join. And thus it was made sure that when the upper court received the case, it came to them purged of mere questions of general reasoning, with all the inferences of fact stated.

It will easily be perceived that a demurrer upon evidence left open no question whatever in the law of evidence, that is to say of the admissibility of evidence; but only, like other demurrers, questions of substantive law. As the facts out of which these questions of law arose were supposed to be admitted, so all questions relating to the evidence of those facts had become immaterial.[678]

This piece of machinery had come to seem a clumsy, dilatory, and expensive one. It stopped the trial, and required an entry on the record of all the evidence. And so, when once the demurring party was driven from his vague expectations of getting something out of a court, in the considering of his evidence, which he might not get from a jury; when once it was forced clearly upon his attention, that, not only did a demurrer upon evidence commit

---

[678] "For a demurrer upon evidence goes to the law upon the matter, and not to the truth of the fact, for it admits that to be true, but denies the operation of the law thereupon." Lewis *v.* Lark, Plowden, 403, 411 (1571); Fitzharris v. Boiun, 1 Lev. 87 (1662); Gibson *v.* Hunter, 2 H. Bl 187 (1793).

him irrevocably to all those inferences from the evidence which were most unfavorable to him, but that he must set these conclusions all down in writing beforehand, then this ancient instrument of justice fell wholly into disuse in England.[679] It had survived its usefulness and must give place to shorter and more efficient ways of serving the necessities of a new generation. It had come into existence at a time when the general introduction of witnesses to the jury and the requirement that evidence must be given to them publicly in open court, had wrought the first revolution in this great mode of trial. As that change had given new effect to the attaint by making it certain that the jury were not ignorant of the matters presented to them, so the demurrer upon evidence had operated still further to moderate their "unchartered freedom." It enabled a party to secure definiteness to the body of evidence which he had to reckon with. By admitting all that his adversary alleged, setting it down upon the record and appealing to the law as arising out of these facts and the just inferences from them, he escaped from the operation of a jury's caprice, and from any resort on their part to that unknown mass of possible knowledge which continued for centuries to be open to them. True, no man. could be compelled to give up a jury, while anything remained to be tried; but when he had put in his evidence and stopped; and when his adversary had admitted it all, and all that legitimately followed from it, there was nothing to go to a jury; he

---

[679] For the misconception sometimes entertained as to the length to which the admissions of a demurrer upon evidence went, see the discussion in Cocksedge *v.* Fanshaw, 1 Dong. 119 (1779-1783). In that case Davenport, for the party demurring, "insisted that, although a demurrer to evidence admits the truth of all the particular facts, it does not admit the conclusions in point of fact, more than those in point of law, which the party offering the evidence contends for. . . . That, in this respect, the effect of such a demurrer differs from a special verdict, and that it may be used where the party demurring is unwilling to trust the jury with the inference in point of fact."As to the effect of the rule in Gibson *v.* Hunter, see Lord Blackburn's remarks in the House of Lords, in Sewell *v.* Burdick, 10 App. Cas. 74, 99 (1884). Of the famous opinion of Chief Justice Eyre Lord Blackburn says: "He explains it [the demurrer], and states his very confident expectations (which have been justified by the result) that no demurrer on evidence would again be brought before the House."An unfortunate and never corrected misprint in the opinion of C. J. Eyre may properly be mentioned here. At p. 207 of 2 H. Blackstone, where the opinion reads: "If the party who demurs will admit the *evidence* of the fact, the evidence of which fact is loose and indeterminate," etc. Obviously the word "evidence," above printed in italics, should be "existence."

might justly be required to join in the demurrer. A jury, in those days, it is true, might, perhaps, out of their own knowledge, supply other facts that would help out this evidence; and so a party might be thought to lose something, when driven to join. But, as Lord Bacon said:[680] "Because the jury is not compellable to supply the defect of evidence out of their own knowledge, though it be in their liberty so to do, therefore the law alloweth a demurrer upon evidence also."

Lasting over into an age when the attaint was obsolete; when juries could no longer act upon what was privately known to them, but only on what was publicly given in court; when their excesses in dealing with evidence were guarded against by new trials, and reservations at *nisi prius,* and a freer use of simple motions to the court; this old demurrer easily submitted to a new shock, and died out. That the rule in Gibson *v.* Hunter was a novelty is fairly plain from the case of Cocksedge *v.* Fanshaw,[681] ten years earlier. The rule was not always followed in this country; but the fact that it was a novelty was sometimes not understood.[682] Here also demurrers to evidence are mainly obsolete; what is called by this name now is often a very different thing.

In handling this keen-edged instrument, it is more than likely that the just line between the duties of court and jury was often overstepped by assuming that what the court thought the right inference was the only one allowable to the jury. Nothing, as has been said already, is more common, even to-day, than the assumption that only a question of law remains, when, in reality, the most important inferences of fact are still to be drawn. In this way much which belongs to the jury remains in the hands of the judges, or passes over to them unnoticed.

And, finally, among the adjustments of procedure by which, through the influence of the judge and the co-operation of the parties, the jury was often partly or wholly eliminated, was a method less remarked than it should be, by practitioners and students of our law. In England, far more commonly than here, the effort has been to shape cases for the appellate court so as to get at the substance of what is in controversy, and so as to settle everything at the appellate

---

[680] *Supra,* 234 n.

[681] 1 Doug. 119 (1779 — 1783).

[682] Patrick *v.* Halleck, 1 Johns. 241 (1806); Whittington *v.* Christian, 2 Randolph, 357 — 8 (1824); Trout *v.* R. R. Co., 23 Gratt. 619 — 20, 635 — 40, (1873). See the cases on this subject in Thayer's Cases on Evidence. 210 — 238

stage and avoid the necessity of a new trial. The great influence of the English judges, powerfully felt all through the trial, has helped to this; and perhaps also it is an indirect result of the English classification of their men of law, by which the barrister, being less intensely committed, as a mere partisan of his client, than here, and less engaged to secure for the client every conceivable loop-hole of possible advantage, and every chance of success, however desperate, is left freer to perceive those public and private considerations that make for an early settlement of any given piece of litigation. Such causes as these, coupled with some accidental reasons, established in England traditional, elastic methods of procedure, which left in the hands of the judges a very great and often unobserved power over ordinary issues of mere fact. Any one who will take the trouble to notice how seldom a bill of exceptions with its narrow question of mere law, and its frequent necessity for a new trial, has ever been resorted to in English practice in recent centuries; and that this method of carrying up questions from the trial court has been wholly abolished in England since 1875; while in this country it has long been one of the commonest instruments of appellate procedure, and to-day flourishes as the great and characteristic one; will be helped not merely to see certain substantial differences between English legal administration and our own, but, what is more to the present purpose, to see the way in which in England, the mother of our own. traditional system, these things have kept in the hands of the judges so great a share of power in determining issues of fact.

An illustration of what is now suggested may be seen in a case which has been already cited.[683] The judges of the Divisional Court, on appeal from the County Court, were of opinion that the judge below should have left the question to the jury instead of deciding it himself. The parties wished the upper court to decide the whole matter and not to send it back for a new trial, and the judges did this — holding that the judge below had, upon the whole, reached the right conclusion. "I wish to say," said Williams, J., "that unless the course we are about to pursue is justified by a rule of practice, it is our duty to send the case back, for we have no right to assume a jurisdiction which does not belong to us. There is a rule which is adopted on motions for a new trial, and upon which we are going to act, that when the cause has been tried and the judges feel

---

[683] Pearce v. Lansdowne, 69 Law Times Rep. 316 (1893).

that they have all the facts before them so that they are entitled to give a judgment that will finally settle the matters in difference between the parties, they are entitled to give such a judgment, although the practice involves, I will not say usurpation by the judges, but a partial transfer to them of the functions of the jury. Here we have got the whole of the plaintiff's duties and the surrounding circumstances admitted." [684]

At common law, besides the right to move the court for a new trial, which came to be recognized as of course, there grew up the practice of reserving questions for the full court in various forms, with authority to make such specified disposition of the case, by nonsuit, or a changed verdict, or a judgment this way or that, as might have been agreed on by counsel, with the approval of the judge. One or two brief and partial, but valuable, expositions of this subject have been made in the opinions of Lord Blackburn; and as it is difficult to find any good account of it in our books, I give from these opinions, in a note, the whole of what that learned judge says about it. [685] These arrangements, and a common habit of courts and

---

[684] For the liberal and elastic rules of English procedure now, see Wilson, Judicature Acts; for example, this: "A new trial shall not he granted on the ground of misdirection or of the improper admission or rejection of evidence, or because the verdict of the jury was not taken upon a question which the judge at the trial was not asked to leave to them, unless in the opinion of the court to which the application is made some substantial wrong or miscarriage has been thereby occasioned in the trial; and if it appear to such court that such wrong or miscarriage affects part only of the matter in controversy, or some or one only of the parties, the court may give final judgment as to part thereof, or some or one only of the parties, and direct a new trial as to the other part only, or as to the other party or parties." Wilson, Judicature Acts (7th ed. 1888), 331, Order xxxix. Rule 6.

[685] So. East. Ry. Co. *v.* Smitherman, a much contested case, where a valuable opinion given in the House of Lords is reported nowhere except in the London Times of July 17, 1883, at page 3; and Dublin, etc. Ky. Co. *v.* Slattery, 3 App. Cas. 1155, 1204 (1878). Both were accident cases. The facts are not important for the present purpose. In the former, in reversing a decision which refused a new trial. Lord Blackburn, whose opinion was concurred in by the other Lords, said: "I think that there has been some misapprehension as to the effect of the alterations in the law introduced by the orders 39 and 40 in the schedule 1 to the Supreme Court of Judicature Act, 1875, and I think it better to begin by explaining what I conceive to be the effect of those orders. At common law all trials by jury were before the court *in banc,* as trials at bar now are. The court took the verdict according to what they thought the effect of the findings of the jury before themselves, and gave what they thought the proper judgment. When trials at *nisi prius* were introduced, at first only in the country before Justices of

Assize, and, at a much later period, in Middlesex and London, where there were no assizes, before the Chief Justices of the Courts of Queen's Bench and Common Pleas and the Chief Baron, — the verdict was taken by the judge who tried the case at *nisi prius,* according to what he thought the legal effect of the findings, but he could not enter judgment. He returned to the court the verdict, and, on the fourth day of term, the verdict, as he returned it, was entered on the record in what was called the *poslea,* and on that the Court *in banc* gave judgment. A practice began at least as early as the beginning of the seventeenth century, by which the court in *bane* would entertain a motion, if made within the first four days of term, while the proceedings were, as it was called, in paper only, to stay the *postea,* and if it was made out that there had been any miscarriage at the trial, to set aside the proceedings at *nisi prius* and grant a new trial. But they could do no more. However clearly it appeared that the verdict ought to have been entered for the other party, the court in *bane* could not enter it. The judge who tried the cause at *nisi prius* might by his notes amend the *postea,* but not the Court. This defect was partially cured by a practice which grew up, by which the judge, with the consent of the parties, for he could not do it without, reserved leave to move in *bane to* enter the verdict the other way. This practice had, before the Common Law Procedure Act, 1852, become the established law. There was no reason why the motion should not, where leave was reserved, be in the alternative to enter the verdict according to the leave reserved, or to have a new trial, on the ground either of misdirection of the judge or anything else which amounted to a miscarriage on the trial. One well-recognized head of miscarriage was when the verdict was against the weight of evidence; where, if the court thought that, though the right direction in law was given, the jury had, either from misapprehension or disregard of the direction, or not properly appreciating and considering the evidence, found a verdict so unsatisfactory that it ought not to stand, and that the question should be submitted to another jury, and for that reason granted a new trial. Now, I think, no doubt was ever entertained, at least, I am not aware of any case in which any was expressed, that the court, in considering whether the verdict was satisfactory or not, looked at everything bearing on the conduct of the jury up to the time when the verdict was finally taken. If, by consent of the parties, anything was reserved for the court, that was to he determined by the court; but, whether it was reserved or not, could not prevent the court from considering how the verdict on other points was obtained, and whether it was satisfactory or not. If there had been a bill of exceptions tendered, the court would not entertain a motion for a new trial on any ground which might have been included in it, unless the bill of exception? was abandoned, but the court would still hear a motion to set aside the verdict as against evidence."For the changes introduced by the Judicature Acts see Wilson, *supra.* In the second of the two cases above named, a few years earlier, Lord Blackburn had discussed the same matters, in a dissenting opinion. He said: "When, as in the present case, there is doubt as to what the proper direction in law is, the judge ought, as far as practicable, to put the case in a proper train for having the verdict entered without any new trial, according to what the law may ultimately be ascertained to be. Down to the beginning of the seventeenth century this could only be done by finding a special verdict; and unfortunately there was so much technical nicety required in framing a special verdict, that it required lawyers to overlook the exact bearing of them on the decisions to which they lead, when these are cited as precedents, have deeply affected the substantive law. Precedents which have turned upon some question of fact, or some limited and incidental principle of procedure, or evidence, or practical sense, have come to stand as settling the main doctrine of substantive law involved in the case. It is obvious, on reflection, that cases may import a very different proposition when they come from the trial court in different ways;

---

great skill and some good fortune to be able to raise the real question on it. At the time I have mentioned a practice began of the court *in bane,* during the first four days in term, whilst the case was yet in the paper, granting, in the discretion of the judges, a new trial, if there appeared to have been any miscarriage on the trial. This was found so very convenient that what at first was only an exercise of the equitable discretion of the courts became a recognized system of law, and it became usual for the judge to give the direction which in his opinion at the trial was the right one, reserving leave to enter the verdict according to what he ought to have directed. This superseded special verdicts where it was not intended to carry the case beyond the court in *bane,* and on these reservations the court *in bane* did not require the same technical precision which had unfortunately become requisite on a special verdict. It looked to the trial to see what was really in dispute, and what the real point was; but till a comparatively recent period the decision of the Court of first instance was final. Now, such a reservation may be taken, as this had been, into a Court of Appeal, and I think if the reservations are treated by the Courts of Appeal, not as special verdicts used to be, having regard to technicalities, but, as justice would seem to require, having regard to the substance of what really took place and was agreed on at the trial, special verdicts will fall into disuse altogether. A jury, no doubt, has the physical power to find a verdict contrary to the direction of the judge, but if that is done it is wrong. And when leave is reserved to enter a verdict according to what is ultimately determined to be the proper direction in law, it is on the supposition that the jurors do their duty and follow that direction."I will add a short passage from a valuable little commentary on the procedure in jury trials in civil cases by a Scotch writer, William Adam, Lord Chief Commissioner under the Act of Parliament (55 Geo. III. c. 42), which first introduced, in Scotland, trial by jury in such cases. "In England," he says, "the course of proceeding by new trial to correct the errors of law by judges presiding at trials by jury, had become prevalent, in consequence of the proceeding by bill of exception creating inconvenience to the judges, under the provisions of the Statute of Westminster. Besides, counsel not being always ready with their exceptions in proper form, trials were thereby delayed; a serious inconvenience when there are many cases to try at a sitting or circuit. To avoid such inconveniences, it was natural that both judges and counsel should prefer proceeding by motion for new trial, by special case, or by reserving the disputed point of law to be decided in the term; the verdict to be entered according to the opinion of the court upon the point reserved." — *A Practical Treatise and Observations on Trial by Jury in Civil Causes,* by William Adam. Edinburgh, Thomas Clark, 1836.

say, for example, on exceptions to a ruling of the judge, involving, as these do, a dry question of law; on a motion, for a new trial, resting, as this may, upon many different grounds, whether of law, or sound reason, or substantial justice, — as, that a particular ruling of the judge was wrong, or that there was no evidence to sustain the verdict, or that it was against the weight of evidence, or on a rule or motion for a nonsuit, which, in Strictness, asks only whether the plaintiff had any case at all, or any evidence at all to go to the jury; or on a special verdict which asks only for the opinion of the court on the law arising out of these specific facts, justly interpreted, — allowing no power to the court to draw inferences of fact; or on a case, stated by agreement of the parties, which asks the same question as that last named, but in practice, at any rate, and, perhaps, in sound theory, permits a little more freedom than the special verdict as touching inferences;[686] or on such a statement, with a power expressly conferred on the court of drawing such inferences as a jury might draw, or accompanied with other special stipulations, such as that the judges shall pass outright on the title or other main question of the case; or on a case tried by the court without a jury, as in the Star Chamber,[687] in equity, and in many cases at law in modern times, where utterances on questions of fact are so easily confounded with rulings on a point of law. And yet nothing is commoner, in opinions of courts, in arguments of counsel, and in treatises, than overlooking all such distinctions, and treating the deliverances of the courts in those different cases, as of similar import and of equal weight, without any regard to the utterly different point which may have been really under consideration.

It has followed from this, not only that cases are cited every day for propositions of substantive law not decided by them, and when they are equally consistent with the contrary proposition, but also that matters of fact, properly, or perhaps carelessly, passed upon by the courts are subsequently treated as thereby, because handled by a judge, made the subject of a rule of law. For instance, in a case [688] where the plaintiff's agent had drawn up and handed to the defendant a memorandum of a sale of goods to the defendants, in which the names of both parties occurred, the general question was,

---

[686] *Infra,* 247 n.

[687] For examples, Twyne's case, 3 Co. 80 b, a source of much confusion.

[688] Durrell *v.* Evans, 1 H. & C. 174; s. c. 31 L. J. Ex. 337.

whether within s. 17 of the English Statute of Frauds, under the special circumstances of the case, the name of the defendant was signed by his authority, or whether the paper was merely an invoice made in behalf of the plaintiff. By consent, a verdict was found for the plaintiff, and leave was reserved to move to enter a verdict for the defendant or a nonsuit. On a rule to that effect, the Court of Exchequer made the rule absolute for a nonsuit. The Exchequer Chamber reversed the judgment and discharged the rule, on the carefully stated ground that the form of this rule presented to them only the question, whether a jury could have found for the plaintiff. Crompton, J., said: "We think that there was evidence (and that is the only point on which we differ from the court below) that Noakes was intended by the defendant as well as the plaintiff to make a record of the contract.... My brother Willes entertains a strong view the same way; and indeed I believe he is of opinion not only that there was evidence to go to the jury, but that the verdict ought to have been for the plaintiff." The other judges limited themselves as Crompton did. Blackburn, J., said: "I cannot, as a matter of course, look at this instrument... as intended only as the vendor's account. Perhaps I should draw the inference that it was; but it is impossible to deny that there was plenty of evidence" the other way. Doubtless in deciding such a case there is a certain amount of discussion and recognition of general legal principles. But when this case comes to be cited for the proposition that "an instrument so drawn as to recognize the obligation, though not for that special purpose, will, if it be delivered to the other party and accepted by him, suffice for a memorandum under the statute,[689] we observe at once that it is overstated; instead of saying "will suffice," the case cannot be put higher than "may suffice."[690]

---

[689] Browne, Stat. Fr. 5th ed. s. 354.

[690] Similar remarks are applicable to such a case as Baldey v. Parker, 2 B. & C. 37, cited generally as the leading case for the ill-founded doctrine, under section 17 of the English Statute of Frauds, that, where a party makes purchases at a shop, for different prices, and has a bill for the whole of them, if each separate parcel costs less than £10, but all together cost more, it is covered by the statute; as to which see Bailey v. Sweeting, 9 C. B. n. s. 843; Leake, Cont. 140; ib. Dig. Cont. 258; Young Mfg. Co. v. Wakefield, 121 Mass. 91; Mills v. Hunt, 20 Wend. 431; Roots v. Dormer, 4 B. & Ad. 77; Jenness v. Wendell, 51 N. H. 63. So, also, in the famous, much misused case of Morton r. Tibbett, 15 Q. B. 428, the whole scope of the decision was truly indicated by the Chief Justice in stating the question: "In this case the question submitted to us is, whether there

By means, then, of these natural and convenient arrangements of common law procedure, questions of fact are often submitted to the judges by consent of the parties. It will easily be seen how propositions may be laid down by judges, in such cases as these, where, by consent, they are playing the part of a jury and are stating the considerations governing them as jurymen, which ought not to pass into the books as rules of law. But very often the peculiar nature of these cases is overlooked, and what is really the utterance of a bench of jurymen is cited as if it were the judgment of a court.[691]

---

was any evidence on which the jury could be justified in finding that the buyer accepted the goods and actually received the same," etc. But, whether from the erode and confused discussion in the opinion itself, or from the carelessness of later judges and text-writers, this case came to stand for very loose doctrines of substantive law, and at last to work permanent and almost irremediable mischief. On the mistaken authority of this case a novel doctrine was imported into the English law, through one or two later cases (Kibble *v.* Gough, 38 L. T. R. 204, 1878; Page *v.* Morgan, 15 Q. B. D. 228,1885); and then, unfortunately, before the correcting forces of the common law, which had begun to operate (Taylor *v.* Place [1893], 2 Q. B. 65), could fully deal with the matter, this error was incorporated into a codification of the law of sale, which Parliament too hastily enacted. Sale of Goods Act; St. 56 & 57 Vict. c. 7 (1894).

[691] Some cases may be added which will illustrate what is here said as to the different ways of bringing a case up, and the importance of remarking the exact way in which the question for the court has been shaped. Collins *v.* Waltham, 151 Mass. 136; Cochrane *v.* Boston, 1 Alien, 480; Forsyth *v.* Hooper, 11 Alien, 419; Jenner *v.* Smith, L. R, 4 C. P. 270; Parker *v.* Wallis, 5 El. & Bl. 21; Goddard *v.* Binney, 115 Mass. 450; Pickering *v.* Busk, 15 East, 78; Shepherd *v.* Harrison, L. R. 4 Q. B. 196; and on appeal *ib.* 498, and L. R. 5 H. L. 116, (compare Stat. 17 & 18 Vict. c. 125, s. 32); Armstrong *v.* Stokes, L. R. 7 Q. B. 508; Mirabita *v.* Imp. Ottom. Bk., 3 Ex. D. 164; Wilmshurst *v,* Bowker, 2 M. &. G. 792, and on app. 7 ib. 882; Smith *v.* Hudson, 6 B. & S. 431; Suydam *v.* Williamson, 20 Howard, 427.As regards the convenient practice of carrying up a case with power to the upper court to draw inferences of fact, it was said by Tindal, C. J., in 1833 that "It is a practice amongst us of a very recent origin. I much question whether any instance can be found at an earlier period than ten years back." Bayley, J., at about the same time, having also been consulted on the subject by the Scottish Lord Commissioner Adam remarked: "Of late years, practically, an incorrect and slovenly mode has been adopted of leaving it to the court to draw such inferences as the court shall think the jury ought to have drawn." Adam, *Trial by Jury,* 390, 392. Both of these judges expressed approval of the views communicated to them by the Lord Commissioner as to the identity, in legal effect, of special cases and special verdicts, and as to the theoretical incapacity of the court in either case, unless expressly authorized, to draw inferences of fact. But the practice of expressly allowing the court to draw such inferences, in the special case, has always continued, and some power of doing this, even where it was not expressly given, has been recognized by high

authority. Baron Parke repeatedly allowed it, and in doing so I can hardly doubt that he represented truly the actual habit of the judges, whether wholly conscious of it or not. Lord Blackburn's intimations on this general subject will have been noticed *(supra,* 243 n.), where he speaks of a real difference in practice between the mode of handling a special verdict and a case reserved, and of the importance of maintaining the difference. In the King *v.* Leake, 5 B. & Ad. 469, Baron Parke (then Parke, J.), in dealing with a case stated, said: "If this were a special verdict I should have thought that both these facts [not expressly stated] should have been found by the jury, and that a *venire de novo* was necessary; but on a special case we are not so strictly bound, and I do not think that we ought to put the parties to the expense of a new trial on that account." And so Parke, J., in Martindale *v.* Booth, 3 B. & Ad. 498, 506, and Littledale, J., in Bailey *v.* Culverwell, 3 B. & Ad. 448, 455. A marked case was Tancred *v.* Christy, 12 M. & W. 316, 324, in the Exchequer Chamber. Below, it had been argued, in 9 M. & W. 438, on a special case. Liberty had been reserved to turn this special case into a special verdict, in order — having regard to the fact that, at this period, the special case was no part of the record — to be able to carry the case on appeal to an upper Court. When it went up we find the court declaring that it was open to the court below to find certain facts, which this court cannot find. "The argument below," said Tindal, C. J., "was on a case reserved and not on a special verdict. So that the court was at liberty to draw, and did draw, inferences of fact. We cannot." And for that reason they ordered a *venire de novo.* Compare Cole *v.* Northwestern Bank, L. R. 10 C. P. 354 (Ex. Ch. 1875), Blackburn, J.: "This is a special case. ... It did not, as originally drawn, give express power to the court to draw inferences of fact; but on that being pointed out during the argument, it was agreed that it was so intended, and that, if necessary, an amendment should be made to give that power.'The same doctrine, in a very unqualified form, was laid down, at common law, in New York. In Johnson *v.* Whitbeck, in a special case, 6 Cowen, 632, 634, the Court, Sutherland, J., said: "The verdict being subject to the opinion of the court, we are substituted for the jury , and have the right to draw the same conclusions from the testimony which the jury in the opinion of the court would have been authorized to draw." And so in Whitney *v.* Sterling, 14 Johns. 215, 217. In a case submitted under the Code, the contrary is held in Clark *v.* Wise, 46 N. Y. 612. And, doubtless, the more usual statement of the common-law doctrine is to the contrary; as in Massachusetts, in Schwarz *v.* Boston, 151 Mass. 226. Compare Cochrane *v.* Boston, 1 Allen, 480; Keegan *v.* Cox, 116 Mass. 289; Old Col. R. R. Co. *v.* Wilder, 137 Mass. 536; Mayhew *v.* Durfee, 138 *ib.* 584. Yet it may reasonably be thought, as was intimated above, that in actual practice there is less precision than such statements would indicate. Even in dealing with special verdicts, there is always, of necessity, the duty of interpreting the verdict; and that shades off imperceptibly into the process of supplying inferences from general experience. See, e. g, Plammer's case (12 Mod. 27, s. c. Kel. (old ed.) 109), and the reasoning there as to what is a sufficient foundation for a legal intendment. And go, when we come to dealing with the case stated, we find a sort of necessary qualification such as this: "Unless upon such facts, with the inevitable inferences, or, in other words, such inferences as the law draws from them, a case is made out," etc. etc. Morton, C. J., in O. C. R. R. Co. v. Wilder, *ubi supra.* The principles applicable to a verdict, the finding of the tribunal which alone has the

Returning now from these long wanderings, it seems plain that the doctrine of our common law system which allots to the jury the decision of disputed questions of ultimate fact, is to be taken with the gravest qualifications. Much fact which is part of the issue is for the judge; much which is for the jury is likely to be absorbed by the judge, "whenever a rule about it can be laid down;"[692] as regards all of it, the jury's action may be excluded or encroached upon by the co-operation of the judge with one or both of the parties; and, as regards all, the jury is subject to the supervision of the judge, in order to keep it within the limits of law and reason.

Before passing from questions of fact, let me turn again for a moment to that class of what are called "mixed questions of law and fact," such as negligence, which are nowadays referred to the jury. We have found no occasion to speak of them as anything other than mere matters of fact. The circumstance that in order to deal with them it is necessary to know what the legal definition is, does not really affect the matter; nor that the definition is more or less difficult to apply.[693] It is sometimes necessary that the jury should be advised as to the ordinary definitions of the dictionaries; but this is needed only to give precision to their inquiry; it does not alter the nature of it. So of any legal definition. The meaning of "burning," in the law relating to arson, is a highly technical one; and so of "breaking and entering," in burglary; because a definition must be given, is it any the less a simple question of fact whether an accused person has burned, or broken and entered a given house? And so of such questions as title to property, or insanity. Equally, where the courts or statutes have fixed the legal standard of reasonable conduct, *e. g,* as being that of the prudent man, and have no exacter rule, the

---

authority, ordinarily, to find the facts, do not fully apply to a special case. This always imports an agreement of the parties; and the Court may properly regard the apparent purpose of the parties in presenting their case, and may govern their action by considering the questions which the parties apparently intended to raise. In principle, however, this power must be a narrow one. It may well be doubted whether any Court, not expressly authorized to do it, can deal with the facts in an agreed statement as freely as a jury may. Some slight and guarded power of drawing inferences of fact is all that can fairly be claimed in such a case, on any sound principle. Such a power May be claimed.

[692] Tindal *v.* Brown, 1 T. R. 167, *per* Lord Mansfield; Holmes' Com Law, 122 — 9.

[693] See, for example, People *v.* Hawking, 109 N. Y. 411; Pearce *v.* Lansdowne, 69 L. T. Rep. 316. *Supra,* 225.

determination of whether any given behavior conforms to it or not is a mere question of fact.[694] It is not a question of law; because there is no rule in question. That in reaching their conclusion the jury must reason, and must "judge the facts," is not material, as we have already seen; always they must do that; the difference, in this respect between these cases of reasonableness and others is simply one of more or less.[695] It is, indeed, to be recognized, as we have seen, that such questions become, from time to time, the subject of more specific legal rule or definition, as in the case of notice of the dishonor of a bill of exchange.[696] But where that has taken place, all that has happened is a change in the legal rule; the rule of "reasonableness" is either displaced or narrowed. When once the exacter rule is known, what is left to be ascertained, in order that the rule may be applied, is none the less a mere question of fact.

A remark of Austin on this subject has been already referred to. He said:[697] "What can be more indefinite... than the expressions *reasonable* time, *reasonable* notice, *reasonable* diligence?... The difficulty... arises from the vagueness, or indefiniteness of the terms in which the definition or rule is inevitably conceived. And this, I suppose, is what people were driving at when they have agitated the very absurd inquiry whether questions of this kind are questions of law or of fact. The truth is that they are questions neither of law nor of fact.... The difficulty is... in determining not what the law is, or

---

[694] Eaton *v.* Southby, Wiles, 131; McLanahan v. Univ. Ins. Co., I Peters, 170, 186; Haskins *v.* Ham. Co., 5 Gray, 432; and as to some similar matters compare Story, J., for the Court, in McLanahan v. The Universal Ins. Co., 1 Peters, 170, 184 (1828): "What is a competent crew for the voyage; at what time such crew should be on board; what is proper pilot ground; what is the course and usage of trade in relation to the master and crew being on board when the ship breaks ground for the voyage, — are questions of fact, dependent upon nautical testimony, and are incapable of being solved by a Court, without assuming to itself the province of a jury, and judicially relying on its own skill in maritime affairs." Irwin *v.* Williar, 110 U. S. 499.

[695] Vaughan, C. J., in Bushell's case (Vaughan, p. 142), in speaking of the ordinary sort of question, says: "The verdict of a jury and evidence of a witness are very different things in the truth and falsehood of them. A witness swears but to what . . . hath fallen under his senses. But a juryman swears to what he can infer and conclude from the testimony of such witnesses by the act and force of his understanding to be the fact inquired after, which differs nothing in the reason, though much in the punishment, from what a judge, out of various cases considered by him, infers to be the law in the question before him."

[696] *Supra,* 215, 226.

[697] Jurisprudence, vol. i. 236 (ed. 1873).

what the fact is, but whether the given law is applicable to the given fact." In this passage the matter seems to be dealt with. too shortly. In such cases not only is it true that the tribunal, jury or court, has occasion to "judge the evidence," and to resort, in doing so, to its fund of general experience, but also it must, as Austin says, apply the law to the facts. That function, it is true, whenever the facts and all just inferences of fact are once ascertained, belongs, in strictness, to the court; and if, at the outset, both sides admit all these things, there is nothing for a jury to do. In such a case the questions raised in the application, of the law to the facts are questions of law; namely, whether there be any rule of law applicable to these facts, any legal consequences attached to them, or any legal implications involved in them; and if so, what? But until they are fully known, the occasion for applying the law to them has not arisen. And whenever a jury has to be called in to ascertain the facts, that body has, almost always, the right to give a general verdict, compounded of law and fact; and so, subject to the instructions of the court, adapted beforehand to different suppositions and contingencies, and subject also to the court's revision of their action, it is, in fact, ordinarily, the jury that has the application of the law to the facts. So that, in this respect also, there is nothing essentially peculiar in this class of cases. "When the rule of law is expressed in a form that takes up into itself a non-legal standard, as, in laying down for a rule of reasonableness, the test of what a prudent man would do in any given circumstances, obviously, before the rule can be applied, this question of what such a man would do has to be answered, — a question of fact, a question for which there is no legal test; and that question, when part of the issue, is properly for the jury.[698] In determining reasonable and probable cause in actions for malicious prosecutions, as we see, it has been retained by the courts;[699] but whenever such questions do go to the jury, the application of the rule of law also falls to their lot, for the reason that this process must await their determination upon disputed facts, and because it is their right, at common law, here as elsewhere, to give a general verdict.

It seems, therefore, to be true, notwithstanding Austin's remark, that questions of reasonable conduct, while requiring a "judgment" of the evidence, and the application of the rule of law to

---

[698] *Supra,* 228.
[699] Supra, 221.

the facts, submit, none the less, to a classification as questions of fact, — sometimes fact for the court, but generally fact for the jury.

VI. As to the other aspect of the maxim, that which excludes the jury from the law, the rule seems to be in a far simpler condition. From the beginning, indeed, it was perceived that any general verdict, such as no disseisin, or not guilty, involved a conclusion of law, and that the jury did, in a sense, in such cases answer a question of law. That was the very ground of some of the arrangements, already mentioned, for removing from them the final question. Moreover, in many criminal cases their verdict could not be controlled. "It was never yet known," said Pratt, O. J.,[700] "that a verdict was set aside by which the defendant was acquitted in any case whatsoever, upon a criminal prosecution." In such cases the judge could not govern their action; he could simply lay down to them the rule of law; and this it was their duty to take from him, and apply it to the fact. Although this might be their duty, yet the jury had the final power, to find the law against the judge's instruction. This power, where it was uncontrollable, has been considered by some to be not distinguishable from a right; and it is not at all uncommon to describe it thus, — as a right to judge of both law and fact.[701]

Even in civil cases it used to be said, in this country, that the jury had the right to judge of the law. In the first trial by jury at the bar of the Supreme Court of the United States, in 1794, in a civil case in which the facts were agreed, Chief Justice Jay nevertheless submitted the case to the jury, and said: "The facts comprehended in the case are agreed; the only point that remains is to settle what is the law of the land arising from those facts; and on that point it is proper that the opinion of the court should be given. It is fortunate... to find the opinion of the court unanimous.... It may not be amiss here, gentlemen, to remind you of the good old rule that on questions of fact it is the province of the jury, on questions of law, it is the province of the court, to decide. But it must be observed that by the same law which recognizes this reasonable distribution of jurisdiction, you have nevertheless a right to take upon yourselves to judge of both, and to determine the law as well as the fact in controversy.... We have no doubt you will pay that respect which is

---

[700] King v. Jones, 8 Mod. 201, at p. 208 (1724); But see *supra,* 175.
[701] Drake v. The State, 53 N. J. Law, 23, a case of criminal libel.

due to the opinion of the court.... But still both objects are lawfully within your power of decision."[702] That seems at the present day a very extraordinary doctrine. It is, perhaps, partly explained by the practical difficulties existing at that period, in controlling the verdicts of juries in trials at bar, and by the lack of learning oil the bench.[703] Chief Justice Shaw, in ail historical sketch of the older practice ill Massachusetts,[704] in speaking of the way in which jury trials were conducted in that State, for a century and more, previous to the establishment of the *nisi prius* system in 1804, says: "During this period, the court was held for all purposes, in each county, by a full bench.... All jury trials were, in effect, trials at bar, and were conducted in the presence of the full court, and not less than three [a majority of the whole] were competent to preside at a jury trial. The necessary consequence of this practice was, that the members of the court were not always unanimous in their opinions upon the questions of law which the case presented.... It not unfrequently happened, therefore, that several different members of the court charged the jury and gave them conflicting and contradictory

---

[702] Georgia v. Brailsford, 3 Dallas, 1.

[703] In the first lecture of James Wilson, as Professor of Law in the college of Philadelphia, in 1790, he remarks: "In many courts — in many respectable courts within the United States, the judges are not, and, for a long time, cannot be gentlemen of professional acquirements. They may, however, fill their offices usefully and honorably . . . notwithstanding. But can they do this, without a reasonable degree of acquaintance with the law? ... In questions of law the jurors are entitled to the assistance of the judges; but can the judges give assistance, without knowing what answers to make to the questions which the jury may propose. Can those direct others who, themselves, know not the road." Wilson, Works (Andrews ed.), i. 10.Wilson was at this time a judge of the Supreme Court of the United States, and, as such, took part in the trial of Georgia v. Brailsford. In a lecture which appears to have been delivered in 1791-2, after laying it down that law is for the court, where it can be separated from the fact, but when it is "inseparably blended" with the question of fact, the judges must inform the jury of the law, and the jury "must pay much regard to the information," he adds: "But now the difficulty in this interesting subject begins to press upon us. Suppose that ... a difference of sentiment takes place between the judges and the jury, with regard to a point of law, . . what must the jury do? The jury must do their duty, and their whole duty: they must decide the law as well as the fact." *Ib.* ii. 220. The doctrine is not here restricted to criminal cases. The lecturer remarks, however, that it is "peculiarly applicable to criminal cases; and from them, indeed, derives its peculiar importance." See Hawles, Englishmen's Right, 20, 21.

[704] Address before the Bar of Berkshire County, Sept. 1830, 9 Pick. 566, 569.

opinions upon points of law.... It followed as almost a necessary consequence of this course of proceeding, that a verdict must be conclusive.... When so decisive an importance was attributed to the verdict of a jury, and when a jury in effect had the power of controlling the court in matters of law, it is natural to believe," etc.[705] It appears here that, in such cases, what was meant by speaking of the right of the jury to decide the law, was, to speak exactly, a power of the jury which it was practically impossible to control. In criminal cases like expressions have frequently been uttered. But in a great proportion of the cases they were probably intended to be understood in a sense similar to that just indicated, — that is to say, they were modes of expressing the doctrine that in the graver criminal cases an acquittal by the jury is final, and cannot be reviewed on any ground, whether of law or fact.[706] It is probably the sound view, at common law, that this power of the jury in criminal cases does not and did not, in any distinct and modern sense, import a right on their part to determine the law. The actual adjustment seems rather to belong among those manifold illogical, but yet rational and useful results, worked out in the course of English history, in all parts of their public affairs, by way of easing up the rigor of a strict application of rules. And such was the conclusion in an elaborate recent judgment of the Supreme Court of the United States. The doctrine is there laid down that the jury must accept the law as given to them by the court.[707]

---

[705] The same state of things formerly existed in New Hampshire. Reporter's Preface to 55 N. H. Rep. 7. For this and other illustrations of the subject in New Hampshire, I am referred by a learned friend to Morison's Life of Chief Justice Jeremiah Smith, pp. 165 — 166, 173, and to the Life of Governor William Plainer, p. 158.

[706] *Supra,* 175 — 179. In Louisiana, where the constitution makes juries judges of law and fact in criminal cases, it is held that they are legally bound to take the law from the court. State *v.* Tisdale, 41 La. An. 338. So in Pennsylvania, Com. *v.* McManus, 14 Pa. 64.

[707] Sparf v. U. S , 156 U. S. 51. The contrary view was maintained in a dissenting opinion of extraordinary learning and great ability by Gray, J., speaking for himself and Shiras, J. For the comments of the court on the case of Georgia *v.* Brailsford, treating it as an anomaly and quoting Curtis, J., as doubting the accuracy of the report, see *ib.* 64 — 65. In the dissenting opinion that case is discussed and the authenticity of the report seems to be vindicated at pp. 154 — 158. See a remarkable collection of authorities in support of the views of Gray, J., in a note to Erving *v.* Cradock, Quincy's Rep. 553, 558 — 572, — understood to have been furnished by that learned judge when at the bar. Compare 1 Bishop Cr.

It seems, then, that whatever be the power over questions of law which has fallen into the hands of juries, in the actual working of our legal machinery, yet it is the duty of the judges, in all cases, to give them the rule, and their duty to follow the rule thus ascertained. We may still quote with approval Hargrave's note on this subject as being an accurate statement of the common law.[708]

Before leaving the grave and complex subject of this chapter, one or two peculiar situations should be shortly mentioned.

In determining the law of the domestic forum, the courts settle all questions relating to the *factum* of the law, *e. g.,* whether, in enacting a statute, a specific requirement of the constitution as to the forms of enactment has been complied with. This is done, it would seem, under the doctrine of judicial notice, or an analogous one; as the judges are chargeable with knowledge of the law, so the ascertaining of it and of whatsoever is requisite to this Knowledge, is wholly for them. Although, in the discussions of tills subject, much is said of the "best evidence" and "conclusive evidence," it seems that judges have a right to resort to any helpful source of information.[709] As regards foreign laws, it is held that the question of their existence is wholly for the jury. This is said, on the theory that such laws are mere matters of fact; and so of the questions incidental to the ascertainment of them. Now, two things seem to be true: that, in an exact sense, these last-named questions are questions of fact, and that equally the same questions about domestic laws are questions of fact; that if the *factum* of domestic law is for the court, equally the *factum* of foreign law should be, — assuming it to be

---

Prac., 3d ed. ss. 977, 983 — 988; 2 Thomp. Trials, s. 2133; Pierce, Life of Sumner, i. 330.

[708] Co. Lit. 155 b, note. Compare what appears to be a part of the verbatim charge to the jury in Salisbury's case, Plowden, 101 (1553), where after laying down the subtle law about malice in murder, the court ends "and therefore you must take the law so." In the French original of the report (ed. 1578) it reads, *et pur ceo, preignez le ley issint.* See Lilburne's case, 4 Howell's State Trials, 1269, 1379, 1380.

[709] Gardner *v.* The Collector, 6 Wall. 499, 511; So. Ottawa *v.* Perking, 94 U. S. 260. Questions, in such cases, as to the finality of the authentication of a statute by officers of the political departments, such as are discussed in Field *v.* Clark, 143 U. S. 649, seem, in reality, to be directed to the scope and limitations of judicial power, and to what, for the purposes of a judicial inquiry, shall constitute a statute. The question is, what is the true point where judicial inquiry should end. Compare French *v* Fyan, 93 U. S. 169; McCormick *v.* Hayes, 159 U. S. 332.

true that it is wanted, in order to determine the rule or law of the case. Such law, as well as the domestic law, should be ascertained by the judge. The circumstance that while the domestic law does not need to be proved by evidence, strictly so called, foreign law must be so proved, is not material. In reason the judges might well enough be allowed to inform themselves about foreign law in any manner they choose,[710] just as the judges of the Federal courts notice without proof the laws of all the States. But if it is required to be proved, it should be proved to the judge.[711] The doctrine, however, that it is for the jury has a wide acceptance; and, so far as it goes, if this is not a qualification of the general principle that the jury are not to answer to law, it is at least a departure from the mode of applying that principle in the case of domestic law; for, as we have seen, a question of fact relating to law, which in the latter case is attracted to the tribunal that deals with law, in the other case is not. Consistency and principle would give the last case also to the judges.

Another situation may be mentioned. The relation of the judge to the jury is often necessarily one of mutual assistance. As the judges give the jury advice, information, and aid, touching the jury's special province, so they call upon the jury for assistance in determining their own questions.[712] The method of the chancery judges, of referring a question for trial to a common-law jury, in order to inform and aid them, giving, however, to a jury's verdict such weight as the judge thinks best, may indicate the nature of this thing. Questions of fact, in equity, are for the judge, but he profits sometimes by the advice of a common-law jury; and the same thing takes place in common law courts under statutory provisions;

---

[710] It was judicially noticed in State v. Rood, 12 Vt. 396.

[711] Pickard v. Bailey, 26 N. H. 152; Lockwood v. Crawford, 18 Conn. 361 (by statute); So. Ottawa v. Perkins, 94 V. S. 260; Story, Confl. Laws, s. 638; 1 Grlf. Ev. s. 486.

[712] With the rule correctly laid down in Gorton v. Hadsell, 9 Cushing, 511, by Metcalf, J.: "It is the province of the judge who presides at the trial to decide all questions as to the admissibility of evidence. It is also his province to decide any preliminary question of fact, however intricate, the solution of which may be necessary to enable him to determine the other question of admissibility" (and so Bartlett v. Smith, 11 M. & W. 483), — compare a more or less common judicial practice of consulting the jury in such cases, as in Bartlett v. Hoyt, 33 N. H. 151, 155, 156; Field v. Tenney, 47 N. H. 513, 521, 522; Com. v. Piper, 120 Mass. 185, 188; and Com. v. Culver, 126 Mass. 464, 466. In some cases, this sort of thing is mere error, and not at all an instance of what is mentioned in the text.

"advisory verdicts" are called for.[713] So the common law judge, in construing a writing, sometimes asks the jury for the mercantile meaning or understanding of it, — not because it is intended to leave to them the decision of the question, but in order to profit by their opinion; just as Lord. Mansfield and others built up the commercial law by taking the opinion of special juries, and their reports as to mercantile usage, and founding rules of presumption upon them when they appeared to be reasonable. To aid them in the construction of writings, judges may well have the evidence of mercantile experts.[714] On the same principle, they may take the opinion of a special jury; and may submit to the jury any proper question, that is to say, any question depending upon a judgment of matters which the jury may fairly be supposed to know more about than. the court. In such cases, also, instead of first receiving the opinion of the jury and then deciding the point, a judge may, of course, leave the question to them with contingent instructions, *e. g.,* that if they find that the usage, custom, understanding, or practice of merchants is so and so, then they shall find so and so as to the interpretation of a certain contract or a certain transaction.[715]

In the great case of Lickbarrow *v.* Mason, where the respective rights were brought in question of an unpaid seller of goods, and of one who, in good faith, without notice and for value, had bought from the first buyer, taking an indorsement of the bill of lading, — after the case had gone to the House of Lords on a demurrer upon the evidence, and had been sent back to a new trial for informality in the demurrer,[716] the jury, at the new trial, in accordance with the judge's request, found a special verdict, stating the facts, and adding the understanding and custom of merchants as to the effect of certain transactions. Thereupon the court, "understanding that the case was to be carried up," gave judgment, without reasons, for the plaintiff, who represented the subvendee.[717]

---

[713] Maier *v.* Lillibridge, 70 N. W. Rep. 1032 (Mich. April, 1897) See, also, Willeford *v.* Bell, 49 Pac. Rep. 6, 7 (Cal., May, 1897).

[714] As in Pickering v. Barkley, Style, 132.

[715] An illustration of this is found in Hawes v. Forster, 1 Moo. & Rob. 368; s. c. Williston, Cases on Sales, 887.

[716] Not (as is often said, even by judges) by reason of any decision on the merits. See Lord Blackburn's exposition of this case in Sewell v. Burdick, 10 Appeal Cases, 74.

[717] 5 T. R. 683.

The case was settled, and was never carried up. Now, as regards the law upon this important point, two thirds of the twelve judges who had been concerned in the case had been against the final opinion of the King's Bench, the one which accorded with the famous advisory opinion of Mr. Justice Buller to the Lords. Yet the law has always been considered as settled in accordance with the *pro forma* judgment in the King's Bench, following the opinion of merchants as given in the special verdict. "It is probable," says Blackburn, "that the finding of the jury of the custom of merchants had great weight."[718] The true significance of such a thing as this, inserting in the verdict the understanding and custom of merchants on a question of doubtful interpretation as to the meaning and legal result of certain commercial transactions, can only amount to a mode of assisting the court by the judgment of experts. The court may follow it, but they need not; it is not a determination which has any binding force; but it does present to the court a fact which may properly weigh with. them in reaching a conclusion, just as the judgment of an expert witness presents to a jury a fact which may properly weigh in reaching their own independent conclusion upon the same point.[719] The value of a knowledge of "the custom among merchants" in interpreting mercantile contracts and transactions had been emphatically recognized by Lord Hardwicke a generation earlier;[720] and "the want of any recent evidence as to the usages of commercial men" is one of the

---

[718] Sale, 288. And so Christian, Bankruptcy (ed. 1814), ii. 406: "As the decision of the Court of King's Bench, . . . though no reason was given, seems to be considered the present law, I presume it arises from the finding of the jury that the property in the goods is transferred by the blank indorsement and transmission of the bill of lading." Regarding it as an original question, both Blackburn and Cliristian agree with the opinion of Lord Longhborough and the majority of the judges, as against Mr. Justice Buller and his court.

[719] Compare the note of the American editor of East's reports at the statement in King *v.* Nicols, 13 East, 411 n , that "this special verdict was removed here," etc.: "This was not a special verdict, properly so called, but rather a special finding of a particular fact, as a guide to the judgment of the court whether, taking the particular fact to be as stated by the jury, they were warranted by the evidence in finding a general verdict of guilty."

[720] Ekins *v.* Macklish, Ambler, 184 (1753); Kruger *v.* Wilcox, 16. 252 (1755); Godfrey *v.* Furzo, 3 P. Williams, 185, 187 (1733). And so in the common-law courts, Fearon *v.* Bowers, 1 H. Bl. 364 n.; and a hundred years before that, Pickering *v.* Barkley, Style, 132.

difficulties complained of in the House of Lords in an important modern case.[721]

A straightforward look at this sort of thing is taken by Lord Esher, in a case involving the construction of a policy of insurance.[722] "Anything," he says, "more informal, inartistic or ungrammatical than those policies or charter parties cannot be found, and until recently whenever a point arose as to their meaning our judges almost invariably took the opinion of the jury upon the question. They did not merely take the evidence of custom, they asked juries what their view of the contract was, and I myself should have been prepared to take the opinion of a jury on this point as a matter of business. It is said that there is this difficulty, that it would be necessary to take the evidence of average adjusters, and that these adjusters have proclaimed that they do not act upon any customs of merchants, but that they endeavor to follow the law. But I should have suggested that merchants should also be called as witnesses, and that the jury should decide after having heard the whole evidence."

The simple truth in such cases appears to be, that the court, whether or not they be quite ready as yet to adopt the opinion which they ask, as giving the legal rule, are wishing to know that opinion, as an aid to them, in laying down the law.[723]

LEGAL REASONING.

---

[721] Glyn & _at. v._ E. & W. I. Dock Co., 7 App. Cas. 591 (1882), _per_ Lord O'Hagan.

[722] Stewart _v._ Merchants' Mar. Ins. Co., 16 Q. B. D. 619, 627; s. c. 34 W. B. 208, 210.

[723] Compare Evans, Decisions of Lord Mansfield, ii. 338, note (m).

CHAPTER VI
THE LAW OF EVIDENCE;
AND LEGAL REASONING AS
APPLIED TO THE ASCERTAINMENT
OF FACTS

I. What is our Law of Evidence? It is a set of rules and principles affecting judicial investigations into questions of fact; for the most part, controverted questions. It is concerned with the operations of courts of justice, and not with ordinary inquiries *in pais;* and even within this limited range, it does not undertake to regulate the processes of reasoning or argument, except as helping to discriminate and select the material of fact upon which these are to operate; these processes themselves go on, after their own methods, even when all the "evidence" is in, or when there is none and all the facts are admitted. They are the same which take place in questions of law upon a demurrer, — those of mere reasoning. But when one offers "evidence," in the sense of the word which is now under consideration, he offers, otherwise than by reference to what is already known, to prove a matter of fact which is to be used as a basis of inference to another matter of fact. He offers, perhaps, to present to the senses of the tribunal a visible object which may furnish a ground of inference; or he offers testimony, oral or written, to prove a fact;[724] for even direct testimony, to be believed or disbelieved, according as we trust the witness, is really but a basis of inference. In giving evidence we are furnishing to a tribunal a new basis for reasoning. This is not saying that we do not have to reason

---

[724] Stephen's limitation of the term "evidence" to (1) the statements of witnesses and (2) documents is too narrow. When, in a controversy between a tailor and his customer, involving the fit of a coat, the customer puts on the coat and wears it during the trial, as in Brown *v.* Foster, 113 Mass., at p. 137, a basis of inference is supplied otherwise than by reasoning or by statements, whether oral or written; and it seems impossible to deny to this the name of "evidence." It is what Bentham called "real evidence," a phrase which imports a very valuable discrimination, when limited to that which is presented directly to the senses of the tribunal. It is not, practically, of much importance when divided further into "reported real evidence," etc. Best, in his treatise, has confused the topic by following Bentham into this sort of refinement, overlooking, probably, for the moment, the fact that Bentham, unlike himself, was engaged in a philosophical discussion and was not writing a law book.

in order to ascertain this basis; it is merely saying that reasoning alone will not, or at least does not, supply it. The new element thus added is what we call the evidence.

It must be noticed, then, that "evidence," in the sense used when we speak of the law of evidence, has not the large meaning imputed to it in ordinary discourse. It is a term of forensic procedure; and imports something put forward in a court of justice. When men speak of historical evidence and scientific evidence, and the evidences of Christianity, they are talking about a different sort of thing. The law of evidence has to do with the furnishing to a court of matter of fact, for use in a judicial investigation. But how "has to do"? It prescribes the manner of presenting evidence; as by requiring that it shall be given in open court, by one who personally knows the thing, appearing in person, subject to cross-examination, or by allowing it to be given by deposition, taken in such and such a way; and the like. It fixes the qualifications and the privilege of witnesses, and the mode of examining them. And chiefly, it determines, as among probative matters, matters in their nature evidential, — what classes of things shall not be received. This excluding function is the characteristic one in our law of evidence.

Observe, at this point, one or two fundamental conceptions. There is a principle — not so much a rule of evidence as a presupposition involved in the very conception of a rational system of evidence, as contrasted with the old formal and mechanical systems — which forbids receiving anything irrelevant, not logically probative. How are we to know what these forbidden things are? Not by any rule of law. The law furnishes no test of relevancy. For this, it tacitly refers to logic and general experience, — assuming that the principles of reasoning are known to its judges and ministers, just as a vast multitude of other things are assumed as already sufficiently known to them.

There is another precept which should be laid down as preliminary, in stating the law of evidence; namely, that unless excluded by some rule or principle of law, all that is logically probative is admissible. This general admissibility, however, of what is logically probative is not, like the former principle, a necessary presupposition in a rational system of evidence; there are many exceptions to it. Yet, in order to a clear conception of the law, it is important to notice this also as being a fundamental proposition. In an historical sense it has not been the fundamental thing, to which the different exclusions were exceptions. What has taken place, in fact, is the shutting out by the judges of one and another thing from time to time; and so, gradually, the recognition of this exclusion under a rule. These rules of exclusion have had their exceptions; and so the law has come into the shape of a set of primary rules of exclusion; and then a set of exceptions to these rules. For example, in the case of hearsay, our courts treat as the affirmative rule the one which excludes hearsay; and in a new case, unless it can be brought within an admitted exception, this is the rule which is applied.[725] And yet, while this is historically true, the main propositions which I have stated should, in the order of thought, be first laid down and always kept in mind as fundamental. If the doing of this shall bring about a restatement of some material parts of the law of evidence, that, perhaps, will only turn out as it should.

In stating thus our two large, fundamental conceptions, we must not fall into the error of supposing that relevancy, logical connection, real or supposed, is the only test of admissibility; for so we should drop oat of sight the chief part of the law of evidence. When we have said that, without any exception, nothing which is not, or is not supposed to be, logically relevant is admissible; and that, subject to many exceptions and qualifications, whatever is logically relevant is admissible; it is obvious that, in reality, there are tests of admissibility other than logical relevancy. Some things are rejected as being of too slight a significance, or as having too conjectural and remote a connection; others, as being dangerous, in their effect on the jury, and likely to be misused or overestimated by that body; others, as being impolitic, or unsafe on public grounds; others, on the bare ground of precedent. It is this sort of thing, as I said before, — the rejection on one or another practical ground, of what is really probative, — which is the characteristic thing in the law of evidence; stamping it as the child of the jury system.[726] The

---

[725] And so Lord Blackburn puts it, at the end of his opinion in the important case of Sturla v. Freccia, 5 App. Cas. 623: "I base my judgment on this, that no case has gone so far as to say that such a document could be received; and clearly, unless it is to be brought within some one of the exceptions, it would fall within the general rule that hearsay evidence is not admissible." Compare the dealing of Erie, C. J., with a rule in the law of sale (Eicholz v. Bannister, 17 C. B. N. s. 708), "beset with so many exceptions that they well nigh eat it up."

[726] It is here that Mr. Justice Stephen's treatment of the law of evidence is perplexing, and has the aspect of a *tour de force*. Helpful as his writings on this subject have been, they are injured by the small consideration that he shows for

the historical aspect of the matter, and by the over-ingenious attempt to put the rules of evidence wholly into terms of relevancy. It is to be observed that by relevancy he always means logical relevancy; the common but uninstructive distinction between legal and logical relevancy is not made by him. This attempt goes far to deprive his work of permanent value; it is impossible thus to take the kingdom of heaven by force. One who would state the law of evidence truly must allow himself to grow intimately acquainted with the working of the jury system and its long history. In the Introduction to the Digest of Evidence, the author says: "The great bulk of the law of evidence consists of negative rules declaring what, as the expression runs, is not evidence. The doctrine that all facts in issue, and relevant to the issue, and no others, may be proved, is the unexpressed principle which forms the centre of, and gives unity to, all these express negative rules. To me these rules always appeared to form a hopeless mass of confusion, which might be remembered by a great effort, but could not be understood as a whole, or reduced to a system, until it occurred to me to ask the question, 'What is this evidence which you tell me hearsay is not?' The expression 'hearsay is not evidence' seemed to assume that I knew, by the light of nature, what evidence was; but I perceived at last that that was what I did not know. I found that I was in the position of a person who, having never seen a cat, is instructed about them in this fashion: 'Lions are not cats in one sense of the word, nor are tigers nor leopards, though you might be inclined to think they were.' Show me a cat, to begin with, and I at once understand what is meant by saying that the lion is not a cat, and why it is possible to call him one. Tell me what evidence is, and I shall be able to understand why you say this and that class of facts are not evidence. The question, 'What is evidence?' gradually disclosed the ambiguity of the word. To describe a matter of fact as 'evidence' in the sense of testimony is obviously nonsense. No one wants to be told that hearsay, whatever else it is, is not testimony. What then does the word mean? The only possible answer is; it means that the one fact either is, or else is not, considered by the person using the expression to furnish a premise or part of a premise from which the existence of the other is a necessary or probable inference, — in other words, that the one fact is or is not relevant to the other. When the inquiry *is* pushed farther, and the nature of relevancy has to be considered in itself, and apart from legal rules about it, we are led to inductive logic, which shows that judicial evidence is only one case of the general problem of science, namely, inferring the unknown from the known. As far as the logical theory of the matter is concerned, this is an ultimate answer. The logical theory was cleared up by Mr. Mill. Bentham and some other writers had more or less discussed the connection of logic with the rules of evidence. But I am not aware that it occurred to any one before I published my 'Introduction to the Indian Evidence Act' to point out in detail the very close resemblance which exists between Mr. Mill's theory and the existing state of the law. The law has been worked out by degrees by many generations of judges who perceived, more or less distinctly, the principles upon which it ought to be founded. The rules established by them no doubt treat as relevant some facts, which cannot be said to be so. More frequently they treat as irrelevant facts which are really relevant; but, exceptions excepted, all their rules are reducible to the principle that facts in issue, or relevant to the issue, and no others, may be proved."It is singular that Stephen should have chosen as a basis for careful

law of evidence is the creature of experience rather than logic, and we cannot escape the necessity of tracing that experience. Founded, as being a rational system, upon the laws that govern human thought, and so presupposing and of necessity conforming to these, it yet recognizes another influence that must, at every moment, be taken, into account; for it is this which brought it into being, as it is the absence of this which alone accounts for the non-existence of it in all other than English-speaking countries, whether ancient or modern. I have already indicated that the main errand of the law of evidence is to determine not so much what is admissible in proof, as what is inadmissible. Assuming, in general, that what is evidential is receivable, it is occupied in pointing out what part of this mass of matter is excluded. It denies to this excluded part, not the name of evidence, but the name of admissible evidence. Admissibility is determined, first, by relevancy, — an affair of logic and experience, and not at all of law; second, but only indirectly, by the law of evidence, which declares whether any given matter which is logically probative is excluded.

Is it then really so, that this great multitude of decisions, emerging day by day, and holding that such and such evidence is or is not admissible, have so little to do with the law of evidence which they are professing to declare? Yes. The greater part of them are really reducible to mere propositions of sound reason as applied to a

---

discriminations so loose a catch as this, that "hearsay is not evidence." Of course it often is evidence, in the sense of being logically relevant; what is meant is, that it is not legally admissible. If the phrase "hearsay is not evidence" is to be used in serious discussion, the term "evidence" must have the purely special sense of that sort of evidence which is legally receivable by the courts. The true statement is, that while hearsay may be evidence, it is not admissible evidence; it is a kind of evidence which is rejected. When the writer says that "the doctrine that all facts in issue and relevant to the issue, and no others, may be proved, is the unexpressed principle which forms the centre of, and gives unity to, all these express negative rules," namely, rules "declaring what, as the expression runs, is not evidence," it is not quite clear what is meant. But certainly the twofold doctrine which is named does not "form the centre of, and give unity to, all these express negative rules," in the sense of supplying the test by which they are applied. Something else has to be taken into account; namely, the many practical considerations which the jury system brought vividly home to the judges, as they shaped our rules of evidence in the daily administration of it. When the writer says that he is assumed to know what "evidence" is, he states what is true enough; the law does take it for granted that people know how to find out what is and what is not probative, as matter of reason and general experience.

point of substantive law or pleading. When a man mistakes his proposition of substantive law and offers evidence to sustain the erroneous view, he is daily told that his evidence is not admissible, when the thing meant is that he is wrong in his notion of the law of damages;[727] or of the legal standard of diligence;[728] or of the scope of the general issue in pleading,[729] or of a plea of payment. In such cases a determination that what is offered in evidence is or is not receivable, means you are wrong in your proposition of substantive law; and, having regard to the. true proposition, your "evidence" (*i. e.,* what you offer as evidence) is logically irrelevant. All such determinations as these, of which there is a vast, uncountable number in our books, while they certainly relate to evidence, and involve questions of law, involve no point at all in the law of evidence.[730]

It seems, then, that our law of evidence, while it is, emphatically, a rational system, as contrasted with the old formal methods, is yet a peculiar one. In the shape it has taken, it is not at all a necessary development of the rational method of proof; so that, where people did not have the jury, or, having once had it, did not keep it, as on the continent of Europe, although they, no less than we, worked out a rational system, they developed under the head of evidence, no separate and systematized branch of the law.

---

[727] Hart v. Pa. R. R. Co., 112 U. S. p. 343.

[728] Grand Trunk Ry. Co. *v.* Richardson, 91 U. S. p. 469.

[729] Marine Ins. Co. v. Hodgson, 6 Cranch, p. 219; Young *v.* Black, 7 *ib.* P. 567; Spooner *v.* Cummings, 151 Mass. 313.

[730] See Holmes, Common Law, 120 — 129. A neat illustration of the common error here referred to is furnished in the very recent case of Richmond B. R. Co. *v.* Tobacco Co., 169 U. S. 311 (1898), in which the opinion would reduce a statutory role as to the liability of carriers to a role of evidence. A statute of Virginia had provided that a carrier taking anything for a point beyond his own terminus should be deemed to assume an obligation for its safe carriage through the whole route, unless at the time of acceptance he were exempted from such liability by a contract in writing. Even if there were such contract in writing, yet in case of loss the carrier was to be liable unless he showed that it did not occur while the thing was in his charge. That is a statutory regulation of the responsibility of carriers; and yet, strangely, it is declared to be too plain for anything but statement that it is a rule of evidence. Perhaps this exposition may be accounted for by the fact that the learned and able judge who gives it was trained in the practice of Louisiana, where common-law rules and principles are much modified or displaced. The same remark, perhaps, may account for the exposition in Coffin *v. U. S.,* 156 U. *S.* 432, and in Bram *v. U. S.,* 168 U. S. 532.

II. And, now, let us bring out into distinct view the element of legal reasoning, — an element common to all rational systems of proof; common also, in rational systems, to all parts of the law, since in administering the law, in all parts of it, this process is forever going on, with all that recognition of a body of commonly known ideas, facts, axioms, and processes of thought which the exercise of this function always and everywhere involves. In seeking to ascertain the unknown from the known, a judicial tribunal is called on to use, apply, reflect upon, and compare a great body of facts and ideas of which it is already in possession, and of which no particle of "evidence," strictly so called, is ever formally presented in court. And then, in addition, it has to be put in possession of new material. It is this necessity, that of furnishing new matter, which gives occasion for rules of evidence. On the other hand, the function of scrutinizing the material which it has once got, of observing its implications, and the effect of one part on another, of comparing and inferring, does not belong to the region of the law of evidence. To the hungry furnace of the reasoning faculty the law of evidence is but a stoker.

Let it be distinctly set down, then, that the whole process of legal argumentation, and the rules for it, essential as these are, and forever pressing upon the attention, are mainly an affair of logic and general experience, not of legal precept. I say mainly, because the reasoning process, in its application to particular subjects, gets always a tincture from the subject-matter. Undoubtedly there are rules of legal practice and procedure, qualifying and restraining the free processes of reason; that it is a proper qualification, when we use the phrase *legal* reasoning; not because, as compared with reasoning in general, it calls into play any different faculties or involves any new principles or methods, or is the creature of technical precepts; but because in law, as elsewhere, in adjusting old and universal methods to the immediate purposes in hand, special limitations, exclusions, and qualifications have to be taken into account. In particular and emphatically, in legal reasoning, such peculiarities spring from the practical aims of a court of justice and the practical conditions of its work; *e. g.,* from the nature of such a tribunal as a jury, and the exigencies of time, place, and subject-matter which control its operations. In dealing with litigation, courts are not engaged in an academic exercise. With them the search for truth is not the main matter; their desire to know this, and their ability to use it, are limited by the requirements of their main business, namely, that of awarding justice, *i. e.,* awarding it so far as they may, under the rules of law, and according to established usages and forms. The doctrine of estoppel, for instance, often makes the actual truth simply irrelevant, because the real question is, "What is it just and lawful that a party should, claim? And again, — whether it be out of regard to the general want of time and convenient opportunity; or to the nature of the questions discussed, and the ordinary methods of mankind in judging of the practical problems of life and. business, and the practical impossibility of running an inquiry out into fine details; or to the nature of our popular tribunal, the jury; or for whatever reason; we have principles of exclusion which limit the inquiry, and so the evidence, to matters that have a clear and obvious bearing and a plainly appreciable weight, as contrasted with what is slight, conjectural, and remote; and to matters which do not unnecessarily tend to complicate and confuse the determination of the issue. These I call principles, rather than rules, because of their necessarily indeterminate form, and their appeal to the general sense and judgment of the tribunal; as contrasted with definite legal rules, in the application of which it is reasonable to expect a near approach to unanimity among competent minds.

We have no treatises and no chapters of treatises that deal separately and specifically with the topic of legal reasoning in the ascertainment of facts. Copious books on Evidence, on Procedure, and on the many branches of substantive law, we have, but none upon the nature and methods of that art by which all the rules of all these various subjects are applied and developed. It is not my purpose now to furnish one, but only to bring this subject out into the light, to mark its characteristics, and to emphasize its separate place and distinctive character.

Why is any such exposition needed? Certainly not, as I have said, because legal reasoning differs in any fundamental respect from any other reasoning, or because lawyers have any peculiar organs or methods for tracking and apprehending the truth. What is called the "legal mind" is still the human mind, and it must reason according to the laws of its constitution. There is a good deal in our ordinary legal phraseology that might seem to discredit this, as when we read of rules that *require* inferences which the principles of sound reasoning neither require nor allow; and of the duty to *weigh* a rule of presumption in one scale and evidence in another.[731] But these are merely phrases; the real thing meant, so far as a clear meaning can be imputed to them, is not what is said.

But while legal reasoning, at bottom, is like all other reasoning, yet a thousand practical considerations come in to shape it. There is one grave reason for discriminating this topic and remarking its characteristic methods and its separate place which has been too little observed, namely, that it has a tendency to run over and mingle with other subjects, and to distress all attempts to clarify them. In particular this has happened with the subject of Evidence. Rules, principles, and methods of legal reasoning have taken on the color and used the phraseology of this subject, and thus disguised, have figured as rules of Evidence, to the perplexity and contusion of those who sought for a strong grasp of the subject. A bastard sort of technicality has thus sprung up, and a crop of fanciful reasons for anomalies destitute of reason, which baffle and disgust a healthy mind. To detach and scrutinize this topic of legal reasoning would tend to relieve our main subject of a great part of its difficulties and ambiguities.

What would be some of the leading matters with which such an exposition would have to deal? It would need, in the first place, to take clearly into account the general scope and purposes of legal reasoning in the ascertainment of facts. This does not, like mathematical reasoning, have to do merely with ideal truth, with mere mental conceptions; it is not aiming at demonstration and ideally exact results; it deals with probabilities and not with certainties; it works in an atmosphere, and not in a vacuum; it has to allow for friction, for accident and mischance. Nor is it, like natural science, occupied merely with objective truth. It is concerned with human conduct, and all its elements of fraud, inadvertence, wilfulness, and uncertainty. Nor, as in history, is the purpose in hand merely that of ascertaining and setting forth the facts, or the habits, of human life and action. In all these fields, not merely is the subject-matter in hand and the purposes, different from those held in view in conducting legal inquiries, but it is handled for the most part under different conditions, and under exigencies of time and place and circumstance that control the general aims in view, and the actual conduct of the proceedings. The peculiar character and scope of legal

---

[731] Stephen, Dig. Ev. Art. I.; *infra,* 337, 561. 18

reasoning is determined, by its purely practical aims and the necessities of its procedure and machinery. Litigation imports, for the most part, as we have seen, a contest, and adversaries. It has in it, therefore, a personal element, and it requires not merely a consideration of what is just, in general, but of what is just as between these adversaries. It has often to be conducted with the aid of a tribunal whose peculiarities in point of number and of physical and mental capacity, and whose danger of being misled must constantly be considered. It must shape itself to various other exigencies of a practical kind, such as the time that it is possible to allow to any particular case, the reasonable limitations of the number of witnesses, the opportunities for reply, and the chance to correct errors. It must adjust its processes to general ends, so as generally to promote justice, and to discourage evil, to maintain long-established rights, and the existing governmental order. The judicial office is really one of administration. Long after the business of legislation passed from the hands of the king, the judicial function remained with him and was exercised by his agents; by judges appointed by' him, and holding office merely at his pleasure. And when men began to talk of the separation of the departments of government it was long before the judicial department took anything like a co-ordinate place. Even when it did take that place, it remained still, by its own nature, merely a branch of public administration.

While all this is true, while legal reasoning in ascertaining facts, as I have said, is an art primarily, and above all, subsidiary to dispensing justice, and not primarily, and above all, subsidiary to truth-seeking; while its search after truth is subordinate to this main purpose; and while it thus develops its own maxims, principles, and rules, growing out of the personal relation of the parties to each other and to the court; out of the general ends which the court has in view, *e. g.,* out of the need, on the one hand, of supporting property and ancient rights, and of adhering to forms and precedents, and out of the need, on the other hand, of adapting procedure and administration to practical exigencies and to the sense of justice and humanity; out of the necessity for decision and for action of some sort; out of the practical limitations of time; out of the practical requirements of good sense; and out of the accumulations of experience in the conduct of trials; — while these are some of the chief characteristics of legal reasoning, it will be noticed that they are only, in the nature of them, so many reasonable accommodations of the general process to particular subject-matters and particular aims. Amidst them all the great characteristics of the art of reasoning and the laws of thought still remain constant. As regards the main methods in hand, they are still those untechnical ways of all sound reasoning, of the logical process in its normal and ordinary manifestations; and the rules that govern it here are the general rules that govern it everywhere, the ordinary rules of human thought and human experience, to be sought in the ordinary sources, and not in law books. And so a knowledge of these processes and methods is presupposed in all judges and lawyers. When Abraham Fraunce, therefore, the friend of Sir Philip Sidney, published, in 1588, "The Lawyer's Logic," it turned out to be only a rather novel sort of treatise on the general subject, illustrated by examples from Plowden's recent volume of 1571, and other law books. He had first written his book under the name of "The Shepherd's Logic," taking his examples from Spenser's poem, "The Shepherd's Calendar," published in 1579. The illustrations differed; the thing illustrated was the same.

We may dismiss, then, any notion that legal reasoning is some non-natural process by which the human mind is required to infer what does not logically follow. Expressions that import this are to be regarded as mere phrases for what may be and should be more accurately stated. The technicalities of legal reasoning merely grow out of the material, the subject-matter, in which it works.

The three chapters next following may indicate more fully the contrivances and methods of legal reasoning, and in some degree illustrate what is here said about it. But enough has already been said to show that one who would understand our law of evidence, must detach, and hold apart from it all that belongs to that other untechnical and far wider subject.

JUDICIAL NOTICE.

CHAPTER VII
JUDICIAL NOTICE

We have observed that not all the matter of fact which courts and juries rest upon, in deciding cases, needs to be communicated to them by the parties. Much, in every case, is known already, and much is common to all cases; such things are assumed, stated and reasoned upon without discussion. Often, also, much of which there might, in point of mere theory, be a doubt, will, as a matter of established practice, be allowed by the court, in the first instance, without formal proof. And there is much which belongs in a dubious and arguable region, as to which a court may or may not proceed in this manner.

The maxim that what is known need not be proved, *manifesta,* [or *notoria] non indigent probatione,* may be traced far back in the civil and the canon law; indeed, it is probably coeval with legal procedure itself. We find it as a maxim in our own books,[732] and it is applied in every part of our law. It is qualified by another principle, also very old, and often overtopping the former in its importance, — *non refert quid notum sit judici, si notum non sit in forma judicii.*[733] These two maxims seem to intimate the whole doctrine of judicial notice. It has two aspects, one regarding the liberty which the judicial functionary has in taking things for granted, and the other the restraints that limit him.[734]

---

[732] Bracton's Note Book, *supra* 13 n.; 7 Co. 39 a — 39 b; 11 Co. 25; State *v.* Intoxicating Liquors, 73 Maine, 279.

[733] Coke, C. J., in an action of slander, Crawford *v.* Blisse, 2 Bul. 150 (1613), quotes this from Bracton, to support the overstrained doctrine of his own day about taking the words charged *in mitiori sensu*

[734] The expression "to take notice of" anything, in our ordinary popular phraseology, imports observing of remarking it. In the legal language of to-day to "take notice" has a meaning correlative to that of giving notice; namely, that of a man's accepting or charging himself with a notification, or with the imputation of knowledge of a thing. But the import of the legal expression to "take judicial notice," as indicating the recognition without proof of something as existing or as being true, seems traceable rather to an older English usage. The word "notice" was formerly often used interchangeably with knowledge, and with our legal term "conusance." In the English of our Bible we read: "Wherefore have we afflicted our souls and thou takest no knowledge?" (Isa. lviii. 3.) "They took knowledge of them that they had been with Jesus." (Acts iv. 13.) So we find in the Norman French of our old reports the expressions take "notice" and take "conusance;" and

What is the nature and scope of this doctrine of judicial notice, and whereabout in the law does it belong? In trying to answer these questions, I propose first to deal briefly with the second one; then to present a number of cases which may furnish illustration, as well as a test and a basis of judgment as regards both questions; then to consider briefly the sort of thing of which courts will take notice without proof, distinguishing also the case of juries; and finally to mention a few discriminations which it is important to keep in mind if one would, make an intelligent application of the principle. The first question will have been answered as we go along.

I. Whereabout in the law does the doctrine of judicial notice belong? Wherever the process of reasoning has a place, and that is everywhere. Not peculiarly in the law of evidence. It does, indeed, find in the region of evidence a frequent and conspicuous application; but the habit of regarding this topic as a mere title in the law of evidence obscures the true conception of both subjects. That habit is quite modern. The careful observer will notice that a very great proportion of the cases involving judicial notice raise no question at all in that part of the law; they relate to pleading, to the construction of the record or of other writings, the legal definition of words, the interpretation of conduct, the process of reasoning, and the regulation of trials. In short, the cases relate to the exercise of the function of judicature in all its scope and at every step. The nature of the process, as well as the name of it, find their best illustration in some of the older cases, long before questions in the law of evidence engaged attention. We are the less surprised, therefore, to find that it was not until Starkie printed his book on evidence, in 1824, that any special mention of this subject occurs in legal treatises on evidence; and that this writer has very little to say about it.[735] The subject of

---

when the reports begin to be translated and published in English, in the seventeenth century and later, we find that the phrase becomes, interchangeably, take notice, take knowledge and take conusance.

[735] Stark. Ev. i. 400 — 405. Bentham, to ba sure, in his "Rationale of Judicial Evidence" (which was not a law book), composed in 1802-1812, and published partly by Dumont in 1823, and in full under the editorship of John Stuart Mill in 1827, had briefly discussed the question (Works, vi. 276, book i. c. 12) how far a judge can pass on questions of fact without "evidence." He concludes, *inter alia,* that a judge should be allowed "at the instance of either party to pronounce, and, in the formation of the ground of the decision, assume, any alleged matter of fact as notorious," subject to the right of the other party to deny the notoriety and call for proof.

judicial notice, then, belongs to the general topic of legal or judicial reasoning. It is, indeed, woven into the very texture of the judicial function. In conducting a process of judicial reasoning, as of other reasoning, not a step can be taken without assuming something which has not been proved;[736] and the capacity to do this, with

---

[736] Stephen (Dig. Ev., 1st and 2d eds., c. vii.) originally dealt with judicial notice under the general head of "Proof," and the special head of "Facts which need not be Proved." For this he was taken to task by an acute critic (20 Sol. Journal, 937), who suggested that since Stephen's art. 93, relating to the burden of proof, declares that whoever desires a judgment as to any legal right depending on the existence or non-existence of facts which he asserts, "must prove that those facts do or do not exist;" and since art. 59 (about judicial notice) declares that some facts asserted by a party need not be proved by him, — the true place for this last was that of an exception to the art. 93. This led Stephen, in his third edition, to change the special head of c. vii. from "Facts which need not be Proved" to "Facts proved Otherwise than by Evidence" (his definition of "evidence," art. 1, being (a) the statements of witnesses in court, and *(b)* documents produced in court), and called forth certain remarks in the preface to the third edition (Little and Brown's ed. (1877) 26: "By proof I mean the means used of making the court aware of the existence of a given fact; and surely the simplest possible way of doing so is to remind the court that it knows it already. It is like proving that it is raining by telling the judge to look out of the window. It has been said that judicial notice should come under the head of burden of proof; hot sorely this is not so. The rules as to burden of proof show which side ought to call upon the court to take judicial notice of a particular fact; but the act of taking judicial notice, of consciously recalling to the mind a fact known, but not for the moment adverted to, is an act of precisely the same kind as listening to the evidence of a witness or reading a document; that is, belongs to the general head of proof." As regards all this, one or two things may be briefly remarked: (a) "The general head of proof," and "the means used of making the court aware of the existence of a given fact," include the whole topic of legal reasoning; they spread far beyond the law of evidence. The same reach belongs to the burden of proof. So that both Stephen and his critic recognize the wide scope of judicial notice. (&) It seems a very inadequate conception of the subject of judicial notice to speak of it as "a means of making the court aware" of a fact; it has to do not merely with the action of the Court when the parties are seeking to move it, but when alone and acting upon its own motion. To read a document in Court, or to listen to a witness there, is to deal with "evidence;" and so when an object is submitted to the judge's inspection in Court. But the true conception of what is judicially known is that of something which is not, or rather need not be unless the tribunal wishes it, the subject of either evidence or argument — something which is already in the court's possession, or at any rate is so accessible that there is no occasion, unless the court ask for it, to use "any means to make the Court aware" of it; something which it may deal with quite unhampered by any rules of law. In making this investigation, the judge is emancipated entirely from all the rules of evidence laid down for the investigation of facts in general. Markby, Notes to Indian Evid. Act. London, Henry Frowde, 1897. (c) There is sometimes

competent judgmeat and efficiency, is imputed to judges and juries as part of their necessary mental outfit.

II. Let me illustrate the subject by a number of classified cases drawn, from all periods of our law. I shall risk a suspicion of pedantry for the sake of emphasizing the main point.

1. Certain cases relating to the pleadings and matters of record. In looking at these the reader will find constant illustration of what has already been indicated, that the right of a court to act upon what is in point of fact known to it must be subordinate to those requirements of form and orderly communication which regulate the mode of bringing controversies into court, and of stating and conducting them. If formal words are necessary, as *felonice, murdravit,* and *burglariter,* in the old private appeals, and in indictments, you must use them. If a certain form of action is necessary, you must resort to it. If a certain order or time of presentation be necessary, you must conform to it. If, as regards the fulness of detail or the precision of allegation, there be any rule of "certainty," you must conform to that. If there be any rule of the substantive law as to what constitutes the actionable or

---

confusion between judicial notice and inspection, or the dealing by a court with what Ben tham calls "real evidence," — a thing submitted directly to the senses of the tribunal; as in Stephenson v. The State, 28 Lid. 272 (1867), where the trial judge had decided the question whether the appellant was over fourteen years of age by simply inspecting him. He certified to the upper court that "as the defendant, being present in court, presented . . . the appearance of a full-grown man, such proof *[i. e.,* other evidence] was not required." Of course this was merely an instance of settling a question by the use of a certain sort of evidence, — and it may be added that it was, at common law, a very familiar way. *Supra,* 21,104. But the upper Court describe the situation as one where "no proof whatever was offered as to the age of the defendant." "The judge was not a witness, and the State is not entitled to avail itself of his knowledge, except upon matters of which the Court takes judicial notice." The real ground of the court's decision here (granting a new trial) appeared to be that when a jury or trial judge decides a question of fact in this way, a party loses the benefit of his exceptions, because there is no way of presenting the evidence to an appellate Court in such a manner as to enable it to judge of "the reasonableness of the impression" made upon the mind of the lower tribunal. It is difficult to assent to the court's conception of what took place at the trial, or their view that it is impossible to have the full benefit of exceptions when the trial Court avails itself of "real evidence." Stephen's illustration of "proving that it is raining by telling the judge to look out of the window," is another instance of the use of real evidence.

punishable thing, or what is a defence, of coarse the pleadings and the record must come up to it. Under this general head may be put the following cases: —

(a) In 1302,[737] in an assize of novel disseisin against John de Wilton, and others, a plea in abatement for misnomer was put forward: *"Westcot.* Sir John answers and says that his name is John de Willington; judgment of the writ.... *Hunt.* Known by this name; ready, etc. Brompton, J. He is known through all England as Willington, and by no other name, and that well know we; and therefore as to John you shall take nothing by your writ." This, as we have it, is giving judgment upon a point of ordinary fact as being notorious.

(b) In 1332 — 3,[738] in a *quare impedit* against the Dean and Chapter of St. Peter's at York, the Dean made no appearance. Counsel stated that he was dead, and then: *"Trewe.*[739] Where notice comes that a man is dead you are not to go to judgment against him. It is a notorious thing that the Dean is dead, and, therefore, you should not go to judgment against him. Herle (C. J.). We cannot go to judgment upon a thing notorious, hut only according to what the process before us is. *Basset.* A *quare impedit* was brought against H. de Stanton,[740] and he died pending the writ, wherefore the writ abated. *Herle.* The writ was not abated by judgment, but the plaintiff waived his writ because he knew that he was dead."

(c) In 1456,[741] in a *quare impedit,* the declaration related to a church in Wales, and the writ was brought in the County of Hereford. *Littleton,* for the defendant, objected that the plaintiff had not stated, either in his account or his writ, that Hereford adjoined Wales, and the law required that the action should be brought in a county adjoining. But the court held with the plaintiff, who insisted that *"prima facie* it will be intended that the County of Hereford adjoins Wales until the contrary is alleged; if the defendant would take advantage of this, he should allege that the County of Hereford is not adjoining, or otherwise it will be taken that it is."

---

[737] Y. B. 30 & 31 Ed. I. 256.

[738] Y. B. 7 Ed. III. 4, 7.

[739] *Semble,* Simon de Trewethosa, a serjeant of the period.

[740] Herle's predecessor as Chief Justice of the Common Pleas.

[741] Y. B. 35 H. VL 30, 35.

(d) In 1552 — 3,[742] in an action of debt upon a statute the defendant demurred to the declaration for misreciting the statute as being of the 32 H. VIII., while in truth it was of the 33 H. VIII. *Sounders,* for the plaintiff, argued: "You judges have a private knowledge and a judicial knowledge *(un pryuate scyence et un iudyciall scyence),* and of your private knowledge you cannot judge.... [And then he recites the story of Gascoigne and Henry IV., in Y. B. 7 H. IV. 41 *(infra,* 291), adding:] But there he could not acquit him and give judgment of his own private knowledge. But where you have a judicial knowledge, there you may, and you may give judgment according to it. As if one be arraigned upon an indictment for an offence which is pardoned by Parliament, there you ought not to proceed in it or give judgment if he is found guilty, because it appears to you by your judicial knowledge that you ought not to arraign him. For the judges ought to take notice *(prender conusance)* of statutes which appear to them judicially, although they are not pleaded; and then the misrecital of that whereof the judges ought to take notice without recital is not material." But the court held that while the plaintiff need not recite the statute "because it is a general statute, and extends to every one of the king's subjects, and the justices are bound to take notice of it; ... [yet] the count should abate for the misrecital.... For declarations ought to have two things; the first is certainty, in order that the defendant may know what he is to answer to; ... the other thing... is truth.... In our case he has grounded his action upon a statute by him recited, where it appears to us judicially that there is no such statute made at that time." Here the court was called upon to take judicial cognizance of the date of a statute, and they did it; but, again, they were restrained from giving the plaintiff any benefit of their knowledge by a rule of pleading. It was not known *in forma judicii.*[743]

(e) In 1588 — 9, in an action of ejectment, there was a special verdict which set forth the founding of a hospital by the name of The Master and Chaplains of the Hospital of Henry the Seventh, late King of England, of the Savoy, and that afterwards the said master and chaplains being seized, etc., leased the same to the defendant by the name of W. H., Master of the Hospital... called the

---

[742] Partridge *v.* Strange, Plow. 77, 83 — 84. It will be remembered that Plowden was first published in French in 1571; the translation first appeared about two centuries later, in 1761.

[743] *Supra,* 277.

Savoy. And afterwards by their true name they leased the same to Thomas Fanshawe the plaintiff's lessor, and the question was whether the lease to the defendant by the name above stated was good.[744] The ground upon which the judges went who decided, in the Exchequer of Pleas, that the first lease was bad, and also those who agreed with them in the Exchequer Chamber, seems to have been that a very high degree of "certainty" was required in such a case.[745] The case is here cited mainly for the high-strung reasoning of Coke in arguing for the plaintiff, in the Exchequer Chamber, against the lease: "If the name given to this hospital upon the foundation of it and the name usurped in the lease be not *unum in sensu* (not in your private understanding as private persons, but in your judicial knowledge upon the record, *quod coram vobis resident,* as judges of record) then this lease is void. For although you as private persons, otherwise than by record, know that the hospital of Savoy and the hospital *vocat le Savoy* are all one hospital, you ought not upon that your private knowledge to give judgment, unless your judicial knowledge agree with it; that is, the knowledge which is out of the records which you have before you. But if the name given upon the foundation and the usurped name be not *idem sensu* in your judicial knowledge, and yon cannot otherwise conceive the identity of these two hospitals nor make any construction to imagine it but by the record, for the record is your eye of justice, and you have no other eye to look unto the cause depending before yon but the record, and to this purpose he cited the case of 7 H. IV. 108 *[sic,* but meaning probably 7 H. IV. 41, — which is thereupon inaccurately stated],.. so in our case, it may be that you in your private knowledge know that the hospital *de la Savoy* and the hospital *vocat le Savoy* is all one; but that doth not appear unto you upon the record which is before you, but it may be, for

---

[744] Marriott *v.* Pascall, 1 Leon. 159; s. c. *sub nom.* Mariot v. Mascal, 1 And. 202, and *sub nom.* Fanshawe's case, Moore, 228. The case was hard fought; in the Exchequer of Pleas it was held (Manwood, C. B., dissenting in a long opinion, preserved in Moore's Reports) that the first lease was had. In the Exchequer Chamber the court discussed it without giving judgment, and were divided in opinion; the full opinion of Anderson (C. J. C. P.) is found in his reports. But the case was finally settled by the parties.

[745] See the quaint, pedantic discourse of Anderson, C. J., on words and names, in his long opinion in 1 And. 208 — 220.

anything that appears in the record, that they are diverse and several hospitals. Therefore the lease is void." [746]

In 1611 an indictment alleged an arrest at London on 18 November "between the hours of five and six in the afternoon." It was contended that the arrest was illegal *as* being in the night, *i.e.,* after sunset, but the court ("all the judges of England and barons of the Exchequer") "resolved that although in truth between five and six o'clock in November is part of the night, yet the court is not bound *ex officio* to take conusance of it, no more than in the case of burglary without these words, *in nocte...* or *noctanter.*" [747]

And again, under this head belong such cases as that of Taylor *v.* Barclay,[748] where, on a demurrer to a bill in equity which alleged that the British Government had recognized the independence of the Federal Republic of South America, the Vice-Chancellor, having informed himself at the foreign office that this was not true, took judicial notice of the fact; and he declined to hold that the admissions of the demurrer extended to what was thus known to the court to be a false allegation.

---

[746] To all this learned triviality add that of Manwood, C. B., in supporting the case of the defendant against another objection, namely, that the lease was bad as omitting the word late *(nuper),* in the designation of King Henry VII. It is intended, he says, that he who speaks of King Henry VII. speaks of the late king of that name, "just as the Dean and Chapter of Carlisle was incorporated by the name of the Dean and Chapter of the Holy and undivided Trinity, of Carlisle; and in the lease they omit undivided, yet was it good enough, . . . and the reason was because by the name of the Trinity the word 'undivided' is as strongly intended as if it were expressed; for everybody knows that the Trinity is undivided, and so in 36 H. VI. the foundation was the Church of St. Peter and Paul the Apostles, and the lease omitted the Apostles, and yet good, for it is intended in the plea, and all know that Peter and Paul were Apostles. So also the lease is good where the foundation is of the Blessed Virgin Mary and Virgin is omitted; yet it is good, for all men well know that Mary was blessed and a Virgin."

[747] Mackelley'a case, 9 Co. 65 a, 67; *ib.* 62. The phrases here are probably those of the first English edition of theas reports in 1658, long after Coke's death in 1633. He published his reports in Norman French. The ninth book appeared in 1613, and the passage above quoted (not to quote it all) reads in the French: *"Le court nest tenus ex officio a prender conusance de ceo nient pluis que in case de burglarie suns ceux paroles in node eiusdem diei,* or *noctanter."* In Trotman's "Epitome" of the first eleven books, published in 1640, this reads (p. 468), *"Court nest ten p prend notice,"* etc.

[748] 2 *Sim.* 213 (1828).

2. A second class of cases relates merely to the construction of writings or the interpretation of words. Here the courts take notice of the ordinary meaning of language and of usual habits of speech; and they formerly took notice, not merely, as now, of the general meaning, but also of the local use of language.[749]

In 1536,[750] in holding good the condition of a bond to pay seven pounds to the obligor's own wife, Fitzherbert, J., says: "The meaning and intent of the parties shall be taken; for I have seen this case adjudged: Two made a contract for eighteen barrels of ale,... and the buyer would have had the barrels when the ale was gone; adjudged that he should not, because it is commonly used that the seller should have them, and it was not the intent of the parties that the buyer should have the barrels but only the ale. Suppose I make a covenant with you that if you, come to my house I will give you a cup of wine; if you come you shall not have the cup, for it cannot be intended *(entend)* that my intent was to give you the cup."

(b) In 1611,[751] on the defendant's demurrer, in an action of debt on a bond, — in passing upon the meaning of these words in the condition, namely, "which should be levied," Fleming, C. J., laid it down that, "as touching construction of words they shall be taken according to the... intent of parties,... and this intention and construction of words shall be taken according to the vulgar and usual sense, phrase, and manner of speech of these words and of that place where the words are spoken." In this case, while there was no averment that the words had any peculiar local meaning, the argument of counsel was in the terms adopted by the court and just quoted, and he illustrated thus: "As in Lincolnshire where eight strikes make a bushel, the judges of the common law are for to take notice of particular usages in several places, as of London measure in buying of cloth there."

And so in 1613 and 1623, in actions on the case (1) for not delivering "20 *Cumbos tritici,*" "though it is not averred by any *Anglice quid est Cumbos,* yet the court ought to take notice thereof, being the phrase of the country of Norfolk and Suffolk and other places, and. there well known;" upon a sale of *"quosdam carrucas signatas, Anglice* car-rooms, though it is not averred what is intended

---

[749] See McGregor *v.* Gregory, 11 M. & W. p. 295.
[750] Y. B. 27 H. VIII. 27, 12.
[751] Hewet *v.* Painter, 1 Bul. 174.

by the word 'car-rooms' nor what it signifies, yet the declaration is good; for it is a phrase in London well known, of which the court ought to take notice, this being a phrase of the country."[752]

(S) There was a set of cases where the courts, for the purpose of checking a particular kind of action, adopted a rule which refused to give effect to the ordinary meaning of words, and persisted for many years in considering only whether they could not be made to bear some other meaning. Actions for defamation, which were a slip transplanted from the popular and ecclesiastical courts, started into such a savage luxuriance of growth in the king's courts, in the sixteenth and seventeenth centuries, that the judges appear to have been frightened.[753] For many years they did their best to discourage the action by applying a rule that the words should be taken *in mitiori sensu.* For example, it was held that it was not actionable, as imputing crime, to say of another,[754] "Thou hast stolen by the highway side," for it might be taken that he came unawares upon some one by the highway, or that he stole a stick under a hedge; or to say,[755] "Holt struck his cook on the head with a cleaver and cleaved his head; the one part lay on the one shoulder and another part on the other," for "the party may yet be living, and it is then but trespass," and again, in 1615 — 16,[756] where one was charged with saying of another, "Thou art a thief, for thou hast stolen me (defendant *innuendo)* a hundred of slafcte," it was held not actionable. The plaintiff's counsel in vain urged that this form of expression was *"le usuall phrase del paies;"* Coke, C. J., answered that he should have averred this, "otherwise we cannot take notice of it, for I do not know that it is a usual phrase in the country. It seems to me that the words are insensible, for it is clear that the first words

---

[752] Rolle's Ab., Court, C. 6, 7. "By car-rooms," adds Bolle, "is intended a mark which the Lord Mayor puts upon a cart."

[753] See Professor Maitland's admirable little paper on "Slander in the Middle Ages," in the Green Bag, ii. 4 (January, 1890). As late as 1671 we find Vaughan, C. J; saying, in King v. Lake (2 Ventris, 28), in an action of slander: "The growth of these actions will spoil all communi-cations; a man shall not say such an inn or such wine is not good. Their progress extends to all professions. . . . The words spoken here have no more relation to the plaintiff's profession, than to say of a lawyer he hath a red nose, or But a little head." Vaughan was dissenting.

[754] Brough v. Dennison, Goldsborough, 143 (1601).

[755] Holt v. Astgrigg, Cro. Jac. 184 (1607).

[756] White *v.* Brough, I Rolle, 286.

are not actionable, *soil.,* thou hast stolen me, 'for it is not felony to steal a man, although it is to steal some women." At Easter, in 1616, plaintiff's counsel again brought up the case and said, *"ceo est un usuall phrase, come en le Scripture,* Fetch me a kidd from the flock."[757] Doderidge, J.: "That is *for* me, and not from me." The counsel urged that either way was good enough for him. Doderidge, J.: "It is uncertain how it should be taken, and therefore the action lies not, for the discredit of such actions;" and judgment was given accordingly against the plaintiff.[758]

The effort of the court in such cases and their point of view may be illustrated by well-known practices of the courts in some classes of modern cases. "Dilatory pleas," said the Supreme Court of Maine, in a recent case,[759] "are allowed because sometimes useful, and promotive of justice. But for the reason that they are often resorted to for inequitable purposes, the law does not favor them;" and thereupon it was held that a plea in abatement was bad which, having begun with praying "judgment of the writ," ended with praying "judg. of said writ." "This abbreviated expression 'judg.,'" said the court, "cannot be accepted for the word 'judgment.' It may stand for other words as well as for that."

In the well-known and sometimes misquoted case of Hoare *v.* Silverlock,[760] the court neatly made a familiar discrimination in applying the doctrine of judicial notice. In an action for libel, in

---

[757] Shakespeare had just died, almost on the first day of this very Easter term. Would Coke, we may wonder, have recognized Prince Henry's description of Hotspur, "He that kills me some six or seven dozen of Scots at a breakfast," or the many other like phrases that are now so familiar to us, — "Rob me the exchequer," "He smiled me in the face," "How this river comes me cranking in," and the like? The Chief Justice might have found his own attitude and that of the courts hit off in the dialogue between Petruchio and his serving man. *"Pet.* Knock me here soundly. *Grumio.* Knock yon here, sir? Why, sir, what am I, sir, that I should knock yon here, sir? *Pet.* Villain, I say, knock me at this gate, and rap me well, or I'll knock your knave's pate. . . . *Pet.* I bade the rascal knock upon your gate, and could not get him for my heart to do it. *Grumio.* Knock at the gate! O heavens! Spake yon not these words plain: 'Sirrah, knock me here, rap me here, knock me well, and knock me soundly'? and come yon now with knocking at the gate?"

[758] Compare also the amusing effort of counsel in Southold *v.* Dounston, Cro. Car. 269 (1633).

[759] Cassidy *v.* Holbrook, 81 Me. 589 (1889), *per* Peters, C. J.

[760] 12 Q. B. 624 (1848). Of the same character is the case of Capital and Counties Bank *v.* Henty, 7 App. Cas. 741, where the question was presented in a similar way, But the judgment was arrested.

saying of the plaintiff in a newspaper that certain persons dealing with her "had realized the fable of the Frozen Snake," after a verdict for the plaintiff, the court declined to arrest the judgment. Lord Denman remarked: "We are not called upon here to take judicial notice that the term 'Frozen Snake' had or had not the meaning ascribed to it by the plaintiff, but to say, after verdict, whether or not a jury were certainly wrong in assuming that those words had the particular meaning."

There is no need to add to this class of cases. Nothing is more familiar[761] than the spectacle of courts construing wills, deeds, contracts, or statutes upon their own knowledge of the import of words; and nothing is more necessary.

3. I will add several miscellaneous cases.

In 1406,[762] in a discussion over arresting judgment on the ground that the facts appeared of record to be otherwise than as the jury had found, Gascoigne, C. J., said: "Certainly if I had been sworn on the same inquest I should, upon the evidence shown on the King's part, nave-found for him [i. e., against the actual verdict]. *Tirwhit.* Sir, suppose a man killed another in your presence and actual sight, and another who is not guilty is indicted before you and found guilty. You ought to respite the judgment against him, for you know the contrary, and to inform the King, that he may pardon *(faire grace). No* more in this case... for you are apprised of the record.... Gascoigne. Once the King himself questioned me as to this case which yon put, and asked me what the law was; and I told him as you say. And he was well pleased that the law was so."[763]

---

761 Nelson v. Cushing, 2 Cush. 519, 533; Atty. — Gen. v. Dublin, 38 N. H. 459, 513; Meyer!;. Arthur, 91 U. S. 570; Tindal, C. J., in Shore *v.* Wilson, 9 Cl. & P. p. 569; Bowes *v,* Shand, 2 App. Cas. 455; Towgood v. Pirie, 35 W. R. 729; Union Pac. R. R. Co. *v.* Hall, 91 U. S. 343.

762 Y. B. 7 H. IV. 41, 5.

763 This was an ancient question. I am indebted to the kindness of Professor Holland of Oxford for a reference to a dispute upon it at Paris in 1166 — 69, by Giraldus Cambrensis, — *utrum judex secundum allegata judicare debeat, an juxta conscientiam.* Gir. Camb. *Opera,* ed. Brewer, Rolls Series, i. 47. Professor Holland adds that "the question was one of those mooted by the Oxford lawyers on the occasion of a royal visit in 1605. Albericus Gentilis was the Regins professor, and the topic was a favorite one with him. It is the subject of Disp. VI. (pp. 72-95) in his *Disputationum Decas Prima,* Londini, Wolfius, 1587, an exceedingly rare book."

A well-known set of cases has to do with the calendar and certain sorts of fact ordinarily given in almanacs. When the books talk about "the calendar," they refer sometimes to the mere order and arrangement of days, and especially saints' days and ecclesiastical feasts, by which the terms and days of court were regulated; and sometimes to the books or written or printed tables in which this order was set down. The courts of necessity recognized without proof the established order and arrangement of days; the phrase was that "the calendar was part of the law of England;" and so it was said of "the almanac."[764] In the multitude and multiplication of saints and saints' days, and the intricacies attending upon the notion of movable feasts, and the arrangement of the Council of Nice fixing Easter by the relation of the moon to a certain date in March, it was no easy matter to find out the details of the calendar for any given year; so that the courts were assisted by written and printed tables of more or less authority. In the Black Book of the Exchequer there is preserved a calendar and a list of dominical letters, dating back, perhaps, as far as 1187.[765] This may well have been the official memorandum of the Exchequer. Since the courts found it convenient or necessary to rely upon such tables, the notion of taking judicial notice of the order of days was easily transferred to the table which set it forth. In 1493 — 4, on a writ of error, a question arose over the continuance of a case to the Monday before St. Boniface's day. There was only one St. Boniface in the "mertlage," and apparently only one was generally recognized; but in the printed calendar there were two. The court finally held the continuance good. I give a translation of this early case in a note. It is curious as showing an early reference in our reports to a *printed* calendar, and as showing the perplexity that such questions might cause at that period.[766] In 1704,[767] when a writ of

[764] Queen *v.* Dyer, 6 Mod. 41 (1703); Page *v.* Faucet, 1 Leon. 242 (1587);s. c. Cro. Eliz. 227; Co. of Stationers *v.* Seymour, 1 Mod. 256 (1677).

[765] Bond's Handy Book of Dates, 68.

[766] Y. B. 9 H. VII. 14, 1. "A writ of error was brought, and error was assigned, in that one brought an action of debt in a court which was grantedby patent, and had a day of continuance till Monday next before St. Boniface's day; and the defendant pleaded, . . . and on Monday next the defendant appeared; found against him; and assigned for error, that St. Boniface's day was past before the day given as 'Monday next before St. Boniface.' In fact, there were two St. Boniface's days in the printed calendar, and in the mertlage only one Boniface. It was moved whether this be error or not. *Kingsmil.* Although there are not two Bonifaces in every book, if there be two Bonifaces, the continuance is good.

inquiry was returnable *tres Trinitatis,* and was returned executed June 14, which was on Monday, the day after the return day, the court held that they must judicially take notice that *tres Trinitatis* was on a Sunday, and equally although it was not assigned for error on the record. "Holt, C. J.: At the Council of Nice they made a calculation movable for Easter forever, and that is received, here in England and becomes part of the law; and so is the calendar established by act of Parliament. And can we take notice of a feast,

---

There are two in the calendar; and the continuance is good and will be referred to the Boniface who is to come and not the one past. There are divers saints who are not in the calendar, and yet a continuance to such and such a day of such and such a saint is good if any such saint there be. As St. Swithin here at Winchester is not in the calendar yet a continuance to this day is good; . . . for if the day be known there, it is enough though it be not in the calendar. (Which the justices agreed to.) They say there are a hundred saints who are not in the calendar; people, also, here in the South do not recognize them; and yet the continuance to one of the days is good. Just so there are two Bonifaces, and the printed calendar proves it. Wherefore, etc. *Huston* [argued] ho the contrary, and [said] in the mertlage there is only one. Hussey [C. J.]. What do you mean by this *mertlage?* What is it? *Huston.* It is a calendar universal in the church of this realm, which priests are bound to keep, and no other *(nient pluis);* and although a new saint were canonized beyond sea, there is no reason why people are bound to recognize him; and so a continuance to inch a saint's day is not good. So here, for in this realm there is only one Boniface, and whether there are [anywhere] two or not, I know not, but it seems not, for he is not in the mertlage. The printed calendar is not to the purpose, and may be false; and maybe there are two Bonifaces beyond sea and only one in England. The judges sent to the Common Bench about the matter. Brian [C. J. C. B.] thought the continuance not good unless two Bonifaces were recognized in England and in the mertlage; or at least recognized, for the printed calendar is of no authority. Vavisor [Justice of the C. B.] to the contrary. And we were in doubt (*fuimus in doubt).* Those in the King's Bench held the continuance good." I have followed an edition of 1597; the Maynard edition appears to have various misprints. For "mertlage" see Dncange; *Martilagium et Martilegium,* and *Matrilogium, pro Martyrologium,* — a martyrology, i. *e.* (as among the books ordinarily kept in churches and monasteries), "a calendar in which were set against particular days the names of the saints and martyrs to be thereupon commemorated." Hubback, Evidence of Succession, 575. For getting on the track of this ecclesiastical slang "mertlage," I am indebted to my late colleague Professor Child, to whose learning and generosity in the use of it his friends were often under obligations.

[767] Harvey *v.* Broad, 6 Mod. 159; s. c. 16. 196. "The Almanack to go by is that which is annexed to the Common Prayer-book." Holt, C. J., in Brough *v.* Perkins, 6 Mod. 81 (1703). And see Tutton *v.* Darke, 5 H. & N. 647; Nixon *v.* Freeman, *ib.* 652. Nowadays, in referring to the almanac, courts have as little thought of any particular edition as they have when they cite the Bible or Æsop's Fables.

without telling what day of the month it is? Shall we take notice of it because you show it on the record and not when we see it as plainly without your telling?" There are also cases where courts judicially notice any common almanacs as being accurate sources of information for such facts as the time of the setting and rising of the sun and moon; or, as it is sometimes put, these courts notice without proof the facts themselves.[768]

In Brown *v.* Piper,[769] on an appeal in equity from a Circuit Court, where the plaintiff asked for an injunction to restrain the defendant from infringing a patent for preserving fish and other articles, the Supreme Court of the United States, having in this case the duty of passing upon facts as well as law, reversed a decree for the plaintiff on the ground that his invention lacked novelty. They adverted to a matter of fact which was nowhere mentioned in pleadings or proof. The patent was for preserving fish and other articles in a close chamber, by a freezing mixture having no contact with the atmosphere of the preserving chamber. The Supreme Court called to mind something which is in all men's knowledge as being old, in daily use, and involving the same principle, namely, the common ice-cream freezer. Of this and of the preservative effect of cold, they said, we take judicial notice, and will deal with it as if set up in the answer and fully proved: "We think this patent was void on its face, and that the court might have stopped short at that instrument, and without looking beyond it into the answers and testimony, *sua sponte,* if the objections were not taken by counsel, well have adjudged in favor of the defendant."

A few years ago, the Court of Appeals of New York,[770] on the question of whether the facts would support the verdict, reversed a judgment for the plaintiff, in an action for personal injuries received while passing through a tunnel on the top of a freight car, in the defendants' service as a brakeman. The height of the tunnel was considerably lessened, in the interior of it, by an arch not visible at the entrance but beginning two hundred feet from it, inside; and of this lessening the plaintiff had no notice. The injuries appeared to have come from striking the plaintiff's head against the arch. But his own testimony was that he was sitting when the accident happened;

---

[768] People *v.* Chee Kee, 61 Cal. 404; State v. Morris, 47 Conn. 179; Munshower *v.* The State, 55 Md. 11; *aliter.* Collier *v.* Nokes, 2 C. & K 1012.

[769] 91 U. *S.* 37; and so Phillips *v.* Detroit, 111 U. S. 604.

[770] Hunter v. N. Y., O. & W. Ry. Co., 116 N. Y. 615 (1889).

and the distance between /the top of the car and the inside of the arch at the top was four feet and seven inches. The trial judge had left it to the jury that, "If the plaintiff was sitting down, it is for you to say whether his head would reach to that height." After verdict and judgment the defendants appealed, and the Court of Appeals put the question thus: "Whether we will accept that finding... or whether we will take judicial notice of the height of the human body and the measurements of its separate parts, and... reverse a judgment that is based upon a finding clearly contrary to the laws of nature." In proceeding to grant a new trial, the court took judicial notice that the average height of man is less than six feet, and the average length of the human trunk to the top of the head is less than three feet, and that men differ in height mainly from a difference in the length of their legs; that this plaintiff could not have struck his forehead against the arch while sitting, unless he were at least nine feet high, and that there is no authenticated instance in human history of any such height; that while the plaintiff may have been a tall man and the jury may properly have acted upon their inspection of him, "a fact so rare in the course of nature should be made apparent, in some way, on the record."[771]

So far these cases have related to the functions of the court. As regards, however, our modern jury, the same considerations apply to them; for now they also are judicial officers, bound to act only upon the evidence which is given to them under the eye of the judge.[772] But as the jury is bound to keep within the restrictions

---

[771] The opinion has an aspect of nicety. Might not the brakeman justly have been regarded by himself and by the jury as "sitting," although at a given moment he was shifting his position, and so raising himself momentarily a foot or two above his sitting height? The tunnel at its entrance was more than four feet higher than the arch, and seemed to allow him a good margin. Two judges, Bradley and Vann, dissented, on the ground that the point on which the decision turns "was not specifically raised at the trial, and it does not necessarily appear that it might not have been obviated if it had been so raised there." On a second trial the brakeman testified that "he rose up as he entered the tunnel," and a new verdict for the plaintiff was not disturbed. 76. 10 N. Y. Sup. 795 (1890).

[772] "A jury," said Mr. Justice Grier, speaking for the Supreme Court of the United States in 1850, has no right to assume the truth of any material fact without some evidence legally sufficient to establish it. It is therefore error in the court to instruct the jury that they may find a material fact of which there is no evidence from which it may be legally inferred. Parks *v.* Ross, 11 How. 362, 373; and see Schmidt *v.* Ins. Co., 1 Gray, 529. This, as we have seen, is a modern doctrine. *Supra, 170.*

imposed upon courts by the principle of judicial notice, so also it has the liberty which that principle allows to courts. The circumstance that the jury is a subordinate tribunal does not change the nature of their office; it merely subjects them in many of the details and particulars of it to the direction of the judge. We find this principle abundantly recognized in our law; as in a case where, on an indictment for the sale of intoxicating liquor, the court below refused the defendant's request for an instruction, that evidence of a sale of gin was not enough, without further evidence that gin was intoxicating; and this refusal was sustained on exceptions. Jurors, said Mr. Justice Metcalf, "are allowed to act upon matters within their general knowledge without any testimony on those matters."[773] On the other hand, the restraining operation of this doctrine was applied by the same court, a little later, to a question about the character of witnesses. The plaintiff in his closing argument appealed to the personal knowledge of some of the jury, that the general character of certain witnesses was "so infamously bad" as to make them unworthy of belief; but the trial judge instructed the jury that they could not act upon such knowledge unless it were testified in court; and this ruling was sustained.[774] In all cases where a jury has to estimate damages and to act upon expert testimony, their power is recognized of bringing into play that general fund of experience and knowledge which in theory is always imputed to them, and on which, in reality, they must in all cases draw. This was formally held in 1881 by the Supreme Court of the United States, in a case where experts had testified to the value of a lawyer's professional services.[775] And the court cited with approval a case in which Chief Justice Shaw, speaking of the question of damages in trover, remarked: "The jury may properly exercise their own judgment and apply their own knowledge and experience in regard to the general

---

[773] Com. v. Peckham, 2 Gray, 514. And he continued, with that well-known touch which gives character to his opinions: "Now everybody who knows what gin is, knows not only that it is a liquor, But also that it is intoxicating. And it might as well have been objected that the jury could not find that gin was a liquor without evidence that it was not a solid substance, as that they could not find that it was intoxicating without testimony to show it to be so. No jury can be supposed to be so ignorant as not to known what gin is. Proof, therefore, that the defendant sold gin is proof that he sold intoxicating liquor. If what he sold was not intoxicating liquor, it was not gin." Compare Hoare *v.* Silverlock, supra, 290.

[774] Schmidt v. Ins. Co., 1 Gray, 529, 531, 535.

[775] Head v. Hargrave, 105 U. *S.* 45.

subject of inquiry.... The jury were not bound by the opinion of the witness; they might have taken the facts testified by him as to the cost, quality, and condition of the goods, and come to a different opinion as to their value." The operation of the same principle in supplementing evidence, came out neatly in a case where woollen, goods of a certain value had been soaked or otherwise injured by salt-water and soda ash, and no admissible evidence was before the jury going to the precise amount of the damage; they fixed it at $500; and the court allowed this to stand, on the ground that they could not say but that the jury might, "as a matter of common experience," find the damage to be not less than the amount named.[776] In an older case the refined. doctrine is put forward, that a jury may be referred to their own knowledge of facts, when once they have been sufficiently proved by admissible evidence, in confirmation of this evidence.[777]

At the end of this collection of instances, illustrating the application of the doctrine of judicial notice through a long period of time and in a wide variety of relations, I will repeat what they help to illustrate, that this topic has its proper place, not in the law of evidence or of pleading, or in any other particular department in our ordinary classification of the law, but wherever the judicial function has a place. And, in particular, as regards the law of evidence, that the question of what the judicial tribunal may or must take knowledge of without evidence or argument, is like another highly important question, viz., what must be proved in order to sustain any particular action; these things are very necessary to be known when one would apply the law of evidence, but they must be learned elsewhere.

III. What are the things of which judicial tribunals may take notice, and should take notice, without proof? It is possible to indicate with exactness only a part of these matters. Some things are thus dealt with by virtue of express statutory law; some in a manner that is referable merely to precedent, — to the actual decisions, which have selected some things and omitted others in a way that is not always explicable upon any general principle; others upon a general maxim of reason and good sense, the application of which must rest mainly with the discretion of the

---

[776] Bradford v. Cunard Co., 147 Mass. 55.
[777] R. v. Sutton, 4 M. & S. 532.

tribunal, and, in any general discussion, must rather be illustrated than defined.

Courts, then, notice without proof: —

(1) Matters, whether of law or fact, which are required by statute to be so noticed, as certain certificates, and attestations of the records and judicial proceedings of the States and Territories;[778] and certain volumes or printed sheets, purporting to be authentic records of law, whether domestic or foreign; and the like.[779]

(2) They notice whatever they have been accustomed to notice in this way, according to the established course 6f the common law and the practice of particular courts; as the authenticity of the signature, seal, and certificate of a notary public, when this certificate purports to be given in the discharge of his ancient international function Of protesting foreign bills of exchange.[780] The recognition by courts of the international relations of their own country, of the great seal, of the names and official signatures and public acts of high public officials, past and present, and the like, may come under this head.[781] The administration of justice is carried on by the sovereign. The sovereign, in the lapse of time, has lost something of his concreteness, where he has not lost it all; but when the king, long ago, sat personally in court, and, in later times, when judicial officers were in a true and lively sense the representatives and even mere deputies of the king, it was an obvious and easily intelligible thing that courts should notice without evidence whatever the king himself knew or did, in the exercise of any of his official functions, whether directly or through other high officers. The same usages of the courts have continued, under the prevalence of legal and political theories very different indeed from those just mentioned, and it is not to be wished that these usages should change. Practical convenience and good sense demand an increase rather than a lessening of the number of instances in which courts shorten trials, by making *prima facie* assumptions, not likely, on the one hand, to be successfully denied,

---

[778] Rev. St. U. S. s. 905; Pub. St. Mass. c. 169, s. 67.

[779] See 2 Tayl. Ev. s. 1527 for illustrations of this; Brady *v.* Page, 59 Cal. 52.

[780] Anonymous, Holt, 296, 297; Pierce *v.* Indseth, 106 U. S. 546.

[781] Wells *v.* Jackson Co., 47 N. H. 235.

and, on the other, if they be denied, admitting readily of verification or disproof.[782]

Some of the usually stated limitations upon the power of taking judicial notice of facts are only explicable on the ground of precedent, and are properly to be referred to this head of the established practice of the courts. It is said sometimes that courts will notice the different counties, but not that any particular place is in a given county, or just where it is.[783] Cases of this class often decide something very different from the broad principle for which they are cited; but in so far as any such doctrine as that last mentioned is true, it must rest merely on authority. The refusing to notice a well-known custom of London, in Argyle and Hunt,[784] is to be regarded in the same light.

(3) Courts notice without proof all, whether fact or law, that is necessarily or justly to be imputed to them, by way of general outfit for the proper discharge of the judicial function. As Lord Mansfield said of underwriters and certain usages which they were bound to know:[785] "If they do not know them they must inform themselves." Among such things are the ordinary usages and practice of their courts; the general principles and rules of the law of their jurisdiction;[786] the ordinary meaning, construction, and use of the vernacular language; the ordinary rules and methods of human thinking and reasoning; the ordinary data of human experience, and judicial experience in the particular region; the ordinary habits of men.[787]

---

[782] In Peltier's case, 28 State Trials, 616 (1803), Lord Ellenborough, in summing up to the jury, said: "That Napoleon Buonaparté was the chief magistrate and first consul of Prance is admitted. And that [France and England were at peace] is also admitted; and, indeed, they were capable of easy proof if they had not been admitted. Their notoriety seems to render the actual proof very unnecessary."

[783] Deybel's case, 4 B. & Aid. 243; Brune v. Thompson, 2 Q. B. 789 But see *infra*, 310.

[784] 1 Strange, 187.

[785] Noble v. Kennoway, 2 Doug. 510.

[786] In a great proportion of the cases that come before the United States courts they may and must take judicial notice of the laws of any State in the Union, *as* well as of the United States. Hanley 11. Donoghue, 116 U. S. p. 6.

[787] "And Holt, Chief Justice, said, that the way 'and manner of trading is to be taken notice of;" Ford v. Hopkins, 1 Salk. 283. In Turley v, Thomas, 8 C. & P. 103, at Nisi Prius, the judge took notice of the [English] role of the road, to tarn to the near hand, and ruled that it applied to riding as well as driving. Of this

(4) And then, finally, there is a wide principle, covering some things already mentioned, that courts may and should notice without proof, and assume as known by others, whatever, as the phrase is, everybody knows.[788] The application of such a principle must, as I have said, leave a great range of discretion to the courts; only in a large and general way can any one say in advance what are and what are not matters of common knowledge. Some such things as the following may be laid down: Whatever a court will notice without proof it may state to the jury, or allow to be stated to it, without proof. Just as it is safe, and even necessary, to assume that juries, witnesses, counsel, and parties, as well as the court itself, all understand the ordinary meaning of language, and have enough capacity, training, and experience to conduct ordinary business, and to understand it when it is talked about, so and upon like grounds it is assumed that they all know certain conspicuous and generally known facts, and are capable of making certain obvious applications of their knowledge. An acquaintance with certain great geographical

---

rule, Christian remarked in 1793 (1 Bl. Com. 12th ed. 74 n.): "The law of the road, namely, that horses and carriages should pass each other on the whip hand . . . has not been enacted by the legislature, and is so modern that perhaps this is the first time it has been noticed in a book of law."

[788] In Texas, in interpreting the statement that a certain person "had been with Sam Houston most of the time and with Davy Crockett," a Court lately said: "It is an historical fact of which courts must take judicial knowledge, that, in the war between Texas and Mexico, Sam Houston held a high military office, and was actively engaged, as a leader in the Texas army." Sargent *v.* Lawrence, 40 S. W. Rep. 1075 (1897). In Lumley v. Gye, 2 El. & Bl. 266 — 7, in a well-known dissenting opinion relating to an opera singer, Coleridge, J., said: "Nor, I think can it be successfully contended that we may not take judicial cognizance of the nature of the service spoken of in the declaration. Judges are not necessarily to be ignorant in court of what everybody else, and they themselves out of court, are familiar with; nor was that unreal ignorance considered to be an attribute of the Bench in early and strict times. We find in the Year Books the judges reasoning about the ability of knights, esquires, and gentlemen to maintain themselves without wages; distinguishing between private chaplains and parochial chaplains from the nature of their employments; and in later days we have ventured to take judicial cognizance of the moral qualities of Robinson Crusoe's 'man Friday' (1 Dow. P. C. 672), and Aesop's 'frozen snake' (12 Q. B. 624). We may certainly therefore take upon ourselves to pronounce that a singer at operas, or a dramatic artiste to the owner and manager of Her Majesty's theatre, is, not a *messor, falcator aut alius serviens* within either the letter or the spirit of the Statute of Laborers. And if we were to hold to the contrary, as to the profession of Garrick and Siddons, we could not refuse to hold the same with regard to the sister arts of Painting Sculpture, and Architecture."

facts will be assumed, as that Missouri is east of the Rocky Mountains,[789] and that "such streams as the Mississippi, the Ohio, and the Wabash for some distance above its confluence with the Ohio, are navigable,"[790] but the point where they cease to be navigable is on a different footing. In Massachusetts it is held that a court may judicially notice that the Connecticut River, above the Holyoke dam, is not a public highway for foreign or interstate commerce.[791] Certain great facts in literature and in history will be noticed without proof; *e. g.,* what in a general way the Bible is, or Æsop's Fables, or who Columbus was; but as to particular details of the contents of these books or of Columbus's discoveries, it may well be otherwise. A knowledge will be assumed of the nature and effects of familiar articles of food or drink in ordinary use, and an infinite number of like matters. Illustrations of this abound in our books; some have already been given; let me add a few others. Where a tobacconist was indicted for illegally keeping his shop Open on Sunday, and sought to bring himself within a statute which permitted "the retail sale of drugs and medicines," without any attempt to show that he sold' — tobacco as a medicine, or kept his shop open for the sale: of it as such, this evidence was excluded; and the jury were charged that "keeping one's shop open to sell cigars on the Lord's Day" would support a conviction. In holding this construction right, the court said:[792] "Some facts are so obvious and familiar that the law takes notice of them.... The court has judicial knowledge of the meaning of common words, and may well rule that guns and pistols are not drugs or medicines, and may exclude the

---

[789] Price *v.* Page, 24 Mo. 65.

[790] Neaderhouser *v.* The State, 28 Ind. 257.

[791] Com. *v.* King, 150 Mass. 221; compare Harrigan *v.* Con. Riv. Co., 189 Mass. 580. So in Talbot *v.* Hudson, 16 Gray, 417, 424, the geographical features of the Concord and Sudbury Rivers were taken to be within the judicial cognizance of the court; *per* Bigelow, C. J.In The Montello, 11 Wall. 411, 414, Field, J., for the court, remarks: "We are supposed to know judicially the principal features of the geography of our country, and, as a part of it, what streams are public navigable waters of the United States. Since this case was presented we have examined, with some care, such geographies and histories of Wisconsin as we could obtain from the library of Congress, to ascertain, if possible, the real character of Fox River, and to render the fiction of the law, as to our supposed knowledge of the navigable streams in that State, a reality in this case." The court found itself unable to decide this point; and the case was remanded for further proceedings.

[792] Com. *v.* Marzynski, 149 Mass. 68, *per* Knowlton, J.

opinion of witnesses who offer to testify that they are.... We are of the opinion that cigars sold by a tobacconist in the ordinary way are not drugs or medicines, within the meaning of those words as used in the statute." In passing on the constitutionality of a prohibitory liquor law, the New York Court of Appeals laid it down as a basis of reasoning that "we must be allowed to know what is known by all persons of common intelligence, that intoxicating liquors are produced for sale and consumption as a beverage; that such has been their primary and principal use in all ages and countries.... It must follow that any... legislation which... makes the keeping or sale of them as a beverage... a criminal offence... must be deemed... to deprive the owner of the enjoyment of his property."[793] On a like question in the Supreme Court of Indiana, one of the majority of the court declared: "The court knows as matter of general knowledge, and is capable of judicially asserting the fact, that the use of beer, etc., as a beverage is not necessarily hurtful, any more than the use of lemonade or ice-cream."[794] The New York Court of Appeals, in declaring unconstitutional an act prohibiting the manufacture of cigars and tobacco in tenement-houses, said: "We must take judicial notice of the nature and qualities of tobacco. It has been in general use among civilized men for more than two centuries. It is used in some form by a majority of the men in this State, by the good and bad, learned and unlearned, the rich and the poor. Its manufacture into cigars is permitted without any hindrance, except for revenue purposes, in all civilized lands. It has never been said... that its preparation and manufacture into cigars were dangerous to the public health. We... are not able to learn that tobacco is even injurious to the health of those who deal in it, or

---

[793] Wynehamer v. The People, 13 N. Y. 378,387 (1855), *per* Comstock, J.

[794] Beebe v. The State, 6 Ind. 501, 519 (1855); and so Klare v. The State, 43 Ind. 483, declining to recognize judicially that common brewers' beer is intoxicating. The "etc." quoted in the text, gives great possible enlargement to the doctrine. The same court judicially knows that whiskey is intoxicating, and allows a jury to finв it so upon their general knowledge (Carmon v. The State, 18 Ind. 450). The Supreme Court of Wisconsin (Briffitt v. The State, 58 Wis. 39) takes judicial notice that "beer," when the word is used alone, imports strong beer, and that such beer is intoxicating; *aliter* in the New York Court of Appeals. Blatz v, Rohrbach, 116 N. Y. 450 (1889).

are engaged in its production or manufacture."[795] So a court will notice, without pleading or proof, that a pile of lumber is likely to attract children to play about it;[796] what is and is not likely to frighten horses of ordinary gentleness;[797] that photography is a proper means of producing correct likenesses;[798] what are the "nature, operation, and ordinary uses" of the telephone;[799] what is the meaning, upon a parcel, of C. O. D.; [800] that steamboats (first-used in 1807) were in 1824 freely employed in transporting merchandise, and not merely passengers;[801] that a post-card is likely to be read by others than the one to whom it is addressed;[802] that coupon railroad tickets for a continuous journey over several different lines were in general use long before March 17, 1885, the

---

[795] Jacob's case, 98 N. Y. 98, 113 (1885). The judges sometimes cover a wide range in their reasonings, and take a very great deal for granted. See, *e. g;* the opinion of Chancellor Walworth on ale and beer, in Nevin v. Ladne, 3 Denio, 437; that of Chancellor Bland on trees and their mode of growth, in Patterson *v.* M'Causland, 3 Bland, 69; and that of Taney, C. J., on negroes, in Dred Scott *v,* Sandford, 19 How. 393.

[796] Spengler *v.* Williams, 67 Miss. 1.

[797] State *v.* Me. C. B. R. Co., 86 Me. 309; Gilbert *v.* R'y Co., 51 Mich. 488, a singular decision.

[798] Udderzook v. Com., 76 Pa. St. 340; Dyson *v.* N. Y. & N. E. R'y Co., 67 Conn. 9, "not hitherto passed upon by this court."

[799] Wolfe *v.* Mo. Pac. R'y Co., 97 Mo. 473.

[800] State *v.* Intoxicating Liquors, 73 Me. 278.

[801] Gibbons *v.* Ogden, 9 Wheat. 1, 220. Such questions relating to new inventions and new usages, must often be answered one way at one time, and in a different way later on. In *Ex parte* Powell, 1 Ch. Div. 501, we find the English Court of Appeal declining to recognize without proof the existence of a certain custom in 1875, while in 1881, in Crawcour v. Salter, 18 Ch. Div 30, the same court holds it to be now so well known that the courts must judicially notice it. For centuries our courts have noticed without proof what the term "o'clock" imports; but when we read (Black Book of the Admiralty, I. 313, note), that "hours of the clock are mentioned [in certain records] in this reign (Richard II.) for the first time, on March 8, 1390," we are reminded that there was a time, in the long annals of these courts, when they would have refused to take judicial notice of this novelty. In 1306 (Y. B. 33 — 35 Ed. I. 122), a defendant, in seeking to remove a default, said that he was detained by floods at a certain point, at noon, the day before. The plaintiff prayed judgment on the ground that the defendant was too late any way, for the place named was fifteen leagues away, and it would have been impossible to get there in season.

[802] Robinson *v.* Jones, 4 L. B. Ir. 391 (1879); and as to telegrams, Williamson *v.* Freer, L. R. 9 C. P. 393 (1874). Post-cards containing certain objectionable matter are declared non-mailable by a statute of the United States of Sept. 26, 1888 (25 St. U. S. 496).

date of a certain patent;[803] what the nature of the business of a mercantile agency is;[804] and that "habitual drunkenness" as a ground for divorce, and being a "habitual drunkard" as a ground for punishment, do not include habitual or common excess in the use of morphine or chloroform.[805]

IV. Some discriminations which must be attended to in applying the principle of judicial notice should now be mentioned.

(1) Sometimes the ultimate fact that is sought to be proved is noticed, and sometimes it is the trustworthiness of a certain medium of proof, and not the thing itself which this tends to prove; as when a notarial seal and signature are taken without proof, or the certificate of a registrar of deeds or other public official. That is to say, the question sometimes concerns an evidential fact and sometimes an ultimate one; whichever it be, it is governed by the same principles. When the statutes of the United States[806] make Little & Brown's edition of the laws and treaties competent evidence of their contents "in all the tribunals and public offices of the United States and of the several States, without any further proof or authentication thereof," the courts are required to take notice of a certain medium of proof as being sufficient. Some of these contents — the public acts — are supposed to be known by the judges without calling for evidence of them; but even as regards these, their discretion in selecting and rejecting modes of proof is here restricted; they cannot reject these volumes. And when, in an interesting case,[807] it was held that although in our courts English statutory law is matter of fact to be pleaded and proved, yet a court will recognize printed books of statutes and printed reports of adjudged cases shown to the satisfaction of the court to be correct — "books of acknowledged or ascertained authority" — as competent evidence of the foreign law, we perceive the doctrine that the court may take judicial notice of a certain means of proving a fact when 'it cannot take notice of the fact itself.[808] The doctrine that almanacs may be referred to in order to ascertain upon what day of the week a given day of a month fell in any year, to learn the time of sunrise or sunset,

---

[803] Eastman *v.* Chic. & N. W. R'y Co., 39 Fed. Bep. 552 (0. C. N. D. 111. 1889).

[804] Eaton Co. *v.* Avery, 83 N. Y. p. 34.

[805] Youngs *v.* Youngs, 130 111. 230; Com. *v.* Whitney, 11 Cush. 477.

[806] R. S. U. S. s. 908.

[807] The Pawashick, 2 Lowell, 142.

[808] And so in Ennis *v.* Smith, 14 How. 426-430.

and the like; and that, in order to prove facts of general history, approved books of, history may be consulted, may also be regarded as illustrating the taking notice of the authenticity of evidential matters, — of certain media of proof.[809] But often, in such cases, the truth is that the court takes notice of the fact itself which these books authenticate; and wherever that is so, a court may refer to whatever source of information it pleases, — the statement that it may consult an almanac or a general history being only an unnecessary and misleading specification of a particular sort of document that may be examined.[810]

(2) It is to be observed that much is judicially noticed without proof, of which the court at a given moment may in. fact know nothing. A statute may have been passed within a few hours or days, and be unknown to the court at the trial; or a given fact as to the international relations of the government may not be in fact known, as in a case before cited, where the judge informed himself by inquiring at the foreign office;[811] or the general meaning of language, where the expression was used in a document of many years ago, may not be known to the court without private study and reflection.[812] In such cases not only may a court, as indeed it must, avail itself of every source of information which it finds helpful, but also, for the proper expedition of business, it may require help from the parties in thus instructing itself.[813]

(3) Taking judicial notice does not import that the matter is indisputable. It is not necessarily anything more than a *prima facie* recognition, leaving the matter still open to controversy. It is true, as regards many of the things which are judicially noticed, that they cannot well be supposed to admit of question; *e. g;* that Missouri is

---

[809] R. *v.* Holt, 5 T. R. 436; R. *v.* Withers, *ib.* 446; Dupays *v.* Shepherd Holt, 296.

[810] Gardner *v.* The Collector, 6 Wall. 499; State *v.* Morris, 47 Conn. 179; People *v.* Chee Kee, 61 Cal. 404. In this last case the almanac used was an ordinary medical advertising almanac, Dr. Ayer's. And so in Quelch's case (14 State Trials, 1083) counsel says, "We shall now (though there be no necessity for it) prove that, ... at the time, . . . her sacred majesty and the King of Portugal were entered into a strict alliance," etc. "Upon this [goes on the report] two London Gazettes . . . were produced and two paragraphs were read."

[811] Taylor v. Barclay, 2 Sim. 213. Compare The Montello, *per* Field, J., *supra,* 303 n.

[812] Atty. — Gen. v. Dublin, 38 H. H. 459.

[813] School Dist. v. Ins. Co., 101 *V. S.* 472; Steph. Dig. Ev., art. 59; Markby, Notes to Ind. EV. Act, 49.

east of the Rocky Mountains, and that Hereford borders on Wales; but the doctrine covers much else. A seal which purports to be the great seal of any State may in fact not be genuine, and so of the certificate and seal of any public official. A sale of tobacco and cigars may be made for medical purposes, although ordinarily it is not. In very many cases, then, taking judicial notice of a fact is merely presuming it, *i. e.,* assuming it until there shall be reason to think otherwise. Courts may judicially notice much which they cannot be required to notice. That is well worth emphasizing, for it points to a great possible usefulness in this doctrine, in helping to shorten and simplify trials; it is an instrument of great capacity in the hands of a competent judge; and is not nearly as much used, in the region of practice and evidence, as it should be. This function is, indeed, a delicate one;[814] if it is too loosely or ignorantly exercised it may annul the principles of evidence and even of substantive law. But the failure to exercise it tends daily to smother trials with 'technicality, and monstrously lengthens them out.

(4) Another thing should be observed, which, often escapes attention, namely, that the thing of which a court is asked to take cognizance without proof, sometimes is a totally different matter from what it appears to be; so that the refusal to notice it is misconceived and misquoted. Thus, in Phillips on Evidence,[815] one reads that "the courts... will not take notice... of any particular city; as, for instance, that Dublin is in Ireland." But the case cited for this decides no such thing; the question was whether a declaration in assumpsit on a bill drawn at Dublin for a certain number of pounds, etc., without any averment to show the facts that it was drawn in Ireland and for Irish currency, could be read as importing those facts, and it was held that it could not. "It is not possible," said Abbott, C. J., "for the court to take judicial notice *that there is only one Dublin in the world."* Again, where a suit was brought in Texas on a promissory note payable at New Orleans, and no averment that this New Orleans was in Louisiana, the defect was supplied by other matter upon the record; but the court thought that it could not

---

[814] The warning is an old one, *Cum multa putentur notoria quæ revera notoria non sunt, prospicere debet judex ne quid dubium est pro notorio recipiat.* Calvinus (A. D. 1600) *sub probatio.*

[815] Vol. I. 466 (10th Eng. ed.), c. x. s. 1, end; citing Kearney v. King, 2 B. & Ald. 302.

judicially know that the note was payable in Louisiana.[816]
Everybody in. this country knows, to be sure, or may know for the
asking, that there is a New Orleans in Louisiana; but few could say
whether there be not another New Orleans in. some other State, or in
a dozen of them. In like manner, in an English case, on a motion to
set aside the service of a summons, as not coil-forming to a statute
requiring the indorsement on it of the name and place of abode of the
attorney suing it out, the actual indorsement was, "Featherstone
buildings, Holborn, in the County of Surrey;" and an objection was
made that, upon the face of it, it was irregular, as it was well known
that this place and street were in Middlesex and not in Surrey. But
Wightman, J.: "I cannot take judicial notice that there is no such
place in the County of Surrey."[817] Another case, in which an English
court is generally quoted as refusing to recognize without evidence
that the Tower of London is in London, may illustrate the need of
scrutiny and discrimination before accepting such paradoxical
statements. The case was on a rule for setting aside a nonsuit and
giving a new trial; which was, in fact, made absolute on paying
costs. But the court refused to do this, as of strict right, or to say that
the court below ought to have taken notice, without proof, that a
certain part of the Tower of London was in the city of London,
instead of being in Middlesex. The point turned upon the fact, that
although, in a popular sense, much of London is in the County of
Middlesex, yet much of it, for judicial and political purposes, is not;
and the line was said to pass through the Tower.[818] The decision,
therefore, is merely that a court is not required to take notice, without
proof, of the precise boundary line of a county; a very different thing

---

[816] Andrews v. Hoxie, 5 Tex. 171. This case was cited by the court in
Ellis v. Park, 8 Tex. 205, to support the holding that they could not take judicial
notice that "St. Louis, Mo.," meant St. Louis in Missouri; but that was a very
different thing, and indefensible. Price v. Page, 24 Mo. 65.

[817] Humphreys v. Budd, 9 Dowl. 1000. And so Bayley, 3., in Deybel's
case, 4 B. & Aid. p. 246.

[818] Brune v. Thompson, 2 Q. B. 789. "This," says Coke, in the Fourth
Institute, 251, "upon view and examination was found out Mic. 13 Jac. regis
[1615], in the case of Sir Thomas Overbury, who was poysoned in a chamber in
the Tower on the west part of that old wall." What is on the west of the wall is
said to be in London, and on the east in Middlesex. And so Coke, Third Inst. 136.
These passages are cited by counsel in 2 Q. B. 789. See Loftie, Hist. London, ii.
136. "London," said Newton, C. J., in 1443 (Y. B. 22 H. VI. 12, 13), "is an entire
body and county by itself, and does not reach beyond Temple Bar. And
Middlesex is an entire county and cannot be in the franchise of London."

from holding that they cannot and should not take notice without proof that an object admitted to be the famous Tower of London is in what is popularly and generally known as London.[819] In another case a learned author[820] seems to misconceive the scope of a Maryland case. "The courts," he remarks, "have refused, more or less capriciously, to take judicial notice of... the meaning of a printer's private mark to an advertisement, thus, 'Oct. 13, 4t,' as indicating the date and term of publication." But on referring to the case cited for this statement we find that the court was not declining to notice the meaning of this expression, but to infer from the use of it that a certain advertisement *actually was published* on the date named, and three times afterwards — where the question was as to the meaning of the record, in determining whether a mortgage had been properly foreclosed.[821] Finally, a case may be mentioned under this head, where a hotel-keeper, now bankrupt, had hired his furniture from a dealer. The furniture was claimed for the creditors, under the English bankrupt law, as having been left in the credit and disposition of the bankrupt; but the dealer claimed on the ground that the custom of letting furniture to hotel-keepers without passing the title to it, was established and generally known. The court, in considering whether they could take notice of this without proof, drew attention to the fact that the real question was not as to the existence of the custom, but whether it had existed so long and had been so extensively acted on, that ordinary creditors of the hotel-keeper, "the wine merchant, the spirit merchant, the brewer, the ordinary tradesman of his town, were likely to know that it exists."[822]

---

[819] Wharton (Ev. i. s. 339, notes) evidently misconceives the decision, when he says that in this case "the court went to the absurd extreme of nonsuiting the plaintiff because he did not prove that the Tower of London was in the city of London."

[820] Wade on Notice (2d ed.), s. 1417. Mr. Wade has a useful collection of cases, and I am indebted to him for several references.

[821] Johnson *v.* Robertson, 31 Md. 476.

[822] *Ex parte* Powell, 1 Ch. Div. 501.

CHAPTER VIII
PRESUMPTIONS

When a learned Italian began a treatise upon Presumptions three hundred years ago, he opened with these words: *Materia quam aggressuri sumus valde utilis est et quotidiana in practica; sed confusa, inextricabilis fere."* These words of Alciatus were put by Best, in 1844, upon the title-page of his early treatise on this subject; and gin the minds of most students of the matter, they have always found a lively echo. Without entering, now, upon any detailed consideration of the mass of legal presumptions, an unprofitable and monstrous task, it may be possible to point out the nature and the place of this topic in our law, and by this means to relieve the subject of much of its obscurity.[823]

1. What is the relation of presumptions to what we call the "law of evidence." They are ordinarily regarded as belonging peculiarly to that part of the law. This appears to be an error; they belong rather to a much larger topic, already briefly considered, that of legal reasoning, in its application to particular subjects. This is

---

[823] The *best* consideration of the subject of presumptions known to me is found in an article in 6 Law Mag. 348 (Oct. 1831). It is, I think, very questionable in many particulars, but I give the main part of it In an Appendix, *infra,* 539. The author dismisses from the subject of evidence proper what are called "presumptions of fact" and also absolute "presumptions of law;" but, erroneously, as I think, he regards disputable presumptions of law not merely as a part of the law of evidence, but as the most important part of it. This writer makes the valuable remark , *(infra,* 549) that "presumptions of law cannot conveniently be treated together under a separate head, but ought to be set forth under the different subjects to which they respectively belong." J. F. Stephen said something similar in 1872 (Introd. to Ind. Ev. Act, 133), and again, in 1876 (lntrod. to Dig. of Evid.); but he still retained in his books on evidence a number of presumptions, and gave, in Article One of his Digest, this definition of the term: ' "A presumption' means a rule of law that courts and judges shall draw a particular inference from a particular fact or from particular evidence, unless and until the truth of such, inference is disproved;" and he allowed a place in the law of evidence to "those [presumptions] which relate to facts merely as facts, and apart from the particular rights which they constitute." He seems to me, here and elsewhere, to have left the subject still in confusion, by not discriminating between rules of reasoning, and the law of evidence. The law has no mandamus to the logical faculty; it orders nobody to draw inferences, — common as that mode of expression is. See, e. y., Austin, Jurisp. i. 507 (London, 4th ed.), and Best, Evid. s. 304.

intimated in the last clause of the partly quoted passage from Alciatus, just referred to, when he goes on to say, *"communisque est et jurisconsultoribus et rhetoribus in genere judiciali."* For reasoning there is no law other than the laws of thought.

Presumptions are aids to reasoning and argumentation, which assume the truth of certain matters for the purpose of some given inquiry. They may be grounded on general experience, or probability of any kind; or merely on policy and convenience. On whatever basis they rest, they operate in advance of argument or evidence, or irrespective of it, by taking something for granted; by assuming its existence. When the term is legitimately applied it designates a rule or a proposition which still leaves open to further inquiry the matter thus assumed.[824] The exact scope and operation of these *prima facie* assumptions are to cast upon the party against whom they operate, the duty of going forward, in argument or evidence, on the particular point to which they relate. They are thus closely related to the subject of judicial notice; for they furnish the basis of many of those spontaneous recognitions of particular facts or conditions which make up that doctrine. Presumptions are not in themselves either argument or evidence, although for the time being they accomplish the result of both. It would be as true, and no more so, to say that an instance of judicial notice is evidence, as to say that a presumption is evidence.[825] Presumption, assumption, taking for granted, are simply so many names for an act or process which aids and shortens inquiry and argument. These terms relate to the whole field of argument, whenever and by whomsoever conducted; and also to the whole field of the law, in so far as it has been shaped or is being shaped by processes of reasoning. That is to say, the subject now in hand is one of universal application in the law, both as regards the subjects to which it relates and the persons who apply it.

Let me now try briefly to explain, illustrate, and make good what is here said. At the outset, we must take notice of a thing which easily escapes attention; namely, that much of the substantive law is expressed presumptively, in the form of *prima facie* rules. This evidential form of statement leads often to the opinion that the substance of the proposition is evidential; and then to the farther

---

[824] As to absolute presumptions, see *infra,* 317, 343 n.

[825] See the very questionable reasoning and conclusions on this subject in Coffin v. *U. S.*, 156 U. S. 432. Compare *infra.* Appendix B.

notion, that inasmuch as it is evidential it belongs to the law of evidence. That is an error. In a reasoned body of law like ours, much of it comes about by "intendments." In applying statutory law also, this takes place,[826] but far less conspicuously than in the common law. If we suppose any fundamental proposition of the substantive law, *e.g.,* that when, in negotiating for a sale of Specific personal property, the event X happens, with the intention of both parties to sell the property, the sale actually takes place, we observe that this comes to be attended by a crop of subsidiary rules, such as that when Y happens, this necessary intention of the parties presumably exists.[827] The question of intention is not closed to evidence by this rule, — the matter lies wholly open; but, in applying the law, a certain *prima facie* effect is given to particular facts, and it is not merely given to them once, by one judge, on a single occasion, but it is imputed to them habitually, and by a rule which is followed by all judges, and recommended to juries; and even laid down to juries as the binding rule of law. Accordingly the substantive law gets into this shape, that when, in a negotiation for a sale of specific personal property, X happens, with the intention, on both sides to sell the property, the sale takes place then; and when Y happens, this intention presumably exists. Or, to put it shorter, "when X and Y happen in a negotiation for a sale of specific personal property, presumably the sale takes place." Blackburn, in stating these rules, calls them rules of construction; that is to say, rules of the substantive law designed to aid in interpreting words and conduct.[828]

In such cases, that which is evidential merely, — that is to say, the foundation of a logical inference as to the existence of one of those ultimate facts to which alone, in the first instance, the substantive law annexes its consequences, — has itself become the subject of a rule of substantive law, and comes to have certain consequences directly annexed to it. By the expedient of making, the

---

[826] For example, *see* Powell *v.* Kempton Park Co., [1897], 2 Q. B. 242.

[827] Blackburn, in his admirable book on Sale, 1st ed., pp. 151-154, gives two such rules, "of which there is no trace in the reports before the time of Lord Ellenborough" (A. D. 1802 — 1818).

[828] "A rule of construction may always be reduced to the following form: certain words and expressions which may mean either X or Y shall *prima facie* be *taken to* mean X. A rule of construction always contains the saving clause: 'unless a contrary intention appear' . . . though some roles are much stronger than others and require a greater force of intention in the context to control them." Hawkins, Wills, Preface.

rule *a prima facie* one, the courts may have seemed to themselves to abstain from legislation, and to be keeping within the region of mere administration of existing law. And yet it is clear that this is true legislation. One may occasionally trace it until it ripens into open and confessed law-giving, as in Dalton *v.* Angus.[829] To say, as sometimes happens, that in such cases there is "a rule of law that courts and judges shall draw a particular inference,"[830] is a loose and misleading expression; for it involves the misconception that the law has any rules at all for conducting the process of reasoning. It would be accurate to say that the rule of law requires a judge to stop short in the process of drawing inferences, or not to enter upon it at all; to assume for the time that one fact is, in legal effect, the same as a certain other. The rule fixes the legal effect of a fact, its legal equivalence with another. And it makes no difference in the essential nature of the rule whether this effect is fixed absolutely or *prima facie: it* gives a legal definition. Such is the nature of all rules to determine the legal effect of facts as contrasted with their logical effect. To prescribe and fix a certain legal equivalence of facts, is a very different thing from merely allowing that meaning to be given to them. A rule of presumption does not merely say that such and such a thing is a permissible and usual inference from other facts, but pit goes on to say that this significance shall always, in the absence of other circumstances, be imputed to them, — sometimes passing first through the stage of saying that it *ought to be* imputed.

I have already said that the nature of these rules is brought out when they ripen from being a mere *prima facie* doctrine into an absolute and incontrovertible one. The familiar doctrine about prescription used to be put as an ordinary rule of presumption; in twenty years there arose a *prima facie* case of a lost grant or of some other legal origin. The judges at first laid it down that, if unanswered, twenty years of adverse possession justified the inference; then that it "required the inference," *i. e.,* it was the jury's duty to do what they themselves would do in settling the same question, namely, to find the fact of the lost grant; and at last this conclusion was announced as a rule of the law of property, to be applied absolutely.[831] It is

---

[829] 6 App. Cas. 740; 2 Greenl. Ev. s. 539.

[830] Stephen, Dig. Ev. art. 1, defining "Presumption."

[831] Dalton *v.* Angus, 6 App. Cas. 740; Wallace *v.* Fletcher, 30 N. H434; 3 Gray's Cases on Property, 127 *et seq.;* Lond. & K W. By. Co. *v.* Com'rs, 75 L. T. R. 629, 632, *per* Wills, J.: "If you are once in the laud of presumptions and

evident, upon reflection, that the rule was always a rule of property, — after it ceased to be a mere statement of a permissible inference, of a mere truth of reason, namely, that this was generally a right and wise conclusion. When the judges advised the jury, and afterwards directed them as a matter of legal duty, to find a lost grant under the circumstances indicated in the rule, they were indeed, dealing with evidential, secondary facts, and they adopted the phraseology of reasoning and drawing inferences. But in reality they were laying down a rule of policy[832] which they themselves had determined to apply, and which they advised, and directed their associates in administration, the jury, — their co-ordinate, and, in a degree, their subordinate associates, — also to apply; a rule which made the twenty years' open and uncontradicted adverse possession a bar. Such advice and such direction is natural and desirable when a presiding learned tribunal is instructing an unlearned one, whose action it has the right to revise; for the administration of the law should be kept consistent. In such cases the judges accomplish, through the phraseology and under the garb of "evidence," the same results that they have long reached, and are now constantly reaching, by the director means of estoppel. The modern extensions of this doctrine broaden the law by a direct application of maxims of justice, — a simple method, and worthy of any judicial tribunal which, rises to the level of its great office; and yet one not quite in harmony with the general attitude of the common-law courts and their humble phraseology in disclaiming the office of legislation. But inasmuch, as every body of men who undertake to administer the law must, in fitting it to the ever-changing combinations of fact that come before them, constantly legislate, incidentally and in a subsidiary way, it is best that this should be openly done; as it is in the cautious reaching out of the principle of estoppel. The same thing has taken place by presumptions, only it was less obvious. By merely handling "evidence," and fixing upon it a given quality, the judges' disavowal of any right to make the law has seemed to moult no feather.[833]

---

things that ought to be supposed (although generally speaking, nobody does suppose that they really exist), I do not see why yon should not presume a grant before the statute of Quio *emptores as* well as after."

[832] See Lord Blackburn in Dalton *v.* Angus, 6 App. Cas. 808 *et seq.;* and Blackburn, J., in Bryant *v. Toot,* L. "R. 2 Q. B. 161, 177. Compare Lindley, L. J., in Saunders r. Saundere, [1897] P. 89, 94.

[833] E. R. Thayer, Judicial Legislation, 5 Harv. L. Rev. 172.

Let me trace the same process in two more instances. It is a rule of presumption that, in the absence of evidence to the contrary, a person shall be taken to be dead, when he has been absent seven years and not heard from. That is a modern rule. It is not at all modern to infer death from a long absence; the recent thing is the fixing of this time of seven years, and putting it into a rule. The faint beginning of it, as a common-law rule, of general application in all questions of life and death, is found, so far as our recorded cases show, in Doe d. George *v.* Jesson,[834] in January, 1805. Long before this, in 1604, the "Bigamy Act" of James I.[835] had exempted from the scope of its provisions, and so from the guilt and punishment of a felon, those who had married a second time when the first spouse had been beyond the seas for seven years; [836] and those whose

---

[834] 6 East, 80.

[835] St. 1 Jac. I c. 11. Best, Ev. s. 409, note, seems to intimate that this may have been an old thing, referring to Thorne v. Rolff, in Dyer's brief report, where something is said of seven years. But the report in Old Benloe, 86, which gives the record, shows that the time was several months less than seven years. Of course the famous number seven (the seven planets, seven wonders of the world, seven deadly sins, seven sleepers, etc.) was likely to be forever suggesting itself. And there were ecclesiastical rules and canons that may well have suggested the time named in the Bigamy Act. In the *"excerptiones"* of Ecgbert, archbishop of York (A. D. 734-766), we read *[Exc.* 124]: "Canon dicit, Si mulier discesserit a viro suo, despiciens eum, nolens revertere et reconciliari viro, *post quinque vel seplem annos* cum consensu episcopi, ipse aliam accipiat uxorem. . . .'" *[Exc.* 125]: "Item, Si cojus uxor in captivitatem ducta fuerit, et ea redimi non poterit, *post annum septimum* alteram accipiat; et si postea propria, id est, prior mulier de captivitate reversa fuerit, accipiat eam, posterioremque dimittat." And so, *vice versa,* if a husband be enslaved. Wilkins, *Concilia,* i. 101, 108 — 109. See also Hart's Ecc. Rec. (2d ed.) 194. Some five centuries later than this, however, it would seem that no such rule governed the courts of common law. At the Easter Term, in 1203, in a dower case, where the question was whether the proceedings should wait until the son, a minor, came of age, it is set up that there is an older son, of age now. "Matilda [the widow], on being questioned, says that she had an elder son, but a certain Abbot, his uncle, took him into parts across the sea, and for seven years past she has not seen him, and she does not know whether he is alive or not. And because she does not know whether her eldest son is living or not, it is considered that the assize do proceed, because Warin [the infant] has an elder brother. 1 Sel. Civ. Pleas (Sold. Soc.), case 156. And in 1201, at the Cornish iter, it was doubted whether an absence for twenty years, unheard of, justified the assumption that a man was dead. 1 Select Civil Pleas (Seld. Soc.), case 190; *ib.* xix.

[836] Without saying anything about a knowledge of the absent party's existence; and so construed as making such knowledge immaterial. 1 Hale, P. C. 693.

spouse had been absent for seven years, although not beyond the seas, — "the one of them not knowing the other to be living within that time." This statute, it may be noticed, did not absolutely treat the absent party as dead; for it did not validate the second marriage in either case. It simply exempted a party from the statutory penalty. Again, in 1667, the statute of 19 Car. II., c. 6,[837] "for redress of inconveniences by want of proof of the deceases of persons beyond the seas or absenting themselves, upon whose lives estates do depend," had provided, in the case of estates and leases depending upon the life of a person who should go beyond the seas, or otherwise absent himself within the kingdom for seven years, that where the lessor or reversioner should bring an action to recover the estate, the person thus absenting himself should "be accounted as naturally dead," if there should be no "sufficient and evident proof of the life," and that the judge should "direct the jury to give their verdict as if the person... were dead." But if the absent party should not really have died, provision was made for a subsequent recovery by him. The effect of this statute, then, was to end, in a specific class of cases, all inquiring into evidence, by a certain, assumption, or, as it is otherwise called, presumption. The rule fixes, for the purpose of a particular inquiry, the effect of specified facts; absence for seven years, unheard of, is to be accounted, as 'regards this particular inquiry, the same thing as death; it is its legal equivalent.

Now, very likely, in practice, similar cases may have been brought within "the equity" of the statute; as Chief Justice Holt, in 1692,[838] is reported to have "held that a remainder-man was within the equity of that law;" but we hear of no suggestion of a general seven-year rule, such as we have now, before 1805.[839] In the case of Doe d. George v. Jesson,[840] there was a rule for a new trial, in an action of ejectment, which turned on the question whether the plaintiff's lessor had entered within the time allowed by the Statute of Limitations; which again turned on the time of the death of the lessor's brother, who had gone to sea and had not been heard of for many years. The Court of King's Bench sustained a ruling that the

---

[837] The ordinary citation. In the "Statutes of the Realm," vol. 5, it is given as 18 & 19 Car. II. c. 11.

[838] Holman v. Exton, Carth. 246.

[839] See, for instance, Rowe v. Hasland, I Wm. Bl. 404 (1762); Dixon v Dixon, 3 Bro. C. C. 510 (1792); Lee v. Willcock, 6 Ves. 605 (1802).

[840] 6 East, 80.

jury must find the time of death as well as they could,... that at any time beyond, the first seven years they might fairly presume him dead; but the not hearing of him within that period was hardly sufficient to afford that presumption. Observe the way in which Lord Ellenborough puts the matter; "As to the period when the brother might be supposed to have died, according to the statute, 19 Car. II., c. 6, with respect to leases dependent upon lives, and. also according to the statute of bigamy (1 Jac. I., c. 2), the presumption of the duration of life, with respect to persons of whom no account can be given, ends at the expiration of seven years from the time when they were last known to be living. Therefore, in the absence of all other evidence to show that he was living at a later period, there was fair ground for the jury to presume that he was dead at the end of seven years from the time when he went to sea on his second voyage, which seems to be the last account of him." This was supporting what the jury had done, on the simple ground that the jury were justified, on the analogy of the two statutes, in finding death by the end of the seven years; and, moreover (looking at Mr. Justice Rooke's ruling, which was not questioned upon this point), that they would not be justified in finding it earlier. It was not laid down that they ought to find death at the end of seven years, or that they must; nor was any rule of presumption put forward; nor, as I say, was it on any such point that the ruling below was questioned in the full bench.

In 1809, at Nisi Prius,[841] in an action against a woman on a promissory note, she pleaded coverture, and proved her marriage; but the husband, had gone to Jamaica twelve years ago, and it was a question how to prove that lie was now living. The defendant insisted that he must be presumed to be alive; but Lord Ellenborough ruled that evidence must be given of his being alive within seven years. This was given, and the defendant had a verdict. In the other case the aim was to prove death; here, life; and here the ruling was that a court cannot assume life now, when all that it knows is that the party has been absent and unheard from for more than seven years. Upon the basis of these cases, there soon appeared in the text-books on evidence, for the first time in 1815, a general proposition that " where the issue is upon the life or death... where no account can be given of the person, this presumption [namely, that a living person

---

'continues alive until the contrary be proved'] ceases at the end of seven years from the time when he was last known to be living, — a period which has been fixed from analogy to the statute of bigamy and the statute concerning leases determinable upon lives."[842] In this form the matter was again put by Starkie, ten years later, in the first edition of his book; and by Greenleaf, and so by Taylor.[843] But the judges as well as text-writers got to expressing what had been put as a cessation of a presumption of life in the form of an affirmative presumption of death; and this was put as a rule of general application wherever life and death were in question. And so Stephen puts it:[844] "A person shown not to have been heard of for seven years by those (if any) who if he had been alive would naturally have heard of him, is presumed to be dead, unless the circumstances of the case are such as to account for his not being heard of without assuming his death." This rule is set down by Stephen among the few presumptions which be thinks should find a place in the law of evidence. Stephen published his Digest in 1876. Here, then, in seventy years, we find the rule about a seven years' absence coming into existence in the form of a judicial declaration about what may or may not fairly be inferred by a jury; in the exercise of their logical faculty; the particular period being fixed by reference to two legislative determinations, in specific cases of a like question; passing into the form of an affirmative rule of law requiring that death be assumed under the given circumstances. This is a process of judicial legislation, advancing from what is a mere recognition of a legitimate step in legal reasoning to a declaration of the legal effect of certain facts.

  In Pennsylvania it is possible to put the finger on the very case that accomplished this legislative stroke. In 1817 [845] the Supreme Court of that State had laid down the duty of a jury to presume death, without any positive proof of it, when an unexplained absence for many years is shown; but they refused to adopt a seven years' rule. "I am not," said Tilghman, C. J., "for fixing any precise period after which a presumption of death rises. But here fourteen years and nine months," etc. But twenty-two years

---

[842] Phil. Ev. i. 152 (2d ed.).

[843] Starkie, Ev. (1st ed.) part iv. p. 458; 1 Gr. Ev. s. 41; 1 Tayl. Ev. (9th ed.) s. 200.

[844] Dig. Ev. art. 99.

[845] Miller v. Beates, 3 S. & R. 490.

later the same court adopted the English rule, although in Pennsylvania there were no statutes like those in England; and they said: "If there is no direct decision, as there is in some of our States, it is because there has been no case requiring it. There is such a case now, and the principle is to be considered as definitely settled."[846] In some States this rule, or the like, has been fixed by statute; but it is no less well established in others where it rests not upon a statute, but a judicial determination.

Again, the nature of such rules and the way in which they spring up, may be illustrated by a short series of modern cases in England. In applications for relief against an alleged interference with ancient lights, the equity courts lay down the test that a new erection must not render the house "substantially less enjoyable." That is the legal rule. In determining whether this amount of interference exists in any given case, it was thought convenient, in 1866,[847] to lay down an auxiliary, *prima facie* rule, on the analogy of a recent statute for regulating the height of buildings on streets, so as to prevent the darkening of opposite houses. This statute had required that no building should be higher than the width of the street, — so as to leave to the opposite neighbors an angle of light of forty-five degrees. Accordingly, on an application for an injunction against continuing a neighboring erection where no question of the street was involved, the Vice-Chancellor adopted and applied this same rule, adding that he had heard from one of the common-law judges that they proposed, in general, to act on that principle. Here was the starting of a rule of practice, — of administration; a rule subsidiary to the general one above given, — a rule of presumption; namely, that in the absence of evidence to the contrary the complainant's property is not substantially less enjoyable when he is left an angle of forty-five degrees of light. This rule had a certain amount of vogue; and it appears to have been creeping into the position of an established *prima facie* rule, and perhaps something more. But in 1873 [848] the Lord Chancellor Selborne denied it this character. "With regard to the forty-five degrees, there is no positive rule of law upon that subject...; but undoubtedly... if the legislature, when making general regulations as to buildings, considered.... then

---

[846] Burr v. Sim, 4 Wharton, 150 (1839).

[847] Beadel v. Perry, L. B. 3 Eq. 465, per Stuart, V. C.

[848] City of London Brewery Co. v. Tennant, L. R. 9 Ch. 212.

the fact that forty-five degrees of sky are left unobstructed may, under ordinary circumstances, be considered *prima facie* evidence that there is not likely to be material injury.... If forty-five degrees are left, this is some *prima facie* evidence of the light not being obstructed to such an extent as to call for the interference of the court, — evidence which requires to be rebutted by direct evidence of injury, and not by the mere exhibition of models." But even in this dubious form the suggestion of any rule at all was afterwards repudiated; and we find the Court of Appeal wholly rejecting it in 1880.[849] "It is no rule of law," said James, L. J., "no rule of evidence, no presumption of law, and no real presumption of evidence except of the very slightest, kind." The Lord Justices Brett and Cotton also denied it the quality of a rule to guide either court or jury. Here, then, is an abortive rule of presumption, the beginning of which, and the end, we can easily trace.[850]

The characteristic of all these instances is the same. Matter, logically evidential, has become the subject of a rule which directly, although only *prima facie,* annexes to it legal consequences belonging to the facts of which it is evidence; and this rule takes its place in the substantive law as a subsidiary proposition, alongside of the main. and fundamental one, as an aid in the application of it. The law, as I have said, is always growing in this way, through judicial determinations; for the application of the ultimate rule of the substantive law has to be made by reasoning; and this process is forever discovering the identity, for legal and practical purposes, of one state of things with some other. Many facts and groups of facts often recur, and when a body of men with a continuous tradition has carried on for some length of time this process of reasoning upon facts that often repeat themselves, they cut short the process and lay down a rule. To such facts they affix, by a general declaration, the character and operation which common experience has assigned to them. Relating, as these declarations do, to specified facts, and

---

[849] Ecc. Com. *v.* Kino, 14 Ch. I). 213; s. c. 28 W. B. 544. See the general criticisms of Brett, L. J., in this case.

[850] *See* Mr. Justice Holmes's interesting comments upon the earlier cases in this series, Common Law, 128. They had attracted my attention quite independently, and I now remark for the first time (since these suggestions were put in print) that he had cited them in a similar line of argument. Perhaps this is only an illustration of that suggestion and stimulus for which go many persons are indebted to this excellent book, although they may have forgotten it.

groups of facts, and certain aspects and consequences of them, they belong to that part of the substantive law which deals with these particular things; and as has been truly remarked,[851] they can be understood only in connection with these branches of the law. They do not belong to the law of evidence. When it is said that if persons contract for the sale of a specific chattel, it is presumed that the title passes; and that when a man voluntarily kills another, without any more known or stated, it is presumed to be murder; and that when a written communication to another is put in the mail, — properly addressed, and postage prepaid, — it is presumed that the other receives it; and that when one has been absent seven years and no knowledge of him had by those who would naturally know, death is presumed; in these cases, rightly considered, we have particular precepts in the substantive law of so many different subjects, — of property, of homicide, of notice, and of persons.

In this way, through rules of presumption, vast sections of our law have accumulated. It is thus, especially, that Lord Mansfield and others conspired with the merchants, and transferred their usages into the law.[852] The essential nature of this process, as I have said, is not at all affected by the fact that these judicial conclusions are only presumptive, and are left open to controversy. That is not an unusual form of legislation, even when men profess to be legislating.

Let me show this by a few instances of admitted legislation running through a dozen centuries, — at times attaching legal consequences to evidential facts absolutely, and at times operating contingently, and leaving these consequences open to counter proof. (1) In an often-quoted passage from the laws of Ine, King of Wessex (A. D. 688 — 725),[853] it is provided that "if a far-coming man or a stranger journey through a wood out of the highway, and neither shout nor blow his horn, he is to be held for a thief, either to be slain or redeemed."[854] (2) In the laws of Cnut (A. D. 1017 — 1035)[855] we read that if a man brings home a stolen thing, and it is put into the wife's chest, of which she has the key, "then she is guilty." And (3)

---

[851] *Supra,* 313 n.

[852] Campbell's Lives of the Chief Justices, iii. 274 — 277 (London ed 1874).

[853] Thorpe, Ancient Laws and Institutes of England, i. 115, c. *20.*

[854] It is interesting, in view of Stephen's definition of a presumption, to find him (Hist. Com. Law, i. 61) calling this "a presumption of law."

[855855] Thorpe, i. 419.

the laws of Ine [856] provide that, "if stolen property be attached with a chapman, and he have not brought it before good witnesses, let him prove... that he was neither privy (to the theft) nor thief; or pay as *wite* (fine) xxxvi shillings." To be found thus in the possession of stolen goods was a serious thing; if they were recently stolen, then was one "taken with the mainour," — a state of things that formerly might involve immediate punishment, without a trial; and, later, a trial without a formal accusation;[857] and, later still, a presumption of guilt which, in the absence of contrary evidence, justified a verdict, and at the present time is vanishing away into the mere judicial recognition of a permissible inference, — as it is stated in Stephen's "Digest of Criminal Law:" "The inference that an accused person has stolen property or has received it, knowing it to be stolen, may be drawn from the fact that it is found in his possession after being stolen, and that he gives no satisfactory account of the way in which it came into his possession."[858] It is to be remembered, of course, that the old modes of trial — the ordeal, the oath, wager of law, battle — differed radically from ours. In a criminal case, when a man was charged with an offence, he might be punished unless he cleared himself. He was offered a certain test, the oath or the ordeal, and if he came out of it well he was cleared; if not, he was punished. With us, if a man be arraigned, he must be proved guilty. If we say that now, in trying a man regularly charged with crime, he is presumed innocent, we should correctly intimate the old system by saying that he was presumed guilty. And so (4) The Assize of Clarendon (1166) required that a person charged under the oath of twelve men of the hundred and four men from each of certain neighboring townships as

---

[856] Thorpe, i. 119.

[857] Staundford, Pl. Cr. 179b; *supra,* 71.

[858] Art. 308. In a note the learned author adds: "As to the rule as to recent possession of stolen goods, many cases have been decided on the subject . . .; but they seem to me to come to nothing but this, that every case depends on its own circumstances," etc. Probably the reason of the existence and persistence of the "presumption" to which Stephen here alludes is found in what I have intimated in the text, namely, the long historical root that the tiling has. It is found probably in all systems of law. See the opinion of Doe, J., in State *v.* Hodge, 50 N. H. 510. For another instance of this fading away of substantive law, through various stages, into mere evidence, see the doctrines as to the crying of the child, in tenancy by the curtesy. Bracton, fol. 438; Co. Lit.1. 1, c. 4, a. 35; and compare Plac. Abb. 267, col. 2 (Hil. 5 Ed. I. A. D. 1276 — 7), with Paine's case, 8 Co. 34, 35; 2 Blackst. Com. 127. See *infra, 333.*

an accused or notorious robber, or the like, should be taken and put to the ordeal of water.[859] (5) By Stat. 25 Jac. I., e. 27,[860] it is enacted that "Whereas... women... delivered of bastard children... secretly bury or conceal the death of their children and... if the child be found dead... allege that the said child was born dead; whereas it falleth out sometimes (although hardly it is to be proved) that the said child... were murdered by the said women... be it enacted... that if any woman... be delivered of any issue of her body... a bastard, and... endeavor privately... so 'to conceal the death thereof, as that it may not come to light whether it were born alive or not, but be concealed... the said mother... shall suffer death as in case of murder, except such mother can make proof by one witness at the least that the child... was born dead."(6) The Puritans of Plymouth, in 1671,[861] "Ordered, that the accusation, defamation, or testimony of any Indian or other probable circumstance, shall be accounted sufficient conviction of any English person or persons suspected to sell, trade, or procure any wine, cider, or liquors as abovesaid, to any Indian or Indians, unless such English, shall upon their oath clear themselves from any such act of direct or indirect selling, trucking, or lending of wine, cider, or liquors to any such Indian or Indians, and the same counted to be taken for conviction of any that trade any arms or ammunition to the Indians." A difficulty in such cases was, that while the matter was very pressing, yet, according to the ideas of that period, they could not swear an unconverted Indian; they seem to have reckoned the Indians' god to be the devil.[862] And the only way to handle such cases as they mentioned in this law — cases of very imperative urgency — was to put the accused to his oath. A similar

---

[859] Stubbs (Select Charters) misconceives the significance of this when he says: "The ordeal in these circumstances being a resource following the verdict of a jury acquainted with the fact could only be applied to those who were to all intents and purposes proved to be guilty." No, the ordeal was strictly a mode of trial. What may clearly bring this home to one of the present day is the well-known fact that it gave place, not long after the Assize of Clarendon, to the petit jury, when Henry III. bowed to the decree of the fourth Lateran Council (1215), abolishing the ordeal. It was at this point that our cumbrous, inherited system of two juries in criminal cases had its origin. *Supra,* 37.

[860] A. D. 1623; modelled, apparently, on an edict of Henry II. of France in 1556, *Recueil des Anciennes Lois Françises,* xiii. 472 — 3.

[861] Plymouth Colony Laws, 290, 7.

[862] See *A Chapter of Legal History in Massachusetts,* 9 Harv. L. Rey. I,5

requirement of "trial by oath" was formerly made in Massachusetts, in cases of usury. "It seems proper to remark," said Chief Justice Shaw, "that trial by jury has been substituted for the old trial by oath under St. 1783, c. 55."[863] (7) And, finally, there is a common enough sort of law nowadays that runs, *e.g.,* in this form: whenever an "injury is done to a building or other property by fire communicated by a locomotive engine of any railroad corporation, the said corporation shall be responsible in damages for such injury, unless they shall show that they have used all due caution and diligence, and employed suitable expedients to prevent such injury."[864]

These are instances of confessed legislation. How do they differ from the rules of presumption established by the judges? Neither the one class nor the other belongs to the law of evidence. Both lay down rules, whether absolute or presumptive, in the nature of substantive law, relating to the various subjects dealt with.

III. Perhaps it may be suggested, as regards judicial rules of presumption, that, when tested by the rules relating to special verdicts, they appear after all to be truly rules of evidence. It was, indeed, long ago held that "request and refusal to deliver [in trover] is good evidence to prove conversion; but if it be found specially, it shall not be adjudged conversion."[865] And yet, the judges said, upon demand and refusal "it will be presumed that he had converted it to his own use and therefore *stabitur presumptioni donec probetur in contrarium.*"[866] Coke, on the same occasion, declared that where a deed of feoffment forty years old is given in evidence at the assizes, and it appears that possession has always gone with it, although livery cannot be proved, he should direct the jury to find it, "for it will be intended; yet if the jury should find these facts Specially, we cannot adjudge it a good feoffment, for want of livery."[867] And so, in

---

[863] Little *v. Rogers, 1* Met 10S.

[864] Gen. St. Vermont, c. 28, s. 78, cited in 91 U. S. p. 456.

[865] Agars *v.* Lisle, Hutton, 10. And gee Ames's Cases on Torts (1st ed.), 891 *et seq.*

[866] Coke, C. J., in Isaack *v.* Clarke, 1 Rolle, at p. 131 (1615); and so he had said in Chancellor of Oxford's case, 10 Co. 53 b, 56 b (1613). In the early cases of Eason *v.* Newman, Cro. El. 495; s. c. Moore, 460 (1595), it was held the other way. In the great case of Isaack r. Clarke, the court was equally divided on it; and in Baldwin *v.* Cole, 6 Mod. 212 (1704), Holt, C.J., said: "The very denial of goods to him that hath a right to demand *them is* an actual conversion, and not only evidence of it, as has been holden."

[867] Isaack *v.* Clarke, 1 Rolle, p. 132.

a leading modern case, as regards the doctrine of prescription and a last grant, it was said by a distinguished judge that "none of them [certain judges] meant to say that a special verdict would have been good which did not in terms find the existence of a grant." And yet there is no doubt that all would agree that a lost grant was presumed in the sort of case then under consideration, by a peculiarly strong rule.[868]

In reality, however, the rules for the construction of special verdicts afford no test for determining the nature of rules of presumption. From the nature of verdicts, the jury must find the ultimate facts and not merely the evidence of them; they must do their own duty of drawing conclusions of fact from the evidence and not leave it to the court to do it. But the rules for the construction of their verdict, for determining what they had and had not found, went on the need of indulgence to juries, and on the danger of subjecting them to an attaint by construction. These rules were rigid and strict *in favor of the jury.* Pleadings were strictly construed against the pleader; but Special verdicts, being "the words of laymen," were more considerately dealt with. "It is a dangerous thing," said Chief Justice Hobart, "to construe a verdict larger or otherwise than upon a sure ground, for it subjects them to an attaint."[869] It is not fatal that they be argumentative, if they find the case in fact clear and without equivocations to common intent.[870] The matter is well summed up in Fulwood's case:[871] "It was said that although verdicts, being the words of laymen, shall be taken according to their meaning, and there need not so precise form in them as in pleading, yet the substance of the matter ought to appear either by express words, or by words equivalent or tantamount, so that there ought to be convenient certainty; which if it be false, the party, for such falsity, may have his attaint." It is, indeed, true, as Doderidge, J., said in his opinion in Isaack *v.* Clarke, that there is no sense in the judges telling a jury that they ought, on their consciences, to find a demand and refusal to be a conversion, and yet themselves, on their

---

[868] Brett, L. J., in Angus *v.* Dalton, 4 Q. B. p. 421; Hill *v.* Corell, I N. Y. 522.

[869] Duncombe *v.* Wingfield, Hob. 254, 263 (1623).

[870] Rowe *v.* Huntington, Vaughan, 66, 75.

[871] 4 Co. 64 b, 65 b (1590 — 1)

consciences, adjudging otherwise.[872] But when the judges lay down to a jury the accepted doctrine about demand and refusal in trover, they are assuming an absence of other evidence. If the jury, in their special verdict, find demand and refusal, and negative other facts to the contrary, their verdict may well be held to amount to a finding of conversion. But if they do not, then sound principles would forbid that conclusion. "We must read all facts," it has been said, in regard to a similar question, "whether in a pleading or a Special verdict, or agreed statement or finding of facts, in the light of rules of law. Presumptions of law are rules of law, whether disputable or the contrary. If the disputable presumption is not contradicted or removed by evidence, it is a rule of law to be applied as inflexibly as a presumption that is indisputable.... In other words, a presumption of law that is disputable, when not changed by evidence, becomes to the court a rule indisputable for the case, and the court is bound to apply it."[873] And so in Paine's case,[874] in a question involving the husband's right as tenant by the curtesy, a special verdict found that " the eldest daughter... had issue which was heard cry and died," — *avoit issue oye wye, etc.* This was treated as a sufficient statement that the issue was born alive; and yet Coke's report (and so Co. Lit. 296) tells us that the thing in question is that the child is born alive, and "the crying of the child is but a proof that it is alive." [875]

---

[872] 1 Rolle, p. 131. N'est reson que nous dirromus al jurors que ils sur lour consciences doint trover ceo destre un conversion et tamen nous adjudgeromus auterment sur nostre consciences demesne.

[873] Kidder o. Stevens, 60 Cal. 414, 449, per Thornton, J. And so Johnson and Trumper's case (1637), 21 Vin. Abr. Trial (A. g), 1, and *ibid.,* various cases in text and margin, under the title "Special Verdict. What shall be a good verdict by intendment."

[874] 8 Co. 34 (1587); 8. c. Anderson, 184.

[875] 8 Co. 34 (1587); a. c. Anderson, 184. Compare the custom as to tithes of milk in Hill *v.* Vanx, 2 Salk. 655, — that the parson should have all the milk, "till a young lamb yeaned should he heard to bleat."In a modem case (Murphy *v.* Bennett, 68 Cal. 528, 531) it is said, "This court may, as an appellate tribunal, infer one fact from another in a special verdict as a finding of facts, where the result is determined by a fixed and certain rule of law." Compare Plummer's case, Kelyng, 109 (old ed.); Oneby's case, 2 Lord Raym. 1485; The Earl of Shrewsbury's case, 9 Co. 46 b, 51 b; Duncombe *v.* Wingfield, Hob. 254, 262; Lyn *v.* Wyn, Bridgman, 122, 151; B. *v.* Huggins, 2 Strange, 882 (1730): "It would be the most dangerous thing in the world if we should once give in to the doctrine of inferring facts from evidence; which is the proper business of a jury and not of the court." Raymond, C. J., in discussing a special verdict. Fabian *v.* Wiston, Savile, 121, 123 (1590), *per* Windham, J.

Of course it must be remembered always that many widely different things are called "presumptions." As regards all that class of things, thus named, which are merely judicial recognitions of what is probable, or permissible in reasoning, or of what is sufficient to support a verdict,[876] these have no quality of substantive law. Furthermore judicial rules of presumption, while in process of gradually growing up and hardening, may have different degrees of force and acceptance at different times; and it may well be that as matter of sound administration the judges will not at all times press their rules and practices equally far, or as far as they legally might. Special verdicts are to be read with reference to the record, and to all appropriate considerations of sense, reason, and law. It is not necessary to assert, nor is it probable, that courts have always observed the true distinctions, and have always abstained from pressing caution beyond its due bounds, and overdoing technicalities. But, allowing for all this, it may probably be laid down as sound in principle and hot contradicted by the cases, that wherever a jury finds facts which, according to the rule adopted by the judges to govern their own conduct and to be laid down to a jury, are stamped with a *prima facie* quality, the court may properly read a special verdict which conforms in its findings to all the suppositions of the rule, as a finding of ultimate facts.[877]

IV. I have been speaking of rules relating to specific facts or groups of facts. But sometimes the suppositions of fact or the situation dealt with are not referable to any one brunch of the law, but spread through several or through all of them. Then you have a general principle or maxim of legal reasoning. There are many of these, which pass current under the name of presumptions, — maxims, ground rules, constantly to be remembered and applied in legal discussion; such as those familiar precepts that *omnia præsumuntur rite esse acta, probatis extremis præsumuntur media,* and the like. Of this nature also is the assumption of the existence of the usual qualities of human beings, such as sanity, and their regular and proper conduct, their honesty and conformity to duty.[878] Often

---

[876] See comments on Doe d. George *v.* Jesson, *supra,* 321.

[877] See Lord Blackburn's intimations as to a needless technicality in dealing with special verdicts, in Dublin Ry. Co. *v.* Slattery, 3 App. Cas. pp. 1204 — 5; supra, 243 n.

[878] *De quolibet homine præsumitur quod sit bonus homo, donec probetur in contrarium.* Bracton, fol. 193.

these maxims and ground principles get expressed in this form of a presumption perversely and inaccurately, as when the rule that ignorance of the law excuses no one, is put in the form that every one is presumed to know the law;[879] and when the doctrine that every one is chargeable with the natural consequences of his conduct, is expressed in the form that every one is presumed to intend these consequences;[880] and when the rule that he who holds the affirmative must make out his case, is put in the form of *præsumitur pro negante.* The form of these statements is often a mere matter of convenience or habit; it means little. In whatever form they are made or ought to be made, their character is the same, that of general maxims in legal reasoning, having no peculiar relation to the law of evidence.

V. If, now, it be asked, What particular effect have rules of presumption in applying the law of evidence? the answer seems to be that they have the same effect (and no other), which they have in all the other regions of legal reasoning. Their effect results necessarily from their characteristic quality, — the quality, namely, which imputes to certain facts or groups of fact a *prima facie* significance or operation. In the conduct, then, of an argument, or of evidence, they throw upon him against whom they operate the duty of meeting this imputation. Should nothing further be adduced, they may settle the question in a certain way; and so he who would not have it settled thus, must show cause. This appears to be the whole effect of a presumption, and so of a rule of presumption. There are, indeed, various rules of presumption which appear to do more than this, — to fix the amount of proof to be adduced, as well as the duty of adducing it. But in these cases also, the presumption, merely as such, goes no further than to call for proof of that which it negatives, *i. e.,* for something which renders it probable. It does not specify how much; whether proof beyond a reasonable doubt or by a preponderance of all the evidence, or by any other measure of proof. From the nature of the case, in negativing a given supposition and calling for argument or evidence in support of it, there is meant such an amount of evidence or reason as may render the view contended

---

[879] "There is no presumption in this country that everybody knows the law; it would be contrary to common sense and reason if it were so." Manie, J., in Martindale *v.* Falkner, 2 C. B. 719, See Lord Esher, in Blackburn *v.* Vigors, 17 Q. B. D. 553, 556 — 562.

[880] 2 Steph. Hist. Cr. Law, 111.

for rationally probable. But beyond that, a presumption seems to say nothing. When, therefore, we read that the contrary of any particular presumption "must be proved beyond a reasonable doubt, as is sometimes said, *e. g;* of the "presumption of innocence"[881] and the presumption of legitimacy, it is to be recognized that we have something superadded to the rule of presumption, namely, another rule as to the amount of evidence which is needed to overcome the presumption; or, in other words, to start the case of the party who is silenced by it. And so, wherever any specific result is attributed to a presumption other than that of fixing the duty of going forward with proof. This last, and this alone, appears to be characteristic and essential work of the presumption. It is the substantive criminal law and the substantive law as to persons respectively that fix the rule about the strength of conviction that must be produced in the mind of the tribunal in order to hold one guilty of crime, or to find a child born in wedlock to be illegitimate.[882]

"While it is obvious, then, that a presumption, *i. e.,* the assumption, intendment, taking-for-granted, which we call by that name, accomplishes, for the moment at any rate, the work of reasoning and evidence, it should be remarked, as I have said before, that neither this result, nor the rule which requires it, constitutes, in itself, either evidence or reasoning. This might seem too plain to require mention if it were not for the loose phraseology in which courts sometimes charge the jury, leaving to it in a lamp "all the evidence and the presumptions," as if they were capable of being weighed together as one mass of probative matter. The error is not limited to trial courts.[883] Such a remark might pass as merely a loose

---

[881] Steph. Dig. Ev. art, 94. "Presumption of innocence. If the commission of a crime is directly in issue in any proceeding, criminal or civil, it must be proved beyond reasonable doubt."

[882] People *v.* Cannon, 139 N. Y. 32, 43, 47. See a note in Chamberlayne'a edition of Best on Evidence, s. 296, in which my friend, the editor, has here and there, by permission, done me the honor of a quotation.

[883] See Appendix B for some notice of the case of Coffin *v. V. S.,* 156 U.S. 432, in which there is presented a wholly untenable exposition of what is called the "presumption of — innocence." It is strangely said in this opinion that "the fact that the presumption of innocence is recognized *as* a presumption of law and is characterized by the civilians as a *presumptio juris,* demonstrates that it is evidence in favor of the accused. For in all systems of law legal presumptions are treated as evidence giving rise to resulting proof to the full extent of their legal efficacy." See *infra,* 568.The operation and effect of rules of this sort may be seen by observing the method of the judges in one or two cases. In an interesting case

and inaccu" rate way of saying that it accomplishes the result of evidence or reasoning, if it were not that sometimes judges go on to declare that the presumption is in itself so much probative matter, to be weighed as against other probative matter, *i. e.,* is evidence in the

---

(Anderson r. Morice, L. B. 10 G. P. 609 [1875]) where a ship partly loaded with a cargo of rice had Bunk, at her anchors, in port, and where the buyers were suing an underwriter, the question was whether the plaintiff had any insurable interest in what was aboard at the time of the loss; whether, as Blackburn, J., put it, if uninsured, he would have suffered any loss from the destruction of this rice. In reaching the conclusion that he would not, that judge reasoned thus: It was the plain intention of the parties that the rice should be at the plaintiff's risk from the time, at any rate, when the lading was complete. Each bag, may have been at his risk as it was put aboard, if this was the intention of the parties. But there is nothing to indicate that the parties had present to their minds any such question as that. "We must collect the intention from the words used, applying to them the general rules which the courts have from time to time adopted, as rules to enable them to ascertain the intention." Now it is a rule that presumably title does not pass before the seller has done what the contract requires of him in order to put the goods into that state in which the buyer is bound to accept them; and in this case completing the lading, so that shipping documents could be made out, seems to be a thing thus required of the vendor. But "this is only a *prima facie* indication of intention, and ... it must yield to anything sufficiently indicating a contrary intention." Yet nothing of that sort appears. Risk and property generally go together. "We . . . proceed on the ground that the *prima facie* rule of construction *[supra,* 316] is that the parties intended that the risk should become that of the buyer, when, and not till, the whole lading was complete, so as to enable the shippers, by getting the shipping documents, to call on the buyer to accept and pay for the cargo; . . . and that there is nothing in this contract to rebut the presumption that such was the intention."Here we have a conclusion of fact reached by applying a *prima facie* rule in the substantive law of sale. *Supra,* 315. Compare this method with that of Lord Coleridge at the earlier stage of Ogg *v.* Shuter, L. R. 10 C. P. 159 (1875), where, in dealing with somewhat related questions, there is no resort to any *prima facie* rule, and the matter is treated as one of mere intention, "on a balance of the various circumstances on one side and the other." This, whether rightly or wrongly applied in the case just referred to, is the method spoken of by Buller, J., in a famous passage in his first opinion in Lickbarrow *v.* Mason, 2 Term Rep. 63: "We find in Snee *v.* Prescott that Lord Hardwicke himself was proceeding with great caution, not establishing any general principle, but decreeing on all the circumstances of the case put together. Before that period [1743], we find that in courts of law all the evidence in mercantile cases was thrown together: they were left generally to a jury, and they produced no established principle. From that time, we all know, the great study has been to find some certain general principles, which shall be known to all mankind, not only to rule the particular case then under consideration, but to serve as a guide for the future. Most of us have heard these principles stated, reasoned upon, enlarged, and explained, till we have been lost in admiration at the strength and stretch of the human understanding."

proper sense of the word, and make this notion the basis of a decision. Such an error is quite too grave and harmful to be overlooked.

VI. The discrimination between presumptions of law and what are infelicitously termed presumptions of fact, however important it may be in pleading or elsewhere, is one of no special significance in the law of evidence; for all presumptions, other than the mere non-technical recognition, by courts, of ordinary processes of reasoning[884] are the subject of rules of presumption, and these rules, of whatever varying degrees of stringency and exactness of application they may be, all of them, belong to the law and are rules of law. They may or may not be enforced by courts in granting a new trial.[885] But the essential character and operation of presumptions, so far as the law of evidence is concerned, is in all cases the same, whether they be called by one name or the other; that is to say, they throw upon the party against whom they work, the duty of going forward with the evidence; and this operation is all their effect, regarded merely in their character as presumptions.[886]

There appear to be two main conceptions, namely: (1) that of such presumptions, intendments, assumptions (whether or not they be founded on the probative quality of the facts which they presuppose), as are made under a requirement of law, or are adopted into and recognized as part of the law; and (2) presumptions not thus required or recognized, but resting merely on the probative quality of the facts which they presuppose. The seven years' presumption of death is an example of the first; of the second, any ordinary antecedent probability may suffice as an illustration, *e. g.,* in a shipwreck, in the absence of other facts, the probability that a strong man who was a good swimmer outlived his companion, a feeble invalid, unable to swim.

---

[884] *Supra,* 313 n.,317,326.

[885] Best, Ev. ss. 314, 321, 323, 327. "We find the same presumption spoken of by judges, sometimes as a presumption of law, sometimes as a presumption of fact, sometimes as a presumption which juries should be advised to make, and sometimes as one which it was obligatory on them to make." The discussion of the general subject of presumptions, in our books, and the attempted classifications, are for the most part singularly ineffective. See, for example, the works of Best and Matthews, and the ordinary treatment of the subject by our courts, *e. g;* by Scott, J., in a sound opinion in Howe *v.* Barret, 28 Mo. 388.

[886] *Supra,* 336.

These last are forever reappearing in the courts, and receiving recognition there, and are thus coming from time to time to have the character of legally recognized presumptions. That which is regularly presumed in trials, and which thus gets to be a commonplace of legal reasoning, becomes, at the same time, the subject of a legal rule of more or less definiteness. Any such presumption which obtains recognition in the courts and is regularly applied by them, and laid down to juries as a precept of legal reasoning, may properly be called a legal presumption, and the subject of a legal rule of presumption.[887]

The quite modern facility in using the contrasted phrases, presumption of law and presumption of fact, has been attended with

---

[887] There is great looseness on this subject in dealing with juries. In an important capital trial in Massachusetts, in 1830 (Com. *v.* Knapp, 9 Pick. 496, 519), it is probable that grave consequences followed from this sort of error; far too serious an emphasis was laid on a matter of mere ordinary probability, by laying it down to the jury as a "legal presumption." In order to convict the defendant, in the case referred to, it was essential to show that he was present at the murder by agreement with the principal; or with his knowledge, aiding and abetting. He had previously conspired with the principal offender, now dead and unconvicted, and at the time of the crime was in a street near by, where he might have given or acted on a signal. He was therefore "present;" but there was no evidence as to his being there by agreement, except the natural probabilities of the situation. The court, however, charged the jury that if the prisoner, being a co-conspirator, was where he could aid at the time of the murder, "then it would follow as a legal presumption that he was there to carry into effect the concerted crime, and it would be for the prisoner to rebut the presumption by showing to the jury that he was there for another purpose, unconnected with the conspiracy." In point of fact, although there was no evidence on the subject, it had been understood between the principal and Knapp that the latter should go home and go to bed. He had done so, but, unknown to the actual murderer, had, in his anxiety, got up again and gone out to the place above named, merely to learn the result. 6 Webster's Works, 49. It seems likely, in this case, that this unexplained use of the term "legal presumption," and this declaration as to the prisoner's duty of rebutting it, contributed materially towards what was felt to be the difficult result of a conviction. In that point of view the case may serve as a conspicuous warning against loose modes of expression very common in our courts. To be sure, the men who were hanged in this case well deserved their fate, — had the law been adequate; but in the next case, where feeling runs high, they may not deserve it.Such rules are frequently misconceived. Forgetting their character as rules operating only in the absence of evidence other than what the facts named in the rule itself present, it is not uncommon to add to a mass of evidence a statement of a rule of presumption which, by the introduction of this evidence, has become inapplicable. The nature of this error has been happily pointed out in the courts of Missouri. See, for example, Morton *v.* Heidorn, 135 Mo. 608 (1896).

some attempt to introduce into our system the niceties of the continental classification of the thousand and one assumptions, positions, presumptions, — on innumerable subjects, — which have a place among the civilians. It has been the old mistake of pouring new wine into old bottles, and old wine into new. The rough and general conception, indeed, of the difference between, their *presumptio juris,* as that which has a place in the law, and so is a rule of law, *on* the one hand; and their *præsumptio hominis,* as that which has no place in the law, and is merely *in arbitrio judicis,* as addressing itself only to the rational faculty, — is indeed sound and helpful. But when our writers or judges undertake to follow the civilians out into such a discussion as the general one, whether presumptions are matter of law or matter of fact, — *Præsumptio an sit quid juris, vel facti,*[888] — and into the subject of conflicting presumptions, — whether *Præsumptio una validior et firmior altera,* and *Quando una præsumptio alteram tollat et diluat,*[889] — the matter becomes very unsuitable to our system of law, and something much more than unprofitable. This puzzling and uninstructive term "presumption of fact" is not found at all in the Roman law, nor is it a leading one among the continental writers. Their contrast, as is said above, is between *presuptio juris* and *presumptio hominis.*[890]

---

[888] Menochius, *de præs.,* lib. I, qu. 11.

[889] *Ib.* qu. 29 and 30. The enormous detail of these continental discussions may be guessed at when it is observed that the treatise of Menochius, an Italian who wrote in the latter part of the sixteenth century *De Præsumptionibus, Conjecturis, Signis, et Indiciis,* has 1167 tall folio pages in double columns and fine print. They are of little if any importance in a system where jury trial prevails.

[890] Divisio quam ipsemet Baldus recenset . . , cum dixit præsumptionem aliam esse legis aliam hominis et præsamptionem illam legis, aliquando esse simpliciter juris, aliquando juris et de jure. Qnam sane divisionem ceteri fere omnes sunt secuti. . . . Rectius itaque ex nos-trorum fere omnium sententia sic nos dividimus præsamptionem, ut una sit juris et de jure, altera juris tantum, tertia vero hominis. Menoch. *de præs;* lib. 1, qu. 2. And so in an Irish case, the earliest case where I have observed these Latin phrases in our books, in 1743 (Annesley *v. An*glesea, 17 St. Tr. 1130, 1430), Baron Mounteney, after some explanations, says to the jury: "These are called presumptions *juris et de jure.* Again there are presumptions of law, as, likewise, what the writers upon this subject call presumptions of man."It should be added that all this phraseology and all the multitudinous details and refinements of the discussions over presumptions, belong not at all to the Roman law or the Corpus Juris. They originated in the continental jurists of a much later time. Ortolan (Hist. Rom. Law, by Prichard and Nasmith, 644), in speaking of absolute presumptions, says:

VII. As to the subject of conflicting presumptions, I have alluded to it as an exotic, ill adapted to an English or North American climate. At common law our principal triers of fact are that changing, untrained body of men the jury, to whom it would be idle to address such speculations on this subject as fill the books of the civilians; the considerations which are to govern and sway their thoughts must be large, simple, untechnical. Nor are these refinements much better adapted to the mental habits of our judges. The jury system has reacted upon them, and upon the body of law which they administer, in a way to keep forever in the foreground, in determining matters of fact, the thought of convenience, and of easily applied principles of practical sense. The continental methods were deeply infected with what has been called " the substitution of arithmetic for observation and reasoning, when estimating the value of evidence." Their writers were dealing with "a system of technical and, as it were, mechanical belief, dependent on the presence of instruments of evidence in some given number; and which has been designated by Bonnier... *systeme qui tarifait les temoignages, au lieu*

"It is this presumption which the commentators have called, in barbarous Latin which never belonged to Roman law, *Prœumptio juris et de jure.* In other cases, where law makes its induction, it allows more or less latitude, that is to say, it permits the parties concerned to question the soundness of the induction. ... It is this presumption that *the commentators* have called, *again on their own sole authority, Præsumptio juris tantum. . . .* Presumptions — that is to say, those conclusions or deductions which are drawn by a process of probable reasoning, as *the result of experience,* from something which is taken for granted — were not classified by the Roman jurists, nor were they treated differently from other forms of proof."It may be well to remember, as I have intimated above, that the present common talk about presumptions as being those of law and of fact, and the introduction of the Latin phrases, are quite modern. The treatises on Evidence before Phillips, in 1814, have, I believe, nothing of it, except that Lofft, in editing Gilbert, in 1791, slightly introduces the phrase presumption of fact. It was not until Greenleaf's Evidence, in 1842, and Best's Presumptions, in 1844, that the phraseology of our textbooks was fairly shaped on the present models. See, however, the discussion of them in 1831, *infra,* 539. That the distinction of presumptions of law and presumptions of fact, so far, at least, as the law of evidence is concerned, is a poor and confusing one, is shown by our cases. It may serve to indicate how likely we are to be misled in adopting continental terms when we observe that the *prœsumptio juris et de jure* was not, with them, what we are generally told to consider it, absolutely and always a conclusive one. Menoch. lib. 1, qu. 60 — 85. That fact may serve to relieve the continental law from the reproach of Austin, when he says: "It is absurd to style conclusive inferences presumptions." Jurisp. i. 507, London, 1873.

de les soumettre à la conscience du juge.[891] But of our system, it has been said by the same writer that "by taking out of the hands of the judge the actual decision on the facts, and the application of the law to them, it cuts up mechanical decision by the roots, prevents artificial systems of proof from being formed, and secures the other advantages of a casual tribunal."[892]

Unfortunately, however, the writer just mentioned has himself tried to introduce into our law parts of that continental method which he so justly condemns.[893] Not much success has attended the attempt, and so far as it succeeds it is not likely to produce anything but harm. In one case, earlier than his time, in 1819, an ill-starred effort was made to use the notion of conflicting presumptions in dealing with a settlement case.[894] Paupers were removed to Twyning as being the wife and children of one Burns. The legality of the order depended on whether a former husband, Winter, was living at the time of the marriage with Burns. The marriage with Winter was about seven years ago. Winter, after living with his wife thereafter for a few months, enlisted as a soldier, went abroad in the foreign service, and was never again heard from. A little more than a year after this enlistment the woman married Burns, had cohabited with him ever since, and had by him the children above named. It was held that the decision below was right, on the ground that it was "a case of conflicting presumptions, and the question is which is to prevail.... The presumption of law is that [Winter] was not alive when the consequence of his being so is that another person has committed a criminal act."

The true analysis of such a case seems rather to be this: We observe that the party seeking to move the court proved the existing marriage (contracted between five and six years ago) and children born of it. On the other side, the only evidence to prove the invalidity of this marriage was the fact of another one, contracted about seven years ago, and the disappearance of the first husband a few months

---

[891] Best, Ev. ss. 71, 69. In the two or three sections of Best which precede and follow these, may be found some brief account of the former artificial method of the Continent.

[892] Ib. s. 85.

[893] *Ib.* ss. 328 — 336, as to conflicting presumptions. He observes (s. 330) that the subject "seems almost to have escaped the notice of the writers on English law."

[894] R. *v.* Twyning, 2 B. & Aid. 386.

thereafter (about a year earlier than the second marriage), on occasion of his enlisting and going abroad in the foreign military service; that husband had never been heard of since. These facts might well seem Inadequate, in evidential force, to impeach the validity of the existing marriage, and the legitimacy of the children. For one thing, the absence, although not long, was upon a dangerous service. Presumptions are displaced or made inapplicable by such special facts. It was not strange, therefore, in 1835, to find the matter handled in a different way.[895] Here the first spouse had been heard from up to twenty-five days before the second marriage as having written to her family at that time, and the court quashed in order which assumed the validity of the second marriage. Lord Denman, C. J., said: "I must take this opportunity of saying that nothing can be more absurd than the notion that there is to be any rigid presumption of law on such questions of fact, without reference to I, accompanying circumstances, such, for instance, as the "age or health of the party.... The only questions in Such cases are, what evidence is admissible, and what inference may fairly be drawn from it."[896]

VIII. It is one of the commonest of errors to misapprehend the scope and limitations of the ordinary rules and maxims of presumption; and to attribute to them a mistaken quality and force. They are, as we have seen, merely *prima facie* precepts; and they presuppose only certain specific and expressed facts. The addition of other facts, if they be such as have evidential bearing, may make the presumption inapplicable. All is then turned into an ordinary question of evidence, and the two or three general facts presupposed in the rule of presumption take their place with the rest, and operate, with their own natural force, as a part of the total mass of probative matter. Of course the considerations which have made these two or three facts the subject of a rule of presumption may still operate, or may not, to emphasize their quality as evidence; but the main point

---

[895] King *v.* Harborne, 2 Ad. & El. 540. Compare State *v.* Plym, 43 Minn. 385.

[896] The sudden emergence, in an English Court; in 1819, of this continental doctrine of conflicting presumptions, may perhaps be accounted for by the influence, in that case, of the counsel whose contention was successful, namely, W. D. Evans. This can hardly be other than the learned translator and editor of Pothier on Obligations, whose acquaintance with continental peculations had been brought into relation with the English law in his valuable Appendix to that work, being the second volume, published in 1806.

to observe is, that the rule of presumption has vanished. For example, in the first of the settlement cases above mentioned the supposed rule of presumption as to the continuance of life for seven years (since repudiated in England)[897] dealt only with the general and colorless supposition of absence not heard from. It did not suppose going abroad in the military service.

A conspicuous illustration of the error now in question may be seen in an observation of Lord Campbell, in a case in the House of Lords in 1849.[898] In a discussion on legitimacy, Lord Campbell remarked: "So strong is the legal presumption of legitimacy that if a white woman have a mulatto child, although the husband is white and the supposed paramour black, the child is presumed legitimate, if there were any opportunities for intercourse." Now there might, without absurdity, be a doctrine which fixed upon a husband, even under such circumstances, the legal responsibilities of a father; according to the rough proverbial wisdom, quoted by a vigorous English judge four or five centuries ago, "who that bulleth my cow the calf is mine." [899] But as the English law actually stands, doubtless Lord Campbell had introduced into his supposition such unusual facts as dissolved and evaporated any rule of presumption. It never was a rule that the mere opportunity for intercourse between an English husband and wife, gave rise to a presumption that he was the father of her child under the specific circumstances named. On the contrary it was a just contention, in North Carolina, in 1872, when a colored child of a white married woman was exhibited to the jury as "proof that it was impossible" that the white husband of the woman could be its father.[900]

IX. It will be profitable to speak of one or two singular cases which illustrate further those aspects of the subject considered in the last two subdivisions of the present chapter.

In an English case, in 1881,[901] the defendant was indicted for bigamy in marrying A in 1880, while his wife B, married by him

---

[897] Nepean v. Doe d. Knight, 2 M. & W. 894; Phene's Trusts, L. R. 5 Ch 139.

[898] Piers v. Piers, 13 Jurist, 569, 572.

[899] Rickhill, J., *"Si cestuy John, fuit deins la mere, issue fuit mulier, et issint heire quant il fuit issue male.* For who that bulleth my cow, the calf is mine." Y. B. 7 H. IV. 9, 13 (1406). Compare Shakespeare, *King John,* Act I. scene 1, where the king is talking with Robert Faulconbridge.

[900] Warlich v. White, 76 No. Ca. 175.

[901] Reg. *v.* Willshire, 6 Q. B. D. 366.

a year before, in 1879, was living. When these marriages and the present life of B had been proved, the defendant on the other hand showed, by the record, his own previous conviction upon an indictment for bigamy; he had married C in 1868, while his wife D, married four years before, was still living. Thus he introduced into the case facts having a tendency to show that B, like several other women in like condition, was not his wife. And so the case was left. How should these facts be treated? On some theory of conflicting presumptions, and their relative force? Or simply by having regard to the evidential quality of the facts, and to the relative duty of the government and the accused, in establishing and defending the case? By the latter method the essential inquiry was (1) whether D, the true and still undivorced wife, was living when B was married? and (2) supposing that matter to be left in doubt, who loses? It may be said that there is a presumption of his own innocence, working in favor of the prisoner, and a presumption of somebody else's life, working against him. But the presumption of innocence means only that the defendant is not to suffer on his trial from being charged with guilt and held on the charge; and that he must not be found guilty on appearances, or suspicions, or anything but evidence establishing guilt beyond a reasonable doubt. And what does the presumption of life mean? In England it is only a general supposition of continuance, applicable to everything which has once been proved to exist — to an orange as well as a man; — a presumption which serves, in reasoning, to relieve from the necessity of constantly re-proving, from minute to minute, this once proved fact of existence.

The presumption of death at the end of seven years had no application in the case under discussion, because that assumes absence *not heard from;* and such an absence was not found here.[902] The government, of course, had to make out guilt beyond a reasonable doubt; the accused needed only to create such a doubt. Guilt depended on whether D, living on April 22, 1868, when C was married, was alive on Sept. 7, 1879, when B was married. The government, to succeed, must satisfy the jury beyond a reasonable doubt of a proposition which included the fact that D was then dead. The accused, to be discharged, must, at least, create a reasonable doubt whether she was then alive.

---

[902] Dowd *v.* Watson, 105 N. C. 476.

In fact, the case was disposed of below by holding that, as the evidence lay, "the burden of proof was on the prisoner," and he was convicted. But on a question reserved "whether he was properly convicted," the conviction was quashed. Lord Coleridge, C. J., talked of conflicting presumptions, and held it wrong to withdraw from the jury "the determination of the fact from these conflicting presumptions.... The prisoner was only bound to set up the life; it was for the prosecution to prove his guilt." Lindley, J., simply put it: "There was evidence both ways: This evidence was not left to the jury, consequently the conviction cannot stand." Hawkins, J. "There was proof that Ellen [D] was alive in 1868; there was a presumption that her life continued. The only evidence to the contrary was that the prisoner presented himself as a bachelor to be married in 1879. Whether that would have satisfied the jury that his former wife was then dead was a question for them to decide, but it was not left to them for decision." Lopes, J. "There was evidence both ways... which should have been left to the jury." Bowen, J., was "of the same opinion." The case, then, was rightly disposed of; and the notion of conflicting presumptions had no real bearing upon it.

Another case covers a point referred to by a distinguished writer on Evidence, as destitute of authority.[903] In Wisconsin a husband, on the death of his wife, claimed, and was at first allowed, in the lower courts, an estate by the curtesy in certain real estate of which she died seized. Under the statutes of Wisconsin his right, as against a daughter of the wife (bearing in this case his name, and born, fully developed, five months after his marriage with her mother, but claiming now to be the daughter of a former husband), depended on the truth of the daughter's contention. Mrs. Shuman had married Ingle in April, 1880, and was divorced from him on November 15, 1884. She married the plaintiff, Shuman, on February 10, 1885, and the defendant was born July 8, 1885, a mature and fully grown child. The divorce from Ingle had been granted on the suit of the husband, begun October 3, 1884, which was undefended. The ground of the application for divorce was desertion, in that the wife had refused sexual intercourse with the husband for nearly two years last past, and declared that she would never again allow it; and the evidence of the husband on the divorce hearing had

---

[903] "I am not aware of any decision *as to* the paternity of a child born say six months after the death of one husband, and three months after the mother's marriage to another." Stephen, Dig. Ev. art. 98 n.

substantiated these allegations. It appeared, however, at the trial of the present case that for several months, before and down to the date of the judgment of divorce, the husband and wife lived in the same house, conversed, ate at the same table, lodged in adjoining rooms, with a connecting door, and had full opportunity for intercourse. The Supreme Court of Wisconsin sustained the rejection by the last court below, of the evidence of the complaint and testimony in the divorce proceedings, and its decision that the defendant, while having the name of the second husband, was the daughter of the first.[904] In a like case it would be easy to suppose the second marriage taking place soon after the death of the first husband, and when the wife was in an advanced state of pregnancy.[905] Or to suppose a prompt second marriage so soon after the first husband's death, that a child might have been begotten in wedlock by either.[906]

To undertake to settle such questions as these (and they they easily be complicated by the introduction of other facts) by

---

[904] Shuman *v.* Shuman, 83 Wis. 250 (1892). See also Shuman *v.* Hard, 79 Wis. 654, where the dates differ slightly. The court, Lyon, C. J., said: "The rules of evidence by which it must be determined whether Frances M. is or is not the lawful issue of the marriage of her mother and Andrew Ingle, are unaffected by the fact that she was born after the marriage of her mother and Alexander Shuman. The last marriage may save Frances M. from being a bastard in case Andrew Ingle is not her father; but the same proof is required to demonstrate that he is not her father, as would be required had the last marriage not taken place, and were she claiming as heir of Ingle."

[905] Compare the case of Gardner *v.* Gardner, 2 App. Cas. 723, where the woman was not married when the child was begotten, and the judges speak of the presumption as being exceedingly strong that the husband was the father of the child.

[906] A case repeatedly put in our books, *e.g.,* in 1347, by R. Thorp, in Y. B 21 Ed. III. 40, where Wilughby, J., follows it up by saying, "I heard the lame case once demanded of Sir William de Bereford, [a justice in the time of Edward I. and II.] — to which of the two husbands he should be adjudged; and ho answered that the son might choose either." And so Co. Lit. 8. In Alsop *v,* Stacy, Palmer, 9; s. o. Cro. Jac. 541, *sub nom.* Alsop v. Bowtrell, a record of 1394 — 5 was cited, where a woman's first husband died, and she married and had a child in two hundred and ninety-one days after the first husband's death, and it was adjudged the child of the second husband. In the principal case the court held a child born of a widow, *un lewd et light damosel,* 290 days after the husband's death to be his child; and Dodridge, J., took a distinction between this case and the other, in that it would make the child a bastard if it should be held otherwise here, while in the other case he would be legitimate either way. As Blackstone permits himself to remark (1 Bl. Com. 459) he would be "more than ordinarily legitimate."

any comparison of the strength of the presumptions would be foreign, to our common-law methods. The bringing forward of unusual facts, as we have seen, often discharges the whole matter from the operation of presumptions, and like Coke's estoppel against estoppel "doth put the matter at large."[907]

X. In closing this long discussion, it may be remarked that the numberless propositions figuring in our cases under the name of presumptions, are quite too heterogeneous and non-comparable in kind, and quite too loosely conceived of and expressed, to be used or reasoned about without much circumspection. Many of them are grossly ambiguous, true in one sense and false in any other; some are not really presumptions at all, but only wearing the name; some express merely a natural probability, and others, for the sake of having a definite line, establish a mere rule of legal policy; very many of them, like the rule about children born in wedlock, lay down a *prima facie* rule of the substantive law, and others, a rule of general reasoning, and of procedure, founded on convenience or probability or good sense; like the wide-reaching principle which "presumes a usual and ordinary state of things rather than a peculiar and exceptional condition,... legality rather than crime, and virtue and morality rather than the opposite qualities; which demands a construction of evidence as well as of written language, *ut res magis valeat quam pereat.*"[908] Some are maxims, others mere inferences of reason, others rules of pleading, others are variously applied; as the presumption of innocence figures now as a great doctrine of criminal procedure, and now as an ordinary principle in legal reasoning, or a mere inference from common experience, or a rule of the law of evidence. Among things so incongruous as these and so beset with ambiguity there is abundant opportunity for him to stumble and fall who does not pick his way and walk with caution.

---

[907] Co. Lit. 352 b. Compare Alciatus, Op. i. 901, 30, *Alia præsumptio aliam tollit;* and ib. iii. 231, 40. See the clear and sensible language of Denio, J., in Caujolle *v.* Ferrie, 23 N. Y. 90, 138, and of Lord Hatherley in Gardner *v.* Gardner, 2 App. Cas. 723, 732.

[908] Per Denio, J., in Caujolle *v. Ferrié* N. Y. 90, 138.

CHAPTER IX
THE BURDEN OF PROOF

Whoever enters on a legal controversy needs to know with precision what is in dispute, in point of substantive law, in point of fact, and in point of form. All this he must know before he reaches the trial. The ascertaining of it belongs, properly, to the period when you state your Case, the period of pleading. It matters not what be the purpose of pleading, whether, as in the Roman system, it be "to give notice to the parties respectively of the facts intended to be proved," or, as at the common law, "to separate the law from the facts, and to narrow the latter down to a single issue, with a view to a trial by jury,"[909] — the rules of correct pleading involve the ascertaining of all these preliminaries. At any rate, they are not to be learned from the law of evidence, which has no precepts at all on these subjects. That brunch of the law is wholly concerned with a later stage of the proceedings, the trial; and with the presentation to the tribunal of evidential matter for enabling it to answer questions which should have been previously ascertained and shaped, and are now-assumed to be known.

The term "burden of proof" designates a topic which, in great part, belongs to this preliminary stage of the proceedings. So far as 'it imports the duty of ultimately establishing any given proposition, the principles which govern it belong wholly to that stage.

But the phrase is an ambiguous one; and its uncertainty runs into and perplexes the subject of evidence, so that the student of that subject needs to reflect carefully on these ambiguities, to perceive the bearing of them, and to have a clear mind about two or three familiar questions relating to the burden of proof, and two or three fallacies about it which are constantly presenting themselves in the proper region of evidence. He would do a great service to our law who should thoroughly discriminate, and set forth the whole legal doctrine of the burden of proof. No such attempt is now to be made. Such a discussion would have to take a wide range, for the subject belongs to universal jurisprudence, and not merely to the law of one people or one age; and the phrase and the things it stands for have a

---

[909] Langdell, Eq. Plead. (2d ed.) a. 34.

long descent. The leading maxims about it (often ill understood) have come from the Roman Law. During the Dark Ages and among our Germanic ancestors it had a different and peculiar application. It was then *the privilege* of proof.[910] With the use of the jury came a new set of ideas and a new system of pleading, very different from those of Rome and modern continental Europe; and gradually, with the slow and strange development of the jury system, and the irregular working out of common-law pleading, there has come into prominence a new set of discriminations. Much that in other times and countries was not the subject of judicial discussion, and remained hidden among the unrecorded details of forensic usage, now, through the working of our double tribunal of judge and jury, and the constant necessity of marking their respective boundaries, and of reviewing, in a higher court, not merely the instructions given by the trial judge to the jury, but the whole conduct of the trial, — comes out into the region of judicial rules and precedents.

Without undertaking to make any direct exposition of this subject, let me now deal with two or three of those incidental matters alluded to above, as being specially important for the student of the law of evidence to consider.

I. In legal discussion, this phrase, "the burden of proof," is used in several ways. It marks, The peculiar duty of him who has the risk of any given proposition on which parties are at issue, — who will lose the case if he does not make this proposition out, when all has been said and done. In saying "the peculiar duty," I mean to discriminate this duty from another one, called by the same name, which this party shares with his adversary. It stands for the duty last referred to, when discriminated from the other one; that is to say, the duty of going forward in argument or in producing evidence; whether at the beginning of a case or at any later moment throughout the trial or the discussion. There is an undiscriminated use of the phrase, perhaps more common than either of the other two, in which it may mean either or both of the others.

As to the first sense of the term, expressing the duty of the *actor, i. e.,* the party having the affirmative of the issue, to establish the proposition at the end of the case, this is an ancient, wide, and

---

[910] See Von Bar's *Beweisurtheil, passim;* Laughlin, *Legal Procedure,* in "Essays on Anglo-Saxon Law;" and Bigelow, Hist. Procedure in England, c. viii.

approved use. It is the sense to which, since the year 1832,[911] the Supreme Court of Massachusetts has sought, with great anxiety, to limit the expression. In 1854[912] it was put thus: "The burden of proof and the weight of evidence are two very different things. The former remains on the party affirming a fact in support of his case, and does not change in any aspect of the cause; the latter shifts from side to side in the progress of a trial, according to the nature and strength of the proofs offered in support or denial of the main fact to be established. In the case at bar, the averment which the plaintiff was bound to maintain was that the defendant was legally liable for the payment of tolls. In answer to this the defendant did not aver any new and distinct fact, such as payment, accord and satisfaction, or release; but offered evidence to rebut this alleged legal liability. By so doing he did not assume the burden of proof, which still rested on the plaintiff; but only sought to rebut the *prima facie* case which the plaintiff had proved." In 1883[913] the Master of the Rolls (Brett) said: "It is contended (I think fallaciously) that if the plaintiff has given *prima facie* evidence which, unless it be answered, will entitle him to have the question decided in his favor, the burden of proof is shifted on to the defendant as to the decision of the question itself. This contention appears to be the real ground of the decision in the Queen's Bench Division. I cannot assent to it. It seems to me that the proposition ought to be stated thus: the plaintiff may give *prima facie* evidence which, unless it be answered, either by contradictory evidence or by the evidence of additional facts, ought to lead the jury to find the question in his favor: the defendant may give evidence, either by contradicting the plaintiff's evidence or by proving other facts; the jury have to consider, upon the evidence given upon both sides, whether they are satisfied in favor of the plaintiff with respect to the question which he calls upon them to answer.... Then comes the difficulty — suppose that the jury, after considering the evidence, are left in real doubt as to which way they are to answer the question put to them on behalf of the plaintiff; in that case also the burden of proof lies upon the plaintiff, and if the defendant has been able, by the additional facts which he has adduced to bring the minds of the whole jury to a real state of doubt, the plaintiff has failed to satisfy

[911] Powers v. Russell, 13 Pick. 69.
[912] Central Bridge Co. *v.* Butler, 2 Gray, 130.
[913] Abrath *v.* N. E. Ry. Co., 11 Q. B. D. 440.

the burden of proof which lies upon him." [914] In New York,[915] Church, O. J., for the court, expresses himself thus: "The burden of maintaining the affirmative of the issue, and, properly speaking, the burden of proof, remained upon the plaintiff throughout the trial; but the burden or necessity was cast upon the defendant, to relieve itself from the presumption of negligence raised by the plaintiff's evidence." In the following passage may be seen a recognition of two meanings of the term. In 1878,[916] Lord Justice Brett remarked, with valuable comments on the case of Watson *v.* Clark,[917] that "The burden of proof upon a plea of unseaworthiness to an action on a policy of marine insurance lies upon the defendant, and so far as the pleadings go it never shifts.... But when facts are given in evidence, it is often said that certain presumptions, which are really inferences of fact, arise and cause the burden of proof to shift; and so they do as a matter of reasoning, and as a matter of fact."[918]

As to the second sense of the term. 'A clear expression of it is found in an opinion of Lord Justice Bowen:[919] "In order to make my opinion clear, I should like to say shortly how I understand the term 'burden of proof.' In every lawsuit somebody must go on with it; the plaintiff is the first to begin, and if he does nothing he fails. If he makes a *prima facie* case, and nothing is done by the other side to answer it, the defendant fails. The test, therefore, as to burden of proof is simply to consider which party would be successful if no evidence at all was given, or if no more evidence was given than is given at this particular point of the case; because it is obvious that during the controversy in the litigation there are points at which the onus of proof shifts, and at which the tribunal must say, if the case stopped there, that it must be decided in a particular way. Such being the test, it is not a burden which rests forever on the person on whom it is first cast, but as soon as he, in his turn, finds evidence which, *prima facie,* rebuts the evidence against which he is contending, the

---

[914] Compare the charge to the jury in Com. *v.* Choate, 105 Mass. 451, 456, and the language of the court in sustaining it, *ib.* 459.

[915] Caldwell v. New Jersey Co., 47 N. Y. 282, 290.

[916] Pickup *v.* Thames Ins. Co., 3 Q. B. D. p. 600.

[917] 1 Dow, 336.

[918] Compare the same judge in Andersen *v.* Morice, L. R. 10 C. P. 58 (1874), Abrath w. No. East. Ry. Co., 11 Q. B. D. 440 (1883), and Davey *v.* Lond. & S. W. Ry. Co., 12 Q. B. D. 70.

[919] Abrath *v.* No. E. Ry. Co., 32 W. R. 50, 53. In the regular report (11 Q. B. D. 440, 455 — 6) the phraseology is slightly, but not materially, different.

burden shifts until again there is evidence which satisfies the demand. Now, that being so, the question as to onus of proof is only a rule for deciding on whom the obligation rests of going further, if he wishes to win." In the Banbury Peerage case,[920] in the course of a question relating to the presumption of legitimacy, the judges were asked by the House of Lords, "Whether in every case in which there is *prima facie* evidence of any right existing in any person the *onus probandi* be always, or be not always, upon the person or party calling such right in question?" They answered, through Mansfield, C. J., "That in every case in which there is *prima facie* evidence of any right existing in any person, the *onus probandi* is always upon the person or party calling such right in question." Stephen [921] lays it down that "The burden of proof in any proceeding lies at first on that party against whom the judgment of the court would be given if no evidence at all were produced on either side, regard being had to any presumption which may appear on the pleadings. As the proceeding goes on, the burden of proof may be shifted from the party on whom it rested at first by proving facts, which raise a presumption in his favor. The burden of proof as to any particular fact lies on that person who wishes the court to believe in its existence...; but the burden may in the course of a case be shifted from one side to the other," etc. An English writer, Best, tells us:[922] "The burden of proof is shifted by those presumptions of law which are rebuttable; by presumptions of fact of the stronger kind; and by every species of evidence strong enough to establish *a prima facie* case against a party."

A few cases may be added which illustrate the common confusion in the use of the expression, A doctrine was formerly laid down in England that in prosecutions under the game laws, the defendant had the burden of establishing that he was qualified. This really rested in part upon the construction of the statutes.[923] But a general principle came to be laid down, that "where the subject-

---

[920] 1 Sim. & St. 153.

[921] Dig. Evid. arts. 95 and 96.

[922] Evidence, s. 273.

[923] The King *v.* Turner, 5 M. & S. 206, 210 (1816): "There are, I think, about ten different heads of qualification enumerated in the statutes. . . . The argument really comes to this: that there would be a moral impossibility of ever convicting upon such an information." *Per* lord Ellenborough. See King *v.* Stone, 1 East, 639 (1801), where the court was divided.

matter of a negative averment lies peculiarly within the knowledge of the other party, the averment is taken as true unless disproved by that party."[924] There is great sense in such a doctrine as indicating a duty of producing evidence, but little or none when it marks a duty of establishing. But by reason of the ambiguity of this phrase, the doctrine is afloat in both senses. That the duty ought to be limited, as a statement of the common law, to that of giving evidence, is plainly shown by the remarks of Holroyd, J.: "In every case the *onus probandi* lies on the person who wishes to support his case by a particular fact which lies more peculiarly within his own knowledge.... This indeed is not allowed to supply the want of necessary proof," etc.[925] A striking instance, at once of a common English sense of the term, and of a confused way of mixing it up with another sense of it, is found in a recent opinion of so great a judge as Lord Blackburn. In an Irish negligence case[926] a very interesting discussion arose as to the relation between court and jury, and the circumstances under which a judge can direct a verdict; incidentally it touched the burden of proof. Lord Blackburn, who held that a verdict should be entered for the defendants, put his view

---

[924] **Greenl. Ev. i. s. 79.**

[925] King v. Burdett, 4 B. & Aid. p. 140 (1820). See also Steph. Dig. Ev. art. 96: "In considering the amount of evidence necessary to shift the burden of proof, the court has regard to the opportunities of knowledge with respect to the fact to be proved which may be possessed by the parties respectively." Compare Best, Ev. ss. 275, 276. Bonnier, *Traité des Preuves* (5th ed.), i. 37 *bis:* "La difficulté de la preuve . . . n'est point un motif suffisant pour intervertir les rôles." And again, s. 49: "C'est toujours an demandeur à prouver, et qu'il pent le faire, même lorsqu'il s'agit d'un fait négatif; il le pourra bien plus facilement si on admet cette sage restriction que, pour rendre la négative définie, il est permis d'obliger la partie adverse à préciser ses prétentious." The sound common-law doctrine, together with a reference to statutes that change it, is found in Wilson v. Melvin, 13 Gray, 73, and Com. v. Lahy, 8 Gray, 459. The question arising under the English Game Laws was afterwards regulated by statute. (1 Tayl. Ev. 9th ed. s. 377, note) Such statutes, exempting one party from the duty of giving evidence in certain cases, or imposing the "burden of proof" on the other, are common enough both here and in England. They might easily give rise to questions of construction as to the meaning of the phrase now under discussion. In dealing with one of these statutes (which had not, however, used the very phrase), it was said by the court in Mugler v. Kansas, 123 IT. S. p. 674, that it simply determined what was *prima facie* case for the government. Compare Peters, C. J., in Buswell v. Puller, 89 Me. 600.

[926] Dublin, etc. By. Co. v. Slattery, 3 App. Cas. 1155, 1201, 1202, 1203, 1208.

thus: To justify this, "it is not enough that the balance of testimony should be overwhelmingly on one side," so that a verdict the other way ought to be set aside, but "the onus must be one way, and no reasonable evidence to rebut it." By "onus" and "onus of proof" Lord Blackburn does not mean the duty of ultimately establishing a proposition; but his use of the term is so connected with that meaning, and with an older doctrine of pleading whereby the general issue did not necessarily mean a negative case, that it will be instructive to quote his words: "It is of great importance to see on whom the onus of proof lies, for if the state of the case is such that on the admissions on the record, and the undisputed facts given in evidence on the trial, the onus lies on either side, the judge ought to give the direction, first, that if there are no additional facts to alter this, the jury ought to find against that party on whom the onus now lies." "I think the recent decision of your Lordship's House in Metropolitan Railway Company *v.* Jackson conclusively establishes this doctrine in cases in which the onus was, on the issue, as joined on the record, on the party against whom the verdict was directed. I am of opinion that it is equally so when a fact found, or undisputed at the trial, has shifted that onus." "The cases in which the principle that the onus may shift from time to time has been most frequently applied, are those of bills of exchange. At the beginning of a trial under the old system of pleading *[i. e; on the general issue]*... the onus was on the plaintiff to prove that he was holder, and that the defendant signed the bill. If he proved that, the onus was on the defendant; for the bill imports consideration. If the defendant proved that the bill was stolen, or that there was fraud, the onus was shifted, and the plaintiff had to prove that he gave value for it. This... depends not on the allegation, under the new system, on the record, that there was fraud, but on the proof of it at the trial." "It was laid down in Ryder *v.* Wombwell that 'there is in every case a preliminary question, which is one of law, namely, whether there is any evidence on which the jury could properly find the question for the party on whom the onus of proof lies; if there is not, the judge ought to withdraw the question from the jury, and direct a nonsuit if the onus is on the plaintiff, or direct a verdict for the plaintiff if the onus is on the defendant,' and this was approved of and adopted in this House in the recent case of Metropolitan Railway Company *v.* Jackson. I have already given my reasons for thinking that the expression, 'the party on whom the onus of proof lies,' must mean, not the party on whom it lay at the beginning of the trial, but the party on whom, on the undisputed facts, it lay at the time the direction was given."

Baron Parke's statement in Barry v. Butlin[927] is well known: "The strict meaning of the term *onus probandi* is this, that if no evidence is given, by the party on whom the burden is cast, the issue must be found against him." This might seem to point to the duty of establishing. Does it? It describes only the duty of one (whoever he may be) having the *onus probandi* (whatever that may be) to produce evidence. Now, as we have seen, a common and approved English conception is that when a party does have this and makes a *prima facie* case, the other party has the *onus probandi;* so that then Baron Parke's remark will apply to him.[928] Baron Parke's expression appears to be consistent with either view, since the duty of beginning and that of finally establishing may, and may not, rest upon different persons;[929] the duty of beginning may be settled by a rule of presumption or a rule of practice that has nothing to do with the duty of establishing. In a Connecticut case[930] the defendant was prosecuted under a statute, for neglecting and refusing to support his wife. At the trial, under the general issue, he set up her adultery. The jury were charged that he had the burden of proof to establish the adultery beyond a reasonable doubt; and a verdict for the State was set aside, and a new trial granted for misdirection. It was laid down by the court (Andrews, C. J.) that the burden of proof is on the government to prove its case in all its parts; that the issue is but one, the defendant's guilt, and that whenever a defence is so proved that a reasonable doubt is caused as to any part of the case, the jury should acquit. But it was also said: "If the defendant relies upon some distinct substantive ground of defence not necessarily connected with the transaction,... as insanity or self-defence, or an *alibi,* or, as in the case at bar, the adultery of the wife, he must prove it as an independent fact.... It is incumbent upon the defendant to establish

---

[927] 2 Moore, P. C. 484; a. c. 1 Curteis, p. 640; and so Metcalf, J., in 6 Cush. p. 319.

[928] Such is Baron Parke's own use of the term in Elkin v. Janson, 13 M. & W. pp. 662-3, and Lord Halsbury's and Lord Watson's in Wakelin v. London, etc. By. Co., 12 App. Cas. 41; where also Lord Blackburn, having read Lord Watson's opinion, remarks: "In it I perfectly agree." See also Stephen, Dig. Ev. arts. 95 and 96, and L. J. Bowen, *supra, 357.*

[929] See *infra,* 377.

[930] State v. Schweitzer, 57 Conn. 532 (1889).

the fact.... All authorities agree that the burden is upon the State to make out its accusation... beyond all reasonable doubt.... When a defendant desires to set up a distinct defence,... he must bring it to the attention of the court; in other words, he must prove it,... that is, he must produce more evidence in support of it than there is against it. When he has done this by a preponderance of the evidence, the defence becomes a fact in the case of which the jury must take notice... and dispose of it according to the rule before stated, that the burden is upon the State to prove every part of the case against the prisoner beyond a reasonable doubt."[931] It is, perhaps, not clear what is meant here. The court avoids saying in terms that the defendant has any "burden of proof," but they seem to say it in substance. If the defendant must establish the insanity or *alibi* by the preponderance of the evidence, he has the burden of proving it. It would seem that the true theory of this case is that the defence has nothing to "prove," but has only to do what the Massachusetts court intimated in one of the cases relied on in this opinion, when it said:

The evidence which tended to prove the *alibi,* even if it failed to establish it, was left to have its full effect in bringing into doubt the evidence tending to prove the defendant's presence at the fire."[932] So here, defendant need not establish the adultery; he need only bring the jury to a reasonable doubt about it; for, according to the theory of the case, that is a reasonable doubt of the defendant's guilt. It "becomes a fact in the case," when there is a reasonable doubt of it.[933]

II. So much for the various meanings of the phrase. And now some explanations as to the relation of the subject to pleading.

---

[931] For this exposition the court cites, among other cases, Brotherton *v.* The People, 75 N. Y. 159, and the charge in Com. *v.* Choate, 105 Mass. 451; and they remark that this last charge was "held to be correct." This is misleading. The Massachusetts court held, in effect, that the charge was inconsistent and in part bad; but that it contained its own antidote, and therefore the verdict might stand.

[932] Com. v. Choate, *ubi supra;* People *v.* Riordan, 117 N. Y. 71; State *v.* Ardoin, 49 La. 1145; State *v.* Howell, 100 Mo. 628, People v; Bushton, 80 Cal. 160. "It is a prisoner's burden, the only burden ever put upon him by the law, that of satisfying the jury that there is a reasonable doubt of his guilt." R. H. Dana, *arguendo,* York's case, 9 Met. p. 98.

[933] See the clear statements in State *v.* Crawford, 11 Kans. p. 44 — 5 (1873), and in Scott *v.* Wood, 81 Cal. 398 (1889). Compare Wilder *v.* Cowles, 100 Mass. 487.

(1) It is important to attend to one or two peculiarities of the Roman law; for that body of law has given us the term *onus probandi* and a variety of maxims about it. Under the system which prevailed in classical times, and for two or three centuries after the Christian Era, — a period which includes the great jurists whose responses are preserved in the "Digest," — the Posetor sent to the judex a formula containing a brief indication of the plaintiff's claim, of the affirmative defence, if any, of the affirmative replication, if any, and so on, — with instructions to hear the parties and their witnesses, and then decide the case. No denials were mentioned in the formula, but each affirmative case was understood to be denied. Then followed a trial of each of these cases separately, — first, the plaintiff's; then, unless that failed, the defendant's; and then, unless that failed, the plaintiff's replication; and so on. What, in our system, is a plea in confession and avoidance, was, in the Roman system, merely a supposition of the truth of the opposite case, and an avoidance of it; nothing was admitted. As illustrating this, I give, in a note, some passages from a clear account of a procedure thought to have "differed but slightly in principle" from that of the period to which I now refer.[934]

Now, under such a method, where there is presented at each stage of the trial only one clear and unchangeable affirmation and denial, the phrase *onus probandi* (and so the leading Latin maxims about it) may have a very simple meaning. The proof, the burden, of proving, belongs to the *actor;* it cannot shift, and cannot belong to

---

[934] Langdell, Equity Pleading (2d ed.), ss. 4 — 14. "There were ... as many stages in the trial as there were pleadings. The first stage consisted of the trial of the plaintiff's case as stated in the libel. For this purpose the plaintiff would first put in his evidence in support of his case, and the defendant would then put in his evidence, if he had any, in contradiction. The evidence bearing upon the libel being exhausted, the next stage was the trial of the exception, which proceeded in the same manner as the trial of the libel, except that the defendant began, he having the burden of proof as to his exception. In this manner the trial proceeded, until all the evidence bearing upon each of the pleas in succession was exhausted, each party being required in turn to prove his own pleading, if he would avail himself of it (a. 8). ... Finally it will be found that all the essential differences between a trial at common law and by the civil law, arise from this, namely, that by the common law a cause goes to trial with everything alleged in the pleadings on either side admitted, except the single point upon which issue is joined, while by the civil law it goes to trial with nothing admitted" (s. 12). This system has largely survived on the continent of Europe, in Scotland, and in our equity and admiralty procedure.

the *reus,* whose function is not that of proving, but the purely negative one of repelling or baffling the adversary's attempts to prove.[935] Consistently with this, however, it may be the duty of the defendant upon any particular point to go forward with evidence; because there may be some presumption which operates as a *prima facie* case on that point, in favor of the party who has the affirmative on the general proposition of the issue, and which, without the production of evidence, accomplishes the result of evidence. In calling this duty of him who has the negative by the name of *probatio* and *onus probandi,* there is in Latin the same ambiguity which we have in English.

The situation is thus indicated by the language of a learned Dutch writer,[936] whose statement I regret to have only in another's translation: "The rule concerning the onus of proof, as to its object, suffers derogation, when, instead of establishing the principal and decisive fact in the cause, one or other of the parties is permitted to refer to other facts from which may be deduced the truth of that which it is sought to prove; in other terms, when the allegations of one of the parties are sustained by a legal presumption. *In such case the relative positions, with respect to the onus of proof, are not transposed;* there is a change only as to the object of proof." And, in a note, the author adds: "This is why the language... of the Dutch Code, 'legal presumption dispenses with all other proof,' is more exact than that... of the French Code, 'legal presumption dispenses with all proof.'"[937]

---

[935] This is equally plain in any simple case under our system, such as Hingeston *v.* Kelly, 18 L. J. n. s. Ex. 360, and Phipps *v.* Mahon, 141 Mass. 471, a like instance, where the thing is well expounded. But in our system the court's revision of the proceedings before the jury is constantly introducing into judicial discussion questions and speculations as to what is called "the burden of proof," which, at Rome, did not thus come out into the light to perplex the simplicity of the subject.

[936] Goudsmidt, *Pandects* (Gould's translation), 317.

[937] Compare the language of an anonymous mediaeval treatise preserved in the Black Book of the Admiralty, supposed to be written by some civilian of the school of Bologna, at about the end of the fourteenth century. "Si neget reus, incumbit probacio. . . . Debet enim actor vel accusator, qui aliquid asseverat, probare, non autem reus qui negat; quia per rerum naturam, id est causarum consuetudinem, inductnm est ut affirmantis, non autem negantis, aliqua sit probacio; nam judices in causis consueverunt imponere onus probandi actori asseveranti, non autem neganti. Hoc tamen verum est, quod aliquando neganti incumbit probacio, ut puta quando presumpcio est pro actore, dicto enim aliquem

But the form of the pleadings may not help to determine the duty of the parties; for there may not be any pleadings. It is possible to conduct legal controversies, as well as others, without any written or recorded pleadings, or in disregard of them. It is often done; the convenient practice of agreeing the facts, whether resting" on a statute[938] or on the practice of the courts, will readily come to mind; in such case, although there is no trial of facts, the question of law remains, and the relative duty of the parties as to the issue. As regards everything following the declaration in civil cases, and the indictment in criminal cases, we are familiar in. modern times with that state of things, — indeed the common law has always known it.[939] An oral plea to an indictment, of not guilty, and a "written general denial have been very common answers, whatever the real nature of the defence on sound principles of pleading. Not long ago it was formally recommended by a committee appointed by the Lord Chancellor and made up of the leading judicial and legal personages in England, that litigation should thereafter be conducted in the High Court of Justice without any pleadings. "The committee," they said, "is of opinion that, as a general rule, the questions in controversy between litigants may be ascertained without pleadings." Then followed the recommendation of a rule that "No pleadings shall be allowed unless by order of a judge."[940] The substitute for pleadings

---

fuisse sanae mentis quando testator, quod tu negas, sed quia quilibet presumitur sanae mentis nisi probetur contrarium, tibi neganti incumbit probacio; et ita presumpcio convertit aliquando onus probandi in negantem, set non omnis presumpcio, quia qui cumplex est presumpcio; de quibus, prosequi longum esset. . . " "The text here," remarks the editor, "is hopelessly corrupt."

[938] *E. g;* St. 15 & 16 Vie. c. 76, s. 46.

[939] Co. Lit. 283.

[940] This interesting document may be found in the London Times for Oct. 8, 1881. It is signed by Lord Coleridge, Lord Justice James, Justices Hannen and Bowen, the Attorney-General (James), the Solicitor-General (Herschell), and others. I will add some passages of the report: "In the year 1879 there were issued in the divisions of the High Court in London writs, 59, 659. Of the actions thus commenced, there were settled, without appearance, 15,372, *i. e.,* 25.68 per cent; by judgment by default, 16,967, *i. e.,* 2834 per cent; by judgment under Order XIV., 4,251, *i.* e., 7.10 per cent; total of practically undefended cases, 36,590, i. e., 61.12 per cent; cases unaccounted for and therefore presumably settled or abandoned after some litigation, 20,804, i. e., 35.10 per cent. The remaining cases were thus accounted for: Decided in court, — for plaintiffs. 1,232; for defendants, 521; before masters and official referees, 512; total, 2,265; that is, 3.78 per cent of the actions brought. From these figures it seemed clear that the writ in its present form was effective in bringing defendants to a settlement at a small cost, and that

which these propositions contemplated was a brief indorsement upon a writ of summons, indicating the nature of the plaintiff's claim, and a brief notice from the defendant of any special defence, such as the Statute of Limitations or payment. Although these suggestions were not in form adopted, yet English common-law pleading has come down to a very simple basis indeed; and so, very widely, in this country.

Whether there be pleadings or not, and whether they be simple or not, you come out, at some stage of the controversy, upon a proposition, or more than one, expressed or implied, on which the parties are at issue, one party asserting and the other denying. An admission may, of coarse, end the controversy; but such an admission may be, and yet not end it; and if that be so, it is because the party making the admission sets up something that avoids the apparent effect of it, as subsequent payment avoids the effect of what shows a claim in contract. When this happens, the party defending becomes, in so far, the *actor* or plaintiff. In general, he who seeks to move a court in his favor, whether as an original plaintiff whose facts are merely denied, or as a defendant, who, in admitting his adversary's contention and setting up an affirmative defence, takes

---

it was unadvisable to make any alteration by uniting it with a plaint or other statement of the plaintiff's cause of action, which would add to the expense of the fist step in the litigation. . . . The committee is of opinion the questions in controversy between litigants may be ascertained without pleadings. In the 20,804 cases which, as appeared from the statistics of 1879, were either settled or abandoned without being taken into Court, it may reasonably be supposed that pleadings were of little use. Of the cases which go to trial it appears to the committee that in a very large number the only questions are: Was the defendant guilty of the tortious act charged, and what ought he to pay for it? or. Did the defendant enter into the alleged contract, and was it broken by him? And in a great many others the pleadings present classes of claims and defences which follow common forms. We may take, for instance, the disputes arising out of mercantile contracts for sale, of affreightment, of insurance, of agency, of guarantee. The cases of litigants, are usually put forward in the same shape, the plaintiff relying on the contract and complaining of breaches; the defendant, on the other hand, denying the contract or the breaches, or contending that his liability on the contract has terminated. The questions in dispute are, as a general rule, well known to the plaintiff and the defendant. It is only when their controversies have to be reproduced in technical forms that difficulties begin." See 4 Harv. Law Rev. pp. 184-185. Compare the provisions of St. 43 Eliz. c. 12 (1601), for the relief of merchants in the matter of insurance. Commissioners were to bear the parties "in a brief and summary course . . . without formalities of pleadings or proceedings."

the rôle of *actor (reus excipiendo fit actor)*, — must satisfy the court
of the truth and adequacy of the grounds of his claim, both in point
of fact and law.[941] But he, in every case, who is the true *reus* or
defendant holds, of course, a very different place in the procedure.
He simply awaits the action of his adversary, and it is enough if he
repel him. He has no duty of satisfying the court; it may be doubtful,
indeed extremely doubtful, whether he be not legally in the wrong
and his adversary legally in the right; indeed he may probably be in
the wrong, and yet he may gain and his adversary lose, simply
because the inertia of the court has not been overcome; because the
actor has not carried his case beyond an equilibrium of proof, or
beyond all reasonable doubt.[942] Whatever the Standard be, it is
always the *actor* and never the *reus* who has to bring his proof to the
required height; for, truly speaking, it is only the *actor* that has the
duty of proving at all. Whoever has that duty does not make out a
prima facie case till he comes up to the requirement, as regards
quantity of evidence or force of conviction, which applies to his
contention; and, of course, he has not, at the end of the debate,
accomplished his task unless he has held good his case, and held it at
the legal height, as against all counter proof.[943] This duty, in the
nature of things, here as well as at Borne, cannot shift; it is always
the duty of one party, and never of the other. But as the *actor,* if he
would win, must begin by making out a case, and must end by
keeping it good, so the *reus,* if he would not lose, must bestir himself

---

[941] Bonnier, *Preuves,* i. s. 36 (5th ed.): "Celui qui doit innover doit
demontrer que sa pretention eat fondee."

[942] Bracton, fol. 239 b.; "Si juratores dubitaverint . . . querens per hoc
nihil consequitur . . . quia quotienscunque dubitatur an quid sit, perinde ert ac si
non esset illud." I have spoken of "the inertia of the court." Of course, from the
court's point of view this question presents itself. What shall we do when we
know not what to do? This has sometimes been answered with much simplicity.
Bonnier, *Preuves,* i. s. 51 (5th ed.), remarks: "Nos anciens auteurs, de leur côt, ont
proposé divers expédients pour résoudre les questions douteuses. Les uns veulent
qu'on tranche le différend par la moitié, ce que Cujas appelle avec raison *anile
judicium.* D'autrea proposent l'emploi dn sort, emploi qui a été réalisé
effectivement en 1644 dans la famenae *sentence des buchettes."* He adds in a
note: "Par un juge de Melle qui avait fait tirer aux plaideurs deux pailles on
buchettes, qu'il tenait entre les doigts. Heureusement pour l'honneur de la justice,
elle a été réformée par le parlement de Paris."

[943] It should be remarked, however, that there is much freedom of
discretion allowed the trial judge in determining when a party may rest for the
time being; and when the other may fairly be called on to explain.

when his adversary has once made out his case, and must repel it. And then, again, the *actor* may move and restore his case, and so on. This shifting of the duty of going forward, with argument or evidence may go on through the trial. Of course, as has been said already, the thing that thus shifts and changes is not the peculiar duty of each party, — for that remains peculiar; *i. e.,* the duty, on the one hand, of making out and holding good a case which will move the court, and, on the other, the purely negative duty of preventing this. It is the common and interchangeable duty of going forward with argument or evidence, whenever your case requires it.

If one asks how he shall know who has the duty of establishing, — the burden of proof in that sense of the term, — he must put this question with reference to some specific proposition. As a general question, it relates to the proposition on which the parties are at issue; and the general answer is that the *actor* has it, the one who holds the affirmative. How, then, shall we ascertain, in any given case, who the *actor* is? As we have seen, the mere form of the pleadings may suffice to tell us. "Where it does not, we must be referred to the principles of pleading; and in attending to these we shall sometimes find ourselves involved in an analysis of the substantive law of the particular case, and perhaps in an inquiry into things obsolete, anomalous, and forgotten. "Undoubtedly," says a learned judge, "many matters which, if true, would show that the plaintiff never had a cause of action, or even that he never had a valid contract, must be pleaded and proved by the defendants; for instance, infancy, coverture, or, probably, illegality. Where the line should be drawn might differ conceivably in different jurisdictions."[944] Clearly one has no right to look to the law of evidence for a solution of such questions as these, and I am not proposing to answer them.[945] It will, however, serve to illustrate the

---

[944] *Per* Holmes, J., in Starratt *v.* Mullen, 148 Mass. 570.

[945] As I have said it would be a great service to the law, if these matters could be thoroughly worked out. My colleague, Professor Langdell, has kindly allowed me the privilege of reprinting here the following pas-cages from a valuable, short treatment of this subject, incidental to his well-known discussion of pleading in equity. I quote from his work on that subject (2d ed.), ss. 108 — 114. It will be observed that his point of view is somewhat different from that taken in the text. "No reliance can be placed upon the form of a plea, even if correctly drawn, for the purpose of determining whether it is affirmative or negative; but the question must be decided in every case upon principle, the test being the burden of proof. That is to say, if the plea amounts merely to a denial,

direct or argumentative, of some fact which the plaintiff must prove in order to obtain relief, whether such fact be alleged in the bill or not, the plea will be negative; for, if the plea be replied to, the only fact to be tried will be the fact thus denied, and as to that the plaintiff will have the burden of proof. The defendant will properly have nothing to prove; and if he puts in any evidence, its object will be merely to show the plaintiff's evidence to be untrue, or, if true, inconclusive. In a word, the fact to be tried constitutes a part of the plaintiff's case. On the other hand, if the plea alleges some fact which is consistent with every fact necessary to be proved by the plaintiff, but which, if true, will till prevent the plaintiff's recovering (and unless such be its effect, the plea will necessarily be bad), in that case the plea will be affirmative; for if it be replied to, the only fact to be tried will be the fact alleged by the plea, and as to that the defendant will have the burden of proof. The plaintiff will have nothing to prove, as all the facts which constitute his cage are admitted by the plea; and if the court decides, upon all the evidence given, that the fact alleged by the plea is not proved, the plaintiff will have a decree upon the facta alleged in the bill and admitted by the plea. In a word, the fact to be tried will constitute a defence in the proper sense of the term 'defence' (*i.e.,* an affirmative defence), and not a part of the plaintiff's case. The question, therefore, whether any particular plea is affirmative or negative, can never be answered intelligently until another question be answered; namely, what facts must the plaintiff prove in order to obtain a decree? The latter question being answered, the former involves no difficulty."How, then, is it to be ascertained whether any particular fact must be proved by the plaintiff to enable him to recover, or whether the contrary must be proved by the defendant to prevent the plaintiff's recovering? If, for example, in an action upon a contract, there be a question whether the defendant was of full age when he made the contract, must the plaintiff prove that he was, or must the defendant prove that he was then an infant? Or if, in an action upon contract, it appear that the defendant made the promise alleged, But do not appear whether he received a consideration for the promise, must the plaintiff prove a consideration, or must the defendant prove that the promise was gratuitous? There is no doubt how these two questions should be answered, namely, that in the former the burden of proof lies upon the defendant, while in the latter it lies upon the plaintiff. But the important inquiry is, why should these two questions be answered differently? It is often said that the burden of proof lies upon the party who holds the affirmative; but, in the two cases just put, each party has an affirmative in form, while in substance the plaintiff has the affirmative in both cases. It is necessary, therefore, to find some other way of distinguishing the two cases; and that is not difficult. Every contract must consist of certain elements prescribed by law. These elements consist of acts done by the parties respectively, and done with a certain intention. Until all of these elements are proved to exist, there is no reason to suppose that there is any contract between the parties, and hence no reason to suppose that the defendant is liable to the plaintiff upon contract. It would be very unreasonable, therefore, to require any proof from the defendant so long as any of the necessary elements of a contract remain unproved by the plaintiff; and one of these elements, in the case of a contract not under seal, is the giving of a consideration by the plaintiff for the defendant's promise. When, however, the plaintiff has proved all the acts required by law for the making of a contract, and these acts have been accompanied by the usual *indicia* of intention to contract, there is a strong probability that the defendant is bound, and it would be very unreasonable to require the plaintiff to go further. If any fact exists, in consequence of which the defendant is not bound, *e.g.,* that he was under twenty-one years of age when he made the t., promise, the defendant should clearly be required to show it. Hence, it is rule that, in all actions upon contract, the plaintiff must prove, first, the making of a contract in fact, *i. e.,* in case of a contract not under seal, [that the defendant promised, and that the plaintiff gave a consideration; for the promise; in case of a contract under seal, that the defendant sealed and delivered to the plaintiff a promise or obligation in writing. Secondly, if the promise was upon a condition or was not to be performed until some; future time, the plaintiff must prove that the condition has been performed of or has happened, or that the time for performance of the promise has arrived. Nothing further need be proved by the plaintiff, unless expressly I required by the agreement of the parties or by a statute; and having proved so much, he will recover unless the defendant establishes an affirmative defence. Such a defence may show that, although the defendant made the promise alleged for the consideration alleged, yet there never was in law any contract, *e. g;* that the defendant was a married woman when she made the promise, or that the promise was declared void by statute for illegality; or it may show that, although there is a contract, yet the defendant is not bound by it (which is commonly expressed by pitying that the contract, though not void, is voidable), e. g., that the promise or the consideration for it was illegal, or that the promise was obtained by fraud or duress, or that the defendant was an infant when he made the promise; or it may show that, although a valid contract was made, yet the plaintiff never had a right of action on it, as it was duly , performed, or was rescinded before breach, or was terminated by the happening of a condition subsequent; or it may show that, although the 'plaintiff once had a right of action, such right has been extinguished , (*e.g.* by a release or by an accord and satisfaction), or that the defendant is protected by statute from being sued upon it, e. g., by the Statute of limitations or by a statutory discharge in bankruptcy."A contract may provide that one of the parties thereto shall not be Mable for a breach of his promise or covenant, except upon the performance of some condition by the other party; or a statute may provide that no action shall lie upon a contract, or even that the contract shall be void, unless some condition specified by the statute shall be complied with; But in neither of these cases will the plaintiff be required to prove compliance with such condition (it being no part of the covenant or promise sued on), unless it clearly appear that such was the intention of the parties to the contract in the one case, or of the legislature in the other. On the contrary, the defendant will be required to show non-compliance with the condition in question as an affirmative defence. . . . ." There has been much difference of opinion upon the question whether the plaintiff, in cases which come within the Statute of Frauds, has the burden of proving that the statute has been complied with. It was formerly held, both by courts of law and courts of equity, that he had, though courts of law committed the extraordinary inconsistency of holding that he need not allege compliance with the statute in his declaration; and this inconsistency was unfortunately not cured by the Hilary Bules. But, if what has been stated is correct, it follows that it is no part of the plaintiff's case to show that the statute has been complied with, but that the defendant must show the contrary as an

nature of the difficulties which have attended the attempt to determine the affirmative in pleading by the method of an analysis of the substantive law, — I need not enlarge on the distresses incident to the obscure effect of forgotten rules and practices, — to look at one or two cases relative to negotiable paper.

In a Massachusetts case, *in* speaking of want of consideration in a promissory note, the court says:[946] "Withput a consideration there is no contract. The question, therefore, whether there was a consideration, is but a form of the question whether a contract was ever made. The burden does not shift. The production of the note, with the signature of the defendant, makes a *prima facie* case against him; and when no evidence is offered to the contrary, the plaintiff will of course prevail. But when evidence is offered by the defendant, and, it may be, by the plaintiff, it all applies to one and the same issue, — was there a consideration? If not, there was no contract. And the burden remains throughout upon him who affirms that a contract was made."

These statements are probably founded in error. Compare the account of the same matter by Lord Blackburn, which is partly

---

affirmative defence, if he would avail himself of the statute; and such is now the rule in England under the Judicature Acts. It should be borne in mind also that this view is independent of the question, whether the statute renders the contract void, in case of non-compliance with its provisions, or merely disables the plaintiff from suing on it."What has been said of actions upon contracts is also true of actions upon torts, *mutatis mutandis, i. e;* the plaintiff must show that the defendant has committed an act which, in the absence of any excuse or justification, constitutes in law a tort to the plaintiff; and he need show nothing more. If any facts existed which rendered the defendant's act justifiable or even excusable, although such facts show that the defendant has in truth committed no tort, yet they constitute an affirmative defence, and hence must be alleged and proved by the defendant."It will have been seen that, in actions upon contract or upon tort, the plaintiff has the burden of proving only that he *once* had a cause of action against the defendant, — not that it continued to exist when he brought his action; and that the defendant always has the burden of proving that a cause of action, which once existed, exists no longer. The reason is that a cause of action does not die a natural death; once created, it continues to exist until some event happens which has the power and the effect of destroying it. Hence, when a cause of action is proved once to have existed, the court must treat it as still existing, until the contrary appears. *De non apparentibus it non existentibus eadem est ratio.*

[946] *Per* Thomas, J., in Crowninshield *v.* Crowninshield, 2 Gray, 524, 531; and so Delano *v.* Bartlett, 6 Cush. 364.

given on a previous page.[947] The document "imports consideration," it is said; which means that a consideration, in such cases, in the regular course of things, is not necessary; or, in other words, as it is expressed by a learned writer, "the modern mercantile specialty" is brought under the doctrine applicable to the older specialty, namely, the rule, as cited from an old case, that whereas, "in debt upon a contract, the plaintiff shall show in his count for what consideration *(cause)* the defendant became his debtor, [it is] otherwise in debt upon a specialty *(obligation),* for the specialty is the contract itself."[948]

In dealing with such questions it has to be remembered, sometimes, as I am reminded by a learned friend, that defences with which we are familiar, and which seem, upon analysis, to be a negation of what is affirmed by an adversary, are really positions which were formerly not allowed to be taken at all in a legal controversy. The long history of equitable defences, such as fraud, and even illegality and failure of consideration, has to be borne in mind;[949] and then it is easy to see why such matters are proper to be alleged and established by him who has been newly allowed the privilege of availing himself of them.

But as time passes and the conceptions on which legal obligation is determined come, from age to age, to rest on a new

---

[947] *Per* Thomas, J., in Crowninshield *v.* Crowninshield, 2 Gray, 524, 531; and so Delano *v.* Bartlett, 6 Cush. 364.

[948] Ames, *Specialty Contracts and Equitable Defences,* 9 Harv. Law Kev. 49. See also the clear assimilation of these classes of documents by one of the judges of the Supreme Court of Massachusetts, Mr. Justice Holmes, in some very trenchant allusions to the famous case of Master *v.* Miller, 4 T. R. 320. He is first speaking of the ordinary specialty: "The contract was inseparable from the parchment. If a stranger destroyed it, or tore off the seal, or altered it, the obligee could not recover, however free from fault, because the defendant's contract, that is, the actual tangible bond which he had sealed, could not be produced in the form in which it bound him. About a hundred years ago Lord Kenyon undertook to use his reason on this tradition, as he sometimes did, to the detriment of the law, and, not understanding it, said he could see no reason why what was true of a bond should not be true of other contracts. His decision happened to be right, as it concerned a promissory note, where again the common law regarded the contract as inseparable from the paper on which it was written; bat the reasoning was general, and soon was extended to other written contracts; and various absurd and unreal grounds of policy were invented to account for the enlarged rule." "The Path of the Law," 10 Harv. Law Rev. 472, 473.

[949] See Ames, 9 Harv. Law Rev. 49 — 59; and compare 6 ib. 344 — 347, and *infra,* 405.

analysis, it would seem that the test of an affirmative case must also change and be made to depend more commonly than. it does now, and more distinctly, on the newly accepted ideas and analysis. Now, and at all times, the tests of justice and practical convenience are legitimate ones, wherever the question is open to debate.

III. Let us look, now, at certain ambiguities and sources of ambiguity.

(a) At the outset, he who has to move the court and establish his case, has also to go forward with the proof of it, unless some presumption or matter judicially noticed, operating like matters already proved, happen to relieve him just at this point; the other party may rest until then, and will win without a stroke if the first remain idle. This duty of beginning is often given as the distinctive test of an affirmative case, — "Which party would be successful if no evidence at all were given."[950] But when the *actor* has gone forward and made his *prima facie* case, he has brought a pressure to bear upon the *reus,* which will compel him to come forward; and he again may bring pressure upon the *actor* that will call him out. This duty of going forward in response to the call of a *prima facie* case, or of a natural or legal presumption, — a duty belonging to either party, — is, in its nature, the same as that which rests upon the beginning party, and which is put as the distinctive test of an *actor;* it is merely a duty of going forward. This fact was perceived; and it led to a modification in the expression of the test. "As, however," says Best,[951] "the question of the burden of proof may present itself at any moment during a trial, the test ought, in strict accuracy, to be expressed thus, namely. Which party would be successful if no evidence at all, or no more evidence, as the case may be, were given?" Now when this has been said and accepted, all notion of a characteristic that is determined by the beginning of the case is thrown away; and so every circumstance that discriminates the *actor* and the *reus.* We are told that we may know him who has the burden of proof by considering whether, at any given moment, a party

---

[950] Amos *v.* Hughes, 1 Moo. & Rob. 464. The right to begin may be fixed by a mere rule of practice. See, *e. g;* in Massachusetts, "the well-settled rule of this court that the plaintiff is to open and close in all cases, without regard to the burden of proof, or to any admission of all the facts necessary to be proved by the plaintiff in opening his case." Page *v.* Osgood, 2 Gray, 260.

[951] Evid. s. 268; and so Bowen, L. J., in Abrath *v.* N. E. Ry. Co., 11 Q. B. D. 440.

would lose if the case stopped then and there. But that test may apply to either party, for it points to a situation in which either may find himself, namely, that of having the duty of going forward. In short, the test for the never changing burden of establishing the proposition in issue, has become good only for the constantly changing burden of producing evidence. This last duty now comes prominently forward, and the other is lost sight of. Meantime, the change is unobserved. And, as we have but one term for the two ideas, it gets used, as we have seen, now for one and now for the other; and, again, in a way which does not discriminate the meaning; and so there is no end of confusion.

     (b) There is much ambiguity in what is said of the "shifting" of the burden of proof. As to this it is vital to keep quite apart the considerations applicable to pleading, and those belonging to evidence. We see that the burden of going forward with evidence may shift often from side to side; while the duty of establishing his proposition, is always with the *actor,* and never shifts. As we have only one phrase for two ideas belonging to two different subjects, we say, as it happens, that the burden of proof does, and does not shift. And then still another ambiguity. The burden of establishing is sometimes called "the burden of proof upon the record;" for it is assumed that the record shows the full allegations of the parties. But, in fact, in our books, the record very often fails to do that; so that when the general issue is pleaded, the denying party has often been allowed, in giving his evidence, to set up affirmative defences. So far as the record shows us anything in such a case, the plaintiff is the *actor,* and the burden of establishing the proposition of the case is upon him. And yet, since his adversary may offer evidence of an affirmative case, and when he does, becomes the *actor,* and so has, with his affirmation, the burden of establishing it, this burden seems to have shifted, because a new proposition has been introduced. But the simple fact is, that under this mode of pleading, as compared with a strictly accurate mode, the time fixed for setting up the affirmative case is different; instead of requiring that it be disclosed before the pleadings are ended, it is allowed to be made known during the progress of the trial; and the sense in which we say that the burden of proof has shifted is that loose sense in which, under a strict rule of pleading, it might be said to shift while the pleadings are going forward, — being first upon the plaintiff, "shifting" to the defendant when he pleads in confession and avoidance, and

remaining fixed at the end where the last purely negative plea leaves it. In both cases the burden of establishing "shifts," only because a new affirmative case has been disclosed, which carries with it the duty of making it out. In reality there is no shifting at all, because the issue is not yet settled. It remains just as true as ever, as regards the issue that the burden of establishing it never shifts; it is always upon the *actor*. It is, therefore, merely a careless mode of expression, — when new issues are allowed to be developed at the trial, — to say that the burden of establishing shifts during the trial. And yet we find that Chief Justice Shaw, in the very act of starting the peculiar practice, which afterwards existed in Massachusetts, of limiting the meaning of the term "burden of proof" to the one meaning of the *actor's* duty of establishing his proposition, expresses himself thus: "Where the party having the burden of proof gives competent and *prima facie* evidence of a fact, and the adverse party, instead of producing proof which would go to negative the same proposition of fact, proposes to show another and a distinct proposition which avoids the effect of it, there the burden of proof shifts, and rests upon the party proposing to show the latter fact."[952] In Massachusetts, they now say that "the burden of proof never shifts."[953]

(c) Another source of ambiguity lies in the relation between the burden of proof, and legal presumptions or rules of presumption. What is true of these phrases in one sense may not be true in another. When it is said that the burden of establishing lies upon the *actor*, this refers, as we see, to the total proposition or series of propositions

---

[952] Powers *v.* Russell, 13 Pick. 69, 77 (1832).

[953] As in 142 Mass. p. 360. But what Chief Justice Shaw *meant,* may till be true, even under the existing practice in Massachusetts, for after the answer there need be no replication, while anything may be proved by the plaintiff at that stage. By the St. 1836, c. 273, special pleas in bar in Massachusetts were abolished in all civil actions, and the general issue substituted. This had been the law as to certain sorts of action before. Of the condition of the law as it stood after this change Mr. B. R. Curtis, afterwards Mr. Justice Curtis, said (Report of Commissioners on the Massachusetts Practice Act, Hall, 139; also in 2 Life of Curtis, 149, 151): "He who now surveys what remains, sees every plaintiff left to inhabit the old building, while all others are tuned out of doors." The "Practice Act" of 1851, prepared by these Commissioners, abolished the general issue in all but real and mixed actions and substituted a stricter system. But this strictness was in part done away the next year, when the first Practice Act was repealed, and a new one enacted. Under this one, now in force, no pleadings are required after the defendant's answer (compare St. 1851, c. 233, s. 28, with St. 1852, c. 312, s. 19); and the old looseness still exists from this point on.

which constitute his disputed case. As when in an action for malicious prosecution[954] the Master of the Rolls said: "The burden of proof of satisfying a jury that there was a want of reasonable care lies upon the plaintiff, because the proof of that... is a necessary part of the larger question, of which the burden of proof lies upon him." Suppose, then, that it be settled in any case, upon the principles, whatever they be, which govern the question, that the burden of establishing a given issue is upon A, and that upon some detail of this issue a rule of presumption makes in favor of A, e. g., that he has to establish a will, and that the presumption of sanity helps him as to this one element of his proposition;[955] or that he has to establish the heirship of a child, including its birth of certain parents, in wedlock, and legitimately, and that the presumption applying in such cases helps him as to the last point; — on the supposition, I say, that in any given case the burden of establishing is thus fixed, and that the presumption thus operates as touching a part only of the total proposition, how does this affect the duty of the *actor?* Of course it does not reach the burden on the whole issue; for this covers not only the presumed thing, but more. Does it then transfer to the other the duty of establishing a part of the issue? If so, we may easily suppose a variety of presumptions operating in the same case which would split up the issue in a manner utterly confusing to judge and jury. What happens in such a case seems rather to be what the Romans called *levamen probationis; i.e.,* the presumption has done the office, as regards a particular fact, *of prima facie* proof; so that the *actor* need not in the first instance go forward as to this matter; his case for all purposes of beginning is proved by this, without evidence, just as it would have been by evidence enough to make a *prima facie* case. Of course he must still meet the defendant's counter proof, and must make good his total proposition not merely at the beginning but at the end of the trial; for "the relative positions as to the onus of proof are not transposed."[956]

   Such is the import of a well-known case, where, in an action of ejectment by an heir-at-law against a devisee, the court held it a misdirection to instruct the jury that while the heir-at-law was entitled to recover unless the will was proved, yet when the

---

[954] Abrath *v.* The N. E. Ry. Co., 11 Q. B. D. p. 451.
[955] Sutton *v.* Sadler, 3 C. B. N. s. 87. Compare *infra,* 382 n.
[956] Goudsmidt, *supra,* 366.

execution of the will was proved the law presumed sanity, and, therefore, the burden of proof shifted and the devisee must prevail unless the heir-at-law established the incompetency of the testator; and, if the evidence made it a measuring cast and left them in doubt, they ought to find for the defendant. The court held, on the contrary, that while the presumption of sanity freed the defendant from the need of proof in the first instance, it did not relieve him of the fixed, unshifting burden of making out his case of a valid will. In this case the court (Cresswell, J.) seemed to think that something turned on the question whether the presumption of sanity be a presumption of law or of fact; and laid it down that it must be regarded, if not as a presumption of fact, "at the utmost as a presumption of law and fact." That inquiry would seem to have been an irrelevant one. There is no rule of legal reasoning which is more commonly called a presumption of law than that which, *prima facie,* attributes sanity to human, beings. That it is a rule of presumption, and a legal rule, there is no doubt. The important question in any particular instance is what is the effect and operation of the rule, not what its name is. And in the case under consideration the result is that where the case is an affirmative one, the effect of this legal rule of presumption, bearing only on a part of the *actor's* case, is that of making out a *prima facie* case on his part, and not, necessarily, that of shifting or otherwise affecting the burden of establishing this part of the case.[957] To the same effect is the clear exposition in a recent opinion of the Supreme Court of the United States, in a criminal case, overruling the doctrine laid down by the Circuit Court. I give this passage in a note.[958]

---

[957] Sutton v. Sadler, 3 C. B. N. S. 87; and so Symes v. Green, 1 Sw. & Tr. 401. So Baxter *v.* Abbot, 7 Gray, 71 (1856), where a decision on an appeal from a decree of a court of probate allowing a will, sustained the ruling (p. 74) that "the burden of proof was on the appellee to show to their [the jury's] reasonable satisfaction that the testator was of sound mind when he executed the instrument in question; that the legal presumption, in the absence of evidence to the contrary, was in favor of the testator's sanity, and that the appellee was entitled to the benefit of this presumption, in sustaining the burden of proof which the law put upon him." "We all agree [p. 83] that it ['the legal presumption'] does not change the burden of proof, and that this always rests upon those seeking the probate of the will." The same general principle is neatly applied in an insurance case by Peters, C. J., in Jones *v.* Gran. St. Ins. Co., 90 Me. 40.

[958] Davis *v. V. S.,* 160 U. S. 469, 485-487 (1895), per Harlan, J. "Upon whom then must the burden of proving that the accused, whose life it is sought to take under the forms of law, belongs to a class capable of committing crime? On principle it must rest upon those who affirm that he has committed the crime for

It is true, then, that presumptions "shift the burden of proof," in a familiar sense of that phrase, importing the duty of going forward in the argument, or in the giving of evidence. That is the only sense of the "burden of proof," in which, having once been fixed, it can ever shift. In this sense presumptions may, of course, relieve, at the outset, him who has the duty of establishing the issue; for both sides, they are, always, *levamen probationis.* In the region

---

which he is indicted. That burden is not fully discharged, nor is there any legal right to take the life of the accused, until guilt is made to appear from all the evidence in the case. The plea of not guilty is unlike a special plea in a civil action, which, admitting the case averred, seeks to establish substantive ground of defence by a preponderance of evidence. It is not in confession and avoidance, for it is a plea that controverts the existence of every fact essential to constitute the crime charged. Upon that plea the accused may stand, shielded by the presumption of his innocence, until it appears that he is guilty; and his guilt cannot in the very nature of things be regarded as proved, if the jury entertain a reasonable doubt from all the evidence whether he was legally capable of committing crime. This view is not at all inconsistent with the presumption which the law, justified by the general experience of mankind as well as by considerations of public safety, indulges in favor of sanity. If that presumption were not indulged the government would always be under the necessity of adducing affirmative evidence of the sanity of an accused. But a requirement of that character would seriously delay and embarrass the enforcement of the laws against crime, and in most cases be unnecessary. Consequently the law presumes that every one charged with crime is sane, and thus supplies in the first instance the required proof of capacity to commit crime. It authorizes the jury to assume at the outset that the accused is criminally responsible for his acts. . . . To hold that such presumption must absolutely control the jury until it is overthrown or impaired by evidence sufficient to establish the fact of insanity beyond all reasonable doubt or to the reasonable satisfaction of the jury, is in effect to require him to establish his innocence, by proving that he is not guilty of the crime charged."And so Brotherton *v.* The People, 75 N. Y. 159 (1878, Church, C. J.), and People *v.* Garbutt, 17 Mich. 9 (1868, Cooley, C. J.); Dacey *v.* The People, 116 111. 555; and a great number of criminal cases in this country holding the like; to the effect that the burden of establishing sanity in an indictment for murder is upon the government, that the presumption of sanity puts upon the defendant the burden of going forward with evidence upon this question, but does not affect the duty of ultimately sustaining sanity; a fact, which, upon the theory of these cases, is none the less a part of the government's case because it is impliedly and not in terms alleged. This doctrine was adopted in Massachusetts as regards the defence of idiocy, an original absence of natural capacity, in Com. *v.* Heath, 11 Gray, 303, (1858); and by Chief Justice Gray and Morton, J., as to insanity in general, in Com. *v.* Pomeroy (Wharton, Homicide (2d ed.), Appendix, 753, 754, 756); and it is now the law in that State. See, e. *g.,* the charge of the jury in the case of Com. *v.* Trefethen in the Boston Daily Advertiser for May 5,1892.

of the law of evidence this appears to be their characteristic function, indeed their only one.

As regards their effect on the duty of establishing, it is not my purpose, as I have already said, to attempt to lay down the rules for ascertaining who has that duty. Udoubtedly it is not the effect of all rules of presumption to fix this, even though they be called presumptions of law.[959] If they do have this effect, it is not because they are presumptions, but because they are rules of law of a certain kind. For example, the doctrine which *prima facie* imputes legitimacy to persons born in wedlock, and requires a great force of reason to overcome this conclusion, seems to import that under all circumstances it shall be adhered to unless the contrary is established; the two situations might have been absolutely identified; but the rule stops short of that. On the other hand, the rule which *prima facie* imputes sanity to human beings, seems only to import the necessity of making this matter fairly disputable, of making it a question in. the case. "What the effect is in any particular rule of presumption, depends on the true analysis and meaning of the rule. The maxim *stabitur presumptioni donec probetur in contrarium* must not be assumed to mean that you are to stand to a presumption until the contrary is established. That may be true in particular instances. But this maxim has in it the old ambiguity as to *probatio* and *probare;* its only universal meaning is that you are to stand to the presumption until there be argument or evidence to the contrary.

IV. I will venture now to add a few suggestions as to a proper terminology for the conceptions indicated by the "burden of proof." It seems impossible to approve a continuance of the present state of things, under which such different ideas, of great practical importance and of frequent application, are indicated by this single ambiguous expression. What can be done? Of courses that are theoretically possible there are three: to abandon the use of this phrase and choose other terms; to fix upon it only one of the two meanings now in use, and find another phrase for the other; or letting it stand as a confessedly indeterminate phrase, often explained by the context, and often good enough for the purpose in hand, to use other phrases whenever it is necessary to be exact. As to the first course, it would be an idle dream to imagine that the phrase could be wholly

---

[959] Menochins, *Praes.* lib. i. qu. 33; compare Best, Ev. ss. 273, 319, 321, s*upra,* 339,381.

banished from legal usage. We might as reasonably expect to exclude it from the common speech of men. Use it we must.

It remains only to choose in what sense it shall be used. Or shall we say here also, that it is hopeless to make a change? It cannot be hopeless. A change is simply necessary to accurate legal speech and sound legal reasoning; and we may justly expect those who have exact thoughts, and wish to express them with precision, to avail themselves of some discrimination in terminology which will secure their end. Particular courts, or judges, or writers may adopt the method of discarding this phrase altogether and substituting other terms; that is an intelligible plan. But if any one prefers to follow the course which is certain to be taken by the current of legal usage, that of retaining the phrase in some sense or other, he will be driven, if he would speak accurately, either to tie up the term to a single meaning, or at least explicitly to recognize its ambiguity by using other phrases when he means to be exact.

If it should be attempted to fix upon the phrase only one of the two meanings above mentioned, and to exclude the other, various considerations might be put forward on either side.

In favor of the meaning of going forward with argument or evidence, it might be said. *(a)* That it is the meaning of the term in common speech. Whoever, men say, asserts a given proposition, has the burden of proof; and whoever supports the proposition by sufficient evidence to make it probable, shifts the burden of proof, and lays it on his adversary. *(b)* That it is also a familiar legal usage, *(c)* That it is the more comprehensive sense, for it includes not merely the duty of meeting a *prima facie* case against you, but also that of meeting a presumption, and that of going forward at the beginning. This last may be put upon the plaintiff by a mere rule of practice,[960] irrespective of his true place in the procedure, or by the considerations which determine whether a case is affirmative or negative; but, however fixed, the duty itself is in its nature merely the duty of going forward with the argument or the evidence, a duty wholly separable from that of finally establishing.

In favor of the other, as an exclusive meaning, it may be said, *(a)* That it is the prominent one in the Roman law, and in jurisdictions which have the Roman procedure, *(b)* That there is a certain body of legal authority for it; *e. g;* it has been adopted as the

---

[960] Dorr v. Bank, 128 Mass. p. 358; Page *v.* Osgood, 2 Gray, 260.

A Preliminary Treatise on Evidence at the Common Law

only proper usage by the Supreme Court of Massachusetts, and, in particular opinions, has been approved by other tribunals and judges.[961] *(e)* That the meaning is a familiar and well-approved one in ordinary legal usage.

But whatever may be thought of the reasons, on one side or the other, and whichever is the better course, the difficulty is well nigh insuperable of driving out either usage. The experience of the Supreme Court of Massachusetts, in its long attempt to limit the meaning to the one usage of the duty of establishing the proposition in issue, is little calculated to encourage such endeavors.

It would seem, therefore, the most practicable suggestion, to submit to what is probably unavoidable, to recognize the phrase as being an indeterminate expression, often convenient, often sufficiently intelligible for the purpose in hand, and too well-established to be wholly got rid of, — and to adopt other terms where it is necessary to mark the discrimination between one meaning and the other. Such a course may reasonably be expected to commend itself to careful thinkers. Whoever has a definite conception to express, and is at the same time aware of the danger of being misunderstood when he uses an ambiguous phrase, will be likely to choose an expression calculated, without danger of mistake, to convey his meaning clearly.[962]

---

[961] See *ante,* 357.

[962] See, e. *g.,* the careful discriminations in Buswell v. Fuller, 89 Me. 600, and Scott *v.* Wood, 81 Cal. 398.As regards the term onus *probandi* in the Roman system, it seems to have had there the same undiscriminated use as with us. According to the Roman conception he who had famished evidence at the outset had famished *probatio.* If counter evidence were offered, he must, indeed, keep up his *probatio;* but the notion of *probare* and *probatio* was answered by a *prima facie* case.I have referred in the text to certain difficulties attending the Massachusetts effort to use the term burden of proof in only one sense. Chief Justice Shaw began it in 1832 (see *ante,* 355), and not, as I venture to think, with a sufficient recognition of the fact that the other use of the phrase was also perfectly well fixed in legal usage, — a use of it in which the thought did not run out into any discrimination about the duty of establishing at the end of the discussion. During the following twenty-eight years of his most valuable judicial life, the Chief Justice was able to hold the terminology of his court with fair success to the new rule, and to establish it in that State. But the example has not been followed. The discrimination has been recognized in other courts, and this meaning allowed, and even preferred, or suggested as the only proper one, in particular opinions; but no other court, I believe, has undertaken systematically to reject the other meaning. It is instructive to remark the troubles that have attended the Massachusetts experiment. In 1840 (Sperry *v.* Wilcox, 1 Met. 267) Chief

V. Whereabout in the law shall we place the doctrine of the burden of proof? I have already indicated the answer. It is common in our system to treat of it in books on evidence, when it is treated of at all; and the result is that it is little discussed, for it does not belong there.[963] It operates in full force both before and after the evidence is in. It belongs under the head of legal reasoning; of reasoning about law as about fact; while the law of evidence relates merely to matter

---

Justice Shaw restates his view, and calls the other use of the word "a common misapprehension of the law on the subject." But in 1842 (Jones *v.* Stevens, 5 Met. 373, 378, Hubbard, J.) the opinion of the court lays down the other doctrine: "The [auditor's] report being made evidence by the statute, it necessarily shifted the burden of proof; for being *prima facie* evidence, it becomes conclusive where it is not contradicted or controlled." In 1S44 (Taunton Iron Co. *v.* Richmond, 8 Met. 434) the reporter, afterwards Mr. Justice Metcalf, gives a decision of the court by Shaw, C. J., that an auditor's report is *prima facie* evidence for the party in whose favor it is made, and adds in his head-note the expression, "and changes the burden of proof." In 1848 (Jennison v. Stafford, I Cush. 168) the court (Metcalf, J.) states that, in a suit by the payee of a promissory note against the maker, "the burden of proof is on the maker" to establish want of consideration. But two years later (Delano v. Bartlett, 6 Cush. 364,368) the statement is that the burden of proof is on the plaintiff, and Fletcher, J., remarks of the previous case that "there is a sentence in this opinion which may be misunderstood [quoting it]. This must be understood to mean that the burden of proof is on the maker to rebut the *prima facie* cage made by producing the note, otherwise the *prima facie* evidence will be conclusive." In this same year, 1850 (Wilde *v.* Armsby, 6 Cush. 314,319), Metcalf, J., for the court, while distinguishing, in the case of an alteration in a writing, between "the burden of proof" and the " burden of explanation," defines the burden of proof in terms borrowed from Baron Parke, but not understood by him or in English legal usage to be limited to the duty of establishing (supra, 362); "The effect . . . would be that if no evidence is given by a party claiming under such an instrument, the issue must always be found against him; this being the meaning of the 'burden of proof.' 1 Curteis, 640." In 1858 (Noxon *v.* De Wolf, 10 Gray, 343, 348), Dewey, J., for the court, remarks upon the fact that the Chief Justice of the lower court had used the phrase in another than "the more precisely accurate use of the term . . . as now held by the court;" but the court concluded that it did not mislead the jury. In 1859 (Morgan *v.* Morse, 13 Gray, 150) the judge below ruled that "the burden of proof was upon the defendant to ... control the auditor's report," and the court is obliged again to set forth the discrimination between "the technical sense" of the burden of proof and the other; and then follows what looks like a confession that an exclusive use of the word had not gained any firm bold in the seven and twenty years since Chief Justice Shaw had begun it: "This mode of using the phrase, though somewhat loose and inaccurate, is quite common, and where not improperly applied to a case, so as to confuse or mislead the jury, cannot be held to be a misdirection."

[963] Bentham, Works, vi. 214. "This topic [the onus *probandi*]... seems to belong rather to Procedure than to Evidence."

of fact offered to a judicial tribunal as the basis of inference to another matter of fact. To undertake to crowd within the comparatively narrow limits proper to the law of evidence the considerations governing the determination of matters of a far wider scope, like those questions of logic and general experience and substantive law involved in the subjects of Presumption, and Judicial Notice, and those other questions compounded of like considerations, coupled with others relating to the history and technicalities of pleading and forensic procedure, which lie at the bottom of what is called by this name of the "burden of proof," — to attempt this is to burst the sides of the smaller subject and to bring obscurity over both. And it is to condemn this topic, so important in the daily conduct of legal affairs, and so much needing a clear exposition, to a continuance of that neglect, and that slight and incidental treatment which it has so long suffered.

CHAPTER X
THE "PAROL EVIDENCE" RULE [964]

Few things are darker than this, or fuller of subtle difficulties. "The admissibility," says a well-known writer, "of extrinsic parol testimony to affect written instruments is, perhaps, the most difficult branch of the law of evidence."[965] The chief reason is that most of the questions brought under this head are out of place; there is a grouping together of a mass of incongruous matter, and then it is looked at in a wrong focus. Because the rules intimated by this title deal with writings, *i. e.,* with things which in their nature are evidence of what they record, it is assumed that they belong to the law of evidence. But in truth most of the matters with which they are concerned — have no special place in the law of evidence; and the way out of these perplexities will be found in clearly recognizing what the law of evidence is, and in eliminating the various parts of the present title which do not belong under that head and allotting them to their proper place.

I. It is necessary to keep in mind a few discriminations, some of which have been repeatedly emphasized already. Let us remind ourselves of them again.

1. Between rules of substantive law and rules of evidence. When the law requires a thing to be recorded, or in writing, or under seal, or attested, these, often, are not requirements of the law of evidence. They are matters of form, required, in some cases, as necessary to the constitution of a thing, as in the case of wills and deeds; in some, that the matter may be available as the ground of an action, as in the case of things included in ss. 4 and 17 of the Statute of Frauds. In any such case they belong to the substantive law of particular subjects; and when testimony or facts offered in evidence are rejected as not conforming to these or the like requirements, it is the substantive law of the case that excludes them.[966] 2. Here also we

---

[964] For common ways of stating what this phrase is thought to cover, see *infra,* 396, 397.

[965] 2 Taylor Ev. (9th ed.) s. 1128.

[966] When a judge says, "I found my judgment on one of the most useful rules in the law, namely, that when parties have put their contract into writing,

must discriminate between different senses of the word "evidence." In the sense which gives name to the great and peculiar department of law known among English-speaking people as their "law of evidence," this word, as we have seen, means testimony, or some matter of fact to be offered to a legal tribunal as a basis of inference to some other matter of fact. It does not include all that relates to the general topic of proof or legal reasoning, or all that is popularly meant by the word "evidence," — all evidential matter, — but only such as it is necessary, to offer for use in court when a tribunal has to ascertain a matter of fact unknown or disputed. The rules of evidence regulate this forensic proceeding; they do not determine questions of mere logic or general experience, or furnish rules for conducting processes of reasoning. To talk of evidence, then, and to settle questions about it, in the mere sense of a logically probative quality or fact, is not to touch upon the region peculiar to the law of evidence; indeed, to talk of It at all, unless with reference to its use for the purposes of litigation, is not to talk of what belongs to this specific department of our law. When we speak of certain writings as "evidences of debt" or ownership, or of writings generally as "written evidence," and with these contrast what is not in writing as "extrinsic evidence" or "parol evidence," we are, for the most part, not using the word "evidence" in any sense apposite to the law of evidence. It is not this head of the law that determines the legal import of a bond, or negotiable paper, or bill of lading. It is not the law of evidence which requires a will, or a deed, or a contract about land, to be in writing, and which determines all the various implications and corollaries of these requirements, — as, *e.g.,* in deciding when the parol or extrinsic matter submitted is or is not consistent with the rule that you must have a writing, a specialty, or an attested document.

3. Furthermore, it is necessary to remember in a thousand cases, when it is said that "evidence is admissible," or the reverse, that this "admissibility" has no necessary relation to the law of evidence. For, in such cases, not merely is it true that the admission or rejection of what is offered may turn wholly on a doubt as to the mere logical quality of what is offered, or as to the true limits of the

---

that writing determines what the bargain is," (Martin, B., in Langton *v.* Higgins, 4 H. & N. 402), — he is not stating a rule of evidence. As to the Statute of Frauds, see Bedell *v.* Tracy, 65 Vt. 494. *As* to the requirement of a seal, see Blewitt *v.* Boorum, 142 N. Y. 357.

governing propositions of substantive law, pleading, or procedure, which in every case must fix the character of what is put forward as being relevant or the reverse; but also, where a declaration as to the admissibility of evidence is clearly not of this sort, yet it is very often merely a single specimen, out of myriads that might be offered, of probative matter *not* excluded by the law of evidence. Such propositions are often put as if they declared a rule or doctrine of that branch of the law. Little reflection is needed to see that such things, mere instances of what is provable, may be but so many illustrations and applications of the fundamental conceptions in any rational system of proof; namely, that what is logically probative, and at the same time practically useful, may be resorted to, unless forbidden by some rule or principle of the law. These instances may be multiplied and heaped up in countless numbers. They are, in fact. And yet, often, he who does this is merely illustrating, perhaps with a benumbing superfluity, the practical working of the principles of reasoning. He is not stating the law of evidence.

4. Another discrimination to be observed is that between documents which constitute a contract, fact, or transaction, and those which merely certify and evidence something outside of themselves, — a something valid and operative, independent of the writing. Brunner, in a learned consideration of the subject of "Documents," has incidentally pointed out this discrimination with precision while speaking of documents in the old Italian law, and of their nomenclature — (1) *carta* or *cartula,* and (2) *notitia* or *memoratorium.* He quotes[967] a Lombard document of the ninth century which sets forth a promise *per wadiam* to give by a document a piece of land in exchange; and goes on to remark that by the Lombard law a binding contract is concluded by the pledge *(wadia);*[968] and that as regards the legal effect of the transaction, the giving of a document is unimportant. The document in such cases is only written testimony of a transaction already valid and complete without it. It is merely an evidence document. "The *carta...* has a twofold office. It is both a means of proof and a means of constituting the transaction which it authenticates. It is used in legal matters which are accomplished only by means of the document. As constituting the contract, it takes the place of the *wadia;* as

---

[967] *Urkunden,* 15 — 17.
[968] 2 gee Essays in Anglo-Saxon Law, 190.

authenticating the contract, it unites with the function of the *wadia* that of the *notitia."* Such documents, he adds, are called "dispositive." "The *carta,* as contrasted with the mere evidence document, is a dispositive document." And, in the Roman law, he names the written will as a dispositive document, and a nuncupative will reduced to writing, as an evidence document.[969]

This distinction finds abundant illustration in our own law, old and new. In 1422[970] a plaintiff sued in account for money received to his use; the defendant pleaded that he had given a deed to the plaintiff testifying the receipt of the money, and insisted that the plaintiff must make *profert* of the deed. Babington, J., at first seemed to agree with the defendant; and he put the case of one owing twenty pounds on a simple contract, and afterwards making a bond for the same twenty pounds; such a one, he said, shall be discharged from the contract by the obligation. Rolfe, counsel for the plaintiff, said the deed merely testifies the receipt. "As to the case you put of a bond, I entirely agree; for the contract and the obligation are two different contracts, and by the greater I am discharged from the less. But in the case of the receipt and the deed which witnesses the receipt, there is but one contract." In 1460,[971] on occasion of a question put to the judges by the Recorder of London, it appeared that one had sued in debt for a sale of cloth, and the defendant would wage his law; upon which the plaintiff set up a custom of London that the defendant should be ousted of his law if the plaintiff put forward "a paper or parchment written and sealed with the defendant's seal, which proves the contract." The plaintiff made *profert* of such a paper, testifying that the defendant had agreed to the contract. Laken, serjeant, said that the action should have been brought on the paper, and not on the contract; but Prisot, C. J., thought otherwise. "The contract," he said, "is not determined by this. It is determined where one makes a bond upon a contract, or if a man recovers in debt upon a contract. Here no bond is shown, but only a paper testifying the contract. If I bail goods by deed indented," he added, "and afterwards bring detinue for them, I am not to count on the indenture, for that is only a thing testifying the bailment. It is the same if I make a contract by deed indented. I shall

---

[969] *Urkunden,* 61.

[970] Y. B. 1 H. VI. 7, 31; Fitz. *Acc.* I; *semble, s. c.* Y. B. 2 H. VI. 9, 5.

[971] Fitz. *Dette,* 68; 8. C. Y. B. 39 H. VI. 34, 46 (ed. 1689). Some older editions of this Year Book omit important parts of the case.

not be compelled to count on the indenture; for the contract is not determined upon the indenture, but continues, and a man may elect how he will bring his action." "To which," adds the reporter, "all the justices agreed."[972]

Whenever, therefore, the law requires, in any transaction, a formal document, the *carta,* it is demanding something more than written evidence; it is making *form* necessary, — as when a seal to a deed is required, or three witnesses to a will. As there is no will without the witnesses, and no deed without the seal, so neither the *carta,* nor any part of it, can exist outside of the writing. And yet, from the nature of it, this sort of writing is also evidence; as they used to say, it "testifies." As contrasted with this sort of thing, it is a *notitia,* a *memora-torium* only, that is called for when the English Statute of Frauds, in ss. 4 and 17, is content with "some note or memorandum in writing" of the agreements there referred to.[973]

II. Leaving, now, these discriminations, and coming to the precept which goes by the name of "The Parol Evidence Rule," it is ordinarily said that in the case of contracts in writing, wills, deeds, and other solemn documents, parol evidence is not admissible to vary or add to their legal effect, or to cut it down; and especially that such evidence of the writer's intention, is not admissible. In this expression, "parol" means what is extrinsic to the writing, and

---

[972] It seems that one might count upon the specialty if he chose, and it "could not be disputed, unless by matter of as high a nature." Fits., *Barre,* 19; s. c. 18 H. VI. 17, 8 (1439).In 1522 — 1523 (Y. B. 14 H. VIII. 17, 6), in a long and interesting case, Brudnel, C. J., said: "Things which pass by parol are made subject to a Condition, as well by parol as in writing; ... for a deed is only proof and testimony of the party's agreement. As a deed of feoffment is only proof of the livery, the land passes by the livery; but when the deed and the livery coexist, it is a proof of the livery." Compare Saunders, J., in considering a deed of lease of land, in Throckmerton *v.* Tracy, Plowden, p. 161 (1556): "And he said he was of the like opinion that Brudnel seemed to be of in 14 H. VIII., that contracts shall be as it is concluded and agreed between the parties, according as their intents may be gathered. . . . And certainly the words are no other than the testimony of the contract."

[973] "The contract itself, and the memorandum which is necessary to its validity under the Statute of Frauds, are in their nature distinct things. The statute presupposes a contract by parol. . . . The contract may be made at one time, and the note or memorandum of it at a subsequent time." — Hoar, J. (for the court), in Lerned v. Wannemacher Alien, 412. That the validity of the contract is not touched by statutes like the English one, But only the remedy, see Townsend *v.* Hargrave, 118 Masg. 325; Maddison v. Alderson, 8 App. Cas. 467, 488 [per Lord Blackburn); Lucas *v.* Dixon, 22 Q. B. D. 357.

"evidence" means testimony or facts, conceived of as tending to show what varies, adds to, or cuts down the writing, or to show the intention. The phrase parol, or extrinsic, evidence stands contrasted with that intrinsic evidence which is found in the writing itself.

Greenleaf's statement of the rule as relating to contracts will serve the present purpose well enough. He says:[974] "When parties have deliberately put their engagements into writing, in such terms as import a legal obligation, without any uncertainty as to the object or extent of such engagement, it is conclusively presumed that the whole engagement of the parties, and the extent and manner of their undertaking, was reduced to writing; and all oral testimony of a previous *colloquium* between the parties, or of conversations or declarations at the time when. it was completed, or afterwards, as it would tend, in many cases to substitute a new and different contract for the one which was really agreed upon, to the prejudice, possibly, of one of the parties, is rejected. In other words, as the rule is now more briefly expressed, 'parol contemporaneous. evidence is inadmissible to contradict or vay the terms of a valid written instrument.'" [975]

It takes but a little attention to the rule thus stated, and the reasons on which it is rested, to perceive that the real aim and substance of it have to do not with excluding evidence, but with preventing the thing itself in aid of which the evidence is offered, namely, the contradicting or varying of the written expression and the written form, by an expression which is not written. If this aim were a legitimate one, as it is in the equitable reformation of documents, the evidence tending to prove 'it would be admissible. It is never the law of evidence that shuts it out, but the substantive law of the topics to which these documents relate.[976]

Another wider statement of the rule is given by Stephen:[977] "When any judgment of any court or any other judicial or official proceeding, or any contract or grant, or any other disposition of

---

[974] Evid. i. s. 275.

[975] "The learned counsel . . . admitted as fully as their opponents could desire, that parol testimony cannot be received to contradict, vary, add to, or subtract from the terms of a written contract, or the terms in which the parties have deliberately agreed to record any part of their contract." *Per* Lord Morris, in Bank of Australia *v.* Palmer, [1897] App. Cas. 540, 545.

[976] 1 Biddle, Ins. s. 523.

[977] Dig. Evid. art. 90.

property has been reduced to the form of a document or series of documents, no evidence may be given of such judgment or proceeding, or of the terms of such contract, grant, or other disposition of property, except the document itself, or secondary evidence of its contents in cases in which secondary evidence is admissible under the provisons herein before contained. Nor may the contents of any such document be contradicted, altered, added to, or varied by oral evidence.

As regards the several parts of this statement of the rule, it may be said, *(1)* That the last sentence, like the propositions of Greenleaf, really forbids, not the evidence, but the thing which is attempted, namely, the varying, contradicting, etc., of what is in writing by what is oral. *(2)* That so far as this statement merely forbids proving the contents of a writing otherwise than by the writing itself, it is covered by the ordinary rule of the law of evidence, applicable not merely to solemn writings, of the sort here named, but to others; known sometimes as the "Best Evidence rule." And *(3)* that in so far as the rule makes the writing the only evidence of the thing it embodies, *i. e.,* of the judgment, the contract, the devise, etc., it is in reality declaring a doctrine of the substantive law of these subjects, namely, in the case of a written contract, that all preceding and contemporaneous oral expressions of the thing are merged in the writing or displaced by it; or, as in the case of wills, that the written form is essential to the legal existence of the thing itself.

Let me illustrate these suggestions by a brief reference to some well-known classes of cases.

1. When it is said of judgments and matters of record generally, that they cannot be "contradicted, added to, or varied by oral evidence," what is generally meant is to express the final and conclusive operation of these things. It is the well-known doctrine as to judgments, in the domestic forum, that they are "as a plea a bar, or as evidence, conclusive, between the same parties, upon the same matter, directly in question in another court," etc.[978] There is no

---

[978] De Grey, C. J., in the advisory opinion of the judges to the House of Lords in the Duchess of Kingston's case, 20 State Trials, 537 n. (1776). Of what are called "interstate judgments" in the United States, it is the rule that "when duly pleaded and proved in a court of that State [i. e., any State in the Union] they have the effect of being not merely *prima facie* evidence, but conclusive proof of the rights thereby adjudicated; and a refusal to give them the force and effect, in

occasion here to go into any full or exact statement of this doctrine. It has certain well-known qualifications. Judgments may be impeached by direct proceedings for that purpose. Moreover judgments of foreign States, and, in a less degree, those of other States of our own nation, are open to impeachment on grounds not applicable to domestic judgments; and, under the Fourteenth Amendment to the Constitution of the United States, even in the domestic forum, the judgments of that forum may be impeached in a manner and on grounds not recognized at common law.[979]

Now, where Such doctrines as these, and the qualifications of them, are expressed in terms of evidence, one must look beneath the form of expression if he would truly understand what is thus phrased. When it is said, e. g., that "if it be a judgment... of a domestic court of general jurisdiction, and the record declares that notice has been given, such declaration cannot be contradicted by extraneous proof.... The judgment... is sustained, not because a judgment rendered without notice is good, but because the law does not permit the introduction of evidence to overthrow that which for reasons of public policy it treats as absolute verity. The record is conclusively presumed to speak the truth, and can be tried only by inspection;"[980] — when that sort of thing is said, the real doctrine is that a certain defence or answer to a domestic judgment is rejected. It is a denial of the right to qualify the full verity and operation of such judgments collaterally, as the phrase is. If this defence or answer were allowed, the evidence would be received. In a suitable direct proceeding, as by a writ of error or a motion to vacate the judgment, there is the right to ask the court that gave the judgment to annul it; and in such proceedings nobody ever heard that extrinsic evidence to prove the facts was not admissible. In any proceeding before any court, wherever such facts are in point of substantive law available, it is a mere matter of course that extrinsic evidence of them is admissible.[981]

---

this respect, which they had in the State in which they were rendered, denies to the party a right secured to him by the constitution and laws of the United States." — *Per* Gray, J., in Huntington *v.* Attrill, 146 U. S. 657, 685.

[979] Needham *v.* Thayer, 147 Mass. 536, overruling Cook v. Darling, 18 Pick. 393; Pennoyer *v.* Neff, 95 U. S. 714 (1877).

[980] Wilcher *v.* Robinson, 78 Va. p. 616.

[981] Carleton *v.* Bickford, 13 Gray, 591; Thompson v. Whitman, 18 Wall 457; Needham *v.* Thayer, 147 Mass. 536; Denton v. Noyes, 6 Johns. 296; compare Post v. Charlesworth, 21 N. Y. Suppl. 168. To the same class of cases

2. In an action for the breach of covenants in a deed, there was a question as to the true boundary of the estate conveyed, and a witness for the plaintiff (the plaintiff's grantor) was allowed to state what was said by the defendant, the original grantor, to be the true boundary, during the negotiations for his own purchase from the defendant. The defendant objected to this "parol evidence," but it was admitted in the Supreme Court of New York. The case ultimately reached the Court of Errors,[982] and the decision was reversed; the Chancellor (Walworth) remarking that the question was not what land Tymason intended to convey to May, but what land is covered by the description in the deed: "It is impossible for me to discover upon what principle May's testimony could be received as legal evidence to support the plaintiff's action.... Our recording Acts would afford no protection whatever to subsequent purchasers if the abuttals and boundaries contained in written conveyances should be considered as referring merely to what was supposed by the immediate parties to be the land described in the deed." In such a case as that it is not the law of evidence that is applied, but the substantive law regulating conveyances, and the substantive law as to the construction and effect of writings. You cannot, says the law, convey land without a deed, and, therefore, yon cannot make "parol" matter operate by way of an addition to the deed, for it lacks the required. form. But were the doing of this allowed, evidence to prove it would be received. It is rejected because if admitted, it could be of no use.

3. It is the Countess of Rutland's case[983] that is so often cited for the rule that "parol evidence is not admissible to vary or add to a writing." But that case, as regards this subject, merely applied a rule as to the declaration of the uses of fines; namely, the doctrine briefly stated in Jones v. Morley,[984] that if the fine be levied pursuant to a covenant declaring the uses, one cannot set up an intervening

---

belongs a doctrine laid down by the Supreme Court of the United States as to the collateral impeachment of patents of land by the United States, refusing, in certain cases, "to permit the validity of the patent ... to be subjected to the test of the verdict of a jury on such oral testimony as might be brought before it. It would be substituting the jury, or the court sitting as a jury, for the tribunal which Congress had provided to determine the question." *Per* Miller, J., in French v. *F*yan, 93 U. S. 169; McCormick v. Hayes, 159 U. S. 332.

[982] Bates v. Tymason, 13 Wend. 300; 14 *ib.* 671.
[983] 5 Co. Rep. 25 (1604).
[984] 2 Salk. 677 (1696 — 7).

oral declaration of uses, or deny the uses declared in the covenant; unless, indeed, there be an intervening declaration by "other matter (than the covenant), as high or higher." Coke's report of the opinion of Popham, C. J., goes on: "For every contract or agreement ought to be dissolved, "by matter of as high a nature as the first deed. *Nihil tam conveniens est naturali æquitati, unumquodque dissolvi eo legamine quo ligatum est.* Also it would be inconvenient that matters in writing made by advice and on consideration, and which finally import the certain truth of the agreement of the parties, should be controlled by averment of the parties, to be proved by the uncertain testimony of slippery memory. And it would be dangerous to purchasers and farmers and all others in such cases if such. nude averments against matters in writing should be admitted."

It is the use of such matter, not the proving of it, that is objectionable; it is the averment of it in pleading, the having an issue on it, the going to the jury with it, that is forbidden. In like manner it is still a doctrine of the substantive law of contracts under seal that is asserted, when, in conflict with some things said in this passage from Coke's Reports, we read in a late case,[985] that "Nothwithstanding what was said in some of the old cases, it is now recognized doctrine that the terms of a contract under seal may be varied by a subsequent parol agreement. Certainly, whatever may have been. the rule at law, such is the rule in equity.... The rule in equity is undoubted." And so in England, under the Judicature Act, a parol agreement" may be applied directly in answer to any proceeding upon the original deed brought contrary to the terms and faith of the agreement; the ancient technical rule of the common law that a contract under seal cannot be varied or discharged by a parol agreement is thus practically superseded."[986] Whichever way the rule be, the law of evidence is untouched. The change relates to the possibility of using the parol agreement; not to the proving of it, but to the use of it as a defence or a ground of action.

4. And so in modern times when, as among "parol" contracts, there was applied, to "parol contracts in writing " the old doctrine and the old remarks about "contracts in writing," meaning sealed writings, — it was still a doctrine of the law of contract. In

---

[985] Canal Co. *v.* Ray, 101 U. S. p. 52 (1879). *26*
[986] Leake, Dig. Cont. 802.

Meres *et al. v.* Ansell *et al.*,[987] the court, without citing any authority, deals with a parol contract in writing as if it were covered by the rules applicable to a sealed contract. The defendants had contracted in writing for an exchange of certain property of theirs for the grass from Boreham Meadow, in the plaintiffs' occupation; the agreement said nothing of a close called Millcroft, which was also in the plaintiffs' possession. The defendants, claiming the grass in Millcroft also, were sued in trespass for acts done there; and upon pleading not guilty and a license, were allowed by Lord Mansfield to prove that at the time of making the writing it was agreed, orally that the defendants should have not only "the hay from off Boreham Meadow, but also the whole possession of the soil and produce both of Boreham Meadow and Millcroft." On a motion for a new trial, on the ground of admitting this "parol evidence," the Court of Common Pleas granted a new trial, declaring "that no parol evidence is admissible to disannul and substantially to vary a written agreement; the parol evidence in the present case totally annuls and substantially alters and impugns the written agreement." Here again the trouble was with the agreement, and not the evidence; it lay in the fact that the form of the agreement was oral. If the agreement could not be used, when proved, evidence of it was, of course inadmissible, but the exclusion is not referable to the law of evidence. The old doctrine, which declared matter "in writing," *i.e.,* under seal, to be of a higher grade than parol, is thus extended, in modern times, to all contracts and solemn instruments which are in writing in our modern sense, *i. e.,* to all of them not oral; it is not now limited to what is by law required to be in writing. This application of the rule rests, in part at any rate, upon a supposed convention or intent of the party or parties in putting the thing into writing.[988]

 In this last case the fourth section of the Statute of Frauds required that either the agreement itself "or some memorandum or note thereof" should be in writing and signed by the party to be charged therewith, or some other person thereto authorized by him. The same statute, in § 17, as regards certain contracts for the sale of

---

[987] 3 Wils. 275 (1771). As to this case, see 2 Evans's Decis. of Lord Mansfield, 302 n.

[988] "We are of opinion that the rule relied on by the plaintiffs only applies where the parties to an agreement reduce it to writing, and agree or intend that that writing shall be their agreement." — Pollock, C. B (for the court), in Harris *v.* Rickett, 4 H. & N. 1.

goods, required, as one of several alternatives, that there be "some note or memorandum in writing;" and in § 5, in the case of all devises and bequests of real estate, that they should be "in writing and signed... and... attested... by three or four credible witnesses." While the statute, in requiring, in § 4, that, if one would bring an action, he should have a writing of the sort named, and, in § 17, a writing or one of the other alternative things, doubtless has an eye to the simplicity and certainty of evidence in court, it is not merely looking out for that. For the writing must exist at the time the action is brought; one obtained after that time, while perfectly answering any requirement of evidence, is not sufficient.[989] The statute, therefore, determines certain prerequisites to the bringing of an action; and when a writing is a prerequisite, it is only putting the same thing in other words to say that nothing but a writing will answer. The real character of the proposition is obscured by phrasing it in terms of evidence; by saying, you cannot "have recourse to parol proof;" and you cannot supplement an insufficient paper "by means of parol evidence, which the statute forbids."[990] The true proposition is one of substantive or procedural law, namely, that a party cannot ground an action upon an oral agreement, unless there be also a note of it in writing, existing when the action is brought.

5. It is in the case of wills, probably, that one may see the most conspicuous illustrations of the errors in question; and Wigram's valuable little treatise[991] gives currency to them. Wigram, as every lawyer knows, made admirable contributions to the subject, but in dealing with construction" and interpretation, he accepted too readily the current language of the books. He puts it (§ 2) as the object of the book to consider "under what restrictions is the admission of extrinsic evidence in aid of the exposition of a will consistent with the provisions of a statute which makes a writing indispensable to the purpose for which the instrument was made." Of construction, and of this famous book, something more will be said later. But it is proper to say here that the real subject of the book concerns the interpretation and construction of wills. It is the same

---

[989] Tisdale v. Harris, 20 Pick. 9, p. 14; Bill v. Bament, 9 M. & W. 36; Gibson v. Holland, L, R. I C. P. I; Lucas v. Dixon, 22 Q. B. D. 357; Re Hoyle, 67 L. T. Rep. 674.

[990] Curtis, J., in Salmon Falls Man. Co. v. Goddard, 14 How. 446.

[991] "An Examination of the Rules of Law respecting the Admission of Extrinsic Evidence in Aid of the Interpretation of Wills."

general topic very ably discussed by Hawking in his well-known treatise,[992] and in an earlier paper,[993] where the nature of the inquiry is described with penetration and accuracy. In that paper the special questions are indicated as being these: What are the limits of inferential interpretation? What constitutes a *sufficient* expression in writing? How far may you supplement the words, the primary expression of the writer's intention, by indications of it drawn from extrinsic sources? And so, in Wigram's book, the chief question is not one of the admission or exclusion of extrinsic evidence; but of the true nature and limits of interpretation, and how far inferences may be drawn from extrinsic facts in aid of it. The law of evidence has little to say in answer to these questions.

6. This same confusion of questions as to what case a man has in point of substantive law, with other questions as to how he may prove it, if he has one, appears in a great variety of other instances. In cases not involving writings, it is easy enough to see that the long, gradual amelioration of law and legal procedure, allowing new grounds of action and defence, enlarging the scope of existing actions, and avoiding circuity, — while it means admitting evidence which could not be given before, yet may involve no change whatever in the law of evidence. New things may be done, and therefore new things may be proved; and if new things may be proved, other new things may be proved by way of meeting them. This was the significance of relief in equity, — what could not be done at law might be done there; and if so, then, of course, pleading and proof must correspond. Yet all this involved no change in the rules of evidence. This, again, is the import of the extension of equitable defences, by statute and at the common law, and even of the whole introduction of new forms of action; namely, that things can now be done which could not be done before; done in one way which, could not be done in. another. Whenever they could be done, of course they could be alleged and proved. In such cases, the new state of things is often expressed by saying that evidence of the new thing is admissible; yet it is plain that this does not touch the real character of the change. A change has taken place in substantive law or procedure; none in the law of evidence.

---

[992] "A Concise Treatise on the Construction of Wills" (1863).

[993] On the Principles of Legal Interpretation, with Reference especially to the Interpretation of Wills, 2 Judicial Soc. Papers, 298; read in 1860 *Infra,* 577.

No less is this true as regards writings, and the same secular process which has liberalized the law relating to them. In Collins *v.* Blantern,[994] as it seems, it was first distinctly held that illegality of consideration, not appearing upon the face of a bond, was a good defence. Such a bond, it was laid down by the court (Wilmot, C. J.), apparently upon a demurrer to the plea, is void by the common law. "The law will legitimate the showing it void *ab initio,* and this can only be done by pleading;... what strange absurdity would it be for the law to say that this contract is wicked and void, and in the same breath for the law to say you shall not be permitted to plead the facts which clearly show it to be wicked and void." And so, fifteen years later, in Pole *v.* Harborn,[995] on a demurrer to a like plea, Lord Mansfield said: "There cannot exist such an absurdity as that a man shall have a good defence to an action, and not be able to show or take advantage of it either by pleading or in evidence.... The foundation is that you shall not by parol impeach a written agreement, and say that the agreement was different; but, the agreement being admitted, the party may come and show circumstances to vitiate the whole proceeding."[996]

---

[994] 2 Wils. 347 (1767); Ames, Specialty Contracts and Equitable Defences, Harv. Law Rev. ix. 49, 52.

[995] 9 East, 415 n.

[996] Six centuries ago the Statute of Fines, 1 Stat. Realm, 128 (1299), after reciting that parties have lately been allowed to set up certain defences to fines, enacts that hereafter no such exceptions or answers, or submitting them to juries, shall be allowed. During the period of the Year Books there was great rigor. "If a man," said Newton, C. J., in 1440 (Y. B. 19 H. VI. 44, 93), "levy a fine of my lands by my name, I shall have no other remedy than a writ of deceit, by which I shall recover damages according to my loss." "To be sure," said Robert Danby, J., in 1455 (Y. B. 34 H. VI. 14, 36), "if there be two Robert Danbies, and one of them make conusance of a matter whereby I am damaged, I can show that I am not the person, but that there is another Robert." (Compare Cary (ed. 1650), 22, in 1602.) And in 1596, about the time that Bacon wrote his famous and much-abused maxim about ambiguities, the new Lord Keeper, Egerton (Hubert's case, Cro. Eliz. 531; s. c. 12 Co. 123), "said that he had always noted this difference: If one of my name levies ft fine of my land, I may well confess and avoid this fine by showing the special matter, for that stands well with the fine; But if a stranger who is not of my name levies a flue of my land in my name, I shall not be received to aver that I did not levy the fine, But another in my name, for that is merely contrary to the record; and so it is of all reconusances and other matters of record." But in this same case, the Star Chamber, "there being then in court the Lord Keeper [Egerton], Popham, Chief Justice, Gawdy, one of the justices of the Queen's Bench, and Walmsley, one of the justices of the

In like manner, when it is a question whether a writing, complete in point of form, was delivered or ever took effect as a contract, deed, or will;[997] whether, if it did, it is voidable for fraud,[998] or amendable for mistake;[999] whether, under a written contract, you

---

Common Pleas, and divers lords," punished one found guilty of procuring the personation of Alexander Gellibrand in a fine of his lands, and ordered that "the fine levied unto him should be void, if it could he so done, by entering a *vacat* upon the roll, or otherwise as the justices of the Common Pleas should best approve; and if it cannot be so made void, that then Hubert, by fine or otherwise, as Alexander Gellibrand should devise, should reconvey the land to him and his heirs in the same manner as it was before, or at the time levied." Popham, C. J., thought a *vacat* might be entered, avoiding the fine, and cited "the case of one Holcomb" where it had been done. The date of this last case was not given. "To warrant this, another precedent was shown, *tempore* Hen. 6." The Lord Keeper, after making the remarks quoted above, added: "But I conceive when the fraud appears to the court, as here, they may well enter a *vacat* upon the roll, and so make it no fine, although the party cannot avoid it by averment during the time that it remains as a record.The direct defence, or "averment," of fraud was distinctly upheld in 1601 — 1602, in Fermor's case, in Chancery (3 Co. 77; 8. C. 2 And. 176, Jenk. 253), where a lessee for years had levied a fine of the lessor's land. The Lord Keeper called for the opinion of the two chief justices; and after conference between them, "they thought it necessary that all the justices of England and barons of the Exchequer should be assembled for the resolution of this great case." The question, as Andersen's report tells us, was whether the plaintiff was barred by the fine, and if so, whether he could have relief in Chancery. The chief justices and all the others agreed that the fine did not bar the plaintiff. "And as to that which was objected, that it would be mischievous to avoid fines on such bare averments, it was answered that it would be a greater mischief ... if fines levied by such covin and practice should bind."Such a determination may well have been helped by the practice in Chancery of relieving against fraud in such cases by ordering a reconveyance. A cage of that sort is reported as of May, 1595 (Welby v. Welby, Tothill, 99; 1 Cruise, Fines, 3d ed. 349).Of course, in allowing new defences at law as against these solemn and sacred assurances, or new relief in equity, the substantive law of fines was changed; and, this being so, it followed, as a mere matter of course, that the new matter could be pleaded and proved.

[997] Pym *v.* Campbell, 6 E. & B. 370; Blewitt *v.* Boorum, 142 N. Y. 357, an interesting case; *per* Peckham, J.

[998] Barnesly *v.* Powell, 1 Ves. 284; State *v.* Cass, 52 N. J. Law, 77.

[999] Baker v. Paine, 1 Ves. 456 (1750): "How can a mistake in an agreement be proved, but by parol evidence ? *Per* Lord Hardwicke. Goode *v.* Riley, 153 Mass. 585. *Per* Holmes, J., who remarked: "It is not necessarily fatal that the evidence is parol which is relied on to show that the contract was not made as it purports on the face of the document to have been made. There was a time when a man was bound if his seal was affixed to an instrument by a stranger, and against his will. But the notion that one who has gone through certain forms

can set up a substituted time of performance;[1000] whether, in case of a deed or written transfer, absolute in form, you can show that it was given as a security merely;[1001] whether, under any circumstances, an indorser of negotiable paper in blank may set up an oral agreement that he was not to be under the usual obligations of such an indorser;[1002] whether a principal not named is bound by an agreement in writing made by his agent, orally authorized, or can recover on it, — when under seal or not under seal;[1003] whether and how far you can "annex incidents" orally to a contract in writing;[1004] and whether and how far, after an agreement in writing, you can use a contemporaneous oral, "collateral," contract, as it is called;[1005] — all these questions, and many more of the same sort, although persistently thrown into the form of whether parol evidence be admissible for such purposes, really present no point in the law of evidence. The true inquiry is, whether certain claims or defences be allowable. If relief can be had in such cases, the law of evidence has nothing to say as to any kind of evidence, good under its general rules, which may be offered to prove these things. In so far as extrinsic facts are a legal basis of claim or defence, extrinsic evidence is good to prove them.

7. It will help to place the class of questions now under discussion in their right point of view if it be observed that the older law and the older decisions relating to them, were often mainly concerned in keeping matters out of the hands of juries. This motive

---

of this sort, even in his own person, is bound always and unconditionally, gave way long ago to more delicate conceptions."

[1000] Cummings v. Arnold, 3 Metcalf, 486.

[1001] Brick v. Brick, 98 U. S. 514; Campbell v. Dearborn, 109 Mass. 130

[1002] Martin v. Cole, 104 U. S. 30.

[1003] Briggs v. Partridge, 64 N. Y. 357. "It is ... difficult," says the court, "to reconcile the doctrine here stated with the role that parol evidence is inadmissible to change, enlarge, or vary a written contract." This form of expression disguises the true difficulty, that of allowing a recovery or a liability upon facts which only appear extrinsically, — a difficulty in point of substantive law. Once get over that, and the law of evidence interposes no obstacle.

[1004] Brown v. Burne. 3 El. & Bl. 703. Compare a discussion as to this sort of thing, where the contract was oral, in Gilbert v. McGinnis, 114 Ill. 28.

[1005] Chapin v. Dobson, 78 N. Y. 74; Emmett v. Penoyer, 151 N. Y. 564; Naumberg v. Young, 44 N. J. Law, 331. The last case puts forward a doctrine which appears to he an extreme and impracticable one. Compare Browne on Parol Evidence, c. xii.

appears in the language of the Statute of Fines,[1006] and in that of the Lord Keeper quoted above,[1007] and it seems to have had its place in bringing into existence the English Statute of Frauds.[1008] As to fines, any notion that absolutely and under all circumstances a fine or any other matter of record was beyond attack, belongs to a ruder period of jurisprudence than any known to our records; always there was power in the Crown, or "the king in parliament," or a regular power in the judges, to vacate and annul such matters;[1009] and when these things could be done, of course the evidence was receivable which was necessary in establishing the facts upon which the court was to act. But a jury, in the days when they went on their own knowledge and were not regularly aided by testimony, when the doctrine of new trials had not developed, and the main hold upon the jury was through the attaint, was quite too rude a tribunal to deal with this sacredest thing in the law. It would have been preposterous to let in such a body to revise the action of the judges in making record of what was done and established before them. Such things seemed less intolerable, as time went on and jury trial developed; and, accordingly, modifications of the rule came in.

It is an entire misconception to think of these things as involving any doctrine in the law of evidence.

III. Something has already been said of interpretation and construction. A great part of the space ordinarily given in books on evidence to the so-called "Parol Evidence Rule" is confusedly occupied by this subject.[1010]

"The construction or interpretation of written contracts," says Leake,[1011] "consists in ascertaining the meaning of the parties as expressed in the terms of the writing, according to the rules of grammar, and subject to the rules of law." In this statement two or three things should be noticed, namely, that no distinction is made

---

[1006] *Supra,* 407 n.

[1007] Gellibrand's case, supra, 407 n.

[1008] *Supra, 407 n.*

[1009] See a case in 1220 (2 Bract. Note Book, case 107), long before the Statute of Fines, where a collusive fine was quashed. See also 1 *ib..* Index, sub *voc.* Deceit.

[1010] "Perhaps," says Stephen (Dig. Evid., note to Art. 91, relating to the interpretation of documents), "the subject-matter of this article does not fall strictly within the law of evidence."

[1011] Dig. Cont. 217.

between construction and interpretation;[1012] that the process is said to be that of ascertaining the meaning of the parties so far only as it is expressed in the writing; and that the controlling authority is recognized of rules of language and rules of law. As regards these controlling rules and principles it has been well said: "All latitude of construction must submit to this restriction; namely, *that the words may bear the sense* which, by construction, is put upon them. If we step beyond this line, we no longer construe men's deeds, but make deeds for them."[1013] Obviously, this is no rule of evidence; it is one of the limitations upon the process of construction; nor does it change the real nature of this limitation when courts inadequately express it by saying that "evidence is not admissible" to prove what is thus excluded.[1014]

To say that the words must be capable of bearing the sense imputed to them, is to recognize that there must be what is called "a sufficient expression." How do we find out whether there be a sufficient expression? Not merely, in case of a real question, by contemplating the words of the text; but also by comparing them with persons, facts, and things outside. They are the words of a particular person, one or more; and the question is, what do his words mean? what is the meaning of the words, in his mouth? Whatever technical rules there be for construing legal language, whatever legal rules for construing ordinary language, whatever *prima facie* rules and presumptions, — these must all be allowed their proper application; and, at the end of it all, the sound judgment of the trained judicial mind, and, perhaps, the practical experience of a jury, must be appealed to. There must be no addition to the text of what is not in it. But when is a thing "in it"? It may be said to be there when a mind fully informed, and doing no violence to the rules of language and of legal construction, may reasonably find it there. This question is discussed by Wigram in connection with his third proposition;[1015] and his answer is, "The court... must be satisfied...;

[1012] It appears that neither common usage nor practical convenience in legal discussions supports the distinction, taken by Dr. Lieber in his "Legal and Political Hermenentics" (c. 1, § 8; c. 3, § 2), between interpretation and construction. I shall not discriminate them.

[1013] Eyre, C. B., in Gibson *v.* Minet, 1 H. Bl. p. 615 (1791); cited and applied in United States *v. U.* P. R. R. Co., 98 U. S. 86.

[1014] Black *v.* Batchelder, 120 Mass. 171.

[1015] Extrins. Ev. pl. 126 — 129.

and no other rule can in the abstract be laid down." It is a question more deeply considered by Hawkins,[1016] who gives the same answer.

One thing, however, is certain, and it is excellently brought out by Hawkins, — no man or court is competent or fully equipped for dealing with this question who has not carefully reflected upon the nature and necessary imperfections of language, and of all written expression. Such a person in approaching the question will remind himself that he has no right to expect more of written language than it is capable of, or more care in the use of it than fallible creatures, subject to time and accident, can reasonably supply. For a consideration of this aspect of the subject I must refer the reader to the discussion above referred to. By leave of the learned author, I have inserted it in an appendix.[1017] He has well pointed out that owing to these imperfections of language, to the facts that it is not, in itself, a perfect "code of signals," and that it is not used with perfect accuracy, there arises a necessity to look for other indications of intention, outside the text. "Interpretation," he says, "is a collecting of the intent from all available signs or marks, and an inquiry into the existence of a sufficient expression of that intent in the single set of signs called language.... The possibility of proceeding in the inquiry after the writer's meaning beyond the point at which the meaning of the words fails, is dependent on the assumption that a perfect written expression is not essential to the legal validity of the writing.... A law... which enjoined a perfect written expression, would, be impossible to be obeyed, and the command which gives rise to the necessity of the latter, in a legal writing, must be interpreted according to its spirit.... The question... is not what the writer meant, but what he has authorized the interpreter to say it is probable was his meaning. But if there be a total absence, not merely of intent, but of *indicia,* of marks or signs from which it is reasonably to be collected,... it is clear the process of interpretation must stop for want of materials.... The meaning of the words... is important in two ways: as a sign of the intent, and as a condition necessary to the legal validity of the writing. As a sign of the intent, it has yielded so far as to admit of other marks or signs being combined with it; as a legal requirement, its necessity

---

[1016] Princ. of Legal Interp., 2 Jurid. Soc. Papera, 298; *infra,* 577.
[1017] *Infra,* 577.

remains.... [Interpretation is] a process of reasoning from probabilities, a process of remedying by a sort of equitable jurisdiction, the imperfections of human language and powers of using language, a process whose limits are necessarily indefinite, and yet continually requiring to be practically determined; — and not... a mere operation requiring the use of grammars and dictionaries, a mere inquiry into the meaning of words."

Among these extrinsic facts, these outward "marks and signs," from which, as thus explained, in connection with the words of the document, and not from these words alone, the intention embodied in the written expression is to be collected, there is one thing which cannot, under our law, be used, namely, extrinsic expressions of the writer as to his intention in the writing. This is usually and rightly regarded as an excluding rule of evidence.

Of this single limitation upon the free and full range among extrinsic facts, in aid of interpretation, the writer from whom I have just quoted points out, as others have done, that it does not rest upon any lack of materiality and probative value in such direct statements of intention, but upon the impolicy and danger of using them. After mentioning that the preamble of a statute is constantly referred to in aid of the interpretation of the enactment, he neatly adds, that this fact "would, one should have thought, have prevented its ever being supposed that intention, *qua* intention, was a matter with which the interpreter had no business to concern himself."[1018] Of course, as was just said, there are reasons for rejecting such extrinsic expressions; and yet in other systems of law they are not wholly rejected, but only "subjected to severe scrutiny."

Let us trace the development and illustrate the character of some of these matters in the case of wills. In so far as it was true, before and after the Statute of Wills, in 1540,[1019] that writing was not legally necessary to a will, no doctrine about writings had any necessary application to these dispositions of property. Doubtless, wills very often were in writing, when this form was not legally necessary; and then, of course, there was scope for such a doctrine.[1020] The Statute of Wills, in allowing, generally, a devise of

---

[1018] 2Jurid. Soc. 314; *infra,* 591.

[1019] Stat. 32 H. VIII. c. 1; and compare Stat. 34 & 35 H. VIII. c. 5 (1542 — 1543).

[1020] *As* regards the earlier usages in the matter of putting wills in writing, see 1 Swinb. Testaments, ii. 5; 2 Black Book Adm. 71; Y. B. 20 & 21

lands, required writing, but it did not require signature.[1021] The Statute of Frauds (§ 5), in 1676, in the case of wills of real estate, added the requirements of signature and attesting witnesses; but as to personalty (§§ 19 — 23), it required no more than writing. It was not until the "Wills Act," in 1837,[1022] that the same formalities were necessary, in England, for all wills.

1. In 1568,[1023] where a man had devised land to his nephew, and the nephew died, leaving a son, and the testator thereafter orally told the son that he should have all which the will had given his father, it was held that the son took nothing. "All," said the court, "that can make the devise effectual ought to be in writing.... No will is within the statute but that which is in writing; which is as much as to say that all which is effectual and to the purpose must be in writing, without seeking aid of words not written." In 1587,[1024] where one had left land to the heirs of the body of his eldest son, and if he die without is — sue, to his two daughters in fee, — on the death of the testator, the eldest son was living, and also a son of his, who was tenant in the action. The defendant's witnesses swore to declarations of the testator that the daughters were to have nothing so long as the eldest son had issue of his body; "but the court utterly rejected the matter."

2. In a famous case, in 1591,[1025] there was a question upon a devise by Sir Thomas Cheyney, made in 1558 — 9, to his son Henry and the heirs of his body, remainder to Thomas Cheyney of

---

Edw. I. 264; 1 Calendar of Wills, London Court of Busting, Introduction, pp. xliv, xlv, and *passim.*

[1021] See a case in Keilwey, 209, pi. 9 (1557 — 1558), where one Atking, being called to prepare a last will for Henry Browne, took full notes, carried them home, and wrote out the will, finishing it before twelve o'clock at noon. On carrying this to Browne's house to read and deliver it to him, within half an hour after twelve, he found that the testator had died at twelve. "The clear opinion of all the justices was that this was a good will in writing, made according to the statute of the year 32 H. VIII." In like manner, to-day, undoubtedly, there exists a contract in writing, if the parties so arrange, without signature. Blackburn, Sale, 1st ed. 43, 44.

[1022] Stat. 1 Vict. c. 26, § 9.

[1023] Brett v. Rigdon, Plowd. 340.

[1024] Challoner *v.* Bowyer, 2 Leon. 70.

[1025] The Lord Cheyney'a case, 5 Co. 68. In the statement of this case in Moore, 727, the report is more detailed, more intelligible, and apparently more accurate; but the decision is not given. Coke's report, for the purposes which he has in hand, appears to be substantially accurate.

Woodley and the heirs male of his body, on condition "that *he or they, or any of them,* shall not alien, discontinue," etc. In the Court of Wards the question was whether this condition extended to the son of the devisor and his heirs, or only applied to Thomas Cheyney of Woodley and his heirs. This sort of question was an old one.[1026] As against those claiming under Henry, the question was whether the opposing party "should be received to prove by witnesses that it was the intent and meaning of the devisor to include his son and heir within these words of the condition (he or they),... but Wray and Anderson, Chief Justices, on conference had with other justices, resolved that he should not be received to such averment out of the will, for the will concerning lands, etc., ought to be in writing, and the construction of wills ought to be collected from the words of the will in writing, and not by any averment out of it; for it would be full of great inconvenience that none should know by the written words of a will what construction to make or advice to give, but it should be controlled by collateral averments out of the will."

The reader will observe the reasons here given namely, as wills of land must be in writing, so the construction of them must be collected from the written words, and not by any averment outside of them; — since people should be able to understand and give advice upon wills from the written words. This offer is not conceived of as in the earlier cases, just cited, as putting forward extrinsic matter which is contrary to the words of the will, or which adds to them, and asking to have effect given to it as if it were duly written out as a will; but as offering it, in aid of construction, in a case where a will uses words which, on their face, admit of either application, yet fix upon neither. It should be observed that we do not know just how this question came up; all that is said in either report is that "it was a question." Nor are we told what the facts were which were offered in order to prove "the intent and meaning." But the subsequent discussion seems to identify the offer, in legal effect, with that of direct statements of intention; for, as contrasted with this case, it is presently said, that in equivocation of names, "he may produce witnesses to prove his father's intent, — that he thought the other to be dead, or that he, at the time of the will named, named his son John the younger, and the writer left out the addition of the younger." It is also to be observed that the judges identify the question of evidence

---

[1026] *Infra,* 423 and note.

with that of pleading; it is "an averment out of the will" that is bad, *i. e.,* an allegation in pleading. To say that you cannot have an averment of facts is to say that you cannot have an issue on it, you cannot go to the jury on it. Here, the question being whether the party "should be received to prove by witnesses" the intent of the devisor, the answer is that he cannot, because he may not have such an averment, *i. e.,* he cannot, in such a case, found any claim on the intent. We may observe, then, that the difficulty is not conceived of as one in the law of evidence, — as, indeed, we might be pretty sure it would not be, at so early a period.

But there is more in this report. It became necessary to discriminate that exceptional case above alluded to, familiar in all systems of law. For centuries there had arisen certain familiar questions of ambiguity. In matters of record, in specialties, and in other writings, there had often been occasion to deal with the problem of a name or description equally fitting two or more persons, places, or things. The wrong man having the right name was often in trouble. He had been arrested and brought into court on an *exigent* in outlawry; or, in the case of a fine or a common recovery, he had had his land claimed by another; or he was sued on a bond given by another; or himself claimed a devise intended for another. These situations and the like are familiar all through the Year Books.[1027] The doctrine has already been mentioned[1028] that although, if a man were to levy a fine on my lands in my name, I should lose my land, yet if there were two of my name "I can show that I am not the person, but that there is another." Under such circumstances one of the persons could be subtracted from the operation of the fine, because this still left it operative upon another; this averment could "stand with the words." Long before that, the civilians, also, like the dramatists, had sharpened their wits upon complicated imaginary mischances of such personages. For example, a scholastic question was put forward thus: There were two brothers, of the same name, and extraordinarily like each other. Each begat a boy, so like his cousin that neither of the fathers knew them apart, they had the same name, and each was loved and treated as his

---

[1027] Walter Brunne's case, Pl. Ab. 280, col. 1 (1287); Fitz. Ab. *Feff.* 56; s. c. 47 Ed. III. 16, 29 (1373); Y. B. 11 H. VI. 13 (1432); Coteler v. Hall, 5 Ed. IV. (Long Quint) 40 b, 1465; s. c. *ib* 48 b, 54 b, 74 b, 80 b, 90,97 b, and Y. B. 5 Ed. IV. 6, 6; Y. B. 11 H. VII. 6, 4 (1496).

[1028] *Supra,* 407 n.

own by both fathers. By and by, both boys went to Bologna as students; one died there: both the fathers died; the surviving boy returned home and laid claim to the inheritance of both the fathers, as having reckoned each of them to be his own, and having been treated by each as his son. The question was whether he could have both inheritances, or neither, or either one. The matter is discussed at length all ways, and finally it is resolved thus: As a matter of strict law he can have neither, because he does not clearly make out his claim. But on equitable grounds he shall have that inheritance which seems most likely to be his.[1029]

The established doctrine in our law, in this class of cases, was that the intention should govern. Clearly, only one person or thing was intended. Either one was adequately described if taken alone, but neither was discriminated; an infirmity in the written expression left it uncertain which was meant. This was a strait from which there was no outlet; unless, indeed, you looked beyond the paper, and gave effect to extrinsic matter in aid of construction. So far, therefore, as men dreamed of interpreting records or any other writings without using extrinsic matter as a lamp to read them by, here was a situation that forever tended to undeceive them.[1030]

[1029] Azo, *Quæstiones,* ed. Landsberg (Freiburg, 1888), 38 — 44, II. Azo it will be remembered, was a famous professor of law at Bologna, at the beginning of the thirteenth century, and the source of much that is found in Bracton; as may be seen in Maitland, *Select Passages from Bracton and Azo;* being vol. viii. of the Selden Society Publications.

[1030] There were other provocations in the same direction. It was clearly recognized in slander, whether written or oral, that the meaning of words Bay depend upon the circumstances under which they are uttered. In 1S77 (the Lord Cromwell's case, 4 Co. Rep. 11 b, "the first cause which the author of this book, who was of counsel with the defendant, moved in the King's Bench"), the court is reported as saying that "in case of Blander by words, the sense of the words ought to be taken, and the sense of them appears by the cause and occasion of speaking of them. . . . The defendant's counsel have done well to show the special matters by which the sense of this word (sedition) appears upon the coherence of all the words." And Coke goes on to tell his reader to note "an excellent point of learning in actions for slander, to observe the occasion and cause of speaking of them, and how it may be pleaded in the defendant's excuse," and to beware of a hasty demurrer in such cases.In contracts, also, it was always recognized that familiar words may have different meanings in different places, so that "every bargain as to such a thing shall have relation to the custom of the country where it is made" (Keilwey, 87, 3, in the Ex. Ch. in 1505). In Baker *v.* Paine, 1 Ves. p. 459 (1750), Lord Hardwicke, in a mercantile case of sale, remarked: "All contracts of this kind depend on the usage of trade. . . . On mercantile contracts relating to

Coke, in his report of the Lord Cheyney's case, after what is stated above, goes on to deal with this old, familiar instance: "But if a man has two sons, both baptized by the name of John, and conceiving that the elder (who had been long absent) is dead, devises his land by his will in. writing to his son John generally, and in truth the elder is living; in this case the younger son may, in pleading or in evidence, allege the devise to him, and if "it be denied, he may produce witnesses to prove his father's intent, that he thought the other to be dead; or that he at the time of the will made, named his son John the younger, and the writer left out the addition of the younger; for in. 47 Ed. 3, 16 b," etc.; — and then he cites a famous case of two William Peynels, in 1373, and discriminates such cases on the ground that they involve no "secret, invisible averment." "He who sees the will... ought at his peril to inquire which John the testator intended, which may easily be known by him who wrote the will, and others who were privy to his intent." But if the intent be not ascertainable, the will, we are then told, is void for uncertainty; since the law makes no construction in favor of either, giving it to him whom the father intended, "and for want of proof of such intent the will... is void."[1031] This problem and this solution of it were also found in

---

insurances, etc., courts of law examine and hear witnesses of what is the usage and understanding of merchants conversant therein; for they have a style peculiar to themselves, which is short, yet is understood by them, and must be the rule of construction." The development of the mercantile law by the use of special juries in volved a recognition of these same ideas.

[1031] In the Year Book from which Coke cites it, this case is reported substantially as follows: "William, son of Robert Peynel, brings a Scire *Facias* on a fine levied between this Robert and others, by which ... [a manor was granted and rendered] to this same Robert, and William; and the younger son sues the issue of the eldest son. *Fulthorp* (for the defendant) told how the remainder was tailed to his father . . . and Robert died, and his father entered and died seised, and he is now in *as* heir. *Hasty* (for the plaintiff) said that the fine was levied to the intent to give the inheritance to him, and therefore the part of the fine was delivered to him by his father Robert at the time of his death, — making protestation that he did not acknowledge that there was any such William, oldest son of Robert, or that he survived his father, or was seised; for he died in Robert's lifetime. Fyncheden (C. J.). This is only evidence: it cannot make an issue in law or in fact, whether the fine was levied to the intent of giving the inheritance to one or to the other. H*asty* then said that the fine was levied to give the inheritance to him, — making protestation as before. *Persey* (for the defendant), the fine was levied to give the inheritance to our father."Brooke in giving this case (Abr. *Fines,* 28, and *Nosme,* 63), notwithstanding what is said in the report, adds to his

the Roman law. In the Digest we read a response of such as had
been discriminated Cheyney's case; namely, the old instance of
two things or persons of the same name. There, he says, since the
writing is clear upon its face, and the ambiguity only appears
extrinsically, you may remedy it extrinsically, and even by
averring the actual intention of the writer, since the form of the
writing really does describe the thing or person intended. And
then, fancifully, he speaks of another sort of *ambiguitas latens,*
where the same person or thing is designated by different names,
and allows an averment of some extrinsic matter here, such. as
goes to identify the person or thing, but not an averment of
intention, since the intention "doth not stand with the words."

---

memorandum of it: "And go see an issue on the intent; and see 12 H. VII. 6, that
where a man has manors of upper S. and Lower S., and levies a fine of the manor
of S., it shall be taken as that manor of the two about which they conferred and
had conversation, and which the conusor intended to pass. . . . The intent shall be
taken; that is, the manor shall pass which the conusor intended should
pass."Fitzherbert's account of it (*Feff.* 56) is taken from another report. W. here
figures as the son of R. H. *"Ham. (semble,* Hannemere). He shall not have
execution, for R. H. had a son older than yon, named W., who was our father, and
there was a talk between J. and R. H. that W. the oldest son should marry J.'s
daughter, and the remainder be tailed to our father, the oldest, according to the
purport of the fine; and thereupon the fine was levied, and then R. died, and our
father entered, and died seised, and we entered as heir. *Hasty* (for the plaintiff).
The fine was levied to the intent that we should inherit, and thereupon R. H. at the
time of his death delivered us a part of the fine. Fyncheden (C. J.). You shall not
take issue on the intent, for the intent does not lie to averment. But if I lease land
for life, remainder to one W. T. by fine, ad there are two W. T.'s in the country, I
say that he who first happens upon the remainder shall not keep it against the
other, if he cannot prove that the remainder was tailed to him by his name, and
that he was the same person. *Belknup.* We understand that if the remainder he
tailed *to W.* T., and there be two W. T.'s, father and son, the father shall have It.
Fyncheden. He to whom the remainder is tailed shall have it, and no other." The
reporter adds: *"Hasty,* because of the court's opinion, rid, the remainder was
tailed to us as the fine purports. Ready. *Ham. It* was tailed to our father, and not to
you. Ready. *Et alli e contra."*It may be surmised that Brooke misconceives this
case. The court teems clearly to refuse an issue upon intention, and puts the
matter solidly on the question, so far as the pleading goes, "Who is it that the
document calls for?" The court at that period (1373) is not troubling itself to how
the jury is going to deal with the question. Doubtless, if they, w any of them,
should happen to have tidings of any declarations of the writer, these would have
their full natural effect in influencing the verdict. As to putting evidential matter
into the pleadings, and why you should insert it there, and how, and how much,
— a century and a half of curious.

In Edward Altham's case,[1032] in 1610, these distinctions are gone over again; but the word "ambiguity," patent or latent, does not occur, and there is no sign of any knowledge of Bacon's phrases. A case of equivocation in a fine is stated, and an averment of intention. "This averment out of the fine is good,... which well stands with the words." But (citing Year Book cases) a gift to one of the sons of J. S., who has divers, and a limitation to two *et haeredibus,* are uncertain, and void by judgment of law, "and no averment *dehors* can make that good which upon consideration of the deed is apparent to be void."

Bacon's maxim was an unprofitable subtlety. In truth, the only patent ambiguity that was not open to explanation by extrinsic matter was one that, in the nature of things, was not capable of explanation. Anything which was capable of it might be explained, as in the case put by Wigram [1033] of "a legacy to one of the children of A by her late husband B. Suppose, further," he adds, "that A has only one son by B, and that the fact was known to the testator,... no principle or rule of law would... preclude a court from acting upon the evidence of facts by which the meaning of an apparently ambiguous will would, in such a case, be reduced to certainty." [1034] Generally speaking, ambiguities, or any other difficulties, patent or latent, are all alike as regards the right and duty to compare the documents with extrinsic facts, and as regards the possibility that they may vanish when this is done. As to the resort to direct statements of intention, in the one case of "equivocation," namely, where there are more than one whom the name or description equally fits, the right to resort to these declarations in such cases in no way depends on the difference between what is patent and latent.[1035]

[1032] 8 Co. p.155.

[1033] Extr. EV. pl. 79.

[1034] Compare the case put by Elphinstone (3 Jurid. Soc. Pap. 266) of a gift "to my nephew John or Thomas," where, extrinsically, it might appear that the nephew wag known to the testator by both these names. And see the language of Sir Thomas Plumer in Colpoys v. Colpoys, Jacob, p. 463 (1822), declaring that "it has never been considered an objection to the reception of the evidence of ... circumstances that the ambiguity was patent, manifested on the face of the instrument."

[1035] Doe d. Gortl *v.* Needs, 2 M. & W. 129; 1 Jarm. Wills (5th Eng. ed.), 400-401; Browne, Parol Ev. p. v, ss. 49, 126; Graves, Extrinsic Evid., Proc.

The great citation in the discussions of the seventeenth century and the first half of the eighteenth was the Lord Cheyney's case. When Bacon's maxim was first brought to the general notice of the profession, — namely, I believe, about the year 1761, — it appeared no longer in its original character as a maxim relating to averments, *i. e.,* to pleading, but to evidence; and it has since almost always been quoted in this sense. But it has been well remarked by an acute writer that "We should commit an injustice to the memory of our great lawyer and philosopher if we looked upon this valuable fragment as if it purported to be a complete dissertation upon the use of extrinsic evidence in the judicial interpretation of legal instruments.... It is worth while to observe that the immediate subject, both of the maxim and the commentary, is not evidence, but pleading; and although, no doubt, the pleadings would guide the judge as to the issues upon which evidence would be received, they would not necessarily determine the nature of the evidence admissible upon each issue."[1036]

4. It was known that construction must take some account of the things and persons of which the document spoke. To some extent this must always have included the conditions, circumstances, and relations out of the midst of which and with reference to which the writer spoke. But the courts were shy of going far in that direction; indeed of going at all beyond the bounds which, limit the identifying process, that of ascertaining, in the simplest sense, the persons and things named in the writing.

In 1651,[1037] in ejectment, it appeared upon a special verdict that one who had real estate, and also had goods and chattels worth only five pounds, gave to his wife, by will, "his whole estate, paying debts and legacies," and these debts and legacies amounted to forty pounds. It was held that the lands passed, as well as the goods, and ail estate in fee simple. "Hales" (afterwards the Chief Baron and. Chief Justice, Sir Matthew Hale) argued, for the plaintiff, that the intention to devise both lands and goods appeared. by "the ordinary

---

of Va. Bar Assoc. for 1893; Hawking, 2 Jur. Soc. Pap. 324: "This rule is not in any way contained or implied in the maxim of latent and patent ambiguities."

[1036] F. M. Nichols, Extrinsic Evidence in the Interpretation of Wills, 2 Jurid. Soc. Pap. 351, 378 (Dec. 1860).

[1037] Kirman *v.* Johnson, Style, 293. It is noticeable how few the extrinsic facts are in the earlier special verdicts of this sort; *i. e.,* such as supply the Court with the facts needed in construing a document.

manner of speech.... Also, the subject-matter in fact doth prove this to be his intent; and although here is not a collateral averment to prove the intention, but a collateral proof to declare the testator's intent, this may be admitted to ascertain the court of his meaning, as it is in proving an Act of Parliament. In the Lord. Cheyney's case, an averment standing with a will was accounted allowable, though an averment against a will be not," etc.

In 1702,[1038] on a special verdict in ejectment, it was set forth that a widow died seised and possessed of the Bell Tavern and certain leasehold estates; and that her will provided, — "I give, ratify, and confirm all my estate, right, title, and interest which I now have, and all the term and terms of years which I now have, or may have in my power to dispose of after my death, in whatsoever I hold by lease from Sir John Freeman, and also the house called the Bell Tavern, to John Billingsley." This J. B. was the son and heir of the widow's husband, and the son also of the widow, who had another son by a former husband. The husband being seised in fee of the Bell Tavern, had settled it for the use of himself for life, remainder to his wife for life, remainder to his son in tail, remainder to his wife in fee. The question now was what estate John Billingsley took in the Bell Tavern, under the widow's devise, whether a life estate in the reversion, or the fee. A majority of the judges, Powell, Powys, and Gould, held (and it was affirmed afterwards in the Exchequer Chamber and the House of Lords) that he took an estate in fee. They relied in part on the fact that she knew that he was already tenant in tail under the settlement and "could not have intended so vain and useless an estate... as an estate for life after an estate tail."

To us of the present time that decision seems equally good sense and good law. But observe the dissent and the reasoning of Chief Justice Holt, the greatest lawyer of them all. He was unwilling to admit that what appeared upon the interpretation of the words, taken alone, to be a life estate, should become an estate in fee through the interpreter's having examined the terms of the father's

---

[1038] Cole *v.* Rawlinson, 1 Salk. 234; s. c. 2 Lord Raym. 831,3 Bro. P. C. 7. The facts of this case, and the relation of the various parties involved in it to each other, are more fully and, as it would seem, more accurately given in 3 Bro. P. C. 7, where there is a brief account of the arguments of counsel in the House of Lords, but only a bare statement of the result reached by the Lords, in 1705. It appears from this report that Chief Justice Trevor, in the Exchequer Chamber, dissented from the opinion of the majority.

settlement. " Holt, O. J., *contra,* for the intent of a testator will not do, unless there be sufficient words in the will to manifest that intent; neither is his intent to be collected from the circumstances of his estates, and other matters collateral and foreign to the will, bat from the words and tenor of the will itself; and if we once travel into the affairs of the testator, and leave the will, we shall not know the mind of the testator by his words, but by his circumstances; so that if you go to a lawyer, he shall not know how to expound it. Upon the will 'tis so; but upon the matter found in a special verdict, 'tis otherwise; and what if more accidental circumstances be discovered, and be made the matter of another verdict? Men's rights will be very precarious upon such construction. And as for the honesty of the construction, what if the woman paid a good portion, and was purchaser of this reversion, is it not as honest then to construe it in favor of her heir as to expound it in favor of the right heir of the husband? But we must not depart from the will to find the meaning of it in things out of it. 'Tis then a certain rule that to devise lands to H without farther words, will pass but an estate for life, unless there be other words to show his intent, as forever; or unless he devise for some special purpose which cannot be accomplished without a larger estate; and as this is a sure rule, so it holds good as well where the devise is of a reversion as where 'tis of lands in possession, unless he devise it as a reversion, or take notice of a particular estate, for then his intent may appear upon the face of the will itself; but if the words be general, and without regard to the nature of the thing, it is otherwise, for it shall not be construed from the nature of the thing, which is extrinsical, but from the words of the will. Ask a lawyer what passes: he says an estate for life, for he knew not that it was a reversion; and though it be a fruitless estate, and will signify nothing, yet that does not appear till it be found, and therefore when found 'tis not to be regarded."

The Chief Justice here retires into that lawyer's Paradise where all words have a fixed, precisely ascertained meaning; where men may express their purposes, not only with accuracy, but with fulness; and where, if the writer has been careful, a lawyer, having a document referred to him, may sit in this chair, inspect the text, and answer all questions without raising his eyes. Men have dreamed of attaining for their solemn muniments of title such an absolute security; and some degree of security they have compassed by giving strict definitions and technical meanings to words and phrases, and by rigid rules of construction. But the fatal necessity of looking outside the text in order to identify persons and things, tends steadily to destroy such illusions and to reveal the essential imperfection of language, whether spoken or written.[1039]

5. Courts of equity by the end of the seventeenth century, besides looking more freely at extrinsic facts, had begun to use a writer's extrinsic expressions of intention in a much freer way than courts of law. Adhering to the rule that extrinsic intention must not be used to displace or vary that of the writing, they nevertheless found many ways of using it, and even of using the direct oral expression of it. These courts, having no jury, had not before them, in listening to whatsoever evidence might help them, the apprehension so often expressed by the common-law judges that "it is not safe to admit a jury to try the intent of the testator."[1040] It must be remembered what such a fear at that period meant. Not yet had any distinct system of rules for excluding evidence come into existence.[1041] The power of judges to set aside verdicts as being against the evidence had begun to be exercised, but had not got far. The attaint was still the regular way of controlling the jury, and this had practically lost its hold. The jury still held its old character and function, might decide on its own knowledge alone, and, if it heard evidence, might reject it all. This power of the jury, and its exemption from fine and imprisonment for deciding against the evidence, were vindicated in Bushell's case in 1670.[1042] The Statute of Frauds, six years later, relieved against this state of things, by requiring in a great many cases that there should be a writing, or some other specific act or formality, before an action could be brought or a claim established. This had the same effect which attended a requirement of the sixteenth century and later, that in certain cases there should be two witnesses, or at least one witness;[1043] it said, in effect, that it should no longer be true that the

---

[1039] *"The* rule," said Lord Hardwicke, about half a century later, in citing Cole *v.* Rawlinson, "is laid down much too large by Holt." Goodinge. Goodinge, 1 Ves. 231 (1749).

[1040] Powell, J., in Lawrence v. Dodwell, 1 Lutw. 734 (1698).

[1041] *Supra,* 179,180.

[1042] Vaughau, 135.

[1043] Stats. 1 Ed. VI. c. 12, § 22 (1547); 5 & 6 Ed. VI. c. 11, § 12 (1552), requiring two witnesses in cases of treason; and 21 Jac. I. c. 27 (1623), where the mother of a bastard child who conceals its death is punished as for murder, unless

verdict of a jury was enough, whether there were witnesses or not. After the Statute of Frauds, — a very extraordinary enactment to have been passed by an English-speaking community in any age, so comprehensive is it and so far-reaching,[1044] — no jury could find a contract of the sort named in. § 4, unless there were a writing; or one named in § 17, unless there were either a writing or one of the facts there specified; no jury could find a devise of real estate without a signature and witnesses, as required in § 5, or a will of personalty without writing, except under circumstances indicated in §§ 19 to 23. To the most important dealings of men the Statute of Frauds gave new security. It is not probable that so wide-reaching an act could have been passed if jury trial had been on the footing which it holds to-day.[1045] And in construing the statute it was entirely natural that different ideas and methods should prevail in the equity and the common-law courts. "This is not," said an equity court, in 1708,[1046] in considering the question of hearing oral statements of a testator's intention, "like the case of evidence to a jury, who are easily biased by it, which this court is not." In 1736 we read in Bacon's Abridgment[1047] that the rule of rejecting "parol evidence... to control what appeared on the face of a deed or will... has received a relaxation, especially in the courts of equity, where a distinction has been taken between evidence that may be offered to a jury, and to inform the conscience of the court, namely, that in the first case no such evidence should be admitted, because the jury might be inveigled thereby; but that in the second it could do no hurt, because the court were judges of the whole matter, and could distinguish what weight and stress ought to be laid on such evidence."

It was for doing this sort of thing that Lord Hardwicke, in 1742, complained of his predecessor, Cowper (1705 — 1710): "He

---

she prove, "by one witness at the least," that the child was born dead. See Hale's practice under this statute, 2 Hale, Cr. Law, 289; *supra,* 179 n.

[1044] [It] "carries its influence through the whole body of our civil jurisprudence, and is in many respects the most comprehensive, salutary, and important legislative regulation on record affecting the security of private rights." — 2 Kent, Com. 494, note.

[1045] *Supra,* 180. Compare Cave, J., in Hoare *v.* Evans, [1892] 1 Q. B, 593, 597.

[1046] Strode *v.* Russell, 3 Rep. Ch. 169. The Lord Chancellor Cowper appears to be speaking. He was assisted by the Master of the Bolls, Trevor, C. J., and Tracy, J.

[1047] Vol. 2, p. 309.

went upon this ground, that it was by way of assisting his judgment, in cases extremely dark and doubtful.... I was never satisfied with this rule of Lord Cowper's, of admitting parol evidence in doubtful wills; besides, he went farther in the great case of Strode *v.* Russell."[1048] In 1708, Lord Cowper seemed to allow this as a regular practice when the declarations were consistent with the will: "Where the words stand *in equilibrio,* and are so doubtful that they may be taken one way or the other, there it is proper to have evidence read to explain them, and we will consider how far it shall be allowed, and how far not after it is read;... and the distinction in Cheyney's case well warrants the reading of evidence where the intent of the testator is doubtful, as there where a man had two sons, named John, etc., which my Lord Chancellor said differed not from this case, where the words hang in equal balance what settlement he intended."[1049] Cowper had held the same thing in 1705, where a bequest gave all the testator's household goods, as woollen, linen, pewter, and brass whatsoever, except a certain trunk. The writer of the will was offered to show that the testator directed him to insert all his goods, except the trunk; "and my Lord Keeper thought it might [be allowed], notwithstanding the Statute of Frauds and Perjuries, for it here neither adds to nor alters the will, but only explains which of the meanings shall be taken, as in case of a devise to son John where the testator had two of the same name."[1050] And in 1750 — 1751,[1051] Sir John Strange, Master of the Rolls, said: "The distinction as to admitting parol evidence I have always taken to be that in no instance it shall be admitted in contradiction to the words of the will; but if words of the will are doubtful and ambiguous, and unless some reasonable light is let in to determine that, the will will fall to the ground, anything to explain, not to contradict, the will, is always admitted. So it is in the case of having two sons of the same name," etc.

[1048] Ulrich *v.* Litchfield, 2 Atk. 372.

[1049] Strode *v.* Russell, 3 Rep. Ch. 169. This was not a case of equivocation.

[1050] Pendleton *v.* Grant, 1 Eq. Cas. Ab. 230, 2; s. c. 2 Vern. 517, where the gift reads: "I give my household stuff, as brass, pewter, linen, and woollen whatsoever, except a trunk under the chamber window." And so Docksey *v.* Docksey, 8 Vin Ab. 195.

[1051] Hampshire *v.* Pierce, 2 Ves. 216.

In these passages, it will be noticed, the old case of two persons or things of the same name holds the place, not of an exception, as it does now, but of an instance under a general principle. Sometimes this principle seems to have been conceived of as covering all cases of an equilibrium upon the evidence; and sometimes to have been limited to errors or uncertainties as to names and persons; and in such cases resort could be had generally to the testator's oral declarations.[1052] In 1707 a testator had devised an estate, charged with the payment of a debt of, £100 to one Shaw. It turned out that this sum was due, not to Shaw, but to Alice Beck, then the wife of one Fitch. The devisees refused to pay her. In a bill, apparently to enforce payment, the plaintiff was allowed to show by the scrivener that the testator said he meant the £100 which was due Mrs. Fitch; "the Lord Chancellor [Cowper] declaring he saw no hurt in admitting of collateral proof to make certain the person or the thing described."[1053] In 1718, [1054] where a legacy was given, to Mrs. Sawyer, and there was no such person known to the testatrix, it was alleged that she meant Mrs. Swopper; and a master was directed to inquire who was meant, "and whether the testatrix meant Mrs. Swopper." So, in the well-known case of Beaumont v. Fell,[1055] in 1723, where, under a bequest to Catherine Earnley, Gertrude Yardley was allowed to take, evidence was admitted of declarations of the testator that he would do well for her by his will." And Lord Hardwicke, in considering a testator's declarations of his meaning, repeatedly recognized some such rule; as in 1742: "I do not know that upon the construction of a will courts of law or equity admit parol evidence, except in two cases, — first, to ascertain the person, where there are two of the same name, or else where there has been a mistake in a Christian or surname; and this upon an absolute necessity; as in Lord Cheyney's case, where there were two sons of the name of John.... The second case is with regard to resulting trusts relating to personal estate, where a man makes a will and appoints an

---

[1052] See Roberts, Frauds, 16, 17; Wigram, Ext. Ev. pi. 157, 158.

[1053] Hodgson v. Hodgson, 2 Vern. 593; s. c. 1 Eq. Cas. Ab. 231. In the margin to this report it is stated that in Free. Ch. 229, the case is given as one where the testator had given the woman's maiden name, having forgotten that of her husband. But the report in Prec. Ch. does not support this statement.

[1054] Masters v. Masters, I P. Wms. 421.

[1055] 2 P. Wms. 141.

executor with a small legacy, and the next of kin claim the residue."[1056]

In 1749, where there was a legacy to such of a man's nearest relations, as his executors "should think poor and objects of charity," "evidence was then offered of the testator's having poor relations in Salop, and that he knew thereof; to which was objected the rule by Holt, C. J., in Cole *v.* Rawlinson, that the intention of the testator is not to be collected from collateral and. foreign circumstances. Lord Chancellor (Hardwicke): "That rule is laid. down much too large by Holt; for in several cases it is admitted that it must be allowed, namely, where the description or thing is uncertain, (not only "where two of the same name), it must be admitted to show that the testator knew such a person, and used to call her by a nickname. Although parol evidence cannot be read to prove instructions of the testator, after the will is reduced into writing, or declarations whom he meant by written words of the will, yet that is different from reading it to prove that the testator knew he had such relations, to establish which fact it may be read, but not to go any farther. And though this is a nice distinction, yet it is a distinction in the reason of the thing." About a year later,[1057] in construing a gift by will "to the four children of my late cousin Elizabeth Bamfield," it appeared that she had six children, two by a former husband, Poddlecomb, and four by a later one, Bamfield. The Master of the Rolls, Sir John Strange, in dealing with an argument that the word "four" should be rejected, and a counter offer to show the extrinsic declarations of the testatrix, said: "As there is some uncertainty, I have admitted the going into evidence to explain the intent of the testatrix in the expression 'the four.'... The testatrix declared... that she had provided for Mrs. Bamfield's four children. Now though the expression in the will might take those by the first, as well as the second husband, yet this, which I think is proper evidence, shows plainly that her declaration was the four children of Mrs. Bamfield...; which explains what she meant by the four children; but she also puts a negative on the other two;... so that taking this on the face of the will, in which also the circumstances of the

---

[1056] Ulrich v. Litchfleld, 2 Atk. 372. So also in Baylis *v.* Attorney-General, 2 Atk. 239 (1741).

[1057] Hampshire *v.* Pierce, 2 Ves. 216.

family must be taken altogether, it appears clearly that the four children by the second husband were those meant to share the £100."

In some of the cases at this period it may be noticed that the question seems to be made a general one, whether any extrinsic matter, any "parol evidence," any "collateral proof," may be looked at; when, in reality, the question is whether a particular kind of evidence of intention,is receivable, namely, the direct expressions of the writer. This indiscriminate use of the phrase "parol evidence" has always been one of the sources of confusion in dealing with this subject. Often there really is this more general Question; and the question is, whether the text is not governed by some rigid rule, or marked by some peculiarity, such as to make it impossible to help the text by extrinsic matter, — as where words with a technical legal meaning are used, like the word "heirs," or where the absence of such words forbids a given construction, or where there is an ambiguity or imperfection of expression which in its nature is incurable; as a gift "to one of the sons of J. S.," or "to Mr. — —." In such cases, of course, no "parol evidence" can help.

Sometimes, admitting that it is necessary to look into extrinsic facts to some extent, the question is whether you can go farther than to identify the persons and things named in the text.[1058] And then, again, another special question; namely, admitting that you may look into almost all outside facts, the question whether you are forbidden to look at extrinsic evidence of intention. And again, admitting that you may look at extrinsic facts generally, even those tending to prove intention, the question is, whether you can regard the writer's own direct statements of intention. And, unfortunately, in our cases, every one of these discriminated questions is often put as a general question whether parol evidence is admissible.

6. In the eighteenth century two sources are visible of a liberalizing influence in this matter of interpretation: one proceeding from the rising system of commercial law, and the other from the conceptions of the Roman law operating through the ecclesiastical courts and the courts of equity. We see a glimpse of the former in Lord Hardwicke's remark in an important case in 1753.[1059] The plaintiff, who had bought in the market a Navy Bill indorsed by

---

[1058] Holt, C. J, in Cole v. Rawlinson, *ubi supra;* Kurtz v. Hihner, 55 Ill 514; Lord Hatherley in Charter v. Charter, L.r. 7 H. L. 364.

[1059] Ekins v. Maclish, Ambler, 184.

defendant's agent, had been held accountable for it in trover on the ground of lack of authority in the agent; and he now sought and got relief in equity against the verdict and judgment in the King's Bench. One question was on the construction of a letter of attorney, and Lord Hardwieke gave effect to "the custom among merchants, to explain the letter of attorney, as in case of policy of insurance, which could not be otherwise understood. Perhaps the judges of the Court of King's Bench thought the construction to be on the letter of attorney itself without such evidence. In this court it is otherwise.... The credit of the funds depends on the facility of transacting them; and therefore nice and critical construction is not to be put on these powers, either at law or in equity; but the usage must be regarded." We are, of course, very familiar, at the present day, with the liberal methods of the courts in interpreting what Baron Parke called "mercantile short hand."[1060] Of the other influence above mentioned, one may see illustrations, not merely in the whole tendency and general methods of the equity courts, but in their way of dealing with wills of personalty. In a case in 1723,[1061] a legacy to Catherine Earnley was awarded to Gertrude Yardley, on peculiar facts, tending to show very clearly a misapprehension on the scrivener's part in taking down the name "Gatty" Yardley, and an intention on the testator's to name her. There was no person with the name of Catherine Earnley. The Master of the Rolls said: "If this had been a grant, nay, had it been a devise of land, it had been void by reason of the mistake both of the Christian and surname.... However, this being a bequest of a personal thing, a chattel interest, makes it a different case, and as originally a bequest of a legacy was governed by and construed according to the rules of the civil canon law, so shall it be after making the Statute of Frauds, provided there be a will in writing.... The name and not the person is mistaken; and it is very material that here is no such person as Catherine Earnley claiming this legacy." In this case no distinction was taken as to the kinds of evidence of intention; direct oral statements were included with the other facts.[1062]

[1060] Marshall *v.* Lynn, 6 M. & W. 109. See, *e. g.*, Brown *v.* Byrne, 3 El & Bl 703, and Salmon Falls Man. Co. v. Goddard, 14 How. 446.

[1061] Beanmont v. Fell, 2 P. Williams, 141.

[1062] Had there been a jurisdiction for reforming wills, perhaps a question of that sort might have arisen here. See Stephen's recommendation for giving the courts such a power. Dig. of Evid. (3d ed.) Preface, p. xxxvii. For the

7. In one of the cases above mentioned,[1063] Lord Hardwicke mentions a famous sort of instance that figured much in the books for a century and a half, from the English Revolution to the Statute 1 Wm. IV. c. 40, in the year 1830. It was the rule of English law that where a testator left personal estate undisposed of, and appointed an executor, this personage took the surplus. "At law it has been the rule from the earliest period that the whole personal estate devolves on the executor; and if, after payment of the funeral expenses, testamentary charges, debts, and legacies, there shall be any surplus, it shall vest in him beneficially."[1064] On the top of this, however, the equity courts laid down a presumptive rule of construction, that if the will showed a gift to the executor, this indicated a purpose not to give him the surplus; and in such a case he was held, *prima facie,* not entitled to it. A contrary intention might, indeed, be apparent from the whole will; and if it were not, it was allowed to appear by the oral declarations of the testator. Such declarations, it will be observed, supported the general *prima facie* right of an executor; they were only received "to rebut the equity" which denied that right. Although when these declarations were received they might be met by others in a contrary sense, yet no declarations were directly and in the first instance receivable to contradict the general legal right of the executor.[1065] Nor, where the construction of the will was plain against the executor, as in the case, at least in modern times, where the gift was, in terms, for his care and trouble, was any effect at all allowed to extrinsic declarations of intention.[1066] This matter, for the most part, came to an end in 1830 by the Statute 1 Wm. IV. c. 40. The doctrine before that having been that "the executor shall take beneficially, unless there is a strong and violent presumption that he shall not so take,"[1067] now, the statute made him a trustee of the residue for the next of kin, "unless it shall appear by the will or any

---

questions that come up in establishing the *factum of* a will, in courts of probate, see Guardhouse *v.* Blackburn, L. B. 1 P. & D. 109. "The question in such cases," said Sir J. P. Wilde, "is not what intention ought to be assigned to the words of a given written paper, but to what extent does a given written paper express the testamentary intentions of the deceased."

[1063] Ulrich *v.* Litchfield, 2 Atk. 372.

[1064] 2 Williams, Executors, 1327 (5th Am. ed.).

[1065] Lady Osborne *v.* Villiers, 2 Eq. Cas. Ab. 416, 12; Cloyne *v.* Young, 2 ves. 95.

[1066] 2 Langham *v.* Sanford, 17 Ves. 435 (1811).

[1067] Sir William Grant in Pratt *v.* Sladden, 14 Yes. p. 197 (1807).

codicil thereto "that he" was intended to take... beneficially." It will be observed that not merely did the statute change the fundamental rule, but it required that the intention to give to the executor beneficially should, appear by the writing.[1068]

Under this general head of "rebutting an equity" are brought all the other cases of a resulting trust, the presumption against double portions, and the like; and it has even been stated as a general principle that where "the document is of such a nature that the court will presume that it was executed with any other than its apparent intention," the apparent intention may be shown to be the real one.[1069] In such cases the testator's mere extrinsic intention is admitted, not as adding to the document, or varying or contradicting it, or as evidence in aid of interpretation. It comes in as a mere incident to the "equity," as a ground of relief against the operation of a rule which refuses its proper construction to the document.[1070] "In such case," says Jarman, "it does not contradict the will, its effect being to support the legal title of the devisee against, not a trust expressed (for that would be to control the written will), but against a mere equity arising by implication of law."[1071] And mere extrinsic intention, being thus available, in point of substantive law, is provable in any legitimate way. The objections to proving it by direct statements of intention, when offered in aid of interpretation, do not hold here.

8. We have observed that direct statements of intention were formerly used, much more freely than they would be to-day. If the Master of the Rolls, in 1750,[1072] might think it possible, logically, to help himself out of an ordinary uncertainty in such a way as this, why should it not generally be so used, in any like case? Well, evidently, it would be highly dangerous to do it, even for a court of

---

[1068] Williams *v.* Arkle, L. R. 7 H. L. 606; Love *v.* Gaze, 8 Beav. 472.

[1069] Steph. Dig. Ev. art. 91. See also 1 Jarm. Wills (5th Eng. ed.), 390 — 392; Reynolds *v.* Robinson, 82 N. Y. 103; *In re* Atwood's Estate, 14 Utah, 1.

[1070] Of this class of cases Hawkins (Wills, Preface, 2d Am. ed. ix) says: "The anomalous case of what are called 'presumptions' of law are, in reality, rules of construction derived from the civil law, which, having obtained a lodgment in English law, But being disapproved of, have been allowed to retain their own antidote in the shape of the capability of being rebutted by parol evidence, which (in common, however, with other rules of construction) they possessed in the system from which they were originally derived."

[1071] I Wills (5th ed.), 391.

[1072] Hampshire *v.* Pierce, *supra,* 435.

equity, and merely "to inform the conscience" of the judge. And when you come to the jury of a common-law court, it would be dangerous in the extreme. That was reason enough for restraining the use of such evidence. It should, however, be carefully borne in mind that, in the nature of things, it might often fairly help in putting a construction on the text. It was not a denial of their probative quality, as mere handmaids to the text, which still continued, in the main, and with greater rigor, to keep out these extrinsic declarations of intention. This was carefully indicated by Sir John Strange in the case referred to, when, after applying the direct evidence of intention, he comes back and rests it all on the will itself; "so that taking this on the face of the will... it appears clearly," etc. In the same way, under the narrower limitations which soon confined direct evidence of intention in aid of construction, merely to cases of equivocation, the judges of a later day explained this single use of it, — not as adding to the text but as merely evidential. "The intention," said Lord Abinger, for the Court of Exchequer, in 1839, "shows what he meant to do; and when you know that, you immediately perceive that he has done it by the general words he has used, which, in their ordinary sense, may properly bear that construction." "The evidence," said Baron Parke, in 1836,[1073]... "only enables the court to reject one of the subjects or objects... and to determine which of the two the devisor understood to be signified by the description." "Such evidence," said the same judge, in 1833,[1074] "is admissible to show (as Mr. Amos properly pointed out) not what the testator intended, but what he understood to be signified by the words he used in the will." Wigram also,[1075] although laboring over this class of cases, comes out at the same point: "The principle," he says, "upon which they proceed, may, perhaps, be explained; for... although the words do not ascertain the subject intended, they do describe it. The person held entitled in these cases has answered the description in the will. The effect of the evidence has only been to confine the language within one of its natural meanings. The court has merely rejected, and the intention which it has ascribed to the testator, sufficiently expressed, remains in the will.... Or, perhaps,

---

[1073] Doe d. Gord v. Needs, 2 M. & W. 129.

[1074] Richardson v. Watson, 4 B. & Ad. 787.

[1075] Extr. Ev. s. 152.

the more simple explanation is that the evidence only determines what subject was known to the testator by the name or other description he used."

All this may, perhaps, be accepted in a general way, namely, so far as it means that direct statements of intention may really be used as mere aids to interpretation, — absolutely as subordinate and auxiliary to the text; not, in any way, as being given an independent operation, but only as contributing to illuminate the writing and give to that its own true meaning and operation. This, as Lord Hardwicke said of a similar matter,[1076] "although it is a nice distinction, yet it is a distinction in the reason of the thing." But, regarded as furnishing any solid ground of reason for a discrimination between this class of cases and others it is wholly unsatisfactory.

The true reason for this distinction appears to be an historical one. An ancient doctrine of pleading and substantive law relating to documents containing an "equivocation" in names, referred to on a previous page,[1077] was much too old and firmly rooted in the law to allow of even a question about it, — the doctrine that averments were open in such cases, defences to the regular operation of the document, such as were not ordinarily allowed. This doctrine permitted (if not at first, yet later, and as it had come to be administered in the sixteenth century) an inquiry into the real meaning of the writer, as extrinsically ascertained.[1078] And when interpretation came openly to take account of all extrinsic aids, except direct statements of intention; it was then inevitable that an exception to this exception should be recognized in the case of "equivocation," that ancient, continuous, and just class of cases could not be set aside, — reason or no reason. This historical connection of the cases is clearly traceable in our books.

That might seem to be all, in the way of explanation, that need be said about this sort of case. But when attempts to explain it are made such as those above indicated, it is well to test them. It should be remembered that where a man's intention is available his contemporary declaration is good evidence of it.[1079] Hawkins,[1080] after quoting most of the explanations above given, has disposed of

---

[1076] Goodinge v. Goodinge, supra, 434.

[1077] Supra, 417.

[1078] Supra, 420 — 423.

[1079] Infra, 444.

[1080] 2 Jurid. Soc. Papers, 298.

them with a conclusive answer. He had been pointing out the nature of the process of interpretation in general, and added that this case of equivocation, differs in no essential particular from any other case. "What interpretation really does in such a case is to give to the words that meaning which the writer intended that they should have,... to add to the name or description that additional mark or sign, whatever it be, which applies to the person or thing intended, and to that person or thing only; the description is thus rendered a complete description, and the words as interpreted convey a meaning which in and by themselves they are insufficient to convey.... The whole of this reasoning [referring to what is quoted above from Wigram[1081]] may be answered in Sir James Wigram's own words: 'To define that which is indefinite is to make a material addition to the will.' The case of two persons or places bearing the same name is a case where language is imperfect: to adapt an illustration from John Stuart Mill, a name is like the chalk-mark put upon the door in the story of 'The Forty Thieves,' which Morgiana rendered useless by chalking all the doors in the street in precisely the same manner. The result is that to distinguish any one door from the other, an additional mark of some sort must be put upon it, the mark originally used having come to mean either and neither of the objects marked, any one considered in itself, but none as distinguished from the others. It is not true to say, with Lord Abinger, that when you know what the writer meant to do, you perceive that he has done it: on the contrary, you perceive that some Morgiana, as it were, has come in to defeat his intention, and has succeeded in defeating it, unless you will permit some new and additional mark to be put on, which will effectually distinguish the object of the writer's intention from other similarly marked objects, the existence of which he was unaware of or had forgotten."

In point of mere reason, then, it may be said, that, after allowing for the operation of rigid technical rules, or definitions, which leave no room for the play of actual or presumed intention, the process of interpretation may and should take account of every indication of the writer's actual meaning, not excepting his direct statements. And that this is not inconsistent with the rule that no effect is to be given to what is not expressed in the writing. The

---

[1081] *Supra,* 441.

court may still be able to say, and must rigidly hold itself to saying, with Sir John Strange, in Hampshire *v.* Pierce,[1082] that, after all is said and done, it finds the meaning imputed to the words, on the face of the document itself. Always it must be recognized, where a writing is required, that a "sufficient expression" is a condition necessary to legal validity.[1083] That this resort to actual intention might on principle always be had is clear enough, as the learned writer last quoted has remarked, from the use in our own system of the preamble of a statute in interpreting it, from our own established rule in the case of "equivocation," and from the fact that in the Roman law there was no exclusion of the writer's actual intention, or of that best and directest of all evidence of it, his own statement.

What, then, is the true character of this rule of our law which excludes direct statements of intention? Is it a rule of evidence? or a rule of construction or interpretation? It would seem that while it partakes of the character of both, it must hold its place as a rule of evidence. If one were to draw out the whole proposition it would run thus: While in the interpretation of solemn documents by a court, no meaning can be attributed to them which the words may not legitimately bear, and therefore full effect must be allowed to any rules of language or of law which limit and fix their meaning and operation; and while, subject to these rules, the words of the document should be allowed to have the meaning and operation which the writer meant them to have, and therefore the process of interpretation should, subject to these rules, take account of the writer's actual intention; and while the process of proving this intention must be carried on under the ordinary principles and rules of the law of evidence, and these would ordinarily allow, where intention was a fact to be proved, that it be proved by a person's own contemporary declarations;[1084] nevertheless, in the interpretation of solemn documents, this sort of evidence of intention is not permitted, except in the case of equivocation, where the description of a person or thing is "equally applicable in all its parts"[1085] *to* more than one. In other words, while it is true that in talking generally of the use of

---

[1082] *Supra,* 435.

[1083] 2 Jurid. Soc. Pap. 325. "The law . . . requires a sufficient, not a perfect expression." *Ib.* 302.

[1084] Mut. Life Ins. Co. *v.* Hillmon, 145 U. S. 285; Com. *v.* Trefethen, 157 Mass. 180.

[1085] Lord Cairns, in Charter *v.* Charter, L. R. 7 H. L. 364.

intention in aid of construction we are not talking of a question in the law of evidence, but of one in the law of construction or interpretation; namely, what is the object of interpretation, and under what limitations is it to be carried on — yet when we talk of direct statements of intention we are talking of a certain kind of evidence of intention, and so of a special excluding rule of evidence, and of a special exception to this ordinary excluding rule.

9. As regards all extrinsic matter which might help in construing a document, except direct statements of intention, when such matter was used merely as a light to read it by, the courts by the middle of the eighteenth century had in a good degree escaped from the bondage of the earlier days. Allowing extrinsic matter thus freely to be brought into view and used, made it impossible for any man to pretend to construe a fine, a deed, or a will by merely reading it over and dealing with it grammatically. It became more and more evident that such a thing, although talked of, was never done and never possible; and that the recognized enlargement of the field of view, in interpreting writings, like a thousand other enlargements, although it might be dangerous, was necessary.

Accordingly it had become possible for Wigram to lay it solidly down, over seventy years ago,[1086] that, with the exception of direct statements of intention, no extrinsic fact relevant to any legitimate question arising in the interpretation of writings and admissible under the general rules of evidence, could be shut out. The fifth proposition in his little book states, as regards wills, that in order to determine the donec, or the thing given, or the quantity of interest, or any other disputed point respecting which it can be shown that a knowledge of extrinsic facts can in any way aid the right interpretation of the words, a court may inquire into every material fact relating to the matter ill question; and that every claimant under a will has a right to require a court of construction to place itself, by examining extrinsic facts, in the situation of the testator himself.[1087]

But the full light of this principle was lessened by the omission to discriminate exactly between rules of evidence and rules of construction, by the acceptance of various too rigidly expressed

---

[1086] Extrinsic Evidence in Aid of the Interpretation of Wills. In the "Advertisement to the First Edition," dated Jan. 1,1831, the writer states that the book was written in 1826.

[1087] Extrins. Evid. s. 96.

principles or rules of construction, and by the inexact mode in which these were sometimes stated and applied in the cases.

Of course, the logical relevancy of evidence is determined among other things by the rules of construction; evidence ceases to be "material" in the sense of Wigram's proposition, when the object which it is offered to promote is made illegitimate. In such cases we remark that it is the rule of construction which excludes, and no principle in the law of evidence; and yet, carelessly, the difficulty is forever being rested on the entirely secondary ground of admitting or excluding evidence.

Among rules of construction thus taking effect in a disguised form there has survived from the older and more formal conceptions a doctrine, for the most part, tacitly assumed and secretly operating, but kept alive by the ever recurring desire to preserve the written expression in its full operation; namely, that in looking into extrinsic facts in aid of interpretation you shall limit the range of vision as much as possible, and never look at them at all unless it be necessary. This took the form, sometimes, of saying that while you must look outside in order to ascertain and identify the persons and things of which the document speaks, yet, when this is accomplished, you cannot look farther: from that point on, the document must plainly, or at least sufficiently, speak its mind to a competent lawyer, who fixes his eyes on the mere text, or else it must fail of its effect.[1088]

Closely connected with this is the alleged principle that if the identifying process discovers among the persons or things to which the text might be applicable some one, and only one, that is aptly designated, this person or thing alone can be taken to answer the words.[1089] While certain leading rules of construction are obviously sound, — that *prima facie* the language of a document shall have its natural and proper meaning, — technical language its proper technical meaning, and ordinary language its ordinary meaning; that the document must be construed as a whole, and any part be subject to modification so as' to make it consistent with the whole; and that no meaning can be attributed to the words that they will not bear; yet, short of this last extreme, it is still possible to make

---

[1088] See Holt, C. J., in Cole *v.* Rawlinson, supra, 428; also Gibbs, C. J., and Mansfield, C. J., *infra,* 451, 452, note.

[1089] *Infra,* 452 n., 000.

words bear other meanings than the usual and proper ones, in order to avoid absurd or unreasonable results. Just here the principle above mentioned makes itself felt with rigor. We are told that if the words of the document taken as a whole, after the identifying process has been carried through, admit of an appropriate, application, and an application more appropriate to one person or thing than to any other, it must have that application; and of course neither extrinsic facts nor anything else can avail to give them any other. This is the rule that Wigram appears to express so uncompromisingly in his second proposition: "Where there is nothing in the context of a will from which it is apparent that a testator has used the words in which he has expressed himself in any other than their strict and primary sense, and where his words so interpreted are sensible with reference to extrinsic circumstances, it is an inflexible rule of construction that the words of the will shall be interpreted in their strict and primary sense and in no other, although they may be capable of some popular or secondary interpretation."[1090]

It is said, also, that where the text shows on its face an ambiguity it is incurable; or, as Lord Bacon expressed it, *"Ambiguitas patens* is never holpen by averment."

And again it is said that in interpretation no attention can be given to the intention of the writer, but only to the meaning of the words, except in the one case of "equivocation."

Now in so far as any of these things are true, they State no rule of the law of evidence; they simply mark a limit and a rule of the substantive law in carrying on the process of construction or interpretation. By that process some things can be done or attempted, and some cannot. In so far as a thing is forbidden to construction, of course there is no use in trying to give evidence in support of it: the fullest extrinsic evidence, the most convincing and regular aggregation of extrinsic facts, if offered to support an inadmissible contention, is itself inadmissible; but it is so because the contention itself is out of place. The exclusion, then, of extrinsic evidence, that

---

[1090] Extrins. Evid. Prop. II. Wigram closes the sentence thus: "And although the most conclusive evidence of intention to use them in such popular or secondary sense be tendered." In saying this he means, by "evidence of intention," here and always, a particular kind of evidence of intention, namely, direct statements of intention, or what is tantamount to these. Wigram describes this (s. 10) as "evidence which is applied to prove intention itself as an independent fact."

is to say of extrinsic facts which are adapted, in their nature, to aid the pure and simple work of interpretation, comes about largely from the limitation put by the substantive law upon the conduct of this work. It is to be carried on under restrictions and according to rules. Whatever extrinsic matter is kept out by these rules is logically irrelevant. Take, for instance, the case of a gift to the testator's "children," when he has children legitimate and illegitimate. Facts tending very strongly to show that the testator meant to include the illegitimate children are generally irrelevant, because, *prima facie,* the legal definition of the term children excludes illegitimates, and therefore a contrary interpretation is not in general legally allowable.

10. Let me now illustrate the subject by a consideration of a few important modern cases.

(a) In a well-known case, early in this century,[1091] in the Common Pleas the heir-at-law claimed in ejectment against the devisee, certain estates in Devonshire. The will gave "my estate of Ashton in the county of Devonshire." The testator had real estate derived from his father called the "Youlston estate," and other real estate, derived from his mother, called the "Ashton estate," all in Devonshire. The plaintiff claimed all of the "Ashton estate," consisting of various parcels. There was a parish of Ashton. Part of the property claimed was a manor of Ashton, some of which was in Ashton parish and some in another. Part of the property, not in the manor of Ashton, was in the parish of that name; and part of it, not in the said manor, was in other parishes and at various distances, up to fifteen miles,' away from the parish of Ashton. The defendant offered to show the testator's instructions to the scrivener at the time of making his will, to give the defendant his "Ashton estate;" that the testator used to call the estate derived from his father the Youlston estate, and the one coming from his mother the Ashton estate, or Ashton property. A series of annual accounts' of his stewards, beginning with 1785, containing receipts of the testator, were offered, with other evidence, to prove this habit. These accounts were entitled "for Ashton estate," and included items relating to the Ashton manor, and to the other manors outside the Ashton parish. The trial judge received this evidence, under the plaintiff's objection, but subject to the opinion of the court *in banc, —* the verdict (given for the defendant) to stand if the evidence was rightly received; and

---

[1091] Doe d. Chichester v. Oxenden, 3 Taunt. 147 (1810). 29

if it was not, to be entered for the plaintiff, the heir, for so much, if any, as did not in the court's opinion pass by the will. The court held for the plaintiff, that only what was in "the manor or parish of Ashton" passed by the will.

This action was brought in 1809 and decided in 1810. In 1811 the devisee brought an action of ejectment in the King's Bench, claiming the lands outside the parish of Ashton, and offered the same extrinsic evidence. It was rejected and judgment entered for the defendant. On a bill of exceptions the House of Lords affirmed the judgment.[1092]

Now in this case suppose none of the evidence had contained direct statements of the testator's intention; undoubtedly these, as the law then stood and stands now, should have been rejected. But the discrimination was not made in this case between that sort of evidence and. any other; the question was, of admitting any extrinsic evidence. "I do not state the particulars of this evidence," said Gibbs, C. J., in delivering to the Lords the opinion of the judges,[1093] "as the question is whether any evidence at all can be admitted to explain the bequest." That is to say, no kind of extrinsic evidence and no amount of extrinsic evidence is available in such a case; and that means that no matter what the extrinsic facts are, a court cannot construe the will as giving anything beyond "the parish or manor of Ashton." Suppose then it should be proposed to show, not merely that the property in question was habitually called the Ashton estate by the testator, but that it was so called by people in general. That is an extrinsic fact or extrinsic evidence.[1094]

[1092] See Blackburn, J., as to this case in Allgood v. Blake, L. R. 8 Ex. 160.

[1093] Doe d. Chichester v. Oxenden, 4 Dow, 65, 92 (1816).

[1094] In the Atty.-Gen. v. Drummond, 1 Drury & Warren, 356, 367, et seq. (1842), Lord Chancellor Sugden in interpreting a deed containing the words "Christian" and "Protestant dissenter," said: "The Court is at liberty to inquire into all the surrounding circumstances which may have acted upon the minds of the persons by whom the deed or will (for it matters not whether it was one or the other) was executed. . . . The Court therefore has not merely a right, but it is its duty to inquire into the surrounding circumstances, before it can approach the construction of the instrument itself. . . . One of the counsel for the defendants . . . says you are not at liberty to receive any parol evidence whatever. ... He absolutely denies my right, as a judge, to receive parol or extrinsic evidence at all, and then he gives me parol evidence as to the meaning of the term 'Protestant dissenter.' He produces acts of Parliament. . . . This is in my opinion very proper evidence, but is it not, for the purpose for which it is produced, parol evidence?

The doctrine of the judges and the House of Lords would exclude that.[1095] The rule of the case is that the words "my estate *of* Ashton" mean the same as "my estate *at* Ashton;" and therefore, they say, the question is whether, "when lands at a particular place are devised, extrinsic evidence may be received to show that the devisor included lands out of that place." The reason for saying that it cannot is given thus: "The courts of law have been jealous of the admission of extrinsic evidence to explain the intention of a testator.... It is of great importance that the admission of such extrinsic evidence should be avoided where it can be done, that a purchaser or an heir-at-law may be able to judge from the instrument itself what lands are or are not affected by at." In this case there is other property at Ashton which satisfies the description. "I know," says the Chief Justice, "only of one case in which it [extrinsic evidence to explain the intention of a testator] is permitted, that is, where an ambiguity is introduced by extrinsic circumstances. There, from the necessity of the case, extrinsic evidence is admitted to explain the ambiguity. [Then he mentions the case of a gift of an estate of Blackaere, where there are two of them, and a gift to a man's son, John Thomas, where there are two of them; in which cases 'from the necessity of the case evidence is admitted to explain, the ambiguity.'] And so also if one devises to his nephew, William Smith, and has no nephew answering the description in all respects, evidence must be admitted to show which nephew was meant by a description not strictly applying to any nephew. The ambiguity there arises from an extrinsic fact or circumstance, and the admission of evidence to explain the ambiguity is necessary to give effect to the will, and it is only in such a case that extrinsic evidence can be received." [1096]

What is usage but parol evidence? It is parol evidence of facts in order to construe the deed."

[1095] Lord Eldon's final opinion (and no other was given on the part of the Lords) simply concurred in that of Gibbs, C. J., for the judges.

[1096] In like manner, in the earlier case (3 Taunt. 147, 156), the Court (Mansfield, C. J.), after citing cases of two persons or estates of the same name and of persons not exactly answering the description, said: "It is not expressly said in any of these cases that it was necessary to receive the evidence in order to give effect to the will, which would not operate without such evidence. But although this is not said, yet the rule seems to hold. It will be found that the will could have had no operation, unless the evidence had been received. Here, without the evidence, the will has an effective operation; everything will pass

The theory of this decision might be given in the language of the Chief Justice, in an earlier very similar case,[1097] where the court was equally divided, namely, "the question will be whether the words... are so descriptive of locality as to preclude the admissibility of evidence that the testator intended to use them in any other sense;" and in the language of Mansfield, C. J., in the first Oxenden case, given in a note below. But it was a principle of construction that shut out these extrinsic facts; the "evidence" (not discriminating one kind from another) was rejected because it was not relevant to any legitimate contention in the case. No rule of evidence was in question.

(b) Thirty years later the House of Lords, in a similar case, took a different tone.[1098] A testator had described himself as "of Ashford Hall in the county of Salop," and had disposed of "all my estate in Shropshire called Ashford Hall." On a bill filed for the purpose of executing the trust, the question was whether only a certain "capital messuage and mansion house" called Ashford Hall, containing ten or twelve acres, passed, as the defendant, the heir-at-law, contended; or this and other neighboring parcels, comprising in all about a hundred and fifty acres. The court held for the plaintiffs. It was contended, on the authority of the Oxenden case, that as "Ashford Hall" proper answered the call of the will, the words could not have a wider sense put on them. But the Lord Chancellor (Cottenham) said: "The plaintiff... proceeded in the regular course to prove the proposition which he had stated; namely, that the estate was used as one estate, and acquired the name from the former proprietor of the Ashford Hall estate, or the estate of Ashford Hall, and that the testator had himself occupied it as one estate, and had himself called it or described it as the Ashford Hall estate, and that he was in the habit of so doing. Various instances are brought to prove this proposition, and beyond all doubt they do prove it." The opinion goes on to say, that "over and over again" the witnesses say. that the testator did so call it, and they called it so; that the defendant,

---

under it that is in the manor or parish, or what he would naturally call his Ashton estate. This will be an effective operation; and, this being, the case herein differs from all the others; because in them the evidence was admitted to explain that which without such explanation could have had no operation. It is safer not to go beyond this line."

[1097] Whitbread *v.* May, 2 B. & P. 595, 597 (1801), *per* Alvanley, C. J.

[1098] Ricketts *v.* Turquand, 1 H. L. C. 472 (1848).

the testator's eldest son, gives no evidence, and yet "nobody could be more capable of establishing the fact of his father's intention in not describing or intending not to describe the property, as alleged in the bill.... It appears that the testator was in the occupation of this property as one estate, and that he did describe and call it the 'Ashford Hall estate,' or 'the estate of Ashford Hall;' ... they both mean to describe the same thing. Moreover, there is evidence that the heir in his own dealings has so described the whole property.... All we are in search of are the terms by which the testator was in the habit of describing the property.... If he describes land in a particular parish by a particular name) or in a particular locality, you cannot go into evidence to show he meant by the general appellation to include something out of it; you cannot do that without contradicting the express terms used. Here is a term which includes more or less land according to what was meant by the term used, and all we are in search of is the particular meaning of the expression which is used."

Of Doe d. Chichester *v.* Oxenden, Lord Campbell said. (p. 493), that "there the question arose as to the admissibility of parol evidence with regard to the construction of a will, but here parol evidence must inevitably have been admitted." It is not clear what this means. In both cases the effort is to find what meaning should be imputed to the testator's words; in both, and in neither more than in the other extrinsic evidence is required to identify the property. If the range of extrinsic inquiry is to be limited in one case by the principle that you can go no further when once you discover property answering the description in its natural and ordinary interpretation, it seems to apply to the last case as well as to the first. It will be observed that there were two steps taken in the Oxenden case. First the expression, "ray estate of Ashton," the phrase actually used, is identified with "my estate at Ashton," a phrase not used; and second, it is declared that when the will names an existing locality, and no other, you cannot construe it as including what is outside that locality. Both these propositions are questionable. In neither is any rule of evidence involved. As a matter of construction, why declare that "my estate of Ashton" means a locality, — at Ashton, — necessarily and under all circumstances? And if it may, under any circumstances, mean a description of an estate, rather than the name of a locality, the authority of the later case would admit most of the evidence offered in the first one.

(c) In 1820, in an action of ejectment, both parties claimed in the character of devisee.[1099] The devisor had three brothers, Thomas, Richard, and Matthew; and each of them had a son named Simon, living at the testator's death. The will gave a legacy to Thomas, and another, with a life interest in a house, to the daughter of Richard, — and an annuity to the wife *of* Matthew, chargeable on. her husband's share of a tenement called Stone; then came the devise in question, namely, "unto Matthew West-lake, my brother, and to Simon Westlake, my brother's son, all that... tenement called Stone," subject to certain charges. "I likewise give... unto Matthew Westlake, my brother, and to Simon Westlake, jointly and severally alike, all other my [property real and personal], and I appoint them executors of my will." The plaintiff was Simon, son of Matthew. The defendant, Simon, son of Richard, insisted that by the facts above named he had "established a latent ambiguity in the will," and he offered evidence of the testator's declarations that he meant Simon the son of Richard. These were received, but, nevertheless, the verdict was for the plaintiff. On a motion for a new trial, on the ground that the verdict was against the evidence, a rule was refused. The court (Abbott, C. J.) put the opinion on the ground that the case was plain on the construction of the will, and that it was "unnecessary to consider whether this verdict is against the evidence; "for the declarations of the testator should not have been received. No ambiguity arises here, the court said, because," in point of legal construction, when the testator is speaking of his.brother's son, he must be taken to speak of the son of that brother who was then particularly in his mind." Matthew was then in his mind, and so "Simon Westlake, his son, must be the person, intended."[1100]

This decision might, perhaps, rest upon the ground, that direct statements of intention can only be received, even in cases of "equivocation," when, it they are not received, the document will fail from uncertainty. That presupposes that the resources of construction, aided by all admissible extrinsic facts, have been first exhausted. And probably that is the true doctrine about the use of direct statements of intention; the danger and general impolicy of resorting to them is such as to lead courts to postpone them, for a last

---

[1099] Doe d. Westlake *v.* Westlake, 4 B. & Aid. 57.
[1100] See Castledon *v.* Turner, 3 Atk. 257 (1745).

resort. And so, we observe the phraseology in the Oxenden case,[1101] that "the admission... is necessary to give effect to the will;" and in Wigram,[1102] the remark that, "If the words of the will are applicable to any subject, the court is inflexible in applying them accordingly. If inapplicable to any subject, the court declares that the will expresses no certain intention. It is not until this declaration is explicitly made, that the question of admitting evidence of intention *[i. e.,* direct statements of intention[1103]] is ever entertained." And so Jarman: "For there is properly no 'ambiguity' until all the facts of the case have been given in evidence and found insufficient for a definite decision." Therefore, if this case is to be understood as holding that on the facts actually in evidence the construction was sufficiently plain, and the extreme situation which alone justifies a resort to direct statements had not been found to exist, it seems a satisfactory decision.

If, however, as is not unlikely, considering the ideas of the period, the case is to be regarded as holding, generally, in respect to all extrinsic facts, — that the question was to be disposed of on grounds of construction only, *i. e.,* aided only by what had to be introduced in order to identify the persons and things referred to, then it is subject to the same sort of objection that applies in the Oxenden case above referred to. Suppose it had been possible to show the sort of facts that existed in Grant *v.* Grant[1104] and Charter *v.* Charter;[1105] *e.g.,* suppose that the testator had quarrelled with Matthew's son, had had nothing to do with him for many years, or did not know that Matthew had a son; and that Richard's son had long lived with him and was much beloved, and had long managed all his business affairs; and that the testator did not know that Thomas had a son, or that although he knew of Thomas's son, he disliked him and had never spoken with him. Would such facts as these be allowed to influence the construction? If so, of course they would be receivable. It seems plain, first, that, under such circumstances, you could not tell whether the construction actually given to the will was "sensible with reference to extrinsic facts," until you had looked over these facts; and, second, that you might

---

[1101] *Supra,* 452.
[1102] Extr. Ev. pl. 159.
[1103] *Supra,* 448 n.
[1104] *Infra,* 461.
[1105] *Infra,* 463.

easily accumulate such facts as would require a different construction.

(d) Another leading case is that of Abbott v. Middleton,[1106] where, in a suit in equity to ascertain the construction of a will, the House of Lords affirmed a decision of the Master of the Rolls; Lords Cranworth and Wensleydale dissenting. The testator had given an annuity of £2,000 to his wife, and had set apart personal property to provide it. On her death his son was to have the interest of this fund for life, and on his death the principal was to go to his children in such sums as he should by will direct. "But in case of my son dying before his mother, then and in that case" the principal was to be divided between the children of the testator's daughters. Specific gifts of money were made to his only surviving daughter; and also to the children of daughters deceased; with the right of survivorship. To his daughter the gift ran "the sum of [etc.] the interest... for her sole benefit during her life, and the principal on her demise" to go to her children equally. "And in the event of her not leaving issue, then and in that case I will that it shall become the property of," etc. The son was residuary legatee of "all property not disposed of in this document," and the wife and son were executors.

The will was made at the Cape of Good Hope in March, 1834. The son, a captain in the British army, was then unmarried; but he married in. July, 1834, had a son born in May, 1835, and was himself killed in the battle of Inkermann in November, 1854. The testator died in January, 1855, and the testator's wife died soon aftrwards.

One of the testator's granddaughters filed a bill against the above named grandson and others, praying the execution of the will; and the Master of the Rolls, in April, 1856, held that in the events that had happened, the grandson above named took a vested interest in the principal of the fund aforesaid subject to the widow's life interest.

The Lords, in supporting the decision of the Master of the Rolls, were divided three to two. The four opinions. reported were equally divided. Lords Chelmsford (Chancellor) and St. Leonards found in the document, taken as a whole and construed in the light of the facts, a purpose to provide primarily for the benefit of the son and the son's children, if he should have any; and they read the

---

[1106] 7 H. L. C. 68 (1858).

clause "in case of my son dying before his mother," as if it had added "without leaving a child." Lord St. Leonards found no difficulty in collecting the testator's general intention from the whole will taken together. "You are," he said, "by settled rules of law, at liberty to place yourself in the same situation in which, the testator himself stood. You are entitled to inquire about his family, and the position in which he is placed with regard to his property." He doubted whether in this particular case the amount of the property could be looked at. But the Chancellor did consider that.

Lord Cranworth and his associate, in taking the other view, declared that the words used here were perfectly plain and sensible in their ordinary meaning, and denied any right, under these circumstances, to impute to them any other. "The question is," said Lord Cranworth,[1107] "whether we can discover from the intention evinced in this will an absolute necessity for interpolating the words 'without leaving issue' or for construing the words used as meaning that.... Every will must by law be in writing, and it is a necessary consequence of that law that the meaning must be discovered from the writing itself, aided only by such extrinsic evidence as is necessary in order to understand the words which the testator has used. No extrinsic evidence can be necessary here for such a purpose, except the fact that the son was a bachelor, if indeed that is necessary." If the testator's intention really was that the son's children should not take unless he survived his mother, "he could not more aptly have expressed what he intended." The only reason for interpreting the words otherwise is a persuasion "that he meant to say something different from that which he has said.... If the words used are unambiguous, they cannot be departed from merely because they lead to consequences which we regard as capricious, or even harsh and unreasonable." There is no ambiguity here, and the only question is whether on the face of the will we can say that the words "without leaving issue" must be supplied. Lord Wensleydale admits that the strict construction would probably disappoint the real intention of the testator, but he quotes from Wigram, saying that the only question is "what that which he has written really means." It is the rule that the words used must have their "ordinary and grammatical sense,... unless some obvious absurdity, or some repugnance or inconsistency with the declared intentions,... to be

---

[1107] 1 p. 88.

extracted from the whole instrument should follow from so reading it." No such result appears here. The words are clear. That he meant anything different from their plain meaning is conjecture merely. You must make out an inconsistency with the context and a declared intention so plain as to enable you to add the words necessary to reconcile them. "But you certainly cannot find any context here which will have that effect. The Master of the Rolls thinks he can see a repugnance between the gift to the children and the condition to take it away, and therefore introduces the words without issue; 'but I see no such inconsistency."

Now the differences between the Lords here seem to be: 1. As to the discovery of a general intention on the whole will clear enough to govern the form of the particular expressions in question, *i. e.,* as to the actual interpretation of this document as a whole; 2. As to the scope and real nature of the rule of construction, stated in Wigram's second proposition; or, as to the degree of strictness with which it is to be understood and applied; and 3. As to the range of allowable inquiry among extrinsic facts. Lord Cranworth says that you are only to look at extrinsic facts so far as is necessary to enable you to understand the words used, and that here no extrinsic fact is "necessary," except that the son was a bachelor, if even that is necessary. But certainly the extrinsic facts that there was a wife and a son, and a son's son, and that the first survived her son and her husband, were extrinsic facts, not to mention others, that it was "necessary" to look at. And hardly less certain can it be, in point of reason, that because you can find a clear meaning when you have looked at half the extrinsic facts, you are not justified in attributing that to the document, when looking at all of them would clearly give it another meaning. Of this case it seems to be true, as a learned writer has said, that "the remainder of the will contained nothing absolutely inconsistent with the literal construction; and the circumstances of the testator's property presented no difficulty in carrying out the provision so understood. The construction which prevailed depended on an inferential interpretation, in which the circumstances of the testator, as determined by extrinsic evidence, were undoubtedly elements of consideration."[1108] And in reference

---

[1108] Nichols, 2 Jurid. Soc. Pap. 351, 372. The writer, like Hawking before him, uses the phrase "inferential (or logical) interpretation" as contrasted with a merely "grammatical interpretation." *Infra,* 588.

to the questions raised by this case, the same sagacious writer well observes:[1109] "An interpreter, unimpeded by the alleged rule that the strict and primary meaning must, if sensible with reference to extrinsic circumstances, be inflexibly adhered to, may well consider that of two contending constructions the one is more proper, more strictly grammatical, without denying that the words will admit the other signification: he may also perceive that the strictly grammatical sense would not, if adopted, be altogether ineffectual, or lead to an absolutely absurd result; but the greater convenience of the opposing construction, and its more perfect harmony with the conception which he has formed of the testator's plan, may convince him beyond doubt that the less proper sense of the words is the true meaning of the testator. Is it expedient that he should be debarred from this conclusion, and forced to adopt the sense most in accordance with grammatical propriety, provided it is not altogether incompatible with the facts? Is this supposed rule of the English law in fact observed by our own courts?"

(e) There is no lack in our cases to-day of attempts to follow the over-rigid doctrines, and the confused and inaccurate conceptions and phraseology of an earlier period. But a sufficient body of precedents has accumulated to support justcer and truer doctrines.

Grant v. Grant[1110] is such a case; where the Court of Exchequer Chamber, upon a consideration of the extrinsic facts, construed "my nephew, Joseph Grant," to mean not the testator's own nephew of that name, but his wife's nephew, Joseph Grant. "The facts disclosed by the evidence set out in... the special case," said Blackburn, J., "are abundantly sufficient to satisfy any rational person that the testator intended to leave the estate to his wife's nephew. But Mr. Quain insists that it is an inflexible principle of law, that if the words of the will have a strict primary sense, evidence is not admissible to show that the testator meant to use them in any other sense." This suggestion is dismissed with the remark (accompanied by an examination of the cases) that "most if not all" the cases cited in support of it were cases of what Wigram calls "evidence of intention," i.e., of direct statements of intention; and he adds that "there was ample explanatory evidence to warrant the judgment of the court below."

[1109] Nichols, 2 Jurid. Soc. Pap. 371.
[1110] L. R. 5 C. P. 727 (1870).

(*f*) Take, again, a case entitled Allgood *v.* Blake,[1111] where in four actions of ejectment the parties were represented by the ablest counsel. In the Exchequer Chamber, Blackburn, J., in giving the opinion of the court, after stating that in construing a will the court is to put itself in the testator's position, to consider all the material facts and circumstances known to him with reference to which he is to be taken to have used his words, and then to declare "what is the intention evidenced by the words used with reference to those facts and circumstances which were (or ought to have been) in the mind of the testator when he used those words, — quotes Wigram's language as to the question being not what the testator meant, but the meaning of his words, and adds: "But we think that the meaning of words varies according to the circumstances of and concerning which they were uttered.... The general rule, we believe, is undisputed that, in trying to get at the intention of the testator, we are to take the whole of the will, construe it altogether, and give the words their natural meaning, unless, when applied to the subject-matter which the testator presumably had in his mind, they produce an inconsistency with other parts of the will, or an absurdity or inconvenience so great as to convince the court that the words could not have been used in their proper signification.... To one mind it may appear that an effect produced by construing the words literally is so inconsistent with the rest of the will, or produces an absurdity or inconvenience so great as to justify the court in putting on them another signification, which to that mind seems a not improper signification of the words, whilst to another mind the effect produced may appear not so inconsistent, absurd, or inconvenient as to justify putting any other signification on the words than their proper one, and the proposed signification may appear a violent construction. Grey *v.* Pearson is an example of this.[1112] Lord Cranworth, Lord St. Leonards, and Lord Wensleydale laid down the general rules in terms not substantially differing from each other; but when they came to apply them... there was a marked difference in opinion. We apprehend that no precise line can be drawn, but that the court must in each case apply the admitted. rules to the case in hand; not deviating from the literal sense of the words without sufficient

---

[1111] L. B. 8 Ex. 160 (1873); 8. c. below. L. R. 7 Ex. 339.

[1112] 6 H. L. C. 61 (1857). In this case Lords Cranworth (Chancellor) and Wensleydale reasoned as they did, a year later, in Abbott *v.* Middleton; and so did Lord St. Leonards, who now, in the earlier case, was the dissenter.

reason, or more than is justified; yet not adhering slavishly to them, when to do so would obviously defeat the intention which may be collected from the whole will."

(*g*) Add to these cases the neat and excellent handling of a difficult matter in the House' of Lords, in 1874, by Lord Cairns (Chancellor) and Lord Selborne, sustaining the decree below.[1113] All the Lords agreed that direct statements of intention were not receivable in this case. "But, my Lords," said the Chancellor, "there is a class of evidence which in this case, as in all cases,... is clearly receivable. The court has a right to ascertain all the facts which were known to the testator at the time he made his will, and thus to place itself in the testator's position, in order to ascertain the bearing and application of the language which he uses; and in order to ascertain whether there exists any person or thing to which the whole description given in the will can be, reasonably and with sufficient certainty, applied." And thereupon follows a full consideration of all the extrinsic facts that were relevant to the questions in dispute. "The ease, therefore, appears to me to become one of those in which there is an erroneous or inaccurate name, and a description or demonstration sufficiently clear to correct the inaccuracy." Lord Selborne remarked, "The moment we find sufficient reason to conclude that there is really error in the name, the observation... that 'we are always bound to assume that the language of the will is the language of the testator' ceases to be material. It is then... part of the case that a mistake has been made."

(*h*) Another case may be mentioned, that of *In re* The Wolverton Mortgaged Estates,[1114] where a testator bequeathed £600 in trust to pay the income to his daughter for life, and at her death to her children by any husband "other than and except Mr. Thomas Fisher, of Bridge Street, Bath"; and subject thereto, to the testator's son. In Bridge Street, Bath, at the date of the will, there lived a Mr. Thomas Fisher, fifty years old, with a wife and family; one of his sons was named Henry Tom Fisher, a commercial traveller, often at the father's house, who had paid his addresses to

---

[1113] Charter *v.* Charter, L. R. 7 H. L. 364; Lords Chelmsford and Hatherley holding differently.

[1114] 7 Ch. Div. 197 (1877); 8. c. 37 L. T. R. 573, 47 L. J. Ch. 127, 26 W.R. 138.

the daughter. In the year after her father's death the daughter married young Fisher. She had a child by him, and now the question was whether this child was entitled to the benefit of the fund. The child was held not entitled. In other words, Henry Tom Fisher was held to be meant by the will and not his father.

In such a case as this, was a rule to be applied which, in looking outside, excluded from view all else, when once the father was discovered? Perhaps there might be another "Thomas Fisher, of Bridge Street, Bath," — another one exactly answering the call; and such a case must certainly be allowed for. In the search for such a person the son Henry Tom would come to light. When he did, was he to be disregarded? Certainly the father exactly answers the language of the will and the son does not; and it is not absolutely irrational to apply the will to the father, for it is conceivable that the testator might have feared future entanglements between him and the daughter, with or without reason for his fears.

Observe the way in which the court (Malins, V. C.) reached its conclusion. "The executors could not believe that Mr. Thomas Fisher, a married "man, was really intended by the testator.... They inquired further and found a son of his, Henry Tom Fisher, who, by the name of Tom Fisher, was known to the testator. 'Thomas' and 'Tom' are generally forms of the same name, and, though Tom was here the son's Christian name, the names of Thomas and of Tom being in reality only forms of the same name, it is necessary to adduce parol evidence of the 'state of circumstances in which the testator stood when he made his will, to ascertain which of the two Fishers he meant; and to assume that he meant the father, Thomas Fisher, a man then of fifty years of age, with a wife and family, is ridiculous. Tom Fisher had been paying attentions to the testator's daughter, and he strongly objected to her marriage with him.... Then again the two Fishers had the same home, and it was quite competent for the executors to adduce parol evidence to prove which of those two persons was really within the testator's contemplation.... No doubt where one person accurately fulfils the description, and no one else does, you cannot admit parol evidence to show that such person was not intended; but here there are two persons who substantially, though not with perfect accuracy, come within the description of Thomas Fisher of Bridge Street."

Doubtless this was not a case of equivocation, and so not a case for direct statements of intention.[1115] It appears, then, to be a case which, in applying the rule of Wigram's second proposition, holds it only applicable when you have fully examined all relevant extrinsic facts; and decides that when these disclose a high improbability that the will really means the person who is exactly designated, he may give place to another, not exactly indicated, but sufficiently so to take if he stood alone.

(i) Finally, let me mention a hard-fought case in the Supreme Court of the United States, in 1886, where the court, reversing its own previous decision, followed the same principles.[1116] A testator devised to his brother "lot numbered six in square four hundred and three," on a well-known plan of the city of Washington. There was such a lot, belonging to another person. The testator did not own or, so far as appears, contemplate owning it. He did own lot three in square four hundred and six; and the question, as stated in the opinion of the court (Bradley, J.), was "whether the parol evidence offered, and by the court [below] provisionally received, was sufficient to control the description of the lot, so as to make the will apply to lot number 3 in square 406." A minority of four judges declared that this was "an unambiguous devise," and stated their doctrine thus: "If there is any proposition settled in the law of wills, it is that extrinsic evidence is inadmissible to show the intention of the testator, unless it be necessary to explain a latent ambiguity; and a mere mistake is not a latent ambiguity. Where there is no latent ambiguity, there no extrinsic evidence can be received." The fact "that the testator did not own the lot described in the devise, but did own another which he did not dispose of by his will... does not tend to show a latent ambiguity. It does not tend to impugn the accuracy of the description contained in the devise. It only tends to show a mistake on the part of the testator in drafting his will. This cannot be cured by extrinsic evidence."

The theory involved in these statements appears to be that when the language of the will, after persons and things named in it

---

[1115] Charter *v.* Charter, L. R. 7 H. L. 364; Doe d. Hiscocks *v.* Hiscochs, 5 M. & W. 363.

[1116] Patch *v.* White, 117 U. S. 110.

are identified, is susceptible, in point of name and description, of an exact application to an existing thing or person, and only to one, it can have no other, no matter how admissible in itself or how probable another construction might be, in case this exactness of application did not exist; and no matter how irrational the adopted construction may be.

The court, on the other hand, began by looking into all the facts. They found, from the will, that the testator was intending to dispose of all his estate; that in giving the residue he thought that he had disposed of all his real estate, except what the residuary clause dealt with, since therein he called it "the balance of my real estate believed to be and to consist in," etc.; that he was meaning to give a lot which he then owned, and that he meant to give a lot with improvements. It was found that the lot actually named had no improvements on it, and the lot supposed to be meant had them. They also found that lot three was not disposed of by the testator's will, unless it passed by the clause in question. And they also found, that on leaving out the false description enough remained to identify the subject of the gift. The reasoning — of the minority in the case just referred to is what the court puts forward in the well-known case of Kurtz v. Hibner,[1117] where a testator, owning only one eighty-acre tract in a certain township, had called it section thirty-two by mistake, when it really was section thirty-three. In holding that the true section did not pass by the will, the court said:

"There is no ambiguity in this case as is urged. When we look at the will it is all plain and clear. It is only the proof *ailunde* which creates any doubt, and such proof we hold to be inadmissible." The true view of such a case appears to be that there is no question of ambiguity in the matter; there is a mistake; and the question is whether the will, taken as a whole, admits of a construction which will correct the mistake. All extrinsic facts which serve to show the state of the testator's property are to be looked at, and then the inquiry is whether, in view of all these facts, anything passes.[1118] The method of the court in that case is justly discredited. In reality Wigram's book, m 1831, gave it a death-blow.

[1117] 55 Illinois, 514.

[1118] Compare Newburgh v. Newburgh, Sugden, Law of Property, 367; 8. c. 5 Madd. 364; Thayer's Cases on Evidence, 847, 931-933; Fonnerean v. Poyntz, 1 Br. C. C. 472. In the excellent case of Hart v. Talk, 2 De G., McN. & G. 300, the words "the fourth schedule" were read as meaning "the fifth schedule,"

11. In turning from the cases which have now been considered, a few things should be said, even at the risk of repetition.

In all cases, upon offering evidence, two questions may arise: one of its logical relevancy, and another of its admissibility, under the excluding rules of evidence. As regards the subject in hand, — "parol evidence," the use of extrinsic matter to affect documents, — there appears to be no peculiar excluding rule of evidence, except that which shuts out direct statements of the writer's intention; and yet rules are so expressed as to obscure the matter and surround it with mystery. The truth is that the scope of construction and interpretation is, indeed, restricted by certain real or imagined rules, undertaking to fix what meaning can and what cannot be given to certain terms, and what under certain conditions can, and what cannot, be done. As is true in all other cases, these restrictions of substantive law determine the relevancy of what is offered in evidence. It is said, truly, that there are two questions: first, whether "the words are sensible as they stand; and, if [not], whether their meaning is clear in any other sense." Or, as it is elsewhere put, "whether the words... with reference to the facts, admit of being construed in their primary sense; and [if not] whether the intention is certain in any other sense of which the words, with reference to the facts, are capable."[1119] This being so, questions of the admissibility in evidence of extrinsic matter, not being direct statements of the writer's intention, are to be determined, in their order, by the general rules and principles that determine such questions in other cases, namely, the logical principle of relevancy, and the excluding operation of the general rules of evidence. They are questions for the court; and they are to be answered upon a consideration of whatever, being relevant to the particular inquiry, is not excluded by the general principles or rules of evidence. "Whether the words of the will, with reference to the facts, admit of being construed in their primary sense;" or, as elsewhere put by Wigram, whether the "words so interpreted are sensible with reference to extrinsic circumstances," is a question that refers us to the extrinsic facts and to all of them that can help; none are excluded, unless shut out by the ordinary

---

upon a consideration of all the facts and the construction of the whole document. Such cases as Tucker *v.* Seaman's Aid Soc., 7 Met. 188, and Am. Bible Soc. *v.* Pratt, 9 Alien, 109, rest well enough on the weight of the evidence; but in dealing with the principles now under consideration they are open to grave question.

[1119] Wigram, Ext. Ev. pl. 102, 213.

principles and rules of evidence. Before you can tell whether the facts allow of a given construction, you must know what they are. In some cases the court will need to scrutinize and weigh them all and in some their search will be very short. If the words of a gift are phrased in technical terms, such as a gift to a man's "children," and there are legitimate and illegitimate children, the range of inquiry may be narrow, for there is a rigid rule as to the meaning of the term.[1120] If the gift be to a man's "nephew," a less technical term, and there are nephews of himself and of his wife, it may be necessary to travel over all the circumstances and relations of the family.[1121] But there is no peculiar doctrine applicable to this sort of question except the one above indicated. In settling it one needs to ask only for the substantive law, of real property or wills, or what else governs the subject; for the rules of construction; and for the general rules and principles of evidence. And it would seem that no restriction. upon the fulness of the court's examination of extrinsic facts can be laid down which does not grow out of the considerations above indicated.

Accordingly a learned and competent writer[1122] has well suggested that "it is next to impossible to shut out all inference of intention [from extrinsic facts] until the possibility of accepting the terms in their literal signification has been determined. The rule which excludes an inferential interpretation of an unambiguous text, unless the primary sense leads to an inconsistency or absurdity, is found, when liberally construed, to proceed upon premises which, from the nature of the case, are at the outset in dispute. First, the words of the text must be shown to admit only of one meaning; or, at the least, not to be intelligible in a second sense without some sacrifice of their ordinary signification or grammatical construction. Secondly, the proper sense thus ascertained must be in harmony with the context, and with the entire scheme of the instrument. Thirdly, as applied to the testator's circumstances, it must lead to no absurdity or glaring improbability. Now, it is precisely upon these three fields that the battle of interpretation is fought; and it is not until the contest

---

[1120] Dorin v. Dorin, L. R. 7 H. L. 568.

[1121] Grant v. Grant, L. R. 5 C. P. 727; and compare Charter v. Charter L. R. 7 H. L. 364, *per* Lord Cairns and Lord Selborne.

[1122] F. M. Nichols (the editor of Britten), in Extrinsic Evid. in the Interpretation of Wills, 2 Jurid. Soc. 351, 374.

upon these points is decided that it is clearly seen how far the principle is fairly applicable."

And the courts do, in fact, in a great measure, proceed after this method, they do, in fact, look over all the relevant facts; for the court is the tribunal which has to decide on the question of construction and also on the question of the admissibility of evidence to affect construction. The court therefore is, in fact, obliged, by hypothesis at any rate, to consider all the extrinsic facts which are offered. "If evidence manifestly impertinent... be tendered, the court," said Wigram, V. C., "is bound, at once to reject it.... Where the evidence tendered may be material, the practice in equity is usually to admit it (as in this case) in the first instance, and reserve the question of its materiality until the hearing of the cause."[1123]

12. Something more should be said as to Bacon's maxim. Every one knows how much it has figured in the modern cases. But, at first, as I have said, it seems to have lain for more than a century and a half unnoticed by the profession. So far as I have observed, it comes first to light, as a part of our legal literature, in 1761, in a little anonymous book, "The Theory of Evidence," apparently written by Bathurst, then a Justice of the Common Pleas, and afterwards the Lord Chancellor Apsley, — the uncle of Buller. This work became part six of what we know as Buller's "Nisi Prius," abook originally published anonymously, before Buller could have written it, and, in its first edition, sometimes called "Bathurst on Trials." In a slight attempt to give shape to the rules of evidence, it was said in the "Theory of Evidence," that "the fifth general rule is, *Ambiguitas verborum latens verifications suppletur, nam quod ex facto oritur ambiguum verificatione facti tollitur;*" and this was accompanied by further quotations from Bacon, and by a few modern instances, coming down as late as 1751.[1124] There is no indication that the writer, in thus exhuming Bacon's sixteenth century maxim, was aware how he was mingling old conceptions with new and very

---

[1123] Sayer *v.* Sayer, 7 Hare. 377, 380. And so Wig. Ext. Ev. pl. 103. See Lowe *v.* Lord Huntingtower, 4 Rus*s.* 532 n.; s. c. Wig. Ext. Ev. 83 — 89.

[1124] There was, perhaps, a touch of the maxim in Jones *v.* Newman, 1 W. Bl. 60, in 1750, where there were two John Cluers, and the trial judge had refused the offer to prove by parol evidence that the testatrix intended to leave it to John Cluer the son. In granting a new trial the court is reported as saying, "The objection arose from parol evidence, and ought to have been encountered by the same."

different ones. He produced it now as a rule of evidence, and not of pleading. The great name of the author of the maxim gave it credit. It seemed to offer valuable help towards settling the troublesome question as to how far you could go in looking at outside facts to aid in construing a written text. To say that a difficulty which was revealed by extrinsic facts could be cured by looking further into such facts, had a reasonable sound; and when it was coupled with a rule that you could not in any way remedy a difficulty which presented itself on the face of the paper, there seemed to be a complete pocket precept covering the whole subject. When this was found clothed in Latin, and fathered upon Lord Bacon, it might well seem to such as did not think carefully that here was something to be depended upon. The maxim caught the fancy of the profession, and figured as the chief commonplace of the subject for many years. Although Wigram,[1125] seventy years after it was thus brought newly to light, abandoned the use of it, and showed how uninstructive it is, and although the lesson has been abundantly repeated since,[1126] yet it still performs a great and confusing function in our legal discussions.

Bacon, when he spoke of ambiguities patent and latent, meant only a limited sort of thing, namely, what he said, *ambiguity.* But now his maxim came, unfortunately, to be treated as covering the entire subject, and was made to apply to all sorts of defects. It could only do duty as a general exposition by being strangely misinterpreted and strangely misapplied, *e. g;* to the question of filling a blank which a testator had left in his will, or, as we have seen, to the correction of an error, where one thing was expressed, and another meant. If any error of expression was apparent on the face of the document, this was called patent ambiguity, and the courts sometimes undertook to reconcile the correction of it with the maxim which forbade this. The maxim had another singular operation: it was sometimes admitted that defects and errors were not ambiguities, and *for that reason* they were said to be incurable; as when the dissenting opinion in Patch *v.* White,[1127] quoting antiquated expressions, says: "If there is any proposition settled in the law of wills it is that extrinsic evidence is inadmissible to show the intention of the testator, unless it be necessary to explain a latent

---

[1125] Extrins. Ev. pl. 196 — 210. The preface is dated 1st January, 1831.

[1126] Jarman, Wills (5th Lond. ed.), 400 — 401.

[1127] 117 U. S. p. 224.

ambiguity; and a mere mistake is not a latent ambiguity. Where there is no latent ambiguity, there no extrinsic evidence can be received." It became common to say that after identifying the persons and things named in the, document by extrinsic evidence the first inquiry must be as to the existence of a latent ambiguity as shown by this extrinsic evidence; and then, according as this appeared or not, more extrinsic evidence was or was not receivable.

But Wigram accurately pointed out that the phrases latent ambiguity and patent ambiguity were ignorantly used; that a paper is not properly to be called ambiguous simply because the reader of it lacks the needed and attainable outfit of skill and information to read it; that it may be inaccurate without being ambiguous; and that if a court can determine its meaning without any other guide than a knowledge of the facts upon which, from the nature of language, its meaning depends, it cannot truly be called ambiguous. And he added that, "In all cases the application of the extrinsic evidence to which the fifth proposition refers, must precede any declaration which a court can have a right to make that a will is ambiguous."[1128] "The evidence of material facts is, in all cases, admissible in aid of the exposition of a will."[1129]

This remark seems to involve a concession of what is truly the fact, that the real subject of Wigram's book is not any brunch of the law of evidence, but the law of the construction or interpretation of wills; and that the title of it is misleading.

13. In 1833, between the dates of the first and second editions of Wigram's book, came the decision in the Lord Chancellor's court of the case of Miller *v.* Travers, on appeal.[1130] The Vice-Chancellor had decided it below about six months before the first edition was printed, and this decision was at variance with Wigram's conclusions and had given him trouble; he had made it the subject of searching criticism in the first edition. The circumstance that the decision on appeal, given by a distinguished tribunal (the

---

[1128] Pl. 203.

[1129] Pl. 212. The import of the term "material" is indicated at pl. 98 — 100: "In limiting the evidence ... to the material facts, the generality of the proposition contended for, respecting the admissibility of explanatory evidence in aid of the exposition of wills, is in no degree broken in upon. This limit is imposed by the general laws of evidence, and not by any thing peculiar to the subject to which it is here applied."

[1130] 8 Bing. 244.

Lord Chancellor Brougham, aided by Tindal, C. J., and Lyndhurst, C. B.) confirmed Wigram's lately published opinion, naturally gave the case a very conspicuous place in the second edition of the book, — one which it has permanently retained.[1131] It is for this reason, perhaps, more than any other, that the case has occupied so prominent a place in the general discussions of the subject. *So* modern case has figured more conspicuously as an illustration of the parol evidence rule. In reality it decides no point in the law of evidence. The decision is undoubtedly sound, but the reasoning is confused and the real point of the matter is out of focus.

A testator had devised, for the purpose of certain trusts, "all my freehold and real estates whatsoever situate in the county of Limerick and in the city of Limerick." He had no real estate in the county of Limerick, and in the city of Limerick only a small amount — quite disproportioned to the charges laid upon the devised estates. He had considerable estates in the county of Clare, and it was these that he had meant to devise. A draft of the will had been submitted to the testator, and approved and returned by him, in which the devise ran, "all my freehold and real estates whatsoever situate in the counties of Clare, Limerick, and in the city of Limerick." While this was approved by the testator, some changes were ordered in other parts of the will; and the draft, with a statement of the proposed alterations, was sent by the testator's attorney to his conveyancer. The conveyancer, in redrawing the paper, by mistake and without authority, struck out the words "counties of Clare" and substituted therefor, the words "county of.'" "When the testator received the new draft, he did not observe this change; and after keeping the will by him for some time, executed it in this, its final form.

The plaintiff filed a bill "for the purpose of establishing the will... and carrying into execution the trusts thereof." The Vice-Chancellor directed an issue on the question "whether the testator... did devise his estates in the county of 'Clare and in the county of Limerick and in the city and county of the city of Limerick, and either and which of them to the trustees mentioned in his will and their heirs." On an appeal by the heiress-at-law, the Lord Chancellor (Brougham) reversed this decree. In arriving at this result, he had

---

[1131] He devotes to the last decision some twenty pages; more than an eighth of the entire book. In its two stages, this case, including the criticisms on the doctrine of the earlier decision, takes up more than a fifth of the book.

called in Chief Justice Tindal and the Chief Baron, Lord Lyndhurst. The opinion is given by the Chief Justice; the Chancellor contents himself mainly with adopting this opinion and decreeing accordingly.

As the case was decided, there was no question of construction in it; it was expressly declared by the Lord Chancellor and the Chief Justice that, as the case stood, no question was made as to "whether the whole instrument taken together, and without going out of it, was sufficient to pass the estates in Clare." It was an attempt to reform a will by adding to it words omitted by mistake.

"It is not," said the Chief Justice, "simply removing a difficulty arising from a defective or mistaken description; it is making the will speak upon a subject on which it is altogether silent, and is the same in effect as the filling up of a blank which the testator might have left in his will. It amounts, in short,... to the making of a new devise for the testator, which he is supposed to have omitted.... The effect... would be... that all the guards intended to be introduced by the Statute of Frauds would be entirely destroyed, and the statute itself virtually repealed." These difficulties and objections arise in point of substantive law. They are not objections which have their root in the law of evidence or any of its rules. The point of them lies in the fact that the plaintiff is seeking to give the quality and operation of a devise to that which has not the necessary form of a devise. The fatal objection is, not that the plaintiff's evidence is bad, but that his substantive case is bad. What he is trying to do is legally inadmissible; the trouble is not that he is trying to do a permissible thing by means of objectionable evidence. Unhappily for the effect of this case upon the law, it does have in it a suggestion of this last difficulty also: evidence inadmissible under the law of evidence was offered. None the less, however, the true proposition of the case is this: 'Whether the plaintiffs' evidence be good or bad is immaterial; he cannot have an issue, because, however admissible the evidence might be, and however full, it can do him no good. He is seeking to do a thing forbidden, by law, — to give the effect of a devise to that which has not the required form of a devise.

In so far as this case and the issue in question might involve a question of the *factum* of the will, a matter which at that period was open to inquiry at this stage of such a case,[1132] it is to be observed

---

[1132] Ricketts *v.* Turquand, 1 H. L. C. 472.

that the discussion lacked the discrimination of later cases. These recognize the necessity under such circumstances of considering any and all contemporaneous expressions of the testator's intentions.[1133]

In so far as any question of construction was open, it was not discussed and was left undecided. This fact, which is often overlooked,[1134] should be carefully observed in estimating the scope and value of this case. "Some arguments," said the Chief Justice, "were offered by the plaintiff's counsel upon the construction, of the will from the context of the whole instrument; and it was contended that, without the introduction of any extrinsic evidence, the estates in Clare would pass under the will; but as the state of the cause at the time of the hearing did not admit of such discussion, and as the counsel for the defendants' disclaimed entering upon it at present, we have, in fact, not heard the parties on that point, and we therefore think it right to forbear offering any opinion thereon." And the Chancellor, in concurring with the advice of the judges, added the remark: "Whether the whole instrument taken together, and without going out of it, was sufficient to pass the estates in Clare, is a point which has not been argued here, and on which we give no opinion." The case was treated as an attempt to reform a mistake in a will; in other words, as raising the same question which was presented in Newburgh v. Newburgh, at its first stage, and which, in that case, was rightly held in the negative both by the Vice-Chancellor below and by the Lords, as well as by the judges, in a unanimous advisory opinion.[1135] That case was cited as the chief authority in the Chief Justice's opinion in Miller v. Travers.[1136]

And yet the desired result in Newburgh v. Newburgh, defeated on the first contention, was at last accomplished in the

---

[1133] Guardhouse v. Blackburn, L. R. 1 P. & D. 109 (1866). "The court of probate, setting about to ascertain the will of the deceased, could not stir a step in the inquiry, without some proof beyond the mere writing. . . . The truth is that the rules excluding parol evidence have no place in any inquiry in which the court has not got before it some ascertained paper, beyond question binding and of full effect."

[1134] See, e. q., Tucker v. Seaman's Aid Soc., 7 Met. 188, pp. 207 — 208.

[1135] 5 Madd. 364 (1820); s. c. *Dom. Proc.* Sugd. Law Prop. 206.

[1136] "Upon the authority of the cases, and more particularly, of that which is last referred to," says Tindal, C. J., in 8 Bing. 244, referring to Newburgh v. Newburgh.

House of Lords merely by construction.[1137] It might, therefore, with entire consistency, have turned out, when Miller *v.* Travers came to be thoroughly canvassed on the question of construction, that a contrary result should be reached; just as it did turn out that way in Newburgh *v.* Newburgh. In other words, the case in reality is not an authority on the question of construction, or the use of extrinsic facts in aid of construction.[1138]

14. The opinion in Miller *v.* Travers does, however, in a confusing way, talk of construction, and one remark calls for observation at this point. The Chief Justice, after saying that a difficulty or ambiguity introduced by extrinsic evidence may be removed by further evidence upon the same subject, adds that this use of extrinsic evidence is limited to two classes of cases, neither of which includes the present: "But the cases to which this construction applies will be found to range themselves into two separate classes, distinguishable from each other, and to neither of which can the present case be referred. The first class is, where the description of the thing devised, or of the devisee, is clear upon the face of the will; but upon the death of the testator it is found that there are more than one estate or subject-matter of devise, or more than one person whose description follows out and fills the words used in the will. As where the testator devises his manor of Dale, and at his death it is found that he has two manors of that name, South Dale and North Dale; or where a man devises to his son John, and he has two sons of that name. In each of these cases respectively parol evidence is admissible to show which manor was intended to pass, and which son was intended to take. Bac. Max. 23; Hob. Rep. 32; Edward Altham's Case, 8 Rep. 155. The other class of cases is that in which the description contained in the will of the thing intended to be devised, or of the person who is intended to take, is true in part, but not true in every particular. As where an estate is devised called A, and is described as in the occupation of B, and it is found, that though there is an estate called A, yet the whole is not in B's occupation; or where an estate is devised to a person whose surname or Christian name is mistaken; or whose description is imperfect or

---

[1137] "The omission," says Sugden, "was supplied by construction, and the will was supported just as if there had been no mistake." Law of Prop. 207; s. c. Thayer's Cases on Evidence, 847; and on appeal, 931.

[1138] And yet see Lord Brougham's high commendation of the case in Mostyn v. Mostyn, 5 H. L. C. 168 (1854).

inaccurate; in. which latter class of cases parol evidence is admissible to show what estate was intended to pass, and who was the devisee intended to take, provided there is sufficient indication of intention appearing on the face of the will to justify the application of the evidence." [1139]

Here we see again the recognition of that ancient case of the two or more persons or things of the same name, which could not be overlooked, because it had been recognized in our books for centuries; and also, the old familiar recognition of another case assimilated with that, as if governed by a common principle, — namely, that of two or more objects, persons, or things, to neither of which does the description accurately apply, but where either might answer the call if it stood alone. The common quality here is described by saying that there is a latent ambiguity, disclosed by extrinsic circumstances: Being thus disclosed, they say, it may be in like manner removed; and it is allowed thus to be removed "from the necessity of the case." [1140] While to this extent extrinsic facts were allowed to "supplement the evidence of the will itself and the terms of the will itself as to the testator's intention," [1141] beyond these limits it was said here, as in earlier cases, you could not go. In saying this, it will be observed, no discrimination was made between direct statements of intention and any other evidence. Of course in that outer region where all extrinsic matter was condemned there was no good and bad; but within the region where extrinsic matter was available in aid of construction, this same lack of discrimination was found, and it had tended to create a confused impression that where any extrinsic evidence was admissible all was equally admissible. Wigram's book corrected that; and although the judges in Miller *v.* Travers had profited little by this book, if they ever heard of it, the doctrine was soon clearly and permanently recognized in the cases. [1142]

[1139] 8 Bing.244,248.

[1140] Doe d. Chichester *v.* Oxenden, 4 Dow, 65.

[1141] Lord Bussell, C. J., in *In re* Stephenson, 75 L. T. R. 495,496 (1897).

[1142] *E. g.* Doe d. Gord *v.* Needs. 2 M. & W. 129 (1836), and Doe d. Hiscocks v. Hiscocks, 5 M. & W. 363 (1839), Charter v. Charter, L. R. 7 H. L. 364 (1874), that it was only in the one case of equivocation that direct statements of intention could be used.

15. With this discrimination clearly made, and the recognition of the narrow restriction thus put upon the use of direct extrinsic statements of intention, room was left for a juster and more liberal view of the use of extrinsic facts, generally, in aid of construction. The main features of this new gospel were truly set out by Wigram; but he was a pioneer; he was hampered by the supposed necessity of so distinguishing the older cases as not to seem to set them wholly aside; and it may be that he saw some points less clearly than his successors, who, in their studies of the subject, had been emancipated by him, and had begun where he left off. While his phraseology condemned all "evidence of intention," unless where direct statements of intention, were allowed, those who came after him could plainly and openly recognize that much of the allowable use of ordinary extrinsic facts did, in fact, go directly to that point. While he found the use of direct statements of intention in any case difficult to support, they were able to find it always logically good; and only excluded, in general, on grounds of policy; and while he laid down with excessive strictness the just principle that, in general, the natural and ordinary meaning of words should be given to them, and so their technical meaning, when they have any, they were able, and the courts in a fair degree have gradually become able, to apply the principle in a more liberal manner. Wigram had put it, in his second proposition, that if the Context of a will allows it, and if the strict and primary sense of the words is *sensible* with reference to extrinsic circumstances, it is an inflexible rule of construction that they shall be interpreted in that sense and no other. And again,[1143] that "in cases in which the meaning of the words is either settled by decision, or clear upon the will itself, and in which the facts of the case do not necessarily *exclude* the supposition that the words were used in their decided or apparent sense, the second proposition, above stated, leaves nothing to the discretion of a court; and exposition, in the strict observance of that proposition, is safe against the inroads of conjecture." [1144] Thirty years later Hawkins[1145] laid

---

[1143] Pl. 128.

[1144] "The court is bound to construe the words of the will in their strict and primary sense unless the circumstances of the case exclude that sense; and the court is not at liberty to construe the words in any secondary sense, only because the state of the property or other extrinsic circumstances may make it in the highest degree probable that the words were used in such secondary sense." *Per* Wigram, V. C., in Sayer *v.* Sayer. 7 Hare, 377, 381 (1848).

down the main proposition, in this more liberal form, namely, that "the words and expressions used are to be taken in their ordinary, proper, and grammatical sense; — unless upon so reading them in connection with the entire will, or upon applying them to the facts of the case, an ambiguity or difficulty of construction, in the opinion of the court, arises, in which case the primary meaning of the words may be modified... so far as to remove or avoid the difficulty or ambiguity, but no further."

Certainly, however, Wigram's little book, in 1831, went far to clear up the confusion that had gathered over the whole subject. He was led to write it, as he says in the "Advertisement" to the first edition, by being accidentally present at the hearing of the case of Goblet *v.* Beechey, before Vice-Chancellor Leach, in July, 1826, — a case of which he gives some account in an appendix. The book lacks an historical exposition, and, as already said, it does not clearly discriminate those parts of it which belong to the law of evidence from the rest. This is its great defect. The cases, also, are not so thoroughly analyzed, or treated with so free a hand, as might be wished. Owing, furthermore, to the use of an "interpretation clause" near the beginning, and to the use of the phrase "evidence to prove intention," in a special sense, his meaning is often misconceived. It should be added that his conception of the nature of the whole process of interpretation lacks thoroughness.[1146]

But whether explicitly stated by Wigram or not, this book brings out and stamps upon the mind of careful readers two or three things of capital importance: 1. That Bacon's maxim is inadequate and uninstructive; 2. That extrinsic expressions of the writer's intention cannot be resorted to in aid of the exposition of a will, except where a person or thing is described in terms equally applicable to two or more; and 3. That there is no excluding rule of evidence, other than this, peculiar to this subject. The seven propositions which are the substance of the book amount to this: A testator, unless the text, read as a whole, shows the contrary, presumably uses words in their primary sense. If the extrinsic facts of the case allow of the words having this sense, they must have it; if they do not, the words must have such other secondary sense as they

---

[1145] Wills, 2.

[1146] Wigram's book should be supplemented by the excellent paper of Hawkins, inserted *infra.* Appendix B.

are capable of, in view of these facts. If the words are obscure, or unintelligible to the court, resort may be had, in deciphering or translating them, to the aid of competent witnesses. While, as regards persons and things indicated by the testator, and "every other disputed point respecting which it can be shown that a knowledge of extrinsic facts can, in any way, be made ancillary to the right interpretation of a testator's words," a court may look at every extrinsic fact which is not excluded by the general rules of evidence, yet there is one excluding rule of evidence, namely, that not even to save a will from being void for uncertainty can "evidence to prove intention itself" be received, unless in the case of equivocation; namely, where a person or thing is described in terms applicable, equally, to more than one.

And this, it is believed, is the only rule of evidence included in the entire compass of the so-called parol evidence rule.

CHAPTER XI
THE "BEST EVIDENCE" RULE [1147]

"We find, to-day, in our treatises on evidence, a role or principle to which is assigned a great, comprehensive place and scope, quite unparalleled in this part of the law. It is called the rule of the Best Evidence. In Greenleaf's treatise on Evidence, where he follows, with a variation, an earlier writer, it is the last of four great, fundamental rules which are said to govern, the production of testimony.[1148] The first three lay it down (1) that evidence must be relevant to what is alleged in pleading; (2) that it need only prove the substance of the issue; and (3) that the burden of proving a proposition lies on him who affirms it. These three rules, however, are not rules of evidence, but of practice, pleading, or legal reasoning. For, as regards the first two, namely, that the evidence must be relevant to the allegations, and that it is enough to prove the substance of the issue, they simply set up the lists for the contest, define the aims and limits of the dispute, and assert the necessity of logical relevancy — which is a matter of course in a rational system.

[1147] The substance of this chapter and the next was read, as a part of the Storrs Lectures, at the Law School of Yale University, in October, 1896. Although, as originally written, these papers were intended ultimately to take their place here, the immediate occasion for which they were prepared must account for the mode of treatment. For reasons indicated before {supra, 5) I have preferred not to recast them.

[1148] The Law of Evidence is considered by Greenleaf under three heads. Part I. deals with the "Nature and Principles of Evidence;" Part II. with "The Rules which govern the Production of Testimony;" and Part III., with "The Instruments of Evidence." It is Part II. which covers the excluding rules and all the main body of the subject; and in opening this, after a few general remarks, the writer says: "The production of evidence to the jury is governed by certain principles which may be treated under four general heads, or rules. The first of these is, that the evidence must correspond with the allegations and be confined to the point in issue. The second is, that it is sufficient if the substance only of the issue be proved. The third is, that the burden of proving a proposition, or issue, lies on the party holding the affirmative. And the fourth is, that the best evidence of which the case in its nature is susceptible must always be produced." These four topics give name to the first four chapters of Part II.; and then the remaining chapters, five to fifteen inclusive, entitled Hearsay, etc., etc., follow, as if they were merely co-ordinate with what precedes. The treatment is obscure; but evidently Greenleaf's conception of these first four rules is not that they are co-ordinate with the others but that they govern the application of them all.

The rules of evidence are not called into play until all this has been first ascertained. The point to which a party must address himself, the thing that he must prove, being determined, the rules of evidence help to govern the mode in which he proceeds to prove it. As to the third rule, fixing the burden of proof, if this means the duty of establishing the issue by the necessary preponderance of proof, as contrasted with the purely defensive office of keeping an adversary in check, that, as we have already seen,[1149] is a rule fixing responsibility, in all departments of legal reasoning; not merely in trying cases, where alone the rules of evidence have place, but in arguing them when the trial is over, or when, as on agreed facts, there never was any trial. And if the burden of proof means the duty of going forward, and not necessarily the duty of establishing, this is still a rule of practice governing the whole topic of legal reasoning, and in no way peculiar to the law of evidence. He who would apply the rules of evidence with success must, of course, have these three rules carefully in mind. But that is only saying that he must take account of the substantive rights and duties, and of the rules of pleading and procedure pertinent to his contention, and that these must govern and point all his evidence. Of course they must. It is only as he observes them, that he is saved from striking wild.

If, then, among these four all-controlling principles there be any rule of evidence at all, it must be the fourth. What is this rule? Is there to-day, in point of fact, any rule of the Best Evidence which either comprehends, or subordinates and shapes the application of all the rules of evidence? If so, what is it, and how shall we state it? As we find it laid down, it runs that "the best evidence of which the case, in its nature, is susceptible, must always be produced."

Greenleaf devotes a chapter to it,[1150] consisting of sixteen sections. The last thirteen of these are devoted to what are called "the cases which most frequently call for the application of the rule... those which relate to the substitution of oral for written evidence;" that is to say, almost all the chapter is merely a statement of the doctrine that if one would prove the contents of a writing he must produce the writing or legally excuse its absence. That rule, it will be observed, is not regarded as being itself the rule of the Best Evidence, but only an. instance of the application of it.

[1149] *Supra,* c. ix.
[1150] Vol. i. c. 4, ss. 82 to 97 incl.

What, then, do we learn of the rule itself, this great, shaping rule, affecting the production of all testimony? We learn this, that it is a rule which "excludes only that evidence which itself indicates the existence of more original sources of information. But where there is no substitution of evidence, but only a selection of weaker, instead of stronger proofs, or an omission to supply all the proofs capable of being produced, the rule is not infringed."[1151]

We are then told, in a few lines (s. 83), that there are exceptions, such as the case of proving that official character may be shown by proof of acting in the office without producing a man's commission. And lastly (s. 84) it is said that this rule divides evidence into primary and secondary. "Primary evidence is... the best evidence, or that kind of proof which, under any possible circumstances, affords the greatest certainty of the fact in question.... All evidence falling short of this, in its degree, is termed secondary....

[1151] Sect. 82. I give the rest of this section in full: "A fourth rule, which governs in the production of evidence, is that which requires *the best evidence of which the case, in its nature, is susceptible.* This rule does not demand the greatest amount of evidence, which can possibly he given of any fact; but its design is to prevent the introduction of any, which, from the nature of the case, supposes that better evidence is in the possession of the party. It is adopted for the prevention of fraud; for when it is apparent, that the better evidence is withheld, it is fair to presume, that the party had some sinister motive for not producing it, and that, if offered, his design would be frustrated. The rule thus becomes essential to the pure administration of justice. In, requiring the production of the best evidence applicable to each particular fact, it is meant, that no evidence shall be received, which is merely substitutionary in its nature, go long as the original evidence can be had. The rule excludes only that evidence, which itself indicates the existence of more original sources of information. But where there is no substitution of evidence, but only a selection of weaker, instead of stronger proofs, or an omission to supply all the proofs capable of being produced, the rule is not infringed. Thus a title by deed must be proved by the production of the deed itself, if it is within the power of the party; for this is the best evidence, of which the case is susceptible; and its. non-production would raise a presumption, that it contained some matter of apparent defeasance. But being produced, the execution of the deed itself may be proved by only one of the subscribing witnesses, though the other also is at hand. And even the previous examination of a deceased subscribing witness, if admissible on other grounds, may supersede the necessity of calling the survivor. So, in proof or disproof of handwriting, it is not necessary to call the supposed writer himself. And, even where it is necessary to prove negatively, that an act was done without the consent, or against the will of another, it is not, in general, necessary to call the person, whose will or consent is denied."

Evidence which carries on its face no indication that better remains behind, is not secondary but primary."

This is the substance of what this leading author says. Taylor, in his book on Evidence, largely repeats Greenleaf. And Best, in his treatise, sets forth, even more emphatically, the great, overtopping pre-eminence of this supposed rule of evidence. Repeating the expressions of earlier writers and judges, to the effect that "there is but one general rule of evidence, the best that the nature of the case will admit," he adds an exposition of his own, not found elsewhere. The true meaning, he tells us, of "this fundamental principle will be best understood by considering the three chief applications of it." 1. Evidence must come through proper channels; *i. e.,* the tribunal must not go on private information, but on legal evidence. 2. The evidence must be original and not derivative; a principle which covers hearsay, and the rule about proving the contents of a writing. 3. The evidence must have an open, visible, clear connection with. the fact to be proved. And then Best adds that "the true character and value of the important principle now under consideration is, however, more easily conceived than described. In dealing with natural evidence, he says, the connection between the principal and evidentiary facts must be left to instinct; in legal evidence this is replaced by a sort of instinct or legal sense acquired by practice."

This is pretty vague. Best limits the distinction of primary and secondary evidence to writings, *i. e;* to what Greenleaf deals with as the "chief application" of the great rule. And in truth, when we talk of specific rules of evidence, this one, which requires the production of the original document, seems to be about all there is left of the Best Evidence principle.

If that is so, it would be wise to drop the expression, as a name for any definite rule of exclusion, since the rule just referred to has its own sufficient name and place. The vagueness and generality of the accounts given by Greenleaf and Best will be noticed. It seems plain that these writers are trying, what Gilbert vainly tried before them, namely, to reduce to the tangible form of an excluding rule what the older judges had put forward as a shaping principle. Any excluding rule of evidence tends necessarily to sharpness of definition: it is by its nature unfitted for that large function which is assigned, on paper, to the Best Evidence principle. In point of fact, the rule against substitutionary evidence is one of narrow operation.

The language of our law writers comes from an attempt to keep alive a phrase that has lost its original meaning and survived its old function.

Let us look at the history of the matter. How did this rule of the Best Evidence originate? what was its meaning? and what has been its development?

The phrase first appears in our cases, I believe, after the English revolution, in C. J. Holt's time. That is an early period for anything like a rule of evidence, properly so called. Such rules could not well come into prominence, or be much insisted on, while the jury were allowed to find verdicts on their own knowledge; and that power of the jury had been elaborately asserted as a leading ground of the judgment in Bushell's case in 1670, by Vaughan, C. J., speaking for the court. Finding the rule, then, at the end of the seventeenth century, let us trace it down, not too minutely. In the year 1699 —1700, in Ford v. Hopkins,[1152] in allowing a goldsmith's note as evidence against a stranger of the fact that the goldsmith had received money, Holt, C. J., said. that they must take notice of the usages of trade; " the best proof that the nature of the thing will afford is only required." This is the earliest instance of the use of the phrase that I remember. This or its synonyms is repeatedly used by Holt and others. In 1701 counsel argue that certain evidence is "not good, because not the host the nature of the thing will bear, but only circumstantial." Holt, C. J., overruled this contention. Again, in 1709,[1153] on a question of proving the contents of papers sent over from Ireland, by a deposition, or by a witness who had gone to Ireland and verified the copy, it was argued that "the best evidence that can be had must be given." The deposition was held good. Holt, C. J: "The law requires the best evidence that can be had.... But this rule must be interpreted with reference to the witness deposing;" his affidavit is not good if he is here; but if absent his deposition may be good.

The phrase now became familiar, and it continued to hold a great place throughout the eighteenth century. Chief Baron Gilbert introduced the expression into his book on Evidence, and recognized the rule which requires of a party the best evidence that he can

---

[1152] 1 Salk. 283. It will be remembered that money used to be deposited with goldsmiths, and their notes taken as evidence of the deposit.

[1153] Altham v. Anglesea, 11 Mod. 210.

produce, as the chief rule of the whole subject. This book was written at some time before 1726, for that was the date of Gilbert's death; and it was not only the first text-book on the subject, of any importance, but it held its place to the end of the century as the great authority. It is said in Gilbert's book[1154] that "the first, therefore, and most signal rule in relation to evidence is this, that a man must have the utmost evidence the nature of the fact is capable of.... The true meaning of the rule of law that requires the greatest evidence that the nature of the thing is capable of is this, that no such evidence shall be brought which *ex natura, rei* supposes still a greater evidence behind in the parties' own possession and power." "Why did he not produce the better evidence? he asks; and he illustrates by what was always the stock example, the case of offering "a copy of a deed or will where he ought to produce the original."

This principle is the test throughout the book. Sometimes we are told that it is enough if a party offer the best evidence that he can. If a witness fall sick by the way, his deposition may be used, "for, in this case, the deposition is the best evidence that possibly can be had, and that answers what the law requires." That remark carries an important suggestion; it is a generalization of Holt's doctrine in 1709, and adds to the rule of the best evidence an aspect of indulgence, by limiting the operation of its excluding quality. The rule becomes now this: a party must bring the best evidence that he can; and if he does this it is enough. Such a rule as that would have admitted hearsay, if a witness had died. In Bacon's Abridgment, first published in 1736, we are told that " It seems in regard to evidence to be an uncontestable rule that the party who is to prove any fact, must do it by the highest evidence the nature of the thing is capable of." And in a book of very extensive vogue, Buller's Nisi Prius,[1155] this rule figured as "the first general rule of evidence," and Gilbert's language was repeated.

Blackstone, also, in 1768, and in all the editions of his Commentaries, followed Gilbert. "The one general rule," he said, "that runs through all the doctrine of trials is this, that the best evidence the nature of the case will admit of shall always be required, if possible to be had; but if not possible, then the best

---

[1154] 2d ed. 4, 15 — 17.
[1155] Originally published as Bathurst on Trials in 1760. Bathurst wag Bailer's uncle.

evidence that can be had shall be allowed." For, he added, if there be better evidence, not producing it raises a presumption of falsehood and concealment.[1156]

The courts also were using the same and even more emphatic language. In 1740,[1157] Lord Hardwicke declared that "the rule of evidence is that the best evidence that the circumstances of the case will allow must be given. There is no rule of evidence to be laid down in this court but a reasonable one, such as the nature of the thing to be proved will admit of." And in 1792[1158] Lord Loughborough said "that all common-law courts ought to proceed upon the general rule, namely, the best evidences that the nature of the case will admit, I perfectly agree." But the great, conspicuous instance in which this doctrine was asserted and applied was in the famous and historical case of Omichund *v.* Barker, in 1744, growing out of the extension of British commerce in India, where the question, was on receiving in an English court the testimony of a native heathen Hindoo, taken in India, on an oath conformed to the usages of his religion. In this case, Willes, J.,[1159] resorted to this rule, and Lord Hardwicke, sitting as Chancellor, with great emphasis[1160] said: "The judges and sages of the law have laid it down that there is but one general rule of evidence, the best that the nature of the case will allow.... It is a common natural presumption that persons of the Gentoo religion should be principally apprised of facts and transactions in their own country." And so he found a "presumed necessity."

Fifty years later these remarks of Lord Hardwicke were resorted to by Burke, in attacking what he regarded as the too great strictness of the Lords in limiting the testimony at the trial of the impeachment of "Warren Hastings. In 1794, in his Report on the Lords' Journal, Burke dealt with the matter in this resounding declaration:[1161] "At length Lord Hardwicke, in one of the cases the most solemnly argued that has been in man's memory, with the aid

---

[1156] Com. iii. 368.

[1157] Llewellin *v.* Mackworth, 2 Atk. 40; Villiers *v.* Villiers, ib. 71. And he affirmed that the rules of evidence at law and in equity were the same. 2 Ves. 38.

[1158] Grant *v.* Gould, 2 H. Bl. p. 104.

[1159] Willes Rep. p. 550.

[1160] 1 Atk. p. 49.

[1161] Works of Burke (Little & Brown's ed.), xi. 77; Thayer's Cases on Evidence, 732.

of the greatest learning at the bar, and with the aid of all the learning on the bench, both bench and bar being then supplied with men of the first form, declared from the bench, and in concurrence with the rest of the judges and with the most learned of the long robe, the able counsel on the side of the old restrictive principles making no reclamation, 'that the judges and sages of the law have laid it down that there is but one general rule of evidence, — *the best that the nature of the case will admit.'* This, then," added Burke, "the master rule that governs all the subordinate rules, does, in reality, subject itself and its own virtue and authority *to the nature of the case,* and leaves no rule at all of an independent abstract and substantive quality."

This perfectly natural interpretation of Lord Hardwicke's statement, made by a great statesman on a conspicuous occasion was indeed a startling outcome of this doctrine of the Best Evidence. It was thus turned, into a solvent of all the other rules that had been forming; and then, itself was dissolved. Whatever was peculiar in the English law of evidence here of a sudden vanished; and all was reduced to the condition of the continental law, that system where the jury had not survived, and where no law of evidence had grown up.[1162] Burke's sharp attack upon the procedure of the Lords soon led to something that helped to clear the air. His urgent insistence, during the Hastings case, that the House of Lords was not rigidly

---

[1162] Burke was not a lawyer. He began the study of law, but soon abandoned it. It may help to moderate our surprise at such a declaration as this, if we remember that at the period when it was made, the English law of evidence, properly so called, had emerged but little out of the nisi *prius* courts. Sir James Stephen, writing in 1885 (Nuncomar and Impey, i. 121 n.), remarks, "After much study of the law of evidence my opinion is that the greater part of the present law came into definite existence, after being for an unascertainable period the practice of the courts (differing by the way to some extent on different circuits), just about one hundred years ago." Stephen was a liker of paradox; but there is some substantial truth in this remark. To be sore we find Lord Kenyon saying in 1790 (R. *v.* Eriswell, 3 T. R. 707), in holding, where he was one of an evenly divided court, that a sworn statement, before justices, of one now insane and so unable to testify, could not be received, — that "the rules of evidence . . . have been matured by the wisdom of ages, and are now revered from their antiquity," etc. In comparing that statement with Stephen's, a century later, all depends on what is meant when you speak of the rules, or law, of evidence. Lord Kenyon doubtless included those numerous exclusions of evidence, running far back into the Year Books, which go upon grounds of substantive law and pleading, and hold that what is offered does not maintain the issue.

bound, in impeachment trials, by the rules of evidence which governed the ordinary law courts, was sharply controverted by Edward Christian, in 1792, in a pamphlet which was his first legal publication. He was then teaching law at Cambridge, where nine years later he became the first Downing Professor of the laws of England, a chair now honored by the learning and accomplishments of Professor Maitland. Burke, in the House of Commons, in the same year, replied to the positions of Christian; whereupon the latter wrote what he called a "Dissertation upon Evidence before the House of Lords." Although, written in 1792, this was not published until 1820, at a time when the proceedings of the Lords, on occasion, of the purely legislative question of passing a bill of pains and penalties against Queen Caroline, called out from Professor Christian a further brief paper maintaining the same doctrine as applicable to those proceedings, and thus led to the printing of the whole work. In this dissertation, thus appearing to have been written in 1792, Christian introduces a passage about the Best Evidence, afterwards preserved in his notes to the twelfth edition, of Blackstone, in 1794, the year in which Burke's Report on the Lords' Journal is dated. At the passage about the Best Evidence, in Blackstone's third volume, which I have already quoted,[1163] Christian adds the note above mentioned, drawn from his previous answer to Burke:

"No rule of law," he says, "is more frequently cited and more generally misconceived, than this. It is certainly true when rightly understood; but it is very limited in its extent and application. It signifies nothing more than that, if the best legal evidence cannot possibly be produced, the next best legal evidence shall be admitted. Evidence may be divided into primary and secondary; and the secondary evidence is as accurately defined by the law as the primary. But in general the want of better evidence can never justify the admission of hearsay, interested witnesses, copies of copies, etc. Where there are exceptions to general rules, these exceptions are as much recognized by the law as the general rule; and where boundaries and limits are established by the law for every case that can possibly occur, it is immaterial what we call the rule and what the exception."

These keen observations, although attributing to the rules of evidence, rightly so called, much too great an elaboration and

---

[1163] *Supra,* 491.

completeness, nevertheless went to the root of this matter. An old principle which had served a useful purpose for the century while rules of evidence had been forming and were being applied, to an extent never before known, while the practice of granting new trials for the jury's disregard of evidence had been developing, and judicial control over evidence had been greatly extended, — this old principle, this convenient, rough test, had survived its usefulness. A crop of specific rules and exceptions to rules had been sprouting, and hardening into au independent growth. It had become perfectly true that in many cases it made no difference whatever whether a man offered the best evidence that he could or not, — the best evidence that the nature of the case admitted, the best *ex natura rei,* as some judges said, or the best, *rebus sic stantibus,* as others said; — none the less it was, in many cases, rejected. The two or three great specific and typical doctrines, indeed, that had been seized upon and generalized into this dogma of the Best Evidence, remained; the doctrines that depositions of witnesses could not be produced to a jury, if the witness himself could be produced; that writings by which a jury was to be informed, must be submitted to their inspection if possible; that the witnesses to an attested document must be produced if they could be had. But all these doctrines had a footing and characteristics of their own, and each was working out its own discriminations and its own exceptions. The rule, itself, of the Best Evidence, in its twofold aspect, — (1) that every man must bring the best evidence that he could, and (2) that the best he could should be received, — was no longer fit to serve any purpose as a working rule of exclusion. Its continued life, if life it was to have, must be that of a large principle to aid the judges in time to come in justly shaping the development of the existing rules of evidence, and in marking out the lines on which the reform of these rules might safely be conducted at the hands of the judiciary.

But the sagacious observations of Christian were little heeded; they were probably little known. We find Lord Kenyon, at *nisi prius,* in 1797, holding that in determining the conformity of a bushel measure to the regular standard, the bushel measure itself must be produced. "The best evidence the nature of the case would admit of was a production of both measures in court, and a comparison of them before the jury."[1164] And this doctrine, as

---

[1164] Chenie *v.* Watson, Peake's Add. Cas. 123.

applicable to everything, was actually laid down in a treatise in 1820, as a general principle of the English law.[1165] "As the evidence of sense," the writer says, "is undoubtedly the most perfect by which that knowledge can be obtained, so, if the person op object can be brought into the presence of the court, no inferior evidence shall be admitted." In reality no such application of the principle was established in the English law; and this doctrine that the Best Evidence rule applies to things, has been emphatically repudiated by the courts.[1166] Of course I am speaking of definite rules of exclusion; not of arguments as to the moral weight of what is received. Again in 1802, in a famous case involving a very large sum of money, where the plaintiff's witness had died, and the only other person directly cognizant of the facts was the defendant's agent; and where the plaintiff, wishing, naturally, to avoid calling the adversary's man as a witness, rested his case on a variety of circumstances tending to prove it, the Court of King's Bench nonsuited him. Lord Ellenborough said: "The best evidence should have been given of which the nature of the thing was capable. The best evidence was to have been had by calling, in the first instance, upon the people immediately and officially employed in the delivery and in the receiving the goods on board.... And though the one of these persons... was dead, it did not warrant the plaintiff in resorting to an inferior and secondary species of testimony, namely, the presumption and inference arising from a non-communication to other persons on board, as long as the military conductor, the other living witness... concerned in... shipping the goods on board, could be resorted to." This special doctrine, however, has not been generally accepted, and the condemnation of it by Starkie, and Phillips and Amos, in their treatises, no doubt truly represents the law.

But as regards the main rule of the Best Evidence, in its general application, the text-books which followed Gilbert, beginning with Peake in 1801, and continuing with the leading treatises of Phillips in 1814, Starkie in 1824, Greenleaf in 1842, Taylor in 1848, and Best in 1849 all repeat it. But it is accompanied

---

[1165] Glassford on Evidence; originally written as an article for the Supplement to the Encyclopaedia Britannica, but found too long for that purpose, and separately printed.

[1166] Queen v. Francis, L. R. 2 C. C. R. 128 (1874); Lucas v. Williams, 66 L. T. Rep. 706.

now with so many explanations and qualifications as to indicate the need of some simpler and truer statement, which should exclude any mention of this as a working rule of our system. Indeed it would probably have dropped naturally out of use long ago, if it had not come to be a convenient, short description of the rule as to proving the contents of a writing. Regarded as a general rule, the trouble with it is that it is not true to the facts, and does not hold out in its application; and in so far as it does apply, it is unnecessary and uninstructive. It is roughly descriptive of two or three rules which have their own reasons and their own name and place, and are well enough known without it. When explained theoretically, and treated as a working rule, it is restricted to the situation where the evidence which is offered discloses, on its face, that there is something behind it for which it is a substitute.

Let us therefore look at the Best Evidence rule, in its character as a specific rule forbidding substitutionary evidence, *i.e.,* such as shows on its face that there is something director and better behind it. In this sense it is a phrase which has been thought to group under one name at least three other specific rules, namely: (1) If you would introduce before a jury the statements of a witness, you must produce the witness in person; (2) If you would introduce to a jury the contents of a writing, you must produce the writing itself; (3) If you would prove to a jury the execution of an attested document, you must produce the attesting witnesses. In each case secondary modes of proof are allowed under more or less definite circumstances. In each we have the general notion of primary and secondary evidence.

But these three requirements have not a common origin, nor are they in fact the developments of a common principle.

What is the origin, and what has been the shaping influence and development of these several rules?

1. As regards the first of them, which is at the bottom of the great rule against hearsay, we seem to see an indication of its source, when, some five centuries and a half ago, the English Court of Common Pleas was marking off the function of the jurors from that of the attesting witnesses to a deed. It was already, even in those days, an ancient practice, when the execution of a deed was denied, to summon the attesting witnesses with the jury and to send them out to a joint

deliberation.[1167] They were not regularly examined in court. In 1349,[1168] one of these witnesses had been summoned not merely with the jury, but on the jury panel itself. He was ousted, and Thorpe, C. J., said there must be a jury wholly separate from witnesses; and witnesses can only be joined to the jury; and testify to them the fact. It is the jury, itself, he went on, who render the verdict, and not the witnesses; the two have different oaths; the witnesses swear to tell the truth, *i. e.,* what they see and hear; and the jury to say the truth according to the best of their knowledge. This remark imports of course that conclusions from the facts in evidence were only for the jury, and we may see here the roots of the rule against opinion evidence as well as hearsay. This definition of a witness's function, as we have already seen, was a very old one. The formula in the old law for a witness was that he was to state what he had seen and heard, *quod vidi et audivi; de visu suo et auditu.*[1169] To state what some one else had seen and heard, was the function of that some one else and not of the witness. Each person must give his own testimony. And accordingly a century later,[1170] where an essoiner *(i. e.,* the attorney of a party who failed to appear in court at his regular day, and who brought that person's excuse) undertook to give as his principal's reason that lie was in the king's service; and was put under oath, and then, being asked if this were so, said he was so informed, but would not say in terms that he was in the king's service, — Newton, C. J., rejected his statement. "The essoiner," he said, "is sworn, and is not willing to say that the principal is in the service of the king. The statute runs that the essoiner shall testify in court *(testetur in curio);* but this is not testifying." It seems then that repeating hearsay was not regarded as legitimate testifying. Each perceiving witness must give his own testimony.

There had of course always been occasion for witnesses to testify to the judges as in the case of the essoiuer, just mentioned; and for transaction witnesses, *e. g;* persons who had allowed themselves to be called as preappointed witnesses to a sale of goods, or the execution of a deed. These cases and others of the sort run back to a time before the days of juries, and the practices relating to them in the old Germanic law come down into our own. *Nos testes...*

[1167] *Supra,* 97.

[1168] 23 Ass. 11.

[1169] *Supra,* 18.

[1170] Y. B. 20 H. VI. 20, 16.

scimus, et oculis nostris vidimus et bene nobis cognitum est, is one of the old forms.[1171]

Witnesses testifying regularly to juries had probably not yet come upon the scene at the time of the first of the two cases above cited, namely, in 1349. We find them, however, in the next century. Whenever it was that they first appeared, their coming was a very remarkable event. We are to remember that the jury themselves were witnesses, — none the less so because they were also triers. They were the old community witnesses. To allow the transaction witnesses, *e. g.,* witnesses to deeds, to be added to them as helpers was easily and very early done. But centuries had to pass in the use of juries before the idea emerged of regularly allowing parties to bring the ordinary casual witness to testify to these other witnesses, the jury. It was very long indeed before the hint which the case of transaction witnesses was forever making was taken. When it was taken, and when witnesses came to testify freely in public to the jury, — certainly not later than Fortescue's time, in the fifteenth century, — they came in under the old notion and definition of a witness. He was one who testified *quod vidi et audivi* — what he had seen and heard. That excluded hearsay. The existence of juries and the necessity of discriminating the office of a witness from that of a juror, drew attention to the fact that the witness to any particular thing, being one who spoke to the fact that he had seen and heard that thing, or, as Vaughan, C. J., said, in 1670,[1172] "generally, or more largely, to what hath fallen under his senses," contributes to a jury's knowledge, just this and no more. All the rest they themselves were to furnish, such as general knowledge, hearsay, their own private knowledge, including hearsay and inferences from it, and the reasoning and conclusions involved in comparing and digesting all that they knew or had heard from others. Afterwards, as the scope of the jury's function narrowed and they became merely judges on what was furnished them by witnesses, the original discrimination between the jury and the witness lost its old application, and had a new form. Now the contrast was between witnesses, and a jury who were judges, knowing nothing of the fact.

The objection of hearsay, then, goes, fundamentally, to the point that something which should come through an original witness

---

[1171] Brunner, Schw. 54.
[1172] Bushell's case, Vaughan, 135.

is sought to be put in at second hand, by one to whom it has been told, one who is not a witness properly speaking, who did not perceive it and cannot therefore testify to it, but only to the fact that somebody said so. It would operate to nullify the requirement that witnesses should personally appear and testify publicly in court, if the statements of the original perceiver could be got in through another person; and it was always the rule that witnesses should thus publicly appear and testify; as it was the rule that jurymen and judges and parties, or their attorneys, should appear and perform their several functions in public.

In leaving this part of the subject we may remark again the fact that hearsay has not been allowed to figure in English law as good circumstantial evidence; that is to say, the statement of a person not called as a witness is not in general made admissible by the fact that it was given under circumstances which impart to it a special credit. This may, perhaps, come about hereafter. But thus far the course of our law of evidence has been to admit this sort of thing only when these special circumstances were joined to the fact of the original speaker's death, or, in some cases, his other disability. Neither the original speaker's death, alone, nor the highly probative character of the circumstances under which he spoke, alone, are enough; and not the two together except in special cases. This sort of circumstantial evidence is separated from all others in the English law of evidence, is classified as hearsay, and as such is condemned. Such is the emphasis which our law puts upon its hearsay prohibition, an emphasis traceable in its origin and in its continuance to the fact that witnesses at common law testify mainly to juries, persons who were formerly themselves witnesses, and not merely to judges.

2. As regards the requirement that the proof of the execution of an attested document must be by the witnesses if they can be had, this, also, has a clear and very old origin. Such persons belonged to that very ancient class of transaction or business witnesses, running far back into the old Germanic law, who were once the only sort of witnesses that could be compelled to come before a court. Their allowing themselves to be called in and set down as attesting witnesses was understood to be an assent in advance to such a compulsory summons. Proof by witnesses could not be made by those who merely happened casually to know the fact. However exact and full the knowledge of any person might be, he could not, in

the old Germanic procedure, be called in court as a witness,[1173] unless he had been called at the time of the event as a preappointed witness. It was a part of such a system and in accordance with such a set of ideas that witnesses formally allowed their names to be written into deeds in large numbers. When jury trial, or rather proof by jury, as it originally was, came in, the old proof by witnesses was joined with it when the execution of the deed was denied;[1174] and the same process that summoned the twelve, summoned also these witnesses. The phrase of the precept to the sheriff was *summone duodecim* [etc. etc.] *cum aliis.* The presence of these witnesses was at first as necessary as that of the jury. Great delays and embarrassments attended such a requirement where the number of witnesses might be so great; the jury was cumbersome enough anyway. Accordingly, in 1318, the presence of the witnesses was made no longer absolutely necessary; they must still be summoned, but the case might go on without them. After another century and a half the process against the witness became no longer a necessity. It was not issued unless it were called for. After still another century, in 1562 — 3, process against all kinds of witnesses was allowed, requiring them to come in, not with the jury or as a part of the jury, but to testify before them in open court, and then the old procedure of summoning such witnesses with the jury seems to have died out. "Such process against witnesses," says Coke,[1175] referring to the old process, "has vanished." There was never a time when such witnesses, the regular transaction witnesses, could not in one way or the other be summoned and compelled to come in. As regards ordinary witnesses to the jury, compulsory process seems not to have existed before 1562.[1176] Since 1318, the attendance of the transaction witnesses might be dispensed with if they could not be got; but the necessity of summoning them existed for most of this long period. As late as the early part of the eighteenth century it was doubtful whether a deed could be proved at all, if the attesting witnesses came in and denied it.[1177] Half a century later, Lord Mansfield, while reluctantly yielding to what he stigmatized as a captious objection that you must produce the witness, declared that "It is a technical rule that the subscribing

---

[1173] Brunner, Schw. 50, 53.

[1174] *Supra,* 97.

[1175] 1 Inst. 6 b, published in 1628

[1176] St. 5 Eliz. c. 9, s. 6.

[1177] Thayer's Cases on Evidence, 776.

witness must be produced; and it cannot be dispensed with unless it appeared that his attendance could not be produced." And still a generation later, in 1815, Lord Ellenborough, in asserting the same thing, savagely thrust out all arguments against this doctrine, and slammed the door on them. "The rule," he said, "is universal that you must first call the subscribing witness.... If any general rule is to prevail, this is certainly one that is as fixed, formal, and universal as any that can be stated in a court of justice."

The pedigree of this rule is not only clear, it has been repeatedly recognized in our cases.[1178]

3. The third sort of case, that which has always been the chief illustration of the Best Evidence principle, the doctrine that if you would prove the contents of a writing, you must produce the writing itself, also runs back to the old law, existing before witnesses testified to the jury. It is connected with the doctrine of *profert,* in pleading, which required a party relying upon a document, as a ground of action or defence, to produce it bodily to the court. Stephen in his Pleading[1179] gives as the explanation, of the doctrine *of profert,* that it was simply the way of complying with the rule that required an offer of a mode of proof when one pleaded affirmatively. "As the pleader, of that time," he says, "concluded in some cases by offering to prove by jury or by the record; so in others, he maintained his pleading by producing a deed as proof of the cause alleged.... Afterward the trial by jury becoming more universally prevalent, it was often applied (as at the present day) to determine questions arising as to the genuineness or validity of the deed itself so produced, and from this time a deed seems to have been no longer considered as a method of proof distinct and independent of that by jury." Whatever qualifications may be required in accepting this statement, it seems probable that it is substantially true. The use of documents, in pleading and proof, long antedates the use of ordinary witnesses to the jury. The vast majority of documents used in trials in early times were no doubt of the solemn, constitutive, and dispositive kind, instruments under seal, records, certificates of high officials, public registers, and the like. Such

---

[1178] Fox *v.* Reil, 3 Johns. 477, *per* Kent, C. J.; Brigham *v.* Palmer, 3 Alien, 459.

[1179] Tyler's ed. 382, and also note 86.

documents, if the authenticity of them were not denied, "imported verity," as the phrase was, fixed liability and determined rights. As questions were tried by record and by Domesday Book, so they were tried by other documents. As has been said, "If a man *said* he was bound [e. *g;* by a sealed instrument], he *was* bound."' Of course, therefore, whoever would use a document of this character must produce it, just as the court had to have the jury in court, in trial (or proof) by jury, and the record, in trial (or proof) by record. As the trial by jury displaced one after another of the older modes of trial, sometimes these were mingled with it in a confused way. The procedure about joining attesting witnesses to deeds with the jury is probably an instance of this, — a combination of the old trial by witnesses with the newer trial by jury. In the same way, it seems probable, the trial by documents, in fading away into trial by jury, left traces of itself in the doctrine of *profert* in pleading, and, ultimately, in the practice of producing the document itself in evidence to the jury. A doctrine which applied to the solemn and constitutive sort of documents, *i. e.,* to the great mass of those which were used and discussed in courts, might naturally attract to itself and cover all documents; and in later days the rule of evidence firmly holds its place on the ground of its excellent sense and its tendency to promote justice.

These three great illustrations of what is called the Best Evidence rule have, then, no common origin. Each stands on its own bottom and has had its own reasons for existence, and for continuing. To attribute results like these, traceable to the slow working out of ancient customs, methods, and institutions, to the operation of a controlling principle of the "Best Evidence," is to forget the facts and lean on idle theories. This name and classification, moreover, tend to confusion; they seem to mean a great deal, and when they come to be explained, they turn out to mean very little. The term should be discarded, in any sense of a working rule of exclusion; all that it truly imports may be expressed by the simple and useful terms, "primary" and "secondary" evidence, as applied to these several cases. In only one way, as it seems to me, is it possible any longer to use this old phraseology with advantage. It served a useful purpose in the early days of the law of evidence, while the rules of the subject were in their infancy, as a large moral principle and not as a precise legal rule; and so in time to come, as the discretion of courts is enlarged, it may continue to serve a useful purpose as a general principle, offering suggestions to guide the discretion of the courts.

Upon the whole, then, it may be said that the Best Evidence rule was originally, in days when the law of evidence had not yet taken definite shape, a common and useful phrase in the mouths of judges who were expressing a general maxim of justice, without thinking of formulating an exact rule; and that Gilbert, in his premature, ambitious, and inadequate attempt to adjust to the philosophy of John Locke the rude beginnings and tentative, unconscious efforts of the courts, in the direction of a body of rules of evidence, hurt rather than helped matters. By holding up this vague principle as the "first and most signal rule" of an excluding system, and imparting to our law at that period such systematized, and far-looking aims in the region of evidence, he threw everything out of focus. A cheap varnish of philosophy took the place of an ordered statement of the facts. In Gilbert's attempt to deal exactly with the question, he was driven to take away from the large principle of the Best Evidence a chief part of its natural and intended reach, and to turn it into a narrow-declaration that you must not offer anything which itself imports that it is a substitute for something better. Such a reduction was necessary, if one would have an exact rule. But it was not necessary for those larger purposes which thus far it had served. The judges, as often happens, knew what they needed better than the book-writers, even if the book-writer was himself a judge, as Gilbert was. Gilbert's definition was, indeed, one application of the larger principle that they used in licking into shape their new bantling, of a law of evidence; but that was all. And they kept on applying maxims of sense and justice, and this one, among others, in its wide, natural sense, until these hardened into one and another definite and specific rule of *nisi prius* practice, and became our present law of evidence. Lord Hardwicke's utterance about there being but "one rule of evidence, the best that the nature of the case will admit," had no such limited notion as the followers of Gilbert sought to put upon it. It was that same broad, untechnical declaration of a general principle of justice, impossible to be reduced into a definite rule of exclusion, with which Holt and his contemporaries began. The attempt to use it, on the one side, as a denial of the existence of any excluding rule at all, and, on the other, as in itself a definite working rule of wide reach and significance, were both dealt with justly by Christian, a hundred years ago. Our experience since then may show us, I think, that we shall help to clear the subject, and keep our heads clear, if we drop the name and the notion of any specific separate rule of the Best Evidence. In doing that, we need not dismiss the great maxim of fair dealing that animated the judges who brought in this phrase and, in many applications, used it for a century in shaping the law; a principle which says, not that one must always furnish the best evidence, and, in the absence of it, have all else excluded; or, that if one does the best he can, this will always be enough, but that always, morally speaking, the fact that any given way of proof is all that a man has, must be a strong argument for receiving it, if it be in a fair degree probative; and the fact that a man does not produce the best evidence in his power must always afford strong ground of suspicion.

CHAPTER XII
THE PRESENT AND FUTURE OF
THE LAW OF EVIDENCE [1180]

Sir henry maine had occasion, thirty years ago, to make some special study of the English system of Evidence, in attempting to adapt it to the use of his countrymen in governing India. In "letting his intelligence play freely over the subject," he was led to remark that "the theory of judicial evidence is constantly misstated or misconceived even in this country, and the English law on the subject is too often described as being that which it is its chief distinction not to be, — that is, as an *Organon*, — as a sort of contrivance for the discovery of truth which English lawyers have patented." And after pointing out that the law of evidence grew out of the jury system, he adds truly that "the English rules of evidence are never very scrupulously attended to by tribunals which, like the Court of Chancery, adjudicate both on law and on fact, through the same organs and the same procedure."

And yet the system is very highly praised. Why then should it be so quickly abandoned when the jury is gone? If we should take too literally the undiscriminating statements of some writers, we might well wonder that so fine a thing should not always be used. A distinguished author tells us, at the end of a famous treatise:[1181] "The student will not fail to observe the symmetry and beauty of this brunch of the law;... and will rise from the study of its principles convinced, with Lord Erskine, that ' they are founded in the charities of religion, in the philosophy of nature, in the truths of history, and in the experience of common life.' " I think that it would be juster and more exact to say that our law of evidence is a piece of illogical, but by no means irrational, patchwork; not at all to be admired, nor easily to be found intelligible, except as a product of the jury system, as the outcome of a quantity of rulings by sagacious lawyers, while settling practical questions, in presiding over courts where ordinary, untrained citizens are acting as judges of fact. Largely irrational in any other aspect, in this point of view it is full of good sense; — a

---

[1180] As regards the form of this chapter see note at the title of Chapter XI., supra, 484.

[1181] Greenl. Evid. i. s. 584.

good sense, indeed, that occasionally nods, that submits too often to a mistaken application of its precedents, that is often short-sighted and ill-instructed, and that needs to be taken in hand by the jurist, and illuminated, simplified, and invigorated by a reference to general principles.

As regards Erskine's often-quoted remark, given above, quite too large and general a reach has been imputed to it. It was a part of the opening argument in Hardy's case, in 1794, and had reference to the great advocate's unsuccessful contention against one of the most extraordinary, characteristic, and subsequently discredited results of English adjudication. His client was charged with the treason of compassing the King's death, and the overt act of a conspiracy to depose him. Erskine had been inveighing bitterly against a doctrine which the court afterwards enforced against his client in its most uncompromising shape — the doctrine, namely, that in such a case proof of the conspiracy to depose was, in legal effect, proof of compassing the death, and not merely evidence of it; and this by virtue of an indisputable "presumption." "The conspiracy to depose the King," said Eyre, C. J., in his charge to the jury,[1182] "is evidence of compassing and imagining the death of the King, conclusive in its nature, so conclusive that it is become a presumption of law, which is in truth nothing more than a necessary and violent presumption of fact, admitting of no contradiction." Such a doctrine, of course, while exhibiting itself in a dress of evidence and presumption, is, in reality, a very different matter; it is really a precept in the substantive law of treason; grounded, indeed, upon a conclusion of evidence, upon what is usually true in such cases, but none the less a doctrine which has now passed out of the sphere of evidence, and even out of the legitimate sphere of presumption, and has become an incontrovertible rule of the substantive criminal law. As against this hard, judicially-legislated principle, Erskine had contended that the overt act was only a piece of evidence; that the intent to kill the King was to be proved to the jury by evidence which really did convince them beyond a reasonable doubt; that a conspiracy to depose might or might not, according to the circumstances of the particular case, suffice to prove the intent to kill; and that the jury must themselves be satisfied that it did. "My whole argument," he said, in substance, towards the end, "is only

_____

[1182] 24 St. Trials, col. 1361.

that the crime of compassing the King's death must be found by you, really *believed* by you; and beyond a reasonable doubt. You are to go upon the ordinary rules of evidence; not upon precedents coming down from evil times. The rules of evidence as they are settled by law and adopted in its general administration, are not to be overruled or tampered with. They are founded in the charities of religion," etc. In saying this Erskine was not engaged in any general estimate of the English law of evidence; he was pressing home a particular point, and condemning a specific contention; this contention, he said, was barbarous and inconsistent with those general principles which secured to a prisoner the free, unfettered exercise of the jury's judgment, instead of driving them to a verdict by an irresistible legal rule.

I have said that our law of evidence is ripe for the hand of the jurist. I do not mean for the hand of the codifier; it is not; but for a treatment which, beginning with a full historical examination of the subject, and continuing with a criticism of the cases, shall end with a restatement of the existing law and with suggestions for the course of its future development. Such an undertaking, worthily executed, if it should commend itself to the bench, would need only a slight co-operation from the legislature to give to the law of evidence a consistency, simplicity, and capacity for growth which would make it a far worthier instrument of justice than it is.

Let us look at this part of our law, and consider (1) "What, in fact, we have now; (2) What we should have, and how to get it.

I. We have now, as our law of evidence, in the form in which it is ordinarily stated, a set of rules of great volume and complexity, occupying, with the illustrations thought needful for their exposition, twelve hundred and thirty-four octavo pages in Taylor's last (9th) edition of his work on Evidence, — a book which was originally an adaptation of Greenleaf's, but now constitutes the chief English book on the subject. The few principles which underlie this elaborate mass of matter are clear, simple, and sound. But they have been run out into a great refinement of discrimination and exception, difficult to discover and apply; and have been overlaid by a vast body of rulings at *nisi prius* and decisions *in banc,* impossible to harmonize or to fit into any consistent and worthy scheme. A great portion of these rules, as laid down by the courts and by our text writers, are working a sort of intellectual fraud by purporting to be what they are not. To the utter confusion of all orderly thinking, a court is frequently represented as passing on questions of evidence when in reality it is dealing with some other brunch, either of substantive law or procedure. The rules are thus in a great degree ill-apprehended, ill-stated, ill-digested. Sometimes, as in the case of proving attested documents, they have come down out of practices and rules of mediaeval procedure by a slow process of change that has concealed their pedigree and their real nature and basis; and then rules of this sort have come to be applied or refused application merely according to their letter, or according to some false imagination of reasons, with grotesque results, and in a manner fanciful and unintelligent. Sometimes our rules have sprung from following on after some single specific ruling at *nisi prius, wise,* perhaps, in the particular case, but having in it no general element or principle which should make it a precedent; and sometimes, on the other hand, from dealing with such a ruling, as if it were only a narrow and particular precedent, and failing to recognize its true character as illustrating some principle of sense and convenience, fit to be spread into a general application. In part the precepts of evidence consist of many classes of exceptions to the main rules, — exceptions that are refined upon, discriminated, and run down into a nice and difficult attenuation of detail, so that the courts become lost, and forget that they are dealing with exceptions; or perhaps are at a loss to say whether the controlling principle is to be found in the exception or in the general rule, or whether the exception has not come to be erected into a rule by itself. In part, our rules are a body of confused doctrines, expressed in ambiguous phrases, Latin or English, half understood, but glibly used, without perceiving that ideas, pertinent and just in their proper places, are being misconstrued and misapplied.

Let me, in part, illustrate what I mean. There is a great bulk of cases, constantly swelling, which are referred to what is known as the "parol evidence rule." Speaking generally, this rule, relating to documents of the solemn and formal kind, undertakes to secure to them their proper legal operation as against less formal extrinsic acts and utterances of the writer. "Parol contemporaneous evidence," we are told, "is inadmissible to contradict or vary the terms of a valid written instrument."[1183] Now so crudely-conceived and so ill-digested is the mass of matter under this head, which every day and many

---

[1183] Greenl. Evid. i. s. 275, quoting Phil. & Am. Evid.

times a day our courts are called on to interpret and apply, that, in reality, vastly the greater part of it, almost all of it, has no proper place in the law of evidence; being chiefly made up of rules in the substantive law of documents, such as wills and contracts, and of rules of construction and interpretation. What is the result of this? Utter confusion of thought, and frequent injustice in decision. Of course when in reality men are discussing a question in the law of partnership, agency, or bankruptcy; or the ground and scope of equity jurisdiction in dealing with fraud, mistake, trusts, or the reforming of documents; or the rules for the construction, and interpretation of language; and yet, out of an imagination that they are dealing with rules of evidence, go on to clothe their ideas in the phraseology of that subject; although a right result maybe reached, it is not rightly reached, and bewilderment attends the process. There is a question, let us say, of reforming a will by inserting words which are not in it. The decision is disguised by saying that parol evidence is not admissible for this purpose; whereas, if the purpose were legitimate the evidence would be good enough. There is a question of denying operative effect to a contract in writing which has been signed, is in the hands of the other party, and is in form complete. The real question is, Have you a legal ground of action or defence in saying that it was not to go into effect till the happening of some event which has not happened, and was not named in the writing? This is called a question of admitting parol or extrinsic evidence. There is a question of whether you can set up the defence of mistake in a common-law action, or whether you must go into equity. That is called a question of admitting parol evidence. There is a question of whether an undisclosed principal can sue or be sued on a written contract signed only by his agent's name; or whether you can avail yourself of an implied warranty when the contract of sale was in writing and says nothing of a warranty. These are called questions of whether parol evidence is admissible; and if the agreement be under seal, the doctrine that the seal of the agent cannot bind the principal, is disguised by saying that parol evidence is not admissible to make the principal responsible. There is a question, in case of a misdescription in a will, whether a given person may take; and this masquerades under the form of an inquiry whether parol evidence is admissible to correct the mistake.

This error is deeply ingrained in our cases; and it is a subtle one. But you cannot possibly deal thoroughly and scientifically with this part of our law until the error is cast out, until it is purged of that mass of substantive law, and of mere rules of procedure, and reason, and logic which overloads it. There was a time when all that was said or read to the jury was spoken of as said era *evidence at jury.* The contrast in mind when this was said, was between saying something to the court, in pleading (in the days of oral pleading), and saying it to the jury. But now, for two or three centuries, we have been discussing the admissibility of what is offered in evidence, under a new brunch of law, called the rules of evidence; as contrasted with its admissibility under the law of pleading and practice, and the substantive law. The old general question of admissibility has become specialized. If it was said, six centuries ago, that you could or could not say a thing era *evidence al jury,* it was because it was or was not matter to be said in pleading and entered on the record; or else because it was or was not logically relevant and material to the issue between the parties. Nowadays it may be excluded for the reason that, although relevant and material to the issue, and not at all matter of law; although properly addressed to the jury as contrasted with the court, yet it is excluded by this modern set of rules called the law of evidence. It is the characteristic of these rules to shut out what is relevant; not all that is relevant, happily, but some things that are relevant, and notwithstanding they are relevant. There are many reasons for excluding what is offered in evidence, that have no relation at all to the law of evidence.[1184] If a thing be excluded because it is not within the scope of the general issue, it id excluded by the law of pleading; if, under the substantive law of the case, what is offered has nothing to do with the question, then it is the substantive law of the case that excludes; if what is offered has no logical relation to the case, then it is the rule of reason that rejects it; or a party may be estopped from setting up what he offers evidence to prove. But when matter of fact bearing on the issue is excluded for none of these reasons, yet lawfully, it is the law of evidence that is working; as when the question is whether you may offer the sworn affidavit of a trustworthy eye-witness, not personally present in court, or a testator's extrinsic statement, when signing his will, that he meant one person rather than another of similar but not identical name; the exclusion in such cases is made

---

[1184] *Supra,* 269.

by the rules of evidence; what is offered is relevant and material, but still is inadmissible.

It is then fundamental that not all determinations admitting or excluding evidence are referable to the law of evidence. Far the larger part of them are not. An innumerable company of questions, of the sort just alluded to, very often — more often than not, nay, much oftener than not — are dealt with in our text-books and cases as belonging to the law of evidence, when in real truth they ought to be carried to the border line of this subject and respectfully deposited on the other side. Most of the affirmative declarations in our books that evidence is admissible, belong to this class; and a great proportion of those which hold it not admissible. As regards relevancy, in determining merely what is logically relevant to any point and what is relevant according to the standards of general experience, it is not the law that guides us; except, indeed, as it points us for guidance to these universal standards, already known, or ascertainable. For the law, being a human contrivance and outgrowth, resting, as if by gravity, on human nature, human experience, and the principles that regulate human thought, takes all these things for granted. It does not undertake to re-enact them, still less to displace them or to lift itself off this ground by its own boot-straps. To impute to it any such efforts is a suggestion as untrue historically, as these endeavors would be idle and superfluous in point of reason.

There is another great class of cases, germane to these just mentioned, but, unlike them, really belonging to the law of evidence, where the decision turns on the just application of certain large and inexact principles, — principles that may be likened to that which a jury has to apply in determining whether conduct in certain cases conforms to the standard of the prudent man. The law of evidence undoubtedly requires that evidence to a jury shall be clearly relevant, and not merely slightly so; it must not barely afford a basis for conjecture, but for real belief; it must not merely be remotely relevant, but proximately so. Again, it must not unnecessarily complicate the case, or too much tend to confuse, mislead, or tire the minds of that untrained tribunal, the jury, or to withdraw their attention too much from the real issues of the case. Now in the application of such standards as these, the chief appeal is made to sound judgment; to what our lawyers have called, for six or seven centuries at least, the discretion of the judge. Decisions on such subjects are not readily open to revision; and, when revised, they have to be judged of in a large way; this is expressed by saying that the question is whether the discretion has been unreasonably exercised, has been abused. Doubtless, in some classes of such cases, there may have grown up a sub-rule which limits the discretion. In such cases, since there is not an unfettered discretion, an ordinary, additional question of law arises as to the application of this subsidiary rule. But, in general, the question of law is not of the ordinary type, because it ties itself to an outside, non-legal standard, namely, that of good sense, common experience, the sound judgment of men of affairs. When, for example, on a question of negligence in driving a horse across a railroad, you offer evidence of a single instance where a third party drove safely over, at another time, under like conditions; or, in another case, evidence of ten separate instances of doing this; and in both cases it is rejected; it is easy to see that a revising court might properly enough sustain both rejections, while themselves disapproving of both; — sustaining and yet disapproving of the first, because the evidence was slight and conjectural, and yet might be thought by a trial judge sufficiently relevant and helpful; and the second, because, while it seemed, in point of quality, fairly clear and strong and probative, it tended, nevertheless, to confuse the case by its multiplication of instances; and because there were other simpler ways of proof open to the party, such as the opinion of experienced observers, or a view by the judge or jury.

In such cases it is a question of where lies the balance of practical advantage. To discuss such questions, as is sometimes done, on the bare ground of relevancy, — even if we introduce the poor notion of legal relevancy, as contrasted with logical relevancy, — tends to obscure the nature of the inquiry. There is, in truth, generally, no rule of law to apply in answering such questions as whether the evidence, although probative, is too slight, conjectural, or remote; or whether it will take too much time in the presenting of it, in view of other practicable ways of handling the case; or whether it will complicate and confuse the case too much. There is no rule and no principle which forbids delay, tediousness, and complication, pure and simple, and always; what is forbidden is unnecessary complication, delay, and tediousness. These things are discouraged; but often they are unavoidable. When the nature of the issue requires it, enormous dangers of this sort have to be run. Consider the

Tichborne case, the Tilton *v.* Beecher case, the Guiteau case, and the great will case of Wright *v.* Tatham which turned up so often in the English books sixty years ago; or consider any hard-fought case raising the question of insanity. In such controversies a range of inquiry is allowed of almost indefinite width, one which covers the behavior of a party during his whole life, and even travels over into that of all his near relations.

In this region of the law of evidence much confusion results from an inexact apprehension of the nature of the questions, and of the appropriate method of handling them on appeal. Often it is not perceived that what appears to be a mistaken determination of such points at the trial, is simply a more or less important mistake in practical judgment, and not at all a mistake in law. Judges, and whole benches of them, may decide such questions differently, while perfectly agreeing on the rule of law and keeping within it.

There is a great head of the law of evidence, comprising, indeed, with its exceptions, much the largest part of all that truly belongs there, forbidding the introduction of hearsay. The true historical nature of this rule is hinted by the remark of an English court, two centuries ago and over, when they checked the attempt of a woman to testify what another woman had told her. "The court," it was quietly remarked, "are of opinion that it will be proper for Wells to give her own evidence."[1185] That is to say, the objection went to the medium of communication; witnesses before the jury, in giving ordinary testimony, had by that time been allowed for some three centuries; but it must be *un oyant et veyant,* a hearer and seer, as they said in the older Year Books; one who could say, as the witnesses to courts in older times always had to say, *quod vidi et audivi;* it must not be testimony at second hand. When juries, who were themselves, originally, witnesses as well as triers, came to be helped regularly by the testimony of other witnesses, it was only by such as personally knew the truth of what they were saying, and not by witnesses who only knew what some one else had said to them. Juries, indeed, could say what they "knew;" but witnesses to juries could only say what they had seen and heard. In the first half of the fourteenth century we find the judges laying this down as applicable in the instance of attesting witnesses. What it meant was that while juries could form opinions from anything they knew, the verdict being

---

[1185] Eliz. Canning's case, 19 St. Tr. 383, 406.

given at their peril; while they might act on what they had picked up in any way, and on such foundations might form a judgment which would count as knowledge; yet witnesses could not do this, or rather were not to state it if they did; were not to say what they "thought," or "believed," or had heard from others, or had inferred from what we now call circumstantial evidence. This contrast between the function of the jury and that of witnesses, which made it necessary to discriminate and define these points five or six hundred years ago, as regards the preappointed witnesses who went out with the jury, — even before witnesses were ordinarily allowed to testify to juries, — has led to a steady and rigid adherence to the general doctrine of hearsay prohibition.

But there came a large and miscellaneous number of so-called "exceptions." Some of these, in reality, were quite independent rules, whose operation was rather that of qualifications and abatements to the generality of this other doctrine; rules which were coeval with the doctrine itself or much older. For example, it seems always to have been true, in cases of homicide, that the dying declarations of persons killed were reported and acted on in judicial proceedings. We find these used by a complaint witness as far back as 1202,[1186] and used in evidence to the jury in 1721.[1187] Such declarations in early times, and even in late times, had a peculiar credit allowed them. So, in tracing pedigree, the family hearsay seems always to have been resorted to. This matter, before jury trial was developed, used to be "tried" by witnesses, who stated circumstantially how they knew what they said;[1188] and hearsay from the family, if confirmed by circumstances, was, probably, always a basis for their testimony. Family hearsay had the aspect of family reputation; and reputation was often reckoned an adequate ground for judicial action. In the thirteenth century we find a witness, in proving another person's age, giving as the basis of his testimony the fact of the mother's recording the age in the records of a Priory, which record he had seen.[1189] In matters affecting a whole parish or a large number of persons, the hearsay and reputation of those belonging in the given community was always regarded as good.

[1186] 1 Seld. Soc. 11; and see, what looks to be about a quarter of a century later, another case in Pl. Ab. 104.

[1187] R. v. Trantor, 1 Strange, 499.

[1188] *Supra,* 19 — 21.

[1189] Pl. Ab. 293, col. 1.

There was another class of unsworn statements which had always been resorted to in judicial proceedings and admitted to the jury, namely, written ones, — entries in registers, in a parson's books, in the account books of stewards, in a merchant's books, in contracts, deeds, wills, and other documents. Documents had always been shown to juries, — long before witnesses were received to testify to them. In the early days they did not stick, it would seem, at showing the jury any document that bore on the case, without even thinking of how the writer knew what he said. As regards ancient matters, writings very imperfectly authenticated were one of the chief sources of information, and often the only one. It appears, then, that a number of the so-called "exceptions" to the hearsay prohibition came in under the head of written entries or declarations; they came in, or rather, so to speak, stayed in, simply because they had always been received, and no rule against hearsay had ever been formulated or interpreted as applying to them. Such things, continuing at the present day, are, *e. g.,* the admission of old entries and writings in proof of ancient matters, written declarations of deceased persons against interest, and in the course of duty or business; and, to a limited extent, a merchant's own account books to prove his own case, — a thing clearly recognized as customary and allowable in an English statute of 1609, nearly three centuries ago,[1190] but insensibly, and often ignorantly, much qualified afterwards. So also of regular entries in public books, a matter probably never even doubted to be admissible in evidence.

In addition to all these ancient and always approved practices in their simple, original shape, operating as qualifications of the hearsay prohibition, there have come in many extensions of them; as when oral declarations of deceased persons against interest were received, and, in England, even oral declarations of deceased persons in the course of duty or business. And not only has the scope of these old titles been enlarged, but new exceptions have been made; or perhaps they are rather old ones coming to be recognized and formulated; such as those relating to the *res gesta, i. e.,* declarations which are a part of some fact itself admissible, and declarations of present intention or present physical sensation. Such things are the natural development of the subject.

[1190] St. 7 Jac I. c. 12.

Now a great deal of perplexity exists, in the law relating to hearsay, from a failure to understand the scope of these exceptions; and from an uncertainty whether and how far they are to be freely developed, or to be strictly limited, as being mere exceptions, while the main rule itself which prohibits hearsay is expanded. Sometimes one thing is done and sometimes the other. In a leading case in the House of Lords, in 1880, Lord Blackburn, in discussing a question of hearsay and rejecting the evidence, said: "I base my judgment upon this, that no case has gone so far as to say that such a document could be received; and clearly, unless it is to be brought within some one of the exceptions, it would fall within the general rule that hearsay evidence is not admissible."[1191] On the other hand, Sir George Jessel, in a very different tone, in 1876, had declared it to be the court's duty to extend the exceptions to the hearsay rule, out of "regard to the reasons and principles which have induced the tribunals of this country to admit exceptions in the other cases."[1192] It seems a sound general principle to say that in all cases a main rule is to have extension, rather than exceptions to the rule; that exceptions should be applied only within strict bounds, and that the main rule should apply in cases not clearly within the exception. But then comes the question, what is the rule, and what the exceptions? There lies a difficulty. A true analysis would probably restate the law so as to make what we call the hearsay rule the exception, and make our main rule this, namely, that whatsoever is relevant is admissible. To any such main rule there would, of course, be exceptions; but as in the case of other exceptions, so in the hearsay prohibition, this classification would lead to a restricted application of them, while the main rule would have freer course. One mischief about the present state of our law is that it shows a spasmodic and half-recognized acceptance of such a theory in particular instances, while rejecting it generally. For example, there is, sometimes, a tendency to regard a hearsay statement as admissible if it be one of a set of facts giving and reflecting credit, each to the other, — on the principle of what is called circumstantial evidence. This brings in confusion, for our law really goes but a very little way in that direction. No doubt, in point of reason, hearsay statements often derive much credit from the circumstances under which they are

---

[1191] Sturla v. Freccia, 5 App. Cas. 623.
[1192] Sugden *v. St.* Leonards, 1 Prob. Div. 154.

made; say, *e.g.,* from the fact of being made under oath, or under impressive conditions, as being against interest, or made under strong inducements to say the contrary, or as part of a series of statements or a class of them which are usually careful and accurate, and the like; credit amply enough in point of reason to entitle them to be received as evidence, when once the absence of the perceiving witness is accounted for; and it would in reason have been quite possible to shape our law in the form that hearsay was admissible, as secondary evidence, whenever the circumstances of the case alone were enough to entitle it to credit, irrespective of any credit reposed in the speaker. This point of view is forever suggesting itself in that part of the subject relating to declarations which are a part of some admissible fact, — of the *res gesta,* as the phrase is. These are often spoken of as parts of a mass of circumstantial facts described as *res gesta;* all evidential, supporting and supported by each other in their tendency to prove some principal fact; instead of being regarded, as they should be, as parts of that fact itself, *pars rei gestœ,* lying under the curse of hearsay, but received, by way of exception, on account of this special intimacy of connection with the admissible fact. This part of the subject presents an instructive spectacle of confusion, resulting from the desire, on the one hand, to hold to the just historical theory of our cases; and, on the other, to resort to first principles, without being aware of the size and complexity of the task which is thus unconsciously entered upon.

  I need not linger long on the two or three other chief topics in the law of evidence. The rules, roughly thus intimated, which forbid the giving of opinion evidence and of character evidence are leading and important. As to the former it is traceable easily to the same source as the hearsay rule. It was for the jury to form opinions, and draw inferences and conclusions, and not for the witness. He was merely to bring in to the jury, or the judge, the raw material of fact, on which their minds were to work. If the witness spoke directly to the very fact in issue, the jury were to consider whether to believe his statements or not; if to other facts, of an evidential sort, then the jury were to judge of their import and their tendency. The witness was not to say that he "thought" or "believed" so and so; it was for the jury to say what they thought and believed. The witness must say what he had "seen and heard," he was an *"oyant et veunt."* But then, simple as this sounds, the distinction could not serve in many nice and critical inquiries. In the loose and easy administration of the law of trials that existed as long as juries went on their own knowledge, and needed no witnesses or evidence at all, and at a time when, even if they had witnesses, they were at liberty to disregard them and to follow their own personal information, it was possible to get along without nice discriminations; so that the law of evidence had hardly any development at all until within the last two centuries; and it was but slight before the present century. In a sense all testimony to matter of fact is opinion evidence; *i. e.,* it is a conclusion formed from phenomena and mental impressions. Yet that is not the way we talk in courts or in common life. Where shall the line be drawn? When does matter of fact first become matter of opinion? A difficult question; but some things are clear. There are questions which require special training and knowledge to answer them. A jury, unless it be one of experts, and, as such, ill adapted, perhaps, for the general purposes of trials, cannot deal with them. On such questions, then, the ordinary jury may be assisted by skilled witnesses, who give their opinions. There are other questions, not requiring skill or training, but only special opportunities of observation, like handwriting and the value of property, on which opinions of ordinary witnesses having such opportunities may be given. How far does this go? There is much apparent perplexity in the cases. In a very great degree it results from differences of practical judgment in applying an admitted rule, — the admitted rule being that opinion evidence is not generally receivable, and the difference arising from differing judgments as to what is and is not really to be called opinion evidence in the sense of the rule. It has been said, judicially, that "there is, in truth, no general rule requiring the rejection of opinions as evidence."[1193] Without acceding quite literally to that, there is ground for saying that, in the main, any rule excluding opinion evidence is limited to cases where, in the judgment of the court, it will not be helpful to the jury. Whether accepted in terms or not, this view largely governs the administration of the rule. It is obvious that such a principle must allow a very great range of permissible difference in judgment; and that conclusions of that character ought not, usually, to be regarded as subject to review by higher courts. Unluckily the matter is often treated by the courts with much too heavy a hand; and the quantity of decisions on the subject is most unreasonably swollen.

[1193] Hardy *v.* Merrill, 56 N. H. 227, 241.

The rule excluding character evidence, when exactly stated, merely forbids the use of a person's general reputation or actual character, as a basis of inference to his own conduct. For other purposes it is often received, *e. g.,* as tending to prove that a fellow-servant's defects were known to his employer. This rule is modern. In earlier times such evidence was freely used in our courts, as it still is in other than English-speaking countries. Undoubtedly, as a mere matter of reason, it often affords a good basis of inference; and, on the other hand, often, besides tending to surprise a man, and to subject him to the operation of prejudice and malice, it is quite too conjectural and too slight to be safely used, and so comes within the condemnation of a general principle already mentioned.

On the rules regulating the examination of witnesses I will not dwell. They are full of sense, and are few, simple, and easily understood; although, like all rules for strenuous competitive struggles, nothing but practice and the observation of practice can bring them to a man's fingers' ends, or keep them there. Fortunately they allow much more discretion to the judges in administering them than is found in most of the rules of evidence. As to rules for the exclusion of witnesses, they have nearly disappeared. Little remains except what reason requires, namely, the exclusion of persons too young to be trusted, or too deficient in intelligence.

Finally, there are rules relating to documents, — as to the proof of their contents, of their execution, and of alterations in them. Of these a word or two should be said. He who would prove the contents of a writing must produce it bodily to the tribunal; if it is lost or destroyed, otherwise than by evil contrivance of the party offering the evidence, then the contents may be proved by copy or orally. This rule, if wisely applied, is one of peculiar good sense, but there is discordance as to the scope of it, and as to what may excuse one from the application of it. It is obscurely connected with the old law of profert, which required the physical production in court, in the course of pleading, of any document which was the basis of action or defence.

As regards the proof of execution where the document is attested, the rule runs back to the most ancient periods of our law. The document witnesses were formerly summoned with the jury, and joined in their secret deliberations.[1194] This was done until about

---

[1194] *Supra,* 97.

four centuries ago, and perhaps later. From these older periods there survived a rigor of requirement as to summoning the attesting witnesses, and a precedence in that method of proving the execution over all others, which have long been irrational; the law is still encumbered with many troublesome remnants of the old doctrine and many ill-instructed decisions.

As regards the proof of alterations in documents the cases are full of confusion. Fragments of substantive law embarrass the rules of evidence relating to this subject; and it is further intolerably perplexed by a quantity of jargon about presumptions and the burden of proof which often conceals the lack of any clear apprehension of the subject on the part of those who use it, and often disguises the true character of sound decisions.

Such is a rough outline of the chief parts of our law of evidence. Speaking exactly, this part of the law deals merely with the business of furnishing to the tribunal such information as to matters of fact in issue as is needed in order to decide the dispute, or to take any desired action. It assumes a properly qualified tribunal, one that knows an evidential thing when it sees it. It does not re-enact, nor does it displace, the main rules which govern human thought. These are all taken for granted. But it does exclude, by rules, much which is logically probative. It also regulates the production of witnesses, documents, and visible objects offered for inspection as the basis of inference.

The chief defects in this body of law, as it now stands, are that motley and undiscriminated character of its contents which has been already commented on; the ambiguity of its terminology; the multiplicity and rigor of its rules and exceptions to rules; the difficulty of grasping these and perceiving their true place and relation in the system, and of determining, in the decision of new questions, whether to give scope and extension to the rational principles that lie at the bottom of all modern theories of evidence, or to those checks and qualifications of these principles which have grown out of the machinery through which our system is applied, namely, the jury. These defects discourage and make difficult any thorough and scientific knowledge of this part of the law and its peculiarities. Strange to say, such a knowledge is very unusual, even among the judges.

The actual administration of this system is, indeed, often marked by extraordinary sagacity and good sense, particularly in

England. In that country it is uncommon to carry questions of evidence to the upper courts. In England the influence of the judge at *nisi prius* goes to check controversy over points of evidence far more than here, and the relations between bench and bar make this influence generally effectual.[1195] Moreover, owing to that great and just confidence in the capacity of the judges which is felt in England, they are able to exercise a beneficent control over the subject through their extensive power of making rules.[1196]

In our own administration of the law of evidence too many abuses are allowed, and the power of the courts is far too little exercised in controlling the eager lawyer in his endeavors to press to an extreme the application of the rules. Sharply and technically used, these rules enable a man to go far in worrying an inexperienced or ill-prepared adversary, and in supporting a worthless case. Our practice, which shows so little of the sensible moderation of the English barrister, and so little of the vigorous control of the English judge, in handling evidence at the trial, operates in another way to injure the rules of evidence. Here questions of this sort are generally taken up on exceptions, a method, never common in England and now abolished there, which presents only a dry question of law, — not leaving to the upper court that power to heed the general justice of the case which the more elastic procedure of the English courts so commonly allows; and tending thus to foster delay and chicane.

In neither country is the system of evidence consistently administered. Wherever evidence is taken by commission or deposition, the rules of exclusion largely break down; that is to say, in a great proportion of trials where there is no jury, namely, in equity, patent, and admiralty cases, and, more or less, in jury cases at

---

[1195] It surprises English lawyers to see our lively quarrels over points of evidence. One of them writing from New York to the "London Times," some years ago, spoke of being present at the trial of a case of trespass to land between two farmers. It involved questions of old boundaries. "The nature of the case," he said, "made it inevitable that many questions of evidence should be raised. But never, not even in a pedigree case, or an indictment for not repairing a road, did I see so many objections to the reception of evidence taken; and I am inclined to think that points of evidence are discussed far more frequently than is now the case with us." The observation of any one who has watched trials in the English courts will emphatically confirm these impressions.

[1196] See Wilson's Judicature Acts, 7th ed. (1888), *passim;* and see comments in Harvard Law Review, viii. 224, on Order XXX., Rule 7, promulgated in August, 1894.

the common law. In such cases the magistrate who takes the evidence notes any objection that is made, but does not and cannot omit to set down the evidence actually given. There it stands, and it is handed up to the court or jury, and is found on the paper with all the rest of the evidence. In most instances there is small profit in fighting over the admissibility of evidence which is already in, and has once been read by or to the tribunal; under such circumstances the whole doctrine of the exclusion of evidence is in a great degree inoperative.

II. So much for the system of evidence which we have. Let me come to the second question: What should we have, and how may we get it?

We should have a system of evidence simple, aiming straight at the substance of justice, not nice or refined in its details, not too rigid, easily grasped and easily applied. All this is necessary, because it is for use in the midst of the eager competition of trials, where time is short and decisions must be quickly made. Long discussion, and delay for reflection, are impracticable; and in a secondary and incidental part of the law, like evidence, however important it be, — and it is very important, for the putting in or keeping out of evidence means often the difference between gaining your case or losing it, — decisions in the lower court should generally be final.

In the pressure of actual trials, where, often, the interests and passions of men are deeply stirred and all the resources of chicane are called into play and directed by great abilities to obstruct the movements of justice, — the rules of evidence and procedure ought to be in a shape to second promptly the authority of the courts in checking these familiar efforts. In the rulings of judges at the trial much depends on momentary and fleeting considerations, addressed to the practical sense and discretion of the court, and not well admitting of revision on appeal. There are many things in which even now the discretion of the courts goes far. A thousand important matters, of one sort and another, are finally disposed of at the trial, — without the right of appeal. The all-important decision of the jury itself is final, except as the court, for a few reasons, may set it aside, *e. g.,* as being irrational or against evidence. In like manner, in the whole of the secondary and adjective part of the law there should be little opportunity to go back upon the rulings of the trial judge; there should be an abuse, in order to justify a review of them by an appellate court. In order to make this practicable, the rules of evidence should be simplified; and should take on the general character of principles, to guide the sound judgment of the judge, rather than minute rules to bind it. The two leading principles should be brought into conspicuous relief, (1) that nothing is to be received which is not logically probative of some matter requiring to be proved; and (2) that everything which is thus probative should come in, unless a clear ground of policy or law excludes it. And then, as regards the mass of detailed rules, these should mainly be subject at all times to the shaping and controlling power of the highest courts, in the different jurisdictions, in making rules of court. The rules of evidence on which we practise to-day have mostly grown up at the hands of the judges; and, except as they be really something more than rules of evidence, they may, in the main, properly enough be left to them to be modified and reshaped.

But, in doing this, let me hasten to say, it would be necessary at the outset to discriminate between what are really rules of evidence, and what are only nominally such. It would never do to submit to the free control of the judges, through rules of court, the great mass of substantive law that now lies disguised under the name of the law of evidence. It is, indeed, on every ground, high time that this separation were made. It is discreditable to a learned profession to allow the subject to lie in the jumble that now characterizes it in this respect. To do this will tend wonderfully to simplify and clear the subject of evidence as we now have it; and it will also remove a chief objection to certain needed reforms, and especially to this of placing in the hands of the judges a far larger discretion in shaping and modifying the system than is now allowed them. This, then, is the first step to be taken; it is necessary in any event, if we are to have clear ideas on the subject; and it is practicable if undertaken by competent hands.

When once this extrusion of foreign matter is accomplished, the process of simplifying and restating the rules of evidence, in the proper sense of the word, can go forward. To accomplish this, some legislation would probably be necessary. It should take the shape of conferring authority on the courts, or expressly recognizing it as already in them, to change and mould the rules of evidence, subject to such limitations as may seem prudent, — subject only, it might be hoped, to a few large and simple principles which are the skeleton of our present system. We can hardly hope for wisdom enough in the legislature to accomplish in any other way what is needed. Good legislation of any sort, in the way of law reform, is very hard, almost impossible, to get. Yet a small and instructed body of lawyers, in any legislature, can overcome even this difficulty; and such a body, in any community, might well hope to carry through so reasonable a provision as that of charging the courts with a general control over the rules of evidence, when once they themselves were persuaded of the need of it. But I do not forget that, on such subjects as this, the lawyers are often the persons chiefly needing to be roused and convinced, and that this is the greatest obstacle to be overcome. This was strongly put two years ago by a leading member of the bar.[1197] In recommending to a body of young lawyers as their special work, "for all their lives," — aside from the necessary work of their immediate calling, — the great business of "the amendment of the law," using the words in a large sense, the distinguished speaker recognized the fact "that no class in modern society is more conservative, more timid in promoting, more resolute in resisting, alterations in existing law, than the body of which we are members." And after alluding to other possible reasons for what he calls "the dull conservatism of many lawyers," he adds that "there is a timidity born of mere ignorance.... And so it is the narrowness of vision, the imperfect intelligence of many lawyers which makes them... apprehensive of changes which, they think untried experiments." These excellent suggestions point to the chief difficulty in accomplishing such a change as I am proposing, so far as it is dependent on legislation. Yet, as I said, a few enlightened and resolute lawyers, men of recognized legal capacity and character, could, with good fortune, carry through any of our legislatures some such prudent measure of reform as I am suggesting. In Massachusetts we have had a typical illustration of what a well-trained lawyer may do for his profession in the way of law reform, by the simplest methods. Nearly fifty years ago Mr. B. B. Curtis, — who, two years later, in 1851, became Mr. Justice.

Curtis of the Supreme Court of the United States, — being a member of the Massachusetts House of Representatives, introduced a resolution for the appointment of three commissioners "to revise and reform the proceedings in the courts of justice in this

---

[1197] Address by Hon. Theodore Bacon, before the Graduating Class of the Yale Law School, in 1896.

Commonwealth, except in criminal cases, subject to the approval of the legislature." It was unanimously adopted, and Mr. Curtis, with two other leading lawyers of the State, was appointed to the task. In 1851 they prepared the draft of what has since been known as the "Practice Act." The commission proceeded cautiously, in some respects too cautiously, and consulted the bench and bar freely; their measure was accompanied by an admirable report of some twenty octavo pages, understood to have been prepared by Judge Curtis, which has still the merits of a legal classic, giving the reasons for their action.[1198] The bill was but slightly changed by the legislative committees to whom it was referred; and it passed without dissent. It was a careful but radical change of the whole civil procedure of the State at common law. A few changes were made in 1852 by a repeal and re-enactment, but they left the law substantially the same, and Massachusetts has lived under it with success and satisfaction ever since, making only occasional improvements. In Connecticut, in 1879, similar reforms were accomplished under the leadership of a distinguished lawyer, now a member of the Supreme Court of that state;[1199] and other instances might be cited in other States of our country. As for England, everybody knows of the great measures, under the general title of the Judicature Acts, which have been carried through in the last quarter of a century, under the impulse of Lord Selborne.

But even without legislation, the judges have great power over the subject, direct as well as indirect. A system which mainly came into life at their hands and has been constantly moulded by them, by way of administering procedure, they can also largely reshape and recast, if they will. But no court should enter upon this task that is not sure of its ground, that does not pretty well understand the history, nature, and scope of the existing rules, and see pretty clearly where it means to come out. With these preparations, however, the course taken from time to time by the English judges is, in a good degree, open to ours. By using strongly their power to shape the procedure and modify it by rules of court, they can do much directly; and by discouraging an unjust and overstrained application of the rules of evidence, by construing them freely and in a large way, by refusing to interfere with the rulings of

---

[1198] Life of B. R. Curtis, ii. 149.
[1199] Hon. Simeon E. Baldwin.

the lower courts except in cases of abuse or clear and important error, by encouraging a more elastic procedure in shaping questions for the upper court, by recurring always to fundamental principles, and inclining always to give effect to these as against exceptional and special rules, and generally by recognizing, resolutely and persistently, the subordinate, auxiliary, secondary, wholly incidental character and aim of the rules of evidence (properly so called), they can indirectly do a very great deal. Let me, however, repeat again and again, and with emphasis, that I mean, in speaking of the secondary character of the rules of evidence, to refer only to what is properly so called; and let me again and again insist that the body of rules now called by that name should, without needless delay, be purged of that spurious matter, *rudis indigestaque moles,* belonging to the substantive law, to the general rules of legal reasoning, and to other parts of the law of procedure, of which I have repeatedly spoken.

What about the jury? some one may ask. If our present system of evidence has been called out by the jury, and we still have that, why must not the law of evidence continue? That suggests the question, whether the jury itself must continue? The jury system is already much modified. The experience of England, Massachusetts, and some other States, where for some years, in most civil cases, no person has a jury trial unless he asks for it before a certain time, has been satisfactory. This has worked a great cutting down in the number of jury trials. It appears to me that, with or without the aid of changes in constitutional provisions, more may well be done in reducing the number of jury trials in civil and criminal cases. Personally I should think that it was not wise to abolish jury trial in civil cases, — of course not in criminal cases, — but only that it should be restricted still farther. Indeed, in civil cases, I would restrict it narrowly, for it appears to me, among other things, to be a potent cause of demoralization to the bar. In so far as it has been or may be restricted, the objections to any changes in our system of evidence which are founded on its relation to jury trial are lessened.

But apart from all that, it may be said, truly, that juries are now much less helped and restrained by the judicial contrivances which find expression in our rules of evidence than is sometimes thought. Judges, to a large extent, sit quiet and let parties try their cases with as loose an application of the rules of evidence as they themselves may wish. Indeed, the waiving of these rules has been judicially declared to be the right of litigating parties in all cases. "As the rules of evidence," said Chief Justice Shaw, in 1848,[1200] "are made for the security and benefit of parties, all exceptions may be waived by mutual consent." Allowing that this is overstated, it may still be insisted that the old conceptions of a jury's incapacity, and of the need of so much exclusion, were overstrained, and that they are largely inapplicable to modern juries.

I will leave aside any question of changing the jury system, and assume that it is to be in no degree restricted. Undoubtedly, at least in my opinion, it will long continue, and should continue, to a greater or less extent. So long as it does, we must have a law of evidence, *i. e.,* a set of regulative and excluding precepts, enforced by the presiding officer of the meeting, namely, the judge. In exercising this function the court must continue to apply certain great principles, such as these: (1) That the jury must, so far as possible, personally see and hear those whose statements of fact, oral or written, they are asked to believe; (2) that witnesses must, so far as possible, testify orally, publicly, under strong sanctions for truth-telling, and that both parties must have full opportunity to examine or cross-examine under the court's supervision; (3) that in the case of writings the jury must, so far as possible, personally and publicly inspect such as they are expected to act upon; (4) that whatever is said or shown to the jury, or privately known to them, bearing on the case, must be said, shown, or stated publicly, in presence of the court and of all parties concerned; (5) that the execution of solemn documents must be clearly shown, and that they must be faithfully construed according to the written terms; (6) that the jury must not be obliged or permitted to listen to what will unduly delay the case, or too much tend to confuse or mislead them; (7) that the jury may be aided by the opinions, on matters of fact, of persons specially qualified, wherever they are likely to be materially helped by it; (8) that the court must have power to review and set aside the verdict of the jury, in order to prevent gross injustice, and secure conformity to the rules of law and the requirements of sound reason, — in no case substituting its own judgment for that of the jury, and always exercising a merely restraining power.

[1200] Shaw v. Stone, 1 Cush. 228, 243.

I am assuming that the two fundamental propositions already named[1201] are kept in mind. In giving effect to these and in regulating details, if a few comprehensive, fundamental principles like these, derived from experience and at the bottom of our present system, be followed, construed and applied in a liberal way; and if the application of them be kept steadily under the oversight and control of the court, by being dealt with as rules of court, it appears to me that our system of evidence might be vastly improved, and be made conformable to the changing convenience of mankind.

And now, finally, if it be said that we have not judges fit for the large discretion thus to be confided to them, several things may be said in answer: —

1. That sort of remark about our judges is often made when one has in mind, not the judges of his own courts, or of any courts that he knows most about, but some other judges in some other parts of the country. Admitting that the statement may be true in some places, it is not true of the higher Federal courts anywhere, or of the higher courts in most of our States. It is not true in England. Wherever it is not true, that particular jurisdiction need not be deterred from giving to its highest courts the proposed recognition and enlargement of discretionary power. And the example thus afforded will be likely to help matters elsewhere.

2. If the judges in any place are not fit for any given functions which those in other places exercise with benefit to the community, or which it is thought well to put upon them, that is a reason for changing the breed of judges. And we may remember that, in most of our States, a change, whether for better or worse, is only too quickly and easily possible.

3. The objection, however, may have another answer. Those who make it, forget, for the moment, how much discretion is already reposed in the judges, and exercised by them at every hour of the day and in every part of their functions. In imposing criminal sentences, in punishing contempts, in passing upon motions, in making rules of court and regulating practice and procedure,[1202] in adopting rules of presumption, in determining the limits of judicial notice, in applying

---

[1201] *Supra,* 530.

[1202] See, for example, as I am reminded by my colleague. Professor Smith, himself formerly a distinguished member of the Supreme Bench of New Hampshire, the experience of that State during the administrations of Chief Justice Bell and Chief Justice Doe.

the rules of evidence, and in conducting trials generally, — in discharging these and other duties, a vast discretionary power is everywhere exercised. Men who can safely be intrusted with the discretion which the ordinary exercise of the judicial office imports, every day of the week, are fit to undertake the function that I am now suggesting.

APPENDIX A

[Supra, 313.]

[From the (English) Law Magazine, vi. 348. October, 1831.]

PRESUMPTIONS OF LAW AND PRESUMPTIVE EVIDENCE.

Presumptions are commonly divided by writers on English law, into two classes, namely, presumptions of law, and presumptions of fact.

Presumptions of law are of two hinds. *First,* conclusive or imperative presumptions, that is, legal rules not to be overcome by any evidence that the fact is otherwise. Thus by the statute of limitations, a simple contract debt, not kept up in certain specified manners, is extinguished after a lapse of six years; nor can it be recovered by proving that the sum due has never been paid. So if a man gives a receipt in full under seal, evidence of a prior unsatisfied debt is not admissible.[1203] The cases in which parties are bound by similar admissions, and particularly by admissions on the record, are very numerous. Again, a sane man is presumed to contemplate the probable consequences of his own acts; and this presumption is conclusive, nor may he rebut it by showing that in fact he did *not* foresee them.[1204] So that by this rule a man is made responsible for the consequences of his acts, whether his conduct is marked by heedless negligence, or obstinate rashness. Of the same nature are all rules respecting the limitation of actions and title by prescription, which Mr. Starkie calls *artificial* presumptions;[1205] but they are no more artificial than any other rule of law; and when it is said that twenty years' peaceable enjoyment of an easement raises a presumption of a grant, this is only a clumsy and circuitous mode of expressing the rule that twenty years' peaceable enjoyment gives a *prima facie* title to an easement. It is no more capricious or absurd that this presumption should not apply to a possession of nineteen

---

[1203] 3 Starkie Evid., tit. Receipt.

[1204] *Per* Lord Ellenborough, "It is an universal principle that when a man ig charged with doing an act of which the probable consequence may be highly injurious, the intention is an inference of law resulting from the doing the act." Rex *v.* Dixon, 3 M. & S. 15. See Law Mag. vol. v. p.365.

[1205] 3 Evid. 1235.

years and three hundred and sixty-four days, than that a man should be a minor at the age of twenty years and three hundred and sixty-four days.

In some cases of conclusive legal presumption, a party is said to be *estopped,* and to have created an *estoppel* against himself. An estoppel is when a man has done some act which affords a conclusive presumption against himself in respect of the matter at issue. Thus, if a plaintiff disputes the title of the defendant to certain lands, and it appears that he holds them as tenant to the defendant, this affords a conclusive presumption, which he may not dispute, that his landlord is rightfully entitled: in other words, a tenant is estopped from disputing his landlord's title.

Formerly, all children born in lawful wedlock, if the husband was not impotent, or beyond the four seas during a period exceeding that of gestation, were legitimate; nor could evidence to the contrary be received in a court of law.[1206] The presumption of law was then imperative; whatever might have been the real facts of the paternity, and however clearly they might be proved, still the husband was considered as the father of his wife's children. Since that time, however, the rule has been changed, and probable evidence that the husband was not the father of the child, is admissible.[1207] The presumption, therefore, in this case now belongs to the *second* and more comprehensive kind: i. *e;* when presumptions of law are certain assumptions or legal rules, defining the amount of evidence requisite to support a particular allegation, which facts being proved, may be either explained away or rebutted by evidence to the contrary, but are conclusive in the absence of such evidence. The distinction between the two kinds of legal presumptions is clearly stated by Lord Mansfield in Darwin *v.*

[1206] Co. Litt. 244 a. See the Edinburgh Review, vol. xlix. p. 190.

[1207] "I apprehend the law to be, that the birth of a child during wedlock raises a presumption *(of law)* that such child is legitimate; that this presumption may be rebutted both by direct and presumptive evidence; that under the first head may be classed impotency and non-access, that is, impossibility of access; and under the second, all those circumstances which can have the effect of raising a presumption *(of fact)* that the child is not the issue of the husband." Lord Redesdale in the Banbury Peerage case, Gardner Peerage by Le Marchant, 432. Lord Redesdale, in these remarks, has confounded *direct* and *presumptive* evidence with *certain* and *probable* evidence. Impotency or non-access is only an indirect proof of illegitimacy, although it is a proof which admits of no doubt.

Upton.[1208] "The enjoyment of lights, with the defendant's acquiescence for twenty years, is such decisive presumption of a right by grant or otherwise, that unless contradicted or explained, the jury ought to believe it: but it is impossible that length of time can be said to be an *absolute bar,* like a statute of limitation; it is certainly a *presumptive bar* which ought to go to a jury."[1209] Legal presumptions of this latter kind (which may be termed disputable or rebuttable presumptions) are definitions of the quantity of evidence, or the state of facts, sufficient to make out a *prima facie* case; in other words, of the circumstances under which the burden of proof lies on the opposite party. Of this very extensive class of presumptions a few examples will suffice. Thus, a man is presumed innocent until he is proved guilty; that is, if a man is charged with a crime, he is not bound to prove that he did *not,* but his accuser is bound to prove that he *did* commit it.[1210] Thus, twenty years' peaceable enjoyment of an easement, throws on any claimant the burden of proving that the possessor's title is bad, and that *he has* a better. So it a child is born in wedlock, one who *questions* his legitimacy must disprove it: if a child is born during a divorce a *mensa et thoro,* one, who maintain his legitimacy must prove it. Again, the presumption of law is that a man is alive, unless nothing has been heard of him for seven years, when the presumption is that he is dead: that is to say, if it is averred that a man is dead, the party must prove his assertion; but if nothing has been heard of him for seven years, the opposite party must prove that he is alive. Waste

---

[1208] 2 Saund. 175 b, note.

[1209] "I have known (says Mr. Christian, note to 3 Bl. Com. 369) a witness rejected, and hissed out of Court, who declared that he doubted of the existence of a God and a future state. But I have since heard a learned judge declare at nisi *prius,* that the judges had resolved not to permit adult witnesses to be interrogated respecting their belief of a Deity and a future state. It is probably more conducive to the course of justice, that this should be presumed till the contrary is proved. And the most religious witness may be scandalized by the imputation, which the very question conveys." The establishment of this conclusive presumption would be nearly equivalent to admitting the evidence of Atheists, which is now excluded; as it would be almost impossible to prove the exact state of a man's belief. This change, therefore, as indeed of all the rules of exclusion of evidence, is very desirable, but has not yet been effected.

[1210] In cases of homicide, however, if it merely appears that one man has killed another, he is presumed to be guilty of murder, unless such evidence is produced as will either reduce the offence to manslaughter, or entirely remove its criminality, by justifying or excusing it. See Law Mag vol. v. p. 362.

land which adjoins a road is presumed to belong to the owner of the adjoining enclosed land; whose title is therefore valid, unless some one can show a paramount claim.

The circumstances which will raise such a legal presumption, or, in other words, will impose on the other party the necessity of proving that the fact is *not* so, sometimes differ with regard to the same fact in different issues: that is, evidence which in one issue is sufficient to establish a certain fact, in another is not sufficient. Thus, in settlement cases, proof of a long cohabitation of two persons who passed as man and wife, is sufficient to raise a presumption of marriage, or to compel the other party to prove that there was no marriage. But in trials for bigamy and actions for criminal conversation, proof of an actual marriage is requisite. So likewise, in actions for breach of promise of marriage, a promise on the part of the woman may be proved by outward marks of acceptance, and such a conduct as would be natural towards an accepted suitor. But on the part of the man, such facts will not raise a presumption of a promise, which must be proved by direct evidence.

The question therefore, with regard to the latter kind, or disputable presumptions of law, resolves itself into this: what state of facts being proved or admitted, in other words, what amount of evidence, shall be sufficient to support the allegations of the one party, so as to compel the other party either to disprove or explain them? This question arises, and must be decided by legal rules, in every case which comes before a court of justice. The doctrine of legal presumptions therefore is not a subject which can be treated by itself, as it runs through the whole law of evidence, and is interwoven with its entire texture: in every different subject it must be laid down what amount of evidence is sufficient to raise a presumption, or to show a *prima facie*[1211] case, and to throw on the

---

[1211] *"Prima facie* evidence is that which, not being inconsistent with the falsity of the hypothesis, nevertheless raises such a degree of probability in its favor, that it must prevail, if it be accredited by the jury , unless it be rebutted or the contrary proved." I Stark. Ev. 453. Mr. Starkie has here introduced an unnecessary condition into his definition. *Conclusive* evidence is not inconsistent with the falsity of the hypothesis: so far from it indeed that it is made conclusive for no other reason than because the contrary *may* be proved. The simple account of the matter is, that *prima facie* evidence is that amount of evidence which is sufficient to establish a certain fact: when this amount is fixed by law, the rule to this effect is termed a *presumption of law;* when it is not, it must be left to the jury

opposite side the burden either of proving the contrary, so that the obligation never attaches, or of showing that, though the obligation once attached, he is now released from it. For example, the plaintiff makes a *prima facie* case by proving the defendant's signature to a promissory note; which case the defendant may answer, either by proving that the signature is a forgery, when he would not be liable, or that the note has been paid, when the liability having existed would have been discharged. The rules on the doctrine of legal presumptions, a doctrine not only of universal application throughout the law of evidence, but of the highest importance to the community, may, in many cases, be referred to the four following maxims: — 1st. That no one shall, in the first instance, be called on to prove a negative, or be put on his defence, without sufficient evidence against him having been offered, which, if not contradicted or explained, would be conclusive. 2d. That the affirmative of the issue must be proved; otherwise men might be called upon by a stranger to prove the title to their property, which they might often be unable to do, though the title was in fact good. 3d. That possession is *prima facie* evidence of property. If in all actions founded on a right of property, the plaintiff was forced to prove his title, the security of property would be much diminished by such disclosures, and the uncertainty of litigation much increased. The 4th maxim is commonly expressed in the words *"Omnia præsumuntur rite et solenniter acta," i. e.,* whatever any thing or person appears or professes to be, is considered to be the fact, until the contrary is proved. What could be more dangerous to the quiet enjoyment of property and the peace of society, than a liberty to put any man to the proof that a deed is genuine, that his birth is legitimate, that his marriage is valid? It would be in vain that the law protected the innocent, if any man could be called upon to prove that he was not guilty; or that it protected property, if property could only be held by a continual war of litigation.

If these views with regard to presumptions are correct, it will be impossible to agree with the remarks of Mr. Bentham, who maintains that the contrary of the maxim, that he who makes an averment should prove it, ought to be followed.[1212] What he means is

---

to determine what conclusion is to be drawn from the facts proved, and whether, if uncontradicted or unexplained, they make out the case.

[1212] Bentham on Evidence, by Dumont, book vii. c. 16. The voluminous papers of Mr. Bentham on the subject of evidence were transmitted

not very clear: for it is not to be supposed that a party could be called on to prove that which is against himself, or to give evidence for the affirmative of an issue by which he is to be a loser: that the defendant should prove the plaintiff's case, and the plaintiff the defendant's. Mr. Bentham probably means, that the plaintiff should not be called upon to prove his case, but that the defendant should be first bound to disprove the plaintiff's allegations. If this is Mr. Bentham's meaning, such a rule would, in our opinion, completely destroy the security of property, and especially of chattels or movables; although he is pleased to say that it is recommended by the system of "plain and simple justice and natural procedure." In another place he lays down a rule to the same effect as that just noticed, namely, that "between plaintiff and defendant, the presumption ought to be in favor of the former, to the prejudice of the latter." His chief argument is contained in the following passage. "I am aware that many lawyers lean to the contrary presumption. They are misled by an illusion. A defendant appears to their mind as a man attacked in his right of possession; and the presumption ought to be in favor of the possessor, because the number of lawful possessors is infinitely greater than that of unlawful possessors. But this is not the state of the question. The point is, whether, in cases of disputed possession, the instances in which the party calling the possession in question is in the right do not greatly exceed those in which he is in the wrong." (Book vi. ch. ii.) Undoubtedly they do; and, as we humbly submit, for no other reason than *because* the presumption of law is in favor of the defendant; in other words, *because* the *onus probandi* lies on the plaintiff, who is called on to prove his own case, and therefore would not go into court unless he thinks that that case is good. If the presumption was in favor of the plaintiff, and if the burden of proof lay not on the claimant, but on the possessor, the courts of justice would be besieged by all persons who had any malice to gratify, or enemies to be revenged on; such claimants might at least deprive others of their property, if they did not make a title to it themselves; litigation would be the most

---

to the late M. Dumont, who extracted from them a treatise which lie published in two vols. under the name of *Traite des Preuves Judiciaires.* This work has been translated into English, and published in one vol. (London, 1825). An edition of the papers from which this work was formed was published by Mr. John Mill, in five thick vols. by the name of the *Rationale of Evidence.* We shall have occasion hereafter to refer to both these works.

powerful instrument of oppression, when any man might by any man be put on his defence. Under such a law, a large part of the personal property in the kingdom would soon fall to the crown, as being without an owner: unless, indeed, the rightful owners thought themselves justified in employing false witnesses to defend an honest cause, salving their consciences with the plea that the end sanctified the means.

It should be carefully remarked, that in both kinds of legal presumption there is no *inference;* the rule of law merely applies or attaches to the circumstances when proved, and is not *deduced* from them. Thus where children are born in wedlock, and there was opportunity of access within the period of gestation, the law presumes or assumes their legitimacy; if it is proved that A or B was born under such circumstances, *his* legitimacy is inferred, and must be disproved by those who deny it. But the presumption of law is one of the propositions from which this conclusion is drawn, nor does it appear that the inference itself, or the entire argument, is ever called a legal presumption.

Moreover, in both cases, a presumption of law is an assumption or proposition. In the one case a categorical proposition, or an express rule of law (as, "a discharge in full under seal extinguishes all prior claims of the releasor against the releasee.") In the other case a conditional proposition (in this form, "if there is no proof to the contrary, a man is taken to be innocent"), liable to be overcome by evidence on the other side.

Of these two classes of legal presumption, that relating to *prima facie* cases, or the burden of proof, itself forms an important part of the law of evidence; the other class, however, of conclusive presumptions has not, properly, any particular reference to that subject. Certain facts are by the law made conclusive under certain circumstances: it follows, therefore, of necessity, that evidence is not admissible to contradict or explain them, as they are equally conclusive, explained or unexplained, contradicted or uncontradicted; and that they form a conclusive defence, after the contrary has been proved, as they have no reference to the truth or falsity of the facts which the party who is concluded seeks to establish....

The other brunch of legal presumptions, namely, presumptions which do not conclude the opposite party, if he is in a condition to disprove or explain the facts proved, forms, in our estimation, the most important part of the law of evidence. To define "the nature and amount of the evidence which the law renders sufficient to establish *a prima facie* case, and throw the *onus probandi* upon the other side," [1213] is a work of great difficulty and labor. The subject is, however, one which cannot be conveniently treated by itself, but the rules of which it is composed must be laid down severally under the different issues which arise in courts of law.

Presumption of fact has a totally different meaning from *presumption of law,* and refers not to propositions, but to arguments — not to assuming, but inferring. When evidence is offered which can only be brought to bear on the matter at issue by a process of reasoning, the inference is termed a *presumption of fact.*[1214] The statement on which this inference is founded is termed *presumptive evidence.* Presumptive evidence forms one of the brunches of the division of evidence according to its direct or indirect bearing on the matter at issue. When the witness or documents attests the very fact to be proved, as when a man proves the making of a promissory note by the defendant, who denies that he made it; when a man states that he was stabbed by the prisoner, who is indicted for the stabbing; or the date of a man's death is proved by a monumental inscription, or an entry in a parish book, the evidence is said to be positive or direct. But if the witness or document attests, not the fact to be proved, but something from which that fact may be inferred, the evidence is said to be presumptive or indirect.[1215] A presumption, therefore, in this

---

[1213] Mill, vol. v. p. 610.

[1214] Mr. Phillipps, speaking of presumptions, states that the definition of the civilians is most correct; "Prœsumtio nihil est quam *argumentum* verisimile, communi sensu perceptum, ex eo quod plerumque fit aut fieri intelligitur" (Ev. vol. ii. p. 156); which he translates thus, "A presumption is a probable *inference,* which our common sense draws from circumstances usually occurring in such cases." Yet in another place he speaks of *"true* presumptions" (p. 155); as if an *argument* could be true. The following remarks are attributed to Lord Tenterden in Rex *v.* Burdett, 4 B. & A. 161. "A presumption of any fact is properly an inferring of that fact from other facts that are known; it is an act of reasoning; *and much of human knowledge on all subjects is derived from this source. A fact must not be inferred without premises to warrant the inference;* bat if no fact could thus be ascertained by inference in a Court of law, very few offenders could be brought to punishment." It is difficult to believe that the words In italics were really uttered by Lord Tenterden.

[1215] The distinction between positive and presumptive evidence is most correctly stated by Mr. Bentham. "Evidence (says he) is direct, positive,

sense, or a presumption of fact, can only mean an argument or inference; and presumptive evidence is not evidence taken by itself, but only because, joined to some other general proposition, it tends to prove a certain conclusion. Thus, when it is said that, where a person was found standing over a wounded man with a bloody sword in his hand, there is a presumption (or it may be probably inferred) that the one stabbed the other: the fact that the man was found with a bloody sword has, in itself, apart from its consequence, no weight; but it tends to determine the question at issue, who stabbed the wounded man. So, if the date of a man's birth be at issue, and it is proved that he died in a certain year at a certain age, his age and the time of his death are in themselves indifferent; but they are data to determine the year of his birth.[1216]

---

immediate, when it is of such a nature, that (admitting its accuracy) it brings with it a belief of the thing to be proved. Evidence is indirect, or circumstantial, when it is of such a nature that (admitting its accuracy) it leads to a belief of the thing to be proved only by way of induction (i. *e.* deduction), reasoning, inference." Treatise on Evidence by Dumont, 186 n. This is more accurate than the definition of Mr. Starkie, which excludes all direct documentary evidence; "Evidence (says he) is direct and positive when the very facts in dispute are communicated by those who have had actual knowledge of them by means of their senses, and where, therefore, the jury may be supposed to perceive the fact through the organs of the witness." 1 Ev. 18. Again he says that "it frequently happens that the fact is of a nature imperceptible by the senses, and which cannot be proved but by presumptive evidence." *Ib.* 19, and see vol. ii. 1234. An entry of a birth or marriage in a parish register is direct evidence of such birth or marriage; a deed is direct evidence of the purpose for which it was executed: though these facts are not communicated by witnesses who have had actual knowledge of them by means of their senses. In numberless instances the production of direct documentary evidence is indispensable, and cannot be supplied by direct oral testimony. Thus on a second trial for certain felonies, a certified copy of the record of the former conviction must be produced; nor would the evidence of a person present at that conviction be admissible. It is plain that the directness or indirectness of evidence has nothing to do with its *credibility.* A genuine or forged deed, a tine or perjured witness, may equally attest the fact at issue, or a fact from which it may be inferred.

[1216] The facts themselves are called presumptions by C. B. Gilbert (Evid. 160); but the common usage unquestionably has been, and is, to call the inferences from them presumptions. Thus it is commonly said that we may presume from such circumstances that the prisoner is guilty or innocent, that a man's intention may be presumed from his acts, etc. Thus Mr. Starkie speaks of "facts and circumstances, upon which any reasonable presumption or inference may be founded" (1 Ev. 17); and such is his constant language. The usage of this word by Mr. Phillipps, supported by the authority of Lord Tenterden, was pointed out in a former note.

As in this kind of proof the fact at issue is not attested, but only some *circumstances* from which that fact may be inferred, presumptive evidence is also known by the name of *circumstantial* evidence....

If the foregoing remarks are well founded, it follows:

1. That the two members of the above division of presumptions, namely, presumptions of law, and presumptions of fact, are not properly opposed to each other. Presumption means reasoning in the one, assumption in the other. Presumptions of law are propositions; presumptions of fact are arguments. Moreover, presumptions of fact belong to evidence, or statements, made by witnesses or contained in documents, offered to a court of justice: legal presumptions belong to the law of evidence, or the rules affecting those statements. They cannot, therefore, be species of a common genus.[1217]

2. That legal or artificial presumptions cannot be a species of indirect evidence.[1218] A fact to which a legal presumption will apply, may be established either by direct or indirect evidence: but legal presumptions themselves cannot be a subdivision of evidence, much less of a particular kind of evidence. The very author who has imagined this classification furnishes the best refutation of his own scheme, by observing, that "legal presumptions are mere arbitrary and positive rules of law,"[1219] and consequently neither arguments, nor statements made by witnesses or contained in documents.

3. That presumptions of law cannot conveniently be treated together under a separate head, but ought to be set forth under the different subjects to which they respectively belong. In every subject or issue it should be stated whether any and what evidence will

---

[1217] If the argument founded on the presumption of law was itself called a presumption of law, this division might be correct. In this case, an argument founded on a legal rule with regard to *prima facie* evidence, or the onus *probandi,* would be a presumption of law, and arguments proving or disproving the question at issue would be presumptions of fact. But this does not appear to be the usual sense of the former term. For instance, in the following: "*Where an easement has been peaceably enjoyed for twenty years, a grant is presumed.* A. B. has so enjoyed an easement for this length of time; it must, therefore, be presumed that he had a grant:" it appears that the major premise (marked in italics), and not the whole argument, containing the matters of fact, is called the presumption of law.

[1218] Mr. Starkie, vol. i. p. 446, divides evidence into direct and indirect; and indirect evidence into artificial presumptions and natural presumptions.

[1219] Vol. i. p. 448.

conclude the opposite party, or prevent him from offering evidence in contradiction or explanation (conclusive presumptions of law); and what amount of evidence will be sufficient to establish a presumptive or *prima facie* case, so as to entitle the court to infer the point at issue, and to throw on the other side the burden of proving the contrary (disputable or rebuttable presumptions of law).

4. That natural presumptions, or presumptions of fact, are not properly opposed to legal or artificial presumptions; but are arguments founded on presumptive or circumstantial evidence, which is opposed to direct or positive evidence. Presumptive evidence being that which tends to prove the fact at issue, or from which the fact at issue may be inferred: while direct evidence establishes the fact at issue itself without any process of reasoning.

5. That presumptions of fact, or circumstantial proofs, do not properly belong to the law of evidence. They are arguments, probable, improbable, or certain, involving no consideration of law, equally valid in and out of a court of justice, belonging to any subject-matter, and to be judged by the common and received tests of the truth of propositions and the validity of arguments. "Mere natural presumptions (says Mr. Starkie) are derived wholly by means of the common experience of mankind, from the course of nature, and the ordinary habits of society. Such presumptions are therefore wholly independent of the system of laws to be applied to the facts when established; they remain the same in their nature and operation, whether the law of England, or the code of Justinian, is to decide upon the legal effect and quality of the facts when found." And in another place he justly remarks, that "it would be a vain endeavor to attempt to specify the numerous presumptions with which the knowledge of a jury conversant in the common affairs and course of dealing in society, necessarily supplies them; it is obvious that such presumptions are coextensive with the common experience and observation of mankind."[1220] Nevertheless it is highly useful in treating of this brunch of law, to explain the nature of circumstantial, or presumptive evidence, and to point out the generality of its character and its independence of legal considerations. There are likewise some few general propositions as to matters of fact, universally taken for granted in the administration of the law, and approved by the invariable usage of judges, which may properly be

---

[1220] 3 Stark. Ev. 1245, 1254.

referred to this head. Such for instance is the rule as to the evidence of an accomplice, which, though admissible for the prosecution, is always treated as liable to great suspicion, and juries are recommended to place no faith in it, if not confirmed in some material points by other witnesses. In law the evidence of accomplices is as good as any other evidence; in fact it has been found that their testimony is often unworthy of credit, and on this experience the constant practice of judges is founded.

APPENDIX B

[Supra, 337 n.]

THE PRESUMPTION OF INNOCENCE IN CRIMINAL CASES.

The following pages are taken from a discussion of the subject above named, in a lecture given in the course of the "Storrs Lectures" fur 1896, by the author of the present treatise, before the Law School of Yale University. The immediate occasion for this discussion was found in a remarkable exposition of the subject by Mr. Justice White, put forward in the opinion of the Supreme Court of the United States in Coffin *v. V. S.,* 156 *V. S.* 432 (189,5). The paper now quoted from, after briefly referring to the very harsh nature of the criminal law of England up to the earlier part of this century, and to various humane maxims of the judges, rules of procedure, and practical adjustments which tended to counteract this severity and to make it endurable, proceeded as follows:[1221] —

Always, of course, there was operating in favor of the accused the sound maxim of general jurisprudence that the plaintiff or, rather, the party who seeks to move the court, must make out a reason for his request. This rule is sometimes expressed in the form

---

[1221] In a note it had been remarked: "Our administration of the criminal law to-day, in a period when the substantive law is merciful, is sadly enfeebled by a continuance of some rules and practices which should have disappeared with the cruel laws they were designed to mitigate. I may refer to the refusal of new trials to the government in some classes of cases, to the absurd extreme to which the rule about confessions in evidence is sometimes pressed, to the strained interpretation of the prohibition of *ex post facto* laws and of self-crimination, to the continuation of technicalities of criminal procedure and practice which have lost their reason for existence, and to a superstitious rigor in enforcing these, which still shows itself. In following English precedents in such matters, we forget to supplement them by that saving good sense which appears in the swiftness and vigor of English administration. If we follow English practices we should remember that they are all meant to go together; they may lose their wisdom and good sense when separated. Excellent criticisms upon one aspect of this sort of thing may be found in the dissenting opinion of Peckham, J., speaking for himself and Justices Brewer and White, in Grain v. U. S., 162 U. S. 625, 646, 650. He justly characterizes the result arrived at in the opinion of the court as "most deplorable." Other recent opinions of the same court in criminal cases, such as Bram *v. U. S;* 168 *V.* S. 532, may, perhaps, be thought open to a like condemnation.

of a presumption, *presumitur pro negante;* or, having regard to the Latin terms for plaintiff arid defendant, *actor* and *reus, — presumitur pro reo.* That is a maxim of policy and practical sense; it is not founded on any notion that defendants generally are free from blame. It is a maxim or principle that saves the defendant by the mere inertia of the court, if the plaintiff does not make out his case. This maxim, in this bare form, and without the familiar additional clause as to the greater force of persuasion in criminal cases, always operated for the accused. It is probably true that in the form last given it has sometimes been mistranslated, and given a special application to criminal cases, as if *reus* necessarily meant a person charged with crime, and not merely, as it truly does, a defendant in any sort of a case. The operation and exact scope of this maxim, both in civil and criminal cases, was very neatly expressed by the General Court (the Legislature) of Massachusetts so long ago as 1657, as follows: "Whereas, in all civil cases depending in suit, the plaintiff affirmeth that the defendant hath done him wrong and accordingly presents his case for judgment and satisfaction — it behoveth the court and jury to see that the affirmation be proved by sufficient evidence, else the case must be found for the defendant; and so it is also in a criminal case, for, in the eye of the law every man is honest and innocent, unless it be proved legally to the contrary." [1222]

In this country and in recent times, much emphasis in criminal cases has been put on the presumption of innocence. Always and everywhere great emphasis was placed on the rule that in criminal cases there can be no conviction unless guilt is established with very great clearness — as we say nowadays, beyond reasonable doubt. In civil cases it is enough if the mere balance of probability is with the plaintiff, but in criminal cases there must be a clear, heavy, emphatic preponderance.

Now, what does the presumption of innocence mean? Does it mean anything more than a particular application of that general rule of sense and convenience, running through all the law, that men in general are taken, *prima facie* — *i. e.,* in the absence of evidence to the contrary, to be good, honest, free from blame, presumed to do their duty in every situation in life; so that no one need go forward, whether in pleading or proof, to show as regards himself or another,

---

[1222] Records of Massachusetts, iii. 434 — 435.

that the fact is so, but every one shall have it presumed in his favor? If it does, what is its meaning?

Let us trace the use of this maxim. In recent years, in this country, at the hands of heated counsel and of some judges, it has been given an extraordinary stretch. One may read, for instance, in a late American book on Evidence, the following statement: "The presumption of innocence is not a mere phrase without meaning; it is in the nature of evidence for the defendant; it is as irresistible as the heavens till overcome; it hovers over the prisoner as a guardian angel throughout the trial; it goes with every part and parcel of the evidence."[1223] That "purple patch" is not marked as being quoted from anybody; but in reality, I believe, it was an impassioned utterance of Rufus Choate, one of the most eloquent and successful advocates of his time.[1224] Such a passage as that, gravely woven into the text of a legal treatise, may show the extent to which the presumption of innocence has been overdone in our hysterical American fashion of defending accused persons. But let us observe it in its earlier history. In Bracton, say in 1260, we find it in the most general form — *de quolibet homine presumitur quod sit bonus homo donec probetur in contrarium.*[1225] In a great and famous continental work on Presumptions, by Menochius,[1226] three centuries later, we have the simple phrase: *"Illa pre-sumptio qua dicimus quemlibet presumi innocentem,"* and that is all the emphasis he gives it. In the middle of the next century, the General Court of Massachusetts, in a passage partly quoted before, said, simply and precisely, "It behoveth both court and jury to see that the affirmation be proved by sufficient evidence, else the case must be found for the defendant, and so also it is in a criminal case; for in the eyes of the law every man is honest and innocent unless it be proved legally to the contrary. In criminal prosecutions the presumption is in favor of the defendant, for thus far it is to be hoped of all mankind, that they are not guilty in any such instances, and the penalty enhances the presumption."[1227]

Very little is said about it before this century, and these quotations fairly illustrate the slight emphasis given it, and the part it

---

[1223] Bradner, Evidence, 460.
[1224] Lawson, Pres. Ev. 433 n.
[1225] Bracton, 193.
[1226] 955, col. 1,16.
[1227] *Ubi supra.*

plays. In looking through the arguments of Erskine and Curran and other great lawyers famous for their defence of accused persons, and through the charges of the court given to juries — in the last century and the early part of this, we shall find very little, indeed almost nothing, about the presumption of innocence. But a great deal will be found, a very great emphasis is placed, upon the rule that a party must be proved guilty by a very great weight of evidence. That is the important thing. And I think it will be found that, in English practice, down to our time, the presumption of innocence — except as a synonym for the general principle incorporated in that total phrase which expresses the rule about a reasonable doubt, namely, that the accused must be *proved* guilty, and that beyond a reasonable doubt — plays a very small part indeed.

Take, for example, two famous English cases of this century. In Despard's case[1228] the Attorney-General in his opening argument said: "I am, however, gentlemen, ready to admit what no doubt the counsel for the prisoner would be glad to have brought forward to your attention, that the great depravity which is required to conceive and to execute a crime of such extensive mischief, so far from operating to create any prejudice against the prisoner, ought rather to give him a fairer claim to the utmost benefit of that indulgent and salutary principle of our law, which holds every man to be innocent till he is proved to be guilty; and therefore, he will unquestionably be entitled to that which I am sure he will experience at your hands, that the charge should be well watched, that the evidence should be well sifted, and that your minds should be most satisfactorily convinced of his guilt, before you think of pronouncing a verdict against him." Serjeant Best (afterwards Chief Justice Best), for the defence (col. 437), said: "Gentlemen, having made these observations, I am persuaded it will be unnecessary for me to desire you to do all that men can do to divest yourselves of that prejudice which you feel against a man in his situation; to do all that which the Attorney-General has emphatically and distinctly told you to do — that which the law of this country has told you to do — that, without which there can be no liberty existing in this country — that is, to presume him innocent till guilt is established in evidence; for, until his guilt be made out, not merely by vague and unconfirmed stories told by suspicious witnesses, but by that species of evidence which is

---

[1228] 28 St. Tr. 345, 363 (1803).

required by juries in cases of this sort, it is your bounden duty to presume him innocent." And, again, at the end of his argument (col. 458, 460): "This case is not to be made out by conjecture, you are not to condemn unless all idea of innocence be completely extinguished by the weight of the evidence that has been produced upon the cause.... Remember the maxim of the Attorney-General, that 'in proportion as the crime is enormous so ought the proof to be clear.' "

At the trial of William Palmer for poisoning in 1856, the counsel have nothing to say of the presumption of innocence. And this is what Lord Campbell says in his charge:[1229] "Gentlemen, I must begin by conjuring you to banish from your minds all that you may have heard before the prisoner was placed in that dock.... I must not only warn you against being influenced by what you have before heard, but I must also warn yon not to be influenced by anything but by the evidence which has been laid before you with respect to the particular charge for which the prisoner is now arraigned.... By the practice in foreign countries it is allowed to raise a probability of the prisoner having committed the crime with which he is charged by proving that he has committed other offences — by showing that he is an immoral man, and that he is not unlikely, therefore, to have committed the offence with which he is charged. That is not the case in this country. You must presume that a man is innocent until his guilt is established, and his guilt can only be established by evidence directly criminating him on the charge for which he is tried.... Unless by the evidence for the prosecution a clear conviction has been brought to your minds of the guilt of the prisoner, it is your duty to acquit him. You are not to convict him on suspicion, even on strong suspicion. There must be a strong conviction in your minds that he is guilty of this offence, and if you have any reasonable doubt yon will give him the benefit of that doubt."

That is the simple, intelligible, plain way in which the presumption of innocence is dealt with in important cases in England. The prisoner is, indeed, carefully protected, but his bulwark is not found in any emphatic or strained application of the phrase or the fact of a presumption of innocence.

[1229] Palmer's Trial, 166.

A Scotch case in 1817[1230] should now be mentioned. We shall see hereafter the use made of it in Coffin *v.* U. S. One Andrew McKinley was indicted for administering false oaths. There was a question as to the true interpretation of the oaths, and the counsel for the accused insisted upon his right to have a favorable construction put on them. He said (col. 283): "In all criminal cases everything must be strictly interpreted in favor of the accused and against the prosecutor," and other similar things. The Advocate Depute replied (col. 334): "A great deal was said about the presumption in favor of the innocence of the panel. This is a common topic of declamation,[1231] but I never could understand the presumption of the innocence of a panel. The *onus probandi* lies on the prosecutor, and he must make out his case, but I see no occasion for a presumption of any sort, but what arises from a want of contrary proof. And I know no such doctrine in any work on the criminal law of Scotland." The defence (col. 438-439) declared that "this was the very first time in a criminal case," that the existence of a presumption of innocence had been denied, and referred to the "very obvious and common-place rule of law that in all trials for crimes there is a presumption in favor of innocence which runs through the whole proceedings and is applied to the indictment, to the proof, to the verdict." In deciding the question then under discussion in favor of the prosecution, Lord Pitmilly said (col. 518) that if anything were doubtful about the construction of the oaths " the presumption must be in favor of innocence.... We are not to presume guilt because the prosecutor alleges guilt... and until guilt is established, we must hold the presumption to be in favor of innocence." Lord Justice Clerk said (col. 538), that if the oath were doubtful he was bound "to let the doubt lean in favor of the accused." None of the other judges commented on this subject except the single dissenting judge, Lord Gillies. He said (col. 506) in an emphatic passage that, to be sure, he himself suspected that the oath was as bad as it was contended. "But," he went on, "the presumption in favor of Innocence is not to be redargued by mere suspicion.... The public prosecutor treats this too lightly. He seems to think that the law entertains no such presumption of innocence. I cannot listen to this. I conceive that this

---

[1230] McKinley's case, 33 St. Tr. 275.

[1231] The reader will observe that this is said of Scotland and not of England.

presumption is to be found in every code of law which has reason and religion and humanity for a foundation. It is a maxim which ought to be inscribed in indelible characters in the heart of every judge and juryman, and I was happy to hear from Lord Hermand that he is inclined to give full effect to it.[1232] To overturn this there should be legal evidence of guilt, carrying home a degree of conviction short only of certainty."

It will be noticed, as I said, that this is a Scotch case, and Lord Gillies a dissenting judge. The Scotch law is not the common law, and in Scotch courts the Continental refinements about presumptions are far more familiar than in England. The handling of the matter in this case is indeed very simple, and not at all strained, but the case is not an authority in English law, or at all indicative of any emphasis, even in the Scottish courts, in recognizing the presumption of innocence.

The English conception of the presumption of innocence has been expressed by a writer peculiarly learned in the criminal law, who had devoted much time to the study and exposition of it, and, as a judge, was long engaged in administering it. Fitzjames Stephen, in the second edition of his "General View of the Criminal Law of England," published in 1890, when the author had been eleven years a judge of the Queen's Bench Division, says (p. 183): "I may mention the general presumption of innocence which, though by no means confined to the criminal law, pervades the whole of its administration.... [Here he quotes from his 'Digest of Evidence' the Article which is given below.] This is otherwise stated by saying that the prisoner is entitled to the benefit of every reasonable doubt. The word 'reasonable' is indefinite, but a rule is not worthless because it is vague. Its real meaning, and I think its practical operation, is that it is an emphatic caution against haste in coming to a conclusion adverse to a prisoner. It may be stated otherwise, but not, I think, more definitely, by saying that before a man is convicted of a crime every supposition not in itself improbable, which is consistent with his innocence, ought to be negatived." In his "Digest of Evidence," Article 94, under the title "Presumption of Innocence," he presents as its definition, this: "If the commission of a crime is directly in issue

---

[1232] All that Lord Hermand is reported as saying on this matter is (col. 499) that "Where there is a possibility of a favorable construction for the panel, it ever will receive effect from me."

in any proceeding criminal or civil, it must be proved beyond reasonable doubt. The burden of proving that any person has been guilty of a crime or wrongful act is on the person who asserts it."[1233]

This mode of stating, or indicating the substance of the presumption of innocence as applied in criminal proceedings, is more or less found in our own decisions. Obviously, it is in a very compact form; and it seems plain that such a statement adds something to the mere presumption of innocence, for that, pure and simple, says nothing as to the quantity of evidence or strength of persuasion needed to convict. But as it is stated above, the rule includes two things: First, the presumption; and second, a supplementary proposition as to the weight of evidence which is required to overcome it; the whole doctrine when drawn out being, first, that a person who is charged with crime must be *proved* guilty; that, according to the ordinary rule of procedure and of legal reasoning, *presumitur pro reo,* i. e., *negante; so* that the accused stands innocent until he is proved guilty; and, second, that this proof of guilt must displace all reasonable doubt.

As regards the simple, just, unambiguous rule, which, in requiring proof, thus emphasizes the weight of evidence and the strength of persuasion necessary to make it out in a criminal case, this rule, thus appearing to Stephen to embody and to be identified with the presumption of innocence as applied to criminal cases, is a very ancient one. We read in the *Corpus Juris,* as far back as the fourth century, a direction which is attributed to several emperors in succession: "Let all accusers understand that in bringing up a matter for judgment it must be supported by fit witnesses, *vel apertissimis documentis vel indiciis ad probationem indubitatis et luci clarioribus.[1234]* This passage was cited for the accused in a Scotch criminal case of piracy in 1705;[1235] and scraps of it have lingered long in our own books; as when Coke in his Third Institute, 70, in speaking of treasons, says: "There should be a substantial proof in a cause so criminal where *probationes oportet esse luce clariores,"*

[1233] This article has a second paragraph which runs thus: "The burden of proving that any person has been guilty of a crime or wrongful act is on the person who asserts it, whether the commission of such act is or is not directly in issue in the action." The doctrine here expressed is probably not the law in most parts of this country.

[1234] Cod. iv. 19, 25.

[1235] Captain Green's case, 14 St. Tr. 1199, 1245.

and again, of treason and felony,[1236] that the reason for not allowing counsel to the accused is that, "the testimonies and proofs of offence ought to be so clear and manifest as there can be no defence of it; " and still again, he speaks of the rule of law *quod in criminalibus probationes debent esse luce clariores.* "[1237]

This rule in England was the one constantly pressed; while, as I have said, little or no mention was made, in terms, of a presumption of innocence. This was the chief rule urged in behalf of accused persons by the great advocates in the last century and later, in such cases as those of Lord George Gordon, Hardy, Home Tooke, and others. MacNally, in his "Treatise on Evidence in Criminal Cases," at the beginning of this century, saying little of a presumption of innocence, remarks: "It may also at this day be considered as a rule of law that if the jury entertain a reasonable doubt they should deliver the prisoner."

There is no need to trace it further, for no one doubts that in one form or another it has always continued to be a great and recognized rule. It has, in our inherited system, a peculiarly important function, that of warning our untrained tribunal, the jury, against being misled by suspicion, conjecture, and mere appearances. In saying that the accused person shall be *proved* guilty, it says that he shall not be presumed guilty; that he shall be convicted only upon legal evidence, not tried upon prejudice; that he shall not be made the victim of the circumstances of suspicion which surround him, the effect of which it is always so difficult to shake off, circumstances which, if there were no emphatic rule of law upon the subject, would be sure to operate heavily against him; the circumstances, e. g., that after an investigation by the grand jury he has been indicted, imprisoned, seated in the prisoner's dock, carried away handcuffed, isolated, watched, made an object of distrust to all that behold him. He shall be convicted, this rule says, not upon any mere presumption, any taking matters for granted on the strength of these circumstances of suspicion; but he shall be *proved* guilty by legal evidence, and by legal evidence which is peculiarly clear and strong — clear beyond a reasonable doubt. The whole matter is summed up and neatly put by Chief Justice Shaw in Webster's

---

[1236] Co. 3d Inst. 29, 137.
[1237] *Ib.* 210.

case:[1238] "The burden of proof is upon the prosecutor. All the presumptions of law independent of evidence are in favor of innocence, and every person is presumed to be innocent until he is proved guilty. If upon such proof there is reasonable doubt remaining, the accused is entitled to the benefit of it by an acquittal."

We observe, in this form of statement, that the general rule of policy and sense requiring that all persons shall be assumed, in the absence of evidence, to be free from blame, — appears in the criminal law, on grounds of fairness and abundant caution, in an emphatic form, as the presumption of innocence, and it is there coupled with a separate special rule as to the weight of evidence necessary to make out guilt.

As to the real nature of the rule about a presumption of innocence, an important intimation is contained in Chief Justice Shaw's phrase that, "All the presumptions of law *independent of evidence* are in favor of innocence." That appears to be accurate and exact. The presumption is "independent of evidence," being the same in all cases; and in all operating indiscriminately, in the same way, and with equal force. On what is it founded? On the fact that men in general do not commit crime? On what is the presumption of sanity founded? On the fact that men in general are sane? Perhaps so, as a legislative reason, so to speak, or one of the reasons. But the rule itself is a different thing from the grounds of it, and when we speak of the presumption of innocence or of sanity we are talking of a legal rule of presumption, a legal position, and not of the facts which are the basis of it.

It is important to observe this, because, by a loose habit of speech, the presumption is occasionally said to be, itself, evidence, and juries are told to put it in the scale and weigh it. Greenleaf, in a single phrase, in the first volume of his treatise on Evidence, section thirty-four, a phrase copied occasionally into cases and textbooks, has said: "This legal presumption of innocence is to be regarded by the jury in every case as matter of evidence, to the benefit of which the party is entitled." [1239]This statement is condemned by the editor

---

[1238] 5 Cush. 295, 320.

[1239] Compare the remarks of Clifford, J., in Lilienthal's Tobacco *v. U. S.,* 97 U. S. 237, 267, where an opinion marked by very loose thinking is paraphrasing some unsupported expressions of Wharton on Evidence. It is easy to be misled by the figure of speech about turning the scale. When Greenleaf (Ev. iii. s. 29), in commenting on the difference between criminal and civil cases as to

of the last edition of Greenleaf's book; and in Taylor on Evidence, the great English handbook, which followed Greenleaf's text closely, this passage is omitted, and always has been omitted. In the latter part of Greenleaf's Evidence, Volume III., which deals specifically with criminal cases, it does not appear. It is denied also by Chamberlayne, the careful editor of the works on Evidence of Best and Taylor.

What can such a statement as this mean — that the presumption is to be regarded as evidence? Is it meant that on grounds of natural presumption or inference, innocence is ordinarily found in criminal cases? As to that, if one would see the true operation of natural inference, and natural presumption in criminal cases, and would appreciate how entirely artificial, how purely a matter of policy the whole rule is which bids a jury on the trial to assume innocence, let him turn his attention to the action of courts at other stages than the trial. In State *v.* Mills, 2 Dev. 421 (1830), as illustrating another point then under discussion, the court (Ruffin, J.) said: "After bill found, a defendant is presumed to be guilty to most, if not to all purposes, except that of a fair and impartial trial before a petit jury. This presumption is so strong, that, in the case of a capital felony the party cannot be let to bail." In *Exparte* Ryan, 44 Cal. 555 (1872), a party indicted for attempting to murder a policeman had been held in the lower court in $15,000 bail. On an application to reduce the bail the court (Wallace, C. J.) refused, saying: "I am bound to assume guilt for the purposes of this proceeding, for certainly I have no means of determining his innocence, to say nothing of the principle of law that, except for the purposes of a fair and impartial trial before a petit jury, the presumption of guilt arises against the prisoner on finding the indictment." In the case of In the matter of Henry Alexander, 59 Mo. 598 (1875), a capital case, the

---

the quantity of evidence required, after saying that in the latter it is enough if the evidence preponderates, adds that "in criminal trials, the party accused is entitled to the benefit of the legal presumption in favor of innocence, which in doubtful cases is always sufficient to turn the scale in his favor;" and that it is a rule of criminal law that the guilt of the accused must be fully proved, and then goes on to give the rule about reasonable doubt — it seems fairly clear that he is not thinking of the presumption of innocence itself, as placed in the scale, bat rather of the rule requiring evidence beyond a reasonable doubt, as being placed there; and, of course, that is not so much putting evidence into one scale as saying what evidence shall be put into the other. It is *this rule* that "turns the scale," and in this way.

question was, after repeated trials and disagreements of the jury, whether bail should be allowed. The Constitution of Missouri, it was held, allowed bail, except "when the proof was evident or the presumption great." In allowing it in this case the court (Wagner, J.) said: "The indictment furnishes a strong presumption of guilt.... Hence, in all such cases, there must be facts and circumstances which counteract or overcome this presumption, before bail will ever be admissible." The same doctrine was held in State *v.* Madison County Court, 136 Mo. 323, in which the court (Burgess, J.) quotes with approval the language of the Supreme Court of California in People *v.* Tinker, 19 Cal. 539, that " It [the indictment] creates a presumption of guilt for all purposes except the trial before the petit jury." These cases are the true ones to illustrate the operation of natural presumption and natural inference. Yet, at the trial all such natural probabilities are held off; the board is swept clear of these, and the accused, while kept well guarded, a prisoner, is yet to be treated as if no incriminating fact existed. His record, by a dead lift of legal policy, is now presented as clean and white. Whatever of wrong or guilt is to be inscribed on it must be the result of legal evidence now presented to the jury.

The effect of the presumption of innocence, so far from being that of furnishing to the jury evidence — *i. e.,* probative matter, the basis of an inference — is rather the contrary. It takes possession of this fact, innocence, as not now needing evidence, as already established *prima facie,* and says: "Take that for granted. Let him who denies it, go forward with his evidence." In criminal cases if the jury were not thus called off from the field of natural inference, if they were allowed to range there wherever mere reason and human experience would carry them, the whole purpose of the presumption of innocence would be balked. For of the men who are actually brought up for trial, probably the large majority are guilty. In inquiring lately of a prosecuting officer in Massachusetts for the statistics about this, he replied that out of every one hundred persons indicted for crime in his jurisdiction, twenty were tried and acquitted, twenty pleaded guilty, and sixty were tried and convicted.[1240] Now

---

[1240] In England it was neatly said, a few years ago, by a learned and accurate lawyer: "Law presumes that the prisoner is innocent until he is found guilty, but it were well to wager four to one that the jury will be satisfied of his guilt. In 1883 there were 11,347 persons found guilty against 2,723 found not guilty." Maitland, Justice and Police. Macmillan & Co., 1885.

the presumption of innocence forbids the consideration of such probabilities as are here suggested and says simply this: "It is the right of this man to be convicted upon legal evidence applicable specifically to him. Start then with the assumption that he is innocent, and adhere to it till he is proved guilty. He is indeed under grave suspicion, and it is your duty to test and fairly to weigh all the evidence against him as well as for him. But he is not to suffer in your minds from these suspicions or this necessity of holding him confined and trying him; he is to be affected by nothing but such evidence as the law allows you to act upon. For the purposes of this trial you must take him to be an innocent man, unless and until the government establishes his guilt."

It may be asked: If then a presumption be not evidence, how can you know when it is overcome? That depends on the nature of the case. It is the office of a presumption, as such, to fix the duty of going on with argument or evidence, on a given question; and is only that. As to how much evidence is to be produced, that is another matter. In criminal cases the rule is fixed that the evidence must negative all reasonable doubt; nothing else will make a case which the defendant need meet. Sometimes the presumption calls only for evidence enough to put the question really into the case, to make it really a question; sometimes for a full *prima facie* case. But in no case is there a weighing, a comparison of probative quality, as between evidence on one side and a presumption on the other.

While then it is true that a presumption may count as evidence, and be a substitute for evidence, in the sense that it will make a *prima facie* case for him in whose favor it operates, and while it is true that the facts on which a presumption is grounded may count as evidence, the presumption itself, *i. e.,* the legal rule, conclusion, or position, cannot be evidence. This question was neatly and accurately dealt with by the court in Lisbon *v.* Lyman, 49 N. H. 553 (1870). On an issue as to the emancipation of a minor, the jury were instructed " that there was a presumption that children under twenty-one are not emancipated; that the presumption was not conclusive, and the fact might be shown by proof to be otherwise, but that in deciding what the fact was, the jury would take this presumption into account, as one element of evidence, and weigh it in connection with all the testimony." Doe, J., for the court, said: " The burden was on the plaintiff to prove that when the town was divided, the last dwelling place of Volney was in the defendant's territory. The plaintiff claimed, that Volney, though a minor, had, by emancipation, acquired a right to have a home of his own, free from the control of his father. The emancipation of Volney was set up as an affirmative and essential part of the plaintiff's case; and in that view it was necessary for the plaintiff to prove it. Without any evidence, or with evidence equally balanced, on that point, emancipation would not be proved. The burden of proof was on the plaintiff, and this burden was not sustained unless the plaintiff proved it by a preponderance of all the evidence introduced on the subject. But it was not necessary for the plaintiff to produce anything more than the slightest preponderance; or to produce a preponderance of anything but evidence.... A legal presumption is a rule of law — a reasonable principle, or an arbitrary dogma — declared by the court. There may be a difficulty in weighing such a rule of law as evidence of a fact, or in weighing law on one side against fact on the other. And if the weight of a rule of law as evidence of a fact, or as counterbalancing the evidence of a fact, can be comprehended, there are objections to such a use of it.... A legal presumption is not evidence.... The presumption against the freedom of minors was not an element of evidence; could not be weighed as evidence, and it does not appear that any use could rightfully be made of it in the case. It was put into the scale with the defendant's evidence, where it would be likely to mislead the jury, and give the defendant a material advantage to which he was not entitled."[1241]

[1241] For a different, and, as I must think, a mistaken exposition of the subject, see Barber's Appeal, 63 Conn. 393, 403, 406 (1893). In a probate appeal involving the question of testamentary capacity, after a verdict against the will, it appeared that the charge of the judge below was objected to by the proponents as "confusing and contradictory." Among other things the judge had said to the jury: "If when the whole matter is before you on the evidence given on both sides, it is left uncertain whether or not the testator was of sound mind, then . . . the will should not be sustained. In the course of the trial the balance of evidence may fluctuate from one side to the other, but the burden of proof remains where it was at the outset, upon the advocates of the will, and, unless at the close of the trial the balance is with the advocates of the will, unless the beam of the scale tips down on the side of the advocates of the will, they must fail." The Supreme Court (Fenn, J.) reversed the judgment below, and in the course of a difficult and unsatisfactory exposition of the meaning and application of the term 'burden of proof," the opinion says: "The law presumes every person to be so [of sound mind] until the contrary is shown, and this presumption is of probative force in favor of the proponents of the will. ... In short ... on the whole case the question would be whether the evidence of the contestants sufficiently preponderated over

Upon the whole, then, it seems to be true that the presumption of innocence, as applied in criminal cases, is a form of expression which requires to be supplemented by the rule as to the weight of evidence; that it is merely one form of phrase for what is included in the statement that an accused person is not to be prejudiced his trial by having been charged with crime and held in custody, or by any mere suspicions, however grave; but is only to be held guilty when the government has established his guilt by legal evidence and beyond all reasonable doubt; that the presumption of innocence is often used as synonymous with this whole twofold rule, thus drawn out; that it is a convenient and familiar phrase, and probably a useful one, when carefully explained; but that it has not played any conspicuous part in the development of our criminal law except as expressed in the fuller statement given above. It may be added that the phrase "presumption of innocence," if used to a jury, peculiarly needs to be carefully explained, because of the very great ambiguity connected with the terms "presumption," "burden of proof," and "evidence," and the way in which these abused expressions reflect their own ambiguities upon each other.

---

the rebutting and special evidence of the proponents, including the evidence of the attesting witnesses, to overcome the presumption of sanity which, constituted the proponent's *prima facie* case. In other words, leaving the presumption of sanity out of the case, was there more evidence of insanity than of sanity? So that, putting it again into the case there would still be as much. Then and then only would the scales of justice, to which the court below in the case before us referred, be so adjusted, according to law, that it would be correct to say 'unless at the close of the trial the balance is with the advocates of the will they must fail; it is not sufficient that the scales stand evenly balanced.' "The opinion does not give its reasons fur the statement that the presumption has a probative quality, and can be" weighed in the scale, and the case does not necessarily involve the point above discussed; so that it is quite possible that the above exposition does not carry with it the authority of all the judges of the court. For the true basis and operation of this presumption see Davis *v. U. S.*, 160 U. *S.* 469, 486 (1895): "If that presumption. [of sanity] were not indulged the government would always be under the necessity of adducing affirmative evidence of the sanity of an accused. But a requirement of that character would seriously delay and embarrass the enforcement of the laws against crime, and in most cases be unnecessary. Consequently the law presumes that every one charged with crime is sane, and thus supplies in the first instance the required proof of capacity to commit crime. It authorizes the jury to assume at the outset that the accused is criminally responsible for his acts." Harlan, J., for the court.

Let me return now to the case of Coffin v. U. S.[1242] It will be necessary to consider it in some detail. It came up from the Circuit Court of the United States for Indiana, and was a proceeding against officials of a national bank who were convicted below of wilfully misapplying funds of the bank, and of other related offences. A great number of exceptions were taken to the charge given by the court to the jury. All but two of these were overruled. The principal exception was against the refusal of the judge to charge as he was requested on the subject of the presumption of innocence.[1243] He had been asked to charge that, "the law presumes that persons charged with crime are innocent until they are proved by competent evidence to be guilty. To the benefit of this presumption the defendants are all entitled, and this presumption stands as their sufficient" protection unless it has been removed by evidence proving their guilt beyond a reasonable doubt." The judge refused to give this charge, but instructed the jury that they could not find the defendants guilty unless satisfied of their guilt beyond a reasonable doubt, and he said: "If yon can reconcile the evidence with any reasonable hypothesis consistent with the defendant's innocence, it is your duty to do so. In that case find defendant not guilty. And if, after weighing all the proofs, and looking only to the proofs, you impartially and honestly entertain the belief that the defendant may be innocent of the offences charged against him, he is entitled to the benefit of that doubt, and you should acquit him." In various forms the judge went on to explain what "a reasonable doubt" is, and to make very clear the duty of the jury as to the weight of evidence which they were bound to require before they could find guilt.

The Supreme Court held that there was error in refusing the charge which was desired on the presumption of innocence; and, while recognizing that no particular form of words was necessary, in dealing with this presumption, they held that the error was not made good by anything found in the rest of the charge. The opinion of the court was given by Mr. Justice White, and was not accompanied by any expression of dissent. It declares that the principle that there is a presumption of innocence is "axiomatic and elementary, and its

---

[1242] 156 U. S.432.

[1243] The action of the trial judge is described in the opinion of the upper-court thus: "Whilst the court refused to instruct as to the presumption of innocence, it instructed fully as to reasonable doubt." This statement is not quite exact, as will be indicated later.

enforcement lies at the foundation of the administration of our criminal law." Many citations are given to show that there is a presumption of innocence. The doctrine that guilt can only be found by the clearest evidence is quoted from various writers, and this principle is referred to as being, in the language of the court, one of the "results of this maxim" of the presumption of innocence, but no reason is given for this view other than what will be stated hereafter. The language of Lord Gillies, the dissenting judge in the Scotch case already referred to, McKinley's case, is cited at length, as showing, in the phrase of the opinion, "how fully the presumption of innocence had been evolved as a principle and applied at common law;" but it is not remarked that this is a dissenting opinion, and that the case is a Scotch case, and not one at common law. The opinion then goes on to inquire whether the charge did substantially embody a statement of the presumption of innocence. It is declared that the authorities upon what is a sufficient statement of this presumption are "few and unsatisfactory." Referring to cases in Texas, Indiana, Ohio, Alabama, and California, on one side and the other of the question, to an anonymous article in the Criminal Law Magazine, and to Stephen's statement of the presumption of innocence, and the remarks of Mr. Chamberlayne, the editor of Best, the opinion goes on to say that it is necessary to consider "the distinction between the presumption of innocence and reasonable doubt, as if it were an original question." The question is then put as being "whether the two are equivalents of each other?" and it is proposed to "ascertain with accuracy in what each consists." It may be remarked, at this point, that this form of putting the question, imputes a very fatuous confusion of ideas to those who hold that the rule requiring proof of guilt beyond a reasonable doubt embodies in it all that the presumption of innocence really means. They would hardly agree that they are arguing that the presumption of innocence and reasonable doubt are "equivalents of each other;" or that the achievement of the opinion as it is described in a later case[1244] in saying: "The court drew a distinction between the presumption of innocence as one of the instruments of proof, contributing to bring about that state of case from which reasonable doubt arises, and a condition of mind called reasonable doubt produced by the evidence," — that this feat was either one that required much pains

---

[1244] Cochran v. U. S., 157 U. S. 286, 299.

to accomplish or one that particularly concerned their own contention.

Having thus started on this interesting and important inquiry the opinion proceeds: "The presumption of innocence is a conclusion drawn by the law in favor of the citizen, by virtue whereof, when brought to trial on a criminal charge he must be acquitted unless he is proven to be guilty. In other words, this presumption is an instrument of proof created by the law in favor of one accused whereby his innocence is established until sufficient evidence is introduced to overcome the proof which the law has created. This presumption, on the one hand, supplemented by any other evidence he may adduce, and the evidence against him on the other, constitute the elements from which the legal conclusion of his guilt or innocence is to be drawn." The court then quotes the passage from Greenleaf on Evidence,[1245] upon which I have commented; a passage from Wills on Circumstantial Evidence, stating that there is such a presumption and that it prevails "until destroyed by such an overpowering amount of legal evidence of guilt as is calculated to produce the opposite belief; " another from Best on Presumptions, simply saying that it is *presumptio juris;* another from an anonymous article in the Criminal Law Magazine,[1246] stating that the presumption is "in the nature of evidence in his favor, and a knowledge of it should be communicated to the jury," etc. The opinion then goes on, " The fact that the presumption of innocence is recognized as a presumption of law, and is characterized by the civilians *as presumptio juris,* demonstrates that it is evidence in favor of the accused; for in all systems of law legal presumptions are treated as evidence giving rise to resulting proof to the full extent of their legal efficacy. Concluding then that the presumption of innocence is evidence in favor of the accused, introduced by the law in his behalf, let us consider what is reasonable doubt." We are then told that reasonable doubt is "the condition of mind produced by the proof resulting from the evidence in the cause. It is the result of proof, not the proof itself; whereas the presumption of innocence is one of the instruments of proof going to bring about the proof from which reasonable doubt arises; thus one is a cause, the other an

---

[1245] Grlf. Ev. i. s. 34.

[1246] This appears to have been an advance chapter of Thompson on Trials The passage is found in that work, s. 2461.

effect. To say that the one is the equivalent of the other is therefore to say that legal evidence can be excluded from the jury, and that such exclusion may be cured by instructing them correctly in regard to the method by which they are required to reach their conclusion upon the proof actually before them. In other words, that the exclusion of an important element of proof can be justified by correctly instructing as to the proof admitted." Farther on, the opinion says: "It is clear that the failure to instruct them [the jury] in regard to what that [the presumption of innocence] is, excluded from their minds a portion of the proof created by the law, and which they were bound to consider." And it is added that the judge below in limiting the attention of the jury " ' to the proofs and the proofs only 'confined them to those matters which were admitted to their consideration by the court, and among these elements of proof the court expressly refused to include the presumption of innocence to which the accused was entitled, and which the court was bound to extend him."

The following remarks are also thrown in near the end of the discussion: "The evolution of the principle of the presumption of innocence, and its resultant, the doctrine of reasonable doubt, makes more apparent the correctness of these views, and indicates the necessity of enforcing the one in order that the other may continue to exist. While Rome and the Mediœvalists taught that wherever doubt existed in a criminal case acquittal must follow, the expounders of the common law in their devotion to human liberty and individual rights traced this doctrine of doubt to its true origin, the presumption of innocence, and rested it upon this enduring basis." It would be instructive to know the ground for this statement as to "the expounders of the common law," and the establishing of this "enduring basis." Unless the phrase refers to an occasional loose *dictum* of a law writer or judge in this country, or to an occasional ill-considered judicial opinion here, I know of no ground for it.

Such was the decision, in Coffin v. *U. S.,* so far as relates to the point now under consideration, and such the general course of the exposition. It proceeds, in a word, on the ground that the lower court refused to recognize the presumption of innocence, and thus kept from the jury a piece of evidence in behalf of the accused to which he was entitled. The immediate result of the decision was that it helped to delay the punishment of persona well deserving it, as appeared when the case came back again after another trial, and when all of "very numerous grounds of error" urged by these defendants were overruled.[1247] It is interesting to observe that, at the new trial, the charge, so far as quoted, dealt with the matters now under consideration in this form (p. 881): "The burden of proving Haughey and the defendants guilty as charged rests upon the government, and the burden does not shift from it. Haughey and the defendants are presumed to be innocent until their guilt in manner and form... is proved beyond a reasonable doubt. To justify you in returning a verdict of guilty, the evidence should be of such a character as to overcome this presumption of innocence and to satisfy each one of yon of the guilt of Haughey and the defendants as charged, to the exclusion of every reasonable doubt." This instruction seems to have raised no question. Except as leaving to the jury without explanation two phrases full of ambiguity, namely, "presumption of innocence" and "evidence... to overcome" it, it seems not to differ materially from the former charge. Can it reasonably be supposed that on such a charge anybody would imagine the presumption to be a piece of evidence, to be placed in the scales and weighed against other evidence? Such a charge is only in form an acceptance of the exposition in the former opinion of the Supreme Court; it is lip service.[1248]

That opinion, however, has had an effect outside of the particular case. Its somewhat wider range than common, of reference and allusion, has caused the imputing to it of an amount of learning and careful research to which, when scrutinized, it can lay no claim; and, to be quite just, it does not, in fact, lay claim to it. But it does lay claim to exactness of discrimination, to a searching and fundamental examination of the nature of the questions involved, and to the character of a leading and, in a degree, a final discussion of a peculiarly vexed and difficult subject. This claim must be disputed. What has been said in the earlier pages of this paper will serve to show grounds for denying the truth of the chief historical suggestions of the opinion, and the validity of some of its fundamental conceptions. Instead of settling anything outside of the particular controversy, it leaves matters worse off than before. Its work of mischief may be seen in the use of it in such later cases as Cochran v. U. S.,[1249] U. S. v. Davis,[1250] Agnew v. U. S.,[1251] (I do not

---

[1247] Coffin v. U. S., 162 U S. 664 (May, 1896).

[1248] See also Agnew v. U. S., 165 U. S. 36, 51 (January, 1897).

[1249] 157 U. S. 286 (March 25, 1895).

[1250] 160 U. S. 469.

now speak of the actual point decided in either of these cases), and No. Ca. *v.* Gosnell.[1252] The difficulty with the case is not with the actual decision — namely, that on the point in question a new trial should be granted; that could easily be agreed to, without any serious difference as to the principal matters. The trouble is with the exposition and the reasons. The absence, therefore, of dissent in this case may have very little significance.[1253]

It may readily be admitted, as the event shows, that it would have been practically wiser on the part of the judge below to have given the charge as requested and to have accompanied it with such explanations as would clear away ambiguity and would prevent the jury from misapplying the statements. And, farther than that, it may be true, as a general proposition, that the right should be maintained to have the presumption of innocence, specifically, and by name, drawn to the attention of the jury. If so, it should also be required that it be definitely and accurately explained, so that it be not misused as if in itself it constituted a piece of probative matter to be weighed against other evidence; and again, so that it be not used in a way to prevent the jury from allowing all evidence against the accused to have its full natural effect, all through the case, as it is put in.

[1251] 165 U. S. 36.

[1252] 74 Fed. Rep. 734 (W. D. No. Ca., June, 1896).

[1253] That the exposition and the reasoning in Coffin v. U. *S;* 156 U. S. 432, count for little in the mind of the court, may be seen in Alien v. U. S., 164 U. S. 492, 500 (Dec. 1896). Error was assigned in a refusal to charge that "where there is a probability of innocence, there is a reasonable doubt of guilt." In overruling the exception, the court (Brown, J.), after remarking that in the Coffin case a refusal to charge on the presumption of innocence was held not to be met by a charge that a conviction could not be had unless guilt were shown beyond a reasonable doubt, added: "In the case under consideration, however, the court had already charged the jury that they could not find the defendant guilty unless they were satisfied from the testimony that the crime was established beyond a reasonable doubt; that this meant: 'First, that a party starts into a trial, though accused by the grand jury with the crime of murder, or any other crime, with the presumption of innocence in his favor. That stays with him until it is driven out of the case by the testimony. It is driven oat of the case when the evidence shows beyond a reasonable doubt that the crime as charged has been committed, or that a crime has been committed. Whenever the proof shows beyond a reasonable doubt the existence of a crime, then the presumption of innocence disappears from the case. That exists up to the time that it is driven out in that way by proof to that extent.' The court having thus charged upon the subject of the presumption of innocence could not be required to repeat the charge in a separate instruction at the request of the defendant." Compare Agnew v. U. S *ubi supra.*

Certainly a specific declaration and explanation as to the presumption of innocence would draw pointed attention to those dangers of injury to the accused from mere suspicion, prejudice, or distrust, and to those other grounds of policy which make such judicial warnings important.

Now what, exactly, was it that the judge below said on this subject? He said something which, although quoted, is not commented upon, or, as it would seem, duly appreciated by the court, namely, "If, therefore, you can reconcile the evidence with any reasonable hypothesis consistent with the defendants' innocence, it is your duty to do so, and in that case find the defendants not guilty. And if, after weighing all the proofs, and looking only to the proofs, yon impartially and honestly entertain the belief that the defendants may be innocent of the offence charged against them, they are entitled to the benefit of that doubt, and you should acquit them." This language required the jury, in considering the evidence, to put upon it the construction most favorable to the defendants' innocence. In effect it said to the jury: "So long and so far as yon reasonably can, hold them innocent, assume them innocent, or, if yon please, presume them innocent, for these forms of phrase mean the same thing. Let nothing but legal evidence count against them, look to the proofs and the proofs only, and let not the evidence or any amount of evidence count against them, so long as you can continue as reasonable men to think them innocent."

When the judge below had said that, in addition to further elaborate and confessedly adequate instructions as to the rule which requires a weight of evidence beyond reasonable doubt, I think that it cannot truly be said, as the opinion does say, that "the court refused to instruct as to the presumption of innocence;" and, again, that "among these elements of proof the court expressly refused to include the presumption of innocence." What the judge below did, was to refuse to instruct in the particular form requested; and that sort of refusal is not necessarily fatal; for, as the court in the Coffin case justly says: "It is well settled that there is no error in refusing to charge precisely as requested, provided the instruction actually given fairly covers and includes the instruction asked." The whole question is, then, whether the instruction below fairly covers the instruction asked. The instruction asked was this: "The law presumes that persons charged with crimes are innocent until they are proven by competent evidence to be guilty. To the benefit of this presumption the defendants are all entitled, and this presumption stands as their sufficient protection, unless it has been removed by evidence proving their guilt beyond a reasonable doubt." I think that this charge was, in effect, given when the jury were told that they were to reconcile the evidence with the supposition of the defendant's innocence if it was reasonably possible; to consider nothing but the evidence and only to find the defendants guilty when the evidence proved it beyond a reasonable doubt.

It will be noticed that the charge requested did not ask for any explanation of the presumption of innocence, nor did the charge given make any explanation of it. As the request for a charge did not say that the presumption of innocence was in itself evidence, so the charge given did not deny that it was evidence. Why the jury should presume innocence was not stated in the request for a charge, and in the charge as actually given it was not stated why the jury should construe the evidence favorably to the accused so long as it was reasonably possible to do so. It was not necessary to do it, in either case, for in both cases it was *a rule* that was being laid down to the jury, and the grounds of the rule were not necessarily to be stated. In so far as evidence, in any proper sense of the word, was concerned, no question was made about it, in the talk about the presumption. If it be thought true that the fact that men in general are innocent is the evidential ground for the rule mentioned in the request, or in the charge, it was nothing to the purpose to go into that; for it is merely the legislative reason for laying down such a rule. In so far as the facts on which the rule rests were themselves to be regarded as evidence or a basis for inference in the case, the request draws no attention to them, and the mere omission to charge on them is no legitimate ground of exception — according to a familiar rule on that subject. Moreover, in so far as the fact that men in general are innocent is a ground of inference for the jury it is one to be taken notice of by court, counsel, and jury, without proof, and without anybody's moving them thereto. Certainly there was no refusal of any request to call the attention of the jury to the fact that men in general are innocent; the refusal was one to charge on the presumption of innocence in the form above stated, and that form offered no suggestion whatever as to what the true import of the phrase is. The accused then had no cause of complaint that any request of his counsel was refused.

But now we come to the kernel of the matter, the exposition in the opinion of the meaning of that phrase. Let us look at that. It said that the presumption of innocence is a conclusion drawn by the law by virtue of which, on a trial, the accused must be acquitted unless proved guilty. This, it will be observed, states the presumption as being a legal "conclusion" requiring exactly what was fully set forth by the trial judge. Then we are told that the presumption is an instrument of proof created by law in favor of the accused whereby his innocence is established until sufficient evidence is introduced to overcome the proof which the law has created. Here the presumption becomes an instrument of proof establishing innocence, and is itself proof, created by the law. This presumption, it is said again, supplemented by any other evidence the accused may produce, on the one hand, and the evidence against him on the other, constitute the elements from which the legal conclusion of guilt or innocence is to be drawn. Here the presumption, our "conclusion drawn by the law," our "instrument of proof," our "proof created by law," becomes evidence; *i. e.,* probative matter, to be added to the evidence of the accused, and balanced against the evidence of the government. How the presumption can be weighed and estimated as evidence we are not told.

After some quotations the opinion then says that the fact that the presumption of innocence is a *presumptio juris,* demonstrates that it is evidence in favor of the accused; for, it is added, in all systems of law, legal presumptions are treated as evidence giving rise to resulting proof, to the full extent of their legal efficacy. No authority is given for that statement, and no explanation of what it means; but it is added: "Concluding then that the presumption of innocence is evidence in favor of the accused, introduced by the law in his behalf," etc., etc.; and then later, it "is one of the instruments of proof, going to bring about the proof from which reasonable doubt arises." Again, the exclusion of it is called excluding "legal evidence," excluding "an important element of proof," excluding "a portion of the proof created by law."

To sum it up, the substance of all this is, as I have said before, that the presumption of innocence *is a piece of evidence, a part of the proof, — i. e.,* a thing to be weighed as having probative quality. And the grounds for saying it are: (1) The authority of the phrase in Greenleaf's Evidence, to which I have referred; (2) A similar phrase in an article in the Criminal Law Magazine, that it "is in the nature of evidence; "to which are added (3) a statement in another text-book (Wills' Circumstantial Evidence) that the presumption must prevail till destroyed by such an overpowering amount of legal evidence of guilt as is calculated to produce the opposite belief; and (4) a statement in Best on Presumptions that it is *presumptio juris.* This is the authority, and it is slight indeed. And the opinion adds a strange, unsupported assertion that the recognition of the presumption of innocence as a presumption of law *(presumptio juris)* demonstrates it to be evidence, and that in all systems of law legal presumptions of law are treated as evidence. It is easy to make such au assertion and to leave the matter there. But as one who has long and attentively studied the subject of presumptions, I can only say that I know of nothing to support it in any sense which tends to sustain the reasoning of the opinion. As against such an utterance I will merely quote the statement of one of the most thoughtful writers on this subject:[1254] "Legal or artificial presumptions cannot be a species of indirect evidence. A fact to which a legal presumption will apply, may be established either by direct or indirect evidence; 'but legal presumptions themselves cannot be a subdivision of evidence, much less of a particular kind of evidence." What appears to be true may be stated thus: —

1. A presumption operates to relieve the party in whose favor it works from going forward in argument or evidence.

2. It serves therefore the purposes of a *prima facie* case, and in that sense it is, temporarily, the substitute or equivalent for evidence.

3. It serves this purpose until the adversary has gone forward with his evidence. How much evidence shall be required from the adversary to meet the presumption, or, as it is variously expressed, to overcome it or destroy it, is determined by no fixed rule. It may be merely enough to make it reasonable to require the other side to answer; it may be enough to make out a full *prima facie* case, arid it may be a great weight of evidence, excluding all reasonable doubt.

4. A mere presumption involves no rule as to the weight of evidence necessary to meet it. When a presumption is called a strong one, like the presumption of legitimacy, it means that it is

---

[1254] 6 Law Magazine, 348, 369; *supra,* 539.

accompanied by another rule relating to the weight of evidence to be brought in by him against whom it operates.

5. A presumption itself contributes no evidence, and has no probative quality. It is sometimes said that the presumption will tip the scale when the evidence is balanced. But, in truth, nothing tips the scale but evidence, and a presumption — being a legal rule or a legal conclusion — is not evidence. It may represent and spring from certain evidential facts; and these facts may be put in the scale. But that is not putting in the presumption itself. A presumption may be called "an instrument of proof," in the sense that it determines from whom evidence shall come, and it may be called something "in the nature of evidence," for the same reason; or it may be called a substitute for evidence, and even "evidence" — in the sense that it counts at the outset, for evidence enough to make *a prima facie* case. But the moment these conceptions give way to the perfectly distinct notion of evidence proper — i. *e.,* probative matter, which may be a basis of inference, something capable of being weighed in the scales of reason and compared and estimated with other matter of the probative sort — so that we get to treating the presumption of innocence or any other presumption, as being evidence, in this its true sense, then we have wandered into the region of shadows and phantoms.

APPENDIX C

[*Supra,* 405.]

ON THE PRINCIPLES OF LEGAL INTERPRETATION, WITH REFERENCE ESPECIALLY TO THE INTERPRETATION OF WILLS.

by f. vaughan hawkins, esq.
[From the Juridical Society Papers, ii. 298.]

In bringing the subject of the present paper under the notice of this Society, it may be well to state, that by the Principles of Interpretation I mean the theoretical, rather than the practical, principles: the principles of the Science rather than of the Art. There is obviously both a science and an art of Interpretation. The business of the art is to collect and furnish practical rules and maxims for performing the process of Interpretation, in relation to this or that class of writings upon which it may have to be exercised. The business of the science is to analyze the nature of the process itself of Interpretation, and to discover, by a deductive method, the principles on which it rests, and in conformity with which the proceedings of the art are or ought to be regulated. It is the latter function with which the following observations are concerned; and although I cannot hope to convey a complete sketch of the theory of Interpretation within the limits of this paper, I may be able to lay a foundation on which such a theory may be built.

It would be a waste of time to enlarge on the importance of the scientific study of Interpretation as a branch of law; but it is surprising to find, when one's attention has been called to the subject, how completely it has been broken up into separate divisions, how little light one part of the subject has been allowed to throw upon any other, and how an entirely distinct art has grown Tip for the interpretation of each of the different classes of documents which most frequently require it, all applying unconsciously the same principles, but each refusing to acknowledge its obligations to the rest. Jurisprudence itself is defined by Heineccius to be the art of interpreting the laws: *"habitus practicus leges recte interpretandi, applicandique rite speciebus quibusuis obvenientibus.*"[1255] Treaties, contracts, statutes, deeds, and wills — each of these kinds of writings — have developed a separate set of axioms and canons of construction, while taken together they present an immense mass of materials for constructing the science of interpretation, which has been so imperfectly studied in comparison with the art. Take, for instance, the English law of the interpretation of wills, of which my thesis makes especial mention. The art of interpretation has here been carried to no inconsiderable perfection, and a remarkable uniformity of decision, even in the most perplexing cases, is in practice attained. Nevertheless, it is a branch of the law almost impossible to systematize in its present state, owing to the fact that the principles which have to be applied, and which are practically understood and acted on with tolerable correctness, have never been clearly laid down and exhibited in their relation to each other, but are enunciated in so many ways, with more or less incomplete-ness, and with such varying but always imperfect modes of expression, that the interpretation of an obscure will generally gives rise to an apparent conflict of opposing principles on the most elementary questions of the science of interpretation, and judges in delivering their opinions frequently think it necessary to examine afresh into the truth of the most fundamental axioms, and even come to seemingly opposite conclusions upon them. The practical result is that the *ratio decidendi* is almost impossible to ascertain or to express succinctly, and this branch of the law presents an aggregate of something like twenty thousand cases capable of being cited as authorities, the number increasing annually by hundreds, and the bulk of cases individually increasing rather than diminishing: a state of things which might, I venture to think, be materially altered by a more accurate knowledge of the real nature of the process involved in the interpretation of a will, of the methods employed in it, and of the limits which bound it.

The system of interpretation which comes nearest to a scientific system is that of the Civil Law, based on the Roman Law; and it is advisable to say a few words in passing on the reasons which, in my opinion, prevent that system from being a convenient basis on which to ground the analytical consideration of the subject on which I am about to enter. The Civil Law system of Interpretation

---

[1255] *Elementa Juris Civilis,* sec. 26.

is derived almost entirely from the methods used in the interpretation of Roman written laws. Now, the interpretation of laws in the Roman system of jurisprudence is, I need hardly mention in this Society, highly peculiar. That system extended the limits of logical or inferential Interpretation in a way certainly not applicable to any other class of legal documents than laws, and not to laws even, under a judicial system of a different kind from the Roman. The controversy between the Sabinians and Proculeians, between the logical and grammatical school of interpreters, may appear at first sight to be, and is sometimes referred to as being, identical with that which may be called the fundamental antithesis in legal interpretation generally — the opposition between intention and expression, between the letter and the spirit; but it is in reality something more than this it is a constitutional rather than a legal problem, and resolves itself into the consideration of the proper line of demarcation to be drawn between the functions of the legislator and the judge. That the rules and maxims derived from the interpretation of Roman laws are not applicable to legal documents generally, is forcibly shown by the remark of Savigny,[1256] who says that the excellence of a Roman law lay in its being neither too plain nor too obscure, but expressed in a sort of middling obscurity, *"Auf einen schmalen Raume mittelmässigen Dunkelheit,"* a phrase which sounds ironical, and is manifestly appropriate only to writings which, like Roman laws, and perhaps the sayings of some philosophers, are made avowedly with a view to being interpreted, and not to legal writings in general, which, it will be admitted on all hands, ought to be so plain as not to require interpretation. Hence the Civil Law distinctions of literal, mixed, and rational, restrictive, and extensive interpretation, and the like, are, I think, too special to be taken as the framework of an analysis of interpretation generally, although some of the problems in the subject have never been better discussed [than] by the Roman lawyers, and such passages as the well-known one in the Caecina,[1257] ending with the words, *"Quæ res igitur valuit! Voluntas: quæ si tacitis nobis intelligi posset, verbis omnino non uteremur: quia non polest, verba reperta sunt, non quæ impedirent, sed quæ indicarent voluntatem,"* will always supply a

---

[1256] *Syst. des heut. Röm. Rechts,* sec. 50.
[1257] *Pro Caecina,* cap. 18 *sqq.*

terse and striking quotation to the liberally disposed interpreter of writings of whatever kind.

It would, however, be unjust to omit that the importance of the interpretation of treaties in international law has caused some attention to be given it by writers on that subject; and the chapter on Interpretation in Rutherforth's Commentaries on Grotius, as an analysis of the construction of language, and the chapter on the Interpretation of Treaties in Vattel, as a collection of practical maxims, are more satisfactory perhaps than anything of a similar nature to be found elsewhere. But upon the whole, it seems to me, that the subject is best approached from first principles; and I shall therefore proceed to consider what is the object and the real nature of the process of legal interpretation, by which I mean the interpretation of any document of a legal nature, as a law, a treaty, a contract in writing, a deed, or a will.

It is necessary in the first place to distinguish that which takes place in the interpretation of a legal writing, such as I have mentioned, from that which takes place in the interpretation of written language in the most general form. In the latter case the object is a single one — to ascertain the meaning or intention of the writer — to discover what were the ideas existing in his mind, which he desired and endeavored to convey to us. *"Interpretatio est collectio mentis ex signis maximé probabilibus,"* is the definition of Grotius. It is a collecting of the intent from the most probable signs or marks. The intent of the writer, the ideas existing in his mind, cannot be known to us with certainty: we can only ascertain them to a greater or less degree of probability from outward marks or signs. The language used is one set of marks or signs, whose office it is to convey the writer's meaning; but interpretation, in its most general form, is not restricted to the consideration of the single set of signs which language is, still less is it debarred from giving to those signs any meaning, however discovered, which may accord with the possible or probable intention of the writer. To collect the intent is the sole object of inquiry; and the language, the written expression, is valuable only as a mark or sign of intent, a medium through which it may be collected.

In the interpretation of a legal document, however, we have not indeed a different, but an additional, object of inquiry. We desire not solely to obtain information as to the intention or meaning of the writer or writers, but also to see that that intention or meaning has been expressed in such a way as to give it legal effect and validity; we desire, in short, to know what the writer meant by the language he has used, and also to see that the language used sufficiently expresses that meaning. The legal act, so to speak, is made up of two elements, — an internal and external one: it originates in intention, and is perfected by expression. Intention is the fundamental and necessary basis of the legal effect of the writing; expression is the outward formality annexed by the law, both as a condition proper to ensure due deliberation in the performance of that which is to operate by force of law, and also as a means of securing that the act itself shall be properly evidenced and authenticated. The law, I say, requires a sufficient, not a perfect, written expression. This question will have presently to be considered more in detail; for the present I assume it to be so. To the general object of inquiry, therefore, in all interpretation, the collecting of the intent, there is superadded, in the interpretation of a legal writing, the further object of seeing that there is a sufficient expression of the intent contained in the writing before us. The language or written expression is therefore valuable in a twofold sense. Towards the collecting of the intent it is, as before, valuable as a mark or sign, though not necessarily the only, or even chief, mark or sign, but it may be one among many; it is, secondly, valuable in and by itself, as a condition of legal validity, essential to give effect to the intention. To interpret a legal writing is, therefore, first to collect the intent, to discover the writer's meaning; secondly, to ascertain that that meaning is expressed sufficiently.

But is it indeed true that the object of inquiry is to discover what the writer meant? There are not wanting great authorities, who use language, and that habitually and emphatically, which, taken in its natural sense, would imply that the writer's meaning was not the object of inquiry: which would resolve interpretation into nothing more than an inquiring into the meaning of words.[1258] Lord Denman, for instance, in Rickman v. Carstairs,[1259] says: "The question in this and other cases of construction of written instruments, is, not what was the intention of the parties; but what is the meaning of the words they have used." Lord Wensleydale in very many cases has used the same language. In Doe v. Gwillim,' be says, "In expounding a will, the court is to ascertain, not what the testator actually intended, as

---

[1258] 5 B. & Ad. 663.
[1259] 5 B. & Ad. 129.

contradistinguished from what his words express, but what is the meaning of the words he has used." By the phrase here used, "what the testator actually intended," is of course meant, what he intended, and endeavored to accomplish, — in short, what he meant by the language used, in opposition to the meaning of the language, which, as we shall see, are very different things. I remark this merely because the word intend is perhaps slightly ambiguous, and might be used to mean something which a person had in his mind, but neither did nor endeavored to do. Throughout this paper I use the words, the writer's intention, to denote that which he desired and endeavored to express, although he may not, in fact, have succeeded in properly expressing it; in short, I use it as synonymous with that which the writer meant by the language used, or, yet more shortly, the writer's meaning. Again, in Grey v. Pearson,[1260] Lord Wensleydale says, "The will must be in writing; and the only question is, what is the meaning of the words used in that writing." Lastly, Sir James Wigram, in his treatise on Extrinsic Evidence, of which I shall have more to say hereafter, lays down the proposition at the outset of his book, with perfect distinctness. "The question," says he,[1261] "in expounding a will, is not — what the testator meant, but simply — what is the meaning of his words;" and his discussion of the admissibility or inadmissibility of the various kinds of extrinsic evidence in aid of the exposition of a will, is based entirely on this supposed principle. There appears to me to be in this maxim a fallacy of no small importance; and I conceive it to be impossible rightly to apprehend the true nature of the process of interpretation without a clear appreciation of the difference between these two subjects of inquiry: what the writer meant, and what is the meaning of his words. To understand this, it is necessary to enter, to some slight extent, on the consideration of the theory of language.

We have seen that the interpretation of a legal writing is a collecting of the intent — of what the writer meant, that is — from the marks or signs used, accompanied with an inquiry Into the existence of the other essential element of a sufficient written expression. The instrument of written expression is language; — one particular set of marks or signs, that is, of which the peculiarity is, that a portion of mankind have agreed beforehand to use them

---

[1260] 6 H. L. Cases, 106.
[1261] Page 8, 4th edition [sect. 9].

according to certain definite significations, which significations are known to the interpreter, and constitute the meaning of the words. The person using the language may or may not have used it with the signification thus attached to it by general agreement; in other words, the meaning of the writer may or may not coincide with the meaning of the words. But the meaning of the words is, in theory at all events, a fixed one; it is independent of the writer, and capable of being known by the interpreter, not, like the writer's intent, with a greater or less degree of probability, but with certainty. Now, the result and the object of the introduction of the convention of language, of the use of one set of signs with definite significations attached to them, is to give a special form to the process of interpretation; to reduce interpretation generally from the indefinite office of collecting the intent from all available marks or signs of it, to the simpler and almost mechanical operation of giving to one set of signs their previously known meaning; and to reduce the interpretation of a legal writing from the twofold process of collecting the intent, and seeing that it be sufficiently expressed, to the single operation just now mentioned, which includes both inquiries; for it is manifest, that if the intent can be collected from the single set of signs of which language consists, by giving to those signs their proper meaning, there must be not merely a sufficient, but a perfect, written expression: the meaning of the words wholly coincides with the intention of the writer. The simplification thus effected in interpretation generally, is exactly analogous to that which would take place, if two persons, ignorant of each other's language, having endeavored in the first instance to communicate by means of signs and gestures, were suddenly furnished with a perfect code of signals, and able to use them. In the first case, he who sought to discover the other's meaning was obliged to keep that meaning in view at every step, and to travel continually from the signs to the supposed intention, and *vice versa,* guessing at the meaning of the signs from what lie conjectured to be the intent, and conjecturing the intent from the probable meaning of the signs. By the use of the signals he would be relieved at once from the necessity of keeping the intention in view during any but the first and last steps of the process of interpretation; starting with the assumption that it was the intention of the other to use the signals according to the signification belonging to them in the code, he would proceed to ascertain that signification with entire certainty from the signal-book, and having done so, and finding the meaning intelligible, he would consider his original assumption to be confirmed and raised to so high a degree of probability as to be beyond further question, and would conclude with reason that the meaning of the signals coincided with the meaning of the signaller, which latter had been throughout the ultimate, though not the immediate, object of his inquiry.

Supposing, therefore, language to be a perfect code of signals, and, moreover, to be used with perfect accuracy, so that the meaning of the words, the meaning, that is, obtained by giving to the language used its known and definite signification, was in all cases plain, and intelligible, and appropriate to the circumstances to which it referred, or to which it had to be applied, it would be correct to say, that the object of inquiry in the interpretation of a legal writing was answered by ascertaining merely the meaning of the words; not because the meaning of the words was the ultimate or real object of inquiry, but because the meaning of the writer, which is the real object, would be thereby ascertained to so high a degree of probability, that expediency would not allow it to be questioned by the admission of further evidence, or the inquiry after intention to be prosecuted further. It would not be true to say, as in the passage quoted from Sir James Wigram, that the question was, not what the writer meant, but what was the meaning of his words: it would be true to say that the meaning of his words was so strong a proof of what the writer meant, that the two must conclusively be taken as identical. In other words, interpretation would be inadmissible. That where the meaning of the words is plain, it is not allowable to question its being the meaning of the writer, is a fundamental maxim of all systems of interpretation. *Ubi in verbis nulla ambiguitas, ibi nulla occurrit, voluntatis quæstio,* says the Digest. *Non licet interpretari quæ interpretatione non egent,* is the maxim of Vattel. If, therefore, the dictum, that the meaning of the words is the only question to be considered, be taken merely as a form of stating this maxim, so far it is practically harmless, although theoretically incorrect; but its applicability ceases the moment a difficulty arises: the moment, in short, that interpretation, in the ordinary sense of the word, begins at all.

For what is it that gives rise to all questions of interpretation? Is it not that the meaning of the words fails to express the meaning of the writer? The meaning of the words, their known and definite signification, is ascertained; it proves to be not plain, not intelligible, not appropriate to surrounding facts and circumstances. What is the result? Manifestly the presumption that the meaning of the words was the meaning of the writer is rebutted: it becomes necessary to seek further for that meaning. Interpretation is brought back from the special form which it had assumed through the introduction of the convention of language, and becomes again what it was before, namely, a double inquiry; a collecting of the intent from all available signs or marks, and an inquiry into the existence of a sufficient expression of that intent in the single set of signs called language. The gap left by the partial failure of language to express the intention must be filled up by a direct inquiry into that intention by the help of other marks of it, and the light thus obtained must be combined with the light previously gained by the inquiry into the meaning of the words. It is only this ulterior process, which takes place when the meaning of the words has been ascertained, but proves not to express adequately the meaning, to which the name of interpretation is usually and properly applied.

The failure of language adequately to convey the intention may take place from three causes: first, the imperfection of language in itself, considered as a code of signals, its want of definite signification, and its inadequacy to the expression of every phase of thought; secondly, from the improper and unskilful use of language by the writer; thirdly, from the limited nature of the human mind, incapable of foreseeing all contingencies to which the expression of its intent may require to be adapted, especially if the interpretation of the writing takes place at a period long after that at which it was composed. The imperfection of language itself as an instrument of conveying ideas is to some extent, though by no means completely, treated in the well-known chapters of Locke on the imperfection and abuse of words. In fact, the convention on which usage of language rests is not a single or fixed one, but is the aggregate of an innumerable number of lesser conventions, which intersect and conflict with each other, and are continually shifting and changing from year to year. The usages of the same words at different times, in different places, by different writers, vary greatly. No words but technical words have their connotation or denotation precisely determined by authority; the classification and fixing of meanings belongs to a very important but little studied subject which may be called the theory of dictionaries; but were that theory far more perfect than it is, language would be and would always continue inadequate to meet the perpetually increasing complexities of human circumstances and human thought.

Some, indeed, of the difficulties thus arising may be solved by a more accurate investigation of the meaning of the words. Evidence of usage may cause what appeared at first a doubtful meaning to become a clear one; rules of grammar may disentangle the confusion of a sentence or a paragraph; unusual or technical words may be properly explained. But in general such evidence fails completely to solve the problem; the ambiguity remains, although one side or the other may somewhat preponderate. Here, however, is to be noticed an expedient by which the ambiguities of ordinary language may be to some extent remedied; I mean by an interpretation clause, such as now usually occurs in Acts of Parliament, whereby the writer himself as it were engrafts upon the general agreement which determines the use of language a special agreement of a more limited nature, and enables the interpreter to know with certainty the sense which the writer intended to attach to certain words. Such an interpretation clause may properly be considered as a sort of appendix to the signal-book used by the interpreter, — to adopt my previous illustration, — and the process of interpreting the writing by means of it may be regarded as a part of the process of ascertaining the meaning of the words.

It is essential to remark, that the possibility of proceeding in the inquiry after the writer's meaning beyond the point at which the meaning of the words fails, is dependent on the assumption, that a perfect written expression is not essential to the legal validity of the writing. Permission to collect the intent from other sources than the meaning of the words, implies that something from other sources may be added to that meaning. If, therefore, there were any case in which a perfect written expression were essential, interpretation, properly speaking, could have no place, and the axiom that the sole object of inquiry is the meaning of the words, would there, and there only, be a true one; if the meaning of the words were in any degree ambiguous, obscure, or deficient, the intent must be inoperative. Such an example may perhaps be found in the strictness of construction which the Roman law applied to clauses of exheredation in testaments: such clauses being against the policy of the law, were viewed with disfavor, and the least deficiency of expression rendered them nugatory. This rule of construction has wandered into our law under the guise of the maxim, that the heir is not to be disinherited, unless by express words or necessary implication; but like some others, it has been deprived of its meaning in the process of being transplanted, and exists only as a lifeless and unmeaning relic of a different system of interpretation. The word "necessary," in which the whole force of the maxim originally lay, having been explained away, so as to mean the opposite, not of probability, but of mere speculative conjecture, in which sense it has no more special application to heirs than to next of kin, or any other persons, things, or circumstances. But in fact with no class of writings, nay, with no one writing, is it ever the case that it is inadmissible to travel in search of the intent beyond the mere meaning of the words. We may distinguish analytically the point at which the interpreter ceases to be occupied with the meaning of the words, and begins to take cognizance of other marks or signs of intention; but in practice, the two processes are impossible to separate: and it is hard to say where meaning in the sense of known and definite signification ends, and implication or inference from probable intention begins to be added to it. Ordinary language is full of ellipses and ambiguities, which we solve unconsciously to ourselves by a reference to intention; and in some kinds of writing and speaking suggestion is almost without limit, and the meaning of the words bears a very small proportion indeed to the amount of meaning conveyed or hinted at. A law, therefore, which enjoined a perfect written expression, would be impossible to be obeyed, and the command which gives rise to the necessity of the letter, in a legal writing, must itself be interpreted according to the spirit.

Indeed the process of interpretation bears a strong analogy, and one which I think it is profitable to bear in mind, to the course of equity. What is it but the correcting or supplementing of the language of the writing, which by itself yields no clear meaning, by the aid of other marks or signs of intent; in short, a bringing of the expression into harmony with the probable intention? The resemblance of this definition to the Aristotelian definition of equity, τπαυσρθωμα νσμον η ελλειπι δια τσ καθσλον, is obvious. Interpretation is in truth a species of equity, just as equity may be said to be a liberal interpretation of the law. The object of interpretation is to supply the deficiency of the written expression. It is not a mere collecting of the intent, since intent denuded of expression can have no legal validity; it collects the intent only for the purpose of rectifying the expression, and only so far as that rectification is possible.

Interpretation, which thus occupies itself with the direct search after the intent, for the purpose of bringing the expression into harmony with it, is sometimes called interpretation by inference, "*interpretatio* κατα συλλογινμσν," in opposition to literal interpretation, or the mere determination of the meaning of the words. In fact, however, all interpretation, whether literal or inferential, is a process of inference or reasoning by probabilities; for the intent, which is the ultimate object of inquiry, can never be the subject of immediate knowledge, but must in any case be inferred from one species or other of marks or signs, with a greater or less degree of probability. The difference is that literal interpretation, so far as it succeeds, operates to reduce the inference to a single step, or rather to two steps, the commencing and final ones, while interpretation which is not literal, consists of a chain or series of inferences, which embrace and connect together all the marks or signs of intention which are made use of, every step of the process involving a separate appeal as it were to probability.

It seems surprising that the nature of that interpretation which clears up the ambiguities, or obscurities, or contradictions, of a writing, should be so entirely mistaken as that any one should assert the meaning of words, and not the intention, to be in such a case the object of inquiry. It is curious to what shifts those who maintain this opinion are sometimes driven. A judge[1262] is called upon to interpret a limitation in a will, of leaseholds to A. B., his executors, administrators, and assigns, for his life. The meaning of the words is here ascertained without the slightest difficulty; but when ascertained, it is repugnant and contradictory, and the presumption that the meaning of the words coincided with the writer's meaning is therefore rebutted. Suppose it to be decided that the limitation in question shall confer a life estate, and that the words, "his executors, administrators, and assigns," are only an incorrect mode of intimating that the person in question is to take a beneficial interest, is it possible to avoid seeing that this conclusion does not proceed upon the meaning of the words, but the meaning of the writer; that so far from carrying out to the full the meaning of the

---

[1262] See Morral *v.* Sutton, 1 Phil. 533, and Lord Wensleydale's judgment in that case.

words, it does in fact deprive some of the words used of their proper meaning, and soften them down so as to bring the expression as a whole into harmony with what can be inferred to be the meaning of the person using it?

If the foregoing observations have made clear the nature of the process of interpretation, in the form in which we are considering it, the next point to be observed is the nature of the methods or means which it employs, and the limits of its application.

Of the latter, it is sufficient for the present to say, that since the object of the proceeding is to rectify the expression by the intent, it can be carried no further, on the one hand, than it can be inferred, from the marks or signs indicative of intent, and with a sufficient degree of probability, that the intent exists, and that in a sufficiently definite form; nor, on the other hand, can it be carried on in the entire absence of a written expression, since there must be words which can be so interpreted as to bear the meaning which is inferred to be the writer's meaning, on which the intent can, so to speak, be ingrafted, without too wide a departure from their known signification. And it is also clear that the process in question need not, and cannot be carried beyond the point when the language has been brought into accordance with the probable intent; since it is only through the fact, and to the extent, that there exists a discordance between the language and the intent, between the meaning of the words and the meaning of the writer, that the former becomes subject to alteration: when the language has been interpreted so that the meaning is clear, the presumption that that meaning must be the writer's meaning returns in full force, and the office of interpretation is at an end.

The proposition that interpretation cannot proceed except on the basis of a supposed intent may perhaps be disputed. It may be said, do not a large proportion of the difficulties which occur in the interpretation of written language arise from the fact, that the writer had in fact no intention, at least no definite intention, upon the point on which his language is of doubtful meaning? With some such view I have seen it argued that the word "construction" comes, not from the verb to "construe," i. e., to put together and arrange existing materials, but from the verb to "construct," as if it were a process of supplying new materials, of creation in fact, and not merely arrangement. But this view I take to be philosophically, as well as etymologically, fallacious. I cannot see on what theory of interpretation the interpreter, as such, can have anything to do with that which he is not led to infer from the materials before him to have been the intention of the writer. No doubt the same judicial or other authority which interprets the writing, may also exercise an ulterior and independent power of disposition or enactment over the same subject-matter, as in the case, for example, of what is called *cy près;* or of the application of laws, by a judge authorized to apply the spirit of the law to cases confessedly not within the contemplation of the framer of it; but so far as the process alone of interpretation is concerned, there must, it seems to me, be a basis of inferred intention, to afford ground for any interference with, or modification of, the meaning of the words. It is to be observed, that there may be cases where intention can and must be inferred, although, in fact, there may have been none. The interpreter cannot certainly know whether the intent existed; it is the *indicia* of intent, the marks or signs which afford reasonable presumption of its existence, which he can alone regard, and these he is bound to regard, although, in spite of such indications, there may have been no actual intention. The question in short is, not what the writer meant, but what he has authorized the interpreter to say it is probable was his meaning. But if there be a total absence, not merely of intent, but of *indicia,* of marks or signs from which it is reasonably to be collected, in such a case it is clear the process of interpretation must stop for want of materials; and therefore it is correct to say, that it can be carried only so far as the intent can be collected with sufficient probability.

Passing to the consideration of the means employed to harmonize the expression with the intent, we observe, that this operation by no means involves the rejection, as a mark or sign of intent, of that which had alone been previously employed to determine it, namely, the meaning of the words, their known and definite signification. The presumption that the meaning of the words coincided with the meaning of the writer, has been displaced, so far as to allow of the introduction of other marks or signs indicative of intent, the meaning of the words being taken no longer as an exclusive guide, but coupled with the rest, each receiving such relative weight as it may be fairly entitled to. The meaning of the words is to be varied by the result of all the marks or signs taken together, in which it is itself included. What then are the other marks or signs indicative of intent, other than the meaning of the words? They may be divided, I think, into four classes. Either they may be such as furnish direct evidence as to what the intention is, or they may furnish circumstantial evidence of it, that is, evidence of facts and circumstances from which it is to be collected; and both direct and circumstantial evidence of intent may be contained in the writing itself, or external to it. And first, the case of direct evidence of intent, contained in the writing itself, may be seen in the preamble of a law: an authentic preliminary statement by the writer, of that which he was about to express or attempt to express in the writing to be interpreted. Such evidence of intent, being both unquestionably material, and proved in the strongest manner, is justly regarded as the most valuable in the inquiry. "The rehearsal or preamble of the statute," says Coke, "is a good means to find out the meaning of the statute, and as it were a key to open the understanding thereof." And the constant reference in the interpretation of statutes, to the intention as set forth in the preamble, would, one should have thought, have prevented its being ever supposed that intention, *qua* intention, was a matter with which the interpreter had no business to concern himself.

Secondly, there may be direct evidence of intention not contained in the writing itself, but proved by other means. In the case of a public document, such as a law, this description of evidence is not often likely to be forthcoming. In the case of writings which express the concurrent intent of two or more persons, as treaties or contracts, evidence of intention, contemporaneous with the writing itself, is not often to be procured or depended on; but the subsequent acts of the parties may, in some cases, usefully be taken as a guide. The most common case, however, of this kind of testimony is that of parol declarations of a testator, offered in explanation of the language of his will; a species of evidence plainly the least trustworthy of any, both from the distance of time, the liability to inaccuracy of statement, and last, not least, the possibility of perjury, where detection is impossible; for which reasons such evidence is, in all systems of interpretation, subjected to severe scrutiny, and in our own, with certain exceptions, rejected altogether.

Circumstantial evidence of the intention contained in the writing may be of two kinds. It may be calculated to throw light on the probable nature of the intention, such as is afforded by other dispositions or enactments, provisions or language bearing upon the same or similar subject-matter; or it may tend to show the sense which the writer attached to particular words or expressions, varying in a greater or lees degree from their meaning as determined by usage. Such evidence, so far as it goes, rests upon strong proof, and the maxim, *ex antecedentibus et consequentibus optima fit interpretatio*, "the context is the best interpreter," bears testimony to its value as a mark or sign of intent; yet it may be difficult in many cases to determine how far it is really material. The fourth and last, but not the least important, species of evidence is circumstantial evidence of intention not contained in the writing, such as the facts and circumstances surrounding the writer at the time when he wrote, and facts and circumstances relating to the persons or things the subject-matter of the writing. This description of testimony enters so largely, as an auxiliary to the meaning of the words, into ordinary language, as to be not unfrequently mistaken for a part of that meaning, and not, as it really is, an addition to it. Thus the writer, to whose views I am about to refer more particularly in connection with this part of the subject, Sir James Wigram, says:[1263] "A page of history, for instance, may not be intelligible till some collateral extrinsic circumstances are known to the reader. No one, however, would imagine that he was acquiring a knowledge of the writer's meaning from any other source than the page he was reading, because in order to make that page intelligible he required to be informed to what country the writer belonged, or to be furnished with a map of the country about which he was reading." In what way a knowledge of the country of the writer would contribute to the understanding of a page of history is not, perhaps, obvious; but to take the other case, that of a historical description not intelligible without reference to a map, but intelligible with that assistance, no one who looks into the matter can fail to see that the map helps by conveying a knowledge of some fact or facts, which the writer of the history might have stated, and which, if he had stated, the history would have been intelligible without the aid of the map: in other words, the writing alone does not perfectly express the meaning of the writer, but leaves it to be ascertained partly through the meaning of the words and partly by other evidence. It is true that in such a case as this an ordinary reader does not pause to consider what may be the exact proportions in which the written description and the map respectively help to give him the information he desires: this comes from the distinction originally pointed out in defining the object of legal interpretation as opposed to that of interpretation generally,

---

[1263] Page 77 [sect. 76]

since it is only in the case of a legal writing that it is necessary to ascertain whether the knowledge of the writer's meaning comes from the words alone, with the aid of that evidence which can alone determine their meaning, namely, evidence of usage, or whether it requires to be partly drawn from other sources, which constitute, in the strictest sense of the word, an addition to the document.

Here another objection may be taken notice of. It is said, and by the same writer, that any writing which refers to a person or thing, must at all events require external evidence in aid of its construction, so far as this, to show that a person or thing exists which answers the description in the writing; that such evidence is necessary, although the meaning of the words fully expresses the meaning of the writer, being sufficient to determine the particular person or thing intended without any ambiguity. This, however, is, I think, only a confusion in words. If the subject intended is fully and perfectly described by the meaning of the words of the writing, no difficulty of interpretation ever arises; the words do not require to be interpreted, and the introduction of any kind of evidence of intention would be wholly superfluous. In short, and this expresses the result of the whole matter, whenever any description of evidence is used to put a meaning on the language of the writing, which is not evidence of the conventional meaning of words, and is therefore, directly or indirectly, evidence to prove intention; the cause of the introduction of such evidence is, that the meaning of the words is insufficient to express the probable meaning of the writer, and the purpose for which it is introduced is to supply that explanation, or definition, or qualification which is lacking, and, in every case, to make an addition to the meaning of the words.

Having thus briefly suggested rather than described the four kinds of evidence of intention, which interpretation uses to combine with the original meaning of the words, I come to one of the principal points to which I desire to call attention, namely, that there is nothing in the essential conditions of the problem of the interpretation of a legal writing, if the process be such as I have described it, which excludes from consideration any of these kinds of evidence in its proper place. And, therefore, that if we find one or more of them are considered inadmissible in any particular system of interpretation of one or more classes of writings, the rule of exclusion, and the consequences which flow from it, will form a peculiarity of that system, and must be matter of arbitrary and positive enactment. The contrary to this proposition is the foundation of Sir James Wigram's Treatise on Extrinsic Evidence.

His theory may be stated as follows: "The statute which requires a will to be in writing," he argues,[1264] "precludes a court of interpretation from ascribing to a testator any intention which his written will does not express, and in effect makes the writing the only legitimate evidence of the testator's opinion." "No will is within the statute but that which is in writing; which is as much as to say, that all that is effectual and to the purpose must be in writing, without seeking aid of words not written."

This reasoning, it is observed, if true, would exclude from the inquiry two of the four kinds of evidence of intention; namely, those not contained in the writing itself. It would not exclude evidence of intention derivable from the writing itself, whether direct, as from a recital of intention, or indirect, as from the context. But Sir James Wigram, it seems to me, argues incorrectly from this incorrect premise. Therefore, he says, the only object of inquiry is, not what the writer meant, but what is the meaning of his words: hereby binding himself to the exclusion of all evidence of intention whatever, and letting in nothing but evidence of the meaning of words; that is, evidence of usage. He then, upon this footing, proceeds to divide evidence into two kinds: evidence explanatory of the words themselves, and evidence to prove intention; and argues that the former kind of evidence, *i. e.* evidence explanatory of the words themselves, must be the only admissible one. Under the head, however, of evidence explanatory of the words themselves, Sir James Wigram includes, not only evidence furnished by the context, — though even this, it is plain, can never show what the words mean, but only what the writer meant by them, — but also the very wide and almost unlimited range of evidence embraced within the terms of his fifth proposition, which is this:[1265] —

"For the purpose of determining the object of a testator's bounty, or the subject of disposition, or the quantity of interest intended to be given by his will, a court may inquire into every material fact relating to the person who claims to be interested under the will, and to the property which is claimed as the subject of disposition, and to the circumstances of the testator, and of his family

---

[1264] Page 7 [sect. 9].
[1265] Pages 11 [sect. 17], 65, [Prop. 5].

and affairs, for the purpose of enabling the court to identify the person or thing intended by the testator, or to determine the quantity of interest he has given by his will. The same, it is conceived, is true of every other disputed point, respecting which it can be shown that a knowledge of extrinsic facts can in anyway be made ancillary to the right interpretation of a testator's words."

The concluding part of this canon, it will be observed, reduces the definition to no definition at all; it amounts to saying that everything is admissible in aid of the interpretation of a will which can in anyway be made auxiliary to the interpretation of it. But, in fact, what Sir James Wigram means to include under his fifth proposition, is that kind of evidence which I have called circumstantial evidence of intention not contained in the writing; and it is plain that the admission of this sort of evidence, on the plea of its being explanatory of the words themselves, is the result of that original confusion between the meaning of the words and the writer's meaning, to which I have so often adverted. Such evidence in reality cannot alter the meaning of the words, it can only lead us to infer what the writer meant by them. "Suppose," says Sir James Wigram,[1266] "a testator to devise an estate to A. B., there being two persons, father and son, of the same name, and that the son only was known to the testator. Or suppose a testator resident in India, to bequeath to A. B., who was also in India, some specific chattel, *e. g;* a gold watch, and that the testator had with him in constant use a specific chattel of the kind described, and that he was also owner of another of the same description which he had left in England twenty years before." In these cases, he argues, evidence showing which of the two persons bearing the same name was known to the testator, or which was the gold watch the testator had with him in use, would be evidence explanatory of the words themselves, and therefore admissible. The fallacy here involved is, I think, obvious. The name John Smith, the description "my gold watch," contains in itself, and as part of the meaning of the words, nothing which is applicable to one of the two John Smiths, or of the two gold watches, more than to the other of them; nothing which can decide which of the two the testator intended. Evidence of the facts is in each conclusive as to the writer's "meaning, but it can add nothing to the meaning of the words; the words mean, after the facts are known, precisely what

---

[1266] Page 73 [sect. 73].

they did before, and nothing more. What interpretation really does in such a case, is to give to the words that meaning which the writer intended they should have, or, which is the same thing in effect to add to the name or description that additional mark or sign, whatever it be, which applies to the person or thing intended, or to that person or thing only: the description is thus rendered a complete description, and the words as interpreted convey a meaning which in and by themselves they are insufficient to convey.

Indeed, Sir James Wigram, in arguing against the admissibility of that particular kind of evidence of intention, which he contends to be from the nature of the case inadmissible, conclusively refutes himself. "If," he says, "the just exposition of the statute be, that the writing which it requires shall of itself express the intention of the testator, it is difficult to understand how the statute can be satisfied by a writing merely, if the description it contains have nothing in common with that of the person intended to take under it, or not enough to determine his identity. To define that which is indefinite, is to make a material addition to the will." These words forcibly express what the effect of all interpretation is, which is not merely a determination Of the meaning of words. It is a defining of that which is indefinite; it is adding to the writing that term which is wanting, in order to determine the identity of the person or thing referred to, or whatever it be which is insufficiently expressed by the meaning of the words.

The most surprising part, however, of Sir James Wigram's theory is yet to come. The arguments I have referred to, if they proved anything, would at least prove the inadmissibility of that class of evidence which is farthest removed from the meaning of the words, — I mean direct evidence of intention not contained in the writing. But our system of interpretation confessedly admits that species of evidence, in its most unequivocal form, — parol declarations of what the testator actually intended, — in particular cases, of which the case of homonymous persons or things, of there being two John Smiths, or two manors of Dale, is one. Sir James Wigram endeavors to prove this to be, not an anomaly or an exception to the theory, but entirely in accordance with it. "The cases," he says, "will be found to have reduced the law to a settled principle."[1267] His explanation of these cases is this: "Although," he

---

[1267] Preface to third edition.

says,[1268] "the words do not ascertain the subject intended, they do describe it. The person held entitled in these cases has answered the description in the will. The effect of the evidence has only been to confine the language within one of its natural meantags. The court has merely rejected, and the intention which it has ascribed to the testator sufficiently expressed, remains in the will. An averment to take away surplusage is good, but not to increase that which is defective in the will of the testator. Or, perhaps, the more simple explanation is, that the evidence only determines what subject was known to the testator by the name or other description he has used." He then refers to Lord Wensleydale, who, speaking of such cases, says,[1269] "Such evidence is admissible to show, not what the testator intended, but what he understood to be signified by the words he used in the will." Even Lord Abinger, in Doe v. Hiscocks,[1270] uses similar language. "Thus," says he, "if a testator devise his manor of S. to A. B., and has two manors of North S. and South S., it being clear he means to devise one only, whereas both are equally denoted by the words he has used, in that case there is what Lord Bacon calls an equivocation, *t. e.,* the words equally apply to either manor, and evidence of previous intention may be received to solve their latent ambiguity; for the intention shows what he meant to do, and when you know that, you immediately perceive that he has done it by the general words he has used, which, in their ordinary sense, may properly bear that construction. It appears to us that in all other cases, parol evidence of what was the testator's intention ought to be rejected, upon this plain ground, that his will ought to be made in writing; and if his intention cannot be made to appear by the writing, explained by circumstances, there is no will."

The whole of this reasoning may be answered in Sir James Wigram's own words: "To define that which is indefinite is to make a material addition to the will." The case of two persons or places bearing the same name is a case where language is imperfect: to adapt an illustration from John Stuart Mill, a name is like the chalk mark put upon the door in the story of "The Forty Thieves," which Morgiana rendered useless by chalking all the doors in the street in precisely the same manner. The result is, that to distinguish any one

---

[1268] Page 123 [sect. 152].

[1269] Richardson *v.* Watson, 4 B. & Ad. 800.

[1270] 5 M. & — W. 363.

door from the other, an additional mark of some sort must be put upon it, the mark originally used having come to mean either and neither of the objects marked, any one considered in itself, but none as distinguished from the others. It is not true to say, with Lord Abinger, that when you know what the writer meant to do, you perceive that he has done it: on the contrary, you perceive that some Morgiana, as it were, has come in to defeat his intention, and has succeeded in defeating it, unless you will permit some new and additional mark to be put on, which will effectually distinguish the object of the writer's intention from other similarly marked objects, the existence of which he was unaware of or had forgotten.

To recur to the difficulty originally started by Sir James Wigram, as the foundation of his theory, — that the fact of a written expression being required by law as a condition of the validity of any class of writings, is inconsistent with the admission into the process of interpretation, of any kind of evidence of intention which is not contained in the writing itself, it may be said, I think, in answer to this objection, — first, that the requirement of a written expression is an obligation or command addressed to the writer and not to the interpreter, and with which therefore the interpreter is concerned only indirectly, so far as it imposes on him the duty of ascertaining that the command has been sufficiently complied with — that there exists a sufficient written expression — while it leaves him at liberty to interpret that command in an equitable and liberal spirit, making allowance for the imperfections of language and for the effect of circumstances unknown to the writer in causing his expression to be in fact imperfect, where he thought he had sufficiently expressed himself, as in the case of the two persons bearing the same name, when the writer only knew of the existence of one of them. And, secondly, that so far as the condition of law we are considering is to be regarded as one, compliance with which third parties, whose rights the operation of the writing if valid will affect, have a right to demand, its existence is to be inquired into only when the process itself of interpretation has been duly performed, — and that if a Court of Interpretation decides that the words used may be so interpreted as to bear the meaning which the writer intended them to have, they do to all intents and purposes carry that meaning; and therefore the writing as interpreted does fully express the writer's intention, although without interpretation the meaning would still be, as it was before, imperfectly expressed, ambiguous, and obscure. Or, perhaps, the simplest way of stating the theory is to adopt the analogy already suggested in this paper, and to say that interpretation is a species of equity, which interposes to prevent the mischief which would accrue from a severe and rigorous application of the rule of law, requiring the meaning of the writer to be completely expressed.

It is, indeed, somewhat extraordinary that it should have been supposed that direct evidence of intention, in the shape of parol declarations of a testator, was necessarily inadmissible in the interpretation of a will required by statute to be in writing, when a comparison of other systems of testamentary interpretation, and even a glance at the history of our own system, so evidently proves the contrary. The Roman law, though imposing considerable formalities on testaments, received such evidence without scruple, only requiring it to be strong; and the almost universal ending of the numerous rules of construction in that system is, *"nisi eridentissimis testimoniis probetur aliter sensisse testatorem,"* or similar expressions. Courts of Equity, following the rules of the civil law, down to the time of Lord Cowper, made no objection to receiving the same class of evidence, in doubtful cases; only taking care not to allow it in cases where it might conflict with any of the other classes of evidence of intention, which they justly considered as of higher value. On the other hand, Courts of Law had established another system of rules as to the admissibility of evidence of this description, applying equally in the interpretation of all writings under seal, whether required by law to be in writing or not; and the result of the collision of these different systems of interpretation has naturally been that, after some confusion, a compromise has been arrived at, and the admission of evidence of the kind in question, in the interpretation of wills, is now regulated by rules altogether arbitrary.[1271]

The common-law rules as to the admission of evidence of intention not contained in the writing were two, which are generally included together in Lord Bacon's maxim as to the patent and latent ambiguities, with his comment upon it. As that maxim and comment are perhaps not always properly understood, I will here devote a few words to them. These rules are, as I have said, matters of positive enactment, and Sir James Wigram appears to me to have acted unwisely in rejecting Lord Bacon as his guide, and endeavoring to

---

[1271] [See some other considerations bearing on this, *supra,* 441, 442]

establish them on o *priori* principles, which, as I have attempted to show, are not correct. The rules, which are two, are distinct from each other, and they apply equally to all written instruments, whether required by law to be in writing or not. The maxim, *"ambiguitas verborum latens verificatione suppletur, nam quod ex facto oritur ambiguum verificatione facti tollitur,"* excludes all evidence of intention, direct or circumstantial, not contained in the writing itself, in all cases where the difficulty or problem of interpretation to be solved was such as was apparent on the face of the writing: allowing extrinsic evidence of intention to be introduced only where some fact had to be averred before the difficulty was raised. This, by the help of the system of pleading, operated as a rough and ready rule, which let in such evidence in those cases where perhaps it was most necessary, where the difficulty related to some person or thing the subject-matter of the writing; but it undoubtedly, while adhered to, excluded all that kind of evidence referred to in Sir James Wigram's fifth proposition, namely, surrounding facts and circumstances relating to the testator's family, etc., wherever the will or other writing was ambiguous on the face of it. It would not be difficult to show that the rule has been gradually relaxed, that evidence of facts and circumstances has by degrees come to be considered admissible in all cases, and that the only rule which is practically now operative in limiting the reception of evidence of intention is the second rule, prohibiting admission of direct evidence of intention from extrinsic sources. This rule is not any way contained or implied in the maxim of latent and patent ambiguities, but is stated by Lord Bacon in his comment on that maxim, when he says that intention itself may be averred only in the case of equivocation, that is, of homonymous persons or things; because there and there alone it would stand with the words, would not tend to alter the meaning of the words, that is, but would only add a term to that meaning. The common-law system of interpretation, therefore, with a prudent though perhaps excessive jealousy of the inferior kinds of evidence, admitted evidence of intention not contained in the writing, only where the ambiguity of the writing could not be detected on the face of it, and admitted direct evidence of intention not contained in the writing, only in the case of homonymous persons or things.

The rejection or admission of the various kinds of evidence, of the marks or signs of intent other than the meaning of the words, in the process of inferential interpretation, marks the point at which the methods of interpretation applied to different classes of writings begin to diverge from one another, and their charactsristics will be henceforth determined by the subject-matter of each, and by considerations peculiar to this or that judicial system, rather than by principles common to all. But it is evident that the grand question in each system will be, what is to be the combined effect of all these other kinds of marks or signs of intent, in comparison with the original object of attention, the meaning of the words? How far may the meaning of the words be modified by the indications of intent drawn from these other sources? What, in short, are the limits of inferential interpretation? What is to determine how far we may go in correcting or supplementing the written expression, for the purpose of bringing it into harmony with the probable intention? These limits will be in fact two, which it is desirable to separate, though in practice the distinction between them cannot always be recognized. The meaning of the words, as I originally stated, is important in two ways: as a sign of the intent, and as a condition necessary to the legal validity of the writing. As a sign of the intent, it has yielded so far as to admit of other marks or signs being combined with it; as a legal requirement, its necessity remains. The extent to which interpretation may go in modifying the meaning of the words will depend, therefore, first, upon the strength of the presumption that the meaning of the words alone expresses the meaning of the writer; a presumption which, though partially displaced, is yet only forced back as it were like a spring, and continually tends to return; and, secondly, upon the greater or less latitude allowed in the requirement of a sufficient written expression. The result of these two considerations taken together will determine the relative weight, which, in the interpretation of any particular writing or class of writings, is to be assigned to the letter, to the meaning of the words; and how great the strength of proof of intent must be which can add to or correct it. These things, like the boundaries of the jurisdiction of equity itself, can be fixed only in practice and approximatively; but it is easy to see where some kinds of writings will differ from others. In general, the presumption that the meaning of the words represents the meaning of the writer will be stronger, and require greater cogency in the evidence of intent adduced to vary that meaning, in proportion as the writing is a more formal one, as it presents fewer difficulties and obscurities to the interpreter, and to some extent as the language employed is more technical, and has therefore a more strongly marked and definite meaning. This, of course, would not apply to documents which, as in the case I referred to of laws according to the Roman conceptions of them, were framed for the purpose of being interpreted; whether this were done in order that they might be couched in such general terms as to permit of application to distant and varying circumstances, or whether, like some philosophical or moral writings, they were made designedly obscure, in order to veil the writer's meaning from careless or hostile interpreters. But generally speaking, the more formal the writing, the narrower must be the limits of interpretation. This is evidently the ground for the distinction that deeds are to be less liberally interpreted than wills. The moderate rule of the Digest — *In testamentis plenius voluntates testantium secutamur* — acquires a tinge of contempt in the mouths of clerical judges — *Testamentorum benignœ faciendœ sunt interpretationes propter simplicitatem laicorum;* and no one familiar with the history of will-construction can doubt that the liberality of interpretation which distinguishes the decisions of ancient, as, for instance, of Elizabethan times, was the result quite as much of contempt for the letter, as of reverence for the, spirit. The increased and increasing strictness of construction is in great part due insensibly to the greater precision which the language itself has acquired, and to the more general possession of the power to use it correctly; interpreters are bound to give writers credit for meaning what they say, instead of making them say what it seems probable they would be likely to mean. The other limit of interpretation of which I have spoken is the result of the necessity of there being a sufficient written expression; the meaning of the words cannot be added to or corrected beyond a certain point, or the words cease to be capable of bearing the interpretation to be put on them; and, though the intent may be known, there is no expression in which it can clothe itself. It cannot be too often repeated that legal interpretation is not a mere ascertaining of the intent; it acts only by putting a meaning, consistent with the intent, upon the words. And the answer to the question, What is a sufficient written expression? will vary largely with different classes of writings, and under different systems of jurisprudence. In this respect it is manifest that private documents must be interpreted more strictly than public. A deed or will made by a private person is made with the knowledge of the command of the law, which requires the writer to express himself fully and completely, and gives validity to the instrument only on the condition of reasonable compliance with the demand which it has imposed. On the other hand a document, such as a treaty, which as to its form is almost wholly independent of everything but the will of the contracting parties, leaves the amount of the expression much less determinate; and, although an intention must fail of effect which has no corresponding expression of any kind in the document, yet the interpreter must resort very much to the inferred will of the parties themselves for a criterion of sufficiency of expression, which thus becomes almost merged in the general inquiry after the probable intention — meaning, as I do, by intention, wherever it occurs in this paper, not a mere inchoate act of the mind, that which a person intended to do, but took a step towards doing, but something which as a mental act was complete, and which the writer endeavored to express by the words he made use of, although those words in fact express his meaning more or less imperfectly.

In the interpretation of writings where the latitude allowed to the interpreter is considerable, and particularly where direct evidence of intention not contained in the writing is admitted, the question of what is a sufficient written expression becomes evidently of great practical importance. If a perfectly definite intent can be collected by the aid only of collateral evidence of it, coupled with the meaning of the words, it is probable that the latter element, that of the meaning of the words, bears a sufficiently great proportion to the former, to assure the interpreter that the words will bear the meaning, and express it sufficiently. But this security does not exist where parol declarations of intention, for example, are admissible. The undoubted fact that no general definition of what is in such cases a sufficient expression can be fixed upon beforehand, is made use of by Sir James Wigram as a constant argument against admitting evidence of intention generally. "Once admit," says he,[1272] "that the person or thing intended by the testator need not be adequately described in the will, and it is impossible to stop short of the conclusion that a mere mark will in every case supply the place of a proper description." Surely there is no impossibility such as here contended. It is reasonable to say, that if a testator, for instance, describes a person by his surname and Christian name, that is a sufficient description to satisfy the letter of the law, though it may in

---

[1272] Page 128 [sect. 158].

fact be insufficient completely to identify the person intended. If, on the other hand, a testator should say, "I give so and so to *my son,*" when he has nine sons, it would probably be right to decide that such a description was not a sufficient one, since it was one which the writer must have known, or ought to have known, would prove ambiguous, and to allow of an addition to which by parol testimony would be to offer a great temptation to perjury. It is evident that a line must be drawn somewhere, and when necessary it will doubtless be drawn in practice; but as yet the boundary of testamentary interpretation on this side is somewhat imperfect, and there is no rule forbidding the introduction of parol testimony of intention to fill up even such a manifestly inadequate description as that I have last supposed.

Many questions on the sufficiency of expression arise upon the interpretation of informal writings, as, for instance, contracts, — what part of a contract required by law to be in writing need be expressed in the writing; how far usages and customs of trade may be imported, and the like. In fact, all the most difficult problems of interpretations arise upon the limits of it, upon the extent to which the meaning of words may be modified by other signs of intent; upon the contest, in short, as it is often termed, between the letter and the spirit. Into the principles which questions of this nature involve, I will not at present enter more minutely. They will suggest themselves in relation to the different classes of legal writings to any one who clearly appreciates the real nature of the process of what I have called inferential interpretation, a process in reality simple, and which, like reasoning, is practised correctly every day by persons who have never considered what it is they do when they perform it, but which can never be understood so long as it is confounded with the mere grammar and dictionary operation of ascertaining the meaning of words. One consideration, however, I will not pass over. I mean the great differences which exist in the measure of interpretation as applied under different judicial systems and by different judicial minds, and the consequent necessity for accumulating a certain mass of decisions, in order to supply a uniform standard, and to fix the nearest approach to absolute correctness by striking an average of opinions through a long series of years. It is sometimes said, in relation particularly to testamentary interpretation, that authorities can be of no service: that to quote cases is to construe one man's nonsense by another man's nonsense,[1273] and that all a judge has to do is to read the writing and endeavor to make out from it the meaning of the testator. Now, if interpretation were, like the determination of the meaning of words whose signification is fixed, something that can be done with absolute certainty, in which one man would come to the same conclusion as another, and which is, so to speak, the same all the world over, the study of previous authorities might indeed be unnecessary. But, in truth, it would be as reasonable to say that no authorities were to be consulted on a question of equity; that a judge ought to act upon his own notions of what was equitable; and that as circumstances are infinitely various, one case could never show what it was right to do in another. Experience shows that the limits of interpretation will be fixed at very different points by different persons; and there are perhaps, no legal subject which brings out peculiarities of individual bias and disposition more strongly than difficult problems of construction. By the combined result of the decisions of a succession of judges, each bringing his mind to bear on the views of those who preceded him, a system of interpretation is built up which is likely to secure a much nearer approach to perfect justice than if each interpreter were left to set up his own standard of how far it was right to go in supplying the defective expression, or of what amounted to a conviction of the intent as distinguished from mere speculative conjecture. Rules of construction are matters the expediency of which may be more doubtful; but that principles of construction there must be in every system of rational interpretation, and that these are only to be gathered by a comparison of a large number of important cases, and by striking the average of a large number of individual minds, will not, I think, be denied by any one who considers interpretation to be as I have described it, a process of reasoning from probabilities, a process of remedying, by a sort of equitable jurisdiction, the imperfections of human language and powers of using language, a process whose limits are necessarily indefinite and yet continually requiring to be practically determined, — and not, as it is not, a mere operation requiring the use of grammars and dictionaries, a mere inquiry into the meaning of words.

[1273] ["The nonsense of one man can furnish no rule for understanding the nonsense of another." Dunning (Lord Ashburton), cited is Evans's Decisions of Lord Mansfield, i. 284. — J. B. T.]

979784

Printed in Great Britain by
Amazon.co.uk, Ltd.,
Marston Gate.